SYSTEMS, ORGANIZATIONS, ANALYSIS, MANAGEMENT:

a book of readings

SYSTEMS, ORGANIZATIONS, ANALYSIS, MANAGEMENT:

A book of readings

DAVID I. CLELAND

Associate Professor
Industrial Engineering
Systems Management Engineering
  and Operations Research
School of Engineering
University of Pittsburgh

WILLIAM R. KING

Associate Professor
Graduate School of Business
University of Pittsburgh

McGRAW-HILL BOOK COMPANY

New York   St. Louis   San Francisco   Toronto
London   Sydney

SYSTEMS, ORGANIZATIONS, ANALYSIS, MANAGEMENT:
a book of readings

Library of Congress Catalog Card Number 68–54007

ISBN 07-011312-2

67890 HDBP 765

PREFACE

The title chosen for this book of readings warrants immediate explanation to readers. The four unconnected words—systems, analysis, organizations, and management—are those which best describe the content of the book. It is a book about *systems* and the systems concept applied to *management* and *analysis* in *organizations*. Yet, in our initial discussions concerning a title, each proposed title which incorporated all of these salient aspects seemed tedious and verbose.

An indexing method used in the field of information retrieval provided the resolution of this dilemma. This method, KWIC (key-word-in-context), utilizes the key words of a title as a basis for indexing. Each index entry for a particular title consists of a key word followed by the remainder of the key words in the sequence in which they appear in the title. Thus, any title which we would have chosen using these four key words in the given order would have four index entries in a KWIC system:

systems, organizations, analysis, management
organizations, analysis, management, systems
analysis, management, systems, organizations
management, systems, organizations, analysis

The chosen title is the first of these index entries. It provides the same information about the content of the book which would be provided by an index entry. Hopefully, this will lead to better communication and an avoidance of the problems inherent in the grandiose titles often selected for readings books.

We were led to develop this set of readings after our perception of the inadequacies of most management texts resulted in a book entitled *Systems Analysis and Project Management*. In preparing that text, we drew on the work and thoughts of many of our colleagues both within and outside the field of management. With this task completed, it was suggested that a book of readings developed along similar modern lines would be valuable in several ways. First, it would be an invaluable complement to the basic book in that it would present the views of others in their own words and serve to better demonstrate the biases and personal values inherent in any good book. Moreover, it would permit a wider coverage of applications and ramifications of the systems concepts to which we focus attention.

However, one of the great utilities envisioned for a modern systems-oriented readings book is as *a complement to basic management texts which do not emphasize systems ideas.* We recognize that the treatment of some aspects of management thought and theory in systems-oriented texts such as ours is not as comprehensive as it is elsewhere. In seeking to demonstrate the applicability of modern systems concepts to both the planning and execution functions of management, we necessarily tended to deemphasize many management principles which are not of central importance to this thesis. In doing so, we produced a book which will be too narrow for the tastes of some teachers. Other texts with which we are familiar have similar biases.

On the other hand, a cursory treatment of systems ideas such as is given in most basic management texts is insufficient for the modern manager and student of management. Thus, a valid role for a readings book such as this is as a complementary vehicle to a basic nonsystems text.

We also envision that this book will play a role in the more advanced study of those who are already well versed in basic management ideas and practice. Of course, we sincerely hope that such a value is found by both students and practitioners, for systems ideas will become even more important in everyone's management task in the future than they are today. Particularly, we hope that those managers and management-oriented technical people who did not study systems concepts as a part of their formal training will make use of the wealth of knowledge put forth by management thinkers here.

Our sincere thanks go to the contributors—who are the real authors of the book. In most cases, we present their work in its original published form. In others, revisions have been made to render previously published material more compatible with the form of presentation.

Our contribution to this volume is in the introductory section and the introductions to the other sections. There, we attempt to set the theme for the book and to integrate the various papers into a consistent whole. For any inconsistencies or omissions, we alone are responsible.

The other contribution which we offer was both arduous and rewarding. We spent many months in reviewing the literature of a variety of fields. The piles of journals and individual papers in our offices were the focal point of many derisory comments from our colleagues. But the learning and discussion which the process stimulated was valuable to us, and it enhanced the quality of the papers finally selected. We are quick to point out that any book is the product of the attitudes and prejudices of its editors and that our biases and prejudices may not be particularly worthy ones. It is nonetheless true that according to our consistent criterion of subjective value, the papers which appear here are the best of hundreds which were considered. Unless our values are completely misdirected, the authors should feel a measure of pride in that selection.

The book is an attempt to collect the thought of recognized authorities in various fields as they apply to the modern ideas of systems analysis and management. A cursory examination of the book may lead one to the conclusion that it represents a continuous attack on the "traditional school" of management. On the contrary, our objective has been to continue to build on, rather than tear down, the existing theory of management. The traditional views of management are just as basic to contemporary thought as algebra is important to the study of higher mathematics.

In Section 1, modern organizations are viewed in an overall framework. Emphasis is placed on the differences between organizations of today and yesterday, and attempts are made to predict the form of typical organizations of the future. Section 2 discusses basic systems concepts and applications.

In Sections 3 and 4, the planning function of management is analyzed in both business and governmental contexts. The latter section discusses the planning, programming, and budgeting cycle which has been instituted in the federal government.

Sections 5 and 6 deal with systems analysis —the application of systems concepts and scientific methods to the planning function of management.

Section 7 discusses the recent techniques of management that require the establishment of a management system having no functional or organizational constraints. This new concept of "interorganizational" management, called *project management,* emerged primarily from the needs of the Department of Defense and the National Aeronautics and Space Administration.

Section 8 deals with the question of evaluating organizational progress in the management process. The material examines the use of network analysis and the more traditional control techniques such as Gantt charts and other methods to measure the cost, schedule, and performance factors of organizational activities.

Section 9 introduces what promises to be a useful view of the management process—the charting of interorganizational relationships. The material in this section questions the use of the traditional organizational chart as a means of portraying the functioning of an organization and offers in addition thereto views of modern organizational patterns.

We wish to extend our thanks to Janet Wheeler, Betty Holt, and Pat Doorley Wagel who helped prepare the manuscript and performed many other kind acts of sympathy and assistance. We also wish to thank Lloyd Dunlap, Al Frey, and Jerry Zoffer for having contributed to environments which facilitated the accomplishment of our task. And, of course, we owe our greatest debt to the authors and copyright holders who kindly gave permission for us to use their material. Finally, our families, who are an intrinsic part of each of our undertakings, deserve at least a brief mention for their tolerance of their fathers.

DAVID I. CLELAND

WILLIAM R. KING

CONTENTS

INTRODUCTION

The modern organization—be it governmental, entrepreneurial, or ecclesiastical in nature—is undergoing radical changes in its basic structure, its method of operation, and its outlook on the world around it. This change is a revolutionary one, yet it is so unobtrusive that many people, even those who are a part of large organizations themselves, do not recognize that it is happening.

Since World War II, an ever-changing environment and the consequent changing responses to that environment have become the established patterns for most organizations. In effect, change has become a way of life.

The manifestations of change are apparent in the operations and makeup of virtually all large organizations. The organization's perception of its dynamic environment has resulted in conscious *planning for change,* in lieu of the established pattern of reacting to it. Moreover, new organizational forms have been developed to permit more flexible patterns of operation, so that in some of its salient features, the modern organization looks little like its pre-World War II predecessor.

Nowhere is the change which has taken place so apparent as in the organization's decision-making process. Formal *analysis* now plays an important role in decision making where once almost total emphasis was placed on executive judgment, experience, and intuition. The modern approach to decision making complements judgment with objective analysis built on a foundation of mathematics and statistics, thereby permitting a blending of the objective and subjective in a fashion which amplifies the executive's ability to cope with complex decision situations.

To understand the basic changes which are taking place, it is useful to begin by considering the organizational form which once was universal and is still pervasive—the *bureaucracy.*

BUREAUCRACY

The bureaucracy is characterized by a number of fixed jurisdictional areas, each with official duties and with individuals who have authority regarding the discharge of these duties. The "system" operates according to fixed rules of superior and subordinate. Individuals are appointed to official positions by superiors, and their status with respect to subordinates is guaranteed by rules of rank.

Bureaucracy has been the basic pattern of organization found in the traditional model of management. Although the bureaucratic form is usually associated with government organizations, the structure and processes of bureaucracy are found in many contemporary industrial organizations.

The bureaucracy's primary advantages have been argued by Max Weber.

> Bureaucratization offers above all the optimum possibility for carrying through the principle of specializing administrative functions according to purely objective considerations. Individual performances are allocated to functionaries who have specialized training and who by constant practice learn more and more. The "objective" discharge of business primarily means a discharge of business according to *calculable rules* and without regard for persons.[1]

Weber's phrase "without regard for persons" is of central importance to the bureaucratic concept, for the roots of the bureaucracy lie in basic assumptions about people and the way in which they are motivated. The bureaucratic view is that the "passions'" of humans must be strictly controlled by the organization in order to effectively direct their energies toward the accomplishment of the goals of the organization. The motivation of people under bureaucracy theoretically rested principally on economic matters. Frederick Taylor, "the father of scientific management," concentrated his attention on improving the efficiency of the individual in the work situation, to the detriment of the human relations aspect of management. Keith Davis summarizes Taylor's attitude towards the human element by stating: "To Taylor and his contemporaries, human problems stood in the way of production, and so should be removed."[2]

Advocates of the bureaucratic form of organization justified the organizational form and the management techniques in terms of the "principles" of management theory. The principles were often based on a complex of assumptions about organizational goals and processes, often unstated, and lacking empirical validation.

The concept of authority offers a good illustration. Authority is defined by the bureaucracy as the legal power to act. According to the bureaucratic tradition, goals are achieved by making them the explicit responsibility of some executive. Then, if that official is given sufficient legal authority (through a form of documented job description, organizational charter, etc.) and the necessary resources, the goal can be reached, regardless of its complexity. Once the executive determines the direction his organization will take, the process of the day-to-day accomplishment of the objectives becomes a matter of organizational routine. The significance of peer-to-peer and technician-to-generalist relations are neglected.

Of course, it is just not that simple. Rigid authority patterns do not assure the accomplishment of goals. In fact, it has been vividly illustrated that the inflexibility of the bureaucratic system may well not even be a good way of assuring a high *likelihood* of achieving goals. People are indeed important, and their motivations must be accounted for if goals are to be accomplished efficiently.

Perhaps the most incriminating assumption of the bureaucratic model concerns the verticality of the organizational form. When compared to the actual flow of work and organizational deliberations, many of the assumptions surrounding the principles seem to be based on a theoretical model of an organization which does not, in reality, exist. Modern organizations are taking on many different forms, thus testing the bureaucratic model of management which emphasizes the vertical flow of authority and responsibility. Structure in these modern organizations is being subordinated in favor of *processes* or *flows* of resources and relationships necessary to sustain the organization in its competitive environment.

Two primary conceptual developments have contributed to the evolution of modern organizations along nonbureaucratic lines. The first of these developments is the *systems concept*, and the second is the growing awareness of the significance of the organization's *human subsystem*.

[1] *Max Weber*, Essays in Sociology, *edited and translated by H. H. Gerth and C. Wright Mills*, Oxford University Press, Fair Lawn, N.J., 1946.
[2] *Keith Davis*, Human Relations at Work, *McGraw-Hill Book Company, New York, 1967, p. 9.*

THE SYSTEMS CONCEPT

Much has been written and said about the "systems concept" or "systems approach" in organizational thought. Much of this, particularly that said in the context of computer-oriented systems, is cloaked in an aura of mystery and sophistication which is unwarranted. The systems approach is neither new nor sophisticated. Neither is it necessarily related to the quantitative analyses which have made such great use of it.

It would indeed be presumptuous to credit the current generation of academicians and practitioners with the development of the systems concept in management. Although certain contemporaries have made significant contributions in integrating and conceptualizing the systems view,[3] the germ of the idea appeared as early as 1912.[4] Indeed, the use of the concept certainly precedes the use of the word "systems" to describe it.

A system may be defined in dictionary terms as "an organized or complex whole; an assemblage or combination of things or parts forming a complex or unitary whole." Thus, virtually everything is a system. The obvious contexts in which the layman uses the term, e.g., the Mississippi River system, the nervous system, etc., are appropriate to the definition. So, too, the universe is a system and so, too, is every organization a system.

In elementary terms, the systems approach may be thought of as requiring that the manager and analyst *adopt a view of as large a system as is practical.* Carried to the extreme, this says that each manager and analyst should consider their role and the implications of their actions on the universe. The obvious constraint, however, is the phrase "as is practical."

Thus, the systems approach in organizations is the antithesis of the bureaucracy with its neatly defined areas of endeavor and communications through the chain of command. The systems view presumes that interactions at all levels are analyzed and used to the advantage of the total system. Moreover, implicit in the systems approach is a deemphasis of the paro-

chial goals of functional units and a corresponding emphasis on total system performance.

Even management functions themselves have an interrelatedness and thus may be visualized as a system. Planning and organization precede control; yet to control we must have a standard against which to compare results and, when necessary, to correct performance. Development of corporate strategy in the planning process precedes the execution of that strategy; the development of strategy can do little for the organization if there is not a clear understanding as to where the responsibility rests for the execution of the strategy. Of course, the carrying out of the strategy requires different skills. Whereas the development of strategy requires analytical and abstract skills, the execution of the strategy requires administrative and "human" skills. Thus we see the interdependencies that exist in the management process when a parochial view, say in planning, can reduce and even endanger the efficacy of the total management system.

Product Systems

Some illustrations of the systems approach will serve to put the idea into focus. What, for instance, is the systems view of a company's product? The answer to this may be attained by asking about objectives—both the company's and the potential consumer's. If a cosmetics manufacturer thinks of his product objective as "selling face powder" and that of his customer as "buying face powder," he is not taking a systems view. The customer's desire is to buy *beauty* and the skillful manufacturer will therefore make it his objective to sell beauty. Obviously, face powder may be one phase of this, but it is not everything, and in fact, in the context of the views of others toward "beauty," it may play no role at all. Thus, the systems approach to marketing involves a recognition of the basic objectives of the consumer and plans for ways to fulfill those objectives. The skillful marketing system analyst will plan a *product system,* e.g., a complex of interrelated products and lines associated with beauty rather than one product or several unrelated products.

A simple illustration of a product system is the one whose elements are *color-coordinated* bedspreads, draperies and curtains, towels, etc.

[3] *See Richard A. Johnson et al.,* The Theory and Management of Systems, *McGraw-Hill Book Company, New York, 1967.*
[4] *See Henry P. Kendall,* Scientific Management: First Conference at the Amos Tuck School, Dartmouth College, *The Plimpton Press, Norwood, Massachusetts, 1912, p. 13.*

By relating the elements one to the other via their complementary function *and* their esthetic appeal, the marketing planner creates a system and takes advantage of the relationships among the elements of the system to increase total sales.

Organizational Systems

The systems approach to organization involves a view of as large a system as feasible in terms of its components and their relationships. In directing and operating an *organizational system,* the manager is faced with a desire for *overall effectiveness* coupled with conflicting *organizational goals.* Thus, each of the functional units of a large company has its own parochial goals, which may well be incompatible with one another. Perhaps the production department wishes to manufacture large quantities of few items in order to reduce costly machine setups and idle time, whereas the sales force desires inventories of a wide variety of items so that any order can be rapidly filled.

So, too, are there conflicting overall objectives of organizations. For example, a desire for profit and a desire for a satisfied work force are not always compatible since, at the superficial level at least, higher wages presumably contribute to lower profits and greater employee satisfaction.

In applying the systems view of an organization, one studies the constituent elements, e.g., the functional units, *and their relationships* and seeks to integrate them in a fashion which contributes to *overall goals.* (Of course, these overall goals are themselves potentially incompatible, so that some resolution of them must first be made.) Consequently, some functional units within an organization may not achieve their parochial objectives, for what is best for the whole is not necessarily best for each component of the system. Thus, when a wide variety of products are produced in relatively small quantities, the apparent performance of the production department may suffer. Yet, if this leads to greater total revenues because no sales are lost, the overall result may be positive. This simple realization is the essence of the systems viewpoint. Its acceptance and utilization has led many organizations to more effective management decisions and to organizing for the efficient execution of those decisions.

The basic difference between the bureaucratic view and the systems view is the difference between *structure* and *process.* The bureaucracy is a hierarchial structure. The systems view of the organization is one involving a set of *flows,* e.g., of information, people, material, money, and a "stream of projects," that represent the work which the organization performs.

Organizational Subsystems

Constituent elements of a total organization may themselves be viewed as systems. For example, the production subsystem is a system which is itself made up of people, machines, flows of products, flows of information, etc. There is also a marketing and financial subsystem within every business organization. Throughout these realizations of the systems concept lies the recognition that technological and social changes have made our economic and social institutions so complex and interdependent that the interactions among their parts and activities warrant as much attention as do their separate functions. This formal interaction between the parts of a system becomes the basis for the conceptual framework of the systems approach.

Other elements of the organization which cut across functional lines may also be viewed in the systems context. For instance, one may view the management information system of a company—that collection of reports, surveys, and other information which is collected and processed to provide a basis for decision making. The management information system, of course, also includes the people, data-processing equipment, models, etc., which contribute to the flow of information.

Applications of Systems Concepts

The systems concept and the modern ideas of human relations have reached fruition in changing organizations in two major areas of organizational management—planning and execution. The planning or *decision-making* aspect of organizations has been influenced by the systems approach through the application of *systems analysis.* In the execution phase of management, *systems (project) management* has been the focal point for the application of systems concepts.

Systems and planning.   One of the major changes which has occurred in organizational management in the past decade is the increasing emphasis on long-range planning. In a dynamic environment such as that in which most modern organizations function, it is necessary to do more than to react to changes in the environment. Long-range planning as a formal activity within an organization reflects the need for organizations to influence the future and to take advantage of the opportunities which it presents. That such opportunities will be available is self-evident. To plan for them requires an answer to the question: "What business should we be in?"

Planning for change requires viewing the company in the context of the greater system of which it is a part and in estimating future opportunity in terms of present-day decisions. Planning serves as the focus of organizational effort in assessing risk and uncertainty in the future. The proper pursuit of planning requires a flexible organization, particularly in terms of the attitudes and skills of the key executives. An organizational structure that is suitable for one product or market may not be suitable for others. Innovation in all the functional areas of a business can enable the organization to develop a system of plans which will influence its environment; the organization will not merely be responding to what it sees its competitors doing. If the organizational philosophy is based on the main tenets of bureaucracy, with its preoccupation of organizational verticality and fixed personal roles, then adherence to the existing order of affairs can be expected. If, on the other hand, the organizational executives do not want to tacitly accept their fate in the ensuing environment, the organization can influence its future.

In this respect, Dr. Fred Polak developed a theory that the future of a civilization, a country, or a people is determined in large measure by its "images of the future." He contends that it is possible to measure these images of the future, and it may be possible to alter or adjust them, thus guiding a nation's or people's future. According to Polak, if a society has optimistic ideas, dynamic aspirations, and cohesive ambitions, the civilization will grow and prosper. If it exhibits negative trends, uncertain ideals, and hesitant faith, the society is in danger of disintegrating. The idea again is that by thinking about the future, man creates that future according to his image.

The application of these ideas to business follow naturally according to Polak. Indeed, history shows that most great industrial enterprises have grown on the strength of an image of the future held consciously or subconsciously by their leaders.[5]

One of the more dramatic aspects of modern business planning is found in the changing executives' attitudes toward corporate objectives and strategy. Today's corporation faces rapidly changing environmental conditions coupled with intensive competition. The need for the formulation of an explicit corporate strategy has never been more acute. The business firm faces groups of "claimants," each seeking satisfaction of a particular claim. To say that the stockholder's claim of profit is superior to the claim of a customer who seeks the service of a product is to take a position inconsistent with today's social environment. From whose viewpoint should the corporate strategy be developed? The traditional view of a corporation would emphasize the common stockholder. On the other hand, one of the aims of capitalism is to encourage wide distribution of the benefits of political freedom and private property; thus, the claim of creditors, employees, customers, governments, and competitors, to name a few, must be factored into the development of the corporate strategy.

Long-range strategic planning and the systems concept are interrelated through *systems analysis*—the formal analysis of the strategic decisions of the organization. All organizations face a scarcity of resources; there is never enough of the resources required to do everything to the degree which one would like to do it. Thus, money allocated to product development is unavailable for advertising, and salesmen assigned to promote Product A are unavailable for promotion of Product B. The scarcity of resources implies a choice between alternatives, and complex choice situations involving great uncertainties are best handled through a combination of formal analysis and subjective judgment.

The reason for this is pragmatic rather than conceptual. The human mind is quite capable of performing analysis. Hence, it is possible that an individual could apply the systems con-

[5] *Weldon B. Gibson, as cited in "Guideposts for Forward Planning,"* Long-Range Planning for Management, *edited by David W. Ewing, Harper and Row, Publishers, Incorporated, New York, 1958, pp. 488–489.*

cept and perform a total systems analysis on a totally subjective basis. However, it is unlikely that anyone could actually do so in any but the most elemental variety of system. The human mind, as presently developed, can comprehend only so much at one time, and the application of the systems concept in decision analysis requires that many complexities and interrelationships between problem elements be considered. Even if the manager were able to reduce the complexities to manageable proportions by abstracting out all but the salient aspects, he has no guarantee that he can subjectively relate them in a fashion which is either logical or consistent.

Systems analysis is a combination of a set of tools, philosophies, and techniques which is designed to facilitate choices between alternatives in a fashion which maximizes the effectiveness of resources available to the organization. Basic to the analysis is the flow of information available to the firm. This information takes the form of intelligence about costs and the effectiveness of different ways of meeting organizational objectives. The information, both qualitative and quantitative, when properly developed and used by the decision maker, can provide a potent force in ensuring that the total volume of resources is effectively allocated to achieve organizational objectives.

The fields called *operations research, management science,* and *systems analysis* are those whose scopes encompass the application of objective scientific methods to the solution of management decision problems. Practitioners in each of these fields may rely on models—formal abstractions of real-world systems—to predict the outcomes of the various available alternatives in complex decision problems.

Because these models are usually symbolic, it is possible to reduce complex relationships to paper and, using techniques of logic and mathematics, to consider interrelationships and combinations of circumstances which would be beyond the scope of any human. Models permit experimentation of a kind which is unavailable in many environments; one may experiment on the model which describes a system without experimenting on the system itself.

Of course, this does not mean that the decision maker cedes his responsibility for making decisions to some mystical scientific process or that his judgment and intuition do not play a major role in decision making. By

the nature of the mathematics which are available, models have one of the same "deficiencies" as does the human brain in that they are able to consider only a part of the real-world decision problem. Other parts are omitted either as being relatively unimportant, or because they cannot be handled using existing techniques. The difference between explicit models and subjective decision analysis using nebulous "models" which exist in the mind of the manager is one of degree. The *process* is very similar, but explicit models formalize salient characteristics and relationships which may be blurred in the mind of a man. Explicit consideration is given to those aspects of the real-world situation which should be included in the model and those which should be abstracted out. Men tend to include in their "mental models" the first (or last) aspects which occur to them and to exclude others which stretch the bounds of their comprehension. Moreover, once the explicit model has been constructed, the objective approach has the guarantee of logic and consistency, which is not usually a feature of the application of judgment and intuition in problem-solving. The role of the manager's judgment and intuition is merely refocused by the systems approach. It is directed toward those aspects of problems which are best handled subjectively. The use of systems analysis provides insights into the problem in that it focuses attention on the important variables and identifies the areas where subjective judgment is required. The analysis clearly states the areas where judgments have been utilized and leaves them to be challenged and defended as necessary. This permits calm, expert judgment on each specific aspect, rather than gross judgments encompassing factors related to wide varieties of disciplines and areas of experience. The best illustration of this value of scientific problem analysis involves the *evaluative* and *predictive* judgments which are a part of most complex problems. The objective approach clearly separates those judgments related to *the worth of a state of affairs* (evaluative) and those related to *the future course of events* (predictive). In the mind of a decision maker, such judgments often become indistinguishable. For example, the executive concerned with a new product decision problem must necessarily predict the sales level to be anticipated and the worth of that sales level. The predictive aspect is independent of the organization's goals, whereas the evaluative one intrinsically depends on them. If both aspects are considered simultaneously, the executive is likely to become confused and achieve poorer results than he might if the two aspects were treated separately.

Another aspect of the refocusing of the manager's judgment through scientific analysis is that this approach involves utilizing judgment in integrating the results of objective analysis with the predicted effect of unconsidered problem elements, and arriving at a decision based on the totality of available information. In effect, the systems approach to planning may be viewed as a logically consistent method of reducing a large part of a complex problem to a simple output which can be used by the decision maker in conjunction with considerations, in arriving at a "best" decision. It permits him to focus his attention on the aspects of the problem which are most deserving and to restrict the attention which he allocates to those things which are best handled more formally. Such an integration of science and intuition permits consideration of the interrelationships of functional activities. In simple terms, it enables the manager to get the "big picture" in its proper perspective, rather than requiring (or permitting) him to devote attention to relatively minor aspects of the total system.

Systems and execution.   The systems concept has not only caused great changes in the planning or strategic decision-making portion of the manager's function, but has also caused revolutionary changes in the fashion in which decisions are executed. The most striking example of this is the emergence of *project management*. Today certain aerospace companies use project-management techniques in their commercial airplane divisions, and large chemical companies use project methods of management in their R&D activities.

The use of project techniques grew out of the need for a management philosophy to cope with the increasing complexity of product-development activities. Engineering-development contracts have generally increased in scope and have a better-defined beginning and end and more specificity of cost, schedule, and/or technology (performance). The pace of competition in product development requires large capital investment with increased risks

in timing of the product. The organizational arrangement necessary to focus management attention on an *ad hoc* project takes many forms; it essentially consists of *integral teams superimposed on the vertical structure of the organization.* The purpose of these teams is to provide a focal point for pulling together all functional aspects of the project. Yet there is another purpose, albeit subtle, of establishing such teams as a means of providing recognition, security, and a sense of contribution to the members of the unit whose individual efforts might otherwise be lost in the morass of functional bureaucracy.

In today's economy, any going concern is constantly confronted with a "stream of projects" that supplies the work for the members of the organization. Each project is in a different stage of completion; one may be merely a concept undergoing feasibility study, another in development, some in production, and some in the process of being phased out of the product line in favor of newer models. The application of systems ideas to this stream of projects, each with its own problems and peculiarities, implies that an individual be designated as Project Manager, with the responsibility for keeping abreast of all the company's work on that project. Project management, therefore, is a general management activity and includes such functions as planning, organizing, motivating, integrating, directing, and controlling efforts to obtain a specific goal. In many ways, project management is similar to functional or traditional management. The project manager, however, may have to accomplish his ends through the efforts of individuals who are paid and promoted by someone else in the chain of command.

The pacing factor in acquiring a new plant, in building a bridge, or in developing a new product is often not technology but management. The technology to accomplish an *ad hoc* project may be in hand but cannot be put to proper use because the approach to the management is inadequate and unrealistic. Too often this failure can be attributed to an attempt to fit the project to an existing management organization rather than *molding the management to fit the needs of the project.* The project manager, therefore, is somewhat of a maverick in the business world. No set pattern exists by which he can operate. His philosophy of management may depart radically from traditional theory. He may use established principles, but he uses them merely as guides to his thinking, for his way of operating may depart radically from the traditional. Furthermore, his task is finite in duration; when he accomplishes the project objectives, he no longer has a function, but must return to his functional organization or be assigned to manage an oncoming project. He is, in effect, constantly working himself out of a job.

The project manager's position is based on the realization that modern organizations are so complex as to preclude effective management using only traditional organizational structure and relationships. Top management cannot be expected to comprehend all of the details and intricacies involved in the management of each activity, be they weapons systems which are under development, products being marketed, or clients being serviced. Functional units properly give greater concern to their function than they do to individual products or projects. Thus, the need for a manager who can cut across traditional functional lines to bring together the resources required to achieve *project goals* is clear.

Just as the systems viewpoint necessitates consideration of the combined effect and interrelationships of various organizational functions in the manager's planning task, so, too, does it require integration of these functions at the execution level. The project manager is able to operate through the various functional managers in directing the resources which are necessary to the effective pursuance of a project. He is thereby able to focus his attention on *project goals* rather than on parochial production, marketing, or financial goals. As such, he serves as the instrument for implementing decisions in terms of the same structure in which they are made—the system.

THE HUMAN SUBSYSTEM

There is one universal resource found in all organizations—the human element; there are no "peopleless" organizations. Yet if one examines the traditional organizational chart as typical of the reality of organization form, he would reasonably assume that organizations are devoid of the human element. This is so because the pyramidal chart fails to display an adequate abstraction of the true interrelationships of people in their day-to-day activities.

We still depend on the hierarchial model of management as a basis for our organizational models—and in so doing continue to portray the vertical order of affairs and neglect the collateral relationships that make up the work-a-day business world.

In bureaucracy the human resource is viewed as an objective element whose rewards and punishments are based on a standard model of man motivated solely by economic factors and lacking ambition and a sense of responsibility.[6] The human element is looked upon as something which must be controlled via a system of rules, procedures, prescribed roles, and prescribed authority.

The modern view of the human element is vastly different from this view; the multidimensional nature of human motivation is well-recognized and accepted. Individuals are motivated for many reasons besides economic rewards. Social and psychological motivations are important as well. The group in which the individual works is of critical importance to the satisfaction of his desires, for these satisfactions are in the form of self-fulfillment, self-esteem, and the approval and acceptance of the social group. Today's accepted value systems recognize the need for the industrial organization to assume more social responsibility as well as to contribute to the economic well-being of the individual. The values resulting from such a view include the integration of the needs of the individual with the needs of the social group to which he belongs. In turn, by meeting individual needs in terms of human dignity, recognition, and self-actualization, the needs of the organization can be better met.

The increased recognition of the value of the human subsystem as it complements the technical one portends more complexity in the manager's job. This, together with the development of information systems which follow no lines on the organizational chart and the growing interdependence of social and economic relationships, are drastically changing the situation which the manager must face. The pace of technology has made many of our "tried-and-tested" management and organization theories obsolete. In order to survive, the business must prepare to adapt to these changes.

[6] *Fortunately this view has been successfully challenged. One of the best challenges is found in Douglas McGregor,* The Human Side of Enterprise, *McGraw-Hill Book Company, New York, 1960.*

manpower program directed toward establishing and maintaining an adequate and satisfactory work force. The program represents a set of potential values which must be converted through action into actual values in the form of desired human relationships that are conducive to cooperation and coordination of effort.

Transforming the potential of the manpower program is accomplished through a *manpower system*. This is the total flow of work required to make the program operate. It consists, in the main, of a number of inputs and outputs, and a number of sequentially related subsystems, processes, and activities. It provides for information retention and feedback from which the evaluation of results, corrective actions, and innovations may be undertaken and even new plans created. Successful operation of the system depends upon the various interrelated work flow systems that are activated through the release of information and authority.

A total manpower system is comprised of at least five separate subsystems: *employment, development, utilization, compensation,* and *maintenance* (see Figure 10-1). The shaded areas show possible divisions of work between personnel staff specialists and operating managers.

In brief, the climate and the nature of the work to be performed supply us with job-related information about the human requirements—skills, knowledge, attitudes, and performance standards—as well as required nonanimate factors. These inputs provide the means through which manpower is employed and capacities are developed, and through which both are put to best use.

Monetary and other values must be provided for satisfying individual wants and needs. Through safety and medical plans and proper consideration of employee relations, the work force is maintained. Feedback from each of the subsystems or from the total system takes a variety of forms and provides a built-in corrective feature.

The utilization system is perhaps the most vital of the subsystems because the effective use of manpower as a resource actually takes place within it. Herein is the greatest opportunity for professional personnel executives to increase their real value to both employees and managers. They are or should be uniquely qualified to communicate to operating managers by translating the findings of the behavioral science researchers into meaningful everyday language. As a result, leadership styles and expected work group behavior may become more compatible, satisfying, and productive.

A systems-oriented approach to manpower management integrates the role and function of the professional personnel executive with those of operating managers who will benefit most from his support.

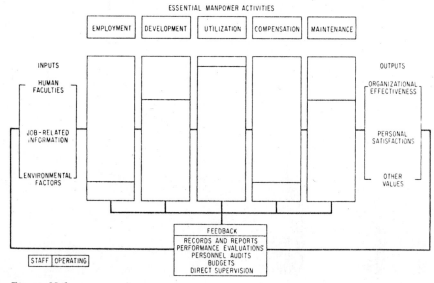

Figure 10-1

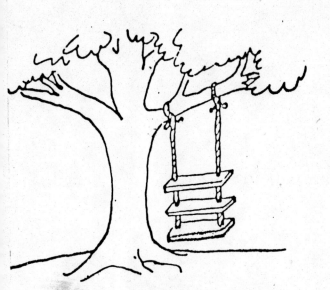

AS MARKETING REQUESTED IT

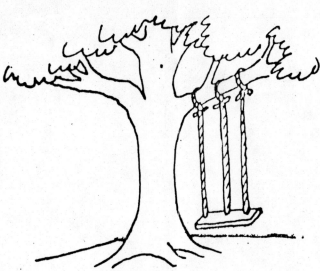

AS SALES ORDERED IT

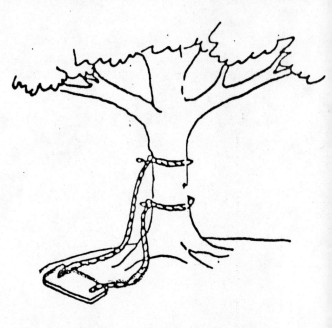

AS ENGINEERING DESIGNED IT

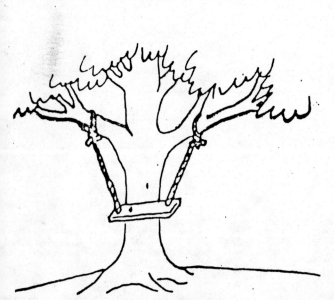

AS WE MANUFACTURED IT

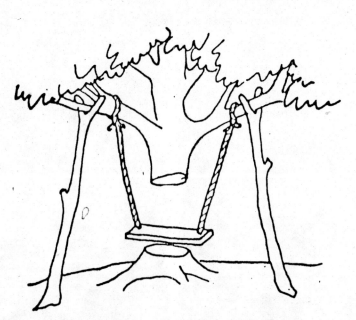

AS FIELD SERVICE INSTALLED IT

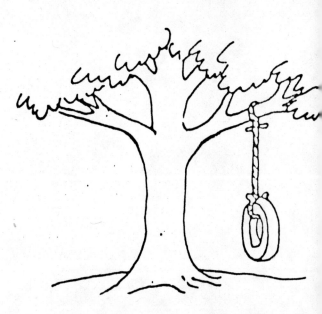

WHAT THE CUSTOMER WANTED!!!

 "COMMUNICATION" MEANS: SAYING AND HEARING HAVE THE SAME MESSAGE

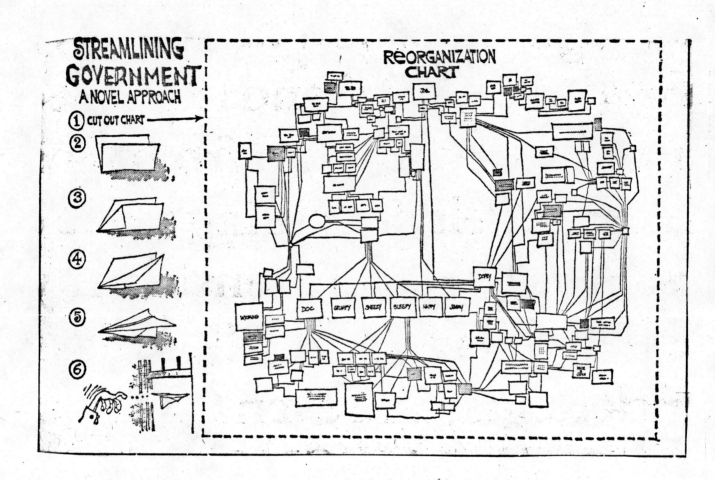

SECTION 1

Modern Organizations

Change has become a way of life in modern organizations. The people who manage these organizations are discovering that the traditional methods of planning and executing decisions, and indeed, the day-to-day organization and operating procedures of the enterprise, were not designed to function in such a climate.

The manager's perception of this dynamic environment has led to the institution of radical changes in organizations to enable them to effectively deal with these changes. These changes have centered around a departure from the traditional vertical structure of organization and have strengthened the role of peer-to-peer relationships that earlier management theory relegated to the "informal" organization. Organizational patterns have emerged which are multidimensional in nature as reflected by the "matrix" form.

The concept of a matrix organization evolves from the imposition of a "stream of projects" on the functionally aligned organization. Of course, "projects" are performed by all organizations whatever their structure may be. For example, the building of a new plant or the development of a new product each may be thought of as a project. However, a project may involve much more elementary activities, such as the gathering of information to complete a questionnaire which an industry association requests. If such a questionnaire must be partially completed by a number of functionaries and departments, it must flow through the organization in much the same fashion as do products, information, etc. This then is the essence of the matrix organization—a stream of ad hoc activities superimposed on the traditional functional organization.

Product management *is a marketing term used to describe an organizational pattern which is analogous to the matrix organization. The product manager is vested with responsibility for a given product or brand. At the extreme, he handles all phases of the marketing of a product—pricing, market research, advertising, promotion, etc. He does this in a fashion similar to the way he would operate his own business, and he is responsible for integrating and coordinating the activities of the functional departments which are concerned with the product.*

The concept of project *management, as it was initially employed in the development of weapons systems, and that of* product *management, which relates primarily to the execution of marketing plans for a product, can be effectively combined in an organization. For example, a project may be established to bring a product idea to marketing fruition. At that point, the life cycle of the project changes and a product manager assumes responsibility for marketing the product. Of course, some of the people may be involved in product management as well as in the project phase. However, many specialists whose talents are needed at one stage of development will not be needed at another, and almost certainly the same specialists will not be needed to execute marketing plans as were needed to develop the product.*

One way of viewing this relationship between project management and product management is in the composition of the project team. As different skills become necessary, the project's complement changes until, as fullscale marketing is embarked upon, most of the original people will no longer be involved. Usually, the project responsibility also transfers at this point from the project leader *to a* product manager.

In this Section, a series of papers which question the traditional model of organizations is followed by an introduction to some of the modern ideas of organizational structure—the "matrix" organization and product management. In the concluding paper, Max Ways considers both the changes which have occurred in today's organizations and the trends which will determine the future structure and operating methods of those enterprises.

READING 1

THE COMING DEATH OF BUREAUCRACY*

Warren G. Bennis

Not far from the new Government Center in downtown Boston, a foreign visitor walked up to a sailor and asked why American ships were built to last only a short time. According to the tourist, "The sailor answered without hesitation that the art of navigation is making such rapid progress that the finest ship would become obsolete if it lasted beyond a few years. In these words which fell accidentally from an uneducated man, I began to recognize the general and systematic idea upon which your great people direct all their concerns."

The foreign visitor was that shrewd observer of American morals and manners, Alexis de Tocqueville, and the year was 1835. He would not recognize Scollay Square today. But he had caught the central theme of our country: its preoccupation, its *obsession* with change. One thing is, however, new since de Tocqueville's time: the *acceleration* of newness, the changing

* Reprinted by permission from Think *Magazine*, published by IBM, copyright 1966 by International Business Machines Corporation.

scale and scope of change itself. As Dr. Robert Oppenheimer said, ". . . the world alters as we walk in it, so that the years of man's life measure not some small growth or rearrangement or moderation of what was learned in childhood, but a great upheaval."

How will these accelerating changes in our society influence human organizations?

A short while ago, I predicted that we would, in the next 25 to 50 years, participate in the end of bureaucracy as we know it and in the rise of new social systems better suited to the 20th-century demands of industrialization. This forecast was based on the evolutionary principle that every age develops an organizational form appropriate to its genius, and that the prevailing form, known by sociologists as bureaucracy and by most businessmen as "damn bureaucracy," was out of joint with contemporary realities. I realize now that my distant prophecy is already a distinct reality so that prediction is already foreshadowed by practice.

I should like to make clear that by bureaucracy I mean a chain of command structured on the lines of a pyramid—the typical structure which coordinates the business of almost every human organization we know of: industrial, governmental, of universities and research and development laboratories, military, religious, voluntary. I do *not* have in mind those fantasies so often dreamed up to describe complex organizations. These fantasies can be summarized in two grotesque stereotypes. The first I call "Organization as Inkblot"—an actor steals around an uncharted wasteland, growing more restive and paranoid by the hour, while he awaits orders that never come. The other specter is "Organization as Big Daddy"—the actors are square people plugged into square holes by some omniscient and omnipotent genius who can cradle in his arms the entire destiny of man by way of computer and TV. Whatever the first image owes to Kafka, the second owes to George Orwell's *Nineteen Eighty-four.*

Bureaucracy, as I refer to it here, is a useful social invention that was perfected during the industrial revolution to organize and direct the activities of a business firm. Most students of organizations would say that its anatomy consists of the following components:

A well-defined chain of command.
A system of procedures and rules for dealing with all contingencies relating to work activities.
A division of labor based on specialization.
Promotion and selection based on technical competence.
Impersonality in human relations.

It is the pyramid arrangement we see on most organizational charts.

The bureaucratic "machine model" was developed as a reaction against the personal subjugation, nepotism and cruelty, and the capricious and subjective judgments which passed for managerial practices during the early days of the industrial revolution. Bureaucracy emerged out of the organizations' need for order and precision and the workers' demands for impartial treatment. It was an organization ideally suited to the values and demands of the Victorian era. And just as bureaucracy emerged as a creative response to a radically new age, so today new organizational shapes are surfacing before our eyes.

First I shall try to show why the conditions of our modern industrialized world will bring about the death of bureaucracy. In the second part of this article I will suggest a rough model of the organization of the future.

There are at least four relevant threats to bureaucracy:

1 Rapid and unexpected change.
2 Growth in size where the volume of an organization's traditional activities is not enough to sustain growth. (A number of factors are included here, among them: bureaucratic overhead; tighter controls and impersonality due to bureaucratic sprawls; outmoded rules and organizational structures.)
3 Complexity of modern technology where integration between activities and persons of very diverse, highly specialized competence is required.
4 A basically psychological threat springing from a change in managerial behavior.

It might be useful to examine the extent to which these conditions exist *right now:*

1 *Rapid and unexpected change*—Bureaucracy's strength is its capacity to efficiently manage the routine and predictable in human affairs. It is almost enough to cite the knowledge and population explosion to raise doubts about its contemporary viability. More revealing, however, are the statistics which demonstrate these overworked phrases:

Our productivity output per man hour may now be doubling almost every 20 years rather than every 40 years, as it did before World War II.
The Federal Government alone spent $16 billion in research and development activities in 1965; it will spend $35 billion by 1980.
The time lag between a technical discovery and recognition of its commercial uses was: 30 years before World War I, 16 years between the Wars, and only 9 years since World War II.
In 1946, only 42 cities in the world had populations of more than one million. Today there are 90. In 1930, there were 40 people for each square mile of the earth's land surface. Today there are 63. By 2000, it is expected, the figure will have soared to 142.

Bureaucracy, with its nicely defined chain of command, its rules and its rigidities, is ill-adapted to the rapid change the environment now demands.

2 *Growth in size*—While, in theory, there may be no natural limit to the height of a

bureaucratic pyramid, in practice the element of complexity is almost invariably introduced with great size. International operation, to cite one significant new element, is the rule rather than exception for most of our biggest corporations. Firms like Standard Oil Company (New Jersey) with over 100 foreign affiliates, Mobil Oil Corporation, The National Cash Register Company, Singer Company, Burroughs Corporation and Colgate-Palmolive Company derive more than half their income or earnings from foreign sales. Many others—such as Eastman Kodak Company, Chas. Pfizer & Company, Inc., Caterpillar Tractor Company, International Harvester Company, Corn Products Company and Minnesota Mining & Manufacturing Company—make from 30 to 50 percent of their sales abroad. General Motors Corporation sales are not only nine times those of Volkswagen, they are also bigger than the Gross National Product of the Netherlands and well over the GNP of a hundred other countries. If we have seen the sun set on the British Empire, we may never see it set on the empires of General Motors, ITT, Shell and Unilever.

3 *Increasing diversity—Today's activities require persons of very diverse, highly specialized competence.*

Numerous dramatic examples can be drawn from studies of labor markets and job mobility. At some point during the past decade, the U.S. became the first nation in the world ever to employ more people in service occupations than in the production of tangible goods. Examples of this trend:

In the field of education, the *increase* in employment between 1950 and 1960 was greater than the total number employed in the steel, copper and aluminum industries.
In the field of health, the *increase* in employment between 1950 and 1960 was greater than the total number employed in automobile manufacturing in either year.
In financial firms, the *increase* in employment between 1950 and 1960 was greater than total employment in mining in 1960.

These changes, plus many more that are harder to demonstrate statistically, break down the old, industrial trend toward more and more people doing either simple or undifferentiated chores.

Hurried growth, rapid change and increase in specialization—pit these three factors against the five components of the pyramid structure

described on page 12, and we should expect the pyramid of bureaucracy to begin crumbling.

4 *Change in managerial behavior*—There is, I believe, a subtle but perceptible change in the philosophy underlying management behavior. Its magnitude, nature and antecedents, however, are shadowy because of the difficulty of assigning numbers. (Whatever else statistics do for us, they most certainly provide a welcome illusion of certainty.) Nevertheless, real change seems under way because of:

a. A new concept of *man,* based on increased knowledge of his complex and shifting needs, which replaces an over-simplified, innocent, push-button idea of man.

b. A new concept of *power,* based on collaboration and reason, which replaces a model of power based on coercion and threat.

c. A new concept of *organizational values,* based on humanistic-democratic ideals, which replaces the depersonalized mechanistic value system of bureaucracy.

The primary cause of this shift in management philosophy stems not from the bookshelf but from the manager himself. Many of the behavioral scientists, like Douglas McGregor or Rensis Likert, have clarified and articulated—even legitimized—what managers have only half registered to themselves. I am convinced, for example, that the popularity of McGregor's book, *The Human Side of Enterprise,* was based on his rare empathy for a vast audience of managers who are wistful for an alternative to the mechanistic concept of authority, i.e., that he outlined a vivid utopia of more authentic human relationships than most organizational practices today allow. Furthermore, I suspect that the desire for relationships in business has little to do with a profit motive per se, though it is often rationalized as doing so. The real push for these changes stems from the need, not only to humanize the organization, but to use it as a crucible of personal growth and the development of self-realization.[1]

The core problems confronting any organiza-

[1] *Let me propose an hypothesis to explain this tendency. It rests on the assumption that man has a basic need for transcendental experiences, somewhat like the psychological rewards which William James claimed religion provided—"an assurance of safety and a temper of peace, and, in relation to others, a preponderance of loving affections." Can it be that as religion has become secularized, less transcendental, men search for substitutes such as close interpersonal relationships, psychoanalysis—even the release provided by drugs such as LSD?*

tion fall, I believe, into five major categories. First, let us consider the problems, then let us see how our 20th-century conditions of constant change have made the bureaucratic approach to these problems obsolete.

1 *Integration.* The problem is how to integrate individual needs and management goals. In other words, it is the inescapable conflict between individual needs (like "spending time with the family") and organizational demands (like meeting deadlines).

Under 20th-century conditions of constant change there has been an emergence of human sciences and a deeper understanding of man's complexity. Today, integration encompasses the entire range of issues concerned with incentives, rewards and motivations of the individual, and how the organization succeeds or fails in adjusting to these issues. In our society, where personal attachments play an important role, the individual is appreciated, and there is genuine concern for his well-being, not just in a veterinary-hygiene sense, but as a moral, integrated personality.

The problem of integration, like most human problems, has a venerable past. The modern version goes back at least 160 years and was precipitated by an historical paradox: the twin births of modern individualism and modern industrialism. The former brought about a deep concern for and a passionate interest in the individual and his personal rights. The latter brought about increased mechanization of organized activity. Competition between the two has intensified as each decade promises more freedom and hope for man and more stunning achievements for technology. I believe that our society *has* opted for more humanistic and democratic values, however unfulfilled they may be in practice. It will "buy" these values even at loss in efficiency because it feels it can now afford the loss.

2 *Social influence.* This problem is essentially one of power and how power is distributed. It is a complex issue and alive with controversy, partly because of an ethical component and partly because studies of leadership and power distribution can be interpreted in many ways, and almost always in ways which coincide with one's biases (including a cultural leaning toward democracy).

The problem of power has to be seriously reconsidered because of dramatic situational changes which make the possibility of one-man

rule not necessarily "bad" but impractical. I refer to changes in top management's role.

Peter Drucker, over twelve years ago, listed 41 major responsibilities of the chief executive and declared that "90 percent of the trouble we are having with the chief executive's job is rooted in our superstition of the one-man chief." Many factors make one-man control obsolete, among them: the broadening product base of industry; impact of new technology; the scope of international operation; the separation of management from ownership; the rise of trade unions and general education. The real power of the "chief" has been eroding in most organizations even though both he and the organization cling to the older concept.

3 *Collaboration.* This is the problem of managing and resolving conflicts. Bureaucratically, it grows out of the very same social process of conflict and stereotyping that has divided nations and communities. As organizations become more complex, they fragment and divide, building tribal patterns and symbolic codes which often work to exclude others (secrets and jargon, for example) and on occasion to exploit differences for inward (and always fragile) harmony.

Recent research is shedding new light on the problem of conflict. Psychologist Robert R. Blake in his stunning experiments has shown how simple it is to induce conflict, how difficult to arrest it. Take two groups of people who have never before been together, and give them a task which will be judged by an impartial jury. In less than an hour, each group devolves into a tightly-knit band with all the symptoms of an "in group." They regard their product as a "masterwork" and the other group's as "commonplace" at best. "Other" becomes "enemy." "We are good, they are bad; we are right, they are wrong."

Jaap Rabbie, conducting experiments on intergroup conflict at the University of Utrecht, has been amazed by the ease with which conflict and stereotype develop. He brings into an experimental room two groups and distributes green name tags and pens to one group, red pens and tags to the other. The two groups do not compete; they do not even interact. They are only in sight of each other while they silently complete a questionnaire. Only 10 minutes are needed to activate defensiveness and fear, reflected in the hostile and irrational perceptions of both "reds" and "greens."

4 *Adaptation.* This problem is caused by

our turbulent environment. The pyramid structure of bureaucracy, where power is concentrated at the top, seems the perfect way to "run a railroad." And for the routine tasks of the 19th and early 20th centuries, bureaucracy was (in some respects it still is) a suitable social arrangement. However, rather than a placid and predictable environment, what predominates today is a dynamic and uncertain one where there is a deepening interdependence among economic, scientific, educational, social and political factors in the society.

5 *Revitalization.* This is the problem of growth and decay. As Alfred North Whitehead has said: "The art of free society consists first in the maintenance of the symbolic code, and secondly, in the fearlessness of revision. . . . Those societies which cannot combine reverence to their symbols with freedom of revision must ultimately decay. . . ."

Growth and decay emerge as the penultimate conditions of contemporary society. Organizations, as well as societies, must be concerned with those social structures that engender buoyancy, resilience and a "fearlessness of revision."

I introduce the term "revitalization" to embrace all the social mechanisms that stagnate and regenerate, as well as the process of this cycle. The elements of revitalization are:

1 An ability to learn from experience and to codify, store and retrieve the relevant knowledge.

2 An ability to "learn how to learn," that is, to develop methods for improving the learning process.

3 An ability to acquire and use feedback mechanisms on performance, in short, to be self-analytical.

4 An ability to direct one's own destiny.

These qualities have a good deal in common with what John Gardner calls "self-renewal." For the organization, it means conscious attention to its own evolution. Without a planned methodology and explicit direction, the enterprise will not realize its potential.

Integration, distribution of power, collaboration, adaptation and *revitalization*—these are the major human problems of the next 25 years. How organizations cope with and manage these tasks will undoubtedly determine the viability of the enterprise.

Against this background I should like to set forth some of the conditions that will dictate organizational life in the next two or three decades.

Dictates Organizational Life

1 *The environment.* Rapid technological change and diversification will lead to more and more partnerships between government and business. It will be a truly mixed economy. Because of the immensity and expense of the projects, there will be fewer identical units competing in the same markets and organizations will become more interdependent.

The four main features of this environment are:

Interdependence rather than competition.
Turbulence and uncertainty rather than readiness and certainty.
Large-scale rather than small-scale enterprises.
Complex and multinational rather than simple national enterprises.

2 *Population characteristics.* The most distinctive characteristic of our society is education. It will become even more so. Within 15 years, two thirds of our population living in metropolitan areas will have attended college. Adult education is growing even faster, probably because of the rate of professional obsolescence. The Killian report showed that the average engineer required further education only 10 years after getting his degree. It will be almost routine for the experienced physician, engineer and executive to go back to school for advanced training every two or three years. All of this education is not just "nice." It is necessary.

One other characteristic of the population which will aid our understanding of organizations of the future is increasing job mobility. The ease of transportation, coupled with the needs of a dynamic environment, change drastically the idea of "owning" a job—or "having roots." Already 20 percent of our population change their mailing address at least once a year.

3 *Work values.* The increased level of education and mobility will change the values we place on work. People will be more intellectually committed to their jobs and will probably require more involvement, participation and autonomy.

Also, people will be more "other-oriented," taking cues for their norms and values from their immediate environment rather than tradition.

4 *Tasks and goals.* The tasks of the organi-

Organic Adaptive Structure

zation will be more technical, complicated and unprogrammed. They will rely on intellect instead of muscle. And they will be too complicated for one person to comprehend, to say nothing of control. Essentially, they will call for the collaboration of specialists in a project or a team-form of organization.

There will be a complication of goals. Business will increasingly concern itself with its adaptive or innovative-creative capacity. In addition, supragoals will have to be articulated, goals which shape and provide the foundation for the goal structure. For example, one might be a system for detecting new and changing goals; another could be a system for deciding priorities among goals.

Finally, there will be more conflict and contradiction among diverse standards for organizational effectiveness. This is because professionals tend to identify more with the goals of their profession than with those of their immediate employer. University professors can be used as a case in point. Their inside work may be a conflict between teaching and research, while more of their income is derived from outside sources, such as foundations and consultant work. They tend not to be good "company men" because they divide their loyalty between their professional values and organizational goals.

5 *Organization.* The social structure of organizations of the future will have some unique characteristics. The key word will be "temporary." There will be adaptive, rapidly changing *temporary* systems. These will be task forces organized around problems-to-be-solved by groups of relative strangers with diverse professional skills. The group will be arranged on an organic rather than mechanical model; they will evolve in response to a problem rather than to programmed role expectations. The executive thus becomes a coordinator or "linking pin" between various task forces. He must be a man who can speak the polyglot jargon of research, with skills to relay information and to mediate between groups. People will be evaluated not vertically according to rank and status, but flexibly and functionally according to skill and professional training. Organizational charts will consist of project groups rather than stratified functional groups. (This trend is already visible in the aerospace and construction industries, as well as many professional and consulting firms.)

Adaptive, problem-solving, temporary systems of diverse specialists, linked together by coordinating and task-evaluating executive specialists in an organic flux—this is the organization form that will gradually replace bureaucracy as we know it. As no catchy phrase comes to mind, I call this an organic-adaptive structure. Organizational arrangements of this sort may not only reduce the intergroup conflicts mentioned earlier; it may also induce honest-to-goodness creative collaboration.

6 *Motivation.* The organic-adaptive structure should increase motivation and thereby effectiveness, because it enhances satisfactions intrinsic to the task. There is a harmony between the educated individual's need for tasks that are meaningful, satisfactory and creative and a flexible organizational structure.

There will also be, however, reduced commitment to work groups, for these groups will be, as I have already mentioned, transient structures. I would predict that in the organic-adaptive system, people will learn to develop quick and intense relationships on the job, and learn to bear the loss of more enduring work relationships. Because of the added ambiguity of roles, time will have to be spent on continual rediscovery of the appropriate organizational mix.

I think that the future I describe is not necessarily a "happy" one. Coping with rapid change, living in temporary work systems, developing meaningful relations and then breaking them—all augur social strains and psychological tensions. Teaching how to live with ambiguity, to identify with the adaptive process, to make a virtue out of contingency, and to be self-directing—these will be the tasks of education, the goals of maturity, and the achievement of the successful individual.

In these new organizations of the future, participants will be called upon to use their minds more than at any other time in history. Fantasy, imagination and creativity will be legitimate in ways that today seem strange. Social structures will no longer be instruments of psychic repression but will increasingly promote play and freedom on behalf of curiosity and thought.

One final word: While I forecast the structure and value coordinates for organizations of the future and contend that they are inevitable, this should not bar any of us from giving the inevitable a little push. The French moralist may be right in saying that there are no delightful marriages, just good ones; it is possible that if managers and scientists continue to get their heads together in organizational revitalization, they *might* develop delightful organizations—just possibly.

I started with a quote from de Tocqueville and I think it would be fitting to end with one: "I am tempted to believe that what we call necessary institutions are often no more than institutions to which we have grown accustomed. In matters of social constitution, the field of possibilities is much more extensive than men living in their various societies are ready to imagine."

READING 2

THE DECLINE OF THE HIERARCHY IN INDUSTRIAL ORGANIZATIONS *

William H. Read

Impact of Technological change on corporate structure

Has today's executive really faced the impact of technological changes on corporate structure and function? Although such changes force industrial leaders to rethink and readjust relationships between manager and manager, manager and specialist, and specialist and specialist, deeply-rooted organizational tradition may make the transition a stressful one.

THE BUREAUCRATIC TRADITION

The bureaucratic tradition, and the set of beliefs that underlie it, emerged from nineteenth century notions about the theory and practice of administration, and has survived since then despite progressive changes in the administrative process. It deals with the nature of authority relations, leader and follower interaction, the division of administration into "higher," "middle," and "lower" management, and the way in which business organizations function.

* Reprinted by permission from Business Horizons, Fall, 1965.

Four interrelated assumptions are contained in the bureaucratic tradition. *First,* the central, crucial, and important business of an organization is conducted up and down the vertical hierarchy. This general process can be described as information organized into certain patterns and passed upward through management levels, while decisions and directives based on this information are passed downward. In this way, according to tradition, organizations function. *Second,* the bureaucratic tradition sees the corporate body as something like the human body in that it has a kind of central nervous system (chain of command) with a spine going up the back, and a brain on top (top management), which does most, if not all, of the directing and steering of important matters. *Third,* the vertical (authority) levels of an organization roughly correspond to levels or gradations of talent and competence. In general, the higher up one goes, the more talent, the more daring, and the more dedication one finds in that organization's mission. *Fourth,* by far the most important single type of relationship in an organization is the superior-subordinate one. If this relationship is healthy and productive, success follows naturally, according to the bureaucratic tradition, since it is in the vertical dimension of organizations that the business is done.

It should be emphasized that however facetiously they have been stated here, these assumptions have provided the philosophical fabric that has united many diverse activities and individuals into what we have come to know as the corporation—people, performing functions, directed toward the achievement of specified goals.

What then is wrong with the bureaucratic tradition? Surely the authority or "line" or administrative system is an absolutely necessary component of a business organization. But is it sufficient? Or rather, is it as sufficient now as it once was? According to some modern scholars of administration,[1] the authority system, the "vertical" of a modern business organization, tends to remain the dominant, at times almost exclusive, structural feature of the modern corporation, long after technological change has created an urgent need for equally powerful organizational machinery to smooth out the lateral flow of decisions, requests, and data.

Perhaps this protest is a bit too strong. But the contemporary business executive should now be willing to entertain the idea that the current system or pattern of managerial action in the modern corporation is rapidly becoming outmoded and considerably overemphasized. Irresistible pressures are now being exerted on corporations, even moderate-sized ones, to change. The pressure stems chiefly from technological change—from the fast-paced revolution in the type and use of hardware, in the type, use, and processing of information, in the systematization and integration of even the simplest jobs and processes and, particularly, in the computerization of an enormous range of business decisions.

These changes are forcing a new appraisal of the relations, authority and otherwise, between people in a modern corporation. Yet many management people are resisting this force—either actively or passively, consciously or unconsciously. Traditions resist change and

so do people; old ways of doing things, established ways of thinking and reacting, are always more comfortable.

A NEW TRADITION

Perhaps then we ought to look again at the bureaucratic tradition, and counter its four major sets of assumptions with a new set. *First,* the central, crucial, and important business of organizations is increasingly shifting from up and down to "sideways"—from the vertical or line organization to the *lateral* or *horizontal.* *Second,* vertical levels of an organization no longer represent roughly the distribution or gradation of talent or brains in an organization. More and more, talent is where you find it, and both talent and creativity are quite often boxed off to one side with only fuzzy provisions for them to function in the mainstream of the organization. The reference here is to highly skilled and talented specialists who have inherited the title "staff group." *Third,* superior-subordinate relationships in an organization, though obviously important, no longer guarantee by their harmony that everything will be all right any more than there is a guarantee that the human body will function effectively with a healthy nervous system but with injured organs.

In a nutshell, the structure of corporations is changing and in fact must change to cope with the impact of complex and sophisticated technological systems. Complex information flow systems, plus the staggering rate of transformation of hand-operated or semi-automatic production and office machinery into automatic, centrally-controlled machine systems, are creating a proliferation of highly skilled specialists, and an even greater proliferation of need for their services. Not only the size, but the skill and influence of these specialized staff groups are deepening and accelerating. The significant point is that these specialists do not fit neatly into a chain-of-command system, cannot easily be lumped together and called "staff," cannot wait for their expert advice to be approved at a higher level, and cannot function effectively if their expertise is shrugged off by recalcitrant old-timers. The corporation manager needs them and needs them badly, just as the expert badly needs the "generalists" among management who can grasp, evaluate, and coordinate specialist work.

These changes now taking place make the

[1] F. J. Jasinski, "Adapting Organization to New Technology," Harvard Business Review, XXXVII, no. 1 (January-February, 1959), 79–86.

effective coordination of specialists the major problem of effective organizational functioning. They are increasingly forcing the manager in the modern corporation to look, work, and think sideways—to establish working relationships laterally with his specialist peers and to de-emphasize vertical relationships with his boss or subordinate.

Some Evidence of Change

For some time now it has been evident that lateral or horizontal relations are more vital to the efficiency of a production organization than was formerly recognized—and that the peer-colleague is the key person in the organizational world of the executive. Yet in our concern for superior-subordinate relations, our heavy emphasis on "man management," and the willingness of industrial leaders to spend enormous sums on human relations training, we have neglected this dimension of organizations.

Some years ago, a group of social scientists conducted an exhaustive study of jobs and worker-supervisor relations in a U.S. automotive plant.[2] They discovered that, contrary to expectations, the boss (foreman) actually did not exert much influence in the workplace. His role was important, but much more as a technician than as a supervisor, much more as a troubleshooter and human monitor of a complex flow system than as a leader. More important than this, though, his major function seemed to be to get the operators fast help when they needed it: help from specialists on or close to his own administrative level—methods men, maintenance experts, and production schedulers. The study indicated that the system itself did a good part of the supervising; the foreman, who had little direct personal contact with the operators, served as liaison between them and the system, and between them and the experts.

A somewhat similar result was seen in a more recent study of manager-worker relations in a textile mill.[3] As mechanization in the mill increased, a corresponding increase occurred in the rate of cross-communication between

supervisors on the one hand and other supervisors and experts on the other. The most important function of the supervisor was not to link management and the worker, not even to coordinate closely with management levels, but to short-circuit and bypass upper-level management in order to get fast, on-the-spot decisions from specialists. The absence of managerial intervention, not the effectiveness of it, was the key to success.

In view of the deeply rooted traditions of administration outlined above, these events represent a staggering change in thinking, action, and decision making in organizations. It means that the classical management function of motivating subordinates, making decisions on the basis of collated data passed upward, and introducing changes in procedure may well be in the process of atrophy. As one writer has recently stated, we are headed for a "working society of technical co-equals" and the "line of demarcation between the leader and the led has (already) become fuzzy."[4]

The Obsolete Square

In this vein, consider a very simple example of old, transitional, and new ways in which decisions, requests for services, and other messages are routed in a production or office department. In the production department of a certain manufacturing organization, a large-scale changeover had been made from semi-automatic to automatic machinery. For maintenance service in all but the simplest problems, prior to the change, the established procedure had been for the operator to route the request upward through his own foreman, who signalled the maintenance chief, who designated the appropriate serviceman (Figure 2-1). This practice was continued after the introduction of high-speed machinery, in order to maintain control, and expensive delays resulted. The routing system, diagramed below, had become obsolete and dysfunctional.

The system was soon streamlined by introducing a diagonal route (Figure 2-2), which eliminated one delay point (the operator's boss) and, incidentally, almost completely bypassed the traditional chain of command.

[2] *C. R. Walker, R. H. Guest, and A. N. Turner,* The Foreman on the Assembly Line *(Cambridge: Harvard University Press, 1956).*
[3] *R. L. Simpson, "Vertical and Horizontal Communication in Formal Organizations,"* Administrative Science Quarterly, *IV (1959), 188–96.*

[4] *J. A. Raffaele, "Automation and the Coming Diffusion of Power in Industry,"* Personnel, *XXXIX (1962), 30.*

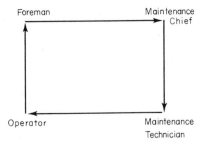

Figure 2-1   The obsolete square.

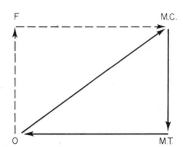

Figure 2-2   The diagonal.

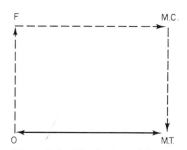

Figure 2-3   The horizontal line.

At present, management is somewhat nervously considering a complete short-circuiting of the command chain in order to eliminate delays and speed the entire process. The horizontal, direct route will have replaced the authority structure in one small segment of the organization.

Figure 2-3 illustrates, however roughly, the crucial importance not only of lowering the coordination function in the organization, but also of developing a formally sanctioned, nonauthority, or semi-authority, relationship between production operator and specialist. The operator must now be more than an operator; he must be an accomplished coordinator.

Horizontal and diagonal coordination, always important, will now be the major human

problem of the new industrial revolution. Yet, unlike the problem of supervision, no clear program, no ideology, and no techniques have been developed for handling it. In many ways, it is a greater problem than that of authority relations, which has occupied management for a century or so. Relations between expert and manager, between expert and expert, and between manager and manager are in some ways more vulnerable than those between boss and subordinate. A major hurdle is presented by the dichotomy between men of thought and men of action (expert and manager), a natural division that rarely exists between a man and his supervisor. Because of radical differences in their training and background, it is very difficult for a production chief to grasp the function and outlook of a system analyst, and vice versa. The problem is even greater with the expert-to-expert relationship, that is, it is even harder for the personnel psychologist to see eye to eye with experts involved in the computerization of an office. Yet both must cope with the problem of radical changes in manpower and skills in a particular office setting.

ALTERNATIVES FOR CHANGE

What broad courses of planning and action are open to industrial leaders in dealing with the impact of technology? The first alternative is to change people: their attitudes, perspectives, and outlooks. The revolution now taking place in our industrial system in both factory and office is going to require a different pattern of management skills. In addition, these changes are going to demand a different type of specialist, with a broader perspective, with as sharp an insight into human and organizational relationships as into mathematical and mechanical ones, and even more crucial, with the vision and wisdom to deal with the greater influence that will be his. Retraining and re-education, then, suggest one major course for preparatory action. The company training classroom and the university campus can be equally effective settings for manager and specialist to interact and to exchange skills and outlooks, with the university offering special short-term training programs.

A second line of preparatory action is to change the form of the organization. The reorganization of tasks, the restructuring of formal organizational relationships, and even the phasing out of some aspects of the traditional hierarchical form of organization have already been accomplished in a few of the more technologically advanced U.S. corporations. In Task Force and Weapons System[5] management, for example, rigid spans of control, and sharp hierarchical leveling, are being abandoned or severely modified in favor of closely coordinated, integrated teams or project groups that cut across functional levels, largely circumvent chains of command, and contain often astounding degrees of skill-mix. The result is a sink or swim confrontation of the problems of horizontal coordination. In an even newer organization form, Rotated Organization Structure (ROS),[6] management functions are completely bifurcated into planning and operating, with rotation, by time period or project, of personnel between these two functions. Thus specialists are *ipso facto* responsible for doing as well as planning. Management generalists, conversely, must plan as well as do.

It is, in short, quite possible that the only truly effective methods for preventing, or coping with, problems of coordination and communication in our changing technology will be found in new arrangements of people and tasks, in arrangements which sharply break with the bureaucratic tradition. In either case, by changing people or changing organizations, a reappraisal of our traditional methods of achieving organizational goals is urgently in order.

[5] *Fremont E. Kast and James Rosenzweig, "Weapons System Management and Organizational Relationships,"* Journal of the Academy of Management, IV (1961), 188–205.

[6] *Ronald J. Ross, "Rotating Planners and Doers,"* Harvard Business Review, XL (1962), 105–16.

READING 3

MATRIX ORGANIZATION *

John F. Mee

A matrix organizational design has evolved in the flow of aerospace technology; changing conditions have caused managers to create new relationships of established organizational concepts and principles. A matrix organization is used to establish a flexible and adaptable system of resources and procedures to achieve a series of project objectives. The figure on the next page is a conceptual framework for a matrix type of organization. It illustrates the coordinated or matrix system of relationships among the functions essential to market, finance, and produce highly specialized goods or services.

From a divisionalized organization structure has emerged a new way of thinking and working to create products dependent upon advanced research and urgency for completion. Time and technology factors forced a more efficient utilization of human talents and facilitating resources.

* Reprinted by permission from Business Horizons, Summer, 1964.

The traditional divisional type of organization permits a flow of work to progress among autonomous functional units of a specific division. A division manager is responsible for total programs of work involving the products of his division. In a matrix organization, the divisional manager has the same responsibility, authority, and accountability for results. Differences occur in the division of work performed as well as in the allocation of authority, responsibility, and accountability for the completion of work projects.

If work performed by an operating division of a company is applied to standardized products or services with high volume, there is no need to consider a matrix organizational design. The total work can flow through the division with each functional group adding its value and facilitation to the completion of the production process. The total work can flow along and among the functional groups of production to a market. The emphasis is on the efficiency of the flow of work.

It is when work performed is for specific

[handwritten notes: NO NEED FOR MATRIX — Standardized Product vs specific project — Need]

project contracts that a matrix organization can be used effectively. If the market for a product is a single customer such as the U.S. Air Force or an industrial firm with a prime governmental contract, the production emphasis changes to the completion of action for a specific work project instead of a flow of work on production programs for product volume. In the illustration of the aerospace division (Figure 3-1), the emphasis is on the completion of specific work projects, namely, Venus project, Mars project, and Saturn project. Additional projects may be added as new contracts are signed by the marketing group. As projects are completed or abolished, they are deleted from the organization; it is a fluid organization.

A matrix type of organization is built around specific projects. A manager is given the authority, responsibility, and accountability for the completion of the project in accordance with the time, cost, quality, and quantity provisions in the project contract. The line organization develops from the project and leaves the previous line functions in a support relationship to the project line organization.

The project manager is assigned the number of personnel with the essential qualifications from the functional departments for the dura-

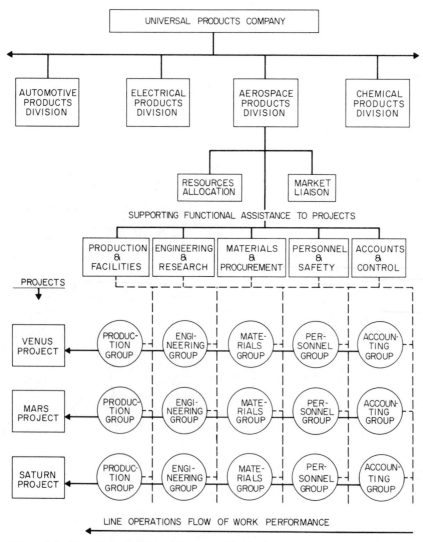

Figure 3-1 Matrix organization. (Aerospace Division).

tion of the project. Thus the project organization is composed of the manager and functional personnel groups. With responsibility and accountability for the successful completion of the contract, the project manager has the authority for work design, assignment of functional group personnel, and the determination of procedural relationships. He has the authority to reward personnel with promotions, salary increases, and other incentives while the project is in progress. He also has the authority to relieve personnel from the functional group assignments. Upon completion of the project, the functional group personnel return to the functional departments for reassignment, or transfer to other divisions or training programs to develop their skills and knowledge. The project manager is also available for reassignment by the division manager or company president.

Management by project objectives or results is paramount to the way of thinking and working in a matrix type of organization. The group organizational personnel perform the line operational work to complete the project. The department functional personnel give support assistance to the line projects such as policy guidance, technical advice, and administrative services. In a matrix organizational chart, the line operations may be illustrated horizontally as the functional groups are aligned to achieve a specific project. The support assistance from the functional departments appears vertically in relationship to the series of projects undertaken by the division.

The concept of a matrix organization entails an organizational system designed as a "web of relationships" rather than a line and staff relationship of work performance. The web of relationships is aimed at starting and completing specific projects. An over-all divisional function of resource allocation for multiple projects determines the priority of resources for specific projects and measures progress against contract requirements.

American managers possess a proud record of ingenuity in creating new organizational schemes to adapt to changing technological and economic requirements. The matrix organizational design is no exception. It permits a higher degree of specialization for human talents with maximum efficiency of operations. New techniques for systems management, information economics, and information systems, as well as improved production planning and control systems, are developing to advance more sophisticated organizational relationships of work, people, and coordinated procedures. Managerial and technical personnel will require new knowledge and skills as well as modified attitudes.

Unless managers and operating personnel are educated and trained to work in the developing organizational designs, they can suffer frustrations, emotional disturbances, and loss of motivation. Working in an environment characterized by change as projects are started and completed is not as comfortable and secure as performing a continuing function in a more stable standardized work flow situation.

Although the matrix organization emerged to improve work performance in the aerospace industry, other alert industrial managers can adapt the concept for uses in new product or market developments in a marketing dominated economy.

READING 4

PRODUCT MANAGEMENT: PANACEA OR PANDORA'S BOX *

Robert M. Fulmer

Despite its climb to popularity during the recent "marketing revolution," product management has failed to satisfy the hopes of some of its more optimistic adopters. The divergence between the highly touted theoretical potentials of product management and the conflict and confusion which occasionally followed its adoption has led some observers and practitioners to conclude that this organizational innovation is an impractical, unworkable, and unrealistic method of centering responsibility for the success of a product or product line. Yet, without question, there are several large, multiproduct companies where product management has provided a remarkably efficient method for coordinating and focusing the functional activities of the firm so as to gain a maximum amount of attention and activity for each product marketed.

How can the same concept be both a panacea and a Pandora's box?   A cursory analysis

* *Reprinted from* California Management Review, *vol. VII, no. 4, Summer, 1965. Copyright 1965 by The Regents of The University of California.*

of published reports and empirical observations of product management in practice reveal that most of the difficulties mentioned revolve around the following problems: authority, selection, and definition.

Authority: how much and what kind?   While it is impossible to give a universal answer to this question, it is unlikely that companies which exact responsibility for total product success without granting commensurate authority can expect the same results as a firm where the product manager is used as a coordinative center of authority to insure unified effort on behalf of each product. Similarly, it is doubtful that a staff assistant, salesman, or clerk can be as effective in working for a product's over-all success as the "president of a company within a company." Yet, positions with such varying degrees of authority are often discussed together under the heading of product management. This article will not attempt to provide an exact recipe for the authority and responsibility to be given product managers, but an overview of the existing spectrum of product-oriented positions will be given and conclusions drawn as to the practicality of this indiscriminate classification.

Selection: traits or training?　Obviously, the ability to delegate authority and exact responsibility will depend on the talents of the employees involved and the degree to which these talents have been cultivated or utilized. There is no magic in the product management concept; consequently, the idea can be no more effective than the men who fill the positions.

Some companies find it desirable to recruit men expressly for development as product managers. Other firms feel that prior experience in one of the company's functional departments is essential. Certain general managerial traits such as the ability to accept responsibility, to think creatively and practically, to act quickly, and to work harmoniously with other departments are necessary. In every instance, a period of training directed toward the requirements of product management will increase effectiveness. Staffing problems are as unique as individual companies; therefore, any detailed analysis would be applicable only in the situation studied. The reservoir of available managerial talent certainly must be considered in any attempt to plan or evaluate the use of product management.

Definition: does everyone understand?　Almost every problem found in product management literature relates, in some way, to improper or misunderstood definitions. A primary step in the solution of difficulties connected with authority delegation and selection is a definite statement of the requirements of the position. With this as a foundation, authority can be delegated and individuals can be selected and trained in view of the requirements. While a general understanding of the terms used in discussing product management is important for all persons interested in this aspect of organization, the need for specificity is paramount for intrafirm understanding. In other words, if a term is misused, it can still prove of value if all personnel within a firm have the same understanding of its meaning.

I will attempt to move toward possible clarifications of these problems by analyzing the various ways in which different practitioners and scholars approach them, discarding the obviously incorrect, and discussing the relative merits of the acceptable theories.

A CONFUSING HISTORY

Origin of product management.　The history of product management provides an interesting insight into its initiating philosophy and can serve as a yardstick by which the later developments may be compared. Product management in its initial form appears to have first been practiced as brand management at Procter and Gamble nearly forty years ago. Since that time, product management has produced an outstanding genealogy (probably including such ramifications as project management, task teams, and, of course, brand management in its various forms). Some of these successors bear little resemblance to the original form of this organizational innovation. Perhaps the multiplicity of members in the product management family has made it difficult to pinpoint the exact birth of the idea. Certainly no aspect of this subject provides a better illustration of the misunderstanding and confusion which pervade the literature. Consider, for example, several absolute statements as to the origin of this idea.

The concept of product management is not new. Probably it originated in the retail trade, in this case in the department stores.[1]

Since the product manager concept was originally developed by General Electric in the early 1950's, most large companies have adopted the approach in one way or another.[2]

The product manager originated accidentally—first as an assistant sales manager with an interest in a particular product or group of products.[3]

An analysis of the concept's history will provide some clues. The product manager's job was created primarily to fill a critical need. In large, multiproduct companies, it has always been difficult to be certain that each product received the attention and support it merited from each of various functional activities of the business, especially manufacturing, marketing, and sales. . . . Therefore, to meet this need, the product manager form of organization was created.[4]

It has been suggested that the rapid expansion of product lines and the need for developing specialized marketing strategies about specific products were the key points indicating a need for the product management function. ... Initially the task of the product manager was one of a coordinator, trying to harmonize the manufacturing and marketing activities associated with his products. Gradually authority was delegated to him to make decisions regarding product improvement, packaging, pricing, field selling, advertising, etc. As authority was increased, the final responsibility for profits and market position was delegated to him.[5]

Often mistakenly thought of as a comparatively new marketing creature, in Procter and Gamble, the brand manager goes back to 1931, when now-chairman Neil McElroy formalized that role in the company.[6]

It is possible that the idea of having one individual with primary responsibility for a group of products originated in the department store; however, the department head of a retail store is no more a product manager than is the production chief of a factory producing similar items or any manager with responsibility for some phase of the life cycle of one or more related products.

General Electric is often credited with ushering in the marketing concept with its reorganization in the early 1950's. While this distinction is somewhat dubious, without question there were companies employing product managers before the 1950's.

The position referred to as "product manager" in some companies may have evolved from "an assistant sales manager with an interest in a particular product or group of products." There is, however, little evidence that this title was so applied before 1928, and, as will be discussed later, there is reason to challenge the accuracy of using the title to describe specialized sales positions.

CREATION OF THE BRAND MAN

Although, and perhaps because, they lack any degree of specificity as to date and source of origin, it is difficult to question the statements cited from Ames or Schiff and Mellman previously quoted. There should be universal agreement that the job of product manager was created to fill the need to provide vigorous product-by-product leadership for multiproduct companies. This view is supported in the *Printers' Ink* article of September 28, 1962, in which Procter and Gamble's Neil McElroy is credited with originating that company's brand-

man organization in 1931. Actually the brand-man system began its evolution in this company even earlier. In January, 1928, Mr. C. C. Uhling was made Procter and Gamble's first brand manager when Lava soap was assigned to him. Later, brand-man assignments were made for Oxydol and Camay.[7] In 1931, the recommendation of McElroy was instrumental in refining the brand-man system and in making it a company-wide concept. This refinement consisted basically in the creation of the brand group hierarchy composed of an assistant brand man, who was to perform much of the detail involved in the management of a particular brand and to serve as an understudy of his superior; the brand man; and the brand-group supervisors, each responsible for reviewing the work of two to four brand managers, who reported to the head of the brand-promotion division.[8] To date, this company has enjoyed almost unparalleled success with little change in orientation or scope of the concept.

It is impossible to determine all the factors which influenced the thinking of those associated with the birth and development of this idea. However, it is possible that the reorganization of Du Pont and General Motors several years before had helped initiate the thought processes which led to this evolution by providing a working example of the product-oriented divisionalization. Ease of coordinating, by brand, the activities of advertising agencies was another possible contributing factor.[9] Certainly, the primary motivation appears to have been the desire to guarantee individual management for each of a number of products.

WHAT DOES THE TITLE MEAN?

What is a product manager?   Perhaps a portion of the problems besetting product management stem from a fundamental lack of understanding or confusion about what is meant by the term. There is a wide spectrum of meanings attached to this term which were not implied at its birth.

One extreme of the range is found in firms such as the National Biscuit Company where one product manager handles everything that pertains to the products except the actual selling—among his responsibilities are product quality, packaging, marketing, advertising, and promotion programs. One product manager handles these responsibilities for Dromedary cake mixes, nut rolls, pimientos, dates, fruits, and peels.[10] In essence this job could be accurately referred to as vice-president of a product division or simply as a division manager; the same holds true where the term "product manager" is used to describe General Electric's general managers. This is somewhat equivalent to calling the head of General Motors' Chevrolet Division a product manager. To avoid confusion, it is wise to differentiate between the titles of the executive who is in charge of a multiproduct division and the manager who has responsibility for a single product.

Examples of companies where real product or brand managers have extensive responsibility would include the following:

> At **Pillsbury,** the man who bears the title, brand manager, has total accountability for results. He directs the marketing of his product as if it were his own business. Production does its job, and finance keeps the profit figures. Otherwise, the brand manager has total responsibility for marketing his product. This responsibility encompasses pricing, commercial research, competitive activity, home service, and publicity coordination, legal details, budgets, advertising plans, sales promotion, and execution of plans.[11]

> Each of **Kimberly-Clark's** brand managers is responsible for drawing up complete marketing programs for his brand. ... In addition (to serving as advertising manager for his product), the brand manager is responsible for recommending marketing objectives for his brand, planning marketing strategy, drawing proposed budgets, initiating new projects and programs, and coordinating the work of all functional units concerned with the production, financing, and marketing of the product.[12]

> At **Colgate-Palmolive,** product managers are responsible for developing plans and programs that will establish brand leadership and enlarge the current and long-range share of market and profits for their brands. These plans include advertising and promotional programs and budgets, selection of distribution channels, forecasts of sales and inventory requirements, forecasts of manufacturing costs, and, as final objectives, projections of profit and share of market on the brands.[13]

> Men employed for this work (at Proc-

ter and Gamble) are trained to accept the responsibility for the effectiveness of the over-all advertising and promotion effort on an important nationally advertised brand. ... These positions involve working with many company departments, including research and development on product development, the sales department on the development of promotions and also with the advertising agency on all phases of consumer planning for the brand.[14]

At the other end of the spectrum from these consumer-oriented producers are some companies such as **Minneapolis-Honeywell** where:

> ... the divisional executives in charge of selling temperature controls to the school market decided to appoint a "product manager" ... who was charged with the broad responsibility of securing more business in this field.... Basically a salesman ... sales management must select its man with great care.[15]

In his study of the semi-conductor industry, Bucklin observed that product managers were frequently required to spend 50 percent of their time in calling on accounts.[16] Ames refers to an anonymous company where a product manager's role is really limited to maintaining sales statistics and performing a variety of high-grade clerical tasks.[17] Mauser makes the general claim that: "Sales managers for products may be given the simple title of product manager."[18]

R. H. Buskirk recognizes the divergent uses of the product manager title and asserts that: "The dimensions of his job vary widely from company to company, sometimes embracing all the activities of product management and sometimes being limited to the sales promotion of the products in his care."[19]

It appears that Professor Buskirk believes that a product manager does not necessarily handle the work of product management, for he defines product management as:

> The planning, direction, and control of all phases of the life cycle of products, including the creation or discovery of ideas for new products, the screening of such ideas, the coordination of the work of research and physical development of products, their packaging and branding,

their introduction on the market, their market development, their modification, the discovery of new uses for them, their repair and servicing, and their deletion.[20]

From a descriptive standpoint, there is no doubt that in many companies "product managers" find their positions much more narrow than the description of product management. A normative view, however, should place considerable emphasis on bringing these two concepts together. The problem of management semantics, eloquently recognized by Col. Lyndall Urwick,[21] will continue to rear its ugly head and breed confusion and misunderstanding as long as commonly used terms such as these two have such a diversity of meaning and application.

While it is impossible to generalize from one article, a recent German publication[22] indicates that such confusion may not be so prevalent in that country. While the brand manager system is practiced only by some companies which are based in the United States and a few German firms in the food, detergent, and electrical industries, it is evidently practiced quite satisfactorily. If the German experience is indeed less chaotic than product management history in the United States, it may be due to the fact that United States companies are not likely to export the concept until they have eliminated most of the major difficulties in domestic practice. Consequently, a descriptive definition of product management in Germany should provide helpful insight into a type considered hardy enough to export. A review of the article suggests the following areas of product management activity:

1 Marketing analysis (product, packaging, price, assortment, channels of distribution).
2 Setting of marketing goals.
3 Long- and short-range planning and budgeting.
4 Coordination of work done by departments within a company as well as by "outsiders" (marketing research, selling, advertising, public relations, production, technical research, financing).
5 Control.[23]

In a report prepared for the Financial Executives' Research Foundation, Schiff and Mellman describe the product manager as "the executive responsible for product manage-ment."[24] This definition may appear to be circular reasoning, but it may be expanded to say that a product manager must manage something; if he does not exercise the managerial functions of planning, direction, and control in relation to the entire scope of a product's immediate existence, he is something less than a product manager and should be appropriately renamed. Though overly simple, this is infinitely superior to saying that a product manager does not necessarily manage a product or that he may manage only one aspect of its existence. This definition does not require that all phases of a product's life cycle (from idea origination to termination of production) be exclusively the domain of one individual, but it does require management as one of the identifying characteristics of a product manager.

The product manager and his authority.

> The (product manager) concept is an organization anomaly in that it violates a proven management precept—that responsibility should always be matched by equivalent authority ... (he is) a member of the management group with high level responsibility for getting a product to market without any line authority over the full range of activities required to get the job done.[25]

An equally extreme position concerning the product manager is taken by R. H. Jacobs who asserts:

> His is not, in essence, a management job but a staff job whose sole responsibility is to secure wider sales of one or more specific items in the line.[26]

Practically speaking, the major problem in applying the product-manager concept may well be how much and what kind of authority to delegate. The quotations cited above indicate that little, if any, line authority is available to the product manager to carry out his myriad responsibilities. Bucklin found that the lack of real authority was the basis for many of the problems encountered by product managers in the semi-conductor firms.[27] *Printers' Ink* reports that, at Merck & Co., "each product manager is a staff member whose primary function is to plan for the growth and profitability of his markets."[28] The same publication generalizes:

> Few companies sharply delineate the product manager's area of operations, as between line and staff function; most of them give him heavy responsibility, though not with commensurate authority.[29]

It is small wonder that the product manager concept has recently been receiving sharp criticism. It is impossible to imagine that a manager can coordinate and manage all aspects of the life cycle of a product with his hands tied in a manner such as described above. Fortunately, this situation is not universal. In those companies which give the product manager the responsibility for product management, there appears to be general agreement that such responsibility must be matched with comparable authority. At least the product manager is not always an "organization anomaly." Professor Edward Bursk has well summarized:

> We have reached the point where we need solid action that cuts across the traditional, functional lines of marketing, finance, manufacturing, research, and so on. Finance may have to consider the desirability of capitalizing initial heavy promotional expenses, manufacturing may have to build inventories faster than is apparently economical. . . . All in all, there must be one man or one office to see that all these steps are taken as part of a unified effort. . . . Those in charge may be merely in a staff capacity, or may have varying degrees of line authority depending on how far this concept (usually referred to as product or brand management) has developed.[30]

In a similar vein, Professor Hepner states that the product manager's job requires that he be endowed with authority to get things done:

> Product managers are a kind of "general manager.". . . The product manager, working under the general direction of a top manager or executive, decides how products shall be made, the quantities to be made, the chains of distribution for each, its packaging, pricing, advertising, and promotion. The product manager is

more than a coordinator—he is the final authority whose decisions affect the profits to be made from his products.[31]

A previous attempt was made to define **product manager** so as to include only those individuals who were responsible for **product management**. At this point, it is proper to add to that definition the requirement that he should also possess adequate authority to handle the needs of his position. This apparently obvious truism has not been universally understood. While this authority cannot be absolute, unlimited, or unchecked, it must exist in sufficient quantity to allow use of the product manager's specialized knowledge and abilities. Bursk's poignant implication that the amount of line authority delegated is an indication of the degree to which the product-management concept has developed should provide real understanding of the product manager's job. There are clearly many companies where the concept, while supposedly employed, is in a state of considerable immaturity.

The product manager in practice. As employed in several companies, the product manager may have line authority in one specialized area of operation—advertising, sales, etc., or perhaps more commonly, general marketing—and functional authority (a slice of delimited line authority which cuts across organizational lines)[32] for the coordination of the activities of other departments **as they relate to his product:** For example, he might be directly in charge of advertising plans for the product and at the same time work closely with liaison members of the sales, market research, legal, art, production, merchandising, and sales promotion, packaging, and public relations departments. In his dealings with these departments, he is able to direct them to supply the services necessary to insure the maximum efficiency of the marketing program for his product. Under most circumstances, the representative of the service department works with several brand or product managers and, with proper planning, should be able to handle their various demands without undue conflict.

AN EXAMPLE

To illustrate, consider a typical situation where a sales force handles all of a division's six products. The very real problem of having all six product managers requesting special emphasis for their products' fall promotion could be handled by coordinative planning or appeal to a final authority. Promotional plans for the year should spell out which brands are free to promote in each selling period. At the time of plan formulation, questions and potential conflicts should be worked out between the individual product managers working in concert with their immediate superior and the division's sales manager. While the product manager focuses the coordination of the company's functional and service activities toward his product, in this case, the marketing division manager would probably hold the final power of decision to insure over-all coordination. Should situations arise during the year which forced deviations from the plan, the division manager would again serve as the ultimate appeal. Similar situations could, of course, be presented that would apply to relations with other functional or service departments.

From the foregoing discussion, it can be seen that, since he cannot hold total line authority such as is exercised by the president of a one-product company or by the division manager of a single-product division, the optimum use of the product manager should come when he is used as coordinating executive in charge of managing all component parts of the marketing mix of one particular product or brand and subject primarily to the final coordination of a superior in charge of the entire division or company.

LIMITS OF AUTHORITY

Functional authority is never absolute; therefore, the product manager does not have complete authority over all departments in the marketing program. In dealing with production, for example, his authority would have to be limited to the range of alternatives considered by production to be technically feasible. The legal department would, of necessity, determine limits to the potential activities of the brand; market research should be free to determine what research projects are practical and likely to provide the desired information; accounting would need the ability to limit activities to the financially feasible, etc. In other words, these departments could and should set parameters of operation within which the

product manager should be free to work and, in turn, to request the services of and/or direct the activities of these departments within the limits which they themselves have set.

The authority level principle[33] (which implies that for any problem there is a level of authority at which a decision can be made for its resolution) provides one remedy for conflicts which might result from this reciprocal interdependence. Many problems can, however, be avoided by careful planning and definition of the product manager's tasks, authorities, and responsibilities.

The product manager—how far from ideal? Paradoxically, the perfect product manager is not a product manager at all. Probably the only person who would completely satisfy the definition given would be the president of a single-product firm. Obviously, the concept has wider applicability than this. Many firms have attempted to approach the ideal by adopting what is frequently referred to as the "little general manager approach." In these cases, however, there must be a "big general manager" to coordinate activities and to resolve conflicts arising from the divergent points of view held by various product managers. Other companies approach the problem by giving product managers authority only to advise. We have indicated in the preceding discussion, however, that staff specialists should not be considered in the same category as the true product manager.

As mentioned above, no product manager can possess final line authority if several executives are employed in this capacity. Similarly, if only staff authority is employed, the product manager is no longer able to manage his product. The answer obviously lies in the judicious delegation of functional authority.

While the specific responsibilities of the product manager will vary according to the needs of a particular situation or the interest of the individual company adopting the concept, the rule of thumb for allocating authority must be that the product manager should always have sufficient authority to discharge the responsibilities associated with or assigned to his position. Unless this basic tenet of management theory is recognized, the product manager can be nothing more than an "organization anomaly" completely incapable of satisfying the demands made of him. This places a large measure of the success of product management in the realm of position description; for without adequate definition at this level, commensurate authority cannot be made available.

A very similar organizational concept, although it usually has an engineering or production orientation rather than a marketing emphasis and is usually less permanent than product management, is project management. Basically,

> Project management is a general management activity encompassing planning, control, supervision, and the engineering or manufacturing involved in producing the end item. . . . The project manager has very specific objectives which, when achieved, mean the end of his function. He usually has no line authority over the organizations producing the items which he must deliver. . . . Communications must be very clear, prompt, comprehensive, and frequently cut across intercompany and intracompany lines.[34]

Baumgartner suggests that although project management had its origin during World War II, it was 1958 before companies began to set up organization structures which superimposed a horizontal project organization on vertical functional lines.[35]

Figure 4-1 shows such an organization cutting across functional lines in order to accomplish project objectives.

A more familiar method of showing the relationship of product and project managers to other departments is the so-called "grid management" approach shown in the simplest form in Figure 4-2.

In project management, as with product management, it is impossible for complete authority to be granted in the various areas of responsibility. But at the same time, absolute responsibility cannot be exacted in these areas.

Figure 4-1 Organizational structure.

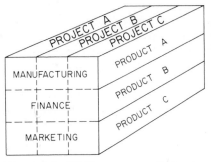

Figure 4-2 "Grid management" structure.

It would be incorrect to refer to a product manager as "ideal" only when he possesses complete line authority for each of his myriad responsibilities; in fact this would be chaotic even if it were possible. A situation is ideal when it functions efficiently in its particular environment.

MEANING VS. APPLICATION

Managers of products, markets, and marketing. Understanding of product management has been substantially clouded by an overlapping of several related terms. Articles referring to the concept have lumped together positions from sales promotion assistants to corporate vice-presidents under the general heading, product management. A primary emphasis of this paper has been to focus attention upon the disparity between the meaning of product management and the misapplication of this term throughout management literature. It is not enough, however, to say that the term has been incorrectly used, or to say that a spade should be called a spade. Some suggestion should be made as to the proper classification of those positions which have been shorn of the "product manager" appellation. Without attempting to use a currently popular buzzword to cover a multitude of positions and without particular emphasis on originality, why not merely call these positions what they are? For example, where one authority states, "Sales managers for products may be given the simple title of product manager,"[36] would it be too homely to refer to this position as a "product sales manager"? Similarly, would it not be preferable to refer to the executive in charge of selling to the school market as a "market manager" since he was "charged with the broad responsibility of securing more business in this field"?[37] Ames' reference to a product manager whose role was limited to keeping sales statistics and performing clerical tasks sounds very much like a "sales department staff assistant."[38]

While it is often correct to refer to a product manager as a marketing manager for a product, frequently his responsibilities are so broad that he is, in effect, the general manager of a "company."

> Companies have adopted the product division approach, centering, in effect, the general management of a "company within a company" on the shoulders of the product manager. He is generally given complete authority to the full extent of his responsibilities and is held accountable for the profit of his division.[39]

In instances such as the one illustrated, the title would more appropriately be "Marketing Manager-Product Division" or "Product Division Manager." (Since the authors had previously referred to the head of product divisions at General Foods, it is assumed that the manager is in charge of several related products. If only one product were in a division, the terms "product manager" and "division manager" could be used interchangeably. Although this situation would seldom occur, the status impli-

cation of the two terms would probably make "division manager" more desirable.)

The *Printers' Ink* product manager who "is interested in developing a broad line of products for use in his markets"[40] is not a true product manager because of his "broad line of products" and his market orientation. He is probably a divisional market manager. Again, the reference to a product manager with 203 products[41] probably refers to a division manager (the article does not indicate if he is a complete marketing manager or is oriented toward a single market).

From this discussion, it is possible to segregate the positions described in the section, "What is a product manager?" into the following titles:

1 **Division manager**—The executive who has the authority and responsibility to manage (or as Buskirk would say, "plan, direct, and control"[42]) the life cycle of a group of related products. (See Figures 4-3 and 4-4.)
2 **Marketing manager**—The executive who has the authority and responsibility to manage all the marketing activities for the products in a company or division. (See Figures 4-3 and 4-4.) In cases where the so-called "marketing concept" is employed, it is common for this official to have line authority over marketing activities and considerable functional authority over production and finance.

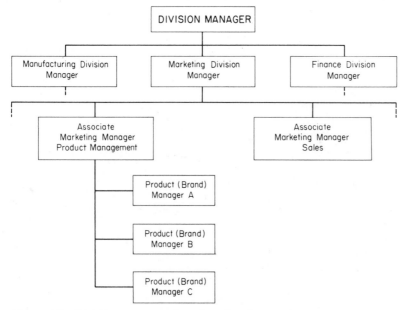

Figure 4-3   Division manager and product/brand manager organization.

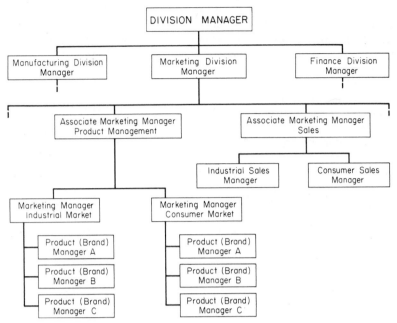

Figure 4-4 Division manager, market manager, and market product manager organization.

3 **Product manager**—The previously mentioned Schiff and Mellman definition should be refined as follows: the executive with primary authority and responsibility for the planning, direction, and control of all phases of a product's current existence. (See Figure 4-3.) This definition does not imply that the product manager has final or unrestricted authority or responsibility for all aspects of a product's life. Under the "marketing concept," however, functional authority belonging to the marketing manager is often delegated to the individual product managers for their products and is, of course, subject to review by the marketing manager.

4 **Market product manager**—This position occurs when "the market manager may be so specialized that he devotes his attention to a single product for a single market."[43] This, however, is unusual. (See Figure 4-4.)

5 **Brand manager**—In most instances today, products are not sold but brands.[44] When purchases of products are made on the basis of brand preference, it is more accurate to refer to the executive responsible for managing the life cycle of the item as a brand manager. This is particularly true when one company markets competing brands within one product category. (See Figure 4-3.)

6 **Product specialist**—Unquestionably, there are instances where a staff position can be a valid way to insure individual attention and interest for each product in a company's line without creating the problems of company-wide coordination which the delegation of extensive functional authority may require. If an individual has only the authority to suggest the marketing program for his product and then must negotiate with the other areas of the company for services to implement these plans, he does not possess a manager's ability to take decisive action and should not be called a product or brand manager. Rather, it seems that the contributions which such a position can offer in some situations could be made with equal effectiveness (and less confusion) if it were recognized as a different variety and called "product specialist."

GUIDELINES

Product management: still no panacea. Without doubt, the practice of product management is replete with potential pitfalls for the unskilled practitioner. The problem of the concept's scope has particularly manifested itself in the areas of authority, responsibility, and definition. A universal answer to the initial question of how much and what kind of authority the product manager should have can still not be given. A safe generalization, however, would be that sufficient authority must be granted to achieve the requirements of the position. A product or brand specialist with only staff authority lacks the quick, decisive power to act which can make the most effective use of his specialized knowledge and interest. Considerable functional authority is often given to the product manager because of his importance as a coordinating influence and because of the need to equate authority and responsibility. In order to avoid, or at least to minimize, conflict, functional authority thus delegated should be subject to over-all coordination one or, at the most, two levels immediately above the product manager.

Obviously, authority cannot be delegated, employees cannot be properly selected or trained, performance cannot be evaluated, and responsibility cannot be exacted until there is agreement on the meaning and scope of the position involved. An attempt has been made to evolve reasonable guidelines for classification of positions in the product management phylum. Operative definitions have been suggested as a means of revealing distinctions in the areas of activity and in the performance expected from various types of product-oriented organizations. Clarity is frequently a function of adequate understanding, and understanding begins with definition. This emphasis on semantics was aptly worded by Confucius: "If names be not used correctly, then speech gets tied up in knots; and if speech be so, then business comes to a standstill."[45]

References

1. "Why Modern Marketing Needs the Product Manager," *Printers' Ink*, CCLXXII (Oct. 4, 1960), 25.

2. Robert W. Lear, "No Easy Road to Market Orientation," *Harvard Business Review*, XLI (Sept.-Oct. 1963), 58.

3. R. H. Jacobs, "The Effective Use of the Product Manager," American Management Association, Marketing Series No. 97, 196, p. 31.

4. B. Charles Ames, "Pay Off From Product Management," *Harvard Business Review*, XLI (Nov.-Dec., 1963), 142.

5. Michael Schiff and Martin Mellman, *Financial Management of the Marketing Function* (New York: Financial Executives Research Foundation, Inc., 1962), pp. 28–29.

6. "What Makes P & G so Successful," *Printers' Ink*, CCLXXX (Sept. 28, 1962), 31.

7. Letter of Dec. 9, 1963, from C. C. Uhling, Manager, Public Relations Department, Procter and Gamble Company.

8. Procter & Gamble, "Intra-Company Product Competition," *Problems in Marketing, No. 2*, Students' Material, 1956, p. 1. Also see Alfred Lief, *It Floats* (New York: Rinehart & Co., 1958), p. 181.

9. Lief, *ibid.*, p. 182.

10. "Product Management: What Does It Mean?" *Sales Management*, April 17, 1959, p. 42.

11. Robert J. Kieth, "The Marketing Revolution," *Journal of Marketing*, XXIV (Jan. 1960), 35.

12. *Printers' Ink*, Oct. 14, 1960, *op. cit.*, p. 26.

13. "Career Opportunities with Colgate-Palmolive Company," a recruiting brochure, p. 4.

14. "Opportunities in Advertising," *What Now?* a Procter & Gamble recruiting brochure, p. 10.

15. R. H. Jacobs, *op. cit.*, p. 16.

16. L. P. Bucklin, "Organizing the Marketing Function in a Growth Industry," *California Management Review*, IV:2 (Winter 1962), 45.

17. Ames, *op. cit.*, p. 141.

18. F. F. Mauser, *Modern Marketing Management* (New York: McGraw-Hill Book Co., 1961), p. 57.

19. R. H. Buskirk, *Principles of Marketing* (New York: Holt, Rinehart, and Winston, Inc., 1961), p. 623.

20. *Ibid.*

21. See Lyndall F. Urwick, "The Problems of Management Semantics," *California Management Review*, II:3 (Spring 1960).

22. E. R. Weger, *Die Absatzwirtschaft*, March 1963, pp. 131–134.

23. W. K. A. Disch, "Review of *Die Absatzwirtschaft*," *Journal of Marketing*, XXVII (Oct. 1963), 116.

24. Schiff and Mellman, *op. cit.*, p. 246.

25. Ames, *op. cit.*, p. 142.

26. Jacobs, *op. cit.*, p. 16.

27. Bucklin, *op. cit.*

28. *Printers' Ink*, Oct. 14, 1960, *op. cit.*, p. 27.

29. *Ibid.*

30. Edward C. Bursk, *Text and Cases in Marketing* (Englewood Cliffs, N.J.: Prentice-Hall, Inc., 1962), p. 499.

31. H. W. Hepner, *Modern Marketing* (New York: McGraw-Hill Book Co., 1955), p. 448.

32. Based on Harold D. Koontz and Cyril O'Donnell, *Principles of Management* (New York: McGraw-Hill Book Co., 1964), p. 272.

33. *Ibid.*, p. 63.

34. J. S. Baumgartner, *Project Management* (Homewood, Ill.: Richard D. Irwin, Inc., 1963), p. 112.

35. *Ibid.*, p. 6. Figure 4-1 is also adapted from this source.

36. Mauser, *op. cit.*, p. 57.

37. Jacobs, *op. cit.*, p. 20.

38. Ames, *op. cit.*, p. 141.

39. H. Lazo and A. Corbin, *Management in Marketing* (New York: McGraw-Hill Book Co., 1961), p. 81.

40. *Printers' Ink*, Oct. 14, 1960, *op. cit.*, p. 27.

41. *Ibid.*, p. 30.

42. Buskirk, *op. cit.*, p. 623.

43. Lear, *op. cit.*, p. 58.

44. See B. Gardner and S. J. Levy, "The Product and The Brand," *Harvard Business Review*, LIII (March-April 1955), 33–39.

45. Quoted by Lyndall F. Urwick, *op. cit.*

READING 5

TOMORROW'S MANAGEMENT: A MORE ADVENTUROUS LIFE IN A FREE-FORM CORPORATION*

Max Ways

What industrialization was to the nineteenth century, management is to the twentieth. Almost unrecognized in 1900, management has become the central activity of our civilization. It employs a high proportion of our educated men and determines the pace and quality of our economic progress, the effectiveness of our government services, and the strength of our national defense. The way we "manage," the way we shape our organizations, affects and reflects what our society is becoming. The essential task of modern management is to deal with change. Management is the agency through which most changes enter our society, and it is the agency that then must cope with the environment it has set in turbulent motion. To carry out its active social role of adaptation, management itself, therefore, must be adaptable. Already the nature of management has undergone drastic alterations. As it stands today on the threshold of the final

third of its first century, modern management seems pregnant with another metamorphosis. It is now possible to see in outline the shapes toward which the next generation of management will tend.

One of the more obvious questions of the last ten years has been whether the number of management men will continue to expand faster than the economy. Will many of the millions now pouring forth from the universities find that management is a contracting job market in which they will be surplus? The question is currently linked with predictions about the computer revolution. Without doubt, computers have taken over some work formerly done by middle management, and are capable of taking over much more. But this fact is only a part of the whole busy scene. Management is still expanding and probably will continue to expand as new tasks are created. Indeed, the new information technology represented by computers is one of the important factors creating the new tasks.

A less obvious question raised by the com-

* Reprinted with permission of Fortune *Magazine,* July 1, 1966.

puters bears on the character, rather than the size, of future management. Will instant access by top management to operational information reverse the trend toward managerial decentralization, which has had the salutary effect of giving more independent scope to more people? It is easy to think of examples where authority now dispersed might be efficiently reconcentrated at the top with the aid of computers. But such reconcentration is not the main trend in organization today. Since the new information technology began coming into use in the Fifties, the trend toward decentralization has probably been accelerated, indicating that there were better reasons for decentralization than the lack of instant information at headquarters. Computers can be used to reinforce either a centralizing policy or its opposite; the probability increases that decentralization will in the coming decades be carried to lengths undreamed of ten years ago.

Much more is involved in these issues than the relative short-run efficiency of men and computers. One can even accept the prediction that the computer revolution will prove to be a more important development than the industrial revolution, and yet see both industrialization and computerization as details in the still broader sweep of a historical era wherein men for the first time deliberately organized their civilization around the processes of social change. In this larger context, both practitioners of management and academic observers of it are developing radically new ideas about what it should and will become. Some of these projections are the more surprising because modern management, in its brief history, has been widely misunderstood. Actual management is already decades ahead of the popular myths about how it works.

THE STAND-INS FOR MR. LEGREE

Assets, they say, make men conservative. Because language, incomparably the greatest in mankind's social assets, changes slowly, we are forced to describe the new and unfamiliar in terms drawn from the old and familiar. Since some change occurs in any period there is always a lag between actuality and the past-bound words we use to describe it. Where change is slow or is confined to a narrow segment of life, this language lag does no great harm. In the fast-changing twentieth century,

however, the language lag causes untold confusion.

Corporations, government agencies, and scientific institutes are really quite different from tribes, families, armies, feudal estates, and monasteries, but our ideas of the newer organizations are distorted by an anachronistic vocabulary drawn from the older group. Business leaders of the late nineteenth century were called "captains of industry" or "robber barons." Government bureaus have "chief." Many present-day organizations still think they operate by "chains of command." From one point of view, management stands in the place of "the owner," a historically familiar figure; it is easy to slip into the habit of talking about a company as if it were merely a complicated kind of plantation with hundreds of "overseers" substituted for Mr. Legree.

As late as the 1920's some American law schools were handling what little they had to say about the internal life of corporations under the rubric of "the law of master and servant." The very word "manager" suggests—even more strongly than "management"—that the basis of the activity is power over other men. (In the 1950's General Electric recognized that a large proportion of the people in management did not, in any literal sense, "manage." G.E. began to speak of management as made up of two groups: managers and "functional individual contributors." The number of "fics," who may be physical or social scientists, lawyers or public-relations experts and who are often future managers or ex-managers, is increasing in nearly all large companies.) In short, the early image of the corporation was heavily loaded on the side of authoritarianism because the early vocabulary pertaining to management came from the patriarchal family, from military organization, from legal concepts of ownership, and from memories of the feudal hierarchy.

Upon this primal image of the corporation some less antique but equally misleading concepts were then superimposed. The science of economics developed in the nineteenth century when the public had become familiar with mechanical principles. Both classical and Marxist economics leaned heavily on mechanical analogies. The economists' model still in service today is a machine. Since humanity is that element in economics least susceptible to mechanical treatment and prediction, economics tends to suppress the human factors. "Economic man" is the most oversimplified of all views of our otherwise interesting species. Man's astounding capacities must be expressed in erglike units, man's even more astounding appetites must be reduced to chilly abstractions resembling Newton's gravitational pull, and man's most profound uncertainties must be ignored because they cannot be quantified. This dehumanized economists' model of the total economy, recast in compact form, merged with the older authoritarian myth of the corporation. The resulting popular image: a kind of life-with-father, automated.

BUREAUCRACY AS A MACHINE

Early in the twentieth century the great German sociologist Max Weber, noting common elements in business organization, government bureaus, and the Prussian military structure, called the new organizational form "bureaucracy." In a bureaucratic system, public or private business was carried out "according to calculable rules and 'without regard for persons.'" Functionaries with specialized training learn their tasks better by practice. "Precision, speed, unambiguity . . . unity, strict subordination, reduction of friction—these are raised to the optimum point in the strictly bureaucratic administration, and especially in its monocratic form." Weber said the new form was succeeding because the "bureaucratic mechanism compares with other organizations exactly as does the machine with the non-mechanical modes of production." Around the same time, Frederick W. Taylor in the U.S. promulgated "scientific management" in which workers were regarded as parts of a corporate machine, the excellence of which was to be measured, of course, by its "efficiency."

It is against this persistent image of dehumanized modern organization that students today react with the sort of castration phobia expressed in the picket-sign slogan: "I am a human being; do not fold, bend, or mutilate." This fear and defiance of modern organization appears in scores of novels and plays, which restate Charlie Chaplin's *Modern Times;* the myth is the root of many anti-business (and some anti-government) attitudes; it even pervades management itself, souring fruitful careers with the sense that life is being sacrificed to a domineering and impersonal organization. The man who says, "I am a cog" does not thereby become a cog—but he may become an unhappy and "alienated" man.

BEYOND EFFICIENCY LIE THE HUMAN QUALITIES

Whatever of truth there once was in the myth of the modern organization as a tyrannical machine has been diminishing for fifty years. The myth never took account of the modern organization's essential involvement in change. As this involvement has deepened, reality and myth have drifted further apart. Around 1900 there was many a one-product manufacturer with a stable technology and a well-defined, reliable market. Such a company could increase its efficiency by routinizing more and more of its decisions into what Max Weber had called "calculable rules." Companies in this situation are exceedingly rare today. In the Sixties, a typical company makes scores, perhaps hundreds or thousands, of products, which it knows it will soon have to abandon or drastically modify; it must substitute others selected from millions of possibilities. Most of the actual and possible products are affected by rapidly changing techniques of production and distribution. Present and prospective markets are enticingly expansive, but fiercely competitive, loosely defined, and unstable.

In this situation, a company cannot be rigidly designed, like a machine, around a fixed goal. A smaller proportion of decisions can be routinized or precoded for future use. The highest activity of management becomes a continuous process of decision about the nature of the business. Management's degree of excellence is still judged in part by its efficiency of operation, but much more by its ability to make decisions changing its product mix, its markets, its techniques of financing and selling. Initiative, flexibility, creativity, adaptability are the qualities now required—and these are far more "human" than the old mechanical desideratum, efficiency.

The institutional system of the Soviet Union has been rigidly organized on the old bureaucratic model. Central authority fixes a definite goal, whether an increase in steel production or a vehicle to reach the moon. Material and human resources are mobilized around that goal. In terms of sheer efficiency certain aspects of the Soviet system work well. Yet we are right in regarding the U.S.S.R. as a "backward" country, and certain Russian leaders are justified in their recent efforts to move toward a more flexible and decentralized system. To cope with a very fluid technological and social environment such as that of the U.S., Soviet management would need much greater emphasis on the specifically human qualities.

Even U.S. governmental institutions, which are years behind our corporations in the evolution of management, are now using flexible approaches inconceivable in the U.S.S.R. The U.S. has consciously embarked on a huge effort to improve the quality of education without defining in any but the vaguest terms what that "improved" quality might be. We assume that through a highly decentralized educational system we may be able to grope our way "forward," step by step, forming new values and new targets as we proceed from choice to choice. In a similar spirit, we have begun an effort to improve the Appalachian region without knowing in advance what we want Appalachia to become. We have no centrally designed plan for Appalachia, but we believe that if the effort is "well managed," in the new (nonbureaucratic) sense of that phrase, a livelier Appalachia may result from the federal government's stimulation of changeful decisions by individuals, communities, and organizations in Appalachia. It is impossible to imagine the U.S.S.R.—or any other organization formed along the old authoritarian, machine-like lines —generating organized activity without first defining "the task."

MANAGEMENT AND CHANGE NEED EACH OTHER

U.S. corporations are pioneering the movement toward the new style of management because they are more heavily engaged than any other category of organization on the frontiers of actual social innovation. It is true, of course, that the main base of modern innovation lies in scientific discovery, most of which is—and all of which could be—carried on independently of business organizations. But the mission of science is to discover new truth; it is not organized to perform the additional and very different work of transforming discoveries into technological inventions; still less is it organized for the third stage of introducing these

inventions into actual use. Usually, scientific discovery is the product of concentrated specialization in a field of study. Innovation, on the contrary, almost always requires various kinds of specialized knowledge drawn from many fields. One of the primary functions of modern management is to assemble various skills and coordinate them in production.

Science and technology, which make possible an ever increasing range of products and services, do not tell us which of these to produce. So another task of management is to mediate between the evolving wants of society and the evolving abilities for satisfying those wants. This mission, performed within a competitive market system, also requires many kinds of specialized knowledge—e.g., market research, cost analysis—and very complex and delicate coordination. The whole process is suffused—as science is not—with questions of *value*, questions of whether the corporation and its customers want A rather than B. The judgments of management are relative and they are often intuitive—i.e., based upon incomplete and perhaps unreliable information. Management's hunger for knowledge on which to base decisions becomes ever stronger, but is fated to be forever unsatisfied. The advance of knowledge does not reduce the remaining body of ignorance because "possible knowledge" is not a finite quantity. In practical affairs, as in science, the more we learn the more questions confront us. Innovation does not wait until risk of failure has been eliminated by complete knowledge; in an era of radical change, management cannot be designed to work like a machine on the assumption that the goals and conditions that determined its design will remain constant.

Although statistical comparisons are impossible, it is almost certainly true that the numbers employed in "management" have been growing more rapidly than the total economy during the past fifty years. If we apply the old bureaucratic machine standards of efficiency we are led to suppose that the vast increase in the numbers of management men represents the wasteful working of Parkinson's Law. But if the prime mission of management is to deal with change, then the size of management should be roughly proportionate to the rate of innovation rather than to the amount of physical output. This explains why the U.S. needs a proportionately larger managerial force than the less lively economy of the U.S.S.R. For years it has been obvious that in numbers and in quality British management was inferior to that of the U.S. and that Britain was not educating nearly enough men to fill its assumed management need. Yet no acute British "shortage" of management personnel exists in the sense that the market there places a very high price in money or prestige on management men; in fact, during the past twenty years a high proportion of men with the kind of training regarded as needed in management have emigrated from Britain, feeling their abilities to be in surplus in a relatively stagnant society. To take a more extreme example, the African nation of Gambia, which produces very few managerial types, would be the world's worst place to look for a job in management.

It appears that the need for management cannot be calculated on a simple supply-and-demand basis, because management creates change and change creates the need for management. As the "inventory" of management people in a society rises (in quantity and quality) the demand for still more management rises with it; or, to put in another way, the rate of innovation and the managerial function are interdependent. Except on a short-range basis or in respect to specific categories of management work, it is pointless to talk about a "shortage" or a "surplus" of managers.

Seen in this perspective, the computer revolution, by powerfully enhancing management's effectiveness in dealing with change, should have the long-range effect of increasing demand for management men. U.S. experience to date seems to support this theoretical expectation. Recruiting for management (of both managers, strictly so-called, and of such "functional individual contributors" as scientists, engineers, accountants) has never been more active, as any reader of newspaper advertisements is aware. More significantly, corporations are making increasing efforts to identify early the men with a high management potential, to train them rapidly, and to promote them to jobs of greater responsibility. This tendency seems especially marked in companies that have been quick to make use of computers. Probably the new information technology has had the effect of breaking bottlenecks that had restrained these companies from generating innovation and coping with the changing environment.

BACK TO THE FAMILY FIRM?

Not everyone expected this expansion of management. In 1958, when the computer revolution was young, two respected observers of management, Harold J. Leavitt and Thomas L. Whisler, wrote for the *Harvard Business Review* a much-discussed article entitled "Management in the 1980's." The article made a persuasive case for the proposition that the new information technology would reverse the trend toward decentralized and "participative" management. Leavitt and Whisler said: "In one respect, the picture we might paint for the 1980's bears a strong resemblance to the organizations of certain other societies—e.g., to the family dominated organizations of Italy and other parts of Europe, and even to a small number of such firms in our own country. There will be many fewer middle managers, and most of those who remain are likely to be routine technicians rather than thinkers." At the end came this portentous note: "We may have to reappraise our traditional notions about the worth of the individual as opposed to the organization."

Seven years later, with much more evidence to draw upon, H. Igor Ansoff, professor of industrial administration at Carnegie Institute of Technology, wrote for the *Harvard Business Review* a sort of answer to Leavitt and Whisler. In "The Firm of the Future," Ansoff said that the right question was not what the new information technology would do to management but "how will the manager use these extraordinarily powerful tools in furthering the objectives of the firm in its environment of the future." Since "the forces which will shape the future firm are already at work ... the shape of the firm in the 1980's ... need not be perceived dimly through a crystal ball [but] can be sketched by analyzing and projecting from the present." He listed three trends in the business environment: (1) *product dynamics*—"the life cycles of products will become shorter"; (2) *market dynamics*—"as superior technology displaces it from its traditional markets, the firm has to fight back by looking for new pastures" and the growing internationalization of markets will add to the competitive "turbulence"; (3) *firm and society*—governmental and social limits on the firm's behavior will increase so that "its search for profit will be strongly affected by an awareness of social consequences." The firm of the future would be able to program many of its activities, thus releasing management to deal with the increasing load of "non-programmable" decisions that would confront it in the new environment.

The manager to match these formidable new conditions would be "broader gauged than his present counterpart." He would need a grip on the firm's technology, but he would also have to deal with problems on "a combined economic-political-cultural level." The new environment would call for more managerial skill in human relations. "Increasing importance will be placed on the manager's ability to communicate rapidly and intelligibly, gain acceptance for change and innovation, and motivate and lead people in new and varying directions." Ansoff was not worried that management might be made obsolescent by new information technology. "The manager of the future will need all the computer help that he can get in coping with the greatly increased complexity of his job."

"MAN IS A WANTING ANIMAL"

The fluid business environment of the future will demand not only a different kind of manager but a different organizational structure. Management's need to keep redefining "the nature of the business" applies not only to the product mix but also to the internal arrangements of the organization. One reason why men and their organizations may fail to adapt is that they cling to erroneous ideas about themselves and/or their situation. The late Douglas M. McGregor, of the Sloan School of Management of M.I.T., believed that the evolution of organizations was being retarded by a set of erroneous beliefs about man and his work which he called Theory X. The average man dislikes work, according to Theory X, and must therefore be coerced, directed, and controlled. He can be made to contribute to the achievement of organizational objectives only by a threat to the supply of his physiological needs. He seeks security and wishes to avoid responsibility for decisions. The old idea of authoritarian, paternalistic organizations fits Theory X; it is better for all concerned if power can be concentrated in the exceptional men at the top, who like responsibility.

Today men respond to certain stimuli that McGregor wrapped in a proposition called

Theory Y. They take for granted the fulfillment of their basic material needs. "A satisfied need," McGregor said, "is not a motivator of behavior. Man is a wanting animal, [and his] needs are organized in a series of levels—a hierarchy of importance." A man whose stomach is satisfied by a secure supply becomes conscious of needs at a higher level. He seeks to feed his ego, which is more insatiable than any stomach, and to achieve a richer sense of his own identity. Many of these higher wants can best be satisfied by the kind of work that has a substantial content of intellectual activity and moral choice. Our society is by no means affluent in providing work of this sort, but more and more men in the professional and managerial category are finding their highest rewards in responsible work itself rather than merely in their pay.

Obviously, an organization based on the assumptions of Theory Y will array itself very differently from the old pyramid, where as much authority as possible was concentrated at the top. A Theory Y corporation would *prefer* to distribute responsibility widely among its managers, even if decision making could be centralized without loss of efficiency. A Theory X organization wants each individual to perform reliably the function assigned to him in the design of the total machine; a Theory Y organization wants an individual to be involved consciously in the relations between what he does and what others are doing; it wants him to seek ways of improving those relations in terms of his own expanding goals and the changing goals of the organization; it wants the individual to participate in setting goals for himself and for the organization.

FAREWELL TO FAUST

What McGregor did was to put a solider and more "human" base under older theories of "participative" management, which had slopped over into the dubious proposition (derisively referred to as "the contented-cow psychology") that the way to make workers efficient was to make them happy. McGregor's Theory Y allows plenty of room for discontent and tension; it provides, however, a realistic way to reconcile the needs of the individual with the objectives of the organization. The individual is no longer seen as entering a corrupt Faustian barter in which he abandons his "soul" in ex-

change for material satisfactions and power—
a deal that will become increasingly repugnant
to the more highly educated men that management will require. In short, the kind of management called for by Ansoff's projection of the
future business environment could be provided
under Theory Y much better than under Theory X.

Warren G. Bennis, McGregor's successor as
chairman of the Organization Studies Group
at M.I.T., asserts in a recent book, *Changing
Organizations,* that during the past decade "the
basic philosophy which underlies managerial
behavior" has made a fundamental shift in the
direction of Theory Y. Bennis discerns the
philosophic shift in three areas:

> 1 A new concept of man, based on in-
> creased knowledge of his complex and
> shifting needs, which replaces the over-
> simplified, innocent push-button idea of
> man.
> 2 A new concept of power, based on col-
> laboration and reason, which replaces a
> model of power based on coercion and
> fear.
> 3 A new concept of organization values,
> based on humanistic-democratic ideals,
> which replaces the depersonalized mech-
> anistic value system of bureaucracy.

Bennis is quick to say he does not mean that
these transformations "are fully accepted or
even understood, to say nothing of implemented in day-to-day affairs." But, "they have
gained wide intellectual acceptance in enlightened management quarters . . . have caused a
tremendous amount of rethinking on the part
of many organizations, and . . . have been used
as a basis for policy formulation by many large-
scale organizations." The shift in philosophy
and the practical predicaments arising out of
twentieth-century changes in the environment
support one another in encouraging management to accelerate its own evolution. Business
organizations, Bennis believes, are leading the
way in replacing the old "bureaucratic mechanism," which was "capable of coordinating
men and power in a stable society of routine
tasks [but] cannot cope with contemporary
realities."

ASSETS NOT ON THE
BALANCE SHEET

The business scene of 1966 shows substantial
evidence to support this view. Some of the evidence lies in what business leaders are saying,
and some in what they are doing. One significant change is the increasing sense that management is the chief asset of the corporation
rather than an overhead expense. "Investment
for modernizing plant and equipment is often
wasted unless there is a corresponding investment in the managerial and technical talent
to run it," says M. J. Rathbone, former board
chairman of Standard Oil (New Jersey). He
notes that the valuation of a corporation's securities is based more upon appraisals of the
quality of its management than upon the
corporation's inanimate assets.

Many advanced companies engage in "total
career development," a conscious policy of
maximizing managerial quality over the long
run by balancing the old criterion of finding
the best man for the job with some consideration of the best job for the development of the
man. This policy is pursued even where it results in some short-run sacrifice of efficiency.
Sears, Roebuck has for many years carried on
an elaborate effort to identify as early as possible those individuals who have a high potential
for development, and to measure as accurately
as possible how they respond to various kinds
of managerial challenges. Polaroid has taken a
further step in the Theory Y direction; instead
of having its top management planning the
paths for executive careers, Polaroid uses a
"posting system" in which its men are encouraged to compete for forthcoming job vacancies.
General Electric's intense concern with the development of managers includes the belief that
the man himself sets the objectives for his career and that the company must make an organized effort to keep open the means by
which an individual can broaden his responsibilities, along lines he chooses himself.

The concern for broadening responsibilities
goes all the way down to men recently recruited from college. Companies have noted
with alarm that many young people, recruited
after considerable effort, quit in the first year
or two. The pay may be satisfactory, but they
complain that their jobs are "too routine," or
"not demanding enough." To meet this criticism, some companies are giving trainees jobs
in which they can make costly mistakes. "There
is no justification left for prolonged training
procedures that prevent people from taking
responsibility," says Frederick R. Kappel, chairman of A.T.&T. "There is no excuse for the
timid doling out of oversupervised little jobs

that allow a person no opportunity to show what he can do." Noting that many youngsters find business goals "too narrow" to fire their imaginations, Kappel counters with a broad one: In the "interaction of science and society," he says, "it is the goal of business management to translate discovery into use. Our job in industry is to assimilate the scientific revolution in such a way that practical values will flow to the public, to society at large, in the most orderly and economical way."

THE WHITE SPACE BETWEEN THE BOXES

The structure of science is loose-jointed, non-pyramidal, non-authoritarian. The same adjectives apply to the structure of modern "society at large." Working between science and society, two fluid and unpredictable worlds, corporations must not let their own structures petrify.

Companies alert to the danger, therefore, have set up continuous reviews of their organization charts. At least one company goes so far as to engage in periodic shake-ups, just to keep its structure from "freezing." A more intelligent way is represented by those companies (including U.S. Rubber and Kimberly-Clark) that have set up permanent analytical staffs to find out how parts of the company actually relate and figure out how they ought to relate. In the search for more flexible structures the old distinctions between staff and line and the old walls between specialists and between departments tend to blur. "The interesting part of the organization chart," says one management consultant, "is in the white space between the boxes. That's where the real activity goes on."

The organizations now evolving on the beliefs of Theory Y represent a shift from a mechanical to an organic model that confronts managers with more subtle and complex challenges. How, for instance, is the unity and coherence of the organization to be maintained in an evolving free-form structure of mobile individuals?

Transitionally, a lot of authority is still concentrated at "the top," but it exists as a reserve to deal with crisis, major internal conflict, and the fundamental decisions affecting the whole organization that cannot, under present conceptions, be made elsewhere. Some management analysts, searching for the shape of the future, are looking intently at large, diversified corporations whose divisions and subdivisions are now competing actively against one another within a loose corporate framework. Can this internal competition be stepped up by rewriting the rules of the game and improving the scoring system? If "the market" is a good way to organize the economy as a whole, why not deliberately make the corporation's internal structure more market-like? At present, the resources of the firm tend to flow toward those divisions where the return on investment has been highest; this "rule" may put too much emphasis on the past. Accountancy, concentrating on the record of what has happened, has not paid enough attention to projecting comparisons between the probable future prospects of several divisions of a company. The Defense Department's work in projecting the comparative cost effectiveness of different weapon systems not yet in being has given business a powerful impetus in the direction of a new kind of accountancy oriented toward the future. Computers, by simulating the results and costs of competing projects, can be of immense help in this kind of accountancy.

Thinking along the lines of an internal corporate market, Professor Jay Forrester of M.I.T. wants companies to get rid of the familiar budget centers, replacing them with profit centers. The budget-center system sets up a conflict between those groups (production, sales, research, etc.) whose interest is to spend and those groups whose function is to restrain spending, such as the controller's office. Because such conflicts can be resolved only at the top of the corporation, the budget-center system perpetuates the authoritarian form of organization. Internal profit centers, on the contrary, demand self-restraint because no group has an interest in spending, as such, or in saving, as such. Every group has an interest in the difference between them—i.e., profit.

Forrester would also break up such central services as purchasing and drafting rooms. Created in the name of efficiency, they can result in "internal monopolies" that tend to become somnolent and unresponsive to the need for change. Moreover, they confuse the accounting system within which internal competition is conducted. The economies of scale that they are supposed to produce are not worth what they cost in deadening the initiative and responsiveness of the corporation.

THE INDEPENDENT PROFESSIONALS

The substitution of structures in which more people exercise self-control fits with the broadest trends in modern society. Professor Bennis believes that "democracy is inevitable" because it "is the only system which can successfully cope with the changing demands of contemporary civilization." By democracy, Bennis means "a climate of beliefs" including "full and free communication, regardless of rank and power; a reliance on consensus, rather than ... coercion or compromise, to manage conflict; the idea that influence is based on technical competence and knowledge rather than on the vagaries of personal whims or prerogatives of power; [and] a basically human bias, one which accepts the inevitability of conflict between the organization and the individual but which is willing to cope with and mediate this conflict on rational grounds."

Not everybody would use the word democracy to describe this set of beliefs, but the contrast between this "climate" and that of the authoritarian machine-like organization is clear. It is also clear that the actual trends in U.S. management are moving in this direction and not back toward the shape forecast by Leavitt and Whisler, "the family dominated organizations of Italy and other parts of Europe."

"Professionalism" is here to stay a while. The scientist, engineer, and lawyer are indispensable to management and so are "professional" communicators and others whose skill lies in the coordination and leadership of specialists. The professional man in management has a powerful base of independence—perhaps a firmer base than the small businessman ever had in his property rights. The highly trained young man entering management today can look for corporate aid in enhancing his competence and hence his base of independence. He need not aspire to becoming *the* top officer of the firm, who holds the only "human" job in an organization conceived on the old line of a machine with all its decision-making initiative concentrated in the "operator" at the top. Today's management recruit can—and, in fact, does—have the more rational and less frustrating ambition of a life of ever widening responsibility and choices. The prospect for a managerial career today is more adventurous than it ever was, because by the year 2000 there will be hundreds of thousands, perhaps millions, of Americans, whose influence on the quality of life in their more fluid society will be greater than that of any past "captain of industry."

Systems Concepts and Applications

The systems concept is much more widely discussed than understood. Probably no concept has ever had more lip service paid to it; undoubtedly few concepts have ever been more widely applied by people who did not know that they were doing so, and perhaps no concept has been more widely ignored by people who should know better.

Virtually anything except the simplest organism can be considered to be a system. The universe is the most general system of which we are all a part. Each system may be made up of subsystems, and in turn, each subsystem can itself be composed of sub-subsystems.

The "systems approach" involves the elementary idea that a system is composed of many interrelated parts; primary concern should therefore be given to the overall effectiveness of the system (rather than to the effectiveness of the respective subsystems) and to the interdependencies of the elements of the system. Of course, this idea is applicable at any organizational level. The marketing department is a system composed of subsystems and the business enterprise is a system of which marketing is a subsystem. In applying systems concepts to such an organization, overall corporate objectives and performance measures need be considered, rather than merely giving consideration to the parochial objectives of the subsystems, e.g., marketing, production, or finance. This may produce an overall result which is distinctly nonoptimal for a subsystem. For example, the corporate decision may be taken that short production runs of many products should be made so that a wide variety of different items will be in stock for sale. The apparent performance of the production department will suffer, since through short runs, they will incur high costs. But, if more sales are produced, the overall net result to the company may be positive.

This Section provides both basic systems concepts and applications of systems ideas in a variety of areas. The emphasis is a pragmatic one since the editors feel that it is at this level that the greatest payoffs are to be gained.

The variety of levels, both conceptual and organizational, at which systems concepts have proved useful, deserves some further emphasis. There is no monopoly on systems ideas at the corporate level. The development of a weapons system requires a management system, for example. The "systems management techniques" (discussed by Morrison) of the Department of Defense serve to illustrate this diversity of levels and variety of system applications.

Taken together, these selections provide sound evidence on which to base a prediction that the use of system ideas will become of increasing significance in both the government and business sectors of our society.

READING 6

THE SYSTEMS CONCEPT * (Systems Simulation)

E. W. Martin, Jr.

The concept of a "system" is getting a great deal of attention in both industrial and academic management circles. Unfortunately, the word has many meanings; for purposes of this discussion, a system is simply an assemblage or combination of things or parts forming a complex whole. One of its most important characteristics is that it is composed of a hierarchy of subsystems. That is, the parts that form the major system may themselves be systems, and their parts may be systems, and so on. For example, the world economy can be considered to be a system in which the various national economies are subsystems. In turn, each national economy is composed of its various industries; each industry is composed of firms; and, of course, a firm can be considered a system composed of subsystems such as production, marketing, finance, accounting, and so on. The systems concept does not provide a set of rules for solving all problems, but it is a useful device for viewing many phenomena. First, it assumes that a system can be understood and that it should be designed to accomplish its purpose. Furthermore, systems concepts emphasize the relationships between the parts and how these relationships affect the performance of the overall system. This viewpoint also allows us to apply knowledge concerning living organisms and complex electronic or mechanized systems to organizational systems. Living organisms are self-adaptive systems in the Darwinian sense; those organisms survive that are able to adapt successfully to their changing environment. Analogously, an organization that wants to be successful in the long run must be capable of adapting to a changing (and perhaps hostile) competitive environment. Perhaps a management task of a higher order is to design the organizational system so that it adapts successfully.

Practical men have long recognized difficulties involved in coping with complex systems, for it is difficult to foresee the consequences of changes in the parts. After making

* Reprinted with permission from Business Horizons, Spring, 1966.

the changes necessary to install and effectively use an electronic computer, for example, many organizations have found that human reactions produce entirely unexpected consequences, which effectively nullify the desired changes.

When we attempt to understand complex systems, problems arise at two distinct levels: the micro level (understanding the basic cause-and-effect relationships governing the performances of the almost elementary subsystems) and the macro level (understanding the effect on systems performance of the complex chains of interrelationships between the elementary subsystems). Historically, we have been able to cope reasonably well with the micro problems by isolating them, studying them in some detail, and building models incorporating the relationships. On the other hand, we have failed miserably at the macro level, frequently by simply ignoring the existence of important relationships.

Some of our difficulties in attempting to educate people for management responsibilities are closely related to these macro systems problems. We can teach individual subjects, but the student frequently cannot integrate his knowledge to form an understanding of the total organization. This failure may occur because a modern business is extremely complex; it also occurs because the process of integration seems to require a high degree of intuition. Even those who do understand the macro aspects of the system do not really know how they do it, and as organizational systems become more complex, the problems of integration may tax the capacity of even the most advanced intuition.

Is there no solution to understanding the operation of complex systems other than through pure intuition or trial-and-error experimentation? One modern approach to problem solving is to build a mathematical model that incorporates the pertinent variables and their interrelationships into a set of equations that can be solved by a computer. Unfortunately, for any complex system, the number of variables and their intricate interrelationships make this approach impossible; the resulting mathematical problem usually can't be solved even by the most powerful computers. Conse-

quently, the mathematical model although quite successful in coping with micro systems problems, has been inadequate in attacking over-all problems.

Fortunately, the combination of the viewpoint of an organization as a system, a model-building approach, and the utilization of powerful computers can be synthesized to produce a technique called (systems simulation,) which shows promise for analyzing and designing complex organization systems. In brief, a simulation model links individual mathematical models (representing the system's micro components or elementary subsystems) with the computer program (incorporating the macro aspects). The simulation model may be operated at a speed that compresses many years of real time into a small amount of computer time; thus a history of performance of the simulated systems under specified conditions can be obtained. The performance of the overall system also can be observed under changes in conditions, changes in characteristics of the individual components, or changes in the interrelationships between the components.

It must be emphasized that the usefulness of systems simulation depends upon our ability to understand the micro components of the system and their basic interrelationships. This is not easy, for we simply do not have a detailed understanding of organizational systems. However, the construction of a model forces us to ask the right questions, and to begin to obtain understanding.

Thus we are led to a final concept of this discussion, that of organizational research and development. This long-range investment of resources (both money and talent) has the objective of understanding the organizational system and improving its performance. Like product R&D, this investment is risky in that it is impossible to predict the outcome with certainty. However, over the past twenty years our aggregate investment in product R&D has completely transformed our economy. It seems likely that long-range and continuous investment in organizational R&D will have a similar revolutionary impact through improved performance.

READING 7

ORGANIZATION AS A TOTAL SYSTEM*

Stanley Young

Increasingly, organizations are being considered from a systems point of view in both a descriptive and normative context.[1] Ashby's work would exemplify some of the descriptive work. System's Development Corporation, Strategic Air Command, and Lockheed are effectively using the systems concept to redesign major phases of organizations in an operational and normative sense.[2] Many companies have expended similar efforts to certain subsystems such as steel-rolling mills and oil refineries.[3]

What appears to be occurring is that our conception of the organization is changing from one of structure to one of process. Rather than visualize the organization in its traditional structural, bureaucratic, and hierarchical motif, with a fixed set of authority relationships much like the scaffolding of a building, we are beginning to view organization as a set of flows, information, men, material, and behavior. Time

and change are the critical aspects. This change in construct will become more pronounced in the future because (and this is an assertion which I will not attempt to defend) I believe the systems approach is more productive. If we consider organization from a normative point of view, there is another reason for this trend which is of more immediate concern and is the working hypothesis of this paper. Only when the organization is designed (Organizational Planning) from a systems orientation will it be able to take full advantage of the new and emerging managerial technologies which include quantitative methods, the computer, information sciences, and the behavioral sciences. Although I will not attempt to prove this proposition in the rigorous sense, the balance of this analysis will be directed toward demonstrating how this might be accomplished.

However, before taking up this thesis, let us note the problems which currently exist that hinder the effective utilization of managerial technology. One problem relates to the absence of a construct as to how the new technology is

* *Reprinted from* California Management Review, *vol. X, no. 3, Spring, 1968. Copyright 1968 by The Regents of The University of California.*

to be used in an integrated and systematic manner; or consider it as the absence of a meaningful gestalt or whole into which such a technology would logically fit. What does exist might be categorized as a tool chest or "bits and pieces" state.

For example, let us suppose that a personnel manager has what he believes is a problem —excessive absenteeism. Given the external and internal environment of the firm, the organizational constraints he has as a manager, and a set of behavioral information and managerial tools, how does he reduce the absenteeism rate? He knows something about psychology— perception, cognition, learning and motivation theory—social psychology, attitude formation, and resistance to change. From sociology he recalls group theory; he can calculate the median, mean and mode, run a correlation and find a derivative. In other words, he is a qualified MBA student. Specifically, what should he do to reduce the absenteeism rate? The students and practitioners are given a tool chest filled with bits and pieces: a little math, a little psychology, a little sociology, and the manager is then admonished to build a better house. How is the application of the technology to be integrated so that the manager can be relatively assured that he is achieving a desired result? What is missing is the bridge or discipline between tools and organizational results. That those of a more traditional bent remain somewhat skeptical of the newer managerial technology is understandable.

Although one can raise many serious questions as to the reality, validity, predictability, and effectiveness of the classical principles approach, nevertheless, it can be said that it roughly holds together as a whole or single unit, and its parts are related in a logical fashion. Starting with the concept of private property and the delegation of authority, the organizational chart is drawn; authority is allocated; a division of labor is specified; the functions of management are outlined and planning, organizing, and staffing are conducted. A certain internal logic is present, not unlike the economist's model of perfect competition. The parts are related to each other in a particular manner. Viewed as a single construct, and traditional model is understandable and .operational to students and practitioners alike.

The same cannot be said for the newer managerial technology. The General Management or Organization Theorist's domain is the whole. One is concerned with the problem of organization space, or the distance between subfunctions, subprocesses, tools, and techniques—the interface problems. To those who are concerned with the whole, the "bits and pieces" approach of the new technology is disconcerting. Where and how do all these parts fit together and what is the relationship between one piece and another? Sprinkling behavioral and quantitative courses about a business curriculum is of questionable effectiveness and has not, I believe, changed the basic manner in which organizations are managed. Therefore, as far as the newer technologies are concerned, a gestalt or general model has been missing which will integrate all the bits and pieces meaningfully. I am suggesting that the systems approach will provide this model.

Another problem which has emerged requiring the organization to be designed as a total system, is that all too frequently the organizational context into which the newer technologies are placed tend to be inappropriate. We are attaching sophisticated techniques to a primitive vehicle, the bureaucratic structure. Organizations should be designed around the technology; technology should not be forced to fit an existing structure. Thus some corporations, to be fashionable, have created operations research departments which, in fact, have been given little or nothing to do. One case was reported in which the primary duty of the O.R. official was to solve the school math problems of the Corporate President's daughter.

In the history of innovation one frequently finds that when a new device is invented, it is attached to the existing model. For example, when the gasoline motor was first invented, it was connected to a buggy. However, as additional innovations occurred, the vehicle itself eventually had to be modified. If advantage was to be taken of additional improvements, obviously one could not unite a 300 horsepower motor to a light shay with wooden wheels and axles. If innovation follows its normal course, we can expect the new managerial techniques to force a modification in the traditional organizational arrangements. This, indeed, has been taking place. The exploitation of the computer, particularly when utilized in an on-line capacity, has led to a weakening or abolishment of the traditional divisional or departmental lines of authority. Improvements in the control and measurement of operations have the same consequences.

The hypothesis that a more sophisticated managerial technology can be fully utilized only when the organization has been designed as a total system, will be examined in accordance with the following model.

In this presentation, my approach will be analytical, or a successive breakdown of the whole into increasingly smaller parts.

ORGANIZATION AS A TOTAL SYSTEM

In Figure 7-1, the business organization is presented in its most simplified form. The basic input is economic resources, the organization is the process, and the output is economic welfare. Other organizations can be represented by changing inputs-outputs. For example, a hospital has a human input (sick patient) and a human output (healthy patient).

In Figure 7-2, the control or feedback mechanism is added to the organization which is represented by management. Or, in terms of control theory, the management segment constitutes the basic control element of the organization. Thus, given a certain welfare objective or expected welfare output (a profit increment),

Figure 7-1   Organization as a system.

actual welfare is measured against expected welfare. If a difference exists, then a problem is indicated. This information is sent to the management segment which formulates a solution that becomes an input in the organization process. This feedback device will operate until the actual and expected welfares are approximately equal.

In Figure 7-3, the control unit is further broken down into a series of parts in order to provide an adaptive capability for the organization.[4] Given a change in certain environmental inputs, one initially has an input analyzer which indicates the nature of such changes. This is an information gathering or sensory device; and somewhat analogously, market research might be so categorized in terms of sensitizing the organization to some of the external variables as accounting functions for the internal changes. One also has a display device or identifier which indicates the state of the organization or any of its subprocesses at any given time. Hence, if the subprocess was a

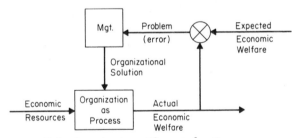

Figure 7-2   Organization with control unit.

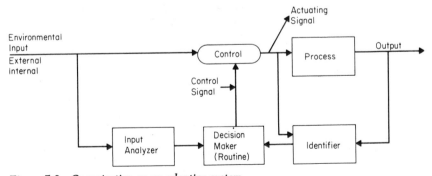

Figure 7-3   Organization as an adaptive system.

production plant, the identifier at a given time might indicate the productive capacity, current running capacity, order backlog, inventory conditions, orders in process, production lines in operation, and machine breakdown. Such information is fed to a decision-making unit along with the information from the environment. We assume that a set of rules has been programmed. One of these rules will be selected, given a particular environmental input, and given the state of the process at some given point of time in order to achieve a certain output.

For example, if the initial input is a large order with a required completion date, the rule may be to go to overtime. This information is called a control signal and is sent to the control unit. The control unit is that element which actually changes the input before it enters the system or the process itself. The order could have been put into a queue. Such information is simultaneously sent to the identifier. Therefore, at any given time, the identifier tells us what inputs have entered the process, the state of the process, and its outputs.

Because the control signal and the control unit are frequently confused, the difference between the two should be noted. The example that is usually given is that of driving an automobile. If one wants to stop an automobile by pressing on the brake pedal, information is

relayed to the brakes of the car. It is not the brake pedal that stops the car, but the brakes which constitute the control unit. Similarly, in a man-to-man system, the control signal, and the control unit might appear as in Figure 7-4.

Let us suppose that the total employee population is the basic system and we want a higher work output. Further assume that we know exactly what the relationship is between need satisfaction input and expected work output. Given the figure for expected work output, the decision-maker will increase or decrease the amount of need satisfaction (for example, money) by a control signal to the financial department where need satisfaction is stored in the form of money. This department would release funds until the expected work output was achieved. The control element constitutes the reservoir and release of funds, not the decision to increase work output, its relay to the employee, or even the decision to pay more. In other words, money may be to the employee what brakes are to an automobile.

For our particular purposes, those subparts of the organizational control mechanism, input analyzer, and so on, give the process an adaptive capability: the ability to adapt the changing inputs in order to maintain a desired or expected output.

In Figure 7-5, the organization is further broken down into a series of major subproc-

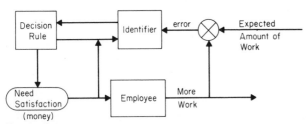

Figure 7-4

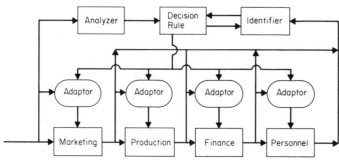

Figure 7-5

esses: marketing, production, and so on, each with its own adaptor. The adaptor consists of an input analyzer, decision rules, identifier, and control for each subprocess. Moreover, it is assumed that each of these subprocesses can be identified and separated from other subprocesses. A super adaptor applies a series of decision rules for subdecision makers to assure appropriate adjustment between processes. It is further assumed that each subsystem's adaptor has this same capability concerning subsubprocesses. Consequently, the production system may have such subsystems as purchasing, inventory control, and maintenance. The inputs and outputs of these subsystems would have to be controlled appropriately with the proper decision rules.

In Figure 7-6, a learning capability in the form of a designer is added to the adaptive system. A learning capability can be thought of as the ability of the system to redesign itself or learn from past mistakes in order to improve system performance. However, although the environmental state of the system and the application of what is thought to be the correct rule is given, the expected output may still not be produced. This indicates design problems.

The designer would receive information as to system performance. Then, in order to increase welfare output, he would attempt to improve the adaptive mechanism by formulating more effective decision rules for the decision-making routine; by improving the identifier in terms of more and better information; by achieving a more rapid response in information from the input analyzer; by improving the sensory devices; and by improving the control mechanism.

In Figure 7-7, we now see the total system in some detail. We have our environmental inputs on the left, both external and internal: psychological, sociological, etc. Two basic subsystems are shown, marketing and production, in which the marketing output becomes a production input. Each of these subsystems has its own adaptor and, although not shown, a coordinating adaptor to integrate the two. Further, each subsystem has its own design capability. The only new feature of the schematic is the box at the top, "Design of System Design." This particular function would integrate the work of subdesigners. For example, if the organization is viewed as an aircraft, design coordination is required for such areas as weight, and structures, air frame, power, and information systems. Moreover, this function would advise as to design technique and strategy, and ideally, one might be able to reach a stage in which the actual design of subsystems could be programmed and routinized.

Thus, in looking at Figure 7-7, we see, in some detail, the organization as a total system that is self-regulating and self-learning and at least partially closed; a system in which the environment can be detailed and in which subsystems are integrated. Further, the adaptor provides for appropriate internal adjustments between subsystems. In other words, the organization, without too much difficulty, can be considered as a total system. All of its essential elements can be incorporated into a design. Also, with an appropriate index, one could detail the subsystems; each subsystem could be broken down into its sub-subsystems, etc. The indexing of the system's subparts schematic to assure appropriate usage is not an insurmountable problem. For example, it is estimated that the blue prints for a new aircraft

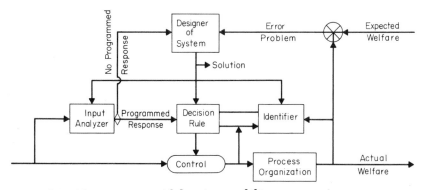

Figure 7-6 Adaptive system with learning capability.

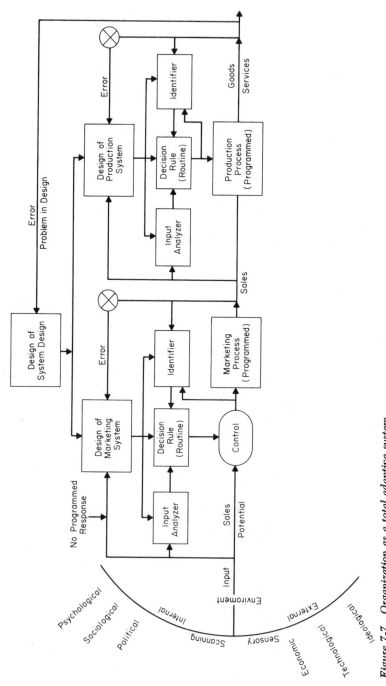

Figure 7-7 Organization as a total adaptive system.

may finally weigh two or three tons—more than the aircraft itself!

SYSTEM DESIGN

In Figure 7-8, we can briefly go through the design process which further analyzes the function of the designer. Given a statement of the problem or the type of system with which one is concerned, the next and key step is the construction of a model of the system. Such a model (which I believe should be essentially stochastic in nature) would stipulate the output, or mission, of the system and the inputs, of which there are three: (1) the input upon which the process is to operate or that input which enters the system, (2) environmental inputs which affect the process, and (3) instrumental or control inputs which modify the operation of the process or the process itself. (This last set of inputs concerns the technology of processing the load inputs.)

For example, in a marketing subsystem, if the initial input is a potential customer, he has to be processed through the subsystem so that a sale is secured. The system's logic relates to the set of decision rules or, given certain inputs, the state of the system and a certain control capability, such as the extent of advertising, what particular decision rule should be utilized to achieve some expected output? Information requirements relate to the classification, amount, and timing of information for the system to operate as expected. Concerning the environmental variables, it is necessary to know what information about which variables should be gathered and how often, how much, and how soon this information has to reach the decision rule.

At the outset, it would be a highly worthwhile investment to construct a fairly complete stochastic model of the proposed system in which output is the dependent variable and environmental and instrumental inputs are the independent variables. For example, one might be concerned with a personnel selection subsystem in which the output is a certain number of qualified employees. The environmental inputs might include labor demand for certain occupations, amount of unemployment, and the number of graduates. The instrumental variables might include the recruiting budget, the number of recruiters, and the training program.

What is being suggested is that it is more efficient to construct one model to which various decision rules can be applied than to construct a new model every time a new decision rule is formulated. With the latter approach, one would always be reconstructing the model when there is a change in tools.

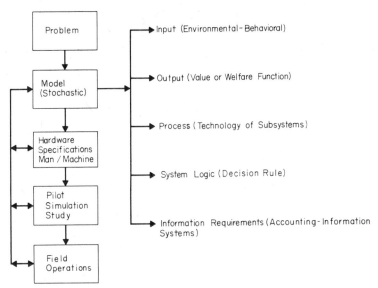

Figure 7-8 System design. For a full explanation of this design process see Harry Goode and Robert Machol. System Engineering. *New York: McGraw-Hill, 1957.*

Assuming the model can be constructed, the research and development begins. One can experiment and try different decision rules and different hardware specifications, which lead to the next two steps in the design process. Given a new rule on a pilot basis, one can apply it to actual hardware. Naturally, one has to be sure that the data from pilot studies are meaningful in terms of the total system with which one is concerned. Experimentation is costly and uncertain, but there is little doubt that the payoff is greater than using an intuitive approach.

If it is successful, the new rule can be applied and data can be fed back regularly to the designer so that he can continually improve and refine his initial model. Although one may begin with a relatively unrefined model, with successive experimentation and field experience, hard data will constantly flow back to the designer. This will enable him to improve his model in terms of the nature of variables, the preciseness of the parameters, and predictability.

As for hardware specifications, apart from the consideration of costs, one is concerned with providing components that will execute the operations as specified. In Figure 7-8, Schematic, the hardware problem how to convert what is essentially a paper model into something that approaches operating reality is of particular concern. (It seems to me that this is the area of greatest deficiency as far as the state of the arts is concerned.) We can construct reasonably good stochastic or econometric models, which can be used to simulate different decision rules, but the conversion of those models into operating reality with appropriate hardware is a different matter.

In operating context, the stochastic model or identifier becomes an information panel for a decision or rule-maker. In terms of hardware, what is needed are information collection or sensory devices which survey the environment and send such data to a central location so that the values of the variables of the model can be displayed. An example of this is the control room in a public utility in which the operator continually watches the changing values of significant variables. Only with such a display can appropriate action be taken. However, wiring such a system is a particularly difficult task.

For example, I am a member of a team that has been given the responsibility of designing a metropolitan poverty program as a total sys-

tem. The primary inputs are poverty families and the output is supposed to be self-sufficient economic units. Although there exists some technical assurance that a stochastic model can be constructed, we have not been able to reach this design step because we are at the very primitive stage of inventing sensory mechanism that will give us some running idea of the nature of our changing inputs. In this instance the changing inputs are the changing mix of the characteristics of our poverty family inputs. This program appears in Figure 7-9.

Another area that requires additional work is the control element, which actually modifies the operation of the system. In a man-to-man system, we do not have sufficient information about which variables to vary and the degree of variation necessary to achieve the desired human behavior. The crude reward and punishment system that we have all too often gives us dysfunctional results. Presumably, in the design process, when serious deficiencies arise, research and development should be directed to those areas.

MANAGERIAL TECHNOLOGY AS UTILIZED IN SYSTEM DESIGN

Although this view of an organization as a total adaptive system and the design process has been brief, perhaps it has been sufficient to indicate how one can take advantage of the newer managerial techniques in the use of system analysis.[5] It is necessary to know where and how these techniques fit in terms of the system presented. As for the behavioral sciences, our environmental inputs or variables are behavioral in nature. To build a model, and eventually a display panel, such knowledge is essential. In the decision box we would utilize our various decision rules such as Linear Programming, Game Theory, Dynamic Programming, and Pert.

Because system design requires eventual concern with a total subsystem such as marketing, we will probably become increasingly concerned with the problem of combining various decision rules. For example, Gerald Thompson has indicated that we must combine appropriate decision rules to achieve the most satisfactory system output. We must know under what conditions it is advisable to move from Linear Programming to rule of thumb and then back to Linear Programming. There is an over-concern with single decision rule,

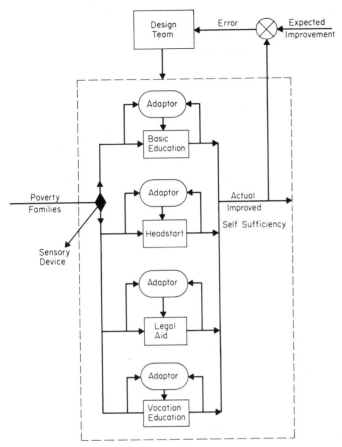

Figure 7-9   Poverty programs system.

and we must learn how to use different combinations of rules under a variety of operating conditions. As Professor Thompson has noted, "We need to develop heuristics about using heuristics. That is, an executive program that would accept a problem and then decide which of a list of heuristics (decision rules) should be employed to give its solution."[6]

The information sciences relate to the input analyzer, collection, manipulation, and relay of information. Here we have all of our data, collection, and processing problems. The control element relates to the relatively new area of control theory; specifically, the direction of human effort. Finally, in designing a specific subsystem, such as personnel or marketing, we should have some knowledge with regard to the technology of these systems. For example, we should be able to use employment· tests correctly in the selection process.

In designing an organization as a total system, it would appear that we would have to be familiar with and capable of using, a wide ar-

ray of reasonably sophisticated managerial techniques and knowledge. The understanding and use of managerial techniques is an integral part of the design process. This is a counter-distinction to the bureaucratic structure, which merely attaches such techniques to the system with little purpose or place.

DESIGN CRITERIA

Design criteria are rules which are utilized to evaluate the acceptability of designs. Given a number of designs, we must determine which one is the best. Although there are numerous rules, the most widely used are measurability, feasibility, optimality, reliability, and stability. We will consider only the first three. Measurability is the system's ability to evaluate its performance. If its performance cannot be measured, a system's desirability or undesirability cannot be established and its particular excellences or deficiencies cannot be known. When models are measurable, the superior system can be inferred from the specific measuring devices used in each. In the model which I have suggested, the identifier as a display panel is the primary measuring mechanism since we would know the actual inputs, process, outputs, and decision rules. If the model is not working as expected, the errors would be fed to the designer on a more or less continual basis so that the system could be redesigned for more effective results.

One of the most serious weaknesses of the bureaucratic design as a management system is that it lacks measurability. When the bureaucratic system is redesigned from a product to a functional arrangement or when the line of command is lengthened by the introduction of additional levels of managers, no measuring devices exist, either in the previous or subsequent design, that will indicate what improvements, if any, have occurred.

Feasibility relates to the question of whether or not the model will operate as planned. A model must be realistic; it must be capable of being installed, of achieving expected payoff, and of performing its task requirements within the environment of the system. If a particular quantitative decision-making tool is suggested, we must be reasonably certain that it can be employed in an operational context.

The use of pilot studies or experimental models relates to the question of feasibility. Given any managerial device, we want to know whether it will increase organizational payoff when it is utilized; whether stockholders, employees, and consumers will be better off than before. Organizations are normative systems. All too often, the student and practitioner are exposed to quantitative manipulations and behavioral research that is interesting, but either no directions are provided as to how these findings are to be incorporated into the operations of the firm, or no measuring devices are suggested that will actually establish the quantity of welfare that the research results will actually produce. Frequently, we are highly impressed with the elegance and sophistication of the research and the virtuosity of the analyst, and then discover that the extent of research usefulness is limited.

The end purpose of the manager, as it is viewed in this analysis, is to design subsystems which will actually increase human well-being. The manager is not, per se, a mathematician, statistician, sociologist, or psychologist. However, he must rely on these disciplines in much the same way as the engineer has to rely on physics.

This does not mean that continuous research is unnecessary in these disciplines, but it does mean that such research will not automatically lead to improvements. It is only when the designer is able to incorporate findings into an operating reality that he can achieve the full value of the research.

A corollary to the feasibility criterion relates to balance between parts of the system. All parts of the system must not only be integrated, but also mutually consistent. We would not put a primitive input analyzer into practice and follow this with a complex regression analysis in the identifier. The final system output would be no more productive than the least productive part of the system. Each part acts as a constraint on all other parts. Consequently, the identifier can never be any better than the input analyzer, and so on.

The absence of integration and/or balance is self-defeating. For example, we frequently find information systems personnel providing voluminous data; that is, the input analyzer is well developed. However, the rest of the system may be missing—there is no identifier, set of decision rules, etc. In other instances, we may have an analysis of the use of a single decision rule, as linear programming, but nothing else.

As long as we find this "bits and pieces" type of analysis, managers will always revert, out of necessity, to the most primitive part of the total system because this part represents the primary constraint. In such a context, increasing sophistication will not meet the criterion of feasibility. Even if it is used, no increment in organizational payoff will result.

For example, in the design of the poverty program system previously mentioned, the staff's initial impulse was to design an econometric model of the program, including exogenous variables. We immediately ran into the constraints of the rest of the system and realized that until we had a relatively effective input analyzer, a set of decision rules, and a control element, we could not move to the sophisticated model we wanted. In other words, when we design a total system, we are generally forced to start with a fairly elementary model. Then, when all the parts are developed, we can progress to a more complex system.

It seems to me that we are overly concerned with the optimality criterion in the "management sciences," while we tend to ignore such other criteria as measurability and feasibility on the assumption that, if one has an optimal solution, there is little else that has to be done. But unless all criteria are considered, we will not get the hoped-for results. To have a solution that is optimum but not feasible is meaningless. Obviously, a solution has to be measurable, feasible, and reliable before we can consider its optimality. For the most part, operating managers stress the feasibility criterion. At the outset, they want something that will work and actually function at this stage. They are not overly concerned with optimality. In dealing with a complex system, I am not sure of what constitutes an optimal solution. Engineers, for example, have told me that they really don't know what an optimal aircraft would be like.

Russell Ackoff has said, "One of the things Operations Research has learned about putting results to work is having considerable effect on its methods. This means the team must either translate elegant solutions into approximations that are easy to use, or side-step the elegance and move directly to a quick and dirty decision rule. Operations Research is learning that an approximation that is used may be a great deal better than an exact solution that is not."[7] Because design methodology imposes a specific discipline on the designer, we can be assured that new techniques will be effectively utilized.

SOME IMPLICATIONS

While this has been a rather broad treatment of the organization as a total system, nevertheless, certain implications can be inferred. First, on a normative basis, organizations should be viewed as a total system if we are to increase organizational output. Different organizations, corporations, universities, poverty programs, and so on, can be so categorized. Further, although this is by and large an article of faith, some empirical evidence does exist; certainly in the area of complex weapons systems. If organizations are viewed as a total system, better results will be obtained. We are in the initial stages of this development and, at this time, we can only block out the basic characteristics of total systems. I am quite convinced, for example, that the poverty program on the local metropolitan operating level can only be designed as a total system.

Second, I have attempted to demonstrate that the systems approach is a highly conducive vehicle for the incorporation of current managerial technologies, unlike the bureaucratic structure. Irrespective of the developing managerial concepts, the bureaucratic structure itself represents such a serious constraint that only minimal advantages would occur.

Third, when viewed in this context, the essential role of the manager is that of designer of organizational or behavioral systems, just as the engineer is the designer of machine systems. The design of a large complex system will, however, necessitate a team effort of mathematicians, psychologists, and information specialists. But, as in the case of large machine systems, system specialists will be required to integrate the team effort. There is little reason why efforts cannot be organized to design a marketing system in the same fashion as the F-111 aircraft was designed.

If we were to speculate about the future, eventually the organization might be divided into two basic divisions, planning and operations. The computer, behavioral scientists, information specialists, and quantitative personnel would comprise the planning unit. This planning division would be comparable to the engineering division currently found in organizations. The organization of the poverty program, for instance, is divided between planning and control on the one hand, and operations on the other. Planning has the primary responsibility of total system design. This unit is an interdisciplinary team under the direction of a systems specialist. This is in contrast to the typical operations research arrangement in which a line manager may use operations research for assistance if he has a problem. In the poverty program, the manager is viewed as the operator of the system developed by the team.

Similarly, if the organization is to fully utilize the systems approach, the first step would be to establish a design team with planning responsibility. Also there is no reason why a particular team has to be concerned entirely with one subsystem, such as marketing or personnel. Once the development work has been done regarding one subsystem, the team should have the capability of designing any other subsystem. In the poverty program, the same team is dealing with headstart, legal aid, health, and manpower training subsystems.

There are educational implications suggested by this analysis; namely, a division of business education into two relatively distinct areas. One would represent the traditional bureaucratic approach and contain the basic principles, material and functional areas. The other would stress the organization as a total system (the alternative to principles), and would be the basic course upon which the newer management technologies (as exemplified by such courses as statistics) would be systematically built and integrated. At the University of Massachusetts, we have moved in this direction on the graduate level.

Thus, rather than offer behavioral and quantitative courses in a curriculum with little rhyme or reason, the new technologies can be integrated in the systems fabric. This is a rational program for the student because he now knows why and where the parts fit, why he has to be able to construct a stochastic model, and so forth.

In all probability, the two basic approaches —bureaucratic and systems—will exist side by side in the curriculum over a number of years. Gradually, however, one would expect the bureaucratic material to be phased out in order to reflect changes in the real world. In form, organizations may continue as bureaucratic structures; in substance, they will take on systems orientation with a continual integration of operations and elimination of authority boundaries.

My final observation concerns the ultimate development in systems. It is hoped that, in the long run, the systems approach will result in a more "human use of human beings" in an organizational setting which the Father of Cybernetics, Norbert Wiener, suggested.[8] The ultimate goal of the designer of man systems is to increase the human welfare of the organization's membership. This will occur because the nature of the design process is to continually create a system that most closely fits the basic material of the system—man himself. I certainly concur with Chris Argris' comments upon the non-human characteristics of bureaucracy.[9]

The ideal organization or system would be a cybernetic one—a self-regulating mechanism in which individuals adjusted and adapted to their environment because they were self-motivated to do so. Such an organization would have the characteristics of the purely competitive economic mode. Yet, if we are to reach such an ideal state, such systems will have to be invented. To observe that the traditional bureaucratic structure has serious drawbacks, or that principles of management are not very rigorous, is not enough. If the present hierarchical scheme is deficient, then only a better one will rectify the situation. There is little question that we are at last in a position to invent better social systems. I have attempted to demonstrate, when we view the organization as a total system, we have taken the first step in this forward direction.

References

1. For example see: Joseph Litterer. *Analysis of Organizations.* New York: John Wiley, 1965. Claude McMillan and Richard Gonzalez. *Systems Analysis.* Homewood, Illinois: Richard Irwin, 1965, chs. 11–14. Ross Ashby. *An Introduction to Cybernetics.* New York: John Wiley, 1958, chs. 10–14. Adrian McDonough, and L. J. Garrett. *Management Systems.* Homewood, Illinois: Richard Irwin, 1964. Richard Johnson, Fremont Kast, and James Rosenzweig. *The Theory and Management of Systems.* New York: McGraw-Hill, 1963 and Stafford Beer. *Cybernetics and Management.* London: English Universities Press, 1959.

2. For example see: G. Donald Malcolm, Alen Rowe, and Larimer McConnell. *Management Control Systems.* New York: John Wiley, 1960.

3. See: Cornelius Leondes. *Computer Control Systems Technology.* New York: McGraw-Hill, 1961, chs. 15–20.

4. For a review of adaptive systems see: Eli Mishkin and Ludwig Braun, Jr. *Adaptive Control Systems.* New York: McGraw-Hill, 1961. John H. Westcott, *An Exposition of Adaptive Control.* New York: Macmillan Company, 1962.

5. For a more complete review, see: Harry H. Goode and Robert Machol. *System Engineering.* New York: McGraw-Hill, 1957.

6. Gerald L. Thompson. "Some Approaches to the Solution of Large Scale Combinatorial Problems." Working Paper. Carnegie Institute of Technology, Pittsburgh, p. 25.

7. Rusel L. Ackoff. "The Development of Operations Research as a Science," in *Scientific Decision Making in Business,* ed. by Abe Shuchman. New York: Holt, Rinehart and Winston, 1963, pp. 59–60.

8. See: Norbert Wiener. *The Human Use of Human Beings.* Garden City, New York: Doubleday and Company, 1954.

9. Chris Argris. *Personality and Organization.* New York: Harper and Brothers, 1957.

A SYSTEMS APPROACH TO RESEARCH MANAGEMENT:
Part 1. Scientific Research*

R. E. Gibson

INTRODUCTION

"Research and development" has now become big business with many complex ramifications within itself and even more complex and far-reaching interactions with the rest of society. According to the estimates made by the National Science Foundation the annual expenditures for R&D in the United States exceeded 11 billion dollars in 1959, were close to 12.5 billion in 1960 and they are still growing. Research and development is now one of the principal components of modern industry[1] and has become a powerful instrument in economic development and in national prestige. International competition in this field is extending and intensifying. The supremacy of the United States is being seriously challenged. The Soviet Union is a prominent challenger in the minds of most of us but the United Kingdom, Sweden, Germany, France, Japan, and Italy are by no means negligible contenders in certain areas and the growing threat of Red China looms in the offing. From a national as well as a private or company viewpoint, it is expedient that we make the fullest use of the potential inherent in our public and private research and development organizations.

This potential is realized through two channels: (1) the intellectual growth of our society, and (2) the growth of modern technology. Although from many points of view the first is the more important, I shall treat it only incidentally in this paper and will concentrate attention on the second, dealing mainly with the role of research and development as components of technology. Because the subject is complicated, we can miss very important points if we attempt to deal with it piecemeal. I shall, therefore, use what may be called a "systems approach" to develop an overall general picture of technology, including research and develop-

* *Reprinted with permission from* Research Management, *vol. V, 1962.*
[1] *In 1960 the expenditures for R&D were made as follows: Government organizations $1.8 billion, Universities $1.0 billion, other non-profit organizations $0.25 billion, Industry $9.4 billion.*

ment and the problems that arise in managing organizations to advance it.

The "systems approach" to a complex subject is a "synthetic" one, as opposed to an "analytic" one. Indeed, we might have called this paper "A synthetic approach to research management" except that the word synthetic emphasizes other meanings, and, therefore, I use the term "systems." Although the words, "system" and "systems," are becoming hackneyed, they do convey an important idea which has proven very fruitful in technical thought and expression. Indeed, the exploitation of this idea is forming the main bridge between the classical sciences of physics and chemistry and the newer sciences associated with biology and medicine. In order to bring out the connotation of the systems approach, I shall discuss what I consider to be some important concepts associated with the term system.

SYSTEMS CONCEPTS

A system may be defined as an integrated assembly of interacting elements designed to carry out cooperatively a predetermined function. Those elements may vary from mechanical components to biological ones, from units in an organization to segments of intellectual activity, but the idea of cooperation with a purpose is always present. Examples include a radio set, an automobile, a guided missile system, an automatic factory, biological organisms ranging from amoeba to homo sapiens, an industrial corporation, a symphony orchestra, a church, a society, a civilization.

The term system conjures up the picture of a group of individual entities, each of which has a peculiar and essential part to play but each of which is entirely dependent for its effectiveness on the communications established between it and its fellows.

Inherent in the idea of a system are the following concepts:

1 The key concept conveyed is a network of elements, each of which develops information peculiar to itself from the inputs it receives, and passes on this information, its outputs, with appropriate *precision* and *timeliness* to the other elements so that they can perform the parts effectively.
2 To be considered a system, an assembly must contain all the sources of significant inputs to its elements. For example, an ani-

mal cannot be divorced from its food supply, a plant from solar radiation, or a factory from its markets.
3 The definition of a system that we have just given emphasizes the importance of objectives or the predetermined functions that the elements of the system are to achieve cooperatively—the stability and breadth of the objective reflects itself in the character of the system designed to carry it out. An objective of ephemeral value tends to produce a flimsy system. However, the objective of the human organism, namely, survival in a competitive and changing world, is one towards which it has worked for millions of years and if we use the term survival to mean that of the race as well as the individual, it seems we have an objective that will challenge our biological system for many years to come.
4 Consideration of a system places the communication lines which link the various elements upon an equal footing with the elements themselves. The ability of these links to transmit timely and precise information, in other words the phasing and band width of the communications, can play a determining role in the growth and functioning of the system.
5 A very important family of communication links are called *feedback links*. When part of the output of a machine or system is applied to affect or control its input, a feedback is established. Familiar examples are the oscillator in a radio transmitter, a governor on a steam engine, automatic control on a radio, the mechanism of balancing, homeostasis, etc., in human beings. It is convenient to distinguish two special cases of feedback, namely, negative feedback and positive feedback. Negative feedback is established when the increase in the output of the system tends to cut down the input, as in the action of a governor on a steam engine. Such feedbacks lead to a condition of equilibrium and are the basis of automatic control. Positive feedback exists when an increase in output acts to increase the input—as in an oscillator. The result is unstable operation. No equilibrium is established, but rather the output of the system increases at an exponential rate. Explosives, epidemics, and the initial growth of populations in an environment of plenty are examples of the working of positive feedbacks.

The phasing or timeliness with which information is transmitted along feedback links is of great importance. Indeed the difference between negative and positive feedback is 180° in phase. Time delays causing phase changes can convert signals intended to produce negative feedback into ones giving positive feedback and vice versa. It can be shown quite simply that positive feedback in a system causes its output to grow exponentially whereas negative feedback leads to stability of control and keeps the system in equilibrium, that is to say prevents its output from growing. In the following discussion I shall refer frequently to the feedbacks in many types of systems; practically all will be positive.

The block diagram so familiar to engineers these days serves to summarize important aspects of the systems approach to complicated subjects. In such a diagram we can divide the subject into definable entities whose internal contents can be treated separately and whose reactions on the operation of the system can be specified through the inputs they require and the outputs they generate. As long as these are kept within tolerances, the exact contents of the blocks are immaterial. With this in mind, we can look at many very different assemblages from the systems point of view. Our system may consist of all those human activities that go to make up a civilization. We may apply it to the individuals that make up society—we may apply it to the brains and skills whose products are research and development. We shall apply it to scientific research—the components or blocks of the system being the ideas

and ratiocinations that go on in one man's mind or in the minds of a number of people. Sometimes the system we are talking about will be composed of tangibles like the people and machines, sometimes of intangibles like ideas, intellectual or manual activities.

DEFINITION OF SCOPE OF RESEARCH MANAGEMENT

Discussion of research management frequently flounders in a morass of arguments between those who claim that management has no place in research and those who claim that unless research is well managed it is ineffective. In order to avoid this type of argument, I should like to comment on the place and scope of management in research operations using the block diagram of technology shown in Figure 8-1 as a frame of reference. Figure 8-1 shows in block diagram form the various activities which make up modern technology.

Scientific Research

Near the bottom of Figure 8-1, we see a block labelled, "scientific research," which is still a very individual activity. It is motivated by curiosity or an uneasy feeling that a discrepancy exists between preconceived ideas and our observations of natural phenomena. Its ob-

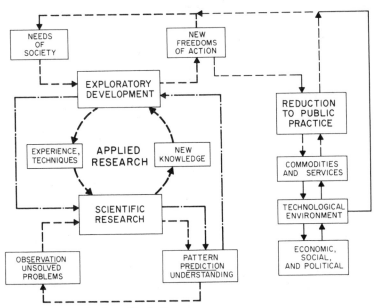

Figure 8-1   Technology block diagram.

jective is understanding or the fitting of new and strange observations into patterns of established fact. In this type of research the role of management is one of complete restraint and noninterference. A decision is made to invest some money in an individual and his assistants in the hope that their talents, intuition, and skill will lead them to the discovery of new and significant knowledge and the broadening of the basis of our understanding of nature. Thereafter they are best left alone.

Exploratory Development

A second activity shown in Figure 8-1 is called "exploratory development" and is the field that used to be the territory of the inventor. Its incentives are the realization that limitations to human activity can be broken down by the application of knowledge and ingenuity to produce new devices, commodities, or services that give us new freedoms of action. The invention of the steam engine, Daimler's invention of a *high speed* internal combustion engine, the Wright Brothers' demonstration at Kittyhawk, Goddard's liquid fuel rockets in 1926—were all events that made available to man new freedoms of action which he has exploited with far-reaching social consequences. In this area, the role of management is a tenuous one and depends primarily on the number of people that are involved in a given exploratory enterprise. Indeed, in both of the activities that I have mentioned, scientific research and exploratory development, it seems that management in the classical sense of the word can play a role only in getting the expeditions started. When, like a band of explorers, they penetrate into the unknown, they are on their own and decisions for action must be taken in the light of the new and strange situations that arise. As the size of the band increases, the need for management goes up, but it is emphasized that the important decisions must be made by those closest to the front line.

Applied Research and Development

In the middle of the diagram is an area entitled "applied research" which bridges the gap between scientific research and exploratory development. Its functions are to provide the exploratory developer with accurate and systematized knowledge and understanding from scientific research, and to carry the unsolved

problems uncovered in the course of a development back to the laboratories for solution and understanding. This is the area in which the large research and development laboratories of government, industry, and nonprofit corporations now operate. It is an area where time scales are important, where the product interacts closely with the environment described in the next paragraph. It is the area to which I shall refer when I speak of management of research and development in this paper.

Reduction to Public Practice

New freedoms of action become effective in society only after they are reduced to public practice and this entails the investment of large sums of money and manpower, an investment which must be amortized by the returns brought in by products. Here, of course, is a place where management, business acumen, and an intimate knowledge of the technological, economic, social, and political environment are of paramount importance. Since the operation of an applied research organization involves expenditures of considerable sums of money and the investment of intellectual and practical talents of a number of scientists and engineers, it becomes important that those responsible for the management of this work also know intimately the interactions of its products or potential products with the technological, political, economic, and social world, and the processes whereby new freedoms of action are reduced to public practice. This knowledge is fundamental to the initiation of research and development programs likely to obtain "profitable" results at the right time. I think, therefore, that we can safely assume that the subject before us is not irrelevant and that management of the right kind has a very important part to play in the realization of the maximum potential inherent in an applied research organization.

The function of research management is to operate effectively the system referred to as applied research in Figure 8-1 and in order that we may see how this may be accomplished, we must understand something about its objectives—the elements it contains, and the interactions among these elements. I propose, therefore, to proceed now with a detailed systematic discussion of the activities which make up modern technology, namely, scientific research, exploratory development, and reduction

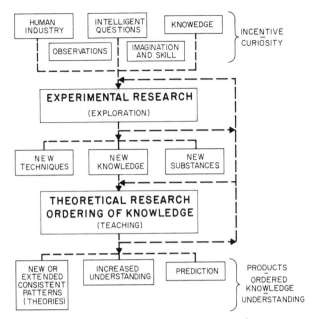

Figure 8-2   Some feedbacks in scientific research.

to public practice with the conviction that a knowledge of the nature of these activities is fundamental to any discussion of their management.

Before doing so, however, it might be wise to say a word or two about "management." The word itself has an unfortunate history. It originally meant training horses to do the exercise of the manége. It still conjures up in the minds of many people a set of manipulations or manipulators promoting the exploitation of human resources for more or less worthy ends. Over the past twenty-five years there has grown up an influential school of thought that regards "management" in the sense of organizing, controlling, and exploiting the brains and skills of people as a profession in itself. The rise of this school parallels that of the rise of the schools of education at the beginning of this century, a movement which placed emphasis on *how* to teach rather than on *what* to teach.

There is no doubt at all that the modern "management" school is making extremely important contributions by attacking objectively the complicated problems that arise when human beings cooperate in a system. It is questioning the dogmas, studying and systematizing the methods of successful practitioners, and evolving new techniques and broadening our basis of understanding. However, along with very sound results there has grown up and

been widely sold a mythology that gives the impression that "professional management" can be substituted for leadership, glib expertise for hard earned experience, and academic formulae for common sense. Discrimination is of the essence in management.

This paper may be regarded as a delineation of my own definition of "management" as applied to an R&D organization or program. What I have in mind is really "leadership" or "generalship" where the prime object of the exercise is to advance technology by means of an organization and the secondary objective is to operate the organization smoothly.

SYSTEMATIC DISCUSSION OF THE COMPONENTS OF MODERN TECHNOLOGY—THEIR INTERACTIONS AND FEEDBACKS

Scientific Research[2]

Figure 8-2 gives a simplified picture of scientific research in block diagram form. The first block in this system is labelled "experimental research." Its inputs are human industry, intelligent questions, existing knowledge, accurate observation of phenomena, imagination and

[2] *This subject is discussed more fully in an article "Cultural Implications of Scientific Research," R. E. Gibson, J. Wash. Acad. Sci. 47, 249 (1957).*

skill—all motivated by curiosity to understand exactly what is going on, through the establishment of valid facts determined by controlled experiments. I cannot dwell here on the immense amount of hard work and ingenuity that must be expended to establish one fact, to be sure that it can be reproduced exactly by any competent observer and that it can be expressed unambiguously in quantitative terms. The outputs of this box are new knowledge, new techniques, new substances.

The second block, of equal or even greater importance than the first, is labelled "theoretical research or the ordering of knowledge." The input to this block is new and old knowledge and the function of this block is to arrange the new facts and the old knowledge in consistent and satisfying patterns which we call theories. Its outputs are new or extended consistent patterns of knowledge—increased understanding that comes when the new and strange are logically related to the old and familiar and the power of predicting new facts by extrapolation from well established theories. In other words, the primary function of this block is to reduce the myriad facts emerging from experimental research to systematic and manageable form.

Figure 8-2 brings out several important feedbacks: the first is the "interplay of experimental theory and experimental practice" to quote Claude Bernard; the second is the feedback from the output to the input of the experimental research box; and the third the feedback from the output of theoretical research not only to its own input but also to the input of the experimental box. These are discussed in more detail in the following paragraphs.

1   From observation and careful study of phenomena or events, facts are obtained which may then be fitted together in an experimental pattern, i.e., a working hypothesis. If the facts fit well into the hypothesis, the latter immediately suggests new subjects for observation or new experiments from which come new facts and so the activity in the circuit builds up, and with it, *confidence in the validity of the facts and the consistency of the theory*. On the other hand, if the facts do not fit into a recognized pattern, one must first make a further study of their validity to ensure that they have not been vitiated by some error (and errors may arise in very subtle ways). At the same time, it may be necessary to reexamine the pattern or theory and, if necessary, modify it to ac-

commodate the new facts. The process is a cyclic one and only when the *facts and the experimental theory fit together* can we be content with either. The product of this circuit is a satisfying pattern or general theory which enables us to understand the phenomena or events in the field of study, which comprehends all the facts, links them with facts from other fields, and enables us to predict verifiable new phenomena or events. The outputs of this circuit are the major theories or patterns which accommodate large bodies of facts such as the Laws of Thermodynamics, the Laws of Motion, the Theory of Relativity, the Quantum Theory, Maxwell's Electromagnetic Equations, the Mendelian Laws.

2   In order to extend and integrate the patterns and to assay* their consistency over wide ranges of facts, it has been found necessary to seek facts in every region susceptible to precise observation. The new substances, instruments, and techniques—we may even include concepts—discovered and developed in the course of one series of researches may be used to explore other new regions for more facts. The build-up in the circuit due to this positive feedback has been most spectacular; indeed the history of natural philosophy is marked by milestones, each indicating the discovery of a new device or technique which opened up to human experience regions that were hitherto inaccessible. These devices were means to an end, but the end would never have been achieved without the means. Telescopes, microscopes, x-rays, radioactivity, alpha-particles, neutrons, cyclotrons, chemical analysis, electronics, highspeed computing machines, have all been means of opening up new continents for valid experiences. The positive feedback from its output to its input gives experimental research an ever expanding potential to break down existing barriers to its own advances.

3   The arrow from the output of theoretical research to the input of the whole system also indicates a positive feedback, the autocatalytic effect of *understanding*. A satisfactory theory or pattern of facts broadens and deepens understanding, pointing the way to new fruitful fields where facts of significance, interest, and potential for application are likely to be discovered. In short, it permits the asking of more *intelligent* questions. It helps research men to make more intelligently the most important decision of all, namely, the choice of problems in which to invest years of their lives. With the aid of new instruments, techniques and methods,

both experimental and theoretical, these decisions may be implemented and the investigators may pursue their researches into new and more complex fields with increasing facility and confidence.

The effects of these feedbacks on the growth of scientific knowledge and understanding have been really extraordinary. It is very difficult to get a quantitative expression of the size and extent of scientific knowledge at any one time but all indices that have been examined indicate that scientific knowledge doubles each 10–15 years and has done so steadily since 1700 [D. J. Price, *Discovery*, 17, 240 (1956)].

There are regions of interest in science where it is not possible to make precise observations or accumulate facts under completely controlled conditions. In such cases the system works in a deductive mode through the feedback from "satisfying patterns" to observation. In cosmogony or petrogenesis for example, it is not practical to build up a theory of the origin of the universe or of rocks from reproducible facts obtained from direct observation of the processes concerned. However, starting from a comprehensive pattern of facts from physics and chemistry and certain assumptions, it is possible to draw a theoretical picture of the origin of the universe or rocks in *sufficient* detail that certain critical consequences which are susceptible to observation may be deduced. Facts extracted from observations may then be compared with those deduced from theory. The history of the sciences I have mentioned shows clearly that as our satisfying patterns grow in depth and breadth, the deductions drawn lead to more and more pertinent and refined observations and our confidence in them grows accordingly. This circuit has found wide application in attacks on complicated problems or those dealing with past or future events. Its power depends on the existence of broadly based, established patterns of facts, a condition which is sometimes not fully appreciated in attempts to apply "scientific methods" in new or complicated fields such as social sciences.

There is one interesting philosophical implication of the role of positive feedbacks in scientific research. When positive feedback exists, we may say that the output is coherent with the input and the subject *grows*. When, however, the outputs of either block are erroneous

(facts being contaminated with error or theories with fallacy) they will be out of phase with the input when fed back; in other words, the outputs and inputs are incoherent in this case. Positive feedback may become negative. We might suggest, therefore, that the criterion of truth can be related to the coherence of the outputs and inputs of these blocks.

Truth leads to rapid growth of knowledge—error leads to stagnation. Examples of incoherence of output and input are not hard to find in the history of science. For example, Lord Kelvin's theory of the cooling of the earth caused a temporary but significant stagnation in the science of geophysics which started again on a rapid growth only after the growing knowledge of radioactivity corrected the error in Kelvin's theory. The struggles of the kinetic theory to explain quantitatively the properties of gases in pre-quantum theory days is another striking example.

It is also interesting to notice two rather important differences between science and art. Positive feedbacks are strong in science and their effects are of greatest significance. In art the feedbacks are quite weak—one masterpiece seldom paves the way for a greater one. The absence of strong positive feedbacks has resulted in the arts growing much less steadily than the sciences. A second difference is to be found in the communications which must be exact and quantitative in science—they need not be so in art.

I cannot leave the subject of scientific research without emphasizing the extreme importance of ordering our knowledge into patterns that make it interesting and manageable. "Order is remembered—chaos is forgotten." Since knowledge grows only in the minds of people, we must recognize the key role of the teacher in ordering new knowledge and experience into interesting and stimulating patterns that excite the interest of the student to assimilate this knowledge in his mind. The teachers who inspire students and write text books systematizing the knowledge in a given field play just as important a role in the advancement of science as do those who discover new knowledge by experimental research. However, it is present day fashion to underrate the former, and the road to academic promotion is paved with reprints without too much regard to their quality. The quality of our scientific education reflects this distressing imbalance.

READING 9

A SYSTEMS APPROACH TO RESEARCH MANAGEMENT:
Part 2. Technology and Its Environment *

R. E. Gibson

INTRODUCTION

In Part 1 of this series [Reading 8] we sketched an outline of technology and its components, pointing out those areas where management has a specific contribution to make. We also discussed in some detail the workings of scientific research as a subsystem in the larger system. An understanding of this subsystem is essential for the intelligent management of any technological enterprise, although the purely management functions associated with this subsystem are more concerned with restraint than action. In this part, we will deal with exploratory development and reduction to practice, and the influence of environment on these activities, noting that this is an area in which management functions play a more fundamental part.

* *Reprinted with permission from* Research Management, *vol. V, 1962.*

EXPLORATORY DEVELOPMENT

In the words of Howard Wilcox, "By exploratory development we mean the practice of investigating, creating, and designing new techniques and devices which promise to break through limitations hitherto set by nature on man's freedom of choice and action." Although the techniques and methods employed in exploratory development are often similar to those employed in scientific research, and there has always been a close connection and interchange of results between the two, their objectives are quite different. Scientific research seeks new and uncontaminated knowledge from which to make patterns of facts and ideas that lead to a deeper understanding of man and his environment. The exploratory developer, sensing the need for a new freedom of choice and action, uses all the knowledge he can glean from any source whatever, and exerts his ingenuity to put it together to give a new device, commodity, technique, or service that supplies this need. In the field of photography the close relation between scientific research and exploratory development is well seen. Actually photography has always been an exploratory development. It has used scientific knowledge wherever available but the exploratory development of new processes and techniques has so outrun the scientific understanding that C. E. K. Mees once remarked, "photography has done more for science than science has for photography."

The general nature of exploratory development is illustrated by the block diagram in Figure 9-1. Its inputs are human industry, existing knowledge, and understanding, existing arts, imagination, and skill; its outputs are new devices and techniques that are capable of giving us new possibilities for action.

It is through this system that human knowledge, imagination, ingenuity, and skill contribute to the material progress of mankind. Exploratory developments such as the domestication of animals, the invention of the sail, the steam engine, the high speed internal combustion engine have literally changed the

ecological patterns of the world and determined the course of civilization. The correlation between the availability of wind driven ships as by far the best means of hauling heavy loads over long distances and the rise of centers of populations adjacent to rivers and sea coasts is ample evidence of this. Exploratory development is a much older activity than scientific research; it goes back to and perhaps even marks the dawn of civilization. For thousands of years it remained the field of the lone inventor or the master artist and his apprentices. The old inventors used whatever knowledge they could find—some of it sound but most of it unsound. Hence, invention was a haphazard game with chances of success rather slim, so that when successful and profitable results were obtained, the techniques and processes were held in tight secrecy. Positive feedbacks were severely limited or nonexistent. The Edisonian method of invention emerged during last century. It was based on empirical knowledge systematically obtained by the combined trial and error of a team of workers. It was successful in its day, but the growth of scientific knowledge

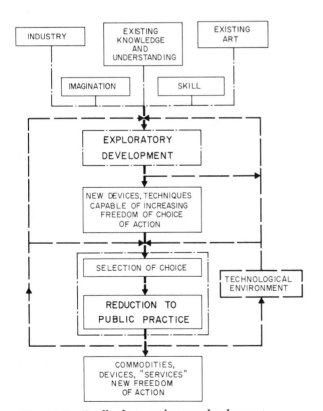

Figure 9-1 Feedbacks in exploratory development.

has brought about its obsolescence. Modern exploratory development now relies heavily on systematic knowledge and understanding, the product of scientific research, and the applied research organization I have described in connection with Figure 9-2 provides its inputs. The arrows on the dashed lines in Figure 9-1 indicate important feedbacks that now exist in exploratory development—all are positive, and our new devices, techniques, and freedoms of choice and action are increasing exponentially.

REDUCTION TO PUBLIC PRACTICE

In the overall realm of technology, the function of the research scientist is to seek and understand new human experiences; that of the exploratory developer is to apply established experience to create new devices and techniques which widen our freedom of choice and action in all fields of human endeavor. However, the selection of courses of action to be taken from the variety of choices available are not made by the scientist or the inventor but by the entrepreneurs of the business, financial, military, and political world. The introduction of a new commodity or service into use by the public at large (reduction to public practice) is an undertaking that requires capital and facilities and in the past has been motivated either by a known demand or by the probability that a demand for a product or a service may be created when it is attractively presented to the public.

Thus, when the potentialities of a new development are demonstrated, a decision to choose it as the basis for a course of action must be taken in the light of the investment in money, manpower, and skill that must be made to prepare it for public use. Its promised performance must be realized with safety, reliability, and ease of operation when it is placed in the hands of the using public. In the absence of other compelling circumstances, its cost must be within the means of potential users and must of course be favorable when compared with competing items designed to do the same job. All these attributes must be engineered into the commodity before it can be said to be *reduced to public practice.* Even then, the economic atmosphere must be such that the demand for the commodity will be large enough to justify the investment in it. The same applies to the introduction of a new service or technique—for example, a new drug or surgical operation must be tested under all conceivable conditions, the results evaluated carefully, and necessary precautions defined. The techniques and methods must be reduced to a routine that

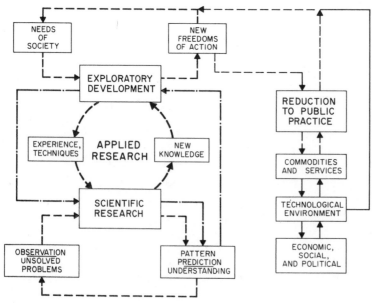

Figure 9-2   Technology block diagram.

can be safely followed by any qualified practitioner. What I have said applies to automobiles, hairdryers, washing machines, television sets, as well as to the practice of medicine, surgery, agriculture, or even the operation of machine tools.

An important factor in determining the reduction to public practice of new knowledge or developments is the "technological environment" prevailing at the time. By "technological environment" I mean the products of former developments that have been reduced to public practice. This comprises the sum total of all the know-how, skills, techniques, tools, materials, and appurtenances that are items of commerce, readily available for producing a new device or perfecting a service so that it can be presented to the using public in simple, reliable, and economical form. For example, if we wish to make a modern loudspeaker cabinet, the technological environment that affects us is the kind of wood we have available, the hand or power tools we have, the screws, the glue, the paint that we can obtain. If we had to cut down a tree, dress it with an adze, drill it with red hot irons and chisels, and hold the pieces together with wooden pegs, the job would be much slower and more difficult than it is when we have plenty of plywood, a well-stocked modern basement fortified by a good neighborhood hardware store. Indeed, it might be so difficult that we would find it impossible.

The interactions between the new development and the "technological environment" give rise to a system of feedback loops as shown in

Figures 9-1, 9-2, and 9-3. A new development not only enriches the technological environment by itself but also by the demands it makes for auxiliary materials, tools, techniques, and so forth. On the other hand, the resources of the prevailing technological environment have a great effect on the speed at which a development is reduced to public practice—a lack of such resources may even prevent the exploitation of a development. It was many years after Newcomen first demonstrated the feasibility of a steam engine that artisans were able to bore a cylinder more than 8 in. in diameter, round enough to accommodate a tight-fitting piston. The introduction of the steam engine into public practice was delayed for a long time. Indeed, one can say without exaggeration that the interactions with the technological environment have played a dominant role in determining the direction of technological progress. The technological environment is only one of the external elements that influence the course of technology. Figure 9-3 shows diagrammatically other environments that influence the direction of technological growth.

The economic environment plays an important role in determining the reduction to public practice of a potential commodity or service. Indeed, in countries encouraging and practicing free enterprise, the operation of the economic feedback loops has played the most important part in determining the direction of technological progress except in time of emergency. The "reduction to public practice" of a new development has depended strongly on its ability

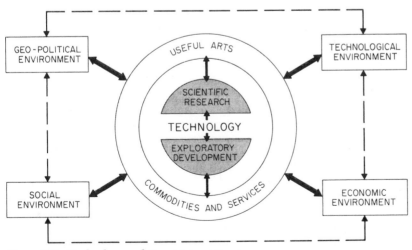

Figure 9-3   Technology and its environment.

to fulfill a need for which people not only *wanted* to pay but for which they *could* pay. The result has been intense efforts to reduce prices without apparent loss of performance, to stimulate wants by advertising, and ability to pay by extension of credit. These factors have had a strong influence on the course technology has taken. On the other hand, a healthy technology has raised its economic environment to a point where standards of living are high and the ability to assimilate more technological developments is correspondingly great.

Recently another feedback has become apparent, or rather, has spread its sphere of influence. I refer to the geopolitical or national prestige feedback. This has existed for centuries in the military sphere where nations whose technology could support development and production of advanced weapons rose to positions of eminence. However, in nonmilitary fields, the economic loop was the determining factor. The competition in space rendered acute by the successful launching of Sputnik I in October 1957 has extended the national prestige value of technological developments beyond the purely military sphere and the geopolitical feedback loop is becoming important in stimulating technological advances. The question of how long the political feedback will be a dominating factor in a free enterprise society is a very interesting one, but somewhat beyond the scope of this paper. It is my opinion, however, that its effects are more likely to grow than to diminish during the next decade.

It will be seen that the successful conduct of modern research and development activities requires that those responsible for planning and execution broaden their thinking to include the whole system shown diagrammatically in Figure 9-3. We cannot think of technology without considering its interactions with the environment of which the four main elements are shown in this diagram. The size and cost of R&D programs and the short time scale between new ideas and new commodities and services demands that the interactions with environment be taken into account even before the initiation of a substantial program.

Probably the most difficult set of problems in the management of research and development is not immediately apparent in an idealized diagram such as Figure 9-3. I refer to those arising from all the noise in the com-

munication links. The signals in the lines to technology from its environments and back again are always buried deep in a background of noise coming from the caprices and conflicts that envelop human beings. The detection of the true meaning of these signals is an art that the research director must learn.

Through scientific research, experience is being accumulated and understood at a rapidly accelerating rate, thereby furnishing an ever growing wealth of organized knowledge for new exploratory developments. Through these exploratory developments, natural limitations to freedom of action are being broken down at an even more rapid rate. The problem is shifting from one of removing limitations to freedom of action, to one of choosing wisely from the plethora of choices presented to us. The technological environment is becoming increasingly richer and consequently the technological problems associated with the reduction of a development to public practice are becoming easier. The time between the completion of a radically new development and its reduction to public practice is shortening to a few years. Over a hundred years elapsed between the first demonstration of Newcomen's engine and the first commercial railroad train. It was 50 years after Faraday first demonstrated a generator of electrical energy that the first electrical generating station supplying power to the public was opened by Edison. It was only 20–25 years after Daimler's invention of a lightweight gasoline engine that the automobile became a reasonably reliable and widely used means of transportation. Within 18 years after Goddard's 200-lb. thrust liquid fuel rocket performed successfully for the first time, the German V-2, with a thrust of 50,000 lb., was being produced in large quantities. Less than three years after the Chicago atomic pile first went critical, large scale atomic piles were operating to produce plutonium and the first bomb had exploded. Within 10 years practical atomic fuel power plants were operating and within 15 years atomic powered submarines were in commission and large-scale atomic plants were providing the public with electric power. Science, technology, and their environments now form an integrated system in which causes in any one part of the system lead rapidly to effects in another. The manager of research must now regard this whole system as his province. Even this is not enough, for technology must now be regarded as a game played in a world arena.

Migration of Technology

Although a technology may be developed and flourish in one particular country, it actually knows no national boundaries. There is a world-wide recognition that technology offers high standards of living and is actually necessary to support the tide of urbanization which is sweeping inexorably over all the world. It is an established fact that any nation which has the will to develop itself technologically can do so, and an increasing number of nations throughout the world are becoming convinced that their only hope for escaping poverty lies in modern technology.

We must, therefore, expect that the rate of growth of world-wide technology will by no means diminish in the future, and that we shall be faced with increasing competition in fields of technology and industry where we have held the leading position.

Indeed, two very old and fundamental limitations to the migration of technology are being removed, namely the limitations imposed by supplies of energy and trained manpower. The effects of the removal of these limitations will be felt more and more strongly in the next decade. With the development of atomic energy and of solar energy, the ready availability of fossil fuels need no longer be the dominant factor in the location of industries. The rapid advances in the field of automatic control, the automatic operation and control of industrial processes are removing the requirements for large numbers of highly skilled workers as a critical factor controlling the technological expansion of a society. Very shortly a handful of highly trained technicians will be able to supply a large population with industrial products. Recognition of the ease with which technology migrates throughout the world and that many of our own developments may be more easily used advantageously by others than by ourselves, with no disruption of vested interests, raises matters of grave concern to those charged with the planning of technological efforts at all levels.

Our vulnerability to the threats of international competition demands more than merely holding a Maginot line of our present industrial might. It requires a dynamic and far-sighted policy to explore new capabilities and objectives in which we can excel for a reasonable length of time. Such policy calls for an increased national investment in scientific research and education, in exploratory development to find new freedoms of action and potential capabilities, and for wise policy planning on the part of the entrepreneurs in the industrial, political, and military world to see new objectives in new capabilities and reduce them to practice at the proper time.

Objectives and Functions of Management of Research and Development

On the basis of the above discussion of scientific research and exploratory development as components of technology and of the relation of technology to society as a whole, it is possible to deduce some of the fundamental functions associated with the management of R&D organizations, for these organizations themselves are systems with communications, feedbacks, coherence and incoherence of inputs and outputs, and with constraints imposed upon them from external organizations in the economic, political, and social world. We have seen that the internal feedbacks in technology are responsible for its exponential growth—the same is true of R&D organizations. We have seen that the external feedbacks existing between technology and its environments are responsible for the *direction* of its growth—the same is true of an R&D organization. Thus, an intimate knowledge of these feedbacks and their implications is an essential part of the equipment of the management of an R&D organization.

Expanding growth is a characteristic of technology and all its components. It seems highly probable that the capacity for expanding growth and change must also be an important characteristic of an R&D organization if it is to remain dynamic and successful. This growth, however, need not be reflected in terms of commonly accepted criteria such as number of staff, floor space, volume of sales, profits, etc., indeed, these may not measure growth but merely inflation. Real growth is measured by the slope of the output curve and significant outputs of lasting value are: (*1*) hardware, exploratory developments that find a permanent place in the useful arts and in public practice, (*2*) patents, (*3*) publications in scientific literature, (4) men of experience and judgment. These outputs are not arranged in order of importance. Their quality and quantity may or may not depend on the size of the organization but they do depend on its vitality and on the functioning of important positive feedbacks associated with internal and external links.

In the first place, a network of communication channels to carry clear, certain, and timely information must be established. This requires a common basis of understanding throughout an organization, not only among groups trained in the same discipline but also among groups and individuals trained in diverse disciplines. An important function of management is to promote this common basis of understanding and a common set of values throughout the organization. Without it, the channels shown in Figure 9-2 are not effective. Vertical channels are essential for spreading a sound knowledge of the objectives throughout the organization and for ensuring that new ideas generated at any level receive prompt attention at the top. Effective horizontal communications are the best assurance of avoiding the negative effects of duplication and enhancing the positive effects of exchanging knowledge and critical discussion. A positive feedback arises from the fact that a basis of mutual understanding promotes better internal communications and better communications broaden the common basis of understanding.

A second feedback that repays attention is that existing between the outputs and the inputs of a group in an organization. This will be positive if the output of the group is of such a quality that it is coherent with the inputs. If, however, the quality and timeliness of the output of a group drops through causes such as sloppy thinking, shoddy workmanship, poor planning, or tardy communications, this feedback ceases and even becomes negative. In most research and development activities, timeliness and clarity of communications are extremely important—the delays in communicating results may well destroy the positive nature of the feedbacks.

It is generally agreed that one of the most baffling problems in the management of research and development is the establishment of criteria for evaluating the productivity of a group or organization. It is suggested that the feedbacks from output to input of the group constitute a focal spot for such an evaluation.

If these are highly positive, the group cannot fail to be productive; if they are low or negative, remedial measures are imperative.

The *external* links involving interactions with the technological, economic, social, and political environments are the channels through which the raw material for policy making flows into an organization. They provide the basis for estimating the compatibility of the products of R&D with the potential and demands of the environment; and of assessing the probability that a development will not only be excellent technically but that it can be reduced to public practice with "profitable" results, using the term in its broadest sense. Because of lead times and "noise," these environmental interactions present particularly difficult problems to the management of R&D organizations who must know not only the present state of environments but must be able to forecast future economic, social, and geopolitical demands years before they become acutely obvious.

These problems are difficult and important enough to warrant the full time attention of a staff group, specializing in a study of environmental interactions and operations analysis or other methods of assessing the relative potential values of different developments. Such staff groups are absolutely essential if the implications of the complex environmental interactions are to be reduced to understandable form.

Probably the chief function of the research manager is to ensure that the organization over which he presides and all its members make the most effective use of time, as measured in years rather than hours. Time is the commodity in shortest supply and is a basis on which all compete on equal terms. The effective use of time not only requires skillful planning, it also requires a scrutiny of all activities in an organization to ensure that they contribute positive feedbacks. If they do not, their usefulness is in question. For example, a reporting system should be such that each stage contributes a real feedback to the previous one as well as a significant communication forward. This feedback should always clarify or add to the ideas of the person writing the report as well as those of the reader.

Summarizing this part we emphasize the following points:

1 A systems approach to the management of research and development focusses the at-

tention of the manager on the formulation of the larger system *in which* he has to operate as well as on the subsystem (laboratory or group) which is his particular responsibility. The larger system must not only contain the subsystem but also *all* the sources of significant information (significant inputs) to the subsystem that influence the outputs of the subsystem. This is essential for recognition of the phase and amplitude of the external feedbacks that determine direction of healthy growth.

2 Systems approach to the management of research and development draws attention to the control of internal feedbacks both in amplitude and phase as a prime function of the management of a program or organization. These are the mechanisms determining growth or stagnation. They provide an index of progress and a point of entry for effective action. They are particularly significant as an index of the health of the overall communications of the organization.

3 The systems approach to research management places utmost emphasis on choice of objectives and the boundary conditions that influence this choice. These conditions arise from internal sources, external sources, and time considerations. The objectives chosen must be within the competence of the organization to deliver at the proper time products that meet the requirements imposed by the environment at that time.

4 Making the most effective use of time is the chief responsibility of research management.

READING 10

A SYSTEMS APPROACH TO MANPOWER MANAGEMENT*

Edgar G. Williams

Automation, data processing, and other technological developments are forcing personnel executives to reappraise their traditional roles and functions. The conventional specialization that has been their stock in trade is proving to be overly microscopic and myopic.

Manpower management must be viewed as a total system, interrelated and interacting with the other systems of work—the creative, the financial, and the distribution systems—with which a business or social institution operates. The ideas that follow attempt to expedite understanding such an approach.

People and their problems absorb much of every manager's time. The responsibility for manpower management in a leadership position cannot be extracted without managerial abdication, although personnel specialists may be assigned some of the work.

Manpower management permeates all organizational levels and units. Competent managers, well-versed in the behavioral and social

* *Reprinted with permission from* Business Horizons, *Summer, 1964.*

sciences, can establish and maintain desirable human relationships that contribute to organizational effectiveness, personal satisfactions, personal growth and development, and productivity and profits.

In any business enterprise, modern manpower management involves four separate but interrelated factors: a manpower philosophy or point of view, the existing personnel climate or environment, the manpower program, and the manpower system.

Concerned with people, their work behavior, and desirable organizational relationships, a *manpower philosophy* consists of fundamental concepts, ideals, principles, and methods relative to manpower resources. Any such system of thought must be suited to the framework of social, economic, technological, and political elements which exist at a particular time and place. This variable combination of internal and external elements that impinge on and influence manpower decisions and actions is the *personnel climate.*

A manpower philosophy adaptable to a particular climate makes it possible to create a

READING 11

DEFENSE SYSTEMS MANAGEMENT: THE 375 SERIES*

Edward J. Morrison

Significant changes have recently been instituted in contracting arrangements between the Department of Defense and the aerospace industry. Through spelling out specific rules and approaches to sharpen systems management, the Department of Defense and the Air Force have taken an important step toward a revision of management practices in that important area. However, the total implications of these changes for aerospace management today, and for government-industry relationships in the future, while still unclear, are likely to be considerable.

Although the exposition of this article is limited to relationships between the Air Force and the aerospace industry, such relationships may prove to be a pattern acceptable to, and adopted by, other governmental agencies in their contracting with private industry. Widespread adoption of these relationships would signal a basic departure from current business

* *Reprinted from* California Management Review, *vol. IX, no. 4, Summer, 1967. Copyright 1967 by The Regents of The University of California.*

practice. Under the new systems management concept:

A new structural relationship has been created in which the Air Force, as a buyer, makes specific management decisions about policy and detailed procedures within aerospace companies that sell defense systems to the Air Force.

The manuals prescribing new systems management concepts and procedures are very large, full of detail, and subject to varying interpretation by officials in government and private contractor organizations. As a result, private contractors may find it difficult to know if they are "in conformance" with new systems management requirements.

Questions may be raised about centralization of power, as government makes industry decisions that were previously made by private contractors.

Managers in private contracting firms may begin to worry more about satisfying government requirements than about producing the most effective weapons systems.

I do not intend to be negatively critical of

the parties involved, but rather seek to examine efforts to date in this field and to point out some of the potential gains and potential problems inherent in such a management accommodation.

A HUGE PLANNING TASK

National defense is a costly business. Maximum efficiency in Department of Defense operations requires a clear statement of national objectives, defense objectives, and a careful consideration of potential weapons systems that will satisfy those objectives. The Department of Defense is concerned with balancing the cost and advantages of any single weapons system against the costs and performance of every other system. This huge planning task must consider short-range requirements as well as those five, ten, or twenty years in the future.

When management decisions involve hundreds of millions, or even billions of dollars, even a small percentage error in estimating by the Department of Defense may result in sizable mistakes. Large sums of money may be wasted if the government finds out, months or years after letting a contract, that the weapons system is not technically adequate or feasible. Also, if there is not a thorough evaluation of the objectives upon which acquisition of a weapons system is made, later examination of these objectives may result in scrapping an entire system into which millions of dollars have been invested. Sophisticated planning tools are required for such a large, important task. For years the government has looked hopefully to private companies in the aerospace industry to develop and standardize management planning and controlling tools throughout the industry; for the most part, standardization did not occur.

During the years since World War II, the Air Force let contracts for weapons systems and utilized a system of Air Force plant representative officers to supervise contractors' performance and to assure conformance to contract specifications and system requirements. Often assistance in this task was hired from technically competent independent firms. However, for a number of reasons, occurring in part from government actions and in part from private contractor practices, serious management and technical problems often beset the achievement of aerospace contract objectives.

In 1964 the Air Force announced a series of manuals that set up a management program designed to enforce consistent management logic and control over acquisition of all future weapons systems to be procured by the Air Force. In its scope and specificity it sounded a significant, and to some an ominous, change in the relationship between government and private business. Public announcements[1] left little doubt that the Air Force was going to try to instill and require the same management discipline in its own Systems Command and in all companies that wish to do business with the Air Force. The tool selected to effect management discipline was a series of Air Force Systems Command Manuals, referred to as the 375 Series.

To those in industry who have expressed fear that government would stifle creativity, government spokesmen replied that they preferred the word "limit" to stifle and then said further that limits should be established to make an innovator conform to the total integrated impact of a program.[2]

The 375 Series was not conceived in a vacuum. Several years of intense management effort in the Department of Defense (DOD) resulted in a more coherent way of doing defense business as well as in the isolation of many problems and problem symptoms. DOD management is concerned with many problems, some of genuine interest to private industry, including:

Excessive growth of program costs.
Serious schedule slippages.
Too frequent redirection and cancellation.
Inadequately defined mission, performance, and operating requirements.
Unrealistic cost and schedule estimates.
Frequent engineering and program management changes.
Inadequate consideration of production unit costs or reliability and the ease of maintenance of hardware.

PROGRAM PACKAGE CONCEPT

In order to combat these problems, the Department of Defense developed a program package concept that relates planning and budgeting to mission-oriented defense requirements. Where previous budgets requested so much for hardware, personnel, operations, etc., the program package concept identifies nine basic defense programs and further segregates each of these into program elements. Each program element is dollar-costed and time-phased functionally. Collectively, these program elements, when costed in a five-year time frame, represent a five-year force structure.[3] This force structure demonstrates the DOD's ability to meet national defense objectives during the next five years. If a new weapons system is to be included and budgeted in the force structure, a program change proposal must first be approved by the Secretary of Defense.

Other concepts were promulgated to facilitate handling the urgencies and complexities of an effective defense posture. The "concurrency concept" stated that several portions of a system can be developed at the same time in order to shorten the time between initiation of a project and its completion. Contract definition has been refined: to speed engineering development by early approval by the Secretary of Defense; to define fully structured fixed price or incentive price contracts; to facilitate system project management; and to extend management planning and control techniques applied to DOD contracts. These changes sound complex (and in operation they are) but later portions of this article should provide some clarification of their nature and effect on the DOD agencies and private contractors doing business with the government.

THE SYSTEM LIFE CYCLE

Phases of a defense system life cycle.   Before discussing the impact of the 375 Series manuals upon government agencies and private contractors, it will be helpful to examine the Defense System Life Cycle in which they are applied. Very briefly a system goes through the following stages:[4]

1 *Concept formulation.* Develop the concept of a system and establish its feasibility.
2 *Contract definition.* Sufficiently define the system and the engineering and development effort necessary.

3 *Acquisition phase.* Physically acquire the system (detail design, development, procurement, and testing).
4 *Operational phase.* Deliver and place the system in use.

As Figure 11-1 indicates, the acquisition and operational phases overlap. As the first end items of hardware and software are developed, produced, tested, and accepted by the Air Force, they are transferred to a using command and made operational with active logistic support. These phases will be covered in more detail.

On July 1, 1965, DOD Directive 3200.9 redefined the relationships and interfaces[5] between government and contractors during the first two phases of a system life cycle. This redefinition is important because it shows the intent of DOD and identifies a complex and somewhat unique relationship between the Air Force as a buyer and the aerospace industry as a seller. As one reads the following paragraphs, it might be interesting to imagine these relationships as if they applied to one's own business' buyer-seller relationships.

Concept formulation.   Completed during this phase are the experimental tests—engineering and analytical studies that provide the technical, economic, and military basis for a decision to develop the equipment or system. Certain steps must be accomplished and demonstrated by a contractor to the Air Force, then by the Air Force to the DOD:[6]

Establish that primarily engineering, rather than experimental, effort is required and that the technology needed is sufficiently in hand.
Define mission and performance envelopes.
Select best technical approaches.
Make thorough trade-off analyses.
Assure that cost effectiveness of the proposed item is determined favorably in relationship to cost effectiveness of competing items (on a DOD-wide basis).

Figure 11-1   Defense system life cycle.

Assure that cost and schedule estimates are credible and acceptable.

One or more contractors may be involved in this concept formulation phase, and one or more contractors may be paid for its work. Obviously, the Air Force Systems Command must be interested in the project if it is to be submitted and recommended to the Office of the Secretary of Defense for consideration. If all of the steps above are accomplished, the Office of the Secretary of Defense may give conditional approval for engineering development and appoint a source selection authority that will eventually make the choice of contractor(s) to define, develop, and produce the equipment or system.

Contract definition.   Having established the desirability and feasibility of a certain weapons concept, the DOD will finance contract definition efforts, usually by two or more contractors, each working in close collaboration with the DOD component having development responsibility. DOD Directive 3200.9 states that after contractors have been selected,

> . . . A fully competitive environment shall be established with the competition in terms of concept, design approach, trade-off solutions, management plans, schedule, and similar factors as well as over-all cost.[7]

The screening and negotiating processes occur in phase A of contract definition (see Figure 11-1). During phase B, the work in the competitive environment described immediately above is done. As a result of phase B, competing contractors each submit a contract definition report and a complete technical, management, and cost proposal for development of the proposed system.

These outputs accomplish the following:[8]

Provide a basis for a fixed price or a fully structured incentive contract for engineering development.
Establish firm and realistic performance specifications.
Precisely define interfaces and responsibilities.
Identify high-risk areas.
Validate technical approaches.
Establish firm and realistic schedule and cost estimates for engineering development (in-

cluding production engineering, facilities, construction, and production hardware that will be funded during engineering development because of concurrency considerations). Establish schedule and cost estimates for planning purposes for the total project (including production, operation, and maintenance).

During phase C of contract definition the proposals submitted by each competing contractor are evaluated by the source selection evaluation board with assistance from the source selection advisory council (cf. DOD Directive 4105.2, April 6, 1965). After the development contractor has been selected, the evaluation board may also recommend what is known as "technical transfusion,"[9] i.e., concepts, management plans, etc., may be taken from one DOD-financed contract definition proposal or another previously contracted technical study and incorporated in another proposal in order to make it stronger. The government may do this since it contracted for unlimited rights to technical data produced in a DOD-financed contract study.

As a result of technical transfusion, the desired changes are incorporated in a contract proposal which is then submitted with a DOD-component recommendation. (Not all proposals are recommended for additional action.) The Secretary of Defense then rules on the recommendation, and, if it is approved, a definite engineering development contract is negotiated and executed, usually with only one private contractor.

Contractor organization.   As a side note, it might be mentioned that three types of contractor organization structures have been considered closely by the Air Force. One type of contractor organization currently in effect is called "functionally oriented" in which the mode of organization is by technical disciplines, such as electrical engineering, mechanical engineering, mathematical department, etc. This type of organization lacks central project control and is not looked on very favorably by the customer (e.g., the Air Force). A second mode of organization is called "fully project oriented," and under this arrangement each project within the contractor's company has its own engineering, manufacturing, and other departments. A third mode of organization is sometimes called a "bi-lateral line" organization (Figure 11-2). It has the strength of a

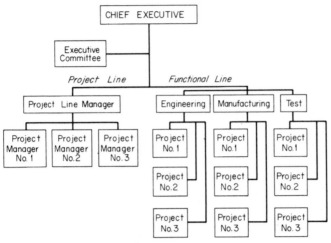

Figure 11-2   Contractor organization: bilateral line.

single project manager within the contractor's firm who is responsible for budget, schedule, and technical performance of each project. Under this type of arrangement the customer (AF) has a single responsible source for contact, and the company may retain the advantages of a concentrated technical discipline within a functional department.[10] In many respects, this type of organization closely parallels the relationship between the systems program office and other participating governmental organizations and civilian contractors. (See AFSCM 375-3, Chapter 3, June 15, 1964.)

Because of the detail specified in the 375 Series manuals, the acquisition and operational phases will be discussed in the following section.

One of the major problems of defense systems management is the immensity of the task. Time spans between system conception and phase-out are often long; many government and private organizations are usually involved. The size of some systems, such as the TFX airplane, is huge, and the technology is often complex. In fact, the same factors that make systems management difficult also make it mandatory.

The Department of Defense has insisted that its systems command be organized to impose more vigorous systems management on their operations. The vehicle for communicating **how** systems management should be performed is the so-called "375 Series." A number of DOD directives and Air Force regulations prescribe and refer to the 375 Series of Air Force Systems Command Manuals, the most important of which are the following:

AFSCM 375-1   Configuration Management
AFSCM 375-3   System Program Office Manual
AFSCM 375-4   System Program Management
AFSCM 375-5   System Engineering Management Procedures
AFSCM 375-6   Development Engineering
AFSCM 310-1   Management of Contractor Data and Reports.

In addition, many other related manuals, program management instructions, AF Headquarters operating instructions, pamphlets, and regulations are relevant to, or prescribe the performance of, systems management. Some of these documents speak solely to government agencies, while others specify required private contractor management practices. In many instances, the systems command requires extensive standard information outputs for all contractors so that it may make valid comparisons. These requirements will affect contractors' internal management information gathering and reporting procedures as well as their management decision-making practices.

The scope and interrelationship of the 375 Series may be seen within the framework of the systems program office which has systems management responsibility for every authorized project (Figure 11-3).

One of the most difficult problems of working with the 375 Series is their sheer size. Moreover, much of the material is covered in

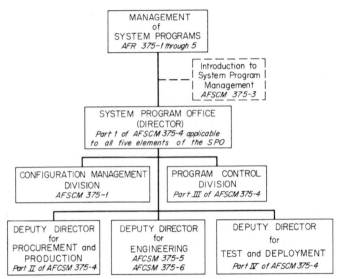

Figure 11-3 Relationship of systems management manuals.

great detail. It is, therefore, difficult for a private contractor to know the extent to which his normal management practices will be affected when he "gets into conformance" with the requirements of the 375 Series.

There is a logic inherent in the manuals, but unfortunately it is not reflected in their numbering system. Perhaps the uninitiated should begin with 375–3, then read 375–4 and DOD Directive 3200.9. The 375–4 manual indicates when other references are necessary to follow the complete sequence of systems management events, and it directs one to 375–1, 375–5, and 310–1 for more detailed explanations of the functions they describe.[11] In this article the manuals are treated in that order, omitting DOD Directive 3200.9 which was covered earlier.

System program office manual, AFSCM 375–3.

This manual contains introductory information and is written in a casual style to familiarize those who may be interested in defense systems management. It discusses basic systems management concepts, systems program office organization, control techniques, functional areas of systems management, and organizational relationships among the various members of the "government/industry team."

System program management procedures, AFSCM 375–4.

Appropriately, AFSCM 375–4 may be considered to be the "parent" manual of this series. This manual establishes the scope, objectives, and procedures for the conceptual, definition, acquisition, and operational phases of a system program. By using the systems program office as a focal point, it prescribes the significant management activities for integrating and fulfilling responsibilities of organizational elements involved in managing a system program. AFSCM 375–4 is a mandatory standard for all future systems command programs and projects.[12]

Part I defines the basic requirements for program control, configuration management, procurement and production, engineering and test, and deployment. These basic requirements are to be implemented by AFSCM 375–1, AFSCM 375–5, AFSCM 310–1, and Parts II, III, and IV of AFSCM 375–4.[13]

A series of "road maps" portrays the sequence of management activities and organizational interaction during the four phases of a system life cycle. These "road maps" are described and explained in considerable detail in the body of AFSCM 375–4, and they provide the reader with the sequential flow of activities involved in systems management. When the details of these activities become too complex, or when higher authority is needed to authorize action, the reader is invited to refer to other documents as appropriate, such as regulations, directives, or further portions of the 375 Series.

By following sequenced events and guidelines described in AFSCM 375–4, as augmented by 375–1, 375–5, and 310–1, program managers should achieve an integrated management information system that will:

Measure progress in meeting program objectives of schedule, cost, and technical performance.

Rank problems in terms of their criticality in meeting program objectives.

Provide each level of management with information in necessary detail for decision-making purposes.

Managing the system life cycle of a defense system of the magnitude of the TFX or the C-5A airplane programs is a Herculean task, and one would expect management guidelines to expand into considerable proportions. The problems of configuration management, systems engineering, and data management are immense.

Configuration management during the definition and acquisition phases, AFSCM 375–1. This function is concerned with identifying, controlling, and accounting for all hardware and facility requirements. During each phase of the life cycle of a system, it is essential to describe fully the picture or profile of each element of the system at that time. These specifications may then be used as a bench mark or baseline against which activities of the next phase may be controlled.

Three major requirements baselines are employed in defense systems management. The contract definition phase is controlled against a **program requirements baseline** which is established by a system specification. During the contract definition phase, hardware and facilities design requirements are further defined and finally established as a **design requirements baseline** against which detailed design and production may be controlled.[14] When the customer formally accepts the first article produced and agrees that it satisfies contractual requirements of technical performance, a third bench mark, the **product configuration baseline,** is established. This baseline is used to control future builds and tests of the article.

During engineering development and production, there are inevitably going to be changes in established baselines. Before such changes may be authorized, each one must be examined to insure that it is compatible with all other system elements, as well as with in-

service equipment. The change must also be timely, feasible, and necessary. Further, any changes that are finally agreed upon must be reflected in the baseline against which they are made.

Another function of configuration management is to report the current status of baselines: of contracts, of specifications, of designs, and of facilities, hardware, and associated software. When the technology of a product is complex, these baselines must be thoroughly defined in detail and the critical interfaces identified to permit control. It is easy to see why electronic data-processing equipment is used to handle the extensive data necessary for effective configuration management. In programs of great complexity or magnitude, it is vital to provide maximum visibility of high-risk technical interfaces and to maintain high standards of technical control.

System engineering management procedures, AFSCM 375–5.   The intent of this manual is to introduce the concept of **total systems design** into Air Force systems command management thinking and into private contractors' engineering organizations. As explained by the manual, total systems design will be accomplished through systems engineering, using a uniform design process. These three terms are further defined and elaborated.

As a result of usage, states the manual, the term "systems" includes:

> . . . prime mission equipment; computer programs; equipment for training, checkout, test, and maintenance; facilities required to operate and maintain the system; selection and training of personnel; operational and maintenance procedures; instrumentation and data reduction for test and evaluation; special activation and acceptance programs; and logistics support for test, activation, and operational aspects of the program.[15]

Obviously, this is a broad definition of the term that necessitates a broad consideration of engineering management problems.

Systems engineering is concerned with deriving a total system design to achieve stated objectives—a single set of optimum outputs based on given inputs. Total systems design includes engineering all system elements and components and their interrelationships for the duration of the total program. Program objectives require that schedule, cost, and technical performance should all be weighed in the evaluation of engineering results.

The manual directs that a uniform design process be followed in systems engineering. It is recognized, in the manual, that:

> No two systems are ever alike in their developmental requirements. However, there is a uniform and identifiable process for logically arriving at systems decisions regardless of systems purpose, size, or complexity. This manual describes and specifies such a process, i.e., a systems engineering management process.[16]

Under this systems engineering management process, there would be an integration of all relevant design disciplines and single control over evaluation of requirements and design. A planned flow of technical information permits dynamic updating of engineering results. Further, basic data would be readily accessible for determining detailed requirements for personnel subsystems, logistics, and procedural publications. The manual prescribes detailed procedures that are designed to facilitate each of the above processes.

By enforcing adherence to this systems engineering management process, the Air Force hopes to achieve several innovations to its past practices, for example:

Develop and identify performance and design specifications before the fact (of detailed design).
Require management to make earlier identification of control, accounting, and system requirements.
Provide a mandatory flow of documentation to the systems command earlier in the program, identifying problem areas and recommending courses of action.
Provide necessary data for making systems management and command decisions.

Generally, systems engineering encourages:

1 Greater visibility of engineering performance.
2 Earlier systems engineering management action.
3 Earlier program management decisions.

Management of contractor data and reports, AFSCM 310–1/AFLCM 310–1.   Although

this manual does not bear the "375 Series" designation, adherence to its specifications is required by AFSCM 375–4 (cf. pp. 57 and 91), as well as AFSCM 375–5 (cf. p. 3). Further, AFSCM 375–3 states that the systems program office is responsible for acquisition of all data, including engineering management, and logistics information and must assure that it is available at the proper time and location. To accomplish this mission, a data management officer is appointed by the system program office.[17]

Data management is a significant and complicated requirement for both the governmental and private contractors. This manual alone is over 1,200 pages long, and is very detailed in its requirements. It specifies types of reports, their form, layout, and contents, and sometimes the size and requirements of each data element included.

Effective performance of data management results in adequate, timely documentation of activities and decisions that have occurred in previous phases of a system life cycle. In fact, contractor data are often a large part of the "product" that is bought under contracts for defense systems. Much work has been done and is being done in this area of data management. However, anyone associated with this function, either in government or out, will agree that much more effort is required before completely meaningful, useful, and manageable systems will be obtained.

CHANGE IN THINKING

From the foregoing exposition, one may discern a major change in the Department of Defense's thinking about systems management. Previous defense contract relationships were characterized by government's stating broader objectives and policies, while leaving the specifics of implementation to private contractors. Determination of satisfactory contractor performance usually came after completion of a project and was accomplished by comparing contract specifications with documentation and hardware performance. In too many instances, the comparisons were inconclusive or less than satisfactory.

Expanded government authority.   Under systems management concepts embodied in the 375 Series, the government's role is considerably enlarged and made much more specific. A systems program director is responsible for program objectives of cost, schedule, and technical performance. He is also responsible for management decisions about specific engineering management disciplines employed by private contractors. He is responsible for detailed management control and reporting procedures and for many other decisions about how well a private contractor's management is doing a job. Under the 375 Series procedures, the government's management authority does not wait until after a product is produced; it works actively while the project is in progress.

Basic structural change.   A realignment of roles played by government agencies and private industry has been described in this article, and this realignment will undoubtedly have significant, lasting effects on the parties involved. Whenever a basic structural change occurs between two large, powerful parties in our economy, one may expect to find significant changes of several kinds. This last statement is predicated on the notion that other government agencies will follow the lead of the 375 Series (such as the National Aeronautics and Space Agency [NASA] is doing with its "500" Series") and that eventually many nonaerospace companies will have to deal with similar requirements imposed by nondefense-oriented governmental agencies that procure private industry goods and services. From observation of the present situation, several problems may result.

THE POSSIBLE CONSEQUENCES

Emerging problems.   It should be obvious that the government enjoys a somewhat privileged relationship as a customer dealing with private business. Typically, a customer buys a product that meets his desired specifications and leaves the process of achieving that product to those who manage the producing organization. By virtue of prescribing extensive management systems and practices that must be followed by companies wishing to do business with it; by reserving (and exercising) the right of review and possible rejection of internal management procedures and operating practices; and by passing technical judgment on the validity, accuracy, and adequacy of technical data, the Air Force places itself in an interesting position. Several possibilities are apparent.

Who is responsible?   Aerospace companies' executives may begin to manage their operations more with an eye to satisfying customer-designed management system requirements than to producing a product they think will perform best in a manner that they feel is most expeditious and most technically fruitful. This reorientation of management attention is more than just a matter of "stifling creativity." It places the right and responsibility for critical management decisions with the Air Force rather than with the contractor. If a wrong decision is made, a forceful argument can be presented that the Air Force had the right of technical review and disapproval and that, in not disapproving, it did, in fact, give tacit approval to the decision in question. This raises a disturbing question of legal liability for payment by the Air Force, even when performance of an end item is not according to prescribed specifications.

Management interpretation.   It is inevitable that a document such as the 375 Series will contain words or paragraphs that are somewhat ambiguous, leaving room for varying interpretation by private contractors or government officials. Examination of current practice shows that variation in interpreting managerial specifications has, in fact, occurred. This variance has the effect of establishing a confusion in personal relationships between a program office and private contractors and may result in some firms being much more controlled than others.

Too much centralization?   A further problem inherent in this customer-contractor relationship may be found in the question of where and by whom technical and management decisions can best be made—the level of decision making inherent in decentralization. Much has been reported in the literature to indicate that decisions should be made as close as possible to the level of occurrence of problems and by people most fully informed about the problems and technically capable of making those decisions.[18] According to this literature, it would seem inadvisable to give the right of review and responsibility for disapproval of problem solutions to an "outside agency" not "in the business" of producing the items in question. Delay of decisions is inevitable. Also, even with technical assistance, it is still difficult to understand fully the intricacies of operating situations and to make better decisions from a remote location and organization that can be made by persons more closely involved in such a situation.

Tons of data—how useful?   In reporting data to the customer, many useless or even dysfunctional reports may be generated and forwarded for review and storage. The massive data requirements for aerospace development, acquisition, and operation would stagger the casual observer and impress even the trained practitioner. The impact of this problem is evidenced by subcontractors who refuse to accept business with aerospace companies because of unrealistic documentation requirements imposed on them. Although discipline in handling data requirements is admittedly necessary, the complexity of this subject area reveals a need for careful analysis and much better systems. One primary danger lies in developing reports that provide prescribed data but that result in little management analysis and decision. Those people involved in electronic data processing, management systems, and contractual data requirements understand the critical nature of this problem far beyond the scope of this article's elaboration of it.

Stifling innovation?   A fundamental question is raised about what is the most fruitful business environment for technical innovation. There seems to be no great customer complaints with technology created under existing management systems; however, greater management control is desired in acquiring systems embodying that technology. The 375 Series inaugurates extensive engineering management controls and a uniform design process, and it remains to be seen whether technical innovation will occur at a satisfactory rate under this system.

In conclusion, one is faced with a certainty and an uncertainty. It is certain that the Department of Defense has expressed its conclusions that previous government/industry relationships were not a satisfactory method of acquiring defense systems. Since the Department of Defense is certainly by far the largest customer for aerospace products, the government has the power to change those relationships. But responsibility must accompany power, and, as government assumes its new management role, it should assume a greater responsibility of some sort toward private industry. It may be concluded that in entering these uncharted relationships the long-run management consequences of changes attempted through application of the 375 Series are still very uncertain.

References

1. Philip Geddes, "Customer Closes Loopholes in Program Management," *Aerospace Management*, April 1964.
2. *Ibid.*
3. *Air Force Systems Command Manual* (AFSCM) 375–4, p. 4, Final Coordination Draft, June 1965.
4. *Ibid.*, p. 1.
5. The word "interface" is a useful part of aerospace industry jargon. The word indicates a meeting or tangency of two or more elements—technical elements or organizational elements—but it does not indicate the nature of the relationship that exists. However, if one is aware of a meeting point, further consideration may be given to defining the nature and criticality of that relationship.
6. DOD Directive 3200.9, July 1, 1965, p. 4.
7. *Ibid.*, p. 6.
8. *Ibid.*, p. 3.
9. *Ibid.*, p. 9 and AFSCM 375–4, p. 85.
10. Some work has been done in describing the nature of matrix organizations; cf. John Mee, "Matrix Organization," *Business Horizons*, VII:2 (Spring 1964), 70–72, and Fremont A. Shull, "Matrix Structure and Project Authority for Optimizing Organizational Capacity" (Business Science Monograph, No. 1, Business Research Bureau; Carbondale, Illinois: Southern Illinois University, n.d.). More work should be done on the effects of such arrangements.
11. AFSCM 375–2 covers management surveys, is not mentioned in AFSCM 375–4, and is not currently in use. AFSCM 375–6 deals specifically with development engineering and will not be covered in this article.
12. Cf. AFSCM 375–4, p.*i.*
13. *Ibid.*, p. 4.
14. AFSCM 375–3, p. 39.
15. AFSCM 375–5, p.*i*, Dec. 14, 1964.
16. *Ibid.*
17. AFSCM 375–3, p. 42.
18. For a discussion of this subject as regards individual firms, see R. C. Davis, *Fundamentals of Top Management* (New York: Harper and Brothers, 1951), pp. 306–316, and Koontz and O'Donnell, *Principles of Management* (New York: McGraw-Hill Book Company, Inc., 1964), chap. 17.

SECTION 3

Planning

Planning involves preparing to meet the future. However, since we shall all meet our future, whatever it may be, and since we are not all planners, a more precise description is necessary. The key word is "preparing." To be prepared to meet the future means that one is able both to adapt effectively and efficiently to the changes which the future will surely bring, but also, that one is able to take advantage of the opportunities which the future presents.

Planning, especially that of the "long-range" variety, is receiving a great deal of attention in the literature of management and associated fields of specialization. Many different views of the planning function are popular, ranging from the simple relationship of planning to forecasting to a view of planning which encompasses a systems view of the management process. The view taken in this section is somewhat temperate but it is more nearly the latter than the former.

Planning is one of the central functions of management. Without planning, it is not possible for the manager to perform his other functions, e.g., organizing, controlling, etc. If the organization has any goal other than self-perpetuation, it is necessary for the manager to direct it toward the future accomplishment of these goals. Indeed, even if self-preservation is the only goal, the organization is more likely to achieve it in a changing environment through planning than it is without planning.

Crucial to the planning function are the organization's objectives. Many large organizations have little idea what their objectives are. Indeed, the idea of an *organization perceiving its objectives really means that the humans who control the organization's destiny do so, and it is vividly clear that many do not. Although an objective of most industrial firms is growth, many have failed to delineate those areas in which growth is both practical and profitable. In failing to do so, they have precluded themselves from taking advantage of the future. As a result, they will be forced to react to a changing environment, and unless they are very fortunate, will be in a position of "catching up" with trends rather than leading them.*

A variety of forces have influenced the planning activities carried on in modern organizations. The Department of Defense embarked on organized planning activities in advance of most industries. Yet, the interplay between government and industry planning is made apparent when one reviews the literature to find papers which emphasize what industry has learned about planning from government (witness the excellent paper by Smalter) and those which treat the impact of industry's planning activities on government. Indeed, both are valid, for the interaction has been great, and the transfer has operated in both directions.

Another major force which has led to increased formal planning emanates from the success achieved by quantitative decision analysis. The fields of concern, e.g., operations research, systems analysis, management science, etc., have demonstrated that analysis can be applied to strategic planning. In doing so, they have provided both techniques to aid planners and a framework on which planning can be performed and evaluated.

During the past few years many companies have established full-time positions with a function variously referred to as "top management planning" or "long-range planning." The continued establishment of these positions indicates that the development of corporate strategy and a system of plans to support that strategy is evolving as a major function in many U.S. Corporations. Although executive personnel have always performed a degree of long-range planning, it is still a rather recent innovation, particularly in the degree of formality being established in organizational arrangements and modus operandi. *The recent furor over long-range planning has produced only a few books; the periodical literature has been enriched with some very perceptive articles on the subject. In this section some of the better articles are reflected; the articles deal with the conceptual framework of long-range planning as well as describing some of the tools that can be used in performing long-range planning.*

READING 12

WHERE LONG-RANGE PLANNING GOES WRONG*

E. Kirby Warren

In comparatively recent years, the emphasis in business planning has moved from adapting to change to actively anticipating and planning for change. With the growth of large corporations and the increased amount, speed, and magnitude of change—economic, social, technological, and competitive—adaptation alone has often proved inadequate to insure corporate survival and profitability.

This is not to say that long-range planning is a new activity; farsighted businessmen have devoted their time and energy to it for at least the last half century. But the increased size and complexity of business have made long-range planning of vital importance in recent years, and companies today ignore it at their peril.

Moreover, the increasing size of corporations—and, indeed, of the economy itself—have taken such planning out of the realm of activities that can be handled informally by a top executive.

* *Reprinted from* Management Review, *by permission of the American Management Association, Inc.,* May, 1962.

tive. The magnitude of the task and the growing number of other responsibilities that must be handled by top management have made it necessary to delegate major portions of the job to other levels of the organization. With this delegation has come the need for more formalized procedures; with it, also, has come the increased danger of error in the performance of any one of its parts or, more important, in the assembly of these parts into a meaningful and integrated whole.

Thus it happens that, at the very time companies are depending most heavily on long-range planning and devoting the greatest efforts to it, they often find that the resulting long-range plans are inadequate, inappropriate, and sometimes extremely harmful to the company.

To see why this should be so, we can take a look at the four major functional parts of long-range planning and see the ways in which the planners involved most often go wrong. Long-range planning can be separated into four basic types of activities that must be performed:

1 Forecasting activities.
2 Budget and financial accounting activities.
3 Setting goals and designing action programs.
4 Direction, supervision, and coordination of planning activities.

FORECASTING

There is a great deal of circularity in the sequencing of these functions, but given a basic sense of the broad goals sought, the first basic phase of long-range planning is forecasting. Despite the difficulties brought on by a rapidly changing business environment, the potential ability to carry out this function has greatly increased in recent years. Not only do improved forecasting techniques enable the planner to make more valid estimates about the future, but there is also considerable increase in the availability of information on virtually every facet of business and economic life. The many surveys and special studies sponsored by governmental agencies provide a wealth of data that not too long ago would have been costly if not impossible for business to obtain. Less directly, government regulations requiring corporations to disclose information that had previously been carefully concealed made still more valuable information available. And the growing sense of professionalism in business management has paved the way for voluntary exchange of business data. Trade associations play an active role in this area by fostering the exchange of information and encouraging the pooling of corporate resources and experience.

Despite these advances, the quality of current long-range forecasting falls considerably short of both what is desirable and what is possible. Time and again, instead of representing estimates of expected or desired future states, given projected internal and external changes, the forecasts or planning assumptions are only mechanical extrapolations of trend.

Rose-colored Glasses

There are two basic causes for this, both stemming from apparent misconceptions about the purpose and nature of forecasting. The fundamental reason for making forecasts is the desire to estimate as accurately as possible the expected outcome of a number of controllable and uncontrollable actions. Despite this, the first major cause of poor forecasting is the feeling of many forecasters that their projections often have to represent what management wants to see, rather than what they are likely to see.

A corporate-level "plans analyst" in one decentralized heavy-industry firm showed unusual candor in confirming this conclusion:

"In many cases, [division planners] show corporate management what they feel corporate management wants to see. They paint a picture that may be unrealistic, but it usually takes two or three years for this to become apparent. Often, they attain their goals for totally different reasons than were planned. Even more often, as might be expected, they fail to realize their objectives.

"Division management seems to take the view that if things don't work out as well as expected, they have the uncertainty of the future to fall back on. At worst, once every three or four years they may get a real going-over, but this is accepted as the price paid for freedom to work on the myriad operational problems faced today, rather than tackle problems that may be several years away."

The Best Guesses

The line of reasoning behind the second form of poor forecasting is more common. One executive explained it this way: "We can estimate what kinds of changes are likely to occur, but for the most part we are just guessing. Rather than base our plans on guesses, we assume that the future will be largely a continuation of current trends. We know that many of our assumptions will prove incorrect, but so would our guesses. This way we have something to start with that can be modified as we approach the time period involved and greater certainty."

This tendency is not limited to estimates of external, uncontrollable variables. One divisional director of research and development pointed out that the work of this group in looking for new products and improving existing product lines, along with work done by product- and market-development groups, was seldom reflected in the division's five-year plan. It was mentioned in the "prose plan" as one of the factors that would produce growth and greater profits, but the tie between this work and action steps to produce such increases was seldom made.

Thus, even the type of change that is quite certain—change the company is actively working on—is often ignored in preparing forecasts and planning assumptions. The usual explanation is that, although change will result, "it is hard to predict the specific impact of this change."

Again, the basic misconception of the purpose of a forecast is evident. Prediction is seldom possible. The purpose of the forecast is to provide the best guesses with regard to the future so alternative plans can be developed. The appropriate alternative can be chosen and modified when the proper time arrives, but current decisions can reflect the best estimates of the future. It is seldom easy to arrive at meaningful estimates, but it is far better to work with even imperfect guesses than with static and unimaginative extrapolations of trend. And the greater the uncertainty of the future, the more does the company need to anticipate possible future changes.

Estimates and Ulcers

The view that to be useful forecasts must be close to certainty has a secondary effect. The men who are actually developing the forecasts often complain that the executives for whom they prepare projections "simply do not understand the nature of forecasting. They don't understand the value of working with alternative estimates of the future. They want *answers*."

With their responsibility for making decisions involving thousands if not millions of dollars, it is not surprising that executives want answers, not estimates. To be sure, they recognize that a long-range forecast is at best a carefully formulated guess, but it is not really surprising that they should rebel at the idea of receiving these guesses in a form that emphasizes their uncertainty.

In an effort to come to grips with this limiting outlook and to improve the quality of long-range forecasting, some companies require that all major forecasts or assumptions be stated in terms of "best," "worst," and "most likely" estimates, and that the ensuing plans be designed to cope with each eventuality.

Basically, forecasting is a technical function performed by specialists. The specialists have developed techniques for producing better forecasts: Great advances have been made in data-processing, storage, and retrieval, and procedures for making decisions under uncertainty are emerging. But for this progress to have meaning, those who direct the technicians must

seek and use true forecasts rather than extrapolations. The importance of this vital element of planning cannot be overemphasized. If preliminary forecasts are inadequate, programs designed to move the company from expected to desired future states will in all likelihood be misdirected.

BUDGETING AND ACCOUNTING

If forecasting receives too little attention in long-range planning, the budgeting and financial accounting function often receives too much. The confusion between budgeting and planning is unfortunately quite common, and the result is most undesirable. If planning and budgeting are viewed as being virtually synonymous, then major portions of the planning responsibility, including much implied objective-setting and program design, may be turned over to the "budgeteers"—men whose financial accounting background often has not prepared them to carry out complete planning jobs.

Budgeting is, after all, largely the translation of objectives and programs into financial form. To turn over major portions of the responsibility for planning to budget specialists is like turning over major portions of the responsibility for international policy-making and speech-writing to the technicians at the United Nations who translate such statements into other languages.

The Budgeteer's Limits

In annual planning, this abandonment of responsibility for objective-setting and program design is somewhat less critical, since much short-term planning is really little more than the allocation of available resources within the framework of existent policy. But for the elements of current decision-making that must reflect change in policy because of environmental changes, and for the aspects of longer-range planning that are designed to alter the company's course, planning must go beyond the limits of the budgeteer.

The Budgeting Job

Budgeting and financial accounting activities constitute only one aspect of long-range planning, but it is an important aspect. The primary function of the budget group is the translation of plans into financial terms. Although many of the financial implications of various objectives and programs are self-evident, a second function of the budget and accounting group is analyzing financial plans and reporting to management on the less obvious indications. A third and related group of responsibilities involves working with division officers to help them achieve their desired goals along desired lines, but in such as way as to produce better-balanced and more desirable financial results.

Members of the units performing these budgetary and financial accounting activities are, as would be expected, men with financial accounting backgrounds. Their leaders are men who have moved up in the financial accounting end of the business, and many have received their basic training in public accounting.

Considerable effort is being expended in many companies to broaden the background of this group, from the individuals working on the detailed elements of the budget up to the controller himself. This effort is certainly commendable, but it does little good if the men involved do not have time to bring this broader viewpoint to bear on their work. There is a tendency in some companies to overload the capacities of those responsible for this work, so that despite their "broadening," they simply do not have time to do more than unimaginative clerical work. Failure to pick out more than the financial errors before departmental plans are summarized places an even greater burden on corporate management with regard to appraisal: By the time plans reach corporate review, only perceptive digging by top management will unearth faulty premises, inadequate program design, or other errors that may be buried in the summary nature of departmental plans.

As is true of forecasting, the greatest single need for improving the quality of budgeting and financial accounting functions is the need for clarifying the true nature of these activities and understanding what should not be done as well as what should be done.

SETTING GOALS AND DESIGNING ACTION PROGRAMS

Commenting on the fairly common problems created by confusing budgeting with planning, particularly when combined with poor forecasting, David Hertz wrote: "Some manage-ments develop 'budgets' based on subjective forecasts and stick to them through thick and thin. Each decision is made in accordance with an arbitrary plan that was established without any forecasting of probable changes in the uncontrollable variables. . . . Does this sound unlikely? It is possible to point out [cases where] the budget called for adding twenty men to several specific companies that had year-to-year budgets for expansion in their product line and [they] proceeded with those plans on schedule, despite clear portents of future difficulties for these products."

Vital Ingredients

This kind of thing occurs when several vital ingredients of planning are left out. When arbitrary objectives are set and budgets are designed to "meet" these objectives, what has not been done is (1) to analyze projections of expected goals in order to realistically set desired goals, (2) to analyze the specific problems standing in the way of filling the gap between expected and desired, and (3) to design a program of *action steps,* not mechanical allocations of wishful thinking, designed to overcome these problems. These three activities comprise the third group of planning functions.

In many cases, programs laid out for years two to five of a five-year plan fail to reflect more than a degree of qualified effort in this area. Because of inadequate forecasting, the best possible picture of the expected future state had not been drawn. Therefore, to begin with, objectives are necessarily arbitrary, since they reflect neither an accurate projection of the external environment nor an accurate projection of internal change. Starting with unsound forecasts and arbitrary goals, it is not difficult to see why less-than-adequate efforts have been made to identify and analyze the problems faced in "filling the gap." What is the gap, after all, other than the distance between desired and expected? If the gap cannot be identified, how can problems and needs be clarified—and, going one step further, how can programs be meaningfully designed?

Obviously, they cannot be, and what results is a vague approximation of long-range plans or merely a stimulus to longer-range thinking. Such a plan is sometimes defended as "a blueprint for what we will do, given a rather conservative allowance for change." But why do you need a blueprint if change is conservative? It may be defended as "a starting point, a point of departure from which we can make changes as the future becomes more certain." But is this doubtful gain really worth the time and expense incurred, when this activity falls so far short of its potential contribution to business management?

Boon or Boondock?

Such poor planning may be defended as a stimulus to reflection, but this also is quite doubtful. If a best effort is made and falls short of perfection, those involved, knowing that their best efforts are expected, will reflect and perhaps be stimulated; but where the best is not demanded and less meaningful efforts are accepted, the first people to realize that "not much is expected of our plans" are those working on them. This is one of the major reasons for poor planning.

A senior staff officer of a large electrical company, commenting on some of the examples of bad five-year planning he had seen, raised the question of whether such planning might not be worse than none: "I am not altogether certain that, when we work with such imperfect devices and accept such poor plans, we may not only be failing to get improved long-range planning, but we may be interfering with those few people whose natural foresight and inclination for future thinking would have been looked to in the past to provide informally what we need in this area."

Who Does What?

Much of the blame for poor objective-setting, inadequate analysis of future problems, and mechanistic program designs has been laid to uncertainty about the future, but it seems likely that the training and ability of the men who are called on to carry out these responsibilities are equally responsible.

The bulk of the long-range planning work should and often does rest with line management. Staff groups do leg work, run down ideas, and occasionally put together program recommendations that are finally decided on by line management, but a major portion of this work usually rests with line officers. There are many cases, however, in which a great deal of the program-design responsibility has been taken over by staff or budget men. Vaguely sketched goals and general strategies are determined by the line manager, and the detail work of indicating how much will be spent in which areas and in what specified ways is left to others. David Ewing has pointed out an important reason: "Long-range planning puts possibly a greater premium on conceptual skills of the manager (as opposed to technical and human-relations skills) than does any other phase of top management. Looked at diagrammatically, a company's long-range plan at any moment would appear as a vast cobweb of short-term and long-term interrelationships between marketing, production, finance, industrial relations, executive development, and all the rest. All of these plans are built on certain assumptions, and the individual plans in turn become premises and assumptions for each other."

How many line managers possess these "conceptual skills"? How many have the experience, breadth of knowledge, attitudes, and time to make use of them? Or, getting closer to the source of the difficulty, how many are hired and promoted with these skills in mind? There is ample evidence that many men charged with long-range planning responsibilities do not possess these attributes to the necessary degree or, if they do, they lack the time or incentive to use them.

Needed Skills

As was the case with the forecasting and financial accounting functions, a necessary first step in improving this third part of long-range planning is the development of a clear sense of what good performance demands. The people performing these activities should possess the skills necessary to analyze the problems involved in moving from the expected to the desired future state in order to identify the specific objectives that need to be realized. They must have the capacity to develop a series of action steps designed to meet these objectives. And they must have the ability to develop alternative programs to meet the contingencies that may arise.

This does not mean that line officers should be chosen solely on the basis of their long-range planning potential. Operational, technical, and administrative skills cannot be overlooked; the line officer must be able to get things done as well as conceptualize and plan. If, in selecting men to fill these posts, a review of their strengths and weaknesses reveals deficiencies in one area or the other, efforts can be made to overcome those weaknesses—either directly or by providing staff assistants in a manner that will assure their use in compensating for these limitations.

DIRECTION, SUPERVISION, AND COORDINATION

Clarifying the nature of these first three groups of long-range planning activities, selecting people qualified to perform them, directing and supervising their efforts, and coordinaitng the separate parts of the plan are among the major responsibilities of those chosen to carry out the fourth aspect of planning.

Although the company president or, in decentralized companies, the division general manager is ordinarily the titular head of division long-range planning, as a matter of fact he usually confines his direct efforts to rather broad and summary analysis and review. He gives direction by decision, supervises by reaction, and coordinates by arbitration, but he is a reactor rather than an active participant in the administrative element of planning. Perhaps all that can be expected of a chief executive or division manager is that he use his influence to stimulate others and support the individual or individuals who play a more direct role in the direction, supervision, and coordination of planning. If this is the case, however, the choice of men to supplement him should be made with a full realization of the responsibilities involved.

Although carrying out these functions necessitates some degree of planning skill, the "director" of long-range planning is not so much a planner as he is a supervisor and coordinator of planning. He will be called upon to advise on planning, but his principal responsibilities are to direct and coordinate its conduct.

The Controller as Director

The job of the planning director in evaluating and coordinating the elements of the long-range plan can be made much easier by effective budget and analysis work. Because of this partial dependency on the budget function, a great many companies and divisions formally or informally turn the direction function over to the head of this group, the controller. There is strong evidence to suggest that although the controller, through his budget and analysis group, can make a significant contribution to planning, he is usually not a good choice to serve as director of long-range planning. Richard G. Martens, an executive with much experience in this field, has presented one of the strongest statements in support of this viewpoint:

> The controller's main job is to see that the resources of the business are conserved and being used efficiently. In accomplishing this task he uses the tools of accounting, auditing, and more recently, budgeting and forecasting. Because of his interest in conservation and efficiency, the controller normally has a functional bias in the direction of saving rather than spending money. His work is primarily with figures and, of necessity, is oriented toward recording and examining the results of past operations. His task is to measure the results of risks taken by other functions of the business rather than to take risks himself. . . . Within such a setting, it is only to be expected that forecasting, as developed by the controller, has tended to be a projection of past trends into the future.
>
> Long-range planning, on the other hand, must contend with the risks of innovation and deal with the exceptional and improbable future. It must be concerned with risk-taking—spending money to make money. The measure of the effectiveness of long-range planning is not efficiency but how well the course of business has been charted on the sea of future risk. Above all, those entrusted with the responsibility for long-range planning must be oriented toward the future—not the past. They must be able to take risk in their stride—not pass the risk to others or act as a passive observer or measurer. The long-range planner must lead—not follow. . . .
>
> Placing the long-range planning function under the average controller will assure its sterility.

Although this may overstate the case, the general conclusion seems justified. Even when an effort has been made to broaden the background and perspective of the controller and his budget and analysis group, they may of necessity continue to be primarily "number" men. If this is not the case, their major work, budget and financial accounting, will suffer.

When the controller assumes responsibility for the direction, supervision, and control of long-range planning, he is charged with what amounts to two somewhat conflicting responsibilities, and the duality of his functions cannot help but reduce his efficiency in one or both areas. On the one hand, he is to direct and assist in planning, and on the other hand he must continue to discharge the control responsibilities that have often led to his being characterized as an "all-seeing eye."

A number of corporate divisions have sought to develop a new post at the division level to relieve the division general manager of a portion of these direction functions. The man chosen, usually called director of long-range planning, is given a very small staff and presumably is expected to act as an extension of the general manager. In some cases, this group also provides assistance in the other elements of long-range planning.

Ideally, the people selected for such posts should possess considerable experience in line operations so they will be regarded as men who know the score. They must also possess the skills and leadership qualities necessary to this vital function. Quite surprisingly, there are many instances in which these factors have been disregarded.

In some cases, the man chosen to serve as planning director and his assistants are younger men who were put in these posts because of the broad experience it would offer them. These key jobs are regarded primarily as good training positions. Perhaps such appointments do provide broad training, but it is virtually certain that they will not provide effective direction and coordination of long-range planning activities.

A somewhat more common type of unfortunate appointment is the assignment of these posts to men regarded as planning theorists. To the men they are supposed to assist in developing plans, they are usually regarded as staff eggheads who are filled with ivory-tower ideas about planning but who lack a working knowledge of practical operating problems.

At the extreme, there are cases where men assigned to this work are generally considered corporate misfits. Although they are talented people in many respects, top management has been unable to find a place for them in either line or other staff positions, and they are put in long-range planning work because "they can stay out of trouble there."

Lack of Concern

The appointment of younger men out to learn the business, planning theorists, or corporate misfits to such vital positions indicates either considerable confusion as to the requirements for such jobs, or, more likely, lack of real concern for long-range planning. There are instances where the division manager or corporate officer who makes the appointment is actually far from convinced that long-range planning is worth the trouble. Where this is the case, formal long-range planning is almost certainly doomed to ineffectuality.

Much vital progress will begin to take place when long-range planning has passed through the early stages of fashionability and is subjected to more objective scrutiny. At that point, planning will no longer be a stylized "must" but will be accepted on its own strengths, and companies that now merely go through the motions will exert more meaningful and effective efforts. Toward this end, an essential first step is a clearer understanding of these four key elements of long-range planning.

READING 13

WHAT ARE YOUR ORGANIZATION'S OBJECTIVES? *
A General-Systems Approach to Planning

Bertram M. Gross

There is nothing that managers and management theorists are more solidly agreed on than the vital role of objectives in the managing of organizations. The daily life of executives is full of such exhortations as:

"Let's plan where we want to go . . ."
"You'd better clarify your goals . . ."
"Get those fellows down (or up) there to understand what our (or their) purposes really are . . ."

Formal definitions of management invariably give central emphasis to the formulation or attainment of objectives. Peter Drucker's (1954) idea of "managing by objectives" gave expression to a rising current in administrative theory. Any serious discussion of planning, whether by business enterprises or government agencies, deals with the objectives of an organization.

* *Reprinted from* Human Relations, *vol. 18, no. 3, 1965 by permission of The Tavistock Institute of Human Relations, London, England.*

Yet there is nothing better calculated to embarrass the average executive than the direct query: "Just what are your organization's objectives?" The typical reply is incomplete or tortured, given with a feeling of obvious discomfort. The more skilful response is apt to be a glib evasion or a glittering generality.

To some extent, of course, objectives cannot be openly stated. Confidential objectives cannot be revealed to outsiders. Tacit objectives may not bear discussion among insiders. The art of bluff and deception with respect to goals is part of the art of administration.

But the biggest reason for embarrassment is the lack of a well-developed language of organizational purposefulness. Such a language may best be supplied by a general-systems model that provides the framework for "general-systems accounting," or "managerial accounting" in the sense of a truly generalist approach to all major dimensions of an organization. It is now possible to set forth—even if only in suggestive form—a general-systems model that provides the basis for clearly formulating the performance and structural objectives of any organization.

Let us now deal with these points separately —and conclude with some realistic observations on the strategy of planning.

THE NEED FOR A LANGUAGE OF PURPOSEFULNESS

Many managers are still too much the prisoners of outworn, single-purpose models erected by defunct economists, engineers, and public administration experts. Although they know better, they are apt to pay verbal obeisance to some single purpose: profitability in the case of the business executive, efficiency in the case of the public executive.

If profitability is not the sole objective of a business—and even the more tradition-ridden economists will usually accept other objectives in the form of constraints or instrumental purposes—just what are these other types? If efficiency is not the only objective of a government agency—and most political scientists will maintain that it cannot be—what are the other categories? No adequate answers to these questions are provided by the traditional approaches to economics, business administration, or public administration. Most treatises on planning—for which purpose formulation is indispensable—catalogue purposes by such abstract and nonsubstantive categories as short-range and long-range, instrumental and strategic (or ultimate), general and specific. One book on planning sets forth thirteen dimensions without mentioning anything so mundane as profitability or efficiency (LeBreton & Henning, 1961). Indeed, in his initial writings on management by objectives, Drucker never came to grips with the great multiplicity of business objectives. In his more recent work Drucker (1964) deals with objectives in terms of three "result areas": product, distribution channels, and markets. But this hardly goes far enough to illuminate the complexities of purpose multiplicity.

Thus far, the most systematic approach to organizational purposes is provided by budget experts and accountants. A budget projection is a model that helps to specify the financial aspects of future performance. A balance sheet is a model that helps to specify objectives for future structure of assets and liabilities. Yet financial analysis—even when dignified by the misleading label "managerial accounting"— deals only with a narrow slice of real-life activities. Although it provides a way of reflecting many objectives, it cannot by itself deal with the substantive activities underlying monetary data. Indeed, concentration upon budgets has led many organizations to neglect technological and other problems that cannot be expressed in budgetary terms. Overconcentration on the enlargement of balance-sheet assets has led many companies to a dangerous neglect of human and organizational assets.

The great value of financial analysis is to provide a doorway through which one can enter the whole complex domain of organizational objectives. To explore this domain, however, one needs a model capable of dealing more fully with the multiple dimensions of an organization's performance and structure. To facilitate the development of purposefulness in each of an organization's subordinate units, the model should also be applicable to internal units. To help executives to deal with the complexities of their environment, it should also be applicable to external competitors or controllers.

THE GENERAL-SYSTEMS APPROACH

As a result of the emerging work in systems analysis, it is now possible to meet these needs by developing a "general-systems model" of an organization. A general-systems model is one that brings together in an ordered fashion information on all dimensions of an organization. It integrates concepts from all relevant disciplines. It can help to expand financial planning to full-bodied planning in as many dimensions as may be relevant. With it, executives may move from financial accounting to "systems accounting." It can provide the basis for "managerial accounting" in the sense of the managerial use not only of financial data (which is the way the term has been recently used) but of all ideas and data needed to appraise the state of a system and guide it towards the attainment of desirable future system states.[1]

Before outlining a general-systems model,

[1] *"General-systems theory" often refers to theories dealing broadly with similarities among all kinds of systems—from atoms and cells to personalities, formal organizations, and populations. In this context the term refers to a special application of general-systems theory to formal organizations— an application that deals not merely with a few aspects but generally with all aspects of formal organizations.*

it is important to set aside the idea that a system is necessarily something that is fully predictable or tightly controlled. This impression is created whenever anyone tries to apply to a human organization the closed or non-human models used by physicists and engineers. A human organization is much more complicated.

Specifically, when viewed in general-systems terms, a formal organization (whether a business enterprise or a government agency) is

1 a man-resource system in space and time,
2 open, with various transactions between it and its environment,
3 characterized by internal and external relations of conflict as well as cooperation,
4 a system for developing and using power, with varying degrees of authority and responsibility, both within the organization and in the external environment,
5 a "feedback" system, with information on the results of past performance activities feeding back through multiple channels to influence future performance,
6 changing, with static concepts derived from dynamic concepts rather than serving as a preliminary to them,
7 complex, that is, containing many subsystems, being contained in larger systems, and being criss-crossed by overlapping systems,
8 loose, with many components that may be imperfectly coordinated, partially autonomous, and only partially controllable,
9 only partially knowable, with many areas of uncertainty, with "black regions" as well as "black boxes" and with many variables that cannot be clearly defined and must be described in qualitative terms, and
10 subject to considerable uncertainty with respect to current information, future environmental conditions, and the consequences of its own actions.

THE PERFORMANCE-STRUCTURE MODEL

The starting-point of modern systems analysis is the input-output concept. The flow of inputs and outputs portrays the system's performance. To apply the output concept to a formal organization, it is helpful to distinguish between two kinds of performance: producing outputs of services or goods and satisfying (or dissatisfying) various interests. To apply the input concept, a three-way breakdown is helpful: ac-

quiring resources to be used as inputs, using inputs for investment in the system, and making efficient use of resources. In addition, we may note that organizational performance includes efforts to conform with certain behaviour codes and concepts of technical and administrative rationality.

These seven kinds of performance objective may be put together in the following proposition:

The performance of any organization or unit thereof consists of activities to (1) satisfy the varying interests of people and groups by (2) producing outputs of services or goods, (3) making efficient use of inputs relative to outputs, (4) investing in the system, (5) acquiring resources, and (6) doing all these things in a manner that conforms with various codes of behaviour and (7) varying conceptions of technical and administrative rationality.

In simplified form, the relations between these categories of performance may be visualized as follows:

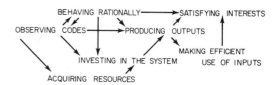

Let us now turn to system structure. The minimum elements in a machine system are certain physical components, including a "governor" (or "selector"), an "effector," a "detector," and lines of communication between them and the environment. For a formal organization these may be spelled out more specifically as subsystems in general, a central guidance subsystem, internal relations among the subsystems, and relations with the external environment. It is helpful at times to consider separately the people and the physical assets grouped together in the subsystems. It may also be helpful to give separate attention to the values held by individuals and the various subsystems.

These seven sets of structural objectives may be put together in the following proposition:

The structure of any organization or unit thereof consists of (1) people and (2) non-human resources, (3) grouped together in differentiated subsystems that (4) interrelate among themselves and (5) with the external environment, (6) and are subject to various values and (7) to such central guidance as may help to provide the capacity for future performance.

In the language of matrix algebra, one can bring the two elements of system performance and system structure together into a 2×1 "nested" vector which may be called the "system state vector." Let P symbolize system performance and S system structure. Then the following sequence of vectors may symbolize changing system states over a period of time:

$$\begin{bmatrix} P \\ S \end{bmatrix}^1 \quad \begin{bmatrix} P \\ S \end{bmatrix}^2 \quad \dots \begin{bmatrix} P \\ S \end{bmatrix}^n$$

The vector is "nested" because both the performance element and the structure element consist of seven subelements and are themselves 7×1 vectors. Each subelement, in turn, is a multidimensional matrix.

The performance vector, it should be noted, includes among its many components the basic elements in income statements and revenue-expenditure budgets. The structure vector includes all the assets (and claims against them) measured in a balance sheet. Indeed, the former may be regarded as a greatly enlarged performance budget, the latter a balance sheet that includes human and institutional assets as well as financial assets. The relations between the two are even closer than those between an income statement and a balance sheet. Almost any aspect of system performance will have some effect on system structure. Any important plans for future performance inevitably require significant changes in system structure. Changes in system structure, in turn, are invariably dependent upon some types of system performance. In everyday affairs, of course, executives often make the mistake of

—planning for major improvements in performance without giving attention to the structural prerequisites, and
—planning for major changes in structure (sometimes because of outworn or unduly abstract doctrines of formal organization) without considering their presumed connection with performance.

The skilful use of a performance-structure model may help to avoid these errors.[2]

The first elements in both structure and performance, let it be noted, are human: people and the satisfaction of people's interests. All the other elements and their many decisions —both financial and technological—are ways of thinking about people and their behaviour. An organization's plans for the future are always plans made by people for people—for their future behaviour and for their future relations with resources and other people. Financial and technological planners may easily lose sight of these human elements. Another virtue of general-systems analysis, therefore, is that it helps to bring together the "soft" information of human relations people with the "hard" data of accountants and engineers.

PERFORMANCE OBJECTIVES

Any one of the seven elements of system performance, as baldly stated above, may be used in a statement of "where we want to go" or as a criterion of "doing an effective job." But none of them is meaningful unless broken down into its subelements. When this is done, indeed, the basic subelements may be rearranged in many ways. There is no magic in any one ordering.

Within the present space limits I shall merely touch upon some of the major dimensions of each element and subelement. Additional details are available in *The Managing of Organizations* (Gross, 1964, Pt. V; Chs. 20–29).

Some random illustrations for both an organization (an aircraft company) and a unit thereof (its personnel office) are provided in Table 13-1. Tables 13-2 and 13-3 provide more detailed illustrations in two areas of special complexity: output objectives and input-output objectives. In these tables "goal" refers to a specific type of subelement and "norm" to a more specific formulation of a goal. To save space, reference to the tables will not be made in the text.

[2] *This performance-structure model represents a major adaptation of what has long been known as "structural-functional" analysis. It is more dynamic than traditional structural-functional analysis, however, since it starts with action (performance) and works back to structure as the more regularized aspect of action. Also, instead of assuming a single function such as "system maintenance," it broadens the idea of function to cover the major dimensions of performance.*

TABLE 13-1   PERFORMANCE OBJECTIVES: SOME GENERAL ILLUSTRATIONS

Performance Objectives	Aircraft Company		Personnel Unit	
	Goals	Norms	Goals	Norms
1. Satisfying Interests				
(a) *Members*	Higher morale	Reducing labour turnover to 6%	Professional prestige	Leadership in professional organizations
(b) *Clientele network*	Meeting airlines' needs	5% rise in total sales	Meeting needs of line	Fewer complaints
(c) *Others*	Investors	Maintaining 3% yield on common stock	Serving all employees	Reducing labour turnover to 10%
2. Producing Output				
(a) *Output mix*	Adding short-range jets	End-product production schedule	New management training programme	End-product services
(b) *Quantity*	Increased market penetration	15% of industry sales	Greater coverage	150 "trainees" per year
(c) *Quality*	Safer planes	Wing improvements	Better designed courses	Better consultants
(d) *Output flow*	Work-flow	Detailed schedules	Work-flow	Detailed schedules
3. Making Efficient Use of Inputs				
(a) *Profitability*	Higher profits on net worth (or total assets)	20% on net worth	—	—
(b) *Costs per unit*	Lower engine costs	8% reduction	Total costs per trainee	$200 per week
(c) *Partial input ratios*	More output per man-hour	10% increase	Teacher costs	$150 per training-hour
(d) *Portion of potential used*	Reducing idle equipment-time	5% reduction	Full participation in training programme	No vacancies
4. Investing in the Organization				
(a) *Hard goods*	Re-equipment programme	Detailed specifications	New files	No vacancies
(b) *People*	Management training programme	50 trainees per year	"Retooling" of old-timers	Participation in "refresher" courses
(c) *Internal units*	Reorganization of personnel unit	Higher status for training section	Maintenance of existing organization	Maintaining present status for training section
(d) *External relations*	More support in Congress	Support by specific senators	More support from "line" executives	Support by specific executives
5. Acquiring Resources				
(a) *Money*	More equity	Selling securities	Larger budget	5% increase
(b) *People*	Better managers	Recruitment programme	More professional staff	Recruitment programme
(c) *Goods*	New machines	Procurement programme	New files	Procurement programme

6. *Observing Codes*				
(a) *External codes*	Obeying anti-trust laws	Competition within limits	Living within budgets	Controls on commitments
(b) *Internal codes*	Obeying company regs.	Control of deviations	Loyalty to unit	Social exclusiveness
7. *Behaving Rationally*				
(a) *Technical rationality*	Aeronautical research	Specific studies	Personnel research	Specific studies
(b) *Administrative rationality*	Formal reorganization	More decentralization	More "democracy"	Monthly staff meetings

TABLE 13-2   OUTPUT PERFORMANCE OBJECTIVES: SOME DETAILED ILLUSTRATIONS

Output Production Objectives	Aircraft Company		Personnel Unit	
	Goals	Norms	Goals	Norms
A. Output Mix	Continued output of long-range jets; New short-range jet; Parts production; Research for government; Advisory services for users	Detailed production schedule	Maintaining personnel records; Recruitment services; Classification system; Job analysis and evaluation; Training programme	Operating programme
B. Output Quality				
1. Client satisfactions				
(a) Presumed results	Planes: Faster, safer flights	Planes: Specific speed and safety standards	Training programme: Better managers	Subsequent performance of trainees
(b) Choices made	Popularity among passengers	Prosperity of airline customers	Popularity of programme	Backlog of applications
(c) Payments given	Rising volume of airline sales	15% of industry sales	Budgets allocated	Specific budget figures
(d) Opinions expressed	Low complaint level	Decline in pilots' complaints	Trainees' opinions	Specific statements
2. Product characteristics	Conformance with specifications	Detailed specifications	Improved curriculum	Emphasis on decision-making skills
3. Production processes	Careful testing	Specific tests	Improved teaching methods	Use of field studies
4. Input quality	Outstanding productive personnel	Acquiring best designers	Outstanding teachers	Acquiring teachers of high repute
C. Output Quantity				
1. Monetary value				
(a) Total sales value	Planes: 15% of industry sales	X million dollars	—	—
(b) Value added	Lower proportion of value added with more sub-contracting	$\dfrac{X}{3}$	—	—
(c) Value added adjusted for price changes	20% beyond 1960	$\dfrac{X \cdot 9}{3}$ (price deflator)	—	
(d) Imputed value of non-marketed output	Advisory services: Input value	Specific cost figures	Input value	Specific cost figures

	Planes: Number to be produced	Detailed production schedule	Training programme:
			—
2. Physical volume			
(a) Tangible units			
(b) Surrogates for intangible services	Advisory services:		
(i) clients	More clients ⎫		More trainees ⎫
(ii) duration	Longer periods ⎬ Specific figures		Longer courses ⎬ Specific figures
(iii) intermediate or subsequent products	Memoranda produced ⎭		Field studies undertaken ⎭
(iv) input value			
	Total costs		Total costs

TABLE 13-3   INPUT-OUTPUT PERFORMANCE OBJECTIVES: SOME DETAILED ILLUSTRATIONS

Efficiency (Input-Output) Objectives	Aircraft Company		Personnel Unit	
	Goals	Norms	Goals	Norms
A. Profitability				
1. *Unit profits*	Short-range jet: higher profits with rising volume	Specific figures	—	—
2. *Total profits*				
Before taxes	Higher profits	10% increase	—	—
After taxes	Higher profits	12% increase		
Total profits	Lower (with replacement of debt by equity)			
3. *Net worth*	Higher	10% decrease	—	—
4. *Total assets*	Higher	10% increase	—	—
5. *Sales*	Lower (with higher volume of sales)	10% decrease	—	—
B. Costs per Unit	New short-range jets: Declining total costs with rising volume	10% decline per unit over first year	Training programme: Rising costs with longer duration and higher quality	20% more per trainee
C. Partial Input-Output Relations				
1. *Labour-output ratios*	For a specific output unit:			
(a) Labour time	More output per direct man-hour	10% increase	More teacher-time per trainee	10% more per trainee
(b) Labour cost	No increase in direct costs	Same	Higher teacher fees	20% more per trainee
	Small increase in direct plus indirect labour costs	5% increase	Higher overhead costs	5% increase
(c) Output per $1 of labour cost	Lower total value	−6%		
	Lower added value	−29%	—	—
2. *Capital-output ratio*	For specific machines: fuller use of rated capacity	Specific figures	Low-cost residential facilities	Specific figures
D. Portion of Output Potential Used				
1. *Waste*	Less scrap material	Specific figures	Less waste	Elimination of unnecessary paperwork
	Better utilization of scrap	Reaching 80% in 2 shifts		
	Fuller use of capacity		Fuller use of computers (on personnel records)	Reaching 35% of capacity
2. *Gap between actual and potential*	Higher fulfilment of profit potential	8% on total assets	Higher fulfilment of service potential	Specific data on quality and quantity of end-products

1. Satisfying Interests

Although the satisfaction of human interests is the highest purpose of any organization, interest-satisfaction objectives (often referred to as benefits, welfare, utility, value, or payoff) are the most difficult to formulate.

First of all, such objectives always involve a multiplicity of parties at interest—or "interesteds." These include the members of the organization, the organization's "clientele network," and other external groups and individuals. They vary considerably in visibility and in the extent to which their interests are affected by an organization's performance.

Second, their interests are usually multiple, often hard to identify, always divergent, and sometimes sharply conflicting. In psychological terms these interests may be described in terms of the human needs for security, belonging, status, prestige, power, and self-development. Many of these needs are expressed in terms of services and goods designed to meet them and the monetary income which, in a market economy, is necessary to provide such services and goods. They may also be expressed in terms of the needs for both employment and leisure. The terms "public interest" or "national interest" are ways of referring to the great multiplicity of interests that many people and groups throughout a society have in common. There are always conflicting views concerning the nature of "public interests."

Third, it is immensely difficult to specify the extent of satisfactions desired or attained. Satisfactions themselves are locked in the hearts and minds of the people whose interests are presumed to be satisfied. They are inextricably associated with dissatisfactions and frustration. The most we can do is use certain indirect indicators expressed in terms of the observable behaviour of the behaviour of "interesteds." Two of the most immediate forms of behaviour are the choices they make (in participating in the organization or using its product) and money they are willing to pay (in the form of consumer purchases, taxes, or dues). Other indicators are their expressed opinions (complaints or praise) and their subsequent behaviour as a presumed result of the satisfactions obtained. Such indicators with respect to clientele satisfactions provide the most important measures of output quality.

2. Producing Output

Output production objectives are much easier to formulate. They may best be expressed in terms of an "output mix" listing the types of services or goods supplied to the organization's (or unit's) clientele. For each type quality and quantity objectives may then be set.

Yet there are at least five major problems in this area. First of all, output quality has many dimensions. As already indicated, clientele satisfaction, the most important dimension of output quality, is exceedingly difficult to measure. Less direct indicators—such as product specifications, production processes, and the quality of input factors—may also be needed. The objective of higher quality often conflicts with the objective of higher quantity.

Second, although monetary aggregates are the only way of measuring total output, they must be used with considerable care. Important distinctions may be needed between the total value of output and value added, between marginal value and total or average value, between different ways of allocating value to time periods. For comparisons over time, adjustments for price changes may be needed; for international comparisons, adjustments in the value of international currencies.

Third, in the case of services and goods that are not sold (and this includes most of the intermediate output within business organizations) the only direct measure of output quantity is physical units. In most instances this means that there is no common denominator for the total quantity of different kinds of unit. All that can be done to aggregate quantity objectives is to use input costs or some administratively determined "price" (as in internal pricing systems) as an indirect quantity indicator.

Fourth, in the case of intangible services there are no physical units that can readily be identified. Here one can set objectives only in terms of such indirect indicators as the number of clients, the duration of services, certain intermediate products that are more tangible, and the volume or value of input factors.

Fifth, considerable confusion may develop between intermediate products and the end-products supplied to an organization's clientele. This readily happens with intangible end-product services that are provided on a

TABLE 13-4   STRUCTURAL OBJECTIVES: SOME GENERAL ILLUSTRATIONS

Structural Objectives	Aircraft Company		Personnel Unit	
	Goals	Norms	Goals	Norms
1. People				
(a) *Types*	Fewer "blue-collars"	Specific manning tables	More professionals	Specific manning tables
(b) *Quantity*	No overall increase	Specific manning tables	Larger staff	4 new positions
(c) *Quality*	Better-educated staff	90% college graduates above supervisory level	Better educational background	All college graduates with a few PhDs
2. Non-human resources				
(a) *Physical assets*	More modern plant	Specific re-equipment programme	More adequate space	5 more rooms
(b) *Monetary assets*	More liquid position	2:1 current liability ratio	Larger reserves	More transferable budget items
(c) *Claims against assets*	Higher ratio of equity to long-term debt	$10 million equity increase	—	—
3. Subsystems				
(a) *Units*	Improved divisional structure	Stronger jet-plane divisions	Improved internal structure	Stronger training group
(b) *Committees*	Improved committee structure	Inter-divisional task force on new jets	Better representation on committees	Participation in jet-plane task force
4. Subsystem relations				
(a) *Cooperation-conflict*	Settlement of inter-divisional disputes	Compromise on jet-plane design	Settlement of inter-unit disputes	Compromise on location of training division
(b) *Hierarchy*	Stronger central control	Fewer levels	Stronger unit position	Direct line to top manager
(c) *Polyarchy*	Dispersed responsibility	New clearance procedures	Dispersed responsibility	New clearance procedures
(d) *Communication*	Better communication among divisions	Weekly paper	Better communication with line executives	Liaison units in line divisions
5. External relations				
(a) *Clients and suppliers*	Better distribution channels for parts	Relations with specific distributors	More support from line executives	Support by specific executives
(b) *Controllers and controllees*	More support in Congress	Support by specific Senators	More support by budget unit	Support for 4 new positions
(c) *Associates and adversaries*	Limits on competition	"Understandings" on division of markets	Rivalry with budget unit	Less budget opposition to training programme funds
6. Values				
(a) *Internal-external orientation*	Public service	Safer planes	Professionalism in personnel management	Advancement of unit's interests

(b) Conformity and individualism	Initiative	Proposing of company policy by divisions	Loyalty to unit	Subordination of external interests
(c) Activism-passivity	Progress	Faster planes	Progress	All-round improvement
7. *System management*				
(a) Higher level	More "professional" approach	Specific planning and control methods	More "human" approach	More emphasis on personnel management
(b) Lower level	More effective supervision	Participatory activation methods	More effective supervision	Better check of supervisors

non-sale basis to an intangible, unorganized, or reluctant clientele. More tangible intermediate products—particularly when supplied by hard-driving, ambitious units—may then receive disproportionate attention. One remedy is to formulate objectives in terms of work-flow—that is, a series of intermediate outputs leading to the production of the organization's end-products.

3. Making Efficient Use of Inputs

When resources available for use as inputs are perceived as scarce, an organization or unit becomes interested in making efficient use of inputs relative to outputs. Since there are many ways of calculating input and output and of relating the two, there are many varieties of input-output performance.

Profitability is the most useful input-output relation, since it provides a common measure of value for both input and output. Profitability measures may be used in many ways, however, depending upon whether one (1) relates profits to net worth, total assets, or sales, (2) focuses on unit profits or total profits, or (3) thinks in short- or long-range terms. Depending upon a variety of techniques for handling difficult accounting problems, they are subject to considerable statistical manipulation. They may also reflect an organization's monopoly power and its ability to obtain subsidies, as well as its efficiency. Nevertheless, in many circumstances—particularly over a long time period—profitability is the best single measure of efficiency, output quantity and quality, and interest satisfaction.

The most generally applicable efficiency objective is attaining the lowest possible total costs for a given unit of output. This cost-accounting measure is an essential instrument in attaining—even in formulating—profitability objectives. It is relevant to non-marketed products as well. In developing cost-accounting goals, however, it is essential not to neglect the quality dimensions of output. In the case of intangible services, as already indicated, the identification of the unit is extremely difficult. Where capital and material inputs are involved, it is necessary to make difficult—and sometimes arbitrary—decisions with respect to depreciation, the distinction between current and capital expenditures, and the value of withdrawals from inventories.

Partial input-output ratios are those relating some measure of input—usually either labour or capital—to some measure of total output. Such a ratio is particularly meaningful when the volume of other input factors may be presumed to remain unchanged. It will be very misleading, however, whenever there is any significant change in any other input factor—as when increased output per employee is counterbalanced, and in fact caused, by increased capital per unit of output.

Another efficiency measure is the proportion of potential actually used. This may be expressed in terms of a reduction in waste, a higher utilization of capacity (potential output), or profits in relation to potential profitability.

4. Investing in the System

In addition to producing current output, an organization must invest in its capacity for future production. Investment objectives involve the expansion, replacement, conservation, or development of assets. They are essential not only for survival, but to prevent decline or promote growth.

The most obvious investment objectives relate to hard goods and monetary reserves. The hard goods may include land, buildings, equipment and machinery, and stocks of materials. The monetary reserves may include cash, deposits, securities, receivables, and any other funds that can be drawn upon.

Less obvious, although equally important, is investment in people, subsystems, subsystem relations, external relations, and the development of values. Investment in the guidance subsystem itself—that is, in the management structure—is particularly important.

In other words, investment performance may deal directly with any element of system structure. Accordingly, the specifics of investment objectives may be presented in the subsequent discussion of system structure.

In general, however, it should be pointed out that investment objectives often mean a diversion of resources from use in current output. Thus there are often important conflicts not only among different forms of investment but between investment and output production.

5. Acquiring Resources

Neither output production nor investment is possible without resources that can be used as inputs. These must be obtained from the external environment or from within the organization. Under conditions of scarcity and competition this requires considerable effort. Thus resource-acquisition objectives usually receive high priority. Indeed, long-range planning is often oriented much more to acquiring resources than to utilizing them.

Organizations that sell their output may acquire external resources from the consumer market (through sales revenue), the capital market (through investment), and banks (through loans). Their sales, investment, and borrowing objectives are closely related to the extent of clientele satisfactions. Organizations and units that do not sell their output must depend mainly upon budgetary allocations.

In both cases monetary terms provide the most general expression of resource-mobilization objectives. But the monetary objectives are meaningful only when they reflect the specific resources to be acquired with money —people, information, facilities, goods, or organizations. In many circumstances it is also necessary to include (1) specifications for the resources desired, (2) specific terms and conditions, (3) selection methods, (4) the maintenance of supply lines, and (5) inspection of resources received.

The logical justification of an organization's "requirements" for additional resources is best provided by a set of objectives that moves back from (1) interest satisfactions and (2) output mix to (3) efficiency and (4) investment. In the budget-allocation process "acquisition logic" also requires efforts to appeal to the interests of those with most influence in the allocation decisions.

6. Observing Codes

Every organization aims at doing things in the "right" way. To some extent the "right" way is set forth in external codes—laws, regulations, moral and ethical prohibitions and prescriptions, and professional principles. It is also determined by the codes of the organization—its written and unwritten rules and rituals.

Some may prefer to think of code observance as a restraint upon efforts to attain other objectives. None the less, a considerable amount of purposeful activity in organizations is involved in containing inevitable tendencies towards code deviation.

The greatest attention is usually given to internal codes. In the case of external codes that are not "internalized," the organization will often tolerate deviation. Indeed, the deception of external inspectors may itself become part of the internal code. Similarly, the deception of the organization's code-enforcement efforts may become part of the internal code of various units. These tendencies towards deviation are facilitated by the difficulty of understanding—or even keeping up with—complex regulations. They are promoted by recurring code conflicts.

These difficulties may be handled only in part by formal enforcement measures. Successful code observance also requires widespread internalization of codes and the continuing adjustment of conflicting and confusing codes.

7. Behaving Rationally

An organization or unit also aims at doing things "rationally." This means the selection of the most satisfactory means of attaining a given set of objectives—from interest satisfaction and output production down to rational behaviour itself. Thus rationality is an all-pervasive instrumental objective.

Perfect rationality is an impossible objective. The instruments of rational calculation—information, knowledge, and skill—are always imperfect. The dimensions of rational behaviour —desirability, feasibility, and consistency—are themselves frequently conflicting. The more desirable objective will frequently be less feasible, the more feasible objective less consistent with other goals, the more consistent objective less desirable.

Technical rationality involves the use of the best methods devised by science and technology. With rapid scientific and technological progress, it is constantly changing. On the one hand, the rational methods of a few years ago may be irrational today. On the other hand, new techniques are often adapted on the basis of "technological faddism" rather than truly rational choice. In either case, there are usually serious disputes among technicians, disputes that cannot be entirely settled within the confines of technical rationality.

Administrative rationality is a much broader type of rationality. It involves the use of the best methods of guiding or managing organizations. This involves the interrelated processes of planning, activating, and evaluating with respect to all significant dimensions of both performance and structure. It provides the framework for resolving technical disputes. Yet administrative rationality, although highly developed on an intuitive basis, still awaits systematic scientific formulation. Many so-called "principles" of administration neglect the major dimensions of performance, deal formalistically with structure, and ignore the relation between the two. Management theory has not yet gone far enough in encouraging managers to think and communicate explicitly in connexion with such delicate subjects as the development and use of power and the management of internal and external conflict.

STRUCTURE OBJECTIVES

In thinking of system structure we should beware of images derived from the "non-human" structure of a building. The structure of an organization is based upon the expectations and behaviour of people and human groups. It has informal as well as formal aspects. It can never be understood (not even in its formal aspects) from an inspection of written decisions alone. It is never free from internal conflicts and inconsistencies. Unlike the frame of a building, it is always changing in many ways. Indeed, structure is merely the more stabilized aspect of activity. It consists of interrelations that provide the capacity for future performance and that can be understood only in terms of performance objectives. Some random illustrations of objectives for structural change are provided in Table 13-4.

1. People

The people in an organization are the first element in an organization's structure. Thus structural objectives may be formulated in terms of the types of personnel, their quality, and their quantity.

Personnel may be classified in terms of specific positions with such-and-such titles, salaries, and perquisites; abilities, knowledge, and interests; experience; educational background; health; and various personality characteristics. Other characteristics relate to age, sex, race, religion, geographical origins. Some combination of these dimensions is usually employed in objectives for recruitment, replacement, and promotion.

The formulation of quality objectives involves consideration of the place of various people within a specific subsystem. Without reference to any subsystem, however, it also involves attention to people's capacity for learning and self-development. It involves objectives for promoting the utilization of such capacity.

The number of people in an organization is one of the simplest measures of its size. Larger numbers are often sought as a prelude to obtaining other assets, as a substitute for them, or as compensation for the lack of quality. Even with high-quality personnel and an adequate complement of non-human resources, larger numbers are often needed to supply essential reserves or the basis of major output expansion.

2. Non-human Resources

With advancing science and technology, non-human resources become increasingly essential as instruments of human activity.

Certain natural resources—if only a piece of land—are an essential foundation of human activity. Physical facilities provide the necessary housing for human activity. Equipment and machinery, particularly when driven by electrical energy, make it possible for people to move or process things with little expenditure of human energy. Data-processing machinery replaces human labour in the processing of information. Thus investment objectives must deal with the structure of these physical assets.

As indicated in the discussion of investment performance, they may also include objectives with respect to monetary assets and—where balance-sheet accounting is used—to the structure of claims against them (liabilities).

3. Subsystems

Within any organization people and non-human resources are grouped together in various subsystems. Each subsystem, in turn, is often subdivided still further. The smallest subdivision is the individual person.

Each subsystem is identifiable mainly by its role or function. The major element in role definition is the output expected from the subsystem. In larger organizations, particularly those based upon advancing technology, role differentiation tends to become increasingly specific and detailed. It also tends to undergo change—but at uneven and varying rates in response to recurring new environmental conditions, new technology, and adjustments in the quantity and quality of the organization's output mix. This means an internal restructuring of the subsystems. With growth of the organization as a whole, the subsystems change in a disproportional manner. Some expand, some decline, and some must be liquidated.

Important distinctions must be made between individuals and roles. People may come and go, while a role remains. Moreover, one person may play a number of roles—that is, "wear many hats." Some roles are substantially developed by the people who play them. Most people are substantially affected by the roles they play.

There are many kinds of subsystem. Some are hierarchically organized units; others are committees. Some are organized to perform functions peculiar to a specific organization; others provide certain kinds of services (personnel, budgeting, accounting, procurement, methods analysis, public relations) that are widely used by many organizations. Some are called "line," others "staff." Some are informal only. The most important subsystem is the management or guidance subsystem (discussed separately under 7 below).

4. Internal Relations

By itself subsystem differentiation is divisive. The system as a whole exists only to the extent that the parts are brought together in a network of internal relations.

The first element in internal relations is co-operation among and within the subsystems. This cooperation must be based upon certain commonly accepted objectives for future performance. Otherwise work-flows will not mesh. A large part of this cooperation may consist of routinized, habitual expectations and activity. At the same time cooperation is always associated with conflict relations within and among subsystems. If carried too far, conflict and tension may impair—even destroy—the internal structure. Within limits they may help to invigorate it.

Hierarchic relations are an indispensable element in the cooperation-conflict nexus. These consist of superior-subordinate relations,

usually confined to certain spheres of behaviour. The lines of hierarchic authority provide formal channels of internal communication and ladders for career advancement. The upper positions in a hierarchy provide valuable points for conflict settlement and important symbols of organizational unity. At the same time, the growing role differentiation in modern organizations leads inevitably towards the subdivision of hierarchic authority and the growth of "multiple hierarchy" (see Gross, 1964, pp. 377–9).

Hierarchy is always accompanied by polyarchy—sometimes referred to as "lateral relations." One form of polyarchy is "joint authority." Thus committee members (often representing different units) may operate together as equals rather than as superiors and subordinates. Another is "dispersed authority." In budget procedures various units negotiate and bargain with each other—at least up to the point where hierarchic authority may be brought into play.

The communication network is an all-pervasive part of internal relations. A critical role in this network is always played by the various lines of hierarchic authority. But many other multi-directional channels and media—some of them informal—are also needed.

5. External Relations

The immediate environment of any organization includes not only individuals but also various groups that may be classified as enterprises, government agencies, and various types of association. The relations between an organization and this immediate environment may be expressed in terms of the roles played by such individuals and groups:

(a) Clients and suppliers
The clients are those who receive, or are supposed to benefit from, an organization's output. The suppliers are those who supply the goods, services, information, or money acquired by the organization.

(b) Controllers and controllees
The controllers are the external regulators or "superiors." The controllees are the organization's regulatees or "subordinates."

(c) Associates and adversaries
The associates are partners or allies engaged

in joint or cooperative undertakings. The adversaries include rivals for the same resources, competitors in producing similar outputs, and outright enemies interested in limiting or destroying the organization's performance or structure.

The same external organization often plays many—at times even all—of these roles. In so doing it will use many forms of external persuasion, pressure, or penetration.

Resistance to external influence usually involves an organization in preventive or counter measures of persuasion, pressure, or penetration. A more positive approach to external relations involves efforts to isolate, neutralize, or win over opponents and build up a farflung structure of external support through coalitions, alliances, and "deals." Such efforts may be facilitated by persuasive efforts aimed at unorganized publics.

6. Values

The individuals and subsystems in any organization are always guided by some pattern of values—that is, general attitudes towards what is desirable or undesirable and general ways of looking at the world. Some of the most important elements in this value structure may be defined in terms of the continua between

(*a*) *Internal and external orientation*
Internal orientation emphasizes the interests of members—in terms of their income, status, power, or self-development. External orientation emphasizes the interests of nonmembers; these may range from investors (owners) to clients to the society as a whole. Some organizations aim at integrating the two sets of values.

(*b*) *Conformity and individualism*
In many organizations conformity is a high value—sometimes to the point of the complete subordination of individual initiative. Nevertheless, highly individualistic values may be hidden behind a façade of superficial conformism.

(*c*) *Passivity and activism*
Among many members or organizations passivity is a highly cherished value. It leads to "playing it safe," "taking it easy," "following the book," and waiting for orders.

Activist values, in contrast, lead to risk-taking, initiative, and innovation. Although apparently conflicting, the two are often intertwined.

Other values relate to freedom and control, authoritarianism and democracy, material and non-material interests, equity and equality, impersonality and particularism, and ascription and achievement.

7. Guidance Subsystem

Some amount of coordinated action is always provided by the autonomous action—both routinized and spontaneous—of an organization's subsystems. But sufficient capacity for effective performance is not possible without the coordinating and promotional functions of a special subsystem with the responsibilty for system guidance, or management. This guidance subsystem is composed of a network extending from a general directorate and top executives down through the middle and lower levels of managerial or supervisory personnel. At any level the members of this subsystem play various roles in decision-making and communication with respect to the making of plans, the activating of people and groups, and the evaluating of plans made and action taken. The interrelation among these roles helps to determine the structure of the guidance subsystem.

An important aspect of management structure is the balance between centralization and decentralization. Both centralization and decentralization may be thought of in terms of the distribution of responsibility and authority by (*a*) vertical levels, (*b*) horizontal levels, and (*c*) geographical location. The extent of centralization or decentralization in any of these dimensions can best be specified with reference to specific roles or functions. The prerequisite for effective decentralization of some functions is the centralization of other functions. With increasing size and complexity, it usually becomes necessary to delegate greater responsibility and authority to lower levels and to field offices. This, in turn, requires the strengthening of certain planning, activating, and evaluating functions *of* the "centre," as well as various horizontal shifts in the centralization-decentralization balance *in* the centre.

Another vital aspect of management structure is its power base. This includes the resources at its disposal. It includes the support it obtains from the membership and major points of internal influence. It includes the support obtained externally—from associates, from clients and suppliers, and from controllers and controllees. Top business executives need support from their boards of directors and banks; government executives from President or Governor, legislators, and external interest groups.

Other important dimensions of management structure relate to managerial personnel and tenure. Admission to the upper ranks of management may be dependent upon a combination of such factors as sponsorship, ability, education, personality characteristics, and social origins. Some top managers seek a self-perpetuating oligarchy, with little or no provision made for inevitable replacement. Others set as major objectives the development of career and recruitment systems that make for high mobility within managerial ranks.

THE STRATEGY OF PLANNING

Planning is the process of developing commitments to some pattern of objectives.

The preceding section set forth the major categories of objectives.

Let us now turn to some of the strategic considerations involved in deriving a pattern from these categories.

1. The Selectivity Paradox

As specialists develop comprehensive ways of looking at systems, they often tend to overemphasize the role of comprehensive objectives in planning. Thus economists often give the false impression that national aggregates of income, product, investment, and consumption are the major goals in national policy-making. In the process of "selling their wares," budgeteers and accountants often give the impression that comprehensive projections of budgets, income statements, or balance sheets can define an organization's major goals. If this approach should be automatically transferred to general-systems accounting, we should then find ourselves recommending that an organization's planners should formulate comprehensive objectives for all the elements of system performance and system structure.

Yet this would be a misleading position. The essence of planning is the *selection of strategic objectives in the form of specific sequences of action to be taken by the organization.* These critical variables must be selected in terms of:

(a) The major interest satisfactions that must be "promised" to obtain external and internal support.
(b) Present, imminent, or foreseeable crises or emergencies. These may require "contingency plans."
(c) Their decisive impact upon preceding, coordinate, or subsequent events.
(d) The long-range implications of action in the present or the immediate future. These are the critical considerations with respect to the "sunk costs" of investment programmes and the immediate steps in extended production processes (such as the building of houses, ships, or aircraft).

With these strategic elements selected, many elements of performance and structure may be detailed in subsystem plans or handled on the basis of current improvisation. A passion for comprehensive detail by either the organization or its subsystems may undermine selectivity. It may easily result in a loss of perspective, in document-orientation instead of action-orientation, and in an information supply that overloads communication channels and processing capacity. It may thus lead to serious waste of resources.

But—and here is the paradox of selectivity—strategic objectives can be selected rationally *only if the planners are aware of the broad spectrum of possible objectives.* Otherwise, objectives may be set in a routinized, arbitrary, or superficial fashion. The very concept of selection implies the scanning of a broad range of possibilities.

The solution to this paradox may be found in the use of general-systems accounting to provide *a comprehensive background for the selection of strategic objectives.*

2. The Clarity-Vagueness Balance

There is no need to labour the need for clarity in the formulation of an organization's objectives. Precise formulations are necessary for delicate operations. They provide the indispensable framework for coordinating complex activity. They often have great symbolic significance.

Yet in the wide enthusiasm for "crystal-clear goals," one may easily lose sight of the need for a fruitful balance between clarity and vagueness. The following quotation is an effort to contribute to this balance through a "crystal-clear" statement on the virtues of vagueness:

> If all the points on a set of interrelated purpose chains were to be set forth with precise clarity, the result would be to destroy the subordination of one element to another which is essential to an operating purpose pattern. The proper focusing of attention on some goals for any particular moment or period in time means that other goals must be left vague. This is even more true for different periods of time. We must be very clear about many things we aim to do today and tomorrow. It might be dangerously misleading to seek similar clarity for our long-range goals.
>
> Apart from its role in helping provide focus, vagueness in goal formation has many positive virtues. It leaves room for others to fill in the details and even modify the general pattern; over-precise goals stifle initiative. Vagueness may make it easier to adapt to changing conditions; ultra-precision can destroy flexibility. Vagueness may make it possible to work towards many goals that can only be attained by indirection. Some of the deepest personal satisfactions from work and cooperation come as by-products of other things. If pursued too directly, they may slip through one's fingers; the happiest people in the world are never those who set out to do the things that will make them happy. There is something inhuman and terrifying about ultrapurposeful action proceeding according to blueprint and schedule. Only vagueness can restore the precious element of humanity.
>
> Above all, vagueness is an essential part of all agreements resulting from compromise. When a dispute is resolved, some degree of ambiguity enters into the terms of settlement. Hence the wide-open language often used in the final language of statutory law. Similar ambiguities are found in most constitutions, charters, declarations of purpose, policy manifestos, and collective bargaining agreements. Certain anticipated situations are always referred to in terms that mean different things to different people, and are valuable because of, not despite, this characteristic. (Gross, 1964, p. 497.)

3. Whose Objectives?

Whose objectives are an organization's objectives?

The crystal-clear answers to this question point to (1) the people who wrote the charter (law or articles of incorporation) under which the organization operates, (2) the holders of formal authority over the organization (legislators or stockholders), (3) the members of the organization as a whole, (4) the organization's specialized planning people, or (5) the organization's top managers.

Yet each of these answers is incomplete. The charter-writers and the holders of formal authority can deal with only a small portion of an organization's objectives. The members, the subsystems, and the specialized planners have or propose many objectives that the organization never accepts. The managers' objectives may be accepted only in part by the rest of the organization. All of these groups have many conflicting objectives.

A better, although vaguer, answer is one that defines an organization's objectives as those widely accepted by its members. These objectives may (to some extent, they *must*) reflect the objectives of charter-writers, the holders of formal authority, and other external groups. They must represent a common area of acceptance on the part of the organization's subsystems and members, albeit within a matrix of divergent and conflicting purposes. The technical planners play a major role in helping to formulate planning decisions. The top managers make (or legitimate) the decisions and play a major role in winning their acceptance throughout the organization. Whether recognized in formal planning procedures or not, the entire management structure is involved *de facto* in the daily operation of formulating and winning commitment to objectives for future performance and structure.

4. Conflict Resolving and Creating

As already indicated, the process of organizational planning involves dealing with many conflicting objectives and with divergent or conflicting parties at interest both inside and outside an organization.

Hence planning—rather than involving nothing but the sober application of technical rationality—is an exercise in conflict management. In this exercise systematic technical calculations are exceedingly valuable as a means both of narrowing areas of conflict and of revealing possibilities for conflict resolution. Yet technical calculations are never enough. Over-reliance upon them can lead to administrative irrationality.

Rational planning, in contrast, requires realistic attention to the power for and against alternative plans. It requires the resolution of conflicts through the use of power in various combinations of persuasion and pressure. It also requires the building of a power base through various methods of conflict resolution. The most widespread mode of conflict resolution is compromise, through which some interests are sacrificed. A more creative—but more difficult—method is integration. This involves a creative readjustment of interests so that all parties may gain and none lose. In some cases, total victory may be obtained for one point of view, with consequent defeat for its opposition. To prevent defeat on some objectives, it is often necessary to tolerate deadlock or avoid an issue entirely. Any real-life planning process may be characterized as *a stream of successive compromises punctuated by frequent occasions of deadlock or avoidance and occasional victories, defeats, and integrations.* All these outcomes lead to new conflicts to be handled by the planners and managers.

Successful planning is often possible only when the key members of an organization see themselves threatened by an imminent crisis. In non-crisis conditions the subsystems tend to move in their own directions. They will most readily accept common objectives when the alternative is perceived as an onslaught of acute dissatisfactions, that is, a crisis. With crisis as the alternative, conflicts may be more quickly and effectively resolved. This is particularly relevant to subsystem resistance against plans for significant structural change.

In developing an organization's purposes, therefore, managers are frequently involved in crisis management. They try to anticipate crises around the corner. They try to respond promptly to crises that emerge. They may even try to create crises by setting high aspirations and accentuating fears of failure. These are delicate activities. For managers without a broad perspective on an organization's performance, structure, and environmental relations, they are dangerous undertakings —with much to be lost on one front as the price of victory on another. Even with such a broad perspective, they involve considerations that may not always be publicly discussed with complete frankness.

Hence a better-developed language of organizational purposefulness will not provide an outsider with a satisfactory answer when he asks a manager, "Just what are your organization's purposes?" The most it can do is help the managers themselves in the difficult and unending process of asking the question and finding workable answers.

References

Drucker, Peter F. (1954). *The practice of management.* New York: Harper.

Drucker, Peter F. (1964). *Managing for results.* New York: Harper & Row.

Gross, Bertram M. (1964). *The managing of organizations* (2 vols). New York: Free Press.

LeBreton, Preston P. & Henning, Dale A. (1961). *Planning theory.* Englewood Cliffs, N.J.: Prentice-Hall.

READING 14

SHAPING THE MASTER STRATEGY OF YOUR FIRM*

William H. Newman

Every enterprise needs a central purpose expressed in terms of the services it will render to society. And it needs a basic concept of how it will create these services. Since it will be competing with other enterprises for resources, it must have some distinctive advantages—in its services or in its methods of creating them. Moreover, since it will inevitably cooperate with other firms, it must have the means for maintaining viable coalitions with them. In addition, there are the elements of change, growth, and adaptation. Master strategy is a company's basic plan for dealing with these factors.

One familiar way of delving into company strategy is to ask, "What business are we in or do we want to be in? Why should society tolerate our existence?" Answers are often difficult. A company producing only grass seed had very modest growth until it shifted its

focus to "lawn care" and provided the suburban homeowner with a full line of fertilizers, pesticides, and related products. Less fortunate was a cooperage firm that defined its business in terms of wooden boxes and barrels and went bankrupt when paperboard containers took over the field.

Product line is only part of the picture, however. An ability to supply services economically is also crucial. For example, most local bakeries have shut down, not for lack of demand for bread, but because they became technologically inefficient. Many a paper mill has exhausted its sources of pulpwood. The independent motel operator is having difficulty meeting competition from franchised chains. Yet in all these industries some firms have prospered—the ones that have had the foresight and adaptability (and probably some luck, too) to take advantage of their changing environment. These firms pursued a master strategy which enabled them to increase the services rendered and attract greater resources.

Most central managers recognize that mas-

* *Reprinted from* California Management Review, *vol. IX, no. 3, Spring, 1967. Copyright 1967 by The Regents of The University of California.*

ter strategy is of cardinal importance. But they are less certain about how to formulate a strategy for their particular firm. This article seeks to help in the shaping of master strategies. It outlines key elements and an approach to defining these. Most of our illustrations will be business enterprises; nevertheless, the central concept is just as crucial for hospitals, universities, and other nonprofit ventures.

A practical way to develop a master strategy is to:

Pick particular roles or niches that are appropriate in view of competition and the company's resources.

Combine various facets of the company's efforts to obtain synergistic effects.

Set up sequences and timing of changes that reflect company capabilities and external conditions.

Provide for frequent reappraisal and adaptation to evolving opportunities.

NEW MARKETS OR SERVICES

Picking propitious niches. Most companies fill more than one niche. Often they sell several lines of products; even when a single line is produced an enterprise may sell it to several distinct types of customers. Especially as a firm grows, it seeks expansion by tapping new markets or selling different services to its existing customers. In designing a company strategy we can avoid pitfalls by first examining each of these markets separately.

Basically, we are searching for customer needs—preferably growing ones—where adroit use of our unique resources will make our services distinctive and in that sense give us a competitive advantage. In these particular spots, we hope to give the customer an irresistible value and to do so at relatively low expense. A bank, for example, may devise a way of financing the purchase of an automobile that is particularly well-suited to farmers; it must then consider whether it is in a good position to serve such a market.

Identifying such propitious niches is not easy. Here is one approach that works well in various situations: Focus first on the industry—growth prospects, competition, key factors required for success—then on the strengths and weaknesses of the specific company as matched against these key success factors. As we de-

scribe this approach more fully, keep in mind that we are interested in segments of markets as well as entire markets.

The sales volume and profits of an industry or one of its segments depend on the demand for its services, the supply of these services, and the competitive conditions. (We use "service" here to include both physical products and intangible values provided by an enterprise.) Predicting future demand, supply, and competition is an exciting endeavor. In the following paragraphs, we suggest a few of the important considerations that may vitally affect the strategy of a company.

ELEMENTS OF DEMAND

Demand for industry services. The strength of the **desire** for a service affects its demand. For instance, we keenly want a small amount of salt, but care little for additional quantities. Our desire for more and better automobiles does not have this same sort of cut-off level, and our desires for pay-television (no commercials, select programs) or supersonic air travel are highly uncertain, falling in quite a different category from that of salt.

Possible **substitutes** to satisfy a given desire must be weighed—beef for lamb, motorboats for baseball, gas for coal, aureomycin for sulfa, weldments for castings, and so forth. The frequency of such substitution is affected, of course, by the relative prices.

Desire has to be backed up by **ability to pay,** and here business cycles enter in. Also, in some industries large amounts of capital are necessarily tied up in equipment. The relative efficiency, quality of work, and nature of machinery already in place influence the money that will be available for new equipment. Another consideration: If we hope to sell in foreign markets, foreign-exchange issues arise.

The **structure of markets** also requires analysis. Where, on what terms, and in response to what appeals do people buy jet planes, sulphuric acid, or dental floss? Does a manufacturer deal directly with consumers or are intermediaries such as retailers or brokers a more effective means of distribution?

Although an entire industry is often affected by such factors—desire, substitutes, ability to pay, structure of markets—a local variation in demand sometimes provides a unique oppor-

tunity for a particular firm. Thus, most drug-
stores carry cosmetics, candy, and a wide
variety of items besides drugs, but a store located in a medical center might develop a
highly profitable business by dealing exclusively with prescriptions and other medical
supplies.

All these elements of demand are subject to
change—some quite rapidly. Since the kind of
strategic plans we are considering here usually
extends over several years, we need both an
identification of the key factors that will affect
industry demand and an estimate of how they
will change over a span of time.

SUPPLY SITUATION

Supply related to demand.   The attractiveness of any industry depends on more than
potential growth arising from strong demand.
In designing a company strategy we also must
consider the probable supply of services and
the conditions under which they will be
offered.

The **capacity** of an industry to fill demand
for its services clearly affects profit margins.
The importance of over- or undercapacity,
however, depends on the ease of entry and
withdrawal from the industry. When capital
costs are high, as in the hotel or cement business, adjustments to demand tend to lag. Thus,
overcapacity may depress profits for a long
period; even bankruptcies do not remove the
capacity if plants are bought up—at bargain
prices—and operated by new owners. On the
other hand, low capital requirements—as in
electronic assembly work—permit new firms to
enter quickly, and shortages of supply tend
to be short-lived. Of course, more than the
physical plant is involved; an effective organization of competent people is also necessary.
Here again, the case of expansion or contraction should be appraised.

Costs also need to be predicted—labor costs,
material costs, and for some industries, transportation costs or excise taxes. If increases in
operating costs affect all members of an industry alike and can be passed on to the consumer in the form of higher prices, this factor
becomes less significant in company strategy.
However, rarely do both conditions prevail.
Sharp rises in labor costs in Hawaii, for example, place its sugar industry at a disadvantage
on the world market.

A highly dynamic aspect of supply is **technology.** New methods for producing established products—for example, basic oxygen
conversion of steel displacing open-hearth
furnaces and mechanical cotton pickers displacing century-old hand-picking techniques
—are part of the picture. Technology may
change the availability and price of raw materials; witness the growth of synthetic rubber
and industrial diamonds. Similarly, air cargo
planes and other new forms of transportation
are expanding the sources of supply that may
serve a given market.

For an individual producer, anticipating
these shifts in the industry supply situation
may be a matter of prosperity or death.

CLIMATE OF INDUSTRY

Competitive conditions in the industry.
The way the interplay between demand and
supply works out depends partly on the nature
of competition in the industry. **Size, strength,
and attitude of companies** in one industry—
the dress industry where entrance is easy and
style is critical—may lead to very sharp competition. On the other hand, oligopolistic competition among the giants of the aluminum
industry produces a more stable situation, at
least in the short run. The resources and managerial talent needed to enter one industry
differ greatly from what it takes to get ahead
in the other.

A strong **trade association** often helps to
create a favorable climate in its industry. The
Independent Oil Producers' Association, to
cite one case, has been unusually effective in
restricting imports of crude oil into the United
States. Other associations compile valuable
industry statistics, help reduce unnecessary
variations in size of products, run training con-
ferences, hold trade shows, and aid members
in a variety of other ways.

Government regulation also modifies competition. A few industries like banking and
insurance are supervised by national or state
bodies that place limits on prices, sales promotion, and the variety of services rendered. Airlines are both regulated as a utility and subsidized as an infant industry. Farm subsidies
affect large segments of agriculture, and tariffs
have long protected selected manufacturers.
Our patent laws also bear directly on the
nature of competition, as is evident in the

heated discussion of how pharmaceutical patents may be used. Clearly, future government action is a significant factor in the outlook of many industries.

CRUCIAL FACTORS

Key factors for success in the industry. This brief review suggests the dynamic nature of business and uncertainties in the outlook for virtually all industries. A crucial task of every top management is to assess the forces at play in its industry and to identify those factors that will be crucial for future success. These we call "key success factors." Leadership in research and development may be very important in one industry, low costs in another, and adaptability to local need in a third; large financial resources may be a *sine qua non* for mining whereas creative imagination is the touchstone in advertising.

We stressed earlier the desirability of making such analyses for narrow segments as well as broad industry categories. The success factors for each segment are likely to differ in at least one or two respects from those for other segments. For example, General Foods Corporation discovered to its sorrow that the key success factors in gourmet foods differ significantly from those for coffee and Jello.

Moreover, the analysis of industry outlook should provide a forecast of the **growth potentials** and the **profit prospects** for the various industry segments. These conclusions, along with key success factors, are vital guideposts in setting up a company's master strategy.

The range of opportunities for distinctive service is wide. Naturally, in picking its particular niche out of this array a company favors those opportunities which will utilize its strength and bypass its limitations. This calls for a candid appraisal of the company itself.

POSITION IN MARKET

Market strengths of company. A direct measure of **market position** is the percentage that company sales are of industry sales and of major competitors' sales. Such figures quickly indicate whether our company is so big that its activities are likely to bring prompt responses from other leading companies. Or

our company may be small enough to enjoy independent maneuverability. Of course, to be most meaningful, these percentages should be computed separately for geographical areas, product lines, and types of customer—if suitable industry data are available.

More intangible but no less significant are the relative standing of **company products** and their **reputation** in major markets. Kodak products, for instance, are widely and favorably known; they enjoy a reputation for both high quality and dependability. Clearly, this reputation will be a factor in Eastman Kodak Company strategy. And any new, unknown firm must overcome this prestige if it seeks even a small share in one segment of the film market. Market reputation is tenacious. Especially when we try to "trade up," our previous low quality, service, and sharp dealing will be an obstacle. Any strategy we adopt must have enough persistence and consistency so that our firm is assigned a "role" in the minds of the customers we wish to reach.

The relationship between a company and the **distribution system** is another vital aspect of market position. The big United States automobile companies, for example, are strong partly because each has a set of dealers throughout the country. In contrast, foreign car manufacturers have difficulty selling here until they can arrange with dealers to provide dependable service. A similar problem confronted Whirlpool Corporation when it wanted to sell its trademarked appliances publicly. (For years its only customer had been Sears, Roebuck and Company.) Whirlpool made an unusual arrangement with Radio Corporation of America which led to the establishment of RCA-Whirlpool distributors and dealers. Considering the strong competition, Whirlpool could not have entered this new market without using marketing channels such as RCA's.

All these aspects of market position—a relative share of the market, comparative quality of product, reputation with consumers, and ties with a distributive system—help define the strengths and limitations of a company.

SERVICE ABILITIES

Supply strengths of a company. To pick propitious niches we also should appraise our company's relative strength in creating goods and services. Such ability to supply services fitted to consumer needs will be built largely on the firm's resources of labor and material, effective productive facilities, and perhaps pioneering research and development.

Labor in the United States is fairly mobile. Men tend to gravitate to good jobs. But the process takes time—a southern shoe plant needed ten years to build up an adequate number of skilled workers—and it may be expensive. Consequently, immediate availability of competent men at normal industry wages is a source of strength. In addition, the relationships between the company and its work force are important. All too often both custom and formal agreements freeze inefficient practices. The classic example is New England textiles; here, union-supported work habits give even mills high labor costs. Only recently have a few companies been able to match their more flourishing competitors in the South.

Access to **low-cost materials** is often a significant factor in a company's supply position. The development of the southern paper industry, for example, is keyed to the use of fast-growing forests which can be cut on a rotational basis to provide a continuing supply of pulpwood. Of course, if raw materials can be easily transported, such as iron ore and crude oil by enormous ships, plants need not be located at the original source.

Availability of materials involves more than physical handling. Ownership, or long-term contracts with those who do own, may assure a continuing source at low cost. Much of the strategy of companies producing basic metals —iron, copper, aluminum, or nickel—includes huge investments in ore properties. But all sorts of companies are concerned with the availability of materials. So whenever supplies are scarce a potential opportunity exists. Even in retailing, Sears, Roebuck and Company discovered in its Latin American expansion that a continuing flow of merchandise of standard quality was difficult to assure, but once established, such sources became a great advantage.

Physical facilities—office buildings, plants, mines—often tie up a large portion of a company's assets. In the short run, at least, these facilities may be an advantage or a disadvantage. The character of many colleges, for instance, has been shaped by their location, whether in a plush suburb or in a degenerating urban area, and the cost of moving facilities is so great that adaptation to the existing neighborhood becomes necessary. A steel company, to cite another case, delayed modernizing its plant so long that it had to abandon its share of the basic steel market and seek volume in specialty products.

Established organizations of highly talented people to perform particular tasks also give a company a distinctive capability. Thus, a good research and development department may enable a company to expand in pharmaceuticals, whereas a processing firm without such a technical staff is barred from this profitable field.

Perhaps the company we are analyzing will enjoy other distinctive abilities to produce services. Our central concern at this point is to identify strengths and see how these compare with strengths of other firms.

FINANCES AND MANAGEMENT

Other company resources. The propitious niche for a company also depends on its financial strength and the character of its management.

Some strategies will require large quantities of capital. Any oil company that seeks foreign sources of crude oil, for instance, must be prepared to invest millions of dollars. Five firms maintain cash reserves of this size, so **financial capacity** to enter this kind of business depends on: an ability to attract new capital —through borrowing or sale of stock—or a flow of profits (and depreciation allowances) from existing operations that can be allocated to the new venture. On the other hand, perhaps a strategy can be devised that calls for relatively small cash advances, and in these fields a company that has low financial strength will still be able to compete with the affluent firms.

A more subtle factor in company capacity is its **management.** The age and vitality of key executives, their willingness to risk profit and capital, their urge to gain personal prestige through company growth, their desire to insure stable employment for present workers— all affect the suitability of any proposed strategy. For example, the expansion of Hilton Hotels Corporation into a world-wide chain certainly reflects the personality of Conrad Hilton; with a different management at the helm, a modification in strategy is most appropriate because Conrad Hilton's successors do not have his particular set of drives and values.

Related to the capabilities of key executives is the organization structure of the company. A decentralized structure, for instance, facilitates movement into new fields of business, whereas a functional structure with fine specialization is better suited to expansion in closely related lines.

PICKING A NICHE

Matching company strengths with key success factors. Armed with a careful analysis of the strengths and limitations of our company, we are prepared to pick desirable niches for company concentration. Naturally, we will look for fields where company strengths correspond with the key factors for success that have been developed in our industry analyses described in the preceding section. And in the process we will set aside possibilities in which company limitations create serious handicaps.

Potential growth and profits in each niche must, of course, be added to the synthesis. Clearly, a low potential will make a niche unattractive even though the company strengths and success factors fit neatly. And we may become keenly interested in a niche where the fit is only fair if the potential is great.

Typically, several intriguing possibilities emerge. These are all the niches—in terms of market lines, market segments, or combinations of production functions—that the company might pursue. Also typically, a series of positive actions is necessary in order for the company to move into each area. So we need to list not only each niche and its potential, but the limitations that will have to be overcome and other steps necessary for the company to succeed in each area. These are our propitious niches—nestled in anticipated business conditions and tailored to the strengths and limitations of our particular company.

An enterprise always pursues a variety of efforts to serve even a single niche, and, typically, it tries to fill several related niches. Considerable choice is possible, at least in the degree to which these many efforts are pushed. In other words, management decides how many markets to cover, to what degree to automate production, what stress to place on consumer engineering, and a host of other actions. One vital aspect of master strategy is fitting these numerous efforts together. In fact, our choice of niches will depend in part, on

how well we can combine the total effort they require.

Synergy is a powerful ally for this purpose. Basically, synergy means that the combined effect of two or more cooperative acts is greater than the sum which would result if the actions were taken independently. A simple example in marketing is that widespread dealer stocks combined with advertising will produce much greater sales volume than widespread dealer stocks in, say, Virginia and advertising in Minnesota. Often the possibility of obtaining synergistic effects will shape the master strategy of the company—as the following examples will suggest.

COMBINATION OF SERVICES

Total service to customer. A customer rarely buys merely a physical product. Other attributes of the transaction often include delivery, credit terms, return privileges, repair service, operating instructions, conspicuous consumption, psychological experience of purchasing, and the like. Many services involve no physical product at all. The crucial question is what combination of attributes will have high synergistic value for the customers we serve.

International Business Machines, for instance, has found a winning combination. Its products are well designed and of high quality. But so are the products of several of its competitors. In addition, IBM provides salesmen who understand the customer's problems and how IBM equipment can help solve them, and fast, dependable repair service. The synergistic effect of these three services is of high value to many customers.

Each niche calls for its own combination of services. For example, Chock Full o' Nuts expanded its restaurant chain on the basis of three attributes: good quality food, cleanliness, and fast service. This combination appealed to a particular group of customers. A very limited selection, crowded space, and lack of frills did not matter. However, if any one of the three characteristics slips at an outlet, the synergistic effect is lost.

ADDING TO CAPABILITIES

Fuller use of existing resources. Synergistic effects are possible in any phase of company operations. One possibility is that present activities include a "capability" that can be applied to additional uses. Thus, American watch companies have undertaken the manufacture of tiny gyroscopes and electronic components for spacecraft because they already possessed technical skill in the production of miniature precision products. They adopted this strategy on the premise that they could make both watches and components for spacecraft with less effort than could separate firms devoted to only one line of products.

The original concept of General Foods Corporation sought a similar synergistic effect in marketing. Here, the basic capability was marketing prepared foods. By having the same sales organization handle several product lines, a larger and more effective sales effort could be provided and/or the selling cost per product line could be reduced. Clearly, the combined sales activity was more powerful than separate sales efforts for each product line would have been.

VERTICAL INTEGRATION

Expansion to obtain a resource.   Vertical integration may have synergistic effects. This occurred when the Apollo Printing Machine Company bought a foundry. Apollo was unsatisfied with the quality and tardy delivery of its castings and was looking for a new supplier. In its search, it learned that a nearby foundry could be purchased. The foundry was just breaking even, primarily because the volume of its work fluctuated widely. Following the purchase, Apollo gave the foundry a more steady backlog of work, and through close technical cooperation the quality of castings received by them was improved. The consolidated set-up was better for both enterprises than the previous independent operations.

The results of vertical integration are not always so good, however; problems of balance, flexibility, and managerial capacity must be carefully weighed. Nevertheless, control of a critical resource is often a significant part of company strategy.

UNIQUE SERVICES

Expansion to enhance market position. Efforts to improve market position provide

many examples of "the whole being better than the sum of its parts." The leading can companies, for example, moved from exclusive concentration on metal containers into glass, plastic, and paper containers. They expected their new divisions to be profitable by themselves, but an additional reason for the expansion lay in anticipated synergistic effects of being able to supply a customer's total container requirements. With the entire packaging field changing so rapidly, a company that can quickly shift from one type of container to another offers a distinctive service to its customers.

International Harvester, to cite another case, added a very large tractor to its line a few years ago. The prospects for profit on this line alone were far from certain. However, the new tractor was important to give dealers "a full line"; its availability removed the temptation for dealers to carry some products of competing manufacturers. So, when viewed in combination with other International Harvester products, the new tractor looked much more significant than it did as an isolated project.

NEGATIVE SYNERGY

Compatibility of efforts.   In considering additional niches for a company, we may be confronted with negative synergy—that is, the combined effort is worse than the sum of independent efforts. This occurred when a producer of high quality television and hi-fi sets introduced a small color television receiver. When first offered, the small unit was as good as most competing sets and probably had an attractive potential market. However, it was definitely inferior in performance to other products of the company and, consequently, undermined public confidence in the quality of the entire line. Moreover, customers had high expectations for the small set because of the general reputation of the company, and they became very critical when the new product did not live up to their expectations. Both the former products and the new product suffered.

Compatibility of operations within the company should also be considered. A large department store, for instance, ran into serious trouble when it tried to add a high-quality dress shop to its mass merchandising activities. The ordering and physical handling of merchandise, the approach to sales promotion, the sales compensation plan, and many other procedures which worked well for the established type of business were unsuited to the new shop. And friction arose each time the shop received special treatment. Clearly, the new shop created an excessive number of problems because it was incompatible with existing customs and attitudes.

BROAD COMPANY GOALS

Summarizing briefly: We have seen that some combinations of efforts are strongly reinforcing. The combination accelerates the total effect or reduces the cost for the same effect or solidifies our supply or market position. On the other hand, we must watch for incompatible efforts which may have a disruptive effect in the same cumulative manner. So, when we select niches—as a part of our master strategy— one vital aspect is the possibility of such synergistic effects.

Master strategy sets broad company goals. One firm may decide to seek pre-eminence in a narrow specialty while another undertakes to be a leader in several niches or perhaps in all phases of its industry. We have recommended that this definition of "scope" be clear in terms of:

Services offered to customers.
Operations performed by the company.
Relationships with suppliers of necessary resources.
The desirability of defining this mission so as to obtain synergistic effects.

But master strategy involves more than defining our desired role in society. Many activities will be necessary to achieve this desired spot, and senior executives must decide what to do first, how many activities can be done concurrently, how fast to move, what risks to run, and what to postpone. These questions of sequence and timing must be resolved to make the strategy operational.

STRATEGY OF SEQUENCE

Choice of sequence.   Especially in technical areas, sequence of actions may be dictated by technology. Thus, process research must precede equipment designs, product specifications must precede cost estimation, and so forth. Other actions, such as the steps necessary to form a new corporation, likewise give management little choice in sequence. When this occurs, normal programming or possibly PERT analysis may be employed. Little room—or need—exists for strategy.

Preordained sequences, however, are exceptional in the master strategy area. A perennial issue when entering a new niche, for instance, is whether to develop markets before working on production economies, or vice versa. The production executive will probably say, "Let's be sure we can produce the product at a low cost before committing ourselves to customers," whereas the typical marketing man will advise, "Better be sure it will sell before tooling up for a big output."

A striking example of strategy involving sequence confronted the Boeing company when it first conceived of a large four-engine jet plane suitable for handling cargo or large passenger loads. Hindsight makes the issue appear simple, but at the time, Air Force officers saw little need for such a plane. The belief was that propeller-driven planes provided the most desirable means for carrying cargo. In other words, the company got no support for its prediction of future market requirements. Most companies would have stopped at this point. However, Boeing executives decided to invest several million dollars to develop the new plane. A significant portion of the company's liquid assets went into the project. Over two years later, Boeing was able to present evidence that caused the Air Force officials to change their minds—and the KC 135 was born. Only Boeing was prepared to produce the new type of craft which proved to be both faster and more economical than propeller-driven planes. Moreover, the company was able to convert the design into the Boeing 707 passenger plane which, within a few years, dominated the airline passenger business. Competing firms were left far behind, and Convair almost went bankrupt in its attempt to catch up. In this instance, a decision to let engineering and production run far ahead of marketing paid off handsomely.

No simple guide exists for selecting a strategic sequence. Nevertheless, the following comments do sharpen the issue:

Resist the temptation to do first what is easiest simply because it requires the least initiative. Each of us typically has a bias for what he does well. A good sequence of activities, however, is more likely to emerge from an objective analysis.

If a head start is especially valuable on one front, start early there. Sometimes, being the first in the market is particularly desirable (there may be room for only one company). In other cases, the strategic place to begin is the acquiring of key resources; at a later date limited raw materials may already be bought up or the best sites occupied by competitors. The importance of a head start is usually hard to estimate, but probably more money is lost in trying to be first than in catching up with someone else.

Move into uncertain areas promptly, preferably before making any major commitments. For instance, companies have been so entranced with a desired expansion that they committed substantial funds to new plants before uncertainties regarding the production processes were removed.

If a particular uncertainty can be investigated quickly and inexpensively, get it out of the way promptly.

Start early with processes involving long lead-times. For example, if a new synthetic food product must have government approval, the tedious process of testing and reviewing evidence may take a year or two longer than preparation for manufacturing and marketing.

Delay revealing plans publicly if other companies can easily copy a novel idea. If substantial social readjustment is necessary, however, an early public announcement is often helpful.

In a particular case, these guides may actually conflict with each other, or other considerations may be dominant. And, as the Boeing 707 example suggests, the possible gains may be large enough to justify following a very risky sequence. Probably the greatest value of the above list is to stimulate careful thought about the sequence that is incorporated into a company's master strategy.

RESOURCE LIMITATIONS

Straining scarce resources.   A hard-driving executive does not like to admit that an objective cannot be achieved. He prefers to believe, "Where there's a will there's a way."

Yet, an essential aspect of master strategy is deciding what can be done and how fast.

Every enterprise has limits—perhaps severe limits—on its resources. The amount of capital, the number and quality of key personnel, the physical production capacity, or the adaptability of its social structure—none of these is boundless. The tricky issue is how to use these limited resources to the best advantage. We must devise a strategy which is feasible within the inherent restraints.

A household-appliance manufacturer went bankrupt because he failed to adapt his rate of growth to his financial resources. This man had a first-rate product and a wise plan for moving with an "economy model" into an expanding market (following rural electrification). But, to achieve low production costs, he built an oversized plant and launched sales efforts in ten states. His contention was that the kind of company he conceived could not start out on a small scale. Possibly all of these judgments were correct, but they resulted in cash requirements that drained all of his resources before any momentum was achieved. Cost of the partially used plant and of widely scattered sales efforts was so high that no one was willing to bail out the financially strapped venture. His master strategy simply did not fit his resources.

The scarce resource affecting master strategy may be managerial personnel. A management consulting firm, for instance, reluctantly postponed entry into the international arena because only two of its partners had the combination of interest, capacity, and vitality to spend a large amount of time abroad, and these men were also needed to assure continuity of the United States practice. The firm felt that a later start would be better than weak action immediately—even though this probably meant the loss of several desirable clients.

The weight we should attach to scarce resources in the timing of master strategy often requires delicate judgment. Some strain may be endured. But, how much, how long? For example, in its switch from purchased to company-produced tires, a European rubber company fell behind on deliveries for six months, but, through heroic efforts and pleading with customers, the company weathered the squeeze. Now, company executives believe the timing was wise! If the delay had lasted a full year—and this was a real possibility—the consequence would have approached a catastrophe.

Forming coalitions.   A cooperative agreement with firms in related fields occasionally provides a way to overcome scarce resources. We have already referred to the RCA-Whirlpool arrangement for distributing Whirlpool products. Clearly, in this instance, the timing of Whirlpool's entrance into the market with its own brand depended on forming a coalition with RCA.

EXAMPLES OF COALITIONS

The early development of frozen foods provides us with two other examples of fruitful coalitions. A key element in Birdseye master strategy was to obtain the help of cold-storage warehouses; grocery wholesalers were not equipped to handle frozen foods, and before the demand was clearly established they were slow to move into the new activity. And the Birdseye division of General Foods lacked both managerial and financial resources to venture into national wholesaling.

Similarly, Birdseye had to get freezer cabinets into retail stores, but it lacked the capability to produce them. So, it entered into a coalition with a refrigerator manufacturer to make and sell (or lease) the cabinets to retail stores. This mutual agreement enabled Birdseye to move ahead with its marketing program much faster. With the tremendous growth of frozen foods, neither the cold storage warehouse nor the cabinet manufacturer continued to be necessary, but without them in the early days widespread use of frozen foods would have been delayed three to five years.

Coalitions may be formed for reasons other than "buying time." Nevertheless, when we are trying to round out a workable master strategy, coalitions—or even mergers—may provide the quickest way to overcome a serious deficiency in vital resources.

THE RIGHT TIME TO ACT

Receptive environment.   Conditions in a firm's environment affect the "right time" to make a change. Mr. Ralph Cordiner, for example, testifies that he launched his basic reorganization of General Electric Company only when he felt confident of three years of high business activity because, in his opinion, the company could not have absorbed all the internal readjustments during a period of declining volume and profits.

Judging the right time to act is difficult. Thus, one of the contributing factors to the multimillion-dollar Edsel car fiasco was poor timing. The same automobile launched a year or two earlier might have been favorably received. But buyer tastes changed between the time elaborate market research studies were made and the time when the new car finally appeared in dealer showrooms. By then, preference was swinging away from a big car that "had everything" toward compacts. This mistake in timing and associated errors in strategy cost the Ford Motor Company over a hundred million dollars.

[margin annotation: Timely Market Research]

A major move can be too early, as well as too late. We know, for instance, that a forerunner of the modern, self-service supermarket —the Piggly Wiggly—was born too soon. In its day, only a few housewives drove automobiles to shopping centers; and those that could afford cars usually shunned the do-it-yourself mode so prevalent today. In other words, the environment at that time simply was not receptive to what now performs so effectively. Other "pioneers" have also received cool receptions—prefabricated housing and local medical clinics are two.

NO SIMPLE RULES

The preceding discussions of sequence and timing provide no simple rules for these critical aspects of basic strategy. The factors we have mentioned for deciding which front(s) to push first (where is a head start valuable, early attention to major uncertainties, lead-times, significance of secrecy) and for deciding how fast to move (strain on scarce resources, possible coalition to provide resources, and receptivity of the environment) bear directly on many strategy decisions. They also highlight the fundamental nature of sequence and timing in the master strategy for a firm.

Master strategy involves deliberately relating a company's efforts to its particular future environment. We recognize, of course, that both the company's capabilities and its environment continually evolve; consequently, strategy should always be based, not on existing conditions, but on forecasts. Such forecasts, however, are never 100 per cent correct; instead, strategy often seeks to take advantage of uncertainty about future conditions.

This dynamic aspect of strategy should be underscored. The industry outlook will shift for any of numerous reasons. These forces may accelerate growth in some sectors and spell decline in others, may squeeze material supply, may make old sources obsolete, may open new possibilities and snuff out others. Meanwhile, the company itself is also changing—due to the success or failure of its own efforts and to actions of competitors and cooperating firms. And with all of these internal and external changes the combination of thrusts that will provide optimum synergistic effects undoubtedly will be altered. Timing of actions is the most volatile element of all. It should be adjusted to both the new external situation and the degrees of internal progress on various fronts.

Consequently, frequent reappraisal of master strategy is essential. We must build into the planning mechanisms sources of fresh data that will tell us how well we are doing and what new opportunities and obstacles are appearing on the horizon. The feedback features of control will provide some of these data. In addition, senior managers and others who have contact with various parts of the environment must be ever-sensitive to new developments that established screening devices might not detect.

Hopefully, such reappraisal will not call for sharp reversals in strategy. Typically, a master strategy requires several years to execute and some features may endure much longer. The kind of plan I am discussing here sets the direction for a whole host of company actions, and external reputations and relations often persist for many years. Quick reversals break momentum, require repeated relearning, and dissipate favorable cumulative effects. To be sure, occasionally a sharp break may be necessary. But, if my forecasts are reasonably sound, the adaptations to new opportunities will be more evolution than revolution. Once embarked on a course, we make our reappraisal from our new position—and this introduces an advantage in continuing in at least the same general direction. So, normally, the adaptation is more an unfolding than a completely new start.

Even though drastic modification of our master strategy may be unnecessary, frequent incremental changes will certainly be required to keep abreast of the times. Especially desirable are shifts that anticipate change before the pressures build up. And such farsighted adjustments are possible only if we periodically reappraise and adapt present strategy to new opportunities.

Master strategy is the pivotal planning instrument for large and small enterprises alike. The giant corporations provide us with examples on a grand scale, but the same kind of thinking is just as vital for small firms.

AN EXAMPLE

A terse sketch of the central strategy of one small firm will illustrate this point. The partners of an accounting firm in a city with a quarter-million population predicted faster growth in data processing than in their normal auditing and tax work, yet they knew that most of their clients were too small to use an electronic computer individually. So they foresaw the need for a single, cooperative computer center serving several companies. And they believed that their intimate knowledge of the procedures and the needs of several of these companies, plus the specialized ability of one partner in data processing, put them in a unique position to operate such a center. Competition was anticipated from two directions: New models of computers much smaller in size would eventually come on the market—but even if the clients could rent such equipment they would still need programmers and other specialized skills. Also, telephonic hook-ups with International Business Machines service centers appeared likely—but the accounting firm felt its local and more intimate knowledge of each company would give it an advantage over such competition. So, the cooperative computer center looked like a propitious niche.

The chief obstacle was developing a relatively stable volume of work that would carry the monthly rental on the proposed computer. A local insurance company was by far the best prospect for this purpose; it might use half the computer capacity, and then the work for other, smaller companies could be fitted into the remaining time. Consequently, the first major move was to make a deal—a coalition—with the insurance company. One partner was to devote almost his entire time working on details for such an arrangement; meanwhile, the other two partners supported him through their established accounting practice.

We see in this brief example:

The picking of a propitious niche for expansion.

The anticipated synergistic effect of combining auditing services with computing service.

The sequence and timing of efforts to overcome the major limiting factor.

The project had not advanced far enough for much reappraisal, but the fact that two partners were supporting the third provided a built-in check on the question of "how are we doing."

References

This article is adapted from a chapter in *The Process of Management,* second edition, Prentice-Hall, Inc., 1967. Executives who wish to explore the meaning and method of shaping master strategies still further can consult the following materials: E. W. Reilley, "Planning the Strategy of the Business," *Advanced Management,* XX (Dec. 1955), 8–12; T. Levitt, "Marketing Myopia," *Harvard Business Review,* XXXVIII:4 (July-Aug. 1960), 45–66; F. F. Gilmore and R. G. Brandenburg, "Anatomy of Corporate Planning," *Harvard Business Review,* XLI:6 (Nov.-Dec. 1962), 61–69; and H. W. Newman and T. L. Berg, "Managing External Relations," *California Management Review,* V:3 (Spring 1963), 81–86.

READING 15

THE CRITICAL ROLE OF TOP MANAGEMENT IN LONG-RANGE PLANNING *

George A. Steiner

There is no substitute for long-range planning in the development of profitable and healthy organizations. It is not, of course, the only requirement, but it is a major one. Too few companies, particularly the smaller and medium-sized ones, and too few government organizations try or do effective long-range planning.

In examining many long-range planning programs, I have come to two major conclusions. First, the fundamental concept of an effective long-range planning program is deceptively simple. Second, creating and maintaining a first-rate long-range planning program is deceptively difficult and demands, for its success, devoted attention by chief executives. I should like to discuss these two points, but first I should like to say a few words about the importance of effective long-range planning.

* *Reprinted with permission from* Arizona Review, *April, 1966.*

IMPORTANCE OF LONG-RANGE PLANNING

There exists in some business and government quarters surprising resistance to developing systematic and comprehensive planning. Naturally there are a great many reasons for such resistance, but failure to grasp the significance of effective planning is more important than it should be.

Several years ago, Mr. S. C. Beise, then President of the Bank of America, observed that for many years before World War II commercial banks did not aggressively seek savings deposits. As a result, the industry did not involve itself importantly in the related field of real estate financing. After World War II building boomed and little financial firms grew dramatically to fill the home financing need.

> Today these once-small savings and loan companies constitute a big industry in the United States and have given banks stiff competition for savings funds.

The commercial banking industry today has made a strong comeback in the fields of savings and real estate lending, but due to its lack of foresight some twenty years ago, the banking industry gave birth to one of its own biggest competitors. I believe the industry has learned its lesson well, and it is one every industry and company should note.[1]

A recent study of the thirteen fastest growing companies in the United States revealed that all give high priority to long-range planning and manage to inspire most levels of managers to think about the future.[2]

Not only are more companies discovering the advantages of comprehensive and effective planning programs, but governments are developing organized long-range planning programs. This movement is particularly rapid among Western European governments and some developing nations. Last August President Johnson dramatically announced that the planning-programming-budgeting system introduced into the Pentagon by Secretary McNamara must be applied throughout the government.

There are many reasons why systematic and structured long-range planning is considered so important by progressive businesses and non-business organizations. Effective planning prevents ad hoc decisions, random decisions, decisions that unnecessarily and expensively narrow choices for tomorrow. Effective planning gives an organization a structural framework of objectives and strategies, a basis for all decision making. Lower-level managers know what top management wants and can make decisions accordingly. But there are also ancillary benefits. An effective planning organization, for example, provides a powerful channel of communications for the people in an organization to deal with problems of importance to themselves as well as to their organization.

It is difficult to exaggerate the importance of effective comprehensive planning to an organization. It has, for many companies, pro-

[1] S. C. Beise, *"Planning for Industrial Growth: An Executive View," remarks before the Milan Conference on Planning for Industrial Growth, sponsored by Stanford Research Institute, 1963, mimeographed.*
[2] *Jack B. Weiner, "What Makes a Growth Company?,"* Dun's Review and Modern Industry, *November 1964.*

vided that margin needed for outstanding growth and profitability.

A CONCEPTUAL MODEL OF LONG-RANGE PLANNING

A conceptual model of planning at a sufficiently low level of abstraction is a guide in establishing a complete system. The words *long-range planning* are useful in emphasizing a time dimension to planning. In describing an effective planning program, however, I prefer to speak of comprehensive, corporate or total planning.

Planning in this sense may be described from four points of view. First, a basic generic view of planning as dealing with the futurity of present decisions. This means that current decisions are made in light of their long-range consequences. It means also that future alternatives open to an organization are examined and decisions made about preferred alternatives. On this basis, guidance is provided for making current operating decisions. There are also many other conceptual views of planning; one concept, for example, recognizes planning as reasoning about how you get from here to there.

Planning is also a process. It is a process which establishes objectives; defines strategies, policies and sequences of events to achieve objectives; defines the organization for implementing the planning process; and assures a review and evaluation of performance as feedback in recycling the process.

Planning may be considered from a third point of view—namely, as a philosophy. Planning has been described as projective thought, or "looking ahead." Planning in this sense is an attitude, a state of mind, a way of thinking.

Finally, planning may be viewed in terms of structure. Long-range planning, as the term is typically used in the business world, refers to the development of a comprehensive and reasonably uniform program of plans for the entire company or agency, reaching out over a long period of time. It is an integrating framework within which each of the functional plans may be tied together and an overall plan developed for the entire organization.

Broadly, this structure includes four major elements (Figure 15-1). The first consists of strategic plans. These are a loose, written and unwritten set of major objectives, strategies and policies. The second is a detailed, uniform

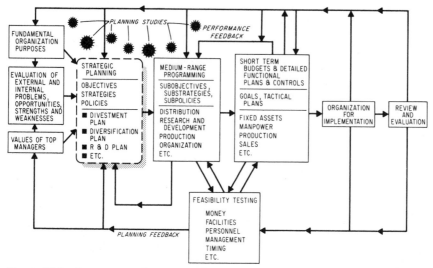

Figure 15-1   A structure and process of business planning.

and a rather complete medium-range set of plans (two to seven, but generally five, years) covering major areas of organizational activity. The third part is short-term plans and budgets. The fourth structural part consists of planning studies which frequently are projections of things to come. A government agency, for example, may make a study of future revenues and demands for funds. A public utility may make population projections for its area. An automobile company may study changing consumer tastes, likely competitor moves and developing automotive technology. Such forecasts are not plans. The results of such studies, however, are important in actually making plans.

Long-range planning as the term is typically used in the business world does not refer so much to the future span of time covered as to the idea of management grappling systematically with future opportunities, problems and alternative courses of action. Many companies typically have the pattern of plans and the concepts of planning already defined. This can be and often is called long-range planning. But I prefer other words to describe this structure.

LONG-RANGE PLANNING IN LARGE AND SMALL BUSINESSES

All companies plan ahead in some degree. But not all have the sort of concept and structure noted here. While statistics on this subject are

rather poor, I think it is probably true that close to a majority of the largest companies throughout the world have some sort of overall business planning program and a staff assigned to help executives do the work. Two years ago I held a research seminar at the Palais de Fontainebleau, France to discuss strategic business planning. About one hundred directors of corporate planning or top line managers of the largest multi-national corporations of the world were present. One of the surprising conclusions reached at the seminar was that, despite the great surface diversities of planning among these companies, there was a large degree of comparability among basic planning definitions, principles, procedures and structures.[3]

There are relatively fewer numbers of medium and small-sized companies with comprehensive planning programs, but their numbers are growing. They are beginning to realize that, despite their limited resources, they have about the same fundamental planning requirements as the larger companies. Their salvation is not to ignore the problem but to develop short-cuts and rough-cut techniques for dealing with it.[4] There are many

[3] *See George A. Steiner and Warren M. Cannon, eds.,* Multinational Corporate Planning *(New York: The Free Press, Spring 1966).*

[4] *For suggestions about how to do this, see Roger A. Golde, "Practical Planning for Small Business,"* Harvard Business Review, *September-October 1964; Myles L. Mace, "The President and*

ways for a small company to get outside help at a reasonable price. Local banks can give advice. Many consulting agencies are available. Even professors are sometimes handy as consultants. Placing on his board of directors some persons who can contribute to long-range planning may also be attractive to a small businessman.

Systematic and reasonably well-structured planning programs are required by all organizations to survive and progress in the most healthy and effective manner. This is not something that only large companies need and are able to do. The requirement for effective planning exists for small companies, trade associations, industrial development agencies and for governments.

Professor Frank Gilmore of Cornell University presents the necessity for better planning in small businesses with this warning:

> The swing to strategic planning in large organizations constitutes a serious threat to small business management. It challenges one of the important competitive advantages which the small company has enjoyed—being faster on its feet than the larger company in adapting to changing conditions. It is perfectly clear that mere adaptation in the short run will no longer suffice. Trends must henceforth be made, not simply coped with.[5]

His point, of course, is that strategic planning among small businesses and smaller nonprofit organizations must accompany the better planning of the larger organizations. Smaller organizations can plan ahead systematically and continuously. First, however, there must be a recognition by the chief executive that this is possible. Then the smaller organization must devise ways and means to perform planning at a cost under benefit.

Naturally, different organizations go about meeting their planning responsibilities in different ways. Many big corporations have a

large central planning staff reporting to the chief executive through a senior vice president. Each of the divisions of such a company may also have a planning staff. At the other extreme are the very small firms where the chief executive does almost all the planning. As firms increase in size, the chief executive may get help by hiring a special assistant, by using his vice presidents in ad hoc advisory planning committees or by using his vice presidents and functional officers as a permanent planning staff to help him develop plans.

In a similar fashion, basic principles essential for effective planning apply to all organizations—large and small, profit and nonprofit. Precisely how the principles are applied, however, does differ among organizations and among problems and over time.

Of cardinal importance in creating and maintaining useful comprehensive planning programs is the role played by chief executives.

TOP MANAGEMENT'S KEY ROLE IN PLANNING

There can and will be no effective long-range planning in any organization where the chief executive does not give it firm support and make sure that others in the organization understand his depth of commitment. Yet one competent observer finds:

> Probably the single most important problem in corporate planning derives from the belief of some chief operating executives that corporate planning is not a function with which they should be directly concerned. They regard planning as something to be delegated, which subordinates can do without responsible participation by chief executives. They think the end result of effective planning is the compilation of a "Plans" book. Such volumes get distributed to key executives, who scan the contents briefly, file them away, breathe a sigh of relief, and observe, "Thank goodness that is done—now let's get back to work."[6]

This, of course, shows a lack of understanding of the planning task and the responsibility of the top executive. Another competent ob-

---

Corporate Planning," Harvard Business Review, *January-February 1965; and Raymond M. Haas, Richard I. Hartman, John H. James and Robert R. Milroy,* Long-Range Planning for Small Business, *Bureau of Business Research, Graduate School of Business, Indiana University, 1964.*
[5] *Frank F. Gilmore, "Strategic Planning's Threat to Small Business," mimeographed, 1966.*

[6] *Mace, op. cit., p. 50.*

server says the matter is not so much a lack of understanding but abdication of responsibility. Professor O'Donnell has said:

> I think one of the outstanding facts about corporate planning at the present is that the presidents of corporations have been ducking their jobs. . . . They seem to be following the practice of setting in a fuzzy way some objectives to be accomplished in the future and establishing a committee, with the staff help of a planning group, to come up with a plan for achieving the objectives. From this point until the plan is presented to him, the president almost abdicates his responsibilities. When the plan is placed on his desk it is often too late for him to exert much influence on it.[7]

It is essential that the chief executive assume primary responsibility for his organization's long-range planning. When he hires an assistant to help him, or establishes a planning staff, he is merely extending his reach. These people are helping him do *his* job. This is a recognition that the world is too large for one man to grasp completely, and that to the extent he can get others to help him he will be more able to examine a wider range of threats to and opportunities for his organization.

Issues concerning the role of the chief executive in the development of plans are subtle and complex. I participated in one conference with chief executives where the major focus was on the relationship of the president with his staff in the development of corporate plans. These executives were dedicated to the idea of comprehensive planning but were uncertain about many matters relating to their participation. The range of alternatives is very wide. Effective planning, for example, requires that the top executive "buy it." He must believe in planning as being important to the success of his enterprise. He must give more than "lip service" to the effort. He must feel committed, and his support must be visible to others in the corporation. By his actions the chief executive will set the psychological climate in which planning is done.

How an executive does these things will depend upon his style of management, the way his company is organized, the personalities involved and his own sense of commitment. For example, if the chief executive devotes most of his attention to short-range problems, this emphasis will not be lost on his subordinates. Even if he is interested in long-range planning, can he find the time to do it properly? I agree partly with Senator Jackson for example, when, speaking about the federal government, he observed:

> . . . I am convinced that we never will get the kind of policy planning we need if we expect the top-level officers to participate actively in the planning process. They simply do not have the time, and in any event they rarely have the outlook or the talents of the good planner. They cannot explore issues deeply and systematically. They cannot argue the advantages and disadvantages at length in the kind of give-and-take essential if one is to reach a solid understanding with others on points of agreement and disagreement.[8]

While this observation does have an important element of truth in it for a large government department or a large multinational business, it has much less for a small enterprise where the chief executive must plan if any planning is to be done. But even in the largest companies and government agencies the chief executives must get involved in the substance of planning. If they do not they will clearly be abdicating one of their major responsibilities. At the very least they will be captives of their planning staffs and thereby lose some element of control of their enterprises.

But the question still exists: how shall the chief executive participate in the substance of planning? There is no simple answer. For the first planning effort, the chief executive of any organization—large or small, profit or non-profit—ought to be deeply involved. Once the planning program has gotten on a solid footing, with periodic cycling, general understanding and acceptance, the chief executive will know more clearly at what points and how much his participation is required. If a company, for example, has just begun the planning process and is pounding out long-

[7] *George A. Steiner, ed.,* Managerial Long-Range Planning *(New York: McGraw-Hill Book Co., Inc., 1963), p. 17.*

[8] *Henry M. Jackson, "To Forge a Strategy for Survival,"* Public Administration Review, *Vol. XIX (Summer 1959), p. 159.*

range objectives, the chief executive should be intimately involved. Once those objectives are established, he must help make and approve strategies to reach them. When this work is done, he may get involved in subsequent cycles of planning only with selected changes in specific objectives and strategies. Both he and his staff will know better with experience what these points are. There is no ready answer for any chief executive, however, to the question of when and how much he can delegate to and rely upon his staff—both line and functional—what are, in the end, his planning responsibilities.

It is not enough that the chief executive participate in the planning exercise. His relationship to it must be visible to others in the organization. By various methods open to him, the chief executive must have others know about and understand his interest in the process.

DEVELOPING THE PLAN

It is a major responsibility of the chief executive to see that the proper planning system is developed and maintained. In this effort, of course, he will have help from subordinates—both line managers and their staffs. But it is his responsibility to make sure that the system is appropriate to his enterprise, and that it is done at a cost (using this word broadly) under benefit which produces optimum values.

Many years ago I had the job of helping an organization develop its first comprehensive planning program. In preparing procedures and suggesting roles of people in the organization I ran into grave difficulties. People were not sure of their responsibilities, or did not want to assume the responsibility I suggested. Different people wanted to do different things which did not necessarily mesh. There were also other points of dispute. To solve the entire problem I prepared a letter for the signature of the chief executive which set forth the essential elements of the planning program, how it should be developed and who was responsible for what. This worked like a charm. From that day to this the top executives of that company have watched over the planning process. It is an outstanding system.

I am not saying, of course, that chief executives must get enmeshed in all the grubby details of a total planning program. What I do say is they must see that the job of planning

the plan is done, that it is appropriate and put into operation.

Clarification of roles of participants in the planning process is important and raises complex issues. For example, since corporate planning staffs are direct aids to the chief executive he must see that their roles are clear and generally understood.

A staff, for example, which fails to distinguish between strategic planning and tactical planning may lose top management if it gets too deeply involved in the details of tactical planning. Top management is interested in both strategic and tactical planning, but principally strategic planning. I once knew a staff that simply could not get itself out of the morass of details involved in short-range tactical planning. It was not long before the top management and its planning staff stopped talking to one another. There have been managers who simply could not differentiate between their responsibilities for strategic as distinguished from short-range tactical planning. Their concentration on the latter got them involved in a sort of Gresham's law of planning: short-range planning tends to drive out long-range planning.

Subtle problems of staff role arise in the development of strategic plans by central planning staffs and plans and operations of divisions. Long-range plans made in one area of a company often make sense only when considered in light of other areas and of the company as a whole. In this light, corporate planning staffs inevitably get involved in this interrelationship. Their role in modification of plans to relate better to the company as a whole may result in bitter conflict with line officers if large issues are involved. No matter how clear staff roles may be this sort of conflict will arise. It is less likely to arise and less likely to be serious if roles are clearly specified and understood.

There is no question about the fact that planning should not be separated from doing. Upon examination, however, this is not as simple as it sounds. In the strategic planning area, for example, plans may be developed for divisional execution, and the divisions may not have much if any participation in their preparation. Even with close line and staff interrelations at central office headquarters, staff inevitably will make decisions. The mere choice of alternatives to present to line managers, for example, may implicitly be decision-making by staff. Problems of drawing a line of demarcation between staff and line decision-making, and planning and operations, vary from case to case in the development of plans, and from time to time. There can be no simple formula. But efforts to clarify staff role can prevent unnecessary conflict.

Even when the staff role is clear, however, difficult problems of relationships may arise. In larger companies with comprehensive planning programs, corporate functional staffs, including long-range planning staffs, review divisional plans at the request of top management. Plans are submitted up the line, but staffs help line managers review them. In one instance a president asked his director of long-range planning to review the plans of a powerful division manager. The president insisted upon a rigorous examination of the plans because of the substantial capital outlays sought by the divisional manager. The planner did so and provided the rationale for rejecting the plans. He was not very happy about his role. He had been cultivating this divisional manager for a long time in order to develop a better planning program in his division and to arrange better communications to help them both do a better planning job. Now the divisional manager felt he had been double-crossed. The corporate planner will have problems in rebuilding his lines of communication with this division.

The planning process is complex. There must be understanding of authority, responsibility, procedures and timing. The chief executive is responsible for seeing that this need is met.

BASE DECISIONS ON PLANS

Comprehensive planning done with and on behalf of top management should result in operating decisions. Without decisions the planning process is incomplete. Failure to take action on prepared plans, or continuous vacillation, will weaken staff efforts. People simply will not be motivated to exert the energy, develop the creativity and use the imagination needed to make quality plans if top management ignores them or cannot seem to act upon them.

In one company I know, one month after a five-year long-range plan had been developed for the first time and approved by top management, the president announced a flat seven percent budget cut for all division budgets. This was his method to reduce costs. The announced reason was the need to bring costs within the year's anticipated revenues. With this announcement, the longer-range projects naturally were abandoned and the benefits of long-range planning cast in grave doubt.

The extent to which divisional line managers make decisions in light of strategic corporate plans raises a different type of problem. In some companies the connection between the corporate strategic plan and the divisional intermediate-range plans is very close. The two may, in effect, be prepared together. In one small company of about five hundred people making a variety of electronics equipment, there was a planning program where strategic plans were developed for the company as a whole and the divisions tied their sub-strategies and detailed long-range plans clearly and closely into the corporate plan. These were intermeshed because the two were done by about the same people and at about the same time. In other instances, the corporate strategic plan constitutes an umbrella under which the divisional plans are made but the interrelationship between the two is rather loose.

A somewhat different type of problem arises very subtly if divisional managers think that corporate planning staffs are making plans for them to execute. It can arise if chief executives do not get involved in the planning and accept staff recommendations without much or any reservation. In such cases divisional managers are likely to take this position to the corporate staff: "You made the plans, now execute them. Don't ask me to."

One of the major attributes of comprehensive corporate planning is that the structure, especially when written, permits managers down the organizational chain to make decisions with a reasonable degree of certainty they are in line with the objectives sought by higher level management. Naturally, if decisions made throughout an organization do not relate to the planning program, it will not be long before the planning program disappears.

This, of course, does not mean blind devotion to plan. Depending upon circumstances, it may be wise for a manager to make decisions which are very different than those planned. Flexibility must be injected into planning. There are a number of techniques to do this. One major method is for the chief executive to inject a philosophy and understanding of flexibility into the planning and operational decision-making process.

In sum, chief executives have an important role in assuring that decisions throughout the organization are made in light of plans and evolving cumstances—not blindly, not without reference to plans, but related meaningfully within a planning framework.

PLANNING TAKES TIME

While conceptually simple, a comprehensive long-range planning program for a large organization cannot be introduced overnight and expected to produce miraculous results immediately. Several years ago I calculated that about five years were required for a medium-sized or large company to develop an effective comprehensive planning system.[9] This was confirmed by another study.[10] Since there is so much more known today about how to develop effective comprehensive planning programs, it is possible to reduce this time span. Much depends upon the organization and what is going on inside it.

Among most initial efforts to develop comprehensive long-range planning programs with which I have been familiar, the first effort

[9] *Steiner, op. cit., p. 19–21.*
[10] *R. Hal Mason, "Organizing for Corporate Planning," Proceedings of the Long Range Planning Service Client Conference, February 7–9, 1962, Menlo Park, Calif., Stanford Research Institute.*

did not produce much of immediate substantive value. Yet, all those involved felt the effort worthwhile. This was so, I found, because the effort introduced a new point of view into the company which appeared to have important possibilities in future planning. It also was seen as a focal point for communicating in a common language about major problems. There are many other reasons why managements have been pleased with the first attempt at long-range planning even though it did not provide immediate substantive values. But first efforts do not always provide important bases for immediate decision.

An effective planning program of one company cannot be lifted intact and applied to another. While the fundamental process and structure may be removed from one company to another, the details of operation will vary. Furthermore, since an organization is a living, dynamic institution in a rapidly changing environment, the procedures for planning change.

RESUME

Two major underlying considerations in the development of effective long-range planning are, first, understanding of an operational conceptual model of plans, and second, understanding and acceptance by the chief executive of his role in creating and maintaining quality planning.

George Humphrey used to say that the best fertilizer ever invented was the footsteps of the farmer. Similarly, the best assurance of effective planning in an organization is the active participation of the chief executive in doing it.

READING 16

THE INFLUENCE OF DEPARTMENT OF DEFENSE PRACTICES ON CORPORATE PLANNING*

Donald J. Smalter

Over the past several years I've conducted a personal study of Department of Defense practices and activities.

My company has no business whatsoever with the Department of Defense, so my interest related strictly to the observation of D-O-D methodologies, their analytical techniques and the usefulness of these to the management of large corporations. In particular, this question puzzled me: Why were many observers labeling Robert McNamara a "great" manager?

I found this: There are *many* significant "values" in observing the D-O-D, as their managerial problems are bigger and more complex. They must, of necessity, formalize and systematize many more of their practices and procedures than managers in smaller organizations.

Some of the concepts and techniques that are useful to industrial corporate planners and managers are:

* *Reprinted with permission from* Management Technology, *vol. 4, no. 2, December 1964.*

1 Strategic planning by missions with special attention to resource allocation, using an annual scheduled planning cycle, linked to the budgeting process.
2 The use of systems analysis and planning, embodying quantitative techniques, incorporating the application of game theory and subjectively judged probabilities.
3 NEEDS research, i.e., formalized study to perceive needs.
4 An approach which might be termed "Management by Priority-of-Challenge."
5 The unique planning/analysis organizational alignment, and its potential applications.
6 The use of logic-sequence network diagrams for project planning and implementation; and finally
7 The utilization of a strategic planning "decision center" in the Pentagon.

Table 16-1 lists inadequacies reportedly found by McNamara and his Assistant Secretary, Charles Hitch, when they assumed their D-O-D responsibilities in January 1961. I compiled this list after reading numerous articles in the public literature. Further, I corresponded briefly with several people in the D-O-D, received literature on their planning process and procedures. Charles Hitch, incidentally, is the Assistant Secretary for Budgeting and Control.

First, McNamara and Hitch claim to have found poor coordination with State Department policies. The D-O-D people apparently had limited liaison with the State Department staff concerning military responses that might be anticipated to be necessary in the various segments of the world—if some specific enemy action occurred. For instance, one of the first things that happened unexpectedly in the Kennedy administration was the Russian erection of the Berlin wall. The late President was reportedly disturbed to find that the military had drawn inadequate contingency plans for the Berlin Wall Crisis.

Next, they concluded that the Pentagon allotted inadequate time for strategy studies of what they should be striving to accomplish. Come budget time each year, there was a tendency for the service heads to allot a billion here, a billion there for continuation of present commitments, without proper analysis of their changing needs. Strategic plans then were assembled in a relatively short period of time, in order to meet budget deadlines.

There was rather poor coordination between strategic planning and functional budgeting, or, in other words, between the long-term mission requirements and the annual budgeting by service branch. The fifth point: There were unilateral service plans and not unified DOD plans, with imbalances in the allocated resources for a given mission. To illustrate: While the Army had a number of divisions on standby at airfields for emergency airlift, the Air Force leadership was dubious about spending their limited funds for airlift capability. They much preferred to use most of their appropriations for nuclear retaliation bombers. Thus, the Air Force possessed far too few planes to airlift these divisions overseas. Another example: The number of bombers, Polaris missiles, and ICBM missiles, all strategic nuclear retaliation devices, were not determined through detailed study, but rather tended to be determined subjectively by the service leadership.

Sixth, the total financial implications of program decisions were poorly determined. For instance: The chiefs-of-staff authorized development of numerous major weapons systems and yet hadn't projected the total cost of *developing* each beyond a year. Further, they had not pre-determined how much it would cost to *operate* these weapons over an extended period of time. Too frequently a poorly conceived project consumed gigantic expenditures. DYNASOAR and SKYBOLT, as examples, are now cancelled.

Seventh, strategic alternatives were selected intuitively, not through dispassionate analysis. The best example to illustrate perhaps would be the B-70 supersonic bomber, a project which made numerous headlines. General Curtis LeMay insisted on vast future reliance on the B-70. But, the chiefs-of-staff had *not* conducted strategy research of the B-70 versus the Polaris missile versus land-based intercontinental missiles. When McNamara assumed responsibility, he initiated the "dispassionate" studies which resulted in a sharply accelerated Polaris program, an expedited, enlarged Minute-Man program, with a drastic cut-back on the B-70 program. This was accomplished through a detailed analysis of alternatives by a section called the Systems Analysis group, primarily an Operations Research type staff.

The eighth point logically follows the previous comment: There was inadequate use of cost/effectiveness as a basis for measurement of weapon system alternatives. Service leadership did *not* possess a sound grasp of the *total* cost for supporting a B-70. The Polaris submarine proved far cheaper to maintain for the same unit of retaliation effectiveness. Prior to this, the Pentagon conducted few, if any studies for cost comparisons of strategic alternatives.

Ninth, there was inadequate DOD analysis on weapon *NEEDS*. Note the emphasis on the word "needs." McNamara found that the initiative for weapons systems ideas was coming mainly from the outside and that the military inside the DOD were not systematically studying their needs to identify new weapon system concepts.

Finally, the span of time to precipitate major program decisions was far too long to satisfy the new Secretary of Defense. In the huge DOD organizational pyramid, specific responsibility tended to be elusive. The Secretary wanted to see decisions faced with much less delay. I'll speak later about this in relation to the Pentagon's decision room, or "BIG BOARD."

Many of these points in Table 16-1 are

TABLE 16-1   DOD SHORTCOMINGS PER McNAMARA & HITCH. . . .

1. Poor coordination with State Department policies.
2. Poor contingency planning for political "upheavals."
3. Inadequate time allotted for strategy studies.
4. Poor coordination between strategic planning & functional budgeting.
5. Unilateral service plans, NOT unified DOD plans.
   —Imbalance in resources for missions
   —Poorly defined missions
6. Financial implications of program decisions poorly determined
   —Poor regard for resource constraints
   —Frequent cancellations of poorly conceived projects
7. Strategic alternatives selected intuitively, NOT thru dispassionate analysis
8. Inadequate cost/effective measurement of weapon system alternatives.
9. Negligible DOD analysis of weapon NEEDS.
10. Long span-of-time to precipitate major program decisions.

criticisms that in an analogous way apply to industrial corporations.

Due to numerous complaints from the military, Secretary McNamara was called before a Congressional Committee to explain his reforms. This is how he stated his philosophy: "We must first determine what our foreign policy is to be, formulate a military strategy to carry out that policy, then build the military forces to successfully conduct this strategy."

He initiated several key organization changes. He enlisted the aid of a scholarly thinker named Charles J. Hitch from Rand Corporation who had studied the Defense Department problems for many years and published several perceptive articles analyzing managerial needs. That move was probably among the more significant he made, for Hitch is Operations Research oriented. Hitch assumed responsibility for the budgeting and operations research functions.

McNamara also created or strengthened several key jobs related to planning. First, the position of Assistant Secretary for Policy Planning and International Security Affairs was provided to better coordinate strategy with State Department policies, to formulate the strategic planning and to determine the broad requirements for conflict contingencies.

Next, he created the high level office of Deputy Assistant Secretary for Systems Analysis. This office and supporting staff were created to make cost-effectiveness studies of major strategic and weapons systems alternatives, using quantitative techniques. Naturally, these mathematical experts, trained in the operations research approach, were sympathetic to the use of computers for solving complex problems.

Further, McNamara and Hitch created the position of Deputy Assistant Secretary for Programming, whose task required maintenance of a "running" five-year program-budget, which would completely reflect all the strategic decisions and all the projected expenditures. This program-budget is updated monthly, based on a managerial system that Hitch created (Reference 1) in which the military may propose "program-changes." These are processed for approval to be inserted into the "running" 5-year plan. This system is a tremendous managerial asset. It did not exist three years ago.

LESSON 1 FOR THE CORPORATE PLANNER

Prior to the McNamara regime, the Army, Navy, Air Force budgeted rather independently and almost ignored coordination of each other's programs. What McNamara instituted was planning by missions, illustrated in Figure 16-1. Key missions were identified, e.g., a nuclear retaliation mission, a "hot-spot response" mission requiring high-capacity airlift of police type forces, etc. In a complete 5-year plan, strategic elements and their supporting expenditures were assembled in what has been popularly termed "mission program-packages." Any mission package-plan then often had elements from the Army, the Navy, and the Air Force. Nuclear retaliation capability serves as a prime example: The Navy possessed the Polaris; the Air Force had the B-70 or other long-range planes, plus Minute-Man and Atlas ICBM's; the Army possessed Pershing missiles with a 400 mile range. The quantity and use of these was planned rather disjointedly. McNamara's staff then determined the *needs* for

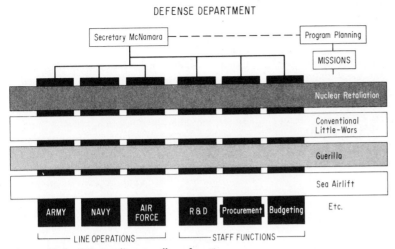

DEFENSE DEPARTMENT

Figure 16-1 Mission "crosscut" on functions.

TABLE 16-2   DEPT. OF DEFENSE FINANCIAL SUMMARY (IN BILLIONS OF DOLLARS)

	FY 1961 Actual	FY 1962 Original	FY 1962 Final	FY 1963 Current Estimates	FY 1964 Budget Estimates
1. Strategic Retaliatory Forces		$7.6	$9.1	$8.5	$7.3
2. Continental Air & Missile Defense Forces		2.2	2.1	1.9	2.0
3. General Purpose Forces		14.5	17.5	18.1	19.1
4. Airlift/Sealift Forces		.9	1.2	1.4	1.4
5. Reserve & Guard Forces		1.7	1.8	2.0	2.0
6. Research & Development		3.9	4.3	5.5	5.9
7. General Support		12.3	12.7	13.7	14.6
8. Civil Defense			.3	.2	.3
9. Military Assistance		1.8	1.8	1.6	1.6
Proposed Legislation for Military Compensation, etc.					.9
Total Obligational Authority	$46.1	$44.9	$51.0	$52.8	$55.2
Less Financing Adj.	−3.0	−1.2	−1.6	−1.5	−1.5
New Obligational Authority	$43.1	$43.7	$49.4	$51.3	$53.7
Adj. to Expenditures	+1.6	+1.0	−1.2	−1.3	−1.3
Total Expenditures	$44.7	$44.7	$48.2	$50.0	$52.4
TOA by Dept. & Agency					
Army	$10.5	$10.6	$12.8	$12.2	$13.1
Navy	12.8	12.5	14.9	15.2	15.5
Air Force	20.1	18.7	20.0	20.9	20.7
Civil Defense			.3	.2	.3
Defense Agencies	.3	.4	.3	1.8	1.9
Retired Pay	.8	.9	.9	1.0	1.2
Military Assistance	1.5	1.8	1.8	1.6	1.6
Proposed Legislation					.9
Total°	$46.1	$44.9	$51.0	$52.8	$55.2

° Excludes cost of nuclear warheads.

any one mission. Such study resulted in significant moves, e.g., a drastic cut-back in B-70 planned expenditures. Table 16-2 illustrates the plan by mission for 1962 as originally budgeted, (Reference 2) and then after hurried study, the whole requirement as rebudgeted. Studies revealed inadequate air and sea-lift forces which needed to be supplemented as well as a certain number of other requirements. Nuclear retaliation capabilities were modified with greater dependence on stationary missiles, cutting out B-70's and Minute-men on railroad cars.

In the middle of Table 16-2 is a comparison of the original budget versus the revised budget. Observe that the Army received more money for limited warfare, and the Air Force was appropriated additional funds for airlift capacity. There were the short-term 1st year changes, and these McNamara initiated promptly after assumption of responsibility. Note that these expenditures are expressed in *billions* of dollars.

What lessons can be gained from this? Permit me to try to clarify the fundamental concept of mission planning. The top management job might best be described as allocating

limited resources, for selected mission purposes in the dimension of *time*. This task may be visualized as a 3-dimensional cube shown in Figure 16-2. (Note my extensive use of colorful visuals. One of the major problems corporate planners must recognize is the necessity to better communicate *concepts* to other executives. We in IMC have used diagrams and charts liberally, as such visuals tend to concisely clarify concepts. Consequently, I highly recommend their use to you. Planners must better communicate the concepts of formal planning and what it can accomplish.) The first time "slice" (vertical) is the annual profit-plan or budget, and the next 5 "slices" are the 5-year corporate program plan.

This conceptualization is useful in clarifying responsibilities to various high-level managers. As illustrated in Figure 16-3, complete program balance is difficult to attain! (This is not meant to be indicative of IMC's true position, but merely serves to illustrate the point).

In examining product-lines or missions, it is often readily apparent that a more adequate job might be done in planning goals and programming expenditures for each different mission.

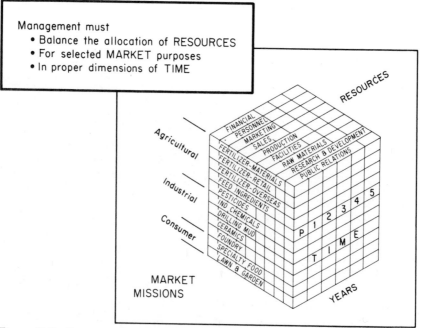

Figure 16-2 Program cube concept with mission, resource, *and* time *dimensions.*

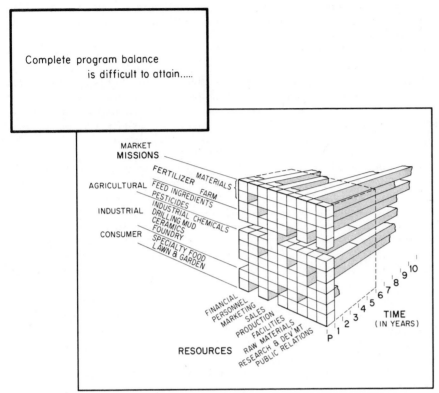

Figure 16-3   An illustration of inadequate program planning.

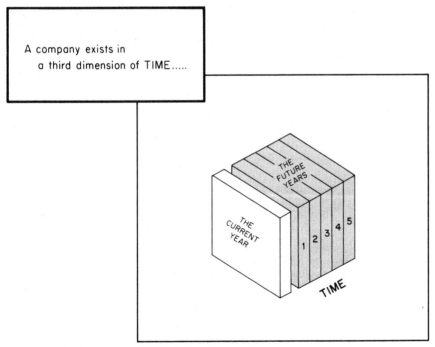

Figure 16-4   Annual time "slices."

Let's segregate the time factor as shown in Figure 16-4, isolating the current year's "slice." How can the annual profit-plan which tends to be a functional budget, be integrated with strategic plans for the 5 years? McNamara organized DOD planning in an annual sequenced relationship, leading up to the deadline date when he had to submit an annual budget to Congress.

In strategic planning then, it is essential to conduct studies on key issues, and this should continue preferably on a year round basis. In the case of the DOD, the program change concept permits monthly changes. As illustrated in Figure 16-5—Annual Planning Calendar, the first phase covers study of the problems, needs, and opportunities as researched and identified. Next, the organization should investigate these issues in detail, and attempt to resolve their strategy, i.e., what they are striving to do. Next, specific targets or goals should be set for a five year plan, followed by preparation of a one year budget. The Defense Department calls this their *planning, programming, budgeting* sequence.

We at IMC essentially adopted the same process: Strategic planning, Step 1; Programming, Step 2; and Budgeting, Step 3. This process has been very useful! As our fiscal year runs from July through June, we present our 5-year plan to the Board of Directors every March. As a result, sales and profit projections in a skeletal plan are already prepared for a detailed 1-year budget. This facilitates the preparation of the 1-year budget or profit-plan on a soundly conceived basis. All the strategic aspects are essentially resolved as ample time has been allotted to the strategic thinking.

With minor imperfections, IMC has operated on this basis for two consecutive years. We pioneered this approach without the benefit of observing the DOD. After studying DOD practice, it sharpened our comprehension, enabling us to do a better job.

Our company identified 9 missions of interest (as shown in Figure 16-6), several where our present involvement was relatively minimal, but our goals ambitious. The DOD coincidentally also has 9. Although IMC has been essentially a mining company, even before we instituted market-mission planning we had significantly progressed toward a greater em-

phasis on market orientation. Examination of our motives and purpose from a mission viewpoint leads to the obvious conclusion that we're in business to serve customers. Consequently, our thinking must be oriented to the market environment, rather than an emphasis on our internal structure and skills. Our thoughts must give dominant attention to the *market* challenges. Corporations possess certain "internal" opportunities (e.g., process cost reduction), but the majority of our opportunities will exist "externally."

With improved insight, we realized our product-markets fell into three distinct market groupings: agricultural, industrial, and consumer. Segmenting this further, we easily identified a prime mission for plant nutrition —or fertilizer, the latter being our largest business, and one with a tremendous demand growth rate. Other missions were also identified, e.g., animal health and nutrition, and foundry supply (as shown in Figure 16-7). Additionally, we were involved in specialty foods and flavors. Ac'cent, a flavor enhancer, is one of our products. This change in perspective influenced our thinking. We found ourselves analyzing possibilities for future growth with a new discernment.

Secretary McNamara initiated planning in "program-packages" around his DOD missions. His method is to maintain a book in which all pertinent master plans are contained. Plans for any given mission are in this book on his desk. Though it is under security restrictions, we can speculate on its contents. What might be in such a book and what should an analogous industrial program-package contain? First, a program-package ought to possess a *charter* which states the scope of the mission as well as the objectives to be fulfilled. What is the vital difference between objectives and goals? Objectives are timeless, immeasurable, without quantification. Goals are measurable and possess a time parameter as well. In addition, the charter should contain a "product-line concept" as cited in Table 16-3. Many commercial development authors profess that a product-line should establish its own "ecological niche" in the market place, i.e., that management should strive to offer unique customer values. What proprietary directions for growth are desirable? What pioneering aims are sought?

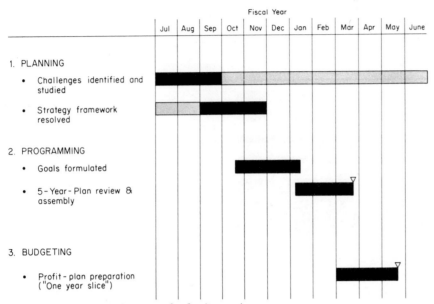

Figure 16-5 Annual planning calendar (3 steps).

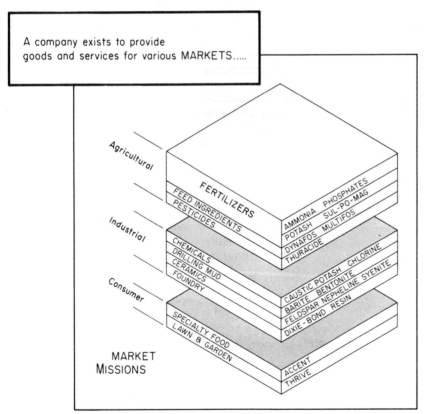

Figure 16-6 Horizontal mission "slices."

INTERNATIONAL MINERALS & CHEMICAL CORPORATION

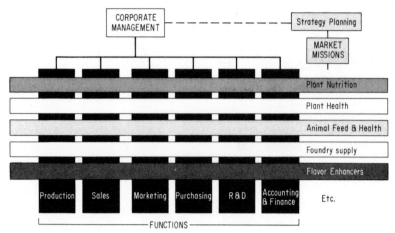

Figure 16-7   IMC mission "crosscut" on functions.

TABLE 16-3   MISSION ''PROGRAM-PACKAGE'' PLANNING CHECKLIST

CHARTER
Scope/Purpose/Objectives
Product-Line Concept
    Unique "values" offered
    Proprietary Directions
    New-Frontier Aims

POSITION (Present & Future)
Industry Structure & Character
Profit Sources
Product Life-Cycle Status
Market Share & Area
Capacity Utilization etc.

ATTRIBUTES (or Capabilities)
Strengths
Weaknesses

ENVIRONMENT (Present & Future)
Market Demand Outlook
Competition and Price
Distribution Channels
Changing Technology
Economy Trends
Regulatory Constraints
Community Constraints

IMPACT ON IMC
Problems & Needs ⎫
Threats   ⎬ Priorities in Response?
Opportunities ⎭

MOMENTUM—PRESENT OPERATIONS
Prospects/Goals
Premises
P&L Summary

**BUSINESS DEVELOPMENT ACTION—
PROGRAMS**
Response to Attributes ⎫
                    ⎬ How?
Response to Challenges ⎭
Alternatives Considered/Selected
Resource "Handling"
    Capital Projects
    Geographical Expansion
    Raw Material Needs
    Services & Merchandising
    Acquisition Goals
    Financial Demands

TECHNICAL PROGRAM
Support
    Cost reduction
    Product improvement
    Sales service
    Market application development
Innovative

ORGANIZATION—NEEDS & PLANS

GOALS
Sales   ⎫
       ⎬ Performance (& Comparison w/others)
Profits ⎭

QUESTIONS: Completeness? Soundness? How
    Execute?

Next, it's desirable to understand your basic *position* through conduct of an audit. What's your participation in the industry structure? Where are the greatest profit margins? What's the product life-cycle status of each product? What market share do the products possess? How well are existing capacities being utilized? Next, the relevant *environment* must be examined. It's vital that management look outward to be aware of the rapidly changing environment in which the company exists. What is the market demand outlook for the product-line?

What are the present distribution channels, and the possibilities of advantageously altering those channels? What impact is changing technology going to have? In the Annual Planning Calendar, the first step involves the creation of a technological forecast as well as a market audit/forecast. These analyses lead to the identification of corporate *attributes,* i.e., strengths and weaknesses in resources and capabilities.

We must then ascertain our relative position in this ever-changing environment. What are the problems, needs, threats, and opportunities? What are the most important challenges?

Next, we must establish what our *momentum* is going to achieve. What are the prospects anticipated? Are we going to have continued growth? Or do we have some major product that will become obsolete? What are the premises or assumptions behind this projection? A profit and loss summary based on our momentum must then be assembled on a year-by-year basis. In business and sales development, what will we be striving to accomplish above and beyond our momentum? How will we respond to our attributes? How will we respond to the challenges that we have identified? But, most importantly, how will we manipulate our limited resources for maximum profit? What capital investments should we make and where? Which should have priority? What degree of raw material insurance is desirable? This question is particularly vital to a mining company because of limited mineral reserves. What are the financing demands from this total program?

What level of technical expenditures is justified, both for product-line support, and for innovative possibilities? What program balance is desirable? Are there any "gaps" in the total program? Next, what are the organizational needs, training plans, and recruiting requirements? And finally, what are the goals for sales and profits? Most important, what's the performance level of return on investment, return on sales, so that we may compare one mission versus the other? What's the return on the incremental investments that we're planning to install, so that we can determine in which mission our capital will be most productive? In review, the manager should ask himself: Is it complete? Is it soundly conceived? How satisfactorily is the organization prepared to execute the plans?

Our planning organization at the corporate-level issues to the various divisions a "call" for plans and goals with guideline formats. It is preferable *not* to *do* the planning, but to assist, guide, and stimulate those who must execute mission strategy. Our staff does work closely with division planners in attempting to resolve appropriate courses of action. An indispensable component of our corporate planning and development division is a sizeable operations research department. In particular, the use of operations research tools and techniques must be initiated at the corporate level first in order to demonstrate to others their usefulness.

The "program-package" contents then as finally condensed and assembled contains about 9–10 pages for each mission:

1 The charter and mission attributes.
2 The company's relative position summarized.
3 The future environment described.
4 A summary of strategy statements, i.e., what we're striving to accomplish.
5 Specific sales goals, the capital allocations, and the anticipated performance.
6 Acquisition criteria, and prospects ranked in order of priority.
7 A sequenced action-plan; and finally,
8 What we term our "green-arrow" diagram.

(It is simply a means to illustrate the items this program supports plus an identification of other corporate activities which are synergistically linked, e.g., logistical investment opportunities.)

Studies of the *process* of planning in the DOD also have been of great assistance. Two professors from Cornell, F. E. Gilmore and R. G. Brandenberg analyzed the thought process used by the Army War College, (Reference 3), and constructed a network diagram for analogous corporate mission planning.

Though not utilized precisely as designed, it has been of significant help in understanding the total corporate planning process. The fundamental step-by-step procedure is as follows: First, what are the challenges facing the corporation? Next, how do these affect our missions, e.g., what justification is there to add new missions? What are the desired missions? What are the attainable goals to be sought? What are the competitive strategies to follow? And finally, what action-plans are necessary to implement these strategies?

The term strategy has been used repeatedly here. What do we mean? It may be defined simply as: "How best to deploy limited resources in order to maximize profits in the changing environment, against competition, in pursuit of goals." Note the resemblance to the military definition of strategy.

This definition is useful to our understanding of the planning task in a number of ways. The planner must determine how to allocate (and even control) the way resources are used. Figure 16-8 illustrates resources as the vertical slices of the cube.

Management has these four fundamental strategies at its fingertips: diversification; product development; market development; market penetration, per Figure 16-9. Around these fundamentals, we at IMC have created a system of plans, which illustrates the interrelationships and hierarchy of these plans. This system helps to clarify the jurisdictional authority and responsibility within the total plan. Fundamental function however, of the corporate planning organization is a "call" for sales and profit goals to be sought by the divisions for present products. This is accomplished in the programming (2nd) phase of the annual corporate planning calendar.

In the task of resource allocation, we, as managers, must maneuver these resources, allocating them rationally to the different market or product missions. With which ones must the corporate planner be most concerned? The

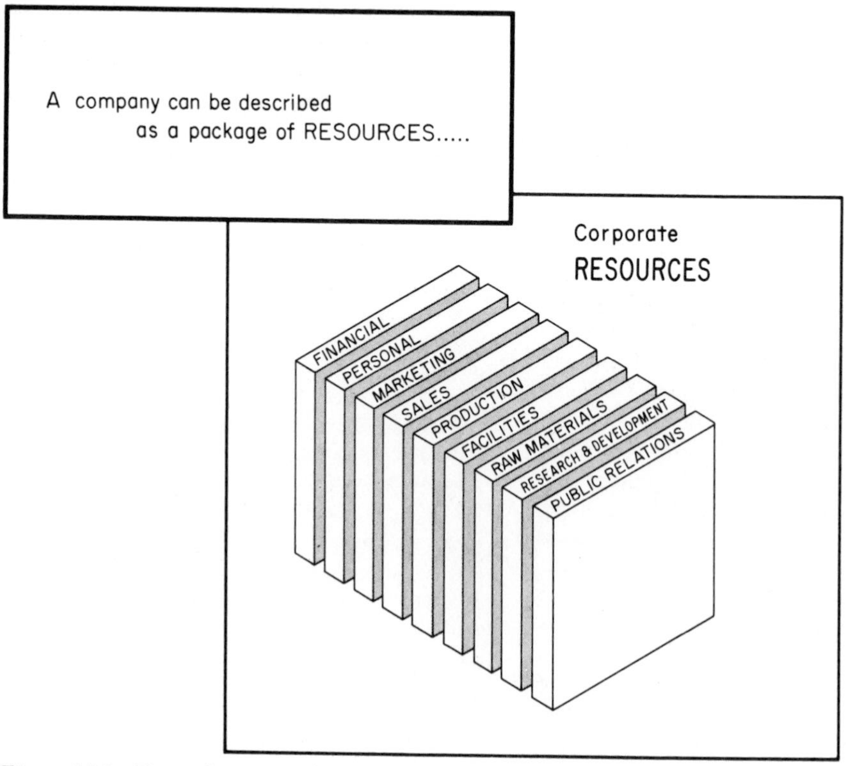

Figure 16-8   Vertical resource slices.

TABLE 16-4 RESOURCE ALLOCATIONS

MUST BE ESTABLISHED FOR—

ACQUISITION CAPABILITIES

NEW CAPITAL INVESTMENTS AND
JOINT VENTURES

R&D PROGRAM EMPHASIS
  POSTURE   OFFENSIVE
             DEFENSIVE

MARKETING EMPHASIS
  MOST PROFITABLE PRODUCTS
  UTILIZE INCREMENTAL CAPACITY

MANPOWER FOR NEW BUSINESS
DEVELOPMENT

most critical are listed in Table 16-4. First, where will we strive to make acquisitions? (Obviously, we can't consummate acquisitions in *all* fields.) Second, which missions deserve the lion's share of our capital investment monies? Next, where are we going to place our emphasis in R&D, and in marketing? Where will we allocate expensive business development people with their creative, entrepreneurial talent?

Certainly, one of the more important allocation tasks is capital budgeting. All capital plans are processed through our department before they're scheduled for review and final approval by executive management. Our budgeter-planner reviews all major proposals with appropriate experts. If necessary, projects are postponed, revised or perhaps cancelled.

The Capital budgeting problem may be best illustrated per Figure 16-10. A corporation has a limited source of funds and MUST try to obtain the best possible rate-of-return. The corporate planner must determine where the funds cut-off line should fall. He must pose this question: Does the corporation possess ample opportunities to warrant moving this cut-off out to the right. If not, why not?

IMC then has been utilizing the mission concept, finding it quite useful in turning our thinking "outward" to the ever-changing environment.

LESSON 2 FOR THE CORPORATE PLANNER

Another of the DOD approaches useful to industry planners is their application of operations research principles to complex strategy research questions. Within 3 weeks after Robert McNamara assumed his Secretary of Defense duties, he produced what are popularly called his "76 trombones." These were seventy-odd questions, each beginning with "why." Why are you doing this? Why couldn't it be done in a cheaper, more effective way? He assigned responsibility for each question, asked for the answers within 3 weeks. These were important fundamental questions. From these answers he concluded that changes were urgently needed.

Much publicity was produced recently when McNamara questioned the need for air-

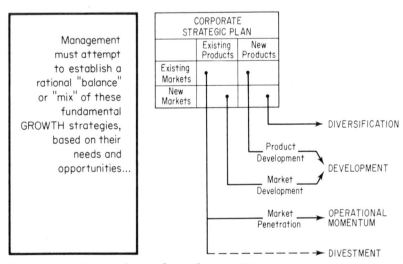

Figure 16-9 Four fundamental growth strategies.

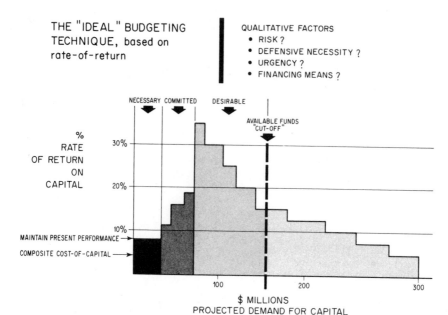

THE "IDEAL" BUDGETING
TECHNIQUE, based on
rate-of-return

QUALITATIVE FACTORS
• RISK ?
• DEFENSIVE NECESSITY ?
• URGENCY ?
• FINANCING MEANS ?

NECESSARY COMMITTED   DESIRABLE

AVAILABLE FUNDS
"CUT-OFF"

%
RATE
OF RETURN
ON
CAPITAL

30%

20%

10%

MAINTAIN PRESENT PERFORMANCE →
COMPOSITE COST-OF-CAPITAL →

100   200   300

$ MILLIONS
PROJECTED DEMAND FOR CAPITAL

Figure 16-10

craft carriers suggesting their vulnerability perhaps outdated their usefulness. He turned the operations research group to studying this query. Naturally, Navy top leaders were terribly upset. I do not know what the answer proposed or concluded. Obviously, the Defense establishment is not going to abandon aircraft carriers tomorrow, although, they may have some longer-term plans. But, McNamara did ask that and similar questions on military strategy, weapons systems cost/effectiveness, and administrative cost reduction.

The following quotation is taken from one of the research articles (Reference 4) on Mc-Namara:

> McNamara is called the virtual master of the Defense Department, the greatest managerial genius of our times.

What is his secret? Answer: The question *Why*, sent to his staff and the military with a deadline for the answers. The study of these questions, mainly strategic in nature, and the asking of more questions, keeps these people thinking and responding with adequate programs. Part of the McNamara technique is to write his questions and insist on written answers. The Secretary maintains on his desk a black, looseleafed notebook containing his annual list of 120 of the most basic questions.

Each February they go out to his advisers. The answers are due the end of the summer, when they will be the basis of his changes in the five year program-budget.

This question posing is a very useful managerial tool. Some of the problems are so complex that McNamara assigns them to a study group, the operations research group. This small group is headed by Dr. Alain Enthoven, who recently has attained much prominence. His title is Deputy Assistant Secretary of Defense for Systems Analysis.

Recently, Dr. Enthoven (Reference 5) cited his fundamental task as:

> Systems Analysis can best be described as a continuing dialogue between the policy maker and the systems analyst, in which the policy-maker (Mc-Namara), asks for alternative solutions to his problems; while the analyst attempts to clarify the conceptual framework in which the decisions must be made, to define alternative possible objectives and criteria, and to explore in as clear terms as possible (and quantitatively), the cost and effectiveness of these courses of action.

That quotation seems particularly descriptive and clear. Fortunately, IMC's chairman and chief executive officer, a graduate Industrial Engineer, sympathizes and understands the values of applying mathematics to complex business problems. IMC has used these techniques in mine planning for more than a decade. We next turned the application of quantitative analysis to marketing strategy questions. As shown in Figure 16-11, an econometric model was created for world phosphate rock supply-demand about three years ago. To gather the required inputs, skilled people were actually sent over to North Africa, to Jordan, to Morocco and other sources where phosphate is mined. A geologist was even assigned to view operations in the South Sea Islands of the Pacific. With input facts gathered from many sources, we estimated our competitors' costs and volumes from numerous mining sources distributed to markets in 45 countries. From this analysis, we ascertained our delivered cost advantages in certain markets. It would have been nearly impossible to have assimilated or manipulated this information without our computer.

The Defense Department civilian staff has been severely criticized on their extensive use of computers for problem solving. To place the use of computers in proper perspective, this quotation by Assistant Secretary of Defense Charles Hitch (Reference 6) in response to that criticism seems particularly apropos:

It cannot be stated too frequently or emphasized enough that economic choice is a way of looking at problems and does not necessarily depend on the use of any analytical aids. Computational devices are quite likely to be useful in analysis of complex problems, but there are many problems in which they have not proved particularly useful, where, nevertheless, it is rewarding to array alternatives and think through their implications in terms of objectives and cost. Where mathematical models and computations are useful, they are in no sense alternatives to, or rivals of good intuitive judgment. They supplement and complement it. Judgment is always of critical importance in designing the analysis, choosing the alternatives to be compared, and selecting the criterion.

LESSON 3 FOR THE CORPORATE PLANNER

Fundamental to the planning task is an understanding of the stepwise thought process to be applied in problem solving. Table 16-5 "Commander's Estimate of Situation" (Reference 7) stems from an Army field manual. It addresses itself to mission planning as a commander analyzes a given situation; identifies

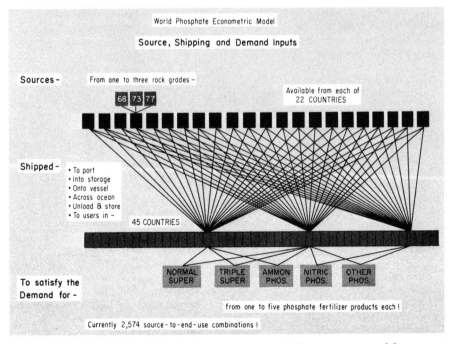

Figure 16-11 Illustration of inputs and parameters for world econometric model.

the possible alternatives; compares these courses-of-action; determines the best, and translates this into an action-plan. An unqualified comprehension of these steps is quite essential.

Table 16-6 illustrates the "attack" procedure of operations researchers in solving a problem.

There are other analogous problem solving techniques: as shown in Table 16-7, the weapons systems analyst solves his problems by starting with an identification of military needs.

Systems engineers have developed the most sophisticated methodology. After looking at all the thought processes that various disci-

TABLE 16-5   COMMANDER'S ESTIMATE OF SITUATION

1. MISSION
   task statement & purpose

2. THE SITUATION & COURSES-OF-ACTION
   gather relevant facts
   list difficulties
   list feasible courses-of-action

3. ANALYSIS OF OPPOSING COURSES-OF-ACTION
   deduce consequences
   determine strengths & weaknesses inherent in each course-of-action

4. COMPARISON OF COURSES-OF-ACTION
   deduce relative merits

5. DECISION
   select best alternative
   translate into complete statement
     who
     what
     when
     where
     how
     why

TABLE 16-6   EXAMPLES OF STEPS IN PROBLEM SOLVING BY VARIOUS DISCIPLINES

Major Steps	Military Strategy	Operations Research
1	—	—
2	Situation observed	—
3	—	Problem identification
4	Mission description	Problem formulation
5	Situation objectives	Construct model
6	Identify all feasible courses of action	Derive model solution
7	Analysis of each course	Test model & solution
8	Compare	—
9	Decision on best	Establish controls
10	—	Report results
11	—	—
12	Action-plan assembled	—

TABLE 16-7   ADDED EXAMPLES OF STEPS IN PROBLEM-SOLVING

Major Steps	DOD Weapons Systems	Systems Engineering
1	(Strategy & Tactics Analysis)	—
2	—	Environmental/Needs Research
3	Military need identified	Unsatisfied need identified
4	Need specified	Problem definition
5	Objectives defined	Select objective criteria
6	Concept proposals solicited	System synthesis alternatives
7	Conceptual & feasibility studies	Systems analysis
8	Cost/effectiveness comparison	Comparison
9	Selection of best	Selection
10	System Package-Plan defined	Communicating results in prospectus
11	—	—
12	Action-Planning	Action-Planning

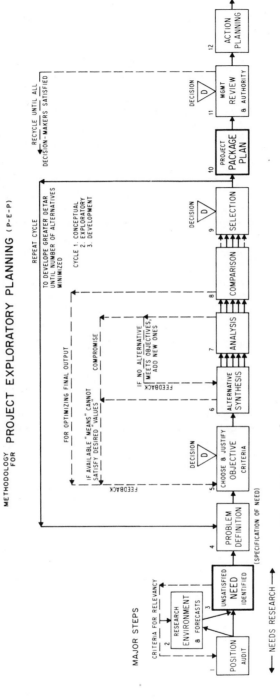

Figure 16-12   A derived problem-solving procedure.

plines apply to the solution of problems, the systems engineering technique was most valuable, as was the military strategy approach. But, the facet with particular merit is comprehension of the "needs research" concept (Reference 8).

Where does the definition of a problem, need, or opportunity begin? At what starting point? Usually it begins by perceptual awareness of the company's position or capability; this awareness plus an imperfect knowledge of the environment precipitates the identification of a problem or opportunity as illustrated in Figure 16-12, "Methodology for Project Exploratory Planning (P-E-P)."

Preferably, relevant facts pertaining to the company's position in the forecasted environment must be examined to identify a problem, need, or opportunity. This might be termed *needs* research. The word "challenge" is more suitable as it covers all the terms: problems, needs, threats, and opportunities.

In Step 5, objectives must be precisely chosen and justified. Step 6 is the process of creating and/or inventing alternatives; Step 7 and 8, their analysis and comparison; Step 9, the selection of the best course-of-action; Step 10 requires the assembly into a "package-plan;" Step 11 is the final decision point before proceeding. The final step is action-planning/scheduling, a useful point to apply network planning techniques.

IMC's Corporate Planning & Development Division organization was designed on the basis of a sound understanding of this process. Emphasis should be on the establishment

of priorities, more clearly demonstrated in Figure 16-13, "Management by Priority-of-Challenge" where the managerial problem is linked with the determination of budget levels. Figure 16-14 shows the organization and broad responsibilities of our planning and development division, a sizeable corporate-level staff division, employing 25 professionals. Notice that the first department consists of an environment analysis group, with primarily market-research type skills.

The second department, strategic planning primarily provides leadership to the assembly of IMC's 5-year plan. Next, a venture development group which endeavors to precipitate appropriate projects, particularly those that the operating divisions are not organized to execute. Finally, a management planning department, which predominantly performs operations research type studies. This division, with its complement of high caliber people is having a sizeable impact on the corporation's activity. Note the striking similarities between this organization and those in Mc-Namara's DOD.

LESSON 4 FOR THE CORPORATE PLANNER

The use of logic sequence network diagrams provides yet an additional lesson from the study of DOD planning techniques. We are in the midst of building a $58 million plant, as a joint venture with Standard Oil of California and E. I. D. Parry of India on the east coast of India. In order to more efficiently execute

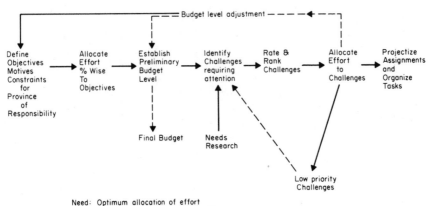

Figure 16-13   Management by "priority-of-challenge."

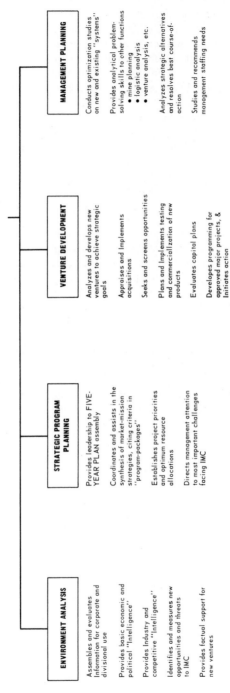

CORPORATE PLANNING & DEVELOPMENT DIVISION

Provides environment "Intelligence" and measures Impact on IMC

Develops strategic plans responsive to challenges

Determines optimum resource allocations

Seeks and develops new venture opportunities

Monitors performance, precipitating responsive decision-making

ENVIRONMENT ANALYSIS

Assembles and evaluates Information for corporate and divisional use

Provides basic economic and political "Intelligence"

Provides Industry and competitive "Intelligence"

Identifies and measures new opportunities and threats to IMC

Provides factual support for new ventures

STRATEGIC PROGRAM PLANNING

Provides leadership to FIVE-YEAR PLAN assembly

Coordinates and assists in the synthesis of market-mission strategies, citing criteria in "program-packages"

Establishes project priorities and optimum resource allocations

Directs management attention to most important challenges facing IMC

VENTURE DEVELOPMENT

Analyzes and develops new ventures to achieve strategic goals

Appraises and Implements acquisitions

Seeks and screens opportunities

Plans and Implements testing and commercialization of new products

Evaluates capital plans

Develops programming for approved major projects, & Initiates action

MANAGEMENT PLANNING

Conducts optimization studies on new and existing "systems"

Provides analytical problem-solving skills to other functions
• mine planning
• logistic analysis
• venture analysis, etc.

Analyzes strategic alternatives and resolves best course-of-action

Studies and recommends management staffing needs

Figure 16-14 Functions and responsibilities—corporate planning and development.

this project in its early phases, we created a network task sequence for the general manager. Say for example, the first task is approval by the Indian government for a license; the next task may be hiring a sales manager; the next, to conduct a market seeding program, and so on. These steps are predetermined for him in the necessary sequence and inter-relationship. It gives the manager a discipline of stepwise tasks as he progresses in the construction of the plant and effectively marketing its output. This technique is an adaptation of a similar method devised by Boeing Aircraft and the Air Force (Reference 9) for more effective contract liaison, re: Figure 16-15.

Network sequence diagrams· have an added advantage when used to minimize time through the use of the well publicized Navy PERT or critical-path planning techniques. For example, we have utilized this in the case of an ammonia plant we recently built on the Mississippi River, Nitrin, Inc., a $22.5 million joint venture with Northern Natural Gas of Omaha. This is the technique first created and used in development of the Polaris Missile.

Note that we *not* only sequence planned the construction of the plant, but, also scheduled

all merchandising programs, and a build-up of the market distribution system.

LESSON 5 FOR THE CORPORATE PLANNER

Now for the last lesson from the DOD management. In the huge, complex organization of the DOD, McNamara perceived the necessity to expedite decision making. There were excessive committee meetings, too many reports being passed around, tending to delay decisions on program changes. Consequently, a specially designed room was created under the management of the Office of Programming, who are also in charge of maintaining the "running" 5-year plan. In this room are four Vu-graph type projectors that display against 4 adjacent screens, as shown in Figure 16-16. On one side of the room is a tramrail which brings forward on floor-to-ceiling charts, the approved program package data. On the opposite side, the tramrail displays added posters that relate to the specific elements under examination. The decision-making party sits in the center area, and can refer to the side panels for perspective data. The visualization is flexible and provides needed support for the proposal or problem under examination.

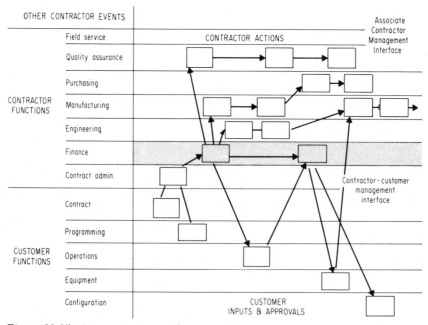

Figure 16-15 Management event-logic network.

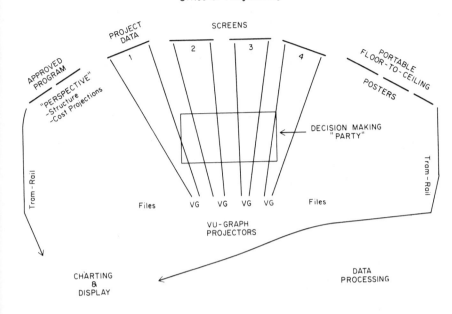

Figure 16-16

There is a computer located behind the projectors in the preparation area which also contains the charting and display requirements. The DOD planners assert that they have the capability, if somebody asks a resource allocation trade-off question, to run it through the computer, type the answer, prepare a visual, and project it back on the screen in seven minutes time.

It can be safely claimed that there are many values in observing DOD management practices. Lesson 1, mission planning, its application, and the organization related to it are useful concepts. Lesson 2, there are significant values in observing the use of quantitative analyses techniques in response to posed questions. Lesson 3, there are values in Needs Research as an unrecognized starting point for problem solving. Lesson 4, logic sequence networks are valuable tools for project execution and coordination. Lesson 5, decision making "centers" are worthwhile devices for expediting review/approval decisions in complex organizations.

Yes, our Defense Department is still providing useful "spin-offs" for industrial application.

References

1. "Programming System for Office of Secretary of Defense"; OASD (c) Programming, Directorate for Systems Planning, 25 June 1962.

2. *Missiles and Rockets Magazine,* Vol. 12, No. 12, March 1963, page 30.

3. Gilmore, F. F. and Brandenburg, R. G., "Anatomy of Corporate Planning"; *Harvard Business Review,* Vol. 40, No. 6, Nov./Dec. 1962, page 61–69.

4. "Secretary McNamara's One Magic Word"; *This Week Magazine,* 4 August 1963.

5. "The Whizziest Kid"; *Time Magazine,* 28 June 1963.

6. Hitch, Charles J., "The New Approach to Management in the U. S. Defense Department"; *Management Science,* Volume 9, No. 1, October 1962, page 1–8.

7. *Defense Department Staff Officers' Field Manual,* FM 101–5, (1960 edition), page 142.

8. Smalter, D. J., "Management by Priority-of-Challenge"; *Chemical Engineering Progress,* Vol. 60, No. 6, June 1964, page 25–27.

9. Kast, F. E., et al., "Boeing's Minuteman Missile Program," *Science Technology, and Management,* McGraw-Hill Book Company, 1963, page 233.

PLANNING, PROGRAMMING, AND BUDGETING

Elements of several basic concepts—the systems view, long-range planning, and formal decision analysis—have been combined into a framework for decision-making at the highest levels of the Federal government. The institution of a planning, programming, and budgeting system (PPBS) in the Federal government resulted from its successful application in the Department of Defense. Subsequently, these ideas have been adopted at the state, city, and other governmental levels. In business similar ideas have been applied using terms dictated by the firm's product orientation.

The concept of planning-programming-budgeting puts organizational strategy into the proper context. Long-range planning should encompass all the functional areas of the enterprise; the concept of a program and a budget facilitates the relating of objectives and the means of attaining these objectives. Also, planning-programming-budgeting forces recognition of what the organization is trying to achieve both in near-term and long-term, and the alternative ways of achieving ends.

The PPBS was instituted in the Federal government to obviate management difficulties which are succinctly spelled out by the original government directive:*

---

* Bureau of the Budget Bulletin 66–3, "Planning-Programming-Budgeting," October 12, 1965.

> ... *program review for decision-making has frequently been concentrated within too short a period; objectives of agency programs and activities have too often not been specified with enough clarity and concreteness; accomplishments have not always been specified concretely; alternatives have been insufficiently presented for consideration by top management; in a number of cases the future year costs of present decisions have not been laid out systematically enough; and formalized planning and systems analysis have had too little effect on budget decisions.*

Essential to the Federal government's PPBS is an output-oriented program structure *which provides data on all of the activities of each agency and which spells out the relationship of each to overall objectives. Complementing this program structure are* analyses *and* comparisons of alternative objectives and of alternative ways of achieving objectives. *The third essential element of PPBS is a* time cycle *which provides analytic results, information, and recommendations at a time which facilitates decision-making.*

The other aspect of timing which is critical to PPBS is the compilation of the costs and benefits derived from various activities over a meaningful time span. This means that projections of future costs and benefits must be made. More importantly however, it means that these factors need be considered at the time at which programs are to be embarked upon. *PPBS provides the framework through which such timely consideration can be given to program decisions.*

READING 17

A CONCEPTUAL FRAMEWORK FOR THE PROGRAM BUDGET*

Arthur Smithies

I. BUDGETING, PROGRAMMING AND POLICY

The need for program budgeting arises from the indissoluble connection between budgeting and the formation and conduct of national policy, or the policy of a state, a city, or a town, as the case may be. Governments, like private individuals or organizations, are constrained by the scarcity of economic resources at their disposal. Not only the extent to which they pursue particular objectives, but the character of the objectives themselves, will be influenced by the resources available. On the other hand, the extent to which the government desires to pursue its objectives will influence the resources it makes available to itself by taxation or other means. Budgeting is the process by which objectives, resources, and the interrelations among them are taken into account to achieve a coherent and com-

* Reprinted with permission from The RAND Corporation, RM-4271-RC, September, 1964, The RAND Corporation, Santa Monica, California.

prehensive program of action for the government as a whole. Program budgeting involves the use of budgetary techniques that facilitate explicit consideration of the pursuit of policy objectives in terms of their economic costs, both at the present time and in the future.

To be more specific, a modern government is concerned with the broad objectives of Defense; Law and Order; Health, Education and Welfare; and with Economic Development, together with the conduct of current business operations, notably the Post Office. No government, whatever its resources, can avoid the need for compromises among these objectives. No country can defend itself fully against all possible external threats. It takes certain risks with respect to defense for the sake of increasing the domestic welfare of its citizens. It must also compromise between the present and the future. The more actively it promotes defense and welfare at the present time, the more it may retard the long-run economic development of the country, by curtailing both private and public investment in the future. The country will be frustrated in the pursuit of all its objectives if it neglects the effective maintenance of law and order. Yet, compromises are made in this area also. No country supports a police force that will detect every crime, and no country enforces every law up to the limit.

Moreover, the character of each major program will depend on the total resources the government can appropriate to its purposes. A small country (at the present time) cannot afford nuclear weapons. Few countries can, or at any rate do, attempt to educate as wide a segment of their population as does the United States. However, countries may vary in their willingness to pursue their national objectives. With much smaller natural resources, the Soviet Union is prepared to make efforts comparable to the United States in both the fields of defense and education.

The task of making the necessary compromises among various objectives is the function of budgeting. To make those compromises it is necessary that the various government activities be expressed in terms of a common denominator, and the only common denominator available is money. It is difficult to compare the relative merits of an additional military division and an additional university. It is often more feasible to compare the relative merits of spending an additional billion dollars in one direction or the other. But to make that comparison it is necessary to know how much an additional billion dollars will add to military strength and how much to university education. While defense and education cannot be measured in simple quantitative terms, quantitative information can throw light on the consequences of spending money in various directions.

There are, however, a multitude of ways in which money can be spent on defense or education. To make intelligent comparisons, each of these major functions must be broken down into meaningful subfunctions. Modern defense at least requires considerations in terms of strategic forces and limited war forces. Education must be broken down at least into primary, secondary, and tertiary education. Major programs should thus be considered in terms of sub-programs, and at the end of the scale one reaches the manpower, material, and supplies used by the government in support of these activities. Such considerations and

calculations should lead to the concept of resources (money) used in optimal ways to achieve policy objectives.

Some government decisions relate only to the immediate future in the sense that if they turn out to be wrong, they can be readily reversed. Others, however, relate to a distant future that can be only dimly foreseen. Pure research, particularly, is in this category, since its consequences are in the nature of the case unknown. But governments nevertheless must make critical decisions with respect to the resources they devote to particular kinds of research as well as to research in the aggregate. At a lower order of difficulty, critical decisions with respect to transportation, resource development and the development of weapons systems relate to the next decade rather than the next year. Budgeting is essentially a matter of preparing for the future, but modern budgeting involves long-range projections into a highly uncertain future.

The basic point of view of this Memorandum is that a government can determine its policies most effectively if it chooses rationally among alternative courses of action, with as full knowledge as possible of the implications of those alternatives. The requirement of choice is imposed on it by the fact that any government is limited by the scarcity of resources. It is fundamental to our culture that rational choice is better than irrational choice. The government must choose not only among various courses of government action, but also between the government's total program and the private sector of the economy. The task of choice is not rendered easier by the fact that a substantial part of the government's program is designed to affect the future performance of the private economy.

Programming and budgeting are the focus of the process of comparison and coordination. In line with the foregoing paragraphs it involves:

1 Appraisals and comparisons of various government activities in terms of their contributions to national objectives.
2 Determination of how given objectives can be attained with minimum expenditure of resources.
3 Projection of government activities over an adequate time horizon.
4 Comparison of the relative contribution of private and public activities to national objectives.

5 Revisions of objectives, programs, and budgets in the light of experience and changing circumstances.

These operations are inherent in any budgetary process. Program budgeting involves more explicit recognition of the need to perform them than has been traditional. It also involves the application of new analytical techniques as an aid to the exercise of the human judgment on which choices must ultimately rest.

It should be clear from this statement of the budgetary problem that the traditional distinction between policy-making and budgeting, or between setting of goals and deciding on how to attain them, is inadequate and misleading. While the government can have a general desire and intention to defend the country, it cannot have a defense objective that is operationally meaningful until it is aware of the specific military implications of devoting resources to defense; and as part of that awareness, it should know the consequences of using defense resources in alternative ways. The question of allocative efficiency is thus intimately bound up with the question of the determination of goals. An adequate programming system must serve both purposes.

Governments can differ by temperament and institutional arrangements in the relative weights they give to the formulation and pursuit of goals, and the attainment of efficiency in the sense of minimizing costs of particular activities. A "crash program" devised with scant attention to efficiency may reach the moon in 1970. Preoccupation with efficiency may delay the successful event until 1980. However, crash programs can fail utterly, through lack of consideration of factors that would emerge in deliberate analysis.

Even in World War II, however, the overriding condition of scarcity placed limits on the pursuit of military abundance. As mobilization proceeded, competition between military output and civilian supply became acute. While many public and private investment projects could be deferred, supplies of canned foods, clothing, and transportation had to be maintained for the sake of the war effort itself. Basic materials—notably steel, copper, and aluminum—and manpower were closely allocated. Special programs were set up for rubber and petroleum. Even though allocation through financial controls receded into the background, the need for efficient allocation asserted itself strongly in other ways.

On the other hand, the successful strategy of World War II consisted of producing more of everything that was needed, so that military commanders could concentrate on military victory unhampered by the limitations of scarcity.

The United States, nevertheless, had options denied to most other countries. The political radical can deride preoccupation with efficiency as a delaying tactic. Conservatives can emphasize it for the same reason. Other countries have less freedom of choice. The plans of many of the underdeveloped countries have been frustrated through failure to pay attention to the elementary economics of choice. Considerations of comparative advantage have been ignored as encouraging indiscriminate *import* substitution. Public enterprises have been inefficiently planned and operated. As a result of such experiences, realization is dawning that, from the point of view of development, the basic principles of efficient allocation cannot be ignored.

Since all governments are confronted with the problem of scarcity, the logic of the decision-making process is independent of the form of government, even though outcomes may differ widely. All governments are concerned with defense, welfare, development, and law and order. In an authoritarian government initial preferences among these objectives depend on the ambitions and values of a central authority. But authority is constrained to those among them by resource limitations, and by the fact that any authority is less than absolute in its ability to enforce its will on the people.

In a democratic government the process is more indirect. Democracies also depend on leadership, but they depend on democratic consent. Leaders must educate and respond to public opinion. They must propose programs that will serve the national interest and also maintain them in power. Whichever of these objectives is uppermost in their minds, the basic task of allocation remains; and its performance reflects the combined judgment of the leadership and the public, concerning the contribution of government expenditures to national objectives. The thesis of this Memorandum rests on the assumption that society benefits to the extent that such choices are made in the light of the fullest possible information concerning their implications.

II. PROGRAM BUDGETING IN THE FEDERAL GOVERNMENT

For half a century there has been dissatisfaction in the United States with traditional budgetary methods, and some notable improvements have been made. A brief survey of that history will help to indicate the possibilities, as well as the difficulties, of further improvement.

Traditionally, budgeting has been conducted in terms of executive departments and their subdivisions. The traditional method of reviewing a department budget is to scrutinize proposed increases or decreases in objects of expenditure, with particular emphasis on personnel of various grades, and with emphasis on supplies and equipment as the activities of the department dictate. Such a system has advantages from the point of view of administrative control and, in highly simplified situations, could meet the requirements set out above. To the extent that every department or subdivision performed an identifiable function, the total expenditures, and particularly changes in them, might serve as rough indicators of the government's program. In the pre-World War II Army, numbers of officers and men were better indicators than they are today. In the Department of Justice, changes in the number and grades of lawyers in the various divisions are some indication of changes in the orientation of the policy of the department. If such indicators are relied on, the task of the budget reviewer is simply to see to it that the Army does not house itself too comfortably or that the lawyers do not have too many secretaries.

The traditional method is not and never has been adequate. The name of a department or a bureau is not sufficient to describe what it does. Nor are numbers or types of personnel employed an adequate measure of the functions they perform. Furthermore, the traditional budget period of a single year throws little light on the significance of expenditures whose effects may be spread over the next decade.

The inadequacies of the traditional system, however, have long been apparent. As early as 1912, President Taft's Commission on Economy and Efficiency recommended drastic changes in existing procedures. The Commission stated:

> The best that a budget can do for the legislator is to enable him to have expert advice in thinking about policies to be determined. His review of the economy and efficiency with which work has been done should be based on facts set forth in the annual reports of expenditures which would supplement the budget.
>
> To the administrator (i.e., the head of an executive department) the advantage to be gained through a budget is the ability to present to the legislature and to the people, through the Chief Executive or someone representing the administration, a well-defined, carefully considered, lucidly expressed welfare program to be financed, and in presenting this, to support requests for appropriation with such concrete data as are necessary to the intelligent consideration of such a program.
>
> To the Executive (i.e., the President) the advantage to be gained lies in his ability to bring together the facts and opinions necessary to the clear formulation of proposals for which he is willing actively to work as the responsible officer. To the people the advantage is the fact that they are taken into the confidence of their official agents. Therein lie the practical use and purpose of the budget.

Consequently, the Commission proposed first, a comprehensive executive budget (which had not previously existed); secondly, a classification of the budget in terms of programs or functions, and also a classification based on the distinction between capital and current items; and, thirdly, thorough and systematic review of the budget *after the fact*. These innovations were to be added to the traditional budget, and resulted in a proposal of extraordinary complexity.

While the Commission laid the foundation for all subsequent reforms, the political climate of the time did not permit action. In fact, nothing was done until 1921, when the drive for economy after World War I produced the

Budget and Accounting Act of that year, which required the President to submit a comprehensive executive budget, and set up the Budget Bureau as the staff agency to assist him. The comprehensive budget was an essential step in achieving the comparison of alternatives in the executive branch, but the Act left departmental budgets and procedures for preparing them unchanged.

Further progress toward a program budget was delayed until after World War II, when the movement again gained impetus—a generation after the Taft Commission. In 1949 the Hoover Commission recommended that "the whole budgetary concept of the federal government should be refashioned by the adoption of a budget based upon functions, activities, and projects: this we designate a 'performance budget'." The recommendation was made a legislative requirement by the National Security Act Amendments of 1949 and the Budgeting and Accounting Act Procedures Act of 1950. The Second Hoover Commission in 1955 recommended a "program budget" and proposed improvements in the government accounting system that would facilitate budgeting on a cost basis.

The result has been significant change and improvement in the presentation and the format of the federal budget, and the change in format has produced a significant change in the methods by which the budget is prepared and considered both in the Executive Branch and with Congress. The old "greensheets" of detailed personnel requirements, which once formed the central pivot of budget examination, have now receded into the background, and are now included merely as an appendix to the President's Budget.

In the immediate postwar period, and of course before, personal services were the heart of the matter. Budget examination in both the Executive Branch and the Congress consisted mainly of "marking up" the greensheets. Even in a construction agency like the Bureau of Ships of the Navy, procurement of material appeared on a one-line item in the President's Budget, while details of personal services occupied 300 lines. Classification by activities was rudimentary; and in many bureaus at the present time the budget for each bureau is classified by objects and by significant activities.

The recent changes in classifications are by no means formalities. They reflect changes in the approach of budget officers and congressional committees to their tasks of review and appraisal. Able and conscientious efforts are being made throughout the government to appraise activities in terms of their effectiveness in promoting national objectives. In this respect the idea of program budgeting has been accepted in principle. The main problem at the moment is not to inject a new idea, but to improve on what has already been done, and there is still abundant room for improvement.

In two major respects there is still need for reconsideration or revision of previous practice. In the first place, programs or activities are still propounded and considered mainly within the limits of the existing bureaus or departments in which they occur. Even if two or more bureaus or departments conduct activities that are essentially complementary or competitive with each other, those activities are not considered together. To take some obvious examples: In agriculture, the price support program has to contend with a wheat surplus. At the same time, its research program is devising methods for increasing wheat production! At the departmental level, the failure to achieve coordination among the water-resource programs of Interior, the Corps of Engineers, and Agriculture has been a long standing embarrassment to the government. The President's Budget Message, however, is arranged in terms of major programs that cut across department lines. For instance, all expenditures in natural resources are grouped as a single major program, irrespective of what department conducts them. But this does not mean that decisions are made in a similar way.

A second major defect of the present budget is its short time span of one year. It is still mainly concerned with appropriations and expenditures for the succeeding year, and contains figures only for the year just completed, estimates for the current year, and for the year to which it relates. This may be adequate for many administrative activities, but, as pointed out above, it is thoroughly inadequate for procurement of long-lead items and for construction projects. Whether projections over a number of years should be published in the formal budget is an open question. But there can be little doubt that they should be available to the executive and congressional authorities who review the budget.

The Defense Budget is a special case that will be discussed in detail later. At this stage, it will suffice to indicate with great brevity what has been done since World War II. Despite the creation of the Department of Defense in 1947, the defense budget consisted essentially of budgets for the three separate Services. The total arrived at by the President and the Secretary of Defense was shared among the Services according to some fairly arbitrary formula, rather than by consideration of the contribution of the Services to the defense program as a whole or by consideration of programs that cut across Service lines.

In 1949, Congress ordered so-called "performance budgets" to be submitted for each Service. Prior to that time, budgets had been prepared for the Army and the Navy, based on estimates made by their technical services. In the Army, for instance, separate budgets were prepared for the Quartermaster Service, the Transportation Service, the Ordnance Service, and so forth. Such an arrangement had little merit from the point of view of determining requirements with reference to the mission of the Army.

The new "performance" budget adopted a new classification, which is now in use. The major headings are Military Personnel; Operation and Maintenance; Procurement; Military Construction; and Research, Development, Test and Evaluation.

From the point of view of relating the budget to national strategy, this arrangement has little apparent advantage over the old one. A budget constructed on these lines does not permit the Secretary of Defense or the President to tell what provision is being made to increase capacity to defend the United States, to engage in operations in Asia, and so forth. However, this budget is an improvement in some respects. It corresponds to major areas of general staff responsibility.

Moreover, it also makes some distinction between the present and the future. Military personnel and operation and maintenance are mainly concerned with current operation. Procurement and construction mainly relate to the investment in equipment for the future, while research and development relates to the more remote future. Thus, if each of the Services had a clear cut mission, a projection of the present budget over, say, a five-year period could give a coherent picture of military costs for each mission. There would still remain the vital problem of assessing the military effectiveness of the costs incurred.

In 1961, a major change was made by adding a programming system to the existing budget system. Since then decisions have been made on the basis of five-year programs relating to the defense program as a whole, regardless of Service distinctions. These decisions are subsequently translated into the existing annual budget categories for each Service. During the process of translation and compilation of the budget, minor but not major revisions are made. The President's Budget is presented on both a program basis and on a conventional basis for the budget period. The five-year projections are not published for general use.

The major programs are Strategic Retaliatory Forces, Continental Air and Missile Defense Forces, General Purpose Forces (including most of the Army and the Navy), Airlift and Sealift Forces, Reserve and National Guard Forces, Research and Development, and General Support. In addition, Retired Pay, Civil Defense, and Military Assistance are included as separate programs.

Budget and Program procedures in the Defense Department will be, the subject of a separate paper. For the present, we shall be concerned with the logic of the program structure that has been adopted, as a complicated and revealing case study of the nature, the possibilities, and the limitations of program budgeting.

III. WHAT IS A PROGRAM?

In the federal government, the terms "program," "performance," "activity" and "function" are all used more or less interchangeably. While there may be shades of difference among them, there is no consistent pattern. Research, for instance, may be designated by some organizations as an activity and by others as a program. Program and performance are often used synonomously. But the federal budget often uses the term "program and performance." The performance budget of the Defense Department does not correspond to the present program structure. These ambiguities and inconsistencies of language reveal the ambiguities of the underlying situation. As we shall see, there are a number of criteria for the designation of an operation as a program. The defense program structure itself reveals a variety of criteria which will be discussed in a moment. Meanwhile light may be shed on the problem by beginning with a hypothetical example outside government.

Consider the question of the organization of a highly integrated automobile manufacturer, which not only produces automobiles, but also produces rubber, iron and steel. The objective of the corporation is to maximize its profits. But it is hard to imagine its conducting its operations simply by reference to that objective. If it produces several brand names, it is likely to have a separate program and separate organizations for each of them. Each brand name presumably is intended to appeal mainly to a separate section of the market. Or the company may, as General Motors does, put brands in active competition with each other.

Programming of final products is hardly likely to be sufficient. Increased demands for rubber and steel from the top do not immediately evoke increases in supply; this may not be forthcoming unless capacity to produce steel and rubber has been built in anticipation of increased demand for automobiles. Consequently the corporation would probably have both a steel and a rubber program that would attempt to anticipate final demands. Moreover, there would be no point in having separate steel and rubber programs for each of the final products. Errors could be avoided and economies achieved by having single organizations supply steel and rubber to the several final product divisions. Furthermore, those concerned with the manufacture of final products are unlikely to be expert in steel and rubber technology. The effective division of labor commends a vertical division of functions.

The long run future of the organization will depend on the research and development it conducts. Some research and development may be connected with specific brands, the production of which can be anticipated; in that event it can be included in the final product programs. But some research is of common benefit to all final products, and some will relate to the models of the future that will come into production beyond the horizon of

any feasible production plans. Consequently, a separate research program is likely to be called for.

It should be noted from this example that the question of programming and that of organization are closely connected. A central management might control the entire operation, in which case the separate programs would aid it in its thinking about its problems. What is more likely is that the need to program will also pattern the administrative shape of the organization and will dictate some decentralization of authority.

Another example from outside government, very different from the corporation, is a liberal arts college. Its objectives are not to make money, and not directly to equip its students to make money. It does not measure its success by the incomes subsequently earned by its alumni—although it is not entirely uninterested in that subject. For objectives, it must rely on general statements, such as the advancement of knowledge and equipping its students for citizenship in a free society. Such general statements do not tell it what to teach or what to investigate. And it would not accept the view that its function is simply to teach students what they want to learn. Yet the college resources are limited. It must allocate its resources.

It solves its problems by setting up programs that it believes will throw light on its objectives. It thinks of its faculty as concerned broadly with science and the humanities, and with teaching and research within these categories. While it cannot define its objectives *precisely*, it believes that their attainment will be furthered by its performance in these areas.

The college begins with some allocation and then from year to year considers reallocations that it believes will further its (undefined) objectives. It may be able to make sensible choices among alternative courses of action, even though its objectives are not clearly defined.

In pursuing its policies, the administration of the university is subject to a number of constraints. It has to persuade its students to accept the relative emphasis it gives to science and the humanities, and its faculty the allocation between teaching and research. Otherwise, it may lose both students and faculty in competition with other institutions.

The programming problems of the college are not unlike those of government in fields such as defense or welfare. When government undertakes to produce the marketable goods, its problem is closer to that of the private business.

Let us now examine the new program structure of the Department of Defense. While we do not know precisely why that particular structure was adopted, it is instructive to guess at the possible reasons.

The structure clearly derives from the strategic doctrine that distinguishes between general war and limited war; and the view that the use of large strategic weapons for limited purposes is "unthinkable." It implies that one of the main programming tasks is to achieve the most effective balance between strategic and limited war forces.

Strategic Retaliatory Forces qualifies as a program for a number of reasons. First, it is directly related to a major objective of defense policy, and, in principle, requirements for these forces can be calculated from knowledge of the enemy threat and of the capability of our own weapons. Secondly, the program can be neatly broken down into a number of program elements—Polaris, Minuteman and manned bombers. These elements are to a large degree substitutes for each other, so that there is a problem of determining an optimum mix of the elements. Thirdly, the program cuts across service lines. The program concept thus serves as an instrument of coordination of the services.

Continental Defense could be regarded as an element of strategic deterrence. The main purpose of it at the present time is to protect and to warn the strategic forces; and when force requirements are reduced, the better the forces are defended. However, if extensive and effective defense of cities ever becomes a reality, continental defense would have more meaning as a separate program, although still linked to strategic concepts.

General Purpose Forces occupy about 35 per cent of the budget and include the forces designed to meet non-strategic attacks in the Western Hemisphere, in the Far East, in Southeast Asia—in fact, all over the world. The threat is not clearly defined, and neither are the requirements for meeting it. Clearly this program is of a very different character from the other two, and does not lend itself readily

to analysis either in terms of its components or of its contribution to defense objectives. One possibility of improvement that suggests itself is that the program should be broken down on a regional basis; but this meets with the serious objection that forces can be transferred from one region to another, and one cannot predict whether threats will appear in isolation, in sequence, or simultaneously.

Airlift and Sealift is logically a component of general purpose forces. It is designed to increase mobility and hence permit economies with respect to the size of forces. It is presumably considered as a separate program because its components, airlift and sealift, should be considered as substitutes for each other, and the best mix should be achieved.

Research and Development is allocated to particular programs when it can be directly related to them. It is properly considered separately when it is conducted for purposes beyond the horizons of other programs.

The large item General Support, which includes nearly 30 per cent of the budget, includes not only items such as general overhead which in its nature cannot and should not be allocated to specific programs, but also an amount which it has not yet proved feasible to allocate.

Other programs such as Reserves and Military Assistance have presumably been considered separately for administrative or political reasons.

These comments on defense programming are not intended to disparage the important advances that have been made. They are intended, rather, to indicate the difficulties and the variety of criteria involved in breaking up a highly complicated operation into neat program categories.

Almost all the difficulties of devising a satisfactory program system arise in the field of international relations (apart from defense); and because of the complexity of the problem, budgeting and programming in this area is still in an unsatisfactory condition.

In the first place, the objectives of foreign policy are diverse, complicated, and amorphous. Only a few years ago the situation seemed simpler. Foreign policy appeared to consist of containing Russian expansion in Europe, ostracizing China, and promoting economic development elsewhere. With that degree of simplification three major programs suggest themselves. Political and military means would implement the first two, and economic aid the third. At the present time, Russia must be distinguished from the Eastern European Communist countries, which also must be distinguished from each other; our allies trade with China; Russia and China are active in the underdeveloped countries, and for our part, sharp distinctions must be drawn among Asia, Africa, and Latin America. Foreign programs must be devised with the realization that a simple foreign policy doctrine is not available.

A second major difficulty is that foreign policy cuts across department lines; not only the Department of State and the Department of Defense, but the AID agency, the Department of Agriculture, the Treasury, the Department of Commerce, the Tariff Commission, and a growing number of international agencies are concerned with it. Moreover, especially in the economic area, there is an intimate relation between foreign and domestic policy. A serious depression in the United States would be more harmful to underdeveloped countries than calling off the entire aid program.

A third difficulty, which is closer to the province of this Memorandum, is the age-old conflict between the regional and the functional point of view. Or more accurately, should a regional or country breakdown be the primary classification, with the functional breakdown secondary, or should it be the other way around? Emphasis on the functional approach tends to center authority in Washington, and creates confusion in the field. Emphasis on the country approach may produce coherence in the field and confusion in Washington. Advocates of either emphasis are encountered with strong counter arguments. Administration must be based on one approach or the other. But in the purpose of planning for the future, perhaps both should run in awkward double harness.

Quite different problems and approaches occur in connection with the programming of resource development, such as power, navigation, and flood control. Such activities are designed mainly to improve the economic performance of the country in the future. Unlike defense or foreign policy, they are intended to produce economic benefits. The difficulties arise because they must be formulated in the context of a mixed economy; and in most cases there are direct or indirect private alternatives which are not subject to government planning. (Even though navigation is the exclusive province of the government, there are private transportation alternatives to inland waterways.)

The programming method used by the Government is to attempt to assess the costs and benefits of individual projects, in comparison with private and other public alternatives. The program, then, consists of the most meritorious projects the budget will accommodate. Meritorious projects excluded from the budget provide arguments for increasing its size, in the same way that excluded defense or foreign aid activities provide a case for increasing those segments of the budget.

There are difficulties inherent in the specific project approach. The attempt is to apply profit criteria to public projects, analogous to those used in valuing private projects. This involves comparison of monetary values of present and future costs and benefits. But, in many important cases, such as urban highways, recreation parkways, free bridges, and flood control dams, the product of the government's investment does not directly enter the market economy. Consequently evaluation requires imputation of market values. For example, the returns on a bridge have been estimated by attempting to value the time saved by users. Such measurements necessarily contain a strong element of artificiality.

In other cases, the purposes of government investment are to alter the character of the market economy, either for the nation as a whole or for particular regions within it. In such cases, returns should be measured in terms of the market values that will exist as a result of the investment, rather than those that prevail before it is undertaken. This difficulty has led economists and planners to attempt to construct "shadow" prices as a basis for their measurements.

In still other cases, government undertakes investments that require a longer view of the future than private enterprise is willing to undertake. It is therefore prepared to accept a lower rate of return than that which is yielded by private investment in other directions. But how much lower the return should be is not revealed by market prices.

These remarks indicate that project evaluation cannot be achieved entirely by objective economic analysis. In most cases, there is a strong political element in the choice of projects. To serve the national interest, such choices should be made in the light of overall policies with respect to economic development. Attempts to build up such policies from the consideration of particular projects seem to give undue scope for the influence of particularistic political interests, and do not appear to add to the formulation of inherent national objectives. The question is therefore raised whether, in fields such as transportation and natural resources, overall programs should not be formulated into which particular projects can be fitted.

If so, what should such programs contain? Description of an area as an activity or a program implies that its components are more closely in competition with each other than they are with elements outside the program. Should urban transport be placed more closely in competition with international transport than with other aspects of urban development? Should international transport be regarded as a component of transportation or foreign trade, or both? In much current discussion, it seems to be taken for granted that transportation is a natural program category. But that conclusion is by no means obvious.

Similar problems and difficulties arise in connection with other fields such as education, health, and welfare. Some aspects of education and health are designed to increase the economic effectiveness of the labor force. Others are designed to enrich the social and intellectual lives of individuals. Education in particular is held essential for the political health of the country. Possibly the economic aspects of education and health should be considered not only as components of education and health generally, but also as parts of a national manpower program.

In the United States, in particular, there is a further major difficulty connected with activities in the resource and welfare fields. The activities of the federal government are designed to supplement those of the private economy, or to supplement and stimulate state and local governments. Should plans in these areas relate to the nation as a whole, covering the activities of the private economy and all levels of government? To what extent should the federal government attempt to implement such overall plans by controls over the private economy or conditional grants-in-aid to other levels of government? Presumably our belief in the competitive market economy and our commitment to the federal system preclude thorough-going resort to central planning and control in any important area. The federal government is thus faced with a dilemma with which it must live as best it can.

This discussion shows that designation of activities as programs is no easy or trivial matter. The way in which a program structure is set up for the government as a whole or for any major segment can have a profound effect on the decisions that are reached, so that the design of programs should be regarded as an important part of the decision-making process. The following paragraphs indicate some of the criteria that should be taken into account.

1 An important criterion for a program structure is that it should permit comparison of alternative methods of pursuing an imperfectly determined policy objective. Thus the need for public assistance can be clarified and analyzed by breaking the problem down into the needs arising from old age, economic dependence, physical disability, and unemployment. Limited resources prevent provisions for all cases under these categories. Despite the absence of a clear cut concept of social welfare, a satisfactory comparison among these various categories must be formed.

2 Even though objectives may be clearly defined, there are usually alternative ways of accomplishing them. Thus Airlift and Sealift is designated as a separate program, largely because a requirement can be accomplished by various combinations of air and sea transports.

3 Programs may also consist of a number of complementary components, none of which can be effective without the others. A health program requires doctors, nurses, and hospitals in the right proportions.

4 A separate program may be needed where one part of an organization supplies services to several others. Economies are likely if a department has a single computer operation rather than separate ones in each bureau. Since the acquisition of computer facilities is likely to have an appreciable lead time, departmental planning is likely to require that computers be budgeted as a separate program, even though they are far removed from the end objectives of the department.

5 An organization's objectives may require it to adopt overlapping structures. This need is evident in foreign affairs where both geographical and functional programs are required. It is also evident within the country, where regional as well as national requirements must be considered.

6 A further criterion relates to the time span over which expenditures take effect. The uncertainties of the future usually preclude firm estimates of requirements for government services beyond a limited period, say five years. Yet, research and development and investment must be undertaken to provide for a longer-run future. Even where such activities can be identified with some major program, they should be dealt with as separate sub-programs, since the uncertainties of the longer-run future should affect the character of the activities undertaken. In other cases, such long range activities may not be identifiable with any current end product program. In that event, it is obvious that they should be dealt with separately. In fact, differences in time spans of various activities may be the leading characteristic of an organization's program structure. A growing undertaking may think primarily in terms of the division of its functions among production, investment, and research and development.

The need for programming arises from the limitations of human beings and the obstinacy of the physical environment. In the first place, it is not sufficient to invoke the Constitution and seek to promote the general welfare. The general welfare can only be understood in terms of components and by choosing among them. Secondly, the process of relating ends to means is immensely complicated in a modern society. The process must be broken down into a hierarchy of optimizations and suboptimizations. Thirdly, results cannot be achieved instantaneously, and frequently long lead times are involved. Moreover, resources once committed to a purpose are not readily transferable elsewhere. Consequently, programming is required.

A general distinction that may be useful is that between the final and intermediate programs of an organization. Final programs can be regarded as those that contribute directly to its general objective. Intermediate programs are operations singled out for treatment as programs that contribute to final programs in the immediate or remote future. Thus in the

Department of Defense, strategic forces, general purpose forces and possibly air defense can be considered final, while all others are intermediate. From the point of view of the government as a whole, however, defense becomes the final program and its components intermediate.

IV. PROGRAM PREPARATION, APPRAISAL, AND ANALYSIS

Preparation

Up to this point in the discussion, programming and budgeting have not been distinguished from each other, and program budgeting has been regarded as a budgetary process that pays due regard to policy objectives, costs, and time dimensions. We must now modify these simplifications and regard programming and budgeting as different but complementary components of the same operation. Every organization, in or out of government, finds it necessary to have an annual budget which represents a detailed and feasible plan of action for the ensuing year. Every organization, however, must look beyond the next year, even to make coherent plans for that year. An explicit projection beyond the end of the following year will be called a program. Programs and budgets should clearly be consistent with each other. Departures of the budget from the program call for revisions of the program, and program revisions call for changes in the budget.

In some instances, budgeting and programming may be identical processes. In the Anti-Trust Division of the Department of Justice, for instance, the basic cost factor is the number and types of lawyers employed. The requirement derives from the vigor of the government's enforcement policy, and the nature of the cases that fall within its net. Anti-trust cases cannot be disposed of in one year; consequently, budgeting must look beyond a single year. Apart from the fact that typewriters and secretaries can be adequately dealt with on an annual basis, there is unlikely to be any difference between the requirements of effective programming and effective budgeting.

In other cases, programming and budgeting methods should differ markedly. Consider, for instance, the Federal Prison System. The system should program for a number of years, because it must have a cell for every prisoner. The number of prisoners will depend on future crime rates and enforcement policies. If techniques of detention, punishment and correction remain the same, the program and its cost can be derived from the expected number of prisoners, changes in price levels, wage rates, conviction costs, and so forth. Further refinements should take into account change in prison methods that could lead to economies or increased costs: changes in length of sentences, the effects of civil rights legislation, of abolition of capital punishment, and so forth. Program estimates of this character require human abilities, research methods and procedures far different from those required to produce a detailed estimate of cost for the ensuing year. While next year's budget should be derived from the program and consistent with it, it should also be separate.

In contrast to the prison system, programming for defense is vastly more complicated. Defense consists of a number of major programs that are in competition with each other for the resources available for defense, and whose program elements are in competition with each other. The President and the Secretary of Defense should be able to decide whether an increase in one area should result in contraction in another or an increase in the total size of the budget. Changes in external threats, technology, management techniques, and strategic doctrine all demand that programs be subject to continual revision. Consequently, it is clear that programming in defense and other agencies responsible for interrelated programs should be a highly centralized operation, carried out by flexible methods and capable of rapid revision. But the centralized operation should not be permitted to occur in a vacuum. Its success will depend heavily on the extent to which ideas and experience at all levels of the Department can be fed into it.

Ideally, the process of revision should be continuous and comprehensive. Every year should, in principle, be the first year of a new program. The need for comprehensive revision derives from the fact that the elements of a program are frequently highly interdependent. Revision of any one element should call for reconsideration of all others. In practice com-

prehensiveness may be too costly in time, effort, uncertainty, and confusion. However, the built-in tendencies towards rigidity in any system must be guarded against. In this respect a centralized programming system is likely to be more flexible than a conventional budget system, which is particularly responsive to the forces of inertia throughout the organization.

The need for flexibility has an important bearing on the time span that programs should cover. The very existence of a program implies some loss of flexibility. By reason of having adopted it, the organization reduces its freedom to do something different in future years, since a conscious act of revision is required. On the other hand, investment projects, to say nothing of research and development, undertaken now must be based on some view of a highly uncertain future. Time spans should be long enough but not unnecessarily long.

The dilemma could be partially resolved if programs could be expressed in terms of ranges rather than single figures. If the ranges included genuine upper and lower limits, it would become clear that projection beyond a limited period was not operationally meaningful. Ranges and more elaborate methods for taking uncertainty into account have been frequently advocated, but rarely adopted. One approach is to program for limited time horizons, but to recognize that important items in the program will yield their benefits beyond the horizon. The imposition of a horizon and the knowledge that there is something beyond it should stimulate the design of projects that can be adapted to conditions that at the present time can be only dimly foreseen.

Appraisal

Both the usefulness and feasibility of programming depend on one's ability to appraise and analyze past experience. The directions and techniques of future policy depend critically on the quantitative and the qualitative data derived from the past. Rational planning can be applied to new departures, such as ballistic missiles, only to the extent that they are comparable with something that was done in the past. The cost-effectiveness of missiles could be appraised initially only by comparison of their expected performance with that of the manned bomber. Once missiles exist, new generations could be compared with their predecessors.

Fortunately for the ordinary conduct of life, dramatic breaks with the past are rare. The decision to construct the atomic bomb was such an example. It may have been thought at the time that comparison with the destructive power of high explosives afforded a basis for comparison. But subsequent experience has shown how naive were simple and vulgar criteria such as "a bigger bang for a buck." However, once the world became imprisoned in the atomic age, the feasibility of rational calculation began to assert itself within that world. We are now at the dawn of the space age. Rational processes do not tell whether we should go to Mars at all or how soon we should get to Mars. Once we are there, we may be able to think more clearly about Venus.

Even though the adoption of space exploration as a goal may not be a matter of rational calculation, problems of efficiency arise as soon as the goal is adopted. The resources that the government is prepared to devote to its pursuit are limited by competing claims on the budget. The efficiency with which the operation is carried out may mean the difference between success and failure, given the constraint on available resources. Even though the objective differs from anything that has been undertaken in the past, experience with the design of research, development, and investment in other areas that were once new can be highly useful and relevant.

Consequently, a successful decision-making process depends heavily on systematic and thorough accumulation of evidence about the past as a guide to the future. A knowledge of the past is necessary not only to provide experiences analogous to those of the present but to point to methods of improving on past performance.

While this point may seem obvious, it nevertheless needs emphasis. Governments seem prone to two kinds of error in this connection. On the one hand past experience is simply reproduced through failure to analyze its relevance for the present. One striking example is provided by the Korean war mobili-

zation—both the pattern of government organization and the long range strategy, such as building up an industrial base. Preparations for the long-run future (as distinct from merely fighting the Korean engagement) showed remarkably little awareness of the nature of nuclear war—although we were already in the atomic age. The reason was that those who were called upon to organize the Korean undertaking had little to go on except their World War II experience. No systematic attempts had been made to appraise that experience and adapt it to future requirements. But governments also tend to make the opposite kind of mistake, by failing to recognize that history does afford instances of problems closely analogous to those of the present. The United States is not exempt from these tendencies. The government does not preoccupy itself extensively with historical analyses.

In the budgetary area, narrowly defined, recording one aspect of the past has been an important preoccupation. Budgeting has been traditionally associated with accounting. But government accounting systems have been largely designed to check on the honesty of officials and to limit their exercise of discretion. This type of accounting has in turn been reflected in traditional methods of budgeting for the future. As in business, the government in recent years has recognized the need for cost accounting. Improvements have been most marked in the corporation area. They are far less evident among the regular departments and agencies. But it is doubtful whether any accounting system will provide all the cost information needed for adequate program analysis.

Reporting on costs, however, is only one side of the problem. Equally important, and far more difficult, are the questions on the benefit side. How well is a long range research program succeeding? Is public health being improved, or is it deteriorating? Does the fact that we have no war mean that potential enemies are being deterred by our forces? How do we compare a world with foreign aid with a world without it? Can such questions as these be answered systematically? Or must detailed information on costs be associated with crude intuition on benefits? This may be true. The assessment of benefits depends largely on judgment and intuition, rather than on precise measurement.

Analysis

When attention moves from the past to the future, two major questions arise separately or in combination. First, how effective is a program in attaining its intended objective; and second, can existing program results be accomplished at lower cost? These questions attempt to draw a distinction between the *effectiveness* of a program in achieving its objective and the *efficiency* with which it is carried out. For instance it may be possible to consider the effectiveness of the antitrust program under the present organization of the division. It should also be possible to decide whether the same results could be more efficiently achieved by reorganizing the division. For instance, efficiency may be increased by having fewer senior lawyers and more assistants, or vice versa.

The distinction between effectiveness and efficiency, when it can be made, is useful for analytic purposes. But in important instances, the distinction is arbitrary, and possibly misleading. Consider an analogy from the market economy. If an automobile is perfectly standardized, it is possible to consider separately the demand for it and the cost of production. But suppose a new technology produces a different kind of car that has greater consumer appeal. The distinction between efficiency and effectiveness becomes much more difficult. If the technology produced helicopters that displaced automobiles it might be meaningless. In these circumstances, total value produced must be compared with total costs. The number of cars loses significance as a precise measurement. It becomes instead an index of automobile transportation. As such, of course, it may have significant uses.

Likewise in government, the feasibility of distinguishing between effectiveness and efficiency depends on the possibility of quantitative measurement of programs. Such measurement is possible in a limited number of cases. Electric power can be measured in kilowatts. Volume of mail handled may be a useful measure of the activities of the Post Office, although the citizen may disagree as he waits impatiently for his mail. Miles of highway constructed again is a measure, but one wants to know where the highways lead to. Numbers of children educated is a significant figure, but is not a measure of the quality of education.

In other areas, notably defense, and law and order, this type of cardinal measurement is clearly impossible. Nevertheless, it may still be possible to apply the criterion "more or less" to a program. Even though strategic deterrence cannot be measured in any units, it still seems meaningful to say that deterrence has increased, decreased or remained the same. If this is possible, the efficiency of the program at any level can be examined separately.

The possibility of ordinal measurement can be increased if trade-off factors can be established among various program components. The effectiveness of airlift and sealift will depend on the numbers of troops transported and the speed of the operation. Experience and analysis may show that to transport 100,000 men in one month is preferable to transporting 200,000 in two months. One may, therefore, be able to say that "airlift and sealift" has increased or decreased, even though the composition of the program has changed materially.

The concepts of efficiency and effectiveness have been emphasized because they serve to indicate the areas where objective analysis may be possible and those where it is not.

The efficiency concept implies that measures taken to achieve economies will not affect the attainment of the objectives of the program, when it is carried out at a given level. Consequently, efficiency can be dealt with by analytical methods. The relatively new techniques of operations research and cost-effectiveness analysis (as usually conceived) are all concerned with efficiency questions.

The distinction between effectiveness and efficiency must, however, be used with extreme care. Measures that purport to increase efficiency may have pronounced effects, good or bad, on effectiveness. Government economy campaigns, for instance, often reduce effectiveness, sometimes intentionally, in the guise of eliminating waste. On the other hand, the elimination of undeniable waste may improve the effectiveness of government operations generally. With respect to particular programs, increasing the number of students per teacher will affect the quality of education. On the other hand, removal of cumbersome equipment from aircraft on grounds of efficiency may have unforeseen beneficial effects in terms of range and maneuverability. Where such possibilities exist, questions of cost and effectiveness become thoroughly intermingled.

Economic factors probably dominate the cost side of the government's activities, but there are non-economic costs as well. Probably the most decisive objection to a civil defense program has been not its economic costs, but the destruction of social values it might involve. The destruction of the beauty of the countryside by superhighways, and of cities by freeways, represents non-economic costs that are too infrequently recognized. In some cases, the final purpose of a program, insofar as the government is concerned, is to produce outputs with economic value. Government production of marketable electric power is a clearcut example. But as was pointed out above, the purported economic valuation of many government activities necessarily involves political judgments concerning critical elements in the valuation.

Many government activities are designed to yield both economic and non-economic returns. Education is a good example. One of its objectives undoubtedly is to produce an enterprising and skilled labor force that will contribute to economic prosperity. Another is to preserve and enlarge the cultural heritage of the country, and, hopefully to sustain its capacity to govern itself, despite technological advance. Another example is public health. Reduction of working time lost by sickness is one of its benefits. But measures to reduce suffering in old age are not undertaken for economic reasons. The idea of economic measurement has great attractiveness because of the analytic possibilities, especially to economists, that it offers. But it is a perversion of human values to push it into areas where it does not belong.

Even where the effectiveness of programs can be measured in terms of money, that is not the end of the story; they must be undertaken or not undertaken in competition with other programs that are not so measurable. The President, for instance, may have to decide whether to spend his marginal billion dollars on a new (measurable) dam or on (non-measurable) hospitals for the aged. Such decisions are necessarily political. Also within

major programs, choices are frequently political rather than technical. There is no purely technical basis for deciding the relative emphasis that should be given to strategic deterrence compared with limited war capabilities. In agriculture, the decision to support agricultural incomes at some desired level is a political rather than a technical matter.

Some authorities argue that political choices can best be made if politicians listen merely to voices in the air, observe straws in the political wind, or regard their occupation as an amusing bargaining game. Our position is that political choices can be improved if politicians are aided by information and technical analysis concerning the probable consequences of their acts. The technician may be able to point out that some courses of political action will not yield the results desired. For instance, in a poor country overemphasis on welfare, compared with development, may destroy the country's chances of both welfare and development.

Ultimately decisions are made by individuals, groups, or legislative bodies exercising their informed judgment. One can hope that such decisions will be improved if they are made in the light of all available evidence and the evidence is marshalled in an orderly way. Furthermore, such procedure may help to avoid the political bargaining and logrolling that mars rather than makes the political process.

There is a useful parallel to be drawn between political and legal processes. The decisions of judges or juries cannot be appraised by objective standards. They depend on adversary procedures that follow well-established rules. If those rules are violated, decisions are upset on appeal. Otherwise, they stand.

A programming approach to government decision-making can be thought of as an adversary process. Decision-making is arranged so as to permit the competition of ideas, in the light of which decision-makers make choices among relevant alternatives.

V. PROGRAMMING AND ORGANIZATION

Our discussion has indicated that there is a close connection between programming and organization. Programs cannot be formulated or carried out unless they are under the direction of a responsible authority. Also, programs cannot be compared and related to each other except by a superior authority responsible for all of them. The question then arises whether the considerations that determine the best program structure for the government are an equally good guide to its organizational structure. Or are there additional or alternative criteria that should govern its pattern of organization? Since differing programming and organizational structures are found to give rise to conflict, there should clearly be no unnecessary incompatibility between them.

At the highest executive level, there is no incompatibility. The President is the head of the administrative executive branch, and since the Budget and Accounting Act of 1921, it has been definitely established that he is responsible for recommending a comprehensive program to the Congress.

There should be a strong presumption that the responsibilities of executive departments should be determined by program criteria. Each department should be assigned responsibility for closely related programs that serve the same general objective. The department head in his recommendations to the President should be personally responsible for achieving the best comprehensive program within the scope of his jurisdiction.

Within departments, the organization of bureaus, divisions and sections should be organized on a programmatic basis unless there are good reasons for departing from that rule.

Unfortunately, the problem is not as simple as this. There are good reasons why the requirements of effective administration may diverge from those of effective programming. There are also reasons, not necessarily good, why, in fact, programming cuts across administrative lines rather than coincides with them.

1 The existing organization of the government has deep historical roots which the strongest President (to say nothing of the Congress) is reluctant to disturb violently. Although Presidents have been repeatedly granted reorganization powers, they have been disinclined to use those powers to make major changes.

2 There may be strong arguments for not disturbing the historical situation, even though contemporary programming requirements seem to demand it. There are many propo-

nents of the virtues of competition among the military services, provided the competition is given coherence by a programming system. Moreover, today's programming structure may not be suitable for tomorrow. Stability in the organization may be worth the price of some inconsistency with the structure that contemporary logic seems to require.

3 When overlapping program structures are required, the organization cannot do full justice to both of them. This difficulty is particularly evident when the regional-functional issue arises.

4 A particular activity may be concerned with more than one program, in which case it cannot be assigned without question to one department. The Corps of Engineers is an essential part of military defense, even though its main peacetime concern is civil works. It should not necessarily be transferred to the Department of the Interior, even though that transfer might improve resource programming. The Department of Agriculture has important international as well as domestic activities. Those activities should not necessarily be transferred to the Department of State. International agricultural programs may be evolved more effectively in an agricultural rather than a foreign service environment.

5 The organization required for effective administration of programs may differ from that required for effective formulation. Good administration may require the setting up of a separate research department, even though all the research done in it can be identified with other programs. Efficiency may be increased by having scientists working together, under the supervision of scientists rather than by having them scattered through a departmental bureaucracy. In the case of the Post Office, questions relating to construction, mail deliveries and technical improvement can be formulated on a functional and nationwide basis. Yet the administration of the Post Office must necessarily be decentralized on a regional and local basis. Furthermore, a single general counsel's office, a single supply organization, and a single carpool is likely to be enough for one department—simply on grounds of administrative efficiency.

These examples suffice to indicate that apart from the forces of tradition and inertia, the criteria for programming and those for effective organization do not coincide, and may diverge materially. Conditions will differ from department to department. In some instances programming may be a highly centralized operation only indirectly concerned with administration. In simpler situations there need be no incompatibility. In still others, programs are intended to overcome the organizational incongruities that cannot feasibly be altered.

The distinction between programming and administration is not as clear-cut as it may appear at first sight. Administration does not consist simply of carrying out directives. In fact, successful administration implies the exercise of discretion by administrators, hopefully in the direction of measuring the efficiency of their operations. Their operating experience should be brought to bear on future program and policy decisions. Moreover, a powerful administrator has his own ideas concerning future policy, and may not willingly accept the views of planners and programmers. He may even have useful ideas to contribute. It is hard to conceive of the three military services carrying out their missions successfully if they had no ideas on national strategy. A central planning organization is unlikely to be successful if it is insulated from operating experience.

Where programming and administration diverge, the way in which the organization as a whole works thus depends largely on the means employed to ensure that administrators in fact carry out programs. The mere announcement of a program, however well conceived, is not enough. The world is full of national planning organizations that have remarkably little influence on powerful departments. The critical factor is the head of the organization. Without his authority and support, departments or bureaus are likely to go their own way. Moreover, programming, as Defense Department experience has shown, can be a potent instrument for increasing the authority of the department head. In fact, some uneasy critics of Defense Department programming allege that that is its main purpose.

Our main concern in the present discussion is the role that the annual budget can play in synchronizing administration with program decisions. The structure of the budget and the financial controls embodied in it can make for harmony and discord. If, for instance, appropriations are made to separate bureaus, as

they used to be, the bureaus acquire a large degree of autonomy and freedom from central control. On the other hand, if they are made to the secretary of a department, and he is free to allocate them at his discretion, he is provided with a powerful instrument of coordination. These matters will be discussed in the next section.

VI. PROGRAMMING AND THE ANNUAL BUDGET

Most governments, as well as other organizations, find it necessary to have an annual, or at most a biennial, budget, even though a coherent program may require projections over a much longer period. Governments are concerned with the immediate impact of their budgets. They may attach importance to a budgetary rule, such as a requirement of budget balance, or they may be concerned with the short-run economic impact of the budget. Furthermore, governments require budgets to be prepared with a degree of detail that would be meaningless if extended over a number of years. Although much has been done since 1950 to eliminate irrelevant detail from the budget, effective administration still requires an impressive amount of it. Thus the budget is to be distinguished from a program with respect both to its detail and its time horizon. The need for greater detail also means that it should be prepared by methods that differ from, but are consistent with, those used in programming.

Budget Preparation and Consideration

If programs are reviewed annually in the manner we have proposed, the annual budget process would result in a more detailed and precise estimate of the costs of the first year of the continually updated program.

The traditional method of preparing the annual budget has been to begin with initial requests from organization units in terms of their objects of expenditure. In some cases this operation has broken down under its own weight. In defense, for instance, budget preparation is in fact largely centralized, even though all installations go through the motions of the traditional method. In other and simpler situations, where there is no conflict between programs and organization, budget and program preparation can be part of the same operation.

In general, budgeting should be associated both with the programming process and with the traditional organization unit method. For the program itself to be realized it must be supported by the financial controls of the budgetary process. On the other hand, the methods of cost estimation by factors that are necessary for a central operation are not precise enough for the preparation of administrative budgets. Factors cannot be satisfactorily used to provide precise estimates of requirements for personnel, office supplies, foreign travel and the like. Moreover, commitment to factors such as those implied by military tables of organization tend to prevent improvements in organization. On the other hand, they may prevent Parkinsonian expansion.

One possibility would be to use centralized methods to arrive at a first approximation to the budget on a program basis. Tentative allocations among organization units could then be made. They would then submit their detailed budgets in the form of revisions to the initial allocations. These revisions would then form the basis of a second approximation to the budget submitted by the department to the President and by him to the Congress.

A more radical departure from traditional budget practice would be to rely entirely on centralized methods for the preparation of the President's budget. This would mean that both the President and the Congress would have to consider the budget in programmatic terms, through lack of any other kind of information.

After the budget was enacted by Congress, the various bureaus would then submit their budgets as part of a separate administrative budget process. This would be an internal affair whereby the Secretary of the department arrived at a final allocation of funds.

This suggestion is not as radical as it sounds. Already, in the Department of Defense, money is allocated after enactment of appropriations through an internal funding program. This is necessary because the detailed estimates that go into the budget have already become out of date one year later, when the budget goes into operation.

Objection would be raised, however, that elimination of detail from the budget would deprive the Congress and the Budget Bureau of an opportunity to review matters such as personnel which have always been one of its main preoccupations. The answer to this objection is that the Congress could still require full reporting by organization units. They could review performance after the fact, and the impressions made by this review would naturally influence attitudes towards appropriation ratios for the future. In fact, appropriation hearings now are as much concerned with review after the fact as with consideration of next year's estimates. Progress in the direction we suggest is not out of the question.

Appropriations should, in general, be made for major programs and perhaps some of their major subdivisions, and within programs separate appropriations would probably be desirable for research and development, construction, major procurement, and for current operations. Those for current operations could be made for obligation within the financial year. For long-lead items, however, longerterm funding would be necessary in order to facilitate effective programming. However, in fluid situations, where the program structure is and should be subject to change, a more stable appropriation structure may be desirable. The Department of Defense retains its old appropriations side by side with its new program system. Whether this should be a transitional or a permanent arrangement remains to be seen.

Fund Allocation: Consumer Budgeting

Designation of appropriations for such purposes, however, does not settle the question of how the funds are allocated within a department. There can be no question but that appropriations should be made to the Secretary of the department and that he should have considerable freedom to transfer funds among closely related activities. Where programs cut across departmental lines they can be made either to the head of the major department concerned, or to the President.

The need for freedom to transfer has already been recognized. Before World War II there were more than 2000 separate appropriation items in the Federal Budget. By the Act of 1950, the President was given authority to simplify the budget, and consequently by 1955 the number of items for the whole government had been reduced to 375, implying a great increase of freedom to transfer among activities. Agreement to this change represents recognition by Congress that it cannot achieve economy by highly specific appropriations. Rather it must rely on considerable discretion of administrators to achieving economy in a time sense, by attempting to allocate funds in order to achieve efficiency.

The question that is still unsettled is how funds should be allocated within departments. Here there are two broad alternatives: consumer allocation and supplier allocation. With consumer allocation the final user of the goods gets the money initially and he "purchases" from the supplier. The supplier gets money only for working capital and long-run capital purposes. With supplier allocation, the supplier gets all the money, but is required to supply on requisition to the user—without a financial transaction taking place. With the first system the commander of a fleet would get the money and he would purchase from the Naval supplying bureaus. Under the present system the money is allocated to the bureaus and they supply ships, men, guns, and ammunition to the fleets.

Commanders of fleets and armies, in time of war, have more important concerns than finance. But in other areas, including many defense activities, the principle of consumer allocation has important advantages. It gives the ultimate user some freedom to choose among alternatives, and, hence, to economize. He also has a financial opportunity to influence the type of product supplied to him. While he is not allowed to make a personal profit, he has some of the incentives of a private business man.

Supplier allocation, on the other hand, tends to neglect questions of cost-effectiveness and, hence, encourages inefficiency. In the absence of compelling reasons to the contrary, such as those already noted, the consumer principle is generally preferable.

Applying that principle means that funds should be allocated initially to the directors of final programs. They should purchase from organization units or from the directors of intermediate programs. Funds provided directly to the latter would be for capital purposes.

With such a system, financial controls could help in implementing program decisions, and in achieving coordination in the face of the inevitable divergences between the organizational structure and the programming structure.

Obligations and Expenditures

Annual budgeting has always involved a dilemma. The principal concern of those concerned with fiscal policy has been the total level of expenditures, which in conjunction with the yield of taxation leads to surpluses, deficits, or budget balance. Yet the primary instrument of control available to the government has been the granting of obligational authority, or appropriations. An appropriation gives an administrator authority to incur obligations either by the letting of formal contracts, or by making more informal commitments to spend money.

Especially where procurement is concerned, expenditures made in any year result largely from earlier obligations and from still earlier grants of obligational authority. Similarly, obligational authority granted this year may only result in expenditures in future years. Consequently, efforts by the President or the Congress to regulate annual expenditures are frequently frustrated because control actions are not taken long enough in advance. Or else those efforts must be concentrated on those obligations that do result in expenditures in the very near future.

Program budgeting could assist annual budgeting by giving a time profile of the government's activities. Ideally, programs should be prepared for a number of years in advance in terms of the obligational authority to be requested, the obligations to be incurred and the expenditures to be made in each of the future years. In these circumstances, future expenditures could be foreseen and a more firm basis for control would exist.

Some critics of the present budgetary process have urged that attention should be focused on still another concept: costs incurred during the year rather than on cash expenditures. Such costs would emphasize resources consumed during the year—e.g., equipment spares and spare parts used in a maintenance activity, regardless of the year in which they were procured. Thus, account would be taken of beginning and year-end inventories. Costs incurred may give a clearer picture of program progress than do expenditures. On the other hand, cash expenditures may be more relevant for fiscal policy. Choice between these concepts is of secondary importance, however, compared with the need to relate them to prior obligations and appropriations.

Concluding Comments

The effectiveness of the programming-budget system will depend strongly on the staff arrangements made to carry it out. The first point to emphasize is that the entire operation must be the personal responsibility of the executive head of the organization. No one at a lower level has the authority or the right or the ability to acquire the knowledge required to perform the necessary tasks of coordination. This point was explicitly and emphatically recognized with respect to the President in the Budget and Accounting Act of 1921. The Budget Bureau has no authority except as a presidential staff agency. To underline the point, the Budget Director is not subject to Senate confirmation, and as a further indication of his staff position he was provided with a lower salary than befitted his importance.

Similarly at the departmental level, the Secretary must be responsible for both programs and budgets, for the same reasons.

The second point to stress is that programming, budgeting, and review after the fact are separate but highly interrelated operations. Programming is concerned with policy objectives, long-range projections and analytic methods that go far beyond the scope of traditional budgetary procedures. Programming, however, may remain merely a useful academic exercise unless it is implemented through the budget, which should provide an essential link between policy and administration. Finally, both programming and budgeting depend in essential ways on the information that can only be obtained through perceptive reviews of past performance, which require the exercise of analytic skills that go far beyond usual concepts of government accounting.

A conceptual framework for program budgeting will not in itself achieve the desired results. The objectives can only be achieved through the exercise of a wide variety of human skills of the highest caliber.

READING 18

PROGRAM BUDGETING AND THE SPACE PROGRAM *

Murray L. Weidenbaum

The implementation of the Planning-Programming-Budgeting System (PPBS) by all major Federal Government agencies presents both important opportunities and major problems to the Nation's space program. The first part of this paper describes the main features of the PPBS effort. The second part analyzes possible applications to and impacts on space activities.

THE PLANNING-PROGRAMMING-BUDGETING SYSTEM [1]

Economists have long been interested in identifying policies that would promote economic welfare by improving the efficiency with which a society uses its resources, particularly in the public sector. For many years, the Corps of Engineers and the Bureau of

° *Reprinted from Walter R. Johnson (ed.),* The Management of Aerospace Programs, *vol. 12 of the American Astronautical Society Science and Technology Series, 1967. With permission of the author and the American Astronautical Society.*

Reclamation have applied benefit/cost analysis to evaluate prospective projects. Despite important difficulties, such as choosing an appropriate discount rate which would correspond to a realistic estimate of the social cost of capital, the use of benefit/cost analysis has improved the allocation of government resources. It has served as a partial screening device to eliminate obviously uneconomical projects—those whose prospective gains are less than estimated costs. Perhaps the overriding value has been to demonstrate the possibility of making objective analyses of essentially political actions, thus narrowing the area in which political forces operate.

A related development has been the application of cost/effectiveness analysis to military budget decision-making. For military programs, ordinarily the benefits or results cannot be expressed in dollars terms. However, the end objective, such as the capability to destroy X number of enemy targets under stipulated conditions, can be expressed in quantitative terms. Hence, the alternative ways of achieving the objective—Y bombers versus Z missiles or some combination—can be priced out and a least-cost solution arrived at.

This latter approach has been at the heart of the Planning-Programming-Budgeting System introduced in the Pentagon. It clearly has been the success of the Pentagon approach which has led to adoption of a government-wide PPBS effort. A fundamental shift has occurred in military resource allocation methods. Previously, each service competed for a larger share of the defense budget and, within the service totals, strategic weapons such as ICBM's competed for funds with tactical programs. Under the new system, close substitutes for performing the same or similar missions are compared with each other, although different services may be involved.

In August 1965, President Lyndon Johnson required each large Federal agency to set up a PPBS activity. Through this combination of planning and budgeting, it was hoped that broad national goals would be identified, specific government programs related to them, and the most economical method of carrying them out arrived at. Four major steps are being taken to accomplish this rather tall order.

Identifying national goals.   The specific goals which are deemed appropriate for the Federal Government to be seeking will be selected, in the light of a comprehensive evaluation of national needs and objectives.

Relating broad goals to specific programs. Specific alternative programs which may help to achieve the broad national goals and objectives will then be examined. The ones that appear to be most promising, given the various constraints under which the government operates, will have to be selected. Many government agencies have little discretion in selecting the optimum combination of programs which can assist in achieving broad national goals in their area of operations. They often find vague or conflicting congressional guidance on goals but clear and precise legislative directive as to which specific programs—and in what amounts—are to be conducted. The task here may be to infer the goals from the specific programs and then develop new or improved means of achieving these goals.

Relating programs to resource requirements. Specific costs of alternative programs will then

need to be estimated, in order to compare their efficiency in achieving the goals. To those acquainted with benefit/cost or cost/effectiveness analysis, this will be no minor achievement in many elusive program areas.

Relating the resource inputs to budget dollars.   Finally, the manpower facilities, and other resource requirements will need to be translated into budget dollars, so that decisions can be made to implement the PPBS plan through the budget process.

The main product of PPBS is designed to be a comprehensive multi-year Program and Financial Plan for each government agency, which will be updated periodically and systematically. This Plan will show projected outlays for each major program area of an agency or department. Hence, determining the output-oriented categories is an important step.

Many difficulties are involved in measuring the output of a government program. Conceptually, only the end-product should be measured rather than intermediate outputs. For example, in the post office, the end product might be the number of letters delivered, and not the number of times these letters were handled at the various post offices.

Similarly, in the case of hospital programs it might be possible to look at output in terms of patient-days. However, the mission of a hospital might be described better as proper treatment of patients. Within a broad framework, the mission of a health program might be viewed as maintenance of good health and the output measure might reflect days of good health rather than incidents of illness.

The Federal agencies are encouraged to consider comparisons and possible trade-offs among program elements which are close substitutes, even though the activities may be conducted in different agencies. This is an attempt to introduce some competition among programs and hopefully to achieve greater effectiveness from budgetary outlays.

Table 18-1 is a hypothetical sketch of this new approach. Transportation is a good example of a major program category which consists of a variety of activities in different departments, with little attention to gaps or overlapping functions or conflicting objectives.

The major agencies involved are the Department of Commerce (Bureau of Public Roads and the Maritime Administration), the Federal Aviation Agency, the Department of

TABLE 18-1   ILLUSTRATIVE OUTLINE OF A NATIONAL TRANSPORATION PROGRAM

Elements	Fiscal Years
	1967, 1968, 1969, 1970, 1971, 1972

General Inter-City Transport

Interstate Highways
  Interstate Highway Program
  Primary System Highways

Domestic Water Transport
  Inland Waterways Facilities
  Maritime Programs

Aviation
  CAB Subsidies to Airlines
  FAA and NASA Aircraft Technology

Urban Commuter Transportation
  Urban Highway Systems
  Urban Transit Systems

Rural Access
  Secondary System-Roads
  Forest, Public Lands, National Parks Roads
  Aid to Local Service Aviation

Military Standby Transportation

the Army (Corps of Engineers, civil functions), the Department of Agriculture (Forest Service), The Department of the Interior (National Park Service), the Treasury Department (the Coast Guard), the Department of Housing and Urban Development (mass transit assistance program), and regulatory agencies, such as the ICC, CAB, and Federal Maritime Board. Significantly, only a few of these agencies are scheduled to be absorbed by the proposed Federal Department of Transportation.

Table 18-2 illustrates the possible specific elements which might comprise one of the

TABLE 18-2   ELEMENTS OF A TRANSPORTATION PROGRAM CATEGORY: URBAN COMMUTER TRANSPORTATION

Urban highways
Passenger-miles carried
Ton-miles of freight carried
Number of miles of way completed
Number of miles of way placed under construction

Urban transit systems
Passenger-miles carried
Number of passenger miles carried
Number of miles of way completed
Number of miles of way placed under construction

From the above information, some comparisons might be made between urban highways and urban transit systems in terms of:
  1. Capital cost per mile of way.
  2. Operating cost per mile of way.
  3. Average commuter travel time per mile of way.

transportation subcategories, urban commuter transportation. These elements may vary from the number of miles of way placed under construction (a measure of capital investment) to the number of passenger-miles carried (a measure of output). Tables 18-1 and 18-2 are indicative of the broader horizons of the new breed of governmental budgeteers and represent an initial step along a relatively new path in governmental resource allocation.

IMPACTS OF PPBS ON THE SPACE PROGRAM

The formal transition to PPBS should be relatively straightforward for the major space agencies. Both the Department of Defense and NASA already develop their budget proposals around programs and specific systems. Certainly the task would seem to be less formidable than for agencies in such elusive areas as justice, social welfare, and beautification. For example, a basic program breakdown of NASA outlays already is contained in the Budget document and can be developed into a rudimentary program budget (see Table 18-3).

Identifying national space goals.   Nevertheless, the complete adaptation of the PPBS mechanism and concepts might create or highlight important policy problems for the space program. It might be helpful to return to each of the four major steps of PPBS described earlier. The first step is "identifying national goals." Two basic and quite different approaches have been suggested for identifying the goals relevant to the space program.

The first approach is that of the recent report of the Senate Committee on Aeronautical and Space Sciences[2] which, although dealing with aeronautics, may be almost equally relevant. The Committee states that "national aeronautical goals (for our purposes, we may substitute 'astronautical goals') support, and interact with, a group of more general goals." Four so-called more general goals are identified: national transportation goals, national defense goals, social and economic development goals, and international relations and prestige goals. From this point of view, space exploration would be considered essentially as an intermediate good, a step toward achieving other, more fundamental goals.

The second approach to identifying national space goals is that of the National Planning Association contained in a recent study by Leonard Lecht.[3] In identifying the major American goals and objectives, Lecht lists space research along with national defense, consumer living standards, and other fundamental needs of our society. He states that, "There is general agreement in the United States that a sustained space research program is an important and continuing national objective" (p. 277).

That these are two different approaches to space goal-setting may be seen by reference to some of the fundamental questions involved in budgeting for space programs. For example, are Project Apollo and the develop-

TABLE 18-3   RUDIMENTARY PROGRAM BUDGET FOR NASA IN FISCAL YEAR 1967 (IN MILLIONS)

Activity (Budget Plan)	Appropriation Categories			
	Research and Development	Construction of Facilities	Administrative Operations	Total
Manned space flight	$3,024	$54	$310	$3,387
Scientific investigations in space	530	6	69	605
Space applications	88	—	13	101
Space technology	248	11	192	451
Aircraft technology	33	21	50	104
Supporting activities	325	9	30	364
Total	$4,248	$101	$664	$5,012

Source: Derived from materials in *Budget of the United States Government for the Fiscal Year Ending June 30, 1967*, Washington, U.S. Government Printing Office, 1966, pp. 867, 870, and 872.

ment of a supersonic transport alternative means of achieving a similar goal—successful scientific competition with the communist nations? According to the Senate approach, it would appear that this would be a sensible tradeoff, and that the two programs are to some degree substitutes. Under the NPA approach, this would not be the case. A manned lunar landing would be considered basic to space research while the SST would be treated together with other transportation programs.

However somewhat different results may be obtained in attempting to answer the question: on what basis should space funds be allocated to DoD or NASA? Under our variant of the Senate approach these would not be viewed as substitutable items. Military space programs would be considered to be part of a national defense goal while NASA programs would be related to one or more civilian national goals. Conversely, under the NPA approach both DoD and NASA could be viewed as, at least in some cases, alternative instruments for performing space research and development.

Clearly, the proper identification of the national goals which each Federal agency's programs are designed to serve is fundamental to the effective application of PPBS. Without doing so, the process can readily degenerate into routine filling out of tedious forms. Although the matter of goal-setting is essentially subjective, the present writer opts for the NPA approach to the space program, that it has become an important national objective. On that basis, it may be useful to proceed to the next PPBS steps.

Relating broad space goals to specific space programs. As Margolis and Barro have pointed out, a set of mission categories that is useful in practice must be based on well-defined characteristics of projects at a lower level of abstraction than "ultimate objectives" or "national goals." They call for an "end-product" rather than "end-objective" set of categories, having the following characteristics:

1 They should group projects that are functionally related in an operationally well-defined sense. This might be according to type of payload or region of space in which they operate.
2 They should separate projects that serve distinct concrete objectives. For example,

projects that provide economic benefits or military capabilities should be separated from purely scientific efforts.
3 They should reflect the space program as currently constituted and projected but should be flexible enough to allow for growth in program scope and variety of subjects.[4]

It should be recognized that there may be fundamental limitations to as well as advantages of the Margolis-Barro approach. Their "end-product" categories do provide a method of budget allocations on a program basis which is rather operationally simple and clear cut. However, it hardly is a format for making the key decisions about the scope and structure of the space program. Rather, it requires that these broad "political" decisions already have been made, so that the PPBS technicians can go about their job of precisely costing out launching schedules and tracking facilities requirements.

Indeed, they state that "the whole question of 'space program goals' has been discussed at too vague and abstract a level to be relevant to the program bugeting process, and it has been obscured by public controversies over the wisdom of undertaking particular space missions" (p. 133). In view of the pioneering nature of the Margolis-Barro effort to develop a space program budget, we should be charitable in belaboring their shortcomings. However, it is somewhat disappointing to see the technician lamenting that his chore of choosing between 80% and 85% learning curves is obscured because the nation has not clearly determined that the overall mission is worth undertaking at all.

On a technical basis, the space program may appear to be readily adaptable to PPBS. Witness the ease with which the standard budget materials were able to be converted into at least a rudimentary space program budget (Table 18-3). However, on a substantive basis, it appears that such program budget materials do not throw up the basic policy alternatives for the space program which is at the heart of the PPBS approach—the choice among alternative programs for achieving a given mission. It is only on the basis of alternative choices that benefit/cost or cost/effectiveness analyses can be made to assist the policy makers in their decision-making.

It may be recalled that for the transportation area, the hypothetical program analysis presented choices among modes—air, water, and land—and between systems—highways and mass transit for the urban commuter function (see Tables 18-1 and 18-2). Despite greater sophistication in the important area of cost methodology, available program analyses for space activities do not present such basic choices, but assume that they already have been made. It is the contention of the present writer that following this less ambitious route will result in PPBS degenerating into a low-level accounting operation. Indeed, the desire to fill out the formats neatly should not take priority over the fundamental need to improve the allocation of government resources among alternative uses. Although any first attempts inevitably will be crude, it is suggested that program budgeting for space activities throw up alternatives such as the following:

1 Continuation of the current effort at a manned lunar landing by 1970.
2 A slow-down in the manned lunar program and an expansion in unmanned planetary exploration, both within the same budget total as (1).
3 A slow-down in the manned lunar landing and an expansion in efforts to utilize the fruits of space technology on earth, both within the same budget total as (1).
4 Continuation of the current effort at a manned lunar landing by 1970 and beginning a major effort at exploring Mars, thus raising the space budget substantially above (1), particularly in later years.
5 Continuation of the current manned lunar landing program and a substantial expansion of NASA's aeronautical R&D with the aim of expanding the use of commercial aircraft in short-haul markets and by personal rather than primarily business travelers. This alternative might require levels of budgetary support at various ranges between (1) and (4).

Undoubtedly the above questions require more precise formulation and in some cases detailed development of missions which have been stated too broadly. However, they are designed to indicate the types of basic choices which should not be ignored in the Planning-Programming-Budgeting System but which are the fundamental reason for establishing the detailed budgetary procedures and forms.

Relating space programs to resource requirements.   Given the identification of the specific programs which could help to achieve broad national space goals, the problem of estimating resource requirements would seem to be a less formidable one. Here, the path-breaking work of the Rand Cost Analysis Department[5] reduces this formidable task to relatively manageable proportions. However, important technical problems do arise.

As Margolis and Barro point out, the interdependence among space activities makes it difficult to compute the true incremental cost of carrying out an individual project. It follows from the principle of the learning curve that the cost of hardware items procured for a particular project depends not only on the number of units required by that project but also on the number required by all projects using those particular items. If a project is eliminated and, hence, the demand for a particular hardware item reduced, then the unit cost of the item increases to all other projects that require it concurrently or at a later date.[6]

To further complicate estimating the requirements of space programs, it should be noted that major space vehicle systems and ground installations are often used in many different flight projects. Items that are most likely to have multiple uses—boosters, propulsion systems, launch facilities, tracking networks—have tended to be expensive relative to items that are peculiar to individual projects.[7] No single method among the many suggested for dealing with this problem is really satisfactory. The present procedure whereby such items are segregated into separate categories appears to be as reasonable as any.

The fundamental problem to be encountered at this step of the process perhaps is the fact that, as in the case of defense activities, so much of the results of the space program cannot be expressed in dollar terms. Hence, benefit/cost analyses cannot be made. To some degree, we must be content with relying on Leonard Lecht's conclusion that "The space effort involves the incurring of large expenditures in the present or near future for benefits at a more remote future date which, at best, can be very imperfectly foreseen . . . the unanticipated consequences are likely to exceed in importance those which can be anticipated in advance."[8]

Again relying on the experience of military analysts, cost/effectiveness studies can be utilized at this step of the space PPBS process to identify the least cost alternatives to achieving already-identified space goals.

Relating the space resource inputs to budget dollars.   In a sense, this last step may seem to be a backward taking one. After identifying the total system resource inputs, PPBS now requires that they be reduced to the common and crude denominator of budget dollars. Upon reflection, it can be seen that this is an essential step of the entire process. Supposedly or hopefully the basic program decisions have been made in the context of a complete analysis of the entire system being considered, including its costs and benefits to the nation as a whole as well as to the Federal Treasury.[9] However, for the *results* of the PPBS analysis to become operationally useful in terms of government budget-making and expenditure allocation, they must be incorporated into the formal budget submissions in the customary manner.

Indeed, this may be the fundamental double contribution of PPBS: to make possible the implementation of long-range planning through the budget process, thus giving practical application to the planning and analysis effort and improving the intellectual content of budget-making.

CONCLUSION

By raising fundamental questions concerning the alternative uses of the Federal Government's funds and resources and by providing some concepts and methodology for answering them, the Planning-Programming-Budgeting System is an important attempt both to sharpen the government's budgetary preparation and review process. Perhaps more funda-mental, it ultimately—if carried out in spirit as well as in letter—will increase the benefits achieved by the Nation from its public investments and outlays.

References

1. For a more detailed treatment, see M. L. Weidenbaum, "Program Budgeting: Applying Economic Analysis to Government Expenditure Decisions," *University of Missouri Business and Government Review*, Vol. VII, No. 4, July-August 1966, pp. 22–31.

2. U.S. Senate, Committee on Aeronautical and Space Sciences, *Policy Planning for Aeronautical Research and Development*, Washington, U.S. Government Printing Office, 1966.

3. Leonard A. Lecht, *Goals, Priorities, and Dollars*, New York, Free Press, 1966.

4. Milton A. Margolis and Stephen M. Barro, "The Space Program" in David Novick, editor, *Program Budgeting, Program Analysis and the Federal Budget*, Cambridge, Harvard University Press, 1965, pp. 133–135.

5. Cf. Harold Asher, *Cost-Quantity Relationships in the Airframe Industry*, Santa Monica, Rand Corporation, July 1956; David Novick, *Weapon-System Cost Methodology*, Santa Monica, Rand Corporation, February 1956; David Novick, *System and Total Force Cost Analysis*, Santa Monica, Rand Corporation, April 1961.

6. Margolis and Barro, *op. cit.*, pp. 128–129. The procedure described by Margolis-Barro raises the question of marginal versus average cost pricing. If the canceled project were the marginal recipient and marginal cost pricing were used, there would be no effect on the projects that were higher up on the curve (to the left on a negative sloping improvement curve). However, under an average cost pricing system, the effects would be as they indicate.

7. *Ibid.*, p. 129.

8. Lecht, *op. cit.*, p. 285.

9. Such externalities are dealt with at length in the pertinent economic literature. See the sources cited in (1).

SECTION 5

SYSTEMS ANALYSIS

Systems analysis is the name which has been popularized by Department of Defense analysts for the application of scientific methodology and economic models to the analysis of strategic decision problems. The areas of study called operations research *and* management science *are so closely allied with systems analysis that, although formal distinctions are made between the fields in particular organizations, the exercise involved in making the distinctions is unlikely to be worth the effort.*

Systems analysis involves the evaluation and comparison of alternative ways of achieving objectives on the basis of the resource costs and the benefits associated with each alternative. Critical to this process is the use of models, abstractions of the real world, which can be analyzed in lieu of experimentation in the real world. Through the use of models, the best alternative can be determined, and if the model is a good one, the best alternative as determined from the model will indicate an action in the real world which is a "good" one (if it is not "the" best of all those which are available).

The similarities among the fields variously called systems analysis *and* operations research *are more important than are the differences. However similar are the concepts, the practical differences which have evolved serve to place the role of each in proper focus. First, systems analysis usually is more concerned with the* invention *of new alternatives than is operations research. Many operations researchers have confined themselves to problems involving the comparison of a prescribed set of alternatives whereas systems analysts have set out to develop new ones. Of course, the level of rigor involved in the determination of the "best" alternative is therefore usually lower in the latter case than in the former, but the possibility of finding alternatives which are radically different from and superior to those obvious ones is also greatly enhanced.*

Another practical difference between the fields lies in the nature of the problems which have been attacked. Systems analysts have tended to concentrate on higher-level "ill-structured" problems in which objectives are less precisely defined and less sophisticated analysis is possible. Although all decision-problem analysis relies heavily on the use of human judgment, systems analysts have perhaps made greater use of judgment than have operations researchers.

Systems analysis is an intrinsic part of the Federal government's planning, programming, and budgeting system. Moreover, some variety of formal analysis is a necessary part of the fulfillment of any manager's planning function.

READING 19

SYSTEMS ANALYSIS TECHNIQUES FOR PLANNING-PROGRAMMING-BUDGETING *

E. S. Quade

INTRODUCTION

Broadly speaking, any orderly analytic study designed to help a decisionmaker identify a preferred course of action from among possible alternatives might be termed a systems analysis. As commonly used in the defense community, the phrase "systems analysis" refers to formal inquiries intended to advise a decisionmaker on the policy choices involved in such matters as weapon development, force posture design, or the determination of strategic objectives. A typical analysis might tackle the question of what might be the possible characteristics of a new strategic bomber and whether one should be developed; whether tactical air wings, carrier task forces, or neither could be substituted for U.S. ground divisions in Europe; or whether we should modify the test ban treaty now that the Chi-

* Reprinted with permission from The RAND Corporation, P-3322, March, 1966, The RAND Corporation, Santa Monica, California.

nese Communists have nuclear weapons and, if so, how. Systems analysis represents an approach to, or way of looking at, complex problems of choice under uncertainty that should have utility in the planning-programming-budgeting (PPB) process. Our purpose is to discuss the question of extending military systems analysis to the civilian activities of the government, to point out some of the limitations of analysis in this role, and to call attention to techniques that seem likely to be particularly useful. I will interpret the term "technique" broadly enough to range from proven mathematical algorithms to certain broad principles that seem to be often associated with successful analysis.

Some fifteen years ago a similar extension raised quite some doubt. When weapons system analysts (particularly those at The RAND Corporation) began to include the formulation of national security policy and strategy as part of their field of interest, experienced "military analysts" in the Pentagon and elsewhere were not encouraging. They held that the tools, techniques, and concepts of operations analysis, as practiced in World War II, or of weapons system optimization and selection—in which analysts had been reasonably successful —would not carry over, that strategy and policy planning were arts and would remain so.

Fortunately, these skeptics were only partially right. It is true that additional concepts and methodologies significantly different from those of earlier analysis had to be developed. But there has been substantial progress, and the years since 1961 have seen a marked increase in the extent to which analyses of policy and strategy have influenced decision-makers on the broadest issues of national defense.

Today's contemplated extension to PPB is long overdue and possibly even more radical. Systems analysis has barely entered the domain of the social sciences. Here, in urban planning, in education, in welfare, and in other nonmilitary activities, as Olaf Helmer remarks in his perceptive essay:

> . . . we are faced with an abundance of challenges: how to keep the peace, how to alleviate the hardships of social change, how to provide food and comfort for the inaffluent, how to improve the social institutions and the values of the affluent, how to cope with revolutionary innovations, and so on.[1]

Since systems analysis represents an approach to, or way of looking at, any problem of choice under uncertainty, it should be able to help with these problems.

Actually, systematic analysis of *routine* operations is widespread throughout the civil government as well as in commerce, industry, and the military. Here analysis takes its most mathematical form—and, in a certain sense, its most fruitful role. For example, it may help to determine how Post Office pick-up trucks should be routed to collect mail from deposit boxes, or whether computers should be rented or purchased to handle warehouse inventories, or what type of all-weather landing system should be installed in new commercial aircraft. Such problems are typically an attempt to increase the efficiency of a man-machine system in a situation where it is clear what "more efficient" means. The analysis can often be reduced to the application of a well-

understood mathematical discipline such as linear programming or queuing theory to a generic "model," which, by a specification of its parameters, can be made to fit a wide variety of operations. An "optimum" solution is then obtained by means of a systematic computational routine. The queuing model, for example, is relevant to many aspects of the operations of the Post Office, airports, service facilities, maintenance shops, and so on. In many instances such models may actually tell the client what his decision or plan ought to be. Analysis of this type is usually called operations research or management science rather than systems analysis, however.

There are, however, other decisions or problems, civilian as well as military, where computational techniques can help only with subproblems. Typical decisions of this latter type might be the determination of how much of the Federal budget should be allocated to economic development and what fraction of that should be spent on South America, or whether the needs of interstate transportation are better served by improved high speed rail transport or by higher performance highway turnpikes, or if there is some legislative action that might end the growth of juvenile delinquency. Such problems will normally involve more than the efficient allocation of resources among alternative uses; they are not "solvable" in the same sense as efficiency problems in which one can maximize some "pay-off" function that clearly expresses what one is trying to accomplish. Here rather, the objectives or goals of the action to be taken must be determined first. Decision problems associated with program budgeting are mainly of this type— where the difficulty lies in deciding what ought to be done as well as in how to do it, where it is not clear what "more efficient" means, and where many of the factors in the problem elude quantification. The final program recommendation will thus remain in part a matter of faith and judgment. Studies to help with these problems are systems analyses rather than operations research.°

Every systems analysis involves, at one stage, a comparison of alternative courses of action in terms of their costs and their effectiveness in attaining a specified objective. Usu-

° *For a further discussion of this distinction, see Reference 2.*

ally this comparison takes the form of an attempt to designate the alternative that will minimize the costs, subject to some fixed performance requirement (something like reduce unemployment to less than 2% in two years or add a certain number of miles to the interstate highway system), or conversely, it is an attempt to maximize some physical measure of performance subject to a budget constraint. Such evaluations are called cost-effectiveness analyses.† Since they often receive the lion's share of attention, the entire study also is frequently called a cost-effectiveness analysis. But this label puts too much emphasis on just one aspect of the decision process. In analyses designed to furnish broad policy advice other facets of the problem are of greater significance than the comparison of alternatives: the specification of sensible objectives, the determination of a satisfactory way to measure performance, the influence of considerations that cannot be quantified, or the design of better alternatives.

THE ESSENCE OF THE METHOD

What is there about the analytic approach that makes it better or more useful than other ways to furnish advice—than, say, an expert or a committee? In areas such as urban redevelopment or welfare planning, where there is no accepted theoretical foundation, advice obtained from experts working individually or as a committee must depend largely on judgment and intuition. *So must the advice from systems analysis.* But the virtue of such analysis is that it permits the judgment and intuition of the experts in relevant fields to be combined systematically and efficiently. The essence of the method is to construct and operate within a "model," a simplified abstraction of the real situation appropriate to the question. Such a model, which may take such varied forms as a computer simulation, an operational game, or even a purely verbal "scenario," introduces a precise structure and terminology that serve primarily as an effective means of communication, enabling the participants in the study to exercise their judgment and intuition in a concrete context and in proper relation to others. Moreover,

† *Or, alternatively, cost-utility and cost-benefit analyses.*

through feedback from the model (the results of computation, the countermoves in the game, or the critique of the scenario), the experts have a chance to revise early judgments and thus arrive at a clearer understanding of the problem and its context, and perhaps of their subject matter.‡

THE PROCESS OF ANALYSIS

The fundamental importance of the model is seen in its relation to the other elements of analysis.§ There are five all told, and each is present in every analysis of choice and should always be explicitly identified.

1   *The objective (or objectives).* Systems analysis is undertaken primarily to help choose a policy or course of action. The first and most important task of the analyst is to discover what the decisionmaker's objectives are (or should be) and then how to measure the extent to which these objectives are, in fact, attained by various choices. This done, strategies, policies, or possible actions can be examined, compared, and recommended on the basis of how well and how cheaply they can accomplish these objectives.

2   *The alternatives.* The alternatives are the means by which it is hoped the objectives can be attained. They may be policies or strategies or specific actions or instrumentalities and they need not be obvious substitutes for each other or perform the same specific function. Thus, education, anti-poverty measures, police protection, and slum clearance may all be alternatives in combating juvenile delinquency.

‡ *C. J. Hitch in Reference 3, p. 23, states "Systems analyses should be looked upon not as the antithesis of judgment but as a framework which permits the judgment of experts in numerous subfields to be utilized—to yield results which transcend any individual judgment. This is its aim and opportunity."*
§ *Olaf Helmer in Reference 1, p. 7, puts it this way: "The advantage of employing a model lies in forcing the analyst to make explicit what elements of a situation he is taking into consideration and in imposing upon him the discipline of clarifying the concepts he is using. The model thus serves the important purpose of establishing unambiguous intersubjective communication about the subject matter at hand. Whatever intrinsic uncertainties may becloud the area of investigation, they are thus less likely to be further compounded by uncertainties due to disparate subjective interpretations."*

3 *The costs.* The choice of a particular alternative for accomplishing the objectives implies that certain specific resources can no longer be used for other purposes. These are the costs. For a future time period, most costs can be measured in money, but their true measure is in terms of the opportunities they preclude. Thus, if the goal is to lower traffic fatalities, the irritation and delay caused to motorists by schemes that lower automobile speed in a particular location must be considered as costs, for such irritation and delay may cause more speeding elsewhere.

4 *A model (or models).* A model is a simplified, stylized representation of the real world that abstracts the cause-and-effect relationships essential to the question studied. The means of representation may range from a set of mathematical equations or a computer program to a purely verbal description of the situation, in which intuition alone is used to predict the consequences of various choices. In systems analysis (or any analysis of choice), the role of the model (or models, for it may be inappropriate or absurd to attempt to incorporate all the aspects of a problem in a single formulation) is to estimate for each alternative the costs that would be incurred and the extent to which the objectives would be attained.

5 *A criterion.* A criterion is a rule or standard by which to rank the alternatives in order of desirability. It provides a means for weighing cost against effectiveness.

The process of analysis takes place in three over-lapping stages. In the first, the formulation stage, the issues are clarified, the extent of the inquiry limited, and the elements identified. In the second, the search stage, information is gathered and alternatives generated. The third stage is evaluation.

To start the process of evaluation or comparison (see Figure 19-1), the various *alternatives* (which may have to be discovered or invented as part of the analysis) are examined by means of the *models.* The models tell us what consequences or outcomes can be expected to follow from each alternative; that is, what the *costs* are and the extent to which each *objective* is attained. A *criterion* can then be used to weigh the costs against performance, and thus the alternatives can be arranged in the order of preference.

Unfortunately, things are seldom tidy: Too often the objectives are multiple, conflicting, and obscure; alternatives are not adequate to attain the objectives; the measures of effectiveness do not really measure the extent to which the objectives are attained; the predictions from the model are full of uncertainties; and other criteria that look almost as plausible as the one chosen may lead to a different order of preference. When this happens, we must take another approach. A single attempt or pass at a problem is seldom enough. (See Figure 19-2.) The key to successful analysis is a continuous cycle of formulating the problem, selecting objectives, designing alternatives, collecting data, building models, weighing cost against performance, testing for sensitivity, questioning assumptions and data, re-examining the objectives, opening new alternatives, building better models, and so on, until satisfaction is obtained or time or money force a cutoff.

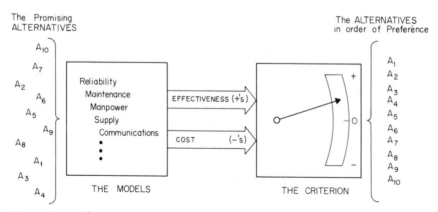

Figure 19-1   The structure of analysis.

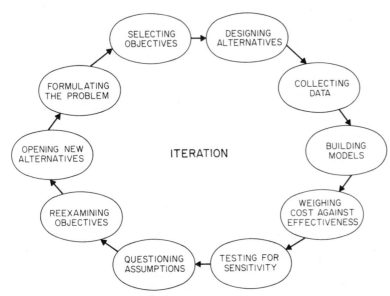

Figure 19-2   The key to analysis.

In brief a systems analysis attempts to look at the entire problem and look at it in its proper context. Characteristically, it will involve a systematic investigation of the decisionmaker's objectives and of the relevant criteria; a comparison—quantitative insofar as possible—of the cost, effectiveness, risk, and timing associated with each alternative policy or strategy for achieving the objectives; and an attempt to design better alternatives and select other goals if those examined are found wanting.

Note that there is nothing really new about the procedures I have just sketched. They have been used, more or less successfully, by managers throughout government and industry since ancient times. The need for considering cost relative to performance must have occurred to the earliest planner. Systems analysis is thus not a catchword to suggest we are doing something new; at most, we are doing something better. What may be novel though, is that this sort of analysis is an attempt to look at the entire problem systematically with emphasis on explicitness, on quantification, and on the recognition of uncertainty. Also novel are the schemes or models used to explore the consequences of various choices and to eliminate inferior action in situations where the relationships cannot be represented adequately by a mathematical model.

Note that there is nothing in these procedures that guarantees the advice from the analysis to be good. They do not preclude the possibility that we are addressing the wrong problem or have allowed our personal biases to bar a better solution from consideration. When a study is a poor one it is rarely because the computer wasn't powerful enough or because the methods of optimization were not sufficiently sophisticated, but because it had the wrong objective or poor criteria. There are some characteristics of a study, however, that seem to be associated with good analysis. Let me identify some of these.

PRINCIPLES OF GOOD ANALYSIS

1 It is all-important to tackle the "right" problem. A large part of the investigators' effort must be invested in thinking about the problem, exploring its proper breadth, and trying to discover the appropriate objectives and to search out good criteria for choice. If we have not chosen the best set of alternatives to compare we will not discover the best solution. But if we have chosen the wrong objective then we might find a solution to the wrong problem. Getting an accurate answer to the wrong question is likely to be far less helpful than an incomplete answer to the right question.

2 The analysis must be systems oriented. Rather than isolating a part of the problem by neglecting its interactions with other

parts, an effort should be made to extend the boundaries of the inquiry as far as required for the problem at hand, to find what interdependencies are important, and to study the entire complex system. This should be done even if it requires the use of purely intuitive judgment.

An interdisciplinary team of persons having a variety of knowledge and skills is helpful here. This is not so merely because a complex problem is likely to involve many diverse factors that cannot be handled by a single discipline. More importantly, a problem looks different to, say, an economist, an engineer, a political scientist, or a professional bureaucrat, and their different approaches may contribute to finding a solution.

3 The presence of uncertainty should be recognized, and an attempt made to take it into account. Most important decisions are fraught with uncertainty. In planning urban redevelopment we are uncertain about city growth patterns, about the extent to which freeways or rapid transit systems will be used, about costs, about tax revenues, about the demand for services. For many of these things, there is no way to say with confidence that a given estimate is correct. The analyst attempts to identify these uncertainties and evaluate their impact. Often he can say the value of a parameter will be more than A but less than B. Sometimes it is possible to indicate how the uncertainty can be reduced by further testing and how long that will take. Most important, the analysis should determine the effect of uncertainty on the answers. This is done by a sensitivity analysis that shows how the answers change in response to changes in assumptions and estimates.*

The study report should include the presentation of a contingency table showing the effectiveness and cost associated with each significant alternative for various future environments and for each set of assumptions about the uncertainties.

4 The analysis attempts to discover new alternatives as well as to improve the obvious ones. The invention of new alternatives can be much more valuable than an exhaustive comparison of given alternatives, none of which may be very satisfactory.

5 While in problems of public policy or national security, the scientific method of controlled repeated experiment cannot be used,

* See, for example, Reference 4, pp. 12–41.

the analysis should strive to attain the standards traditional to science. These are (1) intersubjectivity: results obtained by processes that can be duplicated by others to attain the same results; (2) explicitness; use of calculations, assumptions, data, and judgments that are subject to checking, criticism, and disagreement; and (3) objectivity: conclusions do not depend on personalities, reputations, or vested interests; where possible these conclusions should be in quantitative and experimental terms.

THE MODELS

As mentioned earlier, systems analysis is flexible in the models it uses. Indeed, it has to be. Mathematics and computing machines, while extremely useful, are limited in the aid they can give in broad policy questions. If the important aspects of the problem can be completely formulated mathematically or represented numerically, techniques such as dynamic programming, game theory, queuing theory, or computer simulation may be the means of providing the best solution. But in most policy analyses, computations and computers are often more valuable for the aid they provide to intuition and understanding, rather than for the results they supply.

While a computer can solve only the problems that the analyst knows conceptually how to solve himself, it can help with many others. The objection that one cannot use results which depend on many uncertain parameters represents a lack of understanding of how systems analysis can help a decisionmaker. For a study to be useful it must indicate the *relative* merit of the various alternatives and identify the critical parameters. The great advantage of a computerized model is that it gives the analyst the capability to do numerous excursions, parametric investigations, and sensitivity analyses and thus to investigate the ranking of alternatives under a host of assumptions. This may be of more practical value to the decisionmaker than the ability to say that a given alternative will have such and such a rank with high confidence in a very narrowly defined situation.

The type of model appropriate to a problem depends on the problem and what we know or think we know about it.

For example, suppose we are concerned with long-range economic forecasting or decisions about the development of a national economy. The type of model to use will depend on the particular economy and on the kind of questions that must be answered. If the questions were about the United States, the model might be mathematical and possibly programmed for a computer because of its size and complexity. (By a mathematical model I mean one in which the relationships between the variables and parameters are represented by mathematical equations.) In the case of the United States, because of the vast amount of data available in the form of economic and demographic time series regarding just about every conceivable aspect of economic life, numerous mathematical and computer models have been formulated and used with more or less success.

If we are not able to abstract the situation to a series of equations or a mathematical model, some other way to represent the consequences that follow from particular choices must be found. Simulation may work. Here, instead of describing the situation directly, each element making up the real situation may be simulated by a physical object or, most often, by a digital computer using sets of random numbers, and its behavior analyzed by operating with the representation. For example, we might use computer simulation to study the economy of some Latin American country. The distinction between a computer simulation and the use of a computer to analyze a mathematical model is often a fuzzy one, but the fundamental difference is that in simulation the overall behavior of the model is studied through a case-by-case approach.

For studying the economy of a newly emerging nation such as is found in Africa, where the situation is even more poorly structured and where we have little firm knowledge of existing facts and relationships, a possible approach would be through the direct involvement of experts who have knowledge of the problem.

Ordinarily, we would like to have the judgment of more than one expert, even though their advice usually differs. There are several ways to try for a consensus; the traditional way has been to assemble the experts in one place, to let them discuss the problem freely, and to require that they arrive at a joint answer. They could also be put to work individually, letting others seek methods for the best combined use of their findings. Or they could be asked to work in a group exercise—ranging from a simple structured discussion to a sophisticated simulation or an "operational game"—to obtain judgments from the group as a whole.

This latter approach is a laboratory simulation involving roleplaying by human subjects who simulate real-world decisionmakers. To study the economy of an underdeveloped country the various sectors of the economy might be simulated by specialized experts (see Reference 5). They would be expected, in acting out their roles, not so much to play a competitive game against one another, but to use their intuition as experts to simulate as best they could the attitudes and consequent decisions of their real-life counterparts. For instance, a player simulating a goods producing sector of the economy might, within constraints, shut down or expand manufacturing facilities, modernize, change raw material and labor inputs, vary prices and so on. There would also need to be government players who could introduce new fiscal or monetary policies and regulations (taxes, subsidies, tariffs, price ceilings, etc.) as well as social and political innovations with only indirect economic implications (social security, education, appeals to patriotism, universal military service, etc.) In laying down the rules governing the players' options and constraints and the actions taken within these rules, expert judgment is essential. It is also clear that for this problem political and sociological experts will be needed, as well as economists.

There is, of course, no guarantee that the projections obtained from such a model would be reliable. But the participating experts might gain a great deal of insight. Here the game structure—again a model—furnishes the participants with an artificial, simulated environment within which they can jointly and simultaneously experiment, acquiring through feedback the insights necessary to make successful predictions within the gaming context and thus indirectly about the real world.

Another useful technique is one that military systems analysts call "scenario writing." This is an effort to show how, starting with the present, a future state might evolve out of the present one. The idea is to show how this might happen plausibly by exhibiting a reasonable chain of events. A scenario is thus a primitive model. A collection of scenarios provides an insight on how future trends can depend on factors under our control and suggests policy options to us.

Another type of group action, somewhat less structured than the operational game, attempts to improve the panel or committee approach by subjecting the views of individual experts to each other's criticism without actual confrontation and its possible psychological shortcomings. In this approach, called the Delphi method, direct debate is replaced by the interchange of information and opinion through a carefully designed sequence of questionnaires. At each successive interrogation, the participants are given new refined information, and opinion feedback is derived by computing consensus from the earlier part of the program. The process continues until either a consensus is reached, or the conflicting views are documented fully (see References 6 and 7).

It should be emphasized that in many important problems it is not possible to build really quantitative models. The primary function of a model is "explanatory," to organize our thinking. As I have already stated, the essence of systems analysis is not mathematical techniques or procedures, and its recommendations need not follow from computation. What counts is the effort to compare alternatives systematically, in quantitative terms when possible, using a logical sequence of steps that can be retraced and verified by others.

THE VIRTUES

In spite of many limitations, the decisionmakers who have made use of systems analysis find it extremely useful. In fact, for some questions of national defense, analysis is essential. Without calculation there is no way to discover how many missiles may be needed to destroy a target system, or how arms control may affect security. It may be essential in areas also; one cannot experiment radically with the national economy or even change the traffic patterns in a large city without running

the risk of chaos. Analysis offers an alternative to "muddling through" or to settling national problems by yielding to the strongest pressure group. It forces the devotees of a program to make explicit their lines of argument and talk about the resources their programs will require as well as the advantages they might produce.

It is easy, unfortunately, to exaggerate the degree of assistance that systems analysis can offer the policymaker. At most, it can help him understand the relevant alternatives and the key interactions by providing an estimate of the costs, risks, payoffs and the timespan associated with each course of action. It may lead him to consider new and better alternatives. It may sharpen the decisionmaker's intuition and will certainly broaden his basis for judgment, thus helping him make a better decision. But value judgments, imprecise knowledge, intuitive estimates, and uncertainties about nature and the actions of others mean that a study can do little more than assess some of the implications of choosing one alternative over another. In practically no case, therefore, should the decisionmaker expect the analysis to demonstrate that, beyond all reasonable doubt, a particular course of action is best.

THE LIMITATIONS

Every systems analysis has defects. Some of these are limitations inherent in all analysis of choice. Others are a consequence of the difficulties and complexities of the question. Still others are blunders or errors in thinking, which hopefully will disappear as we learn to do better and more complete analyses.

The alternatives to analysis also have their defects. One alternative is pure intuition. This is in no sense analytic, since no effort is made to structure the problem or to establish cause-and-effect relationships and operate on them to arrive at a solution. The intuitive process is to learn everything possible about the problem, to "live with it," and to let the subconscious provide the solution.

Between pure intuition, on one hand, and systems analysis, on the other, other sources of advice can, in a sense, be considered to employ analysis, although ordinarily a less systematic, explicit, and quantitative kind. One

Jamestown
Classic Collection by Ajax

4075 TISSUE HOLDER (recessed)

IF THERE IS A WOOD MOUNTING BLOCK IN WALL

1. Place tissue holder in 5¼" square wall opening.
2. Use tissue holder as a template to mark screw hole location on wood block in wall.
3. Drill two 1/8" pilot holes in wood block.
4. Place holder in opening and fasten with screws provided.

IF THERE IS NOT A WOOD BLOCK IN WALL

1. Purchase hanger bracket from your hardware dealer. (Be sure to take tissue holder with you for proper fitting)
2. Place hanger bracket into wall opening so that spring is pressing against opposite wall. Spring pressure holds the bracket in place. Center the bracket both vertically and horizontally as shown.
3. Place holder in opening and insert screws (included). Screws engage slots in hanger bracket. Tighten screws.

Mounting Screws Included.

To clean, use a damp cloth with mild soap. Do not use abrasive cleaners as this may permanently damage the finish.

Made and printed in U.S.A.

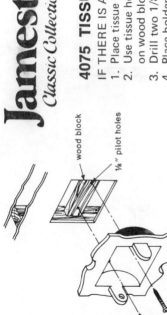

wood block

1/8" pilot holes

hanger bracket with spring

slots in hanger bracket

can turn to an expert. His opinion may, in fact, be very helpful if it results from a reasonable and impartial examination of the facts, with due allowance for uncertainty, and if his assumptions and chain of logic are made *explicit*. Only then can others use his information to form their own considered opinions. But an expert, particularly an unbiased expert, may be hard to find.

Another way to handle a problem is to turn it over to a committee. Committees, however, are much less likely than experts to make their reasoning explicit, since their findings are usually obtained by bargaining. This is not to imply that a look by a "blue ribbon" committee into such problems as poverty or the allocation of funds for foreign aid might not be useful, but a committee's greatest utility is likely to be in the critique of analysis done by others.

However, no matter whether the advice is supplied by an expert, a committee, or a formal study group, the analysis of a problem of choice involves the same five elements and basic structure we discussed earlier.

It is important to remember that all policy analysis falls short of being scientific research. No matter how we strive to maintain standards of scientific inquiry or how closely we attempt to follow scientific methods, we cannot turn systems analysis into science. Such analysis is designed primarily to recommend—or at least to suggest—a course of action, rather than merely to understand and predict. Like engineering, the aim is to use the results of science to do things well and cheaply. Yet, when applied to national problems, the difference from ordinary engineering is apparent in the enormous responsibility involved in the unusual difficulty of appraising—or even discovering—a value system applicable to the problems, and in the absence of ways to test the validity of the analysis.

Except for this inability to verify, systems analysis may still look like a purely rational approach to decisionmaking, a coldly objective, scientific method free from preconceived ideas and partisan bias and judgment and intuition.

It isn't, really. Judgment and intuition are used in designing the models; in deciding what alternatives to consider, what factors are relevant, what the interrelations between these factors are, and what criteria to choose; and in interpreting the results of the analysis. This fact—that judgment and intuition permeate all analysis—should be remembered when we examine the apparently precise results that seem to come with such high precision analysis.

Many flaws are the results of pitfalls faced by the analyst. It is all too easy for him to begin to believe his own assumptions and to attach undue significance to his calculations, especially if they involve bitter arguments and extended computations. The most dangerous pitfall or source of defects is an unconscious adherence to a "party line." This is frequently caused by a cherished belief or an *attention bias*. All organizations foster one to some extent; RAND, the military services, and the civilian agencies of the government are no exception. The party line is "the most important single reason for the tremendous miscalculations that are made in foreseeing and preparing for technical advances or changes in the strategic situation" (Reference 7). Examples are plentiful: the political advisor whose aim is so fixed on maintaining peace that he completely disregards what might happen should deterrence fail; the weaponeer who is so fascinated by the startling new weapons that he has invented that he assumes the politician will allow them to be used; the union leader whose attention is so fixed on current employment that he rejects an automatic device that can spread his craft into scores of new areas. In fact, this failure to realize the vital interdependence among political purpose, diplomacy, military posture, economics, and technical feasibility is the typical flaw in most practitioners' approach to national security analysis.

There are also pitfalls for the bureaucrat who commissions a study or gives inputs to it. For instance, he may specify assumptions and limit the problem arbitrarily. When a problem is first observed in one part of an organization, there is a tendency to seek a solution completely contained in that part. An administrator is thus likely to pose his problems in such a way as to bar from consideration alternatives or criteria that do not fit into his idea of the way things should be done; for example, he may not think of using ships for some tasks now being done by aircraft. Also, to act wisely on the basis of someone else's analysis one should, at the very least, understand the important and fundamental principles involved. One danger associated with analysis is that it may be employed by an administrator who is unaware of or unwilling to accept its limitations.

Pitfalls are one thing, but the inherent limitations of analysis itself are another. These limitations confine analysis to an advisory role. Three are commented on here: analysis is necessarily incomplete; measures of effectiveness are inevitably approximate; and ways to predict the future are lacking.

Analysis Is Necessarily Incomplete

Time and money costs obviously place sharp limits on how far any inquiry can be carried. The very fact that time moves on means that a correct choice at a given time may soon be outdated by events and that goals set down at the start may not be final. The need for reporting almost always forces a cutoff. Time considerations are particularly important in military analysis, for the decisionmaker can wait only so long for an answer. Other costs are important here, too. For instance, we would like to find out what the Chinese Communists would do if we put an end to all military aid to Southeast Asia. One way to get this information would be to stop such aid. But while this would clearly be cheap in immediate dollar costs, the likelihood of other later costs precludes this type of investigation.

Still more important, however, is the general fact that, even with no limitations of time and money, analysis can never treat all the considerations that may be relevant. Some are too intangible—for example, how some unilateral U.S. action will affect NATO solidarity, or whether Congress will accept economies that disrupt cherished institutions such as the National Guard or radically change the pattern of domestic military spending. Considerations of this type should play as important a role in the recommendation of alternative policies as any idealized cost-effectiveness calculations. But ways to measure these considerations even approximately do not exist today, and they must be handled intuitively. Other immeasurable considerations involve moral judgments—for example, whether national security is better served by an increase in the budget for defense or for welfare, or under what circumstances the preservation of an im-

mediate advantage is worth the compromise of fundamental principles. The analyst can apply his and others' judgment and intuition to these considerations, thus making them part of the study; but *bringing them to the attention of the decisionmaker*, the man with the responsibility, is extremely important.

Measures of Effectiveness Are Approximate

In military comparisons measures of effectiveness are at best reasonably satisfactory approximations for indicating the attainment of such vaguely defined objectives as deterrence or victory. Sometimes the best that can be done is to find measures that point in the right direction. Consider deterrence, for instance. It exists only in the mind—and in the enemy's mind at that. We cannot, therefore, measure the effectiveness of alternatives we hope will lead to deterrence by some scale of deterrence, but must use instead such approximations as the potential mortalities that we might inflict or the roof cover we might destroy. Consequently, even if a comparison of two systems indicated that one could inflict 50 per cent more casualties on the enemy than the other, we could not conclude that this means the system supplies 50 per cent more deterrence. In fact, since in some circumstances it may be important *not* to look too dangerous, we encounter arguments that the system threatening the greatest number of casualties may provide the *least* deterrence!

Similarly, consider the objective of U.S. government expenditures for health. A usual measure of effectiveness is the dollar value of increased labor force participation. But, this is clearly inadequate; medical services are more often in demand because of a desire to reduce the every day aches and pains of life. Moreover, we cannot be very confident about the accuracy of our estimates. For example, one recent and authoritative source estimates the yearly cost of cancer to the United States at $11 billion, while another, equally authoritative, estimates $2.6 billion (Reference 8).

No Satisfactory Way to Predict the Future Exists

While it is possible to forecast events in the sense of mapping out possible futures, there is no satisfactory way to predict a single future for which we can work out the best system or determine an optimum policy. Consequently, we must consider a range of possible futures or contingencies. In any one of these we may be able to designate a preferred course of action, but we have no way to determine such action for the entire range of possibilities. We can design a force structure for a particular war in a particular place, but we have no way to work out a structure that is good for the entire spectrum of future wars in all the places they may occur.

Consequently, defense planning is rich in the kind of analysis that tells what damage could be done to the United States given a particular enemy force structure; but it is poor in the kinds of analyses that evaluate how we will actually stand in relation to the Soviets in years to come.

In spite of these limitations, it is not sensible to formulate policy or action without careful consideration of whatever relevant numbers can be discovered. In current Department of Defense practice quantitative estimates of various kinds are used extensively. Many people, however, are vaguely uneasy about the particular way these estimates are made and their increasingly important role not only in military planning but elsewhere throughout the government.

Some skepticism may be justified, for the analytical work may not always be done competently or used with its limitations in mind. There may indeed be some dangers in relying on systems analysis, or on any similar approach to broad decisions. For one thing, since many factors fundamental to problems of Federal policy are not readily amenable to quantitative treatment, they may possibly be neglected, or deliberately set aside for later consideration and then forgotten, or improperly weighed in the analysis itself or in the decision based on such analysis. For another, a study may, on the surface, appear so scientific and quantitative that it may be assigned a validity not justified by the many subjective judgments involved. In other words, we may be so mesmerized by the beauty and precision of the numbers that we overlook the simplifications made to achieve this precision, neglect analysis of the qualitative factors, and overemphasize the importance of idealized calculations in the decision process. But without analysis we face even greater dangers in neglect of considera-tions and in the assignment of improper weights!

THE FUTURE

And finally, what of the future? Resistance by the military to the use of systems analysis in broad problems of strategy has gradually broken down. Both government and military planning and strategy have always involved more art than science; what is happening is that the art form is changing from an ad hoc, seat-of-the-pants approach based on intuition to one based on analysis *supported by* intuition and experience. This change may come more slowly in the nonmilitary aspects of government. For one thing, the civilian employees of the government are not so closely controlled "from the top" as those in the military; also the goals in these areas are just as vague and even more likely to be conflicting.* The re-

---

* James R. Schlesinger in Reference 2 has a slightly different view: "Thus the mere uncovering of ways to increase efficiency is not sufficient. Even where a decision is clear to the disinterested observer, it is difficult to persuade committed men that their programs or activities should be reduced or abandoned. The price of enthusiasm is that those who have a commitment will be "sold" on their specialty and are incapable of viewing it in cold analytical terms. This may be especially true of the military establishment, where the concepts of duty, honor, and country when particularized lead to a certain inflexibility in adjusting to technological change and the new claims of efficiency. But it is also true in the civilian world: for conservationists, foresters, water resource specialists, businessmen, union leaders, or agrarians, some aspects of their value-systems run directly counter to the claims of efficiency. The economic view strikes them all as immoral as well as misleading. (After all, is it not a value judgment on the part of economists that efficiency calculations are important?)

"Even in the case of fairly low-level decisions, if they are political, systematic quantitative analysis does not necessarily solve problems. It will not convince ardent supporters that their program is submarginal. Nevertheless, quantitative analysis remains most useful. For certain operational decisions, it either provides the decisionmaker with the justification he may desire for cutting off a project or forces him to come up with a nonnumerical rationalization. It eliminates the purely subjective approach on the part of devotees of a program and forces them to change their lines of argument. They must talk about reality rather than morality. Operational research creates a bridge to budgetary problems over which planners, who previously could assume resources were free, are forced, willingly or unwillingly, to walk."

quirements of the integrated Planning-Programming-Budgeting system will do much to speed the acceptance of analysis for other tasks, however.

With the acceptance of analysis, the computer is becoming increasingly significant—as an automaton, a process controller, an information processor, and a decision aid. Its usefulness in serving these ends can be expected to grow. But at the same time, it is important to note that even the best computer is no more than a tool to expedite analysis. Even in the narrowest decisions, considerations not subject to any sort of quantitative analysis can always be present. Big decisions, therefore, cannot be the *automatic* consequence of a computer program or of any application of mathematical models.

For broad studies, intuitive, subjective, even ad hoc study schemes must continue to be used—but supplemented to an increasing extent by systems analysis. The ingredients of this analysis must include not only an increasing use of computer-based models for those problems where they are appropriate, but for treatment of the nonquantifiable aspects, a greater use of techniques for better employment of judgment, intuition, and experience. These techniques—operational gaming, "scenario" writing, and the systematic interrogation of experts—are on the way to becoming an integral part of systems analysis.

CONCLUDING REMARKS

And now to review. A systems analysis is an analytic study designed to help a decision-maker identify a preferred choice among possible alternatives. It is characterized by a systematic and rational approach, with assumptions made explicit, objectives and criteria clearly defined, and alternative courses of action compared in the light of their possible consequences. An effort is made to use quantitative methods, but computers are not essential. What is essential is a model that enables expert intuition and judgment to be applied efficiently. The method provides its answer by processes that are accessible to critical examination, capable of duplication by others, and, more or less, readily modified as new information becomes available. And, in contrast to other aids to decisionmaking, which share the same limitations, it extracts everything possible from scientific methods, and therefore its virtues are the virtues of those methods. At its narrowest, systems analysis has offered a way to choose the numerical quantities related to a weapon system so that they are logically consistent with each other, with an assumed objective, and with the calculator's expectation of the future. At its broadest, through providing the analytic backup for the plans, programs, and budgets of the various executive departments and establishments of the Federal Government, it can help guide national policy. But, even within the Department of Defense, its capabilities have yet to be fully exploited.

References

1. Helmer, O., *Social Technology*, The RAND Corporation, P-3063, February 1965; presented at the Futuribles Conference in Paris, April 1965.

2. Schlesinger, J. R., "Quantitative Analysis and National Security," *World Politics*, Vol. XV, No. 2, January 1963, pp. 295–315.

3. Quade, E. S., (ed.), *Analysis for Military Decisions*, Rand McNally, Chicago, 1964.

4. Fort, Donald M., *Systems Analysis as an Aid in Air Transportation Planning*, The RAND Corporation, P-3293, January 1966.

5. Helmer, O., and E. S. Quade, "An Approach to the Study of a Developing Economy by Operational Gaming," in *Researche Operationale et Problems du Tiers-Monde*, Dunod, Paris, 1964, pp. 43–54.

6. Helmer, O., and Norman C. Dalkey, "An Experimental Application of the Delphi Method to the Use of Experts," *Management Sciences*, Vol. 9, No. 3, April 1963, pp. 458–467.

7. Helmer, O., and Nicholas Rescher, "On the Epistemology of the Inexact Sciences," *Management Sciences*, Vol. 6, No. 1, October 1959, pp. 25–52.

8. Kahn, H., and I. Mann, *Ten Common Pitfalls*, The RAND Corporation, RM-1937, July 17, 1957.

9. Marshall, A. W., *Cost/Benefit Analysis in Health*, The RAND Corporation, P-3274, December 1965.

10. McKean, R. N., *Efficiency in Government Through Systems Analysis*, John Wiley & Sons, Inc., New York, 1958.

11. Hitch, C. J., and R. N. McKean, *The Economics of Defense in the Nuclear Age*, Harvard University Press, Cambridge, Massachusetts, 1960.

12. Peck, M. J., and F. M. Scherer, *The Weapons Acquisition Process: An Economic Analysis,* Harvard University Press, Cambridge, Massachusetts, 1962.

13. Ellis, J. W., Jr., and T. E. Greene, "The Contextual Study: A Structured Approach to the Study of Limited War," *Operations Research,* Vol. 8, No. 5, September-October 1960, pp. 639–651.

14. Novick, D., (ed.), *Program Budgeting: Program Analysis and the Federal Budget,* Government Printing Office, Washington, D.C., 1965; and Harvard University Press, Cambridge, Massachusetts, 1965.

15. Mood, Alex M., "Diversification of Operations Research," *Operations Research,* Vol. 13, No. 2, March-April 1965, pp. 169–178.

16. Dorfman, Robert, (ed.), *Measuring Benefits of Government Investments,* The Brookings Institute, 1965.

17. Fisher, G. H., *The World of Program Budgeting,* The RAND Corporation, P-3361, May 1966.

READING 20

THE ANALYTICAL BASES OF SYSTEMS ANALYSIS*

G. H. Fisher

INTRODUCTION

My assigned topic is "The Analytical Bases of Systems Analysis." This subject may be approached from several points of view. The usual one, I suppose, is to translate "analytical bases" into "tools and techniques," and then to proceed to talk about linear programming, Monte Carlo techniques, computer simulation models, and the like. Since a lot has already been written and said on these subjects, I prefer to take a different tack.

I want to focus on a discussion of the role of analysis in the decisionmaking process. This is important because different people in the analytical community have differing views on the matter and depending on which view is held, one can arrive at various alternative conclusions regarding the conceptual and procedural bases for analysis in support of the deci-

* Reprinted with permission of The RAND Corporation, P-3363, May, 1966, The RAND Corporation, Santa Monica, California.

sion process. Let me say at the onset that my views are probably somewhat controversial, and that no doubt many attendees at this symposium will tend to take issue with some of my arguments. This, however, should help stimulate lively discussion!

Let me also emphasize at this point that my remarks are focused primarily on a *long-range-planning military decision context;* but hopefully many of the points made will have more general applicability.

WHAT IS SYSTEMS ANALYSIS?

Before launching into a discussion of the role of systems analysis in the long-range-planning process, I think I had best take a few moments to tell you what the term "systems analysis" means to me. This seems necessary because the term itself apparently has various meanings today; and also there are *other* terms which are sometimes used as being synonomous with systems analysis: e.g., cost-effectiveness analysis, cost-benefit analysis, operations analysis, and the like. Now I do not want to get tangled up in a semantics jungle here. So let me just say that in the context of my talk, systems analysis is an analytical process having the following major characteristics:

1 A most fundamental characteristic is the systematic examination and comparison of alternative courses of action which might be taken to achieve specified objectives for some future time period. Not only is it important to systematically examine all of the relevant alternatives that can be identified initially, but also to *design additional ones if those examined are found wanting.*[1] Finally, the analysis, particularly if thoroughly and imaginatively done, may frequently result in modifications of the initially specified objectives.
2 Critical examination of alternatives typically involves numerous considerations; but the two main ones are assessment of the cost (in the sense of economic resource cost) and the utility (the benefits or gains) pertaining to each of the alternatives being compared to attain the stipulated objectives.
3 The time context is the future—often the distant future (five, ten, or more years).
4 Because of the extended time horizon, the environment is one of uncertainty—very often great uncertainty. Since uncertainty is an important facet of the problem, it should be faced up to and treated explicitly in the analysis. This means, among other things, that wherever possible the analyst should avoid the exclusive use of simple expected value models.
5 Usually the context in which the analysis takes place is fairly broad (often very broad) and the environment very complex with numerous interactions among the key variables in the problem. This means that simple, straightforward solutions are the exception rather than the rule.
6 While quantitative methods of analysis should be utilized as much as possible, because of items (4) and (5),[2] purely quantitative work must often be heavily supplemented by qualitative analysis. In fact, I stress the importance of *good* qualitative work and of using an appropriate combination of quantitative and qualitative methods.

7 Usually the focus is on research and development and/or investment type decision problems, although operational decisions are sometimes encountered. This does not mean, of course, that operational considerations are ignored in dealing with R&D and investment type problems.

THE ROLE OF SYSTEMS ANALYSIS IN THE LONG-RANGE-PLANNING DECISION PROCESS

Given this general conception of systems analysis, let me now turn to a discussion of the role of analysis in the long-range planning-decision process.

I suppose, as analysts, we would always like to try to come up with "preferred solutions" when studying alternative future courses of action. Ideally this means determining *"the optimum"*—that is, the point on some well-defined surface where all the partial derivatives are equal to zero and the appropriate second order conditions prevail. I submit, however, that in most of today's long-range-planning decision problems of any consequence, it is rarely possible to even approach anything like a hard core optimization. Most likely we will be lucky if we can get some notion as to the *signs* of the partial derivatives—i.e., whether we are moving "up the hill," so to speak, toward the saddle point in a maximization problem, or away from the saddle point ("down hill"). In fact, I would even argue that in most studies that I have worked on in recent years, it is often difficult to determine what "hill" we are on, or should be on! This rather crude analogy begins to convey the flavor of my thoughts on the role of analysis in the long-range decision process. Let me now be more specific.

Here I shall take as a text for my remarks the following statements by the Assistant Secretary of Defense, Systems Analysis:

> Ultimately all policies are made . . . on the basis of judgments. There is no other way, and there never will be. The question is whether those judgments have to be made in the fog of inadequate and inaccurate data, unclear and undefined issues, and a welter of conflicting personal opinions, or whether they can be made on the basis of adequate, reliable

[1] E. S. *Quade*, Military Systems Analysis, *The RAND Corporation, RM-3452-PR, January 1963, p. 1.*
[2] *And also because of inadequate data and information sources.*

2 of these positions
— zero analysis
— quantitative

information, relevant experience, and clearly drawn issues. In the end, analysis is but an aid to judgment . . . . Judgment is supreme.[3]

The analyst at this level is not computing optimum solutions or making decisions. In fact, computation is not his most important contribution. And he is helping someone else to make decisions. His job is to ask and find answers to the questions: "What are we trying to do?" "What are the alternative ways of achieving it?" "What would they cost, and how effective would they be?" "What does the decisionmaker need to know in order to make a choice?" And to collect and organize this information for those who are responsible for deciding what the Defense program ought to be.[4]

The Assistant Secretary's remarks pretty much reflect my own views on the subject. I would put the argument in the following manner:

Contrary to what some of the more enthusiastic advocates of quantitative analysis may think, I tend to visualize systems analysis as playing a somewhat modest, though very significant, role in the overall decisionmaking process. In reality most major long-range-planning decision problems must ultimately be resolved primarily on the basis of intuition and judgment. I suggest that the main role of analysis should be to try to *sharpen* this intuition and judgment. In practically no case should it be assumed that the results of the analysis will "make" the decision. The really critical problems are just too difficult, and there are too many intangible (e.g., political, psychological, and sociological) considerations that cannot be taken into account in the analytical process, especially in a quantitative sense. In sum, the analytical process should be directed toward assisting the decisionmaker in such a way that his intuition and judgment are better than they would be without the results of the analysis.

We might say that there are two extreme positions regarding the role of analysis in the decisionmaking process. On the one hand, one might argue that the types of long-range-planning decision problems under consideration here are just too complex for the current state of analytical art to handle. Decisions must be made purely on the basis of intuition, judgment, and experience; i.e., the zero analysis position. At the other extreme are those who tend to think that all problems should be tackled in a purely quantitative fashion, with a view to essentially "making" the decision. Such a view implies explicit (usually meaning quantitative) calculations of cost and utility for all the alternatives under consideration. This may be possible, at times, for very narrowly defined, low level sub-optimization problems; but even this is questionable.

More generally, in dealing with major decision problems of choice, if the analyst approaches the analytical task in an inflexible "hard core" frame of mind, he is likely to be in for trouble. For example, he may soon give up in complete frustration, he may wind up with such a simplified model that the resulting calculations are essentially meaningless, or the result might be that his conclusions are presented two years after the critical time of decision and therefore useless to the decisionmaker.

My viewpoint is that in most cases the relevant range is between the extremes mentioned above, and that in such a context there is a wide scope of analytical effort that can be useful. Furthermore, even when only a relatively incomplete set of quantitative calculations of cost and utility can be made (probably the general situation), much can be done to assist the decisionmaker in the sense that I am using the term assistance. To repeat: The objective is to *sharpen* intuition and judgment. It is conceivable that only a small amount of sharpening may on occasion have a high payoff.

One other point seems relevant here. In that rare circumstance when a fairly complete set of calculations of cost and utility is possible and a resulting conclusion about a preferred alternative reached, it just may be that the conclusion itself may not be the most useful thing to the decisionmaker. In the first place, as pointed out earlier, the analysis usually cannot take everything into account—particularly some of the nebulous non-quantitative considerations. The decisionmaker has to allow for

[3] *A. C. Enthoven, quotation contained in an article in* Business Week, *November 13, 1965, p. 189.*
[4] *A. C. Enthoven, article in* The Armed Forces Comptroller, *Vol. IX, No. 1, March 1964, p. 39.*

these himself. But more important, most high-level decisionmakers are very busy men, with the result that they do not have time to structure a particular problem, think up the relevant alternatives (especially the *subtle* ones), trace out the key interaction among variables in the problem, and the like. This the analyst, if he is competent, can do, and should do. And it is precisely this sort of contribution that may be most useful to the decisionmaker. The fact that the analysis reaches a firm conclusion about a preferred alternative may in many instances be of secondary importance.

WHY IS OPTIMIZATION SO DIFFICULT?

At this point you may well ask the question: "Why is hard core optimization so difficult for the class of decision problems under consideration here?" Part of the answer, of course, is that in dealing with long-range-planning problems major uncertainties are always present; and the theory of choice under conditions of uncertainty does not always give us a definite set of rules to follow. Should we use expected values and ignore variances? Should we take variances into account; and if so, how? Should we use a minimax rule? And so on.

Another part of the answer concerns the basic nature of the decision questions themselves—their complexity and the scenario dependency of assumptions that must be made to formulate and to deal with the questions. Let me illustrate this point by referring to an area where in the past some of us thought that something approaching optimization might be attained. (We could have been wrong, of course; and I suspect we were!) I have in mind the general war problem area.

In the past—and still to a large extent today—general war decision problems have been formulated in terms of a "spasm response" scenario; and analyses of these problems have for the most part been conducted in that context. Spasm response involves a fairly mechanistic set of considerations. One side lets go with all (or a major part) of his strategic forces, and the other side retaliates in kind. Many of the major facets of this problem can be modeled, and numerous sets of quantitative results can be calculated—and have been calculated. Now I do not suppose any of us would argue that

we have ever attained "hard core" optimization in dealing with the spasm response case. There are still major uncertainties involved. But I do think some of us thought we were moving in that direction.

Now let us see what happens when we move away from the spasm response case (today usually called the pure *assured destruction* case) and begin to consider other strategies and scenarios. While not at all underplaying the importance of having an assured-destruction deterrent capability, many people today feel that in addition, other concepts of general war involving *controlled response* capability should be seriously considered. The main idea here is that in future time periods it might be desirable, even mandatory, that the national leaders have a wider range of options available to use in dealing with crisis situations—that is, a wider range than that available from a force mix tailored primarily to the notion of spasm response. Examples of these other options may be summarized under headings like:

1 Damage limiting capability.
2 Coercion and bargaining capabilities to be used in an escalation process stemming from a crisis situation.
3 Intrawar deterrence of countervalue exchanges.
4 War termination.

In addition, we have the problem of the proliferation of nuclear weapons in the future—the "N-country" problem—and the question of what this means for the future force posture of the United States.

Now I obviously cannot get into a detailed discussion of these topics here. Each is a complex subject in itself. But the main point I am trying to make is, I think, clear. Once controlled response strategies and scenarios are taken into consideration, the analytical problems increase astronomically when compared with the spasm response case. The uncertainties compound, scenario dependencies abound, a force mix that might seem preferred in one case might not look so good in another, non-quantifiable variables (e.g., political and psychological factors) are just very important, and the like. In sum, any notion of anything approaching hard core optimization goes out the window; and we begin to wonder whether classical systems analysis can contribute very much in dealing with problems of this kind.

Perhaps something can be done in the way of very low level suboptimizations for small pieces of the total problem. And some of this may be useful to a limited extent. But the long-range force planners have to grapple with the general war *force mix* problem (including force size) for future time periods; and the real question is whether analysis of *some kind* can sharpen the intuition and judgment of the decisionmakers in this complicated area.

I think the answer is probably "yes," but I confess that at this time I cannot be specific as to how analysis might help. At RAND we have just recently launched a major study of the whole question of controlled response in general war. Initially we shall probably experiment with various combinations of the more conventional methods, including war gaming (manual), war game simulations, classical systems analysis, and the like. Here we recognize that any one method alone will not do the job, and we also realize that the political scientists will have to provide a substantial input, particularly in the form of a menu of rich scenarios of various controlled response environments. Our main goal, of course, is to try to come up with some *new* concepts, methods and techniques of analysis, as well as to say something substantive about the complicated issues involved. We may fail, of course; but we think it is very important to give the problem a good try.

Let us turn now to a different problem area: the question of the mobility of the general purpose forces. Here again is a case where one might, at first glance, think that something approaching a reasonably good optimization might be possible. I haven't time to even outline all of the issues involved in this problem. So I shall discuss a few of them (staying within the bounds of an unclassified discussion) to illustrate my point.

Until recently most studies tended to focus on the "big lift" part of the total problem—that is, the intercontinental transportation question. The central issue here, of course, is the preferred mix of airlift, sealift, and prepositioned supplies and equipment. Some very good work has been done in this area, and I think something fairly close to good *sub*optimizations has been attained. However, when one

begins to think more deeply about the *total* problem—the problem the force planners have to grapple with—then questions begin to arise.

Two key factors in the big lift problem are: (1) the high cost of airlift vs. sealift and prepositioning; and (2) the payoff in terms of *very* rapid response time available from force mixes containing a relatively high proportion of expensive airlift capability. So the question of the value of very rapid response is a dominant consideration. However, if one wants to get serious about delving into the matter of quick response, it is immediately obvious that the boundaries of the original problem have to be broadened. Total response time is made up of intra-Z.I. mobility and intra-theater (or objectives area) mobility in addition to the big lift. And there are *interactions among all three*. So we have to look at the total before we know what kind of a response we really have for various alternatives. Here the problem begins to get very complicated. For example, when the intra-objectives area is added to the analysis, things get particularly messy. The ground battle cannot be ignored, nor can the questions of re-deployment and resupply. Furthermore, the final outcomes are just *very scenario dependent*.

Although I have barely scratched the surface, I think I have said enough to illustrate my point: that hard core analysis of the mobility problem facing the long-term planners is very difficult—particularly in an optimization sense. Does this mean that all the study effort expended in this area to date is worthless to the decisionmakers? I think nothing could be further from the truth. Recently, some very interesting work has been done on the intra-theater (or objectives area) mobility problem, to supplement the studies already done in the big lift area. While no over-all "preferred solutions" have been forthcoming, these studies have provided major insights into the key variables involved, some of the more important interrelationships among the variables, the sensitivity of results to variations in key parameters and assumptions, and the like. As a result, I feel that the decisionmakers have a much better basis for their judgments regarding future mobility force mixes than they would have had without the studies. But in my view, this is the real value of analysis. That is my main point.

WHAT CAN BE DONE?

If you agree with even half of what I have said up to this point, you may wonder about whether systems analysis can contribute very much to the long-range planning process in the area of national security—or any other realm, for that matter. Perhaps systems analysts had best apply for job re-training and transfer to other occupations!

I do not think such a conclusion is warranted. Given the appropriate view regarding the role of analysis in the planning decision process, I think that the analyst can pull his own weight many times over in assisting the decisionmakers to sharpen their intuition and judgment. Let me try to illustrate my point by offering some simple examples.

For these examples, I have deliberately chosen "sticky" (but not atypical) problem areas. I have also deliberately chosen what some people might call fairly "low level" examples of analytical work in these problem areas. Actually, I think that in many cases, much more in the way of analysis can in fact be done than is indicated in any illustrations. However, I want to try to make an *a fortiori*

argument, so to speak. If I can show that relatively simple type analyses can be useful, then I shall be well on the way toward demonstrating my point without having to resort to arguments based on more sophisticated forms of analytical effort. Another point is relevant here. In most fast-moving decision environments, the analyst is quite often called on to try to do something useful in a relatively short period of time. Usually this means that he does not have time to structure and carry out a complicated, complete analysis of the problem. He will have to settle for much less if he is to have any impact at all on the decision process.

For a change of pace, let us start out with an example outside the national security area. Suppose that we are concerned with deciding among alternative proposed water resources projects, and that we have a given budget to spend on such projects in the future. The budget is such that all of the proposed projects cannot be undertaken. We therefore want to choose the "preferred mix." Suppose further that we have an analytical staff and that it comes up with a summary of results of systems analyses of the problem in the following format:

TABLE 20-1

	Proposed Projects				
Analytical Factor	1	2	3	4 ... n	

(1) Present worth[a] ($):
    (a) Discounted @ $2\frac{1}{2}\%$ (50 yr)
    (b) Discounted @ 5% (50 yr)
    (c) Discounted @ 8% (50 yr)
(2) Possible variability of outcome:
    (a) "Most likely" range of present worth (low-high $)
    (b) Range of present worth outside of which outcome is "very unlikely" to fall
(3) Effect on personal wealth distribution:
    (a) Number of farms affected
    (b) Average value of land and buildings per farm in the watershed ($)
    (c) Average net benefit per farm owner ($)
(4) Effect on regional wealth distribution:
    (a) Average increase in per family income in the Basin ($)
    (b) Percentage increase in average income in the Basin due to project
(5) Internal rate of return of project (%)[b]

[a] Present value of estimated benefits minus present value of estimated costs.
[b] The rate of discount which reduces present worth to zero.

Assume that in addition to the quantitative data presented in the table, the analytical staff has supplemented the numerical calculations with *qualitative* discussion of some of the more relevant nonquantifiable issues involved in the decision: e.g., political factors, non-quantifiable "spillover" effects, and the like.

Now decision problems regarding alternative water resources projects are usually very complex. The analyst can rarely come up with a preferred solution—particularly in the sense that one mix of alternatives completely dominates all others. I submit, however, that even in such a context, analytical results of the type portrayed above can go a long way toward sharpening the intuition and judgment of the decisionmakers. I think you will all agree that in the above illustrative case, the decisionmakers would be better off if they had the results of the analytical effort than if they did not have such information. Their decision is likely to be a more informed one.

Let me now turn briefly to another example to illustrate a somewhat different point. Actually, I want to show two things with this example: (1) how wrong conclusions can be drawn from a systems analysis—particularly in the face of uncertainty; and (2) how the results of the same study can be interpreted differently, and how the second interpretation can be of assistance to the decisionmakers.

I have in mind here the results and conclusions of a study that was actually performed by one of the military departments in the Department of Defense and submitted to the Secretary of Defense and his staff. We need not get into the substantive national security issues involved in the study to illustrate the methodological points that I want to emphasize.

The structure of the analysis was an equal cost comparison of several alternative future courses of action; that is, for a specified budget level to be devoted to a particular military mission area, the alternatives were compared on the basis of their estimated effectiveness in accomplishing the stipulated task. The final quantitative results took the following form.

The stated conclusion of the study, based almost exclusively on these quantitative results, was that alternative C is preferred over A and B for a wide range of circumstances and contingencies. (The context of the study, I should point out, involved a time period some

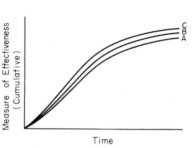

Figure 20-1   Comparison of equal cost alternatives.

10 to 15 years into the future.) Yet the difference in estimated effectiveness of the alternatives (for a constant budget level) was *at most* 15 percent! Now my point is simply that the context of the problem was clouded by so many uncertainties and the model used in the analysis was so aggregative, that calculated differences among the alternatives averaging less than 15 percent *just cannot be regarded as significant.* Thus, the stated conclusions of the study, if taken literally, could in a real sense be misleading to the decisionmakers.[5] In decision problems of this type where uncertainties are very great, the analyst is generally looking for much larger differences among the alternatives being examined. How great? There is no general rule. However, I can say that in the past when experienced analysts have been dealing with problems of this type, differences in the neighborhood of a *factor* or 2 or 3 have been sought. I personally feel that in most long-range planning problems where major uncertainties are present, quantitative differences among alternatives must be *at least a factor of two* before we can even begin to have any confidence that the differences are significant. In any event, when they are smaller than that, the analyst must exercise extra caution in interpreting the results, and he must not make statements that are likely to mislead the decisionmakers.

There is another side to the coin, however. When quantitative differences among alternatives fall within a relatively narrow range, does this mean that the study is of no use to the decisionmaker? Not necessarily. If the

---

[5] *Needless to say, the Secretary of Defense and his analytical staff were not misled in this case. They are too experienced in interpreting the results of analytical studies to be overly impressed by small differences.*

quantitative work has been carried out in a reasonably competent manner and the differences among alternatives do tend to be relatively small, this fact in itself can be of considerable interest to the decisionmaker. This is especially true if sensitivity analyses have been made showing that as key parameters in the problem are varied over their relevant ranges, the final results are still within relatively narrow ranges. Given results of this kind, the decisionmaker can be less concerned about making a mistake regarding the quantitative aspects of the problems, and he may then feel somewhat more comfortable about focusing more of his attention on the *qualitative* factors —political, psychological, sociological considerations. In fact, if the analyst has done a reasonably thorough job, he might include a discussion of these factors in a qualitative supplementation to the purely quantitative part of the study.

The main point here is that while one of the main goals of analysis is to search for "pre-ferred alternatives" characterized by quantitative results *significantly* different (better) from other alternatives, the fact that a strong case cannot be made for a preferred alternative does not mean that the study is worthless. The results, and the sensitivity analysts supporting the results, can still be very enlightening to the decisionmaker. And again I emphasize that this is the main purpose of analysis.

As a final example, let us consider a military decision environment where the analyst is called upon to come up with something in a relatively short period of time in a rather complex problem area. The question is what can be done, if anything? If we take the position that the objective is to provide something that will help sharpen the decisionmakers' intuition and judgment, I think a great deal can be done. Something far short of a type of analysis involving a relatively complete set of calculations of utility and cost may be very useful. For one thing, a mere enumeration of all the relevant alternatives may be very helpful. If

TABLE 20-2   SELECTED DATA BEARING ON UTILITY CONSIDERATIONS FOR ALTERNATIVE SYSTEMS A, B, C, D AND E

	Alternative System				
Description	A	B	C	D	E
Quantitative Information					
Effective range (n mi)					
Cruise speed (kn)					
Penetration speed (kn)					
Warhead yield (MT)					
Circular error probability (CEP)					
Single-shot-kill probability					
Against soft targets					
Against hard targets					
Extended strike option time (days)					
etc.					
Qualitative Information[a]					
"Show of force" capability					
Multi-directional attack capability					
Ground vulnerability					
In-flight vulnerability					
Controlled response capability					
etc.					

[a] Some of these items have quantitative aspects to them; but they are very difficult to assess in a study with a short time deadline.

the analyst can go beyond this and furnish data and information bearing on utility and cost of these alternatives, so much the better.

One thing that can be done is to develop summary analyses of cost and utility and present them along with a qualitative statement of some of the key implications. Examples are contained in Figure 20-2 and Table 20-2.

Figure 20-2 shows total system cost (research and development, investment, and operating cost[6]) vs. force size for several alternative systems. Here some of the alternatives are ground-based missile systems, others are airborne-alert, long-endurance-aircraft systems, with the aircraft serving as missile-launching platforms. In the case of the missile systems, force size means number of missiles in position ready to go. For the aircraft platform systems, force size means number of missiles continuously airborne on station ready to go.

Used in conjunction with data pertaining to utility (as in Table 20-2), system cost vs. force size curves can be useful. For example, suppose that alternatives A and C are in the same ball park with respect to certain key utility variables—say, penetration capability and single-shot kill probability—but that C is clearly more vulnerable to an initial enemy strike than is A. The difference in the system cost curves for A and C in Figure 20-2, then, essentially represents what we pay for getting reduced vulnerability. But there are other ways

to play this game. Suppose the decisionmaker has a given budget (B_0 in Figure 20-2) to spend for supplementation of the already planned strategic forces. For B_0 he can get a force size of F_1 for alternative A, or a much larger force (F_2) of system C. He may judge that the larger force of C may more than compensate for its higher vulnerability. Or he may decide that F_2 of C is roughly equivalent to F_1 of A and decide to go for C for other (qualitative) reasons: e.g., C may have more of a show-of-force capability than A, or be preferable from a controlled response point of view.

In any event, *the decisionmaker is clearly in a better position to sharpen his intuition and judgment if he has the benefit of Figure 20-2 and Table 20-2 than if he did not have them.*[7] This is an illustration example of what was meant earlier when I indicated that there are numerous things that can be done between the extremes of no analysis whatever and "hard core" cost-utility analysis. The above example is certainly far short of the latter; but it nevertheless may be useful.

CONCLUDING REMARK

I see that my allotted time has expired. I hope that my remarks have served to sharpen your intuition and judgment regarding the analytical bases of systems analysis. Thank you.

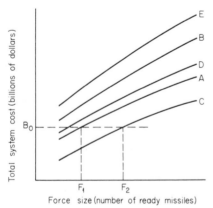

Figure 20-2 Total system cost versus force size for alternative systems A, B, C, D, and E.

[6] *Operating cost is usually computed for a fixed period of years—say, 5 or 7.*

References

Enthoven, A. C., "Decision Theory and Systems Analysis," *The Armed Forces Comptroller*, March 1964.

Fisher, G. H., *The Role of Cost-Utility Analysis in Program Budgeting*, The RAND Corporation, RM-4279-RC, September 1964.

———, *Analytical Support for Defense Planning*, The RAND Corporation, P-2650, October 1962.

Fort, Donald M., Systems Analysis as an Aid in Air Transportation Planning, The RAND Corporation, P-3293-1, March 1966.

Hitch, C. J., *An Appreciation of Systems Analysis*, The RAND Corporation, P-699, August 1955.

[7] *It is assumed, of course, that a textual discussion goes along with the figure and the table, so that the decisionmaker has the benefit of any interpretive comments that the analyst may have.*

————, and R. N. McKean, *The Economics of Defense in the Nuclear Age*, Harvard University Press, Cambridge, 1960.

Hoag, M. W., *Increasing Returns in Military Functions*, The RAND Corporation, P-3309, February 1966.

McKean, R. N., *Efficiency in Government Through Systems Analysis*, John Wiley & Sons, Inc., New York, 1958.

Novick, David, *Program Budgeting: Program Analysis and the Federal Government*, Harvard University Press, Cambridge, 1965.

Prest, A. R., and R. Turvey, *"Cost-Benefit Analysis: A Survey,"* The Economic Journal, December 1965, pp. 683–735.

Quade, E. S. (ed.), *Analysis for Military Decisions*, Rand McNally & Co., Chicago, 1964.

————, *Systems Analysis Techniques for Planning-Programming-Budgeting*, The RAND Corporation, P-3322, March 1966.

————, *Cost-Effectiveness: An Introduction and Overview*, The RAND Corporation, P-3134, May 1965.

————, *Pitfalls in Military Systems Analysis*, The RAND Corporation, P-2676, November 1962.

————, *Military Analysis*, The RAND Corporation, RM-4808, November 1965.

————, *The Limitations of a Cost-Effectiveness Approach to Military Decision-Making*, The RAND Corporation, P-2798, September 1963.

READING 21

SYSTEMS ANALYSIS—CHALLENGE TO MILITARY MANAGEMENT*

Laurence E. Lynn, Jr.

The question is whether . . . judgments have to be made in the fog of inadequate and inaccurate data, unclear and undefined issues, and a welter of conflicting personal opinions, or whether they can be made on the basis of adequate, reliable information, relevant experience, and clearly drawn issues.

Dr. Alain C. Enthoven

Essentially we regard all military problems as, in one of their aspects, economic problems in the efficient allocation and use of resources . . . The job of economizing, which some would delegate to budgeteers and comptrollers, cannot be distinguished from the whole task of making military decisions.

Hon. Charles J. Hitch

* Reprinted with permission of Commandant, U.S. Army Management School, Fort Belvoir, Virginia.

. . . how decisions are reached greatly influences what the decisions are.

Capt. Stanley M. Barnes, USN

SECTION 1 INTRODUCTION

Defense and the nation's resources. To fail to provide an adequate military defense capability for the United States would expose not only this country—its inhabitants, its institutions, and its material wealth—but also the entire non-Communist world to the threat of conquest or destruction.

Annual defense budgets are now in the neighborhood of fifty billion dollars. Yet both despite and because of the enormity of this sum, public debate as to the adequacy of our defenses continues among those who could fairly be said to subscribe to the initial statement of this section. Some regard the current budget as insufficient; criticisms range from "we could do more" to the dramatic claim that the size and composition of the budget represent "unilateral disarmament." On the other hand, it is claimed by some who believe in the need for active defenses that the budget compounds a defense posture which already represents a diabolical overkill capacity far exceeding the requirements of deterrence.

Apparently, then, commitment to the goal of "an adequate defense capability" does not imply a clear-cut policy recommendation. Should we utilize more or less resources than the current budget allows? If so, how much more or less should we utilize, and on what? If not, are the resources obtained with currently budgeted funds utilized in the most effective manner, or should we be allocating more to some activities and less to others? A mere recognition of the need for defense does not automatically provide answers to questions as to what kind of defense and how much of it we need.

This paper focuses primarily on an economic and quantitative approach to defense planning at the national policy level which is known as *systems analysis,* or, what amounts to the same thing, *cost-effectiveness.* As employed by Secretary of Defense McNamara, systems analysis "assists in selecting weapon systems and choosing among alternative courses of action for purposes of designing and procuring a force structure adequate to our needs."[1] A mission-oriented planning, programing and budgeting process has been implemented which facilitates the use of such analyses in defense planning and procurement.

The need for quantitative defense analysis at the national policy level arises from several economic considerations: (a) The resources available for defense are limited. Hence, duplication of effort is a luxury which we can ill afford. Nor can we afford to allow imbalances in our defense capabilities to develop through a lack of effective planning. (b) The point has been reached in weapon system acquisition at which, in general, relatively large increases in expenditure may yield relatively small increments in defense effectiveness. Wasteful commitments of resources to projects with only marginal value must be avoided. (c) Because implementing the rapid developments in mili-

tary technology is both enormously costly and time consuming, great care must be taken to insure sound decisions in the planning stages. It is unnecessarily wasteful to abandon poorly-conceived projects only after large amounts of resources have been expended on them. On the other hand, care must be taken not to abandon promising developments prematurely.

Considerations such as these suggest that defense planning must be vitally concerned with quantitative issues. Decision makers and managers must be concerned not only with whether or not a particular proposal will add to our capabilities, but also, to the greatest extent possible, how much our capabilities will be augmented. It is important as well to know how much a particular proposal will cost and how the cost of augmenting capabilities in this way compares with the costs of achieving similar results in other ways. The availability of such quantitative information, when used properly in light of the many nonquantitative factors that must be considered, can help insure that the total volume of resources available for defense is most effectively employed to achieve military objectives. Systems analysis, which assists in providing and evaluating quantitative information, is properly viewed as effectiveness-maximizing, not cost-minimizing.

The relevance of quantitative analysis is by no means limited to the allocation of resources at the national policy level. Operations research techniques have long been applied to problems concerning the efficient utilization of defense resources at many levels in the defense establishment. The importance of using resources efficiently is growing as rapid changes in weapons technology and the increasing sophistication of strategic and tactical doctrine place ever greater demands upon our defense capabilities. Throughout this paper the logical similarities of systems analysis as used at the national policy level and other quantitative problem-solving approaches used throughout the defense establishment will be stressed.

The objectives of achieving optimum allocation and efficient utilization of defense resources can be justified from another viewpoint: resources devoted to defense represent resources which are not devoted to other desirable uses such as private consumption and investment, expenditures for education, highways, water pollution control, the alleviation of poverty and disease, and the like. Systems

[1] Robert S. McNamara, "Managing the Department of Defense," Civil Service Journal, April-June 1964.

analysis can help insure that what we get in terms of defense for what we give up in terms of other, non-military, objectives is maximized. To put it another way, systems analysis can help insure that given defense capabilities are attained with a minimum sacrifice of other objectives. This is an important economic and social objective. As Kermit Gordon, Director of the Bureau of the Budget, stated, a billion dollars ". . . is a lot bigger in civilian terms than it is in military terms. With it we can underwrite the anti-poverty program for a year."[2] When resources have such a high potential yield in social benefits if devoted to civilian uses, it is incumbent upon defense decision-makers to employ these resources to maximum effect in military uses.

Quantitative analysis and defense planning. This discussion is addressed to all military decision-maker/managers, though its subject matter should be of interest to anyone concerned with defense planning. It is recognized that relatively few military managers are connected with the decision making process at the national policy level at any given time. The probability is increasing, however, that the typical military manager, no matter at what level in the defense establishment he is working, will be in positions to initiate, supervise, evaluate or participate in some phase of quantitative analysis. It is of considerable importance, therefore, that managers obtain sufficient understanding of what is involved in quantitative analysis so that they can effectively confront the needs and issues as they arise. The systems analysis approach is chosen as a fulcrum for the discussion because (1) it is a useful introduction to the application of quantitative reasoning to problems concerning the allocation and efficient utilization of resources at all levels, and (2) it is an essential element in the education of those who want to know more about how and why the tools of the military profession are chosen.

The thesis which emerges in the subsequent discussion can be stated in two parts, as follows:

a. Economic concepts and quantitative reasoning are tools of management. The careful and intelligent application of such concepts

[2] *Quoted by Daniel Lang in "An Inquiry into Enoughness,"* The New Yorker, *10 October 1964.*

and methods in the allocation of limited defense resources among a variety of alternative uses and the efficient utilization of resources in given uses can materially assist the military manager in solving many of the complex problems involved in mission accomplishment and in achieving the most with the resources available to him.

b. The meaningful application of quantitative economic analysis can enhance the role of military judgment and experience in the decision-making process by permitting the decision maker to focus his attention on the essential relationships and critical values of the problem. All military managers need not possess the technical and academic skills of the analysts, though there is a growing need for trained analysts in the military. If the manager will familiarize himself with the analytical approach and know the characteristics of good quantitative analysis, he will be able to communicate effectively with the specialists both to insure the proper consideration of his judgment and ideas in the analyst's work and to incorporate analytical results meaningfully into his decisions.

Section outline.   In Section 2 we will describe more specifically what is meant by systems analysis—also pointing out what is not meant—and why it makes sense to employ it in solving military problems. The logical relationship of systems analysis both to traditional military problem-solving frameworks such as the staff study and the estimate of the situation and to other scientific problem-solving techniques is discussed in Section 3.

SECTION 2
WHAT IS SYSTEMS ANALYSIS?

Some basic ideas.   *Systems analysis/cost-effectiveness is the process by which the costs and effectiveness of alternative courses of action are determined and compared for the purpose of assisting the decision maker in choosing the best course, or combination of courses, of action to accomplish his mission.*

A course of action is the commitment of a volume of resources to some specific configuration or use, where the term resources refers to an aggregation of men, materiel and facilities. A course of action may be a decision to utilize productive facilities to fabricate materials into some particular kind of product or class of products such as weapons or vehicles and to organize these into effective elements of our defense posture. In other problems, a course of action may be a decision to use existing resources in some specified way, perhaps by reorganizing or relocating them, modifying them or augmenting them with additional equipment or personnel. These organized aggregations of resources, designed to perform certain definite missions, can be termed "systems."

The important thing to realize is that a decision to commit resources to some specific use, or to utilize more rather than less resources for a particular use, is simultaneously a decision not to commit these resources to some alternative use or configuration. What these resources would accomplish if committed to other uses represents the opportunities foregone, or *opportunity cost*, of choosing the given course of action.

"Opportunity cost" is not a familiar term in military activities. It is common to think of the costs of a course of action as the resources used up in its undertaking, i.e., the amounts of inputs required. Costs in this sense are generally measured in terms of the dollar value of the resources or in terms of actual manhours, supplies and services of equipment and facilities. But the value of the outputs which these resources could produce if used in some other way is an equally valid way of expressing cost. The user "trades in" or gives up these outputs, or opportunities, in order to undertake the given course of action and gain its output. We generally cannot place a monetary value on the outputs of military activities as can be done in many business problems. But we can approximate the value of military activities by attempting to quantify their effectiveness in achieving designated missions. Thinking in terms of opportunity costs is a way of focusing attention on the fact that there are many effective ways of using resources in accomplishing defense missions. The decision maker must concern himself with these alternatives in order to insure that what is given up by taking a particular course of action is not more important than what is gained.

The cost effectiveness dilemma.
The military decision maker obviously cannot consider the infinitely large number of useful ways that resources can be employed. He must confine

himself to the ways resources can be used to accomplish a given objective or mission in which he is interested. Systems analysis can help the decision maker approach this task systematically by revealing to him the differences in effectiveness associated with differences in resource costs for those courses of action which contribute to the attainment of a given objective or set of objectives. Then it is up to the decision maker to establish a choice criterion which will answer the question: Is the difference in effectiveness which I get by choosing action A instead of action B worth the difference in cost?

The answer to this question is simple if, when comparing two courses of action, for example, greater effectiveness is associated with lower costs. In most problems, however, the decision maker is confronted with the need to make a judgment in cases in which greater effectiveness is associated with higher costs. The decision maker must then attempt to decide whether the more costly alternative adds sufficiently to defense capabilities to make the added expenditure worthwhile.

Systems analysts have a way of making these difficult problems at least manageable. We can illustrate this point with an example. Let two courses of action under consideration be the development and procurement of two alternative surface-to-air missiles for defending against attacking enemy bombers. Missile A might have a higher kill probability than Missile B, but it may also be more expensive to deploy. Missile A might, for example, have a more complex and costly guidance and control system which makes it more accurate when operational. On the other hand, this complex guidance and control system may reduce the probability that Missile A is launched successfully, i.e., reduce its reliability. However, the probability that an air defense missile will kill an attacking enemy bomber is assumed to depend both on accuracy and on reliability, and the greater accuracy of Missile A in our example may be supposed to outweigh its lower reliability.

But consider this hypothetical experiment. Suppose that instead of spending X dollars on Missile A, we spend the same amount on Missile B. That is, suppose that we buy more cheap missiles instead of fewer expensive ones. It might be discovered that the level of effectiveness which can be obtained with these B missiles exceeds the effectiveness obtainable with fewer expensive A missiles. Effectiveness, then, depends not only on reliability and accuracy, but also on the number of missiles that can be launched at an attacker. For a given budget outlay, Missile B is more effective than Missile A.

Exactly the same conclusion would result if, instead of using the conceptual device of a given budget outlay, a given level of effectiveness were specified and the question asked: Which missile system will achieve this effectiveness more economically?

The use of this last conceptual device sounds a little suspicious. It seems to imply that the best system is the cheapest system. Or, alternatively, it may imply that all that must be done is to compute the ratio of effectiveness to cost and the highest ratio wins. No one with any understanding of weapons and technology, or with any concern for the absolute degree of effectiveness of a system, is going to accept such rules of choice.

But something else in the statement must be noted. A given level of effectiveness is specified. This point is of crucial importance. Failure to recognize its implications is the source of a great deal of misunderstanding. A comparison of ratios is meaningless unless the value in the numerator or the value in the denominator of the ratio is held constant.[3] The analyst, when considering ratios, is careful to specify that either effectiveness—the numerator —or cost—the denominator—is the same in all comparisons. This is, as was noted, a conceptual device which clarifies the "more-expensive-but-more-effective" dilemma.

Clearly, if a given level of effectiveness is desired, *all things considered,* the most economical means of achieving it is the best choice. And if the allowable budget outlay is fixed, the decision maker will prefer the system which provides the greater effectiveness, *all things considered,* for that fixed outlay. This is a far different thing than simply comparing cost-effectiveness ratios and picking out the highest one. No competent systems analyst

[3] *If the ratio of effectiveness to cost for one system is greater than that for another system at every level of effectiveness or cost, ratio comparisons will indicate the preferred system but will not indicate how much of it is desirable. The analyst's device must still be employed to answer the latter question.*

advocates the latter procedure. These comparisons could look quite different for different budget outlays, or at different levels of effectiveness. It is up to the decision maker to decide which level of effectiveness he wants, or which budget outlay will be allocated to the problem.

Systems analysts typically use graphs to describe the relationships that have been discussed. In Figure 21-1, effectiveness is measured along the vertical axis and cost is measured along the horizontal axis. Notice the following characteristics of this graph: (1) For any given level of costs, or alternatively, for any given level of effectiveness, development and procurement of Missile B is the preferred course of action, because of the greater number of B missiles that can be successfully launched. (2) Beyond level of cost outlay X, effectiveness is increased only negligibly. This reflects a phenomenon termed *diminishing marginal returns:* in using resources to accomplish given objectives, it is usually the case that ever greater amounts of additional resources must be utilized to obtain given increments of effectiveness. At point X in Figure 21-1, diminishing marginal returns have reached the extent that it simply isn't worthwhile to allocate any more resources to either system.

The word "marginal" is one of the most frequently encountered in a systems analyst's vocabulary. Analysis "at the margin" means considering the impact on effectiveness of adding or subtracting "a little bit more" resources with respect to a given allocation. Consider again point X in Figure 21-1. Adding a little more to budgeted outlay for the two air defense missiles hardly affects the effectiveness of either missile system. Returns "at the margin" are nearly zero. The average returns of the two systems—*total* effectiveness divided by

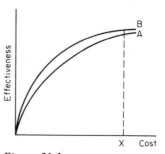

Figure 21-1

total resource outlay—may be impressive. But what the decision maker/manager should really want to know is what happens when he spends a little *more* or a little *less* on the systems. This information will tell him the real impact that extra spending or budget cutting will have on system effectiveness.

By using graphs, the decision maker can visually examine the implications of any budget outlay for optimum force structure, or he can determine approximately how much it costs to attain any specified level of effectiveness. In some cases he may discover that a large increase in outlays on a particular system will produce only a negligible increase in effectiveness. It is likely that these funds would be far better used for some force component which would add materially to defense capabilities. In other cases, it may become apparent that what is being spent yields very little effectiveness and that increased expenditure would increase effectiveness a great deal.

In the particular example under discussion, the systems analyst has provided a particularly useful piece of information to the decision maker. His analysis so far has revealed that Missile B is a better weapon than Missile A in accomplishing the specified objectives. Provided that the objective has been correctly stated, the decision maker now has a basis for making a decision that he probably could never obtain by being able to consider only the statement, "Missile A is both more effective and more expensive than Missile B."

The parametric study. Even the hypothetical example we have been discussing is too simple to be illustrative of many of the problems with which analysis must contend. It may be supposed, for example, that the kind of attack initially envisioned by the analyst was enemy bombers approaching from a high altitude. If, instead, we consider bombers approaching in low altitude attack patterns, the missile with the better guidance and control system might become more effective. Missile A might have a complex over-the-horizon radar which is able to identify and engage targets when Missile B's simpler line-of-sight radar is ineffective. The graphs might appear as in Figure 21-2. The situation is now reversed. If the enemy attacks at low altitudes, Missile A is the preferred weapon at every level of expenditure.

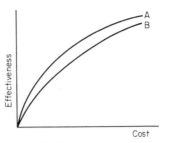

Figure 21-2

Figures 21-1 and 21-2 together represent a highly simplified version of a "parametric study." In each cost-effectiveness graph, a different assumption is made concerning the altitude of the enemy's attack. In technical terms, each assumption concerning the altitude of attack is a parameter with respect to graphs relating the variables cost and effectiveness. For each different assumption concerning altitude, a new graph must be drawn. By comparing these graphs the analyst can get a feel for the sensitivity of his missile comparisons to changing values of the parameter.

The altitude of the enemy's attack is one thing, the timing of his attack quite another. How sensitive are the two weapon systems under analysis to this factor?

Let us suppose that expensive Missile A has a reprograming capability. That is, if the missile fails to fire after the first attempt to launch, steps can be taken to make additional launch attempts possible. The greater the number of times that attempts to launch the missile can be made, the greater the reliability of the system. However, this reprograming capability assumes that time is available to accomplish the necessary actions. The more time that is available after an initial failure to launch, the more attempts to launch that can be made. We may describe the relationship between missile reliability and time as in Figure 21-3.

This consideration enters into the analysis in the following way. Attacking enemy bombers need not arrive over a target area simultaneously. This was assumed to be the case in the preceding analysis. It can be argued, however, that since a large wave of incoming bombers is highly vulnerable to U. S. manned interceptors, the enemy may prefer to time phase his attack. If a non-simultaneous attack is considered to be a possibility, our preference for air defense missiles may be affected

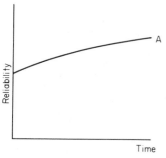

Figure 21-3

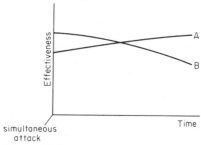

Figure 21-5

just as it was when low altitude attacks were considered. As we have seen, the reliability of Missile A increases with the length of time over which an attack takes place. If we assume that bombers attack over a lengthy time span, the cost-effectiveness graph may appear as in Figure 21-4.

Missile A now is preferred at every level of expenditure over Missile B. The increased reliability of Missile A, resulting from its reprograming capability, and its greater accuracy combine to offset the cost advantage of Missile B. Presumably, there exists some assumption concerning the time phasing of an enemy attack for which we would be indifferent between Missile A and Missile B. In fact, we can construct the following graph: for a given budget expenditure on missiles, and also assuming a high altitude attack, we can describe the relationship between effectiveness and the timing of an attack for both Missile A and Missile B. This graph is presented in Figure 21-5.

For a simultaneous attack, Missile B is more effective. Missile B's margin of superiority gradually is overcome, however, as the amount of time utilized by the enemy in his attack is increased.

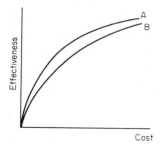

Figure 21-4

"Parameterizing," that is, drawing new cost-effectiveness graphs which incorporate different assumptions concerning factors which may have an important bearing on systems comparisons, is a convenient way of analyzing the sensitivity of the comparisons to these factors. We have discovered in our example that comparisons between Missile A and Missile B are highly sensitive to both the altitude and the time-phasing of the enemy's attack. If we pursued the analysis further, we might find that the comparisons were insensitive to certain other factors.

Such information is of the utmost importance to the decision maker. If analysis reveals that system comparisons are insensitive to certain factors, he need not worry about these factors in making his decision. He will want to focus his attention on those factors which do affect system comparisons. Uncertainty concerning any of these latter factors must weigh heavily on his decision.

Analysis and decisions.   The decision maker now knows that the optimum choice of weapons is strongly influenced by the altitude of attack adopted by the enemy and by the timing of the attack. Since these factors are beyond his control, the decision maker will not want to commit himself to a choice of weapons which is appropriate for only one or two contingencies. He may want to "take out insurance" against the possibility of a variety of contingencies by procuring a mix of weapons. He may now feel he is in a position to go ahead with development and initial investment in both Missile A and Missile B. On the other hand, he may feel that only Missile A should be developed and procured, even though it is an inferior missile under certain contingencies. He may feel, for example, that the existence of a manned interceptor force is sufficient insurance against simultaneous attack. The more sophisticated capabilities of Missile A might make the most valuable additions to air defense.

Note that the decision to procure Missile A, which the hypothetical analysis revealed as a reasonable course of action, is a decision to buy the weapon with the greater unit cost. Systems analysis relates costs to effectiveness for a range of threats. The aim is to find the system which, for a given outlay, best counters these threats. This may be the least expensive weapon, but it may well be the most elaborate and expensive weapon if its effectiveness in countering the threats is sufficiently great.

The decision maker has some ideas, too, as to how his decisions may in fact affect enemy decisions. The deployment of a missile capable of defending against low altitude attacks may mean that the enemy will have to increase his force considerably, at great cost, if he is to penetrate these defenses. Or he may have to employ additional weapons, say ICBMs, to suppress the U. S. defenses and permit penetration by bombers. The enemy may be forced to abandon low altitude attack plans in favor of alternatives which are less costly but also less effective from his point of view.

The graphs and analysis that have been discussed by no means constitute a complete study. No attempts were made to evaluate such innovations as a shoot-look-shoot capability resulting from the use of a radar which is "farsighted" enough to permit us to look and see if an incoming bomber has been destroyed and, if not, to shoot at it again. The effects of varying the number of bombers in an attacking force and their dispersal within an attack pattern were not considered. Nor were varying assumptions concerning the target system which the enemy is attacking treated explicitly. Such factors should be "parameterized" as were altitude and timing. The decision maker may want to see further studies which consider more sophisticated versions of enemy strategy and tactics, perhaps incorporating detailed intelligence information, in order to get a better idea of exactly how much of each type of weapon he will want in the force.

Moreover, effectiveness has been defined in only one of several possible ways: increase the probability of killing attacking enemy bombers. Perhaps the real objective is to limit the damage inflicted on the U. S. population or on its economic strength, and effectively meeting this objective may call for expenditures on passive defense, i.e., blast and fallout shelters, as well as on active bomber defense, or perhaps even increased capability of destroying enemy bombers before they reach the CONUS defenses. Further analysis might clarify these issues in terms of the tradeoffs among costs and effectiveness.

But is all this analysis worthwhile? The decision might have been made without knowing the results of analysis. The decision maker might have announced that Missile A would be developed because it was more accurate and had more sophisticated radar. On the other hand, the decision maker might have decided to go ahead with both missiles because they were both good weapons, and it is always wise to have a diversified arsenal since you never know what the enemy will come up with. It is by no means obvious that either of these decisions, based purely on judgment and experience, is inferior to decisions backed by analysis. Moreover, not so much time and talent has been wasted on studies.

Intuitive judgment does not necessarily produce inferior decisions. Yet two points must be made:

a. The decision maker who has no analysis to assist him may actually have less opportunity to bring his experience to bear on a problem and to exercise effective judgment. Good analysis will have succeeded in identifying the real objectives and key variables of a problem. It will indicate how sensitive the analytical findings are to changes in the values of the key variables or in the assumptions on which the analytical model is constructed. Of vital importance, it will point out remaining areas of uncertainty, which may call for additional information or further study. Uncertainty can never be eliminated when the actions of a devious enemy must be taken into account. Analysis can, however, explicitly identify areas of uncertainty and indicate how the likelihood of mission accomplishment is affected by them. And by bringing these uncertainties into the open, analysis can frequently succeed in squeezing them into the smallest area.

Dealing explicitly with uncertainty—and indicating the relative significance of what we do know compared to what we do not know—is one of the most important contributions of analysis to the decision-making process. Uncertainty as to how an ICBM force would perform in a nuclear exchange, could (and has!) lead to the conclusion that "we can't rely on missiles" or even "missiles have no deterrent value." This type of reaction implies that if we are not completely sure about a future event, we are obliged to be completely unsure. Analysis which reveals that a particular weapon is, on the basis of the best information available, 80% reliable—thus expressing our uncertainty explicitly in the form of a probability—can lead to more fruitful reactions. For example, launching two weapons instead of one can increase reliability to 96%. Design improvements or better maintenance policies might increase the reliability of a given missile. Moreover, the fallibilities of human judgment being what they are, the weapon or alternative we "feel" sure about may be no more reliable in fact than the missile. Explicit treatment of uncertainty will serve the planning process much better than unaided intuitive judgment.

With the aid of analysis, then, the decision maker can focus his attention on clearly-defined issues, utilizing his judgment to evaluate assumptions, criticize the numbers and probabilities the analyst has employed, weigh the uncertainties with which facts and assumptions must be accepted, temper and modify analytical conclusions with experience factors, predict the future consequences of actions taken now, evaluate how and to what extent factors not considered by the analyst should affect the decision. The opportunities which the decision maker has to exercise critical and meaningful judgment, and the likely consequences of his judgments, are much more clearly delineated when major aspects of the problem have been quantified and analyzed.

b. When only intuitive, unsupported judgment is used, the danger exists that the premises and assumptions which the decision maker consciously or unconsciously has in mind, and which may be wholly appropriate in some problems, may lead to conclusions which are far wide of the mark in other problems, and lead to serious imbalances or vulnerabilities in our capabilities. Willingness consistently to draw upon the results of analysis can add an important element of objectivity to the decision-making process (provided, of course, that the military and civilian analysts are encour-

aged to be objective in their analyses). This is important in view of the consequences that can follow on a biased or uninformed decision.

Does the possibility exist, however, that quantitative analysis can lead to worse decisions than those that would be made without it? The answer is yes. One reason is that the analysis may be faulty. A second reason, related to the first, may seem paradoxical. The more the military decision maker/manager fails to exercise his judgment and draw upon his experience in participating in and evaluating analyses, the greater the possibility that analytical results will be misinterpreted, misused, or used indiscriminately to the detriment of national defense.

Analysis cannot, and must not, substitute for military judgment; it can however, serve as an exceedingly valuable input to inform military judgment. However, successful analysis depends on two-way communication between the analyst and the user. The challenge to military decision maker/managers is to become sufficiently conversant with the purpose, scope and methods of systems analysis and the other quantitative problem-solving approaches so that they can communicate effectively with the technically trained analysts.

Challenge to military managers. If what has been said so far is true, the military decision maker/manager, far from being replaced by the analysts, will be confronted with the need both to understand what the analyst is doing and to integrate the results of analysis into the management process. Yet considerable skill and judgment are involved in designing and conducting studies. Establishing quantifiable objectives for a given problem, identifying the courses of action which will accomplish the objectives, and measuring the costs and effectiveness of each course of action are complex and difficult tasks. It may seem to many that a specialist's skills are required if one is to begin to make sense of quantitative analysis and analytical findings.

While there is a rapidly growing need for specially trained military personnel to participate in quantitative analysis, there is perhaps a greater need for managers who are able to supervise or evaluate quantitative analysis, or to envision how quantitative analysis could be useful to them and to initiate the necessary studies. To perform these roles successfully, military managers should be familiar with elementary economic and quantitative concepts, comprehend both the value and the limitations of the scientific approach and know the characteristics of good quantitative analysis. Military managers should be able to evaluate the quality of studies in terms of the measures of effectiveness which are defined, the analytical assumptions, procedures and techniques, the elements included in the cost calculations and choice criteria.

This general ability to evaluate quantitative analysis does not necessarily depend upon formal training in the technical and academic skills of the specialist. The essential requirement is a willingness to learn new concepts and to acquire some new attitudes and to utilize these concepts and attitudes objectively whenever the need or the opportunity arises. As we previously noted, the needs and opportunities may arise not only at the national policy level but at any level in the defense establishment.

Some practitioners have found it conceptually useful to describe the many possible levels of analysis in terms of a hierarchy, as follows (from highest to lowest): system, subsystem, assembly, sub-assembly, component, and part.[4] It is apparent that as we ascend in the hierarchy, we are considering progressively more complex aggregations of resources. Problems can be classified by considering where in the hierarchy of resource aggregation the elements of analysis are to be found.

At lower levels in the hierarchy, problems tend to be relatively narrow in scope and more readily quantifiable. These problems are frequently of a repetitive or routine nature, involving the efficient organization or utilization of the resource elements under study under conditions in which there is general agreement as to what efficiency means. For these reasons, they are frequently amenable to the sophisticated mathematical techniques of operations research or the detailed technical considerations of value engineering. Examples of these types of problems are those concerning optimum maintenance scheduling and procedures, transporting items from a variety of origins to a variety of terminals, managing inventories, loading and unloading cargo vehicles, servicing customers.

This is not the case at the systems analysis level. Earlier we described a system as an integrated organization of men, material and facilities designed to perform some specific service or set of services in support of major defense establishment missions. In systems analysis, as the term implies, systems, taken *in toto*, are the elements of analysis. It is instructive to consider how a system analyst views his task. "We . . . tend to compare a small number of different systems under varying circumstances and objectives. No simple criteria of performance are used. The major attention is focused on uncertainties. A system is preferred when it performs reasonably well under probable circumstances in terms of the high-priority objectives, and yet hedges against less probable or even improbable situations and does more than just pay lip service to medium and low priority objectives."[5]

Far from dealing with routine tasks and/or relatively narrow objectives, systems analysis is concerned with mission accomplishment and broad strategic objectives at the national policy level. At this level there is rarely an accepted view as to the meaning of mission accomplishment or the precise nature of strategic objectives. Thus systems analysis must be centrally concerned with problem definition and the selection of appropriate objectives. It must concern itself with all of the risks, uncertainties and unknowns of contingency planning for national defense.

The challenge to the analyst and the manager at the national policy level is to develop better ways of thinking about problems and assigning better alternatives for handling them, not to acquire technical virtuosity in solving them. The problem orientation of systems analysis and the need to consider a great range of uncertainties and strategies are readily apparent in the hypothetical air defense analysis presented in the previous section.

Many military problems, for example, those involving tactics or the costs and effectiveness of sub-systems such as particular battlefield weapons or support items, occupy an intermediate position in the hierarchy. Such problems frequently involve contingency analysis and hence are influenced by uncertainties and parameters which are difficult to quantify. On the other hand, their scopes are limited relative

---

[4] *I am indebted to Wayne Allen, Member of the Technical Staff at IDA, for helpful discussions on this point.*

[5] *Herman Kahn,* On Thermonuclear War, *Princeton: Princeton University Press, 1961, pp. 119–120.*

to those encountered at the national policy level and the analyst may be able to confine himself to a narrower range of issues and uncertainties and benefit from somewhat better opportunities for agreement on objectives, quantification and even experimental verification of assumptions.

It may be noted finally that problem packages may involve analysis at all levels. Information may be generated by operations analysis and war gaming, with the results serving as inputs to a higher level systems analysis. Extensive interactions among analytical conclusions and techniques at the various levels may take place, and the methodologies may range from intuition to sophisticated mathematical programing.

The importance of making this somewhat artificial distinction among problems is this. The senior military decision maker/manager may become involved in problems at any or all of these levels. Each type of problem may, however, involve different tests of his competence and require different responses and different degrees of personal involvement. In some cases, a few hours of discussion to define the problem may be all that is necessary before it is handed to the experts to arrive at a solution. In others, military assistance may be required in problem formulation, in data gathering and analysis, in constructing new alternatives, problem reformulation and so on. In still others, objective evaluation and critique by military management of completed analysis may be necessary. Some may require experience with equipment performance, logistics, operations; others may involve strategic or doctrinal judgments and insights. All involve the integration of this knowledge and experience with scientific principles of problem solving. It is to prepare him for this varied role that it is necessary for the military manager "to be familiar with the analytical approach, comprehend both its value and its limitations, and know the characteristics and good quantitative analysis." We advocate, in other words, an intuitive understanding on the part of the military of scientific quantitative problem solving.

We will describe more fully the logic of systems analysis in the following section. At this point we want to introduce some general guidelines for the manager to assist him in initiating, supervising, and evaluating quantitative analysis.

Does the Study Ask the Right Questions?

Analytical studies are built around some measure or measures of performance or effectiveness. Measures of effectiveness should accurately describe some desirable military objective. To be truly quantifiable, they must be defined at less than the ethereal level of "winning the war" or "destroying the enemy's will to resist." Beyond this general comment, the narrowness or breadth of the specified objectives depends upon the kind of problem which is subjected to analysis. The higher the level of the problem, the more the analysis should be cognizant of the trade-offs that exist among narrowly-defined objectives. Mobility versus firepower, missile accuracy vs. missile reliability, vehicle land speed vs. the capability of negotiating rugged terrain—desirable capabilities may be competitive rather than complementary, and this must be recognized in good analysis.

Frequently objectives are framed in terms of requirements which are generated by the need or the desire to handle particular contingencies. Studies based on such objectives may lead to recommendations which represent uneconomical uses of defense resources when considering more broadly conceived tactical or strategic missions. Hence measures of effectiveness should be conceptually sound in that they are consonant with strategic and/or tactical doctrine or with general policy directives. Depending, of course, upon the level of the problem, proposed courses of action should be evaluated in terms of their contribution to relatively broadly-defined defense missions. Their capability of handling narrower problems can be evaluated within the more general framework.

It is important to emphasize that careful definition of the questions which a study is to answer is an analytical step in itself. Ideally, optimum solutions are obtained by relating a set of known, defined preferences to a set of available alternatives for satisfying such preferences. The mix of alternatives chosen is that which most fully satisfies preferences. Military analysis cannot be so conceptually neat. It is frequently an iterative procedure, and initial formulations of the problem and the initial list of alternatives to be considered may be revised considerably as analysis proceeds. Yet the tendency to define objectives so that they are in line with *hoped for* outcomes or to define and analyze alternative courses of action in a manner which is slanted toward yielding particular answers, is not likely to produce optimal solutions. These tendencies can be minimized by concentrating on achieving a careful, comprehensive and sound definition of objectives and missions and attempting to evaluate all relevant alternatives impartially in terms of these objectives and missions. If it proves necessary or desirable to revise objectives or design new alternatives, this should be justified by the analysis itself, and successive rounds of analysis should proceed in the same impartial manner.

Are the Answers to the Questions Reasonable in Light of the Evidence?

Closely connected with the definition of objectives is the selection of a criterion or criteria for choosing among courses of action in terms of objectives attainment. Sometimes, through analytical devices such as those described on pp. 219–222 above, the choices can be described in relatively unambiguous terms. For example, the system which provides a satisfactory level of effectiveness at least cost will be chosen. In others, such as our air-defense problem, a variety of characteristics and capabilities must be balanced against a variety of uncertainties and risks. Subjective judgments inevitably enter to resolve complex choice problems. The military manager should determine what the choice criteria are and if they appear to be reasonable and consistent in light of available evidence and the assumptions and procedures of the analysis itself.

Has the Evidence Been Evaluated Objectively, Consistently, and Comprehensively?

The manager must be able and willing to discount or reject study assumptions, analytical techniques and concepts, and interpretations which appear to reflect undue attention to irrelevant considerations, personal prejudices or preconceived opinions. A careful and objective study will make its assumptions explicit and will provide adequate justification for them. The manager should be able to verify from the study report precisely how conclusions were arrived at.

The manager should also examine the content of the study and ask some probing questions. Are the concepts, assumptions and procedures sound? Are they consistent with the specified objectives? Are they sufficiently comprehensive of the key elements of the problem?

If the manager is himself consistent and objective in asking these questions of his analysts and analysis, as well as asking these questions of himself when he is engaged in problem solving, he is beginning to acquire facility in handling quantitative analysis.

Some misconceptions. Though good systems analysis and cost effectiveness studies, properly used, can be a useful input to the decision-making process, some misleading impressions tend to be created when the value to military decision makers of making quantitative estimates of costs and effectiveness is asserted. We label these impressions "misconceptions" and list them as follows:

Misconception 1: Systems analysis requires that all factors within its purview be strictly measurable—factors which are not measurable are ignored.

Systems analysis, indeed all quantitative analysis, presupposes that important elements of military problems can be quantified and that it is desirable to do so. Verbal generalizations are difficult to analyze, compare and apply. Moreover, as we have tried to show, generalizations may lead to erroneous conclusions. Even if intuitive reasoning could tell us which of many courses of action are "better" or "best," the crucial questions are likely to be (a) how much better and under what conditions? and (b) what are the trade-offs in terms of effectiveness and cost among desirable courses of action? What intuitive reasoning and clever insight can do most effectively is handle the non-measurable and non-comparable factors and integrate them with analytical results to produce wise decisions. ". . . the significance of the numbers in an analysis depends upon the importance of effects not encompassed by these numbers, and the recognition of this dependence should not be left to chance. . . . As a minimum (such factors) can be displayed and talked about."[6] They can never be ignored.

Misconception 2: The output of a systems

---

[6] *Charles J. Hitch and Roland N. McKean,* **The Economics of Defense in the Nuclear Age,** *Cambridge: Harvard University Press, 1961, p. 184.*

analysis is a decision as to which of the alternatives considered is "best"—the best alternative is always the one with the lowest cost.

The quality of analysis and its usefulness to the decision maker are not judged on the basis of how many definitive conclusions are contained in it. Definitive answers are much less desirable than a plausible formulation of the problem accompanied by analysis which explores the sensitivity of results to alternative assumptions for a broad range of budget outlays and levels of effectiveness. Good analysis points out those areas which are characterized by a high degree of uncertainty or are in need of further study. Definitive conclusions are the decision-maker's job. He must evaluate the information contained in analysis and arrive at his decision.

A premise of systems analysis is that it is only common sense to consider costs when evaluating alternative ways of achieving given objectives. If a particular objective is agreed upon, and if a given level of effectiveness can be achieved in several ways, it is common sense to prefer the most economical way of achieving this level of effectiveness. The decision maker could use an uneconomical way of achieving his objective, but this would mean that he was using up resources which could be used to better advantage in some other way. But, as we have emphasized, this does not mean that analysis is biased toward cheap weapons. Analysis is biased in favor of effectiveness, and if the procurement of expensive weapons will produce the greatest effectiveness for a given budget outlay, analysis will reveal these weapons to be the preferred choice.

Misconception 3: The techniques of systems analysis, because they are quantitative, are inherently complex and must be performed on computers.

Computers are frequently useful to the analyst. Cost computations, for example, may require the summarization of a large volume of raw data which computers can accomplish quickly and efficiently. Yet the essence of analysis is not the placement of giant computers in a harness of sophisticated mathematical models. Decision makers are more likely to be bounced out of the saddle by failure to assure adequate problem design and definition, or by selection of inappropriate rules of choice and erroneous interpretation of results, than by galloping computers.

Misconception 4: Systems analysis is used when problems are too complicated for ordinary human judgment.

Quantitative reasoning does not require incomprehensible mathematical expressions. A grasp of relatively simple quantitative concepts coupled with an aggressive application of objectivity and common sense can yield good analyses and good interpretations of analyses even when complicated problems are involved. Systems analysis is used whenever a means of making a systematic evaluation of alternatives is desired and whenever the problem lends itself to quantification. The results of analysis are inputs to the decision-making process. But the decision maker is still in control. Systems analysis helps to focus judgment—it does not replace it.

It is reiterated, however, that systems analysis, as any other endeavor undertaken by human beings, can be good or bad, sound or faulty. These are numerous pitfalls in systems analysis which must be carefully and studiously avoided. In fact, good systems analysts are the first to enumerate these pitfalls and point out the consequences of ignoring them. It is entirely disingenuous, therefore, to chronicle these pitfalls and allege them to be "weaknesses" or shortcomings of the systems analysis approach. All systems analysts are not superficial and narrow any more than all doctors are quacks. The basic procedures and characteristics of systems analysis/cost-effectiveness have been shaped by the need to account for complex situations full of pitfalls and problems.

SECTION 3   SYSTEMS ANALYSIS: THE COLD, HARD LOOK

Scientific problem solving and military tradition.   Does the use of quantitative concepts such as those employed in cost-effectiveness analyses represent a revolutionary break with military problem solving traditions embodied in the estimate of the situation and staff research? Have military judgment and experience, which form the backbone of military problem-solving approaches, thus been downgraded?

It must be noted immediately that some types of quantitative analysis, indeed some of the most sophisticated and complex analyses, have been done continuously in the military for over 20 years. Operations research techniques have been applied to military problems since World War II. But these applications were mainly in areas in which there was little serious dispute as to how the problem ought to be defined and no serious doubts that sophisticated techniques were required. Military users of such studies readily conceded the need for highly-trained experts to arrive at the answers.

The controversies have arisen as scientific problem solving approaches have been applied to problems which the military have solved before without experts and without explicit reference to the scientific method. It is in connection with such problems that questions as to the relationships of systems analysis/cost-effectiveness to traditional problem solving approaches, and suspicions as to the confidence being placed in military judgment, arise. Many of these questions are profound and are related to military professionalism in its broadest sense. Still others arise out of misunderstandings or a lack of familiarity with scientific problem solving. We want to begin to shed some light on these issues in this section.

Staff research and systems analysis both begin when problems arise that are too big to be solved by one man using his unaided brain power and paper and pencil. These problems are generally empirical, i.e., arising from observation or experience with some difficulty in planning, operations, procurement or the like. The question becomes one of approach: how are possible solutions to these problems to be determined?

The logic of problem solving. No matter which problem-solving approach is chosen, four phases can generally be identified. In empirical inquiries:

a. The problem must be formulated in a precise manner: Exactly what are the questions which are to be answered? This may involve a statement of objectives to be attained, performance to be evaluated, or perhaps hypotheses to be verified. Whatever form the problem statement takes, it must be consistent with the overall goals or missions of the organization in which the problem has arisen.

b. Data, facts and information which bear upon the questions to be answered must be assembled. The nature of these information "raw materials" is determined both by the

problem and by the prospective methods of evaluation or analysis to be employed. They may consist of numerical information such as design or performance characteristics and descriptive statistics and sets of alternative possibilities for objectives attainments, evaluation of probabilities.

c. Procedures for processing the data and facts so that they relate directly to the problem statement must be decided upon and employed. These procedures may be formal or informal, sophisticated or casual.

d. Conclusions may be arrived at, decisions recommended, or courses of action suggested on the basis of results obtained from the problem solving procedures employed in Step 3 and then communicated to the decision maker.

We may summarize the four phases of empirical inquiry as:

a. Problem Formulation
b. Assembly of Facts
c. Analysis
d. Conclusions and Recommendations

How do traditional staff research procedures, outlined, for example, in Army FM 101-5, relate to this schema? The steps of staff research are study and understanding of the problem (problem formulation); preparation of basic work plan, collection, evaluation and organization of data (assembly of facts); analysis of data (analysis); and the drawing of sound conclusions and the formulation of recommendations (conclusions and/or recommendations). Similarly, the steps in an estimate of the situation can be similarly organized: the mission (problem formulation); the situation and courses of action (assembly of facts); analysis, opposing courses of action, and comparison, own courses of action (analysis); decision (conclusion and/or recommendations).

We can similarly analyze the procedures of systems analysis. According to one description[7] the problem is formulated by describing the context in which it arises, the objectives in tentative form, the criteria needed to determine success or failure, and the hypotheses of action to achieve objectives (problem formulation); the relevant data are sought out as facts,

[7] *Captain Stanley M. Barnes, USN, "Defense Planning Processes,"* U. S. Naval Institute Proceedings, *June 1964, p. 34.*

possibilities, alternatives, and costs (assembly of facts); the application of these data to the problem as formulated, is worked out with models ("a set of relationships, mathematical or logical"), approximations, computation and results (analysis); the results obtained are translated into conclusions after interpretation of the effect of nonquantifiables, incommensurables, and uncertainties (further analysis and conclusions and/or recommendations).

The breakdown of staff research estimate of the situation and systems analysis into the four problem-solving phases is summarized in Table 21-1.

To emphasize the generality of this scheme, it is useful to apply it to more sophisticated and technical problem solving approaches. The basic concepts of operations research have been described as the measure of effectiveness, the model, the role of experimentation, and the necessity for decision.[8] In operations research, the measure of effectiveness describes

[8] *Cyril C. Herrmann and John F. Magee, "Operations Research for Management," in Edward C. Bursk and John F. Chapman, editors, New Decision-Making Tools for Managers, Cambridge: Harvard Univ. Press, 1963, p. 6.*

the extent to which the objectives of the operation are met. Hence a problem formulation phase must clearly establish these objectives or goals. The model "is generally built up from observed data or experience . . ." A careful study of the operation and assembly of relevant facts, perhaps involving experimentation, must precede analysis. A model is constructed which represents those aspects of the operation which relate to effectiveness as defined. The model is then manipulated in the analytical phase to produce information which will be of importance to the decision maker in deciding how best to manage his operation. The operations researcher should finally clearly indicate, on the basis of his analytical findings, how alternative courses of action available to the decision maker are related to the decision maker's goals.

In a similar manner, the procedures for conducting a linear programing analysis can be described as: determination of a measure of effectiveness (problem formulation): determination of alternative means, or processes, of accomplishing the objective and their rates of efficiency, together with the linear constraints binding upon the operation (assembly of facts),

TABLE 21-1

	Staff Research	Estimate of Situation	Systems Analysis
1. Problem Formulation	Study and understanding of the problem	Mission	Formulation: describe problem context, objectives, criteria, hypotheses.
2. Assembly of facts	Preparation of work plan Collection, evaluation of data Organization of data	The situation and courses of action.	Seeking out facts, possibilities, alternatives and costs.
3. Analysis	Analysis of data	Analysis, opposing courses of action. Comparison, own course of action.	Application of data to problem using models, approximations, computations, results. Interpret effects of nonquantifiables, incommensurables, uncertainties.
4. Conclusions and/or recommendations	Drawing of sound conclusions Formulation of recommendations	Decision	Results translated into conclusions.

construction of an objective function and a linear equation system relating the various processes to objectives obtainment subject to the linear constraints (analysis); description of the solution(s) and their implications (conclusions and/or recommendations).

There are no fundamental differences among the various problem-solving approaches, either traditional or scientific, in the logic of what has to be accomplished. The differences are rather in methods—how the problem gets solved—and to some extent, in emphasis. The military manager should desire to find and apply the most effective method or approach for resolving his problems. Systems analysis, or any kind of quantitative approach, is one way—one set of tools and procedures—available to the manager to assist him in making effective plans and good decisions. As we suggested in the preceding section, there is nothing inherent in quantitative analysis which downgrades military judgment or experience. What quantitative analysis brings to the decision-making process are objectivity, a concern for explicit, quantitative treatment of the key factors and relationships in the problem, a belief that costs and effectiveness have to be consid-

ered simultaneously in the decision-making process, and an emphasis on *how* answers are arrived at as opposed to arriving at answers.

Analysis is, as General Decker has put it, *"the cold, hard look which individuals or organizations directly involved in the problem find difficult to take."*[9]

The interrelationships among the many problem-solving methods is depicted in Figure 21-6. Systems analysis and cost effectiveness studies are viewed as integrating, either explicitly or implicitly, four different kinds of inputs: (1) a problem in defense planning which needs to be solved; (2) the judgment and experience of military men, together with their acknowledged background in solving problems; (3) the objective and comprehensive thinking characteristic of scientific quantitative methods; and (4) the results of many other studies dealing with related problems of narrower scope and perhaps using highly sophisticated techniques.

[9] *General George H. Decker, "Costing Strategy,"* Armed Forces Management, *September 1963, p. 40.*

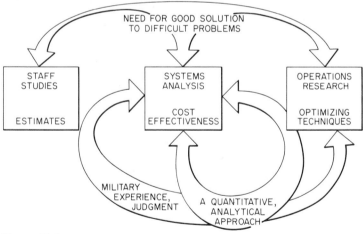

Figure 21-6

SECTION 6

APPLICATIONS OF SYSTEMS ANALYSIS

In this section, system analyses in a number of major decision areas are discussed by the people who were involved in the analyses. Of necessity, the level of formality is higher in a few of these papers than in the rest of the book. However, in no case is any high-level mathematics used, and in all of the papers, the essence of both the problem and the salient analytic aspects can be gained from the informal portions of the discussions.

John Haldi's paper on issues of analysis serves to place in perspective the current and future role of systems analysis in government.

READING 22

SYSTEMS ANALYSIS IN THE WAR ON POVERTY*

Robert A. Levine

Last summer [1965] the Office of Research, Plans, Programs and Evaluation of the Office of Economic Opportunity put together an anti-poverty plan and a four-year program based on that plan, for OEO and for the total War on Poverty of which OEO-funded programs are a part. OEO was probably the first civilian agency to do this. It was done hurriedly with the due date of Labor Day and with a planning staff that did not come on board until the first of July.

I want to share some experiences of this planning process. Although planning of this type was first done by the U.S. Government in 1961, in the Department of Defense, our problems as a civilian agency are quite different from those of Defense.

1 Welfare is easier to define than national security. That is, we know what we mean and can measure what we mean in terms of

° *Reprinted with permission of the author. Paper presented at the 29th National Meeting of the Operation Research Society of America, Santa Monica, California, May 18–20, 1966.*

improvement of people as defined by income and other variables. Deterrence is much more difficult to measure.

2 We had a lot of data to begin with—more than Defense. Good economic data have been gathered and tabulated in this country for 30 years or more, and for the 20 years since the Employment Act of 1946 created the President's Council of Economic Advisers, the data have been quite good. Unfortunately, as most users will testify, these data are almost always out of phase with operational needs. There are problems such as the need for series on time and geographical bases different from the bases on which the data are gathered.

3 Unlike the Defense Department, we play a game against nature which makes our task considerably easier. We do not have to contend with a malevolent enemy.

These first three make our job easier than Defense; the next makes it more difficult, however.

4 Unlike many of the Defense programs, our results are testable. They have not really

been tested yet, although, when the 1965 Current Population Survey reported a drop of one million in the number of poor people from 1963 to 1964, a copy of the release was sent to OEO by a White House staffer who had written across it "nice going Sarge." Unfortunately, the change had taken place before OEO had really gotten into the business. In any case, the results of our activities are testable and are being tested and that means that our concepts will come into direct contact with what one of my colleagues calls the "real world out there." Thus far, deterrence theory has made no such contact.

5 Perhaps our greatest difficulty compared to the Department of Defense is that we started with no long history of accumulated systematic analysis in the field of poverty and social welfare. There had been, of course, much writing by economists and sociologists on related topics, but remarkably little of it systematically related costs and benefits of suggested policies or made systematic comparison of alternatives. The Department of Defense in 1961 had a huge backlog of accumulated analyses and policy recommendations from organizations like RAND, and much of what was done in 1961 and 1962 resulted directly from the intellectual investments started in 1951 and 1952.

I think we in OEO did a good quick planning job in this first year, but it was narrow and shallow because of the time constraints. It was narrow in that we did not consider as many alternatives as we should have; it was shallow because analysis did not go as deep as it should have. But, at least we know where the bodies are buried—we know what shortcuts we took and what simplifications we made.

What I would like to do today is to describe what we did and to draw some conclusions, but first, I want to expose a prejudice. We have done a set of system analyses of which we are pretty proud and I think that systems analysis properly done is bound to improve government planning and operations. Nonetheless, I am a bit skeptical of some of the uses made of systems analysis. For one thing the numbers used in systems analysis are always imperfect and to make decisions on the basis of small quantitative differences derived from very fuzzy inputs is wrong and is dangerous.

If differences are small, then an entirely different basis for decision should be arrived at. Indeed, if quantitative results do not accord with one's intuition, one had better check his numbers very carefully, because by and large intuition is the better guide.

A similar danger is that too much concentration on quantity, as is sometimes the case with systems analysis and systems analysts, can lead to asking the wrong questions. It is all too easy to substitute the concrete for the important, and it is frequently done.

I know some pretty horrible examples of misuse of analysis from my time at RAND and in the Defense establishment, but these are classified Secret, so I will give two other examples of systems analysis badly used.

The first comes from the cost-benefit analysis of water resource projects. (Incidentally, cost-benefit analysis and systems analysis are not identical. Cost-benefit analysis can be an important part of systems analysis but it is not the whole. The imposition of non-quantitative systems on decision making—the construction of qualitative alternatives, for example, can be just as important.) In any case, some work on water resource projects goes into an immense amount of intricate detail to try to establish the interest rate which should be used to discount future benefits from the water in order to match them against current costs of the project. Should it be the interest rate the government must pay for its borrowed funds, should it be the opportunity cost of using the same funds for private capital projects, or what should it be? To me, this whole debate is meaningless when estimates of proper interest rates are very imprecise and the final choice of an interest is arbitrary. If a Go-no-Go decision were made on the basis of such an arbitrary choice of interest rate it would be the wrong decision half the time.

Fortunately, the study I have in mind came out with the answer that at *any* interest rate the particular project under consideration was uneconomical. The costs, no matter how defined, were substantially greater than the benefits. The water system proposed would have provided a major subsidy to agricultural programs which would otherwise have been uneconomic. Now, this is the best use of highly legitimate cost-benefit analysis; the analytical discovery of *large* quantitative differences on the basis of simple generally acceptable *ceteris paribus* assumptions. The project was clearly unjustified.

And to end the story, the uneconomical project was adopted with great popular and political fanfare which shows another sort of limit on the application of cost-benefit analysis.

The second example of the dangers of systems analysis comes from some of our own work in the War on Poverty. Again it is a question of the use of cost-benefit analysis. It illustrates the possible use of quantity to narrow the focus down to the wrong questions. We of course avoided the error, but we could have made it.

In our OEO programs we do much training. For the evaluation of training programs, a frequently used method is that of matching the cost of the program against estimated increases in lifetime earnings derived from the training. If lifetime earnings, discounted properly, are greater than the cost then the training is justified. But for the purposes of War on Poverty training, in order to bring policy logic to this sort of computation, it must be assumed that if a training project is uneconomical—that is, if discounted earnings are less than cost—a preferable alternative would be to provide transfer payments for the less expensive direct support of those who would otherwise have been trained more expensively.

But our objective, as stated by our legislation, is not just removal of people from poverty by simple devices such as transfer payments. We operate under the Economic Opportunity Act and our primary mandate is to provide the opportunity for people to get themselves and their families out of poverty. In this case, therefore, the rationale of transfer payments as an equal-value alternative to training, is incorrect. Even if discounted earnings were less than cost we might want to do the training anyhow because of the social value placed on ending poverty through personal opportunity.

All this, I think, demonstrates some skepticism about classical (10–15 years old) systems analysis as a solution to all problems. Nonetheless, a standard *caveat* of systems analysis is that one should not look for perfect optimum but rather for any available improvement. Let me look now—under this *caveat* about systems analysis being imperfect and sometimes dangerous—to all we did to try to *improve* policy-

making through the use of such an analysis. My last point about the training programs provides a start. To my mind the most important contribution of systems analysis is to demand a definition of objectives, and to make that definition operational. I have already pointed out that in the hierarchy of our objectives, opportunity comes above the direct cure of income-defined poverty as such. But that initial definition of objectives does not end our problem; it begins them.

How do we define the objectives of providing opportunity and reducing poverty? We decided that our major measure would be the number of people moved past a family-income benchmark we call the poverty line. To move people past an arbitrary line is *not* our objective but it is a measure which can be applied to our real objectives. It is a necessary compromise in the name of systematic decision making. So we try to move people by a line. What line? We decided to use an *annual* income measure. This is not completely satisfactory—it ignores assets for example, and thus it includes as poor some people that may be really rich. Similarly by selecting annual income, it ignores those who may have an income in one year that may be atypically low and who may not be really poor at all. We have been struggling with refinements of the definition, but in the meantime, in order to get something done we have made compromises in the name of system and have used annual income. Having decided on income as a measure, we made one immediate advance; we changed from the simple poverty line adopted some years ago by the Council of Economic Advisers of $3,000 for a family and $1,500 for an individual to a more detailed, more variable line. Our current line, adapted from the work of Mollie Orshansky of the Social Security Administration, varies according to family size and according to farm versus non-farm residence. For a non-farm unrelated individual, the poverty line is $1,540, for a four-person family, it is $3,130, and it varies between these numbers and above them up to much larger families (which are too typical among the poor). Farm families are set at 70% of the nonfarm level.

Still more advance is necessary. We are working on regional variations, and in addition there is a question as to whether the poverty line should change over time as it has done in the past. But again in order to get going with our planning, we made the necessary compromise in the name of system.

Another definitional question still bothers us, and this one is also connected with our objectives. An individual and family line is certainly proper for the measurement of those dimensions of the poverty problem which can properly be called individual and family problems. But is such a line relevant to the community problems which Community Action programs (half the OEO total budget in fiscal 1966) are designed to attack? Even in the worst urban slums more than half the residents are above the individual-family poverty lines. Should we not extend our programs to them because of this fact? I doubt it; I feel we may need a different sort of standard to operate on and measure the progress against the problem of the community. For the moment, however, we are still using a single standard, another compromise among detail, system, and the need to get on with the job.

Getting on with the job, the necessary step was to divide this defined poor population into subgroups. Here, one's first intuition about the groups to use is wrong. It's very tempting to use age groups—that is apparently the first impulse of anyone starting into the question. But age groups are not completely workable in terms of the above kinds of problems, and the kinds of programs with which we are trying to attack these problems. Youth—say ages 16–21—is a usable age group, because youth have separately definable problems and we have separately definable programs for these youth. The aged provide another quite distinct and separable group whose needs—primarily for money alone—are distinct from those of the rest of the poor population. Children provide a less tractable group. In part there are separable children's programs, in the education field and elsewhere, but difficulties arise because programs to approach children *as* children are not the only ones. Operationally, a major way to reach a poor child is through his family. And most families understandably have people in a variety of age groups. So families provide another category we must look at and one which is not neatly parallel to the others. And families ought to be further divided between those whose heads are in or should be in the labor force and those who are

out or should be out; the problems and programs are quite different for the two categories. So we end up with a complex and overlapping set of categories—youth, aged, children, labor-force families, non-labor-force families. One really cannot divide the problems of poverty without looking at the programs designed to attack these problems, and we end up with a cross-classified matrix with objective groups on one axis and programs on the other.

Turning to our treatment of programs, what our summer analysis first did was to look at the whole range of existing government programs which might, without too much stretch of the imagination be called poverty programs. We estimated that the Federal Government was spending about $20 billion in this, with state and local governments spending about $10 billion more. The scope of OEO in the overall War on Poverty is indicated in part by the fact that this fiscal year we are disposing of only a billion and a half dollars. In any case what we should have done last summer was to attempt to re-allocate the entire $20 billion of Federal expenditures for greatest effectiveness against poverty. The charge of our legislation is that the Director of OEO should coordinate all anti-poverty programs. Last summer, however, we did not attempt this overall re-allocation because we did not have time. Rather we tried to allocate our own OEO programs and suggested major *additions* to other anti-poverty programs, but made no recommendations for internal re-allocation. Certainly, in our second planning cycle we are attempting the larger job.

To get a handle on programs then, we divided these programs into three functional groups according to the particular portion of the poverty problem that they were designed to attack. This division, a qualitative one, is the guts of our systems analysis. The three functional groups were *jobs, social programs* and *transfer payment* programs. These are three reinforcing categories—three legs on a stool—rather than being alternatives.

The importance of jobs is demonstrated definitionally. If opportunity is our primary objective then, in the American economy and American society as they exist, jobs are the name of the game. Opportunity means opportunity for self support which in turn means the opportunity to work in a useful and gainful job at non-poverty wages. If there are not enough jobs (and there were not at the time this analysis was made, last summer, although this has drastically changed since) we need programs to correct this deficiency. Job programs are important both because they provide immediate concrete and symbolic results from the War on poverty, but they are also vital to the long-run effectiveness of our remedies.

Second in order, although not particularly second in importance, come social programs. These are programs for basic individual and environmental change. We must realize that many of the poor do not have decent jobs because they are not capable of taking and holding decent jobs. Their individual education and training may be too low; their health may be too bad; family situations such as a large family headed by a female may make work difficult; families may be too large even for acceptable work to bring them above the poverty line; people cannot get jobs because of racial discrimination. Therefore in order to make job programs successful we must change the personal, family and environmental factors which make people and families unable to take jobs. These social programs thus reinforce the job programs but the job programs also reinforce the social programs. The worst thing that could happen would be for us to educate and to train people, to change their environments to raise their hopes and then not to fulfill their hopes because there are not enough jobs in the economy.

The third leg is transfer payments—pure money payments for no services rendered. Transfer payment programs are not primarily opportunity. They are recognition that some people cannot use work or training opportunities. The aged can make little fruitful use of such opportunities and the same can be said for many female family heads. Transfer payments also provide interim money for those who are waiting for opportunity programs to pick them up. But in one major way transfer payment programs also do provide opportunity. Money means ability to choose. A man with a family to support may, if given money, have the choice of taking training for a decent job instead of having to grab the first available job of any type in order to feed his family.

This is the structure of our analytical system and note that I have described it without mentioning cost-effectiveness or cost-benefit once. Nonetheless it is systems analysis made systematic by organizing problems and programs into a structure where it becomes possible to examine alternatives and magnitudes in relationship to one another. Of course that is not all of it. Let me give some further examples of the kinds of analysis we did internally within this structure.

1 I have already mentioned the crucial nature of the definition of objectives with Opportunity in the top position, and the quantitative measurement of these objectives, even though this measurement must be oversimplified.

2 We used quantitative analysis to confirm intuitions. Our intuitions told us, for example, that family planning would be a highly cost-effective program. We looked at family planning and discovered that this was indeed the case. Program costs were estimated to be low and effectiveness was estimated to be high. Our estimate is that, had family planning programs for the poor been started a generation ago, there would be about $4\frac{1}{2}$ million fewer poor people in the country today. This is highly cost-effective, although not quite as good as suggested by the summer intern who burst in and told us that a particular family planning program had proved effective after only six months of operation. In any case the family planning case also provides a good example of the political constraints on the uses of analysis. We are pushing ahead with family planning programs, but cautiously.

3 We also used quantity to make at least one discovery we did not expect, although please note that it is a large rather than a small quantitative difference. In the Job category of programs, we started out with the aggregate demand hypothesis that tight overall employment would take care of almost all the job problems of the poor. We made estimates however, of the size and projected changes of unemployment in various categories of the poor and discovered that it just ain't so. Our estimates have since been confirmed by the fact that even at the lowest unemployment rate in 13 years, the poor still do not have enough jobs. On the basis of these estimates we recommended substantial job creation programs, although with unemployment at current levels (much lower than the time we made our proposals) job creation is no longer our major emphasis.

4 We made numerical evaluations of alternative programs. Looking again at the job category, we looked in last summer's con-

text of over four percent unemployment, at job training, aggregate demand programs and housing construction programs and estimated that none of these would provide enough jobs for the poor. We therefore became quite interested in community employment programs to take poor people into useful public service jobs such as teachers' aides, health aides, other subprofessional categories and maintenance jobs as well. This seemed the most cost-effective mode of creating jobs and at the same time it would help fill the vast need in this country for an increase in public services.

5 Our definition of objectives implies that what we are out to do is cure rather than ameliorate poverty and thus in looking for effectiveness, we looked for the causal relationships between various problems and poverty and we looked for fundamental rather than ameliorative programs. Because we had questions about whether things such as poor housing and bad health care caused poverty rather than being spectacular symptoms of poverty, we gave programs in these areas relatively low priority relative to jobs and education—whose causal connection to poverty is clear.

6 We looked for the universes within which our programs could be most effective. The Job Corps technique of intensive training in a residential program is hoped to be successful for a wide variety of youths. Relative to cheaper alternatives, however, we believe its differential effectiveness is likely to be highest for hard core, hard-to-reach youth who simply cannot be reached any other way. And we recommended Job Corps concentration on these. For easier youths, cheaper programs are likely to be more cost-effective. Similarly Community Action can be a useful technique almost anywhere. But it is more likely to be more useful where the poor live among the poor in urban slums and rural depressed areas. In these environments where facilities, surroundings, and neighbors are all likely to be poor, the expenditure of Community Action dollars is likely to be most effective, because there is far more to be done—we are not working at a sparse margin. Because these dollars are limited, we recommend they be confined primarily to such areas of "concentrated" poverty even though they would not be ineffective elsewhere.

7 My last example describes a technique for getting the total budget down to a prescribed level. We used it not necessarily because it was the best technique but because in the short time available to us it seemed the only technique. In retrospect, it may be the best anyhow. Rather than trying to add up programs to reach a certain specified budget level, we started out with what we called an unconstrained budget—unconstrained by fund availability. That is, we estimated how large our programs could be, subjected only to constraints other than dollars, constraints such as the number of doctors available for medical programs. This added up to a sum higher than there was any likelihood of our obtaining. We then cut programs back by priority, cutting out the least cost effective first. We started with programs universes which included all the 34 million poor, then in order to get our budgets down we cut back for example to the hard-core universe of greatest need I have described for Job Corps and the universe of concentrated poverty which is in greatest need of Community Action, for example. We have not considered the general applicability of this sort of method compared to other modes of budget analysis for other programs but it did work well for us.

Let me conclude with two points. First, what I have been talking about is planning analysis and should be carefully distinguished from operations. For example, in talking about concentrated poverty, we defined this poverty to be that which existed in the lowest 25 percent of urban census tracts and the lowest 40 percent of rural counties. This was based on the greatest-need rationale described above, but what we were aiming at was a definition which would enable us statistically to measure the slums and rural depressed areas. For operational purposes, it is necessary to look directly for areas describable as slum or depressed areas, rather than arbitrarily decide on the particular tracts and counties we used for statistical purposes. Census tracts and counties are arbitrary definitions, and the only data currently available for these definitions are from the 1960 Census and are now six years old. The rationale of concentrated poverty by which we arrived at these definitions was not arbitrary, but it is the rationale rather than the superannuated statistics which must be used to apply programs to these areas. For statistical and budgeting purposes, the Law of Large Numbers implies that we are likely to be okay but the Law of Large Numbers cannot be applied to detailed local operations.

More generally, planning does not control operations and one problem we have not yet solved is how to control operations to meet the plan.

Finally let me mention evaluation. The plan I have described is based on theory. For better or for worse, OEO very rapidly built up spending commitments for over one billion dollars which preceded the conclusion of the planning processes described. The planning, however, preceded the first results of the programs so that we planned and allocated on the basis of how these programs *ought* to have worked. This year it is different. We are beginning to get evaluative results on how our programs are working. What we can do now and are beginning to do is much closer to true cost-effectiveness analysis—matching actual effectiveness against actual costs. My skepticism about the over-use of such analysis still applies. Decisions should still be made only on the basis of big quantitative differences and the right questions should be asked whether or not the answer is quantifiable. Now, however, the quantities we are working with are real numbers and not hypotheses, which is a very substantial change. As I have said at the outset, our results are testable. They are being tested, and next year, I may speak with less confidence.

READING 23

A PROPOSED METHODOLOGY FOR COMPARING FEDERALLY ASSISTED HOUSING PROGRAMS *

William B. Ross

Sheerly by coincidence, the launching of the new Federal Department of Housing and Urban Development followed shortly on the heels of the new presidential directive[1] for increased formal emphasis on more precise identification of national goals and on more systematic analysis of alternative means of reaching them most effectively. From the beginning, there have been no illusions either

* Reprinted with permission of the American Economic Association from American Economic Review, vol. LVII, no. 2, May, 1967. The opinions expressed in this article are those of the author and do not necessarily represent those of the Department of Housing and Urban Development. Grateful acknowledgment is extended for comments on an earlier draft to several individuals but especially to Robert C. Caldwell, Charles W. Wiecking and George W. Wright.
[1] *President's Memorandum to Heads of Departments and Agencies, Aug. 25, 1965; U.S. Bureau of the Budget, Bulletin No. 66–3, Oct. 12, 1965, and Supplement to Bulletin No. 66–3, Feb. 21, 1966.*

that the desired objective of effective public administration was a new one or that all the sought-after improvement in the precision and quality of analysis would be achieved overnight—or in a single year—or in a single administration.

The urgency of the presidential instruction was clearly of the "let us begin" variety. But the full burden falls on individual agencies to translate into their own operational setting an analytic approach long pioneered—but still conceded to be in the development stage[2]— in the analysis of defense goals and alternatives. The launching of so many simultaneous diverse efforts—without benefit of the extensive developmental work which preceded the formal Defense Department system—has inevitably resulted in analysis ranging from the un-

[2] *Alain C. Enthoven, "Introduction," A Modern Design for Defense Decision: A McNamara-Hitch-Enthoven Anthology (Washington, Industrial College of the Armed Forces, 1966), p. 7.*

even to the unsatisfactory and, often, to the unproduced. Each agency making this effort faces its own particular version of generalized national goals supported by broad individual program objectives leading to loosely related program activities on which voluminous records are kept on everything but how the program activities support the program objectives and lead specifically and measurably to the fulfillment of concrete national goals.

When everything depends on everything else, it is not immediately clear whether better analysis can be started most effectively: at better specification of national goals; at clearer development of relationships between overall program objectives and national goals; at testing of the relationships between specific program activities and program objectives; or at development of better data on any or all of the preceding relationships.

The present paper is, at best, a progress report on how one analytic staff in one agency is attempting to approach one specific policy problem cycle. The aim of the paper is to describe what we believe to be useful analytic methodology for the federal decision-maker; we try to be explicit about the stages of analysis in which we choose to defer concentration while presenting for critical review those tentative proposals which now appear to us both to be relevant and to lead in useful directions.

Federal Goals in Housing

Since 1949, the nation has had the expressed goal "of a decent home and a suitable living environment for every American family. . . ."[3] The directness, simplicity, grandeur, and scope of this expression have been the envy of presidential speechwriters and of legislative draftsmen ever since. None has topped it, and most have sensed the futility of even trying.

But the process of refining this broad goal into operational terms—even setting aside for present purposes the phrase "a suitable living environment"—is neither direct nor unambiguous. Certainly, the refinement process must consider the broad variety of action programs enacted under the "decent home" banner. Not

[3] *Declaration of National Housing Policy, Section 2, Housing Act of 1949 (Public Law 171, 81st Cong.; 63 Stat. 413).*

all of the relevant programs are the responsibility of the Department of Housing and Urban Development, but even those that are represent a diversity which we feel incapable of encompassing altogether within a single analytic framework.

For initial clarity, we have chosen somewhat arbitrarily to subdivide HUD's housing programs between those which appear to fit most logically under the phrase "to facilitate effective private housing market mechanisms" as distinguished from programs whose ultimate purposes appear to include overt assistance in the provision of housing at below-market costs. This dichotomy is neither a clean one nor of indefinite value. But, for the present, we find it to be a useful distinction.

The "assisted" housing programs are not themselves by any means a homogeneous group. Interpretation and interpolation of recorded legislative histories, inductive reasoning from obvious relationships, and even interrogation of participants in the legislative process all have a part in trying to identify just what unique combination of contributions a particular program was (and is) expected to make toward the overall decent home goal.

Essentially, each well-established federal activity has been the product of a unique, continued exercise in group dynamics involving interaction between (1) proposers of legislation (executive and legislative); (2) subcommittees, full committees, and leadership groups in the legislative process; (3) executive branch program administrators; (4) executive and legislative participants in the budgetary process; and (5) the "target group" of individuals or institutions. The net programmatic result has both the strengths and the weaknesses of the processes of democracy; above all, however, it means that single-dimensional measurement and single-criteria evaluation and even single-disciplinary study are inadequate—or even misleading.

The unraveling of the mixture of motivations and goals is the most difficult and the most critical part of analytic efforts—and, potentially, the most productive. But, the complexity of these patterns means that analysis cannot start at a logical beginning of clear identification of unambiguous goals and proceed in orderly, martial fashion to conclusions. The program grouping with which this paper deals is merely one special case of this problem.

At this stage, for example, we do not find it useful to insist on a direct separation of the income-redistribution goals of housing assistance programs from the development goals—both economic and social—of providing more housing of socially acceptable quality for various population groups. Yet, we cannot ignore the existence of "low" income groups too "poor" to be aided directly through existing housing assistance mechanisms. The evidence of constraints on the utility of functional programs for income-maintenance objectives requires more careful delineation of objectives/means relationships but cannot be regarded as a prima facie case for abandonment.

The Concept of Output

In the past, it would have been relevant, or even necessary, to debate at length whether the "outputs" of housing assistance programs should be quantified in "goods" terms (e.g., units produced) or "service" terms (e.g., unit months of occupancy). This dilemma appears to us to have been resolved by increased reliance on upgrading of existing substandard housing units and by the initiation of new assistance methods which involve temporary support of units for varying periods of time. Thus, for the present, at least, we find it necessary to use output concepts of the flow-of-service in order to compare those programs which we now administer, let alone the infinite varieties of alternative assistance devices which could be considered.

Again, the choice is a tentative one, and the probabilities are high that we will, for some parts of the analysis, need to return to production or "goods" output measurements. For either choice, considerably more thought will need to be given to the "standard-substandard" concepts and definitions.

"Housing Assistance" Programs

Any listing of federal "programs" is tentative and subject to expansion or contraction as analysis focuses, at one stage, on relevant characteristics which require separate consideration of distinctions within an administratively co-hesive program or, at another stage, on characteristics which blur the distinctions between programs administered by totally different organizations or agencies.

With these reservations, we consider that seven administratively separate programs constitute the "assisted housing" category:

1 Low-rent public housing (including new construction; acquisition of new units; acquisition of existing units, with or without rehabilitation; and leasing of existing units).
2 Rent supplements with mortgage insurance (with or without federal acquisition of the insured mortgage).
3 Direct loans at below-market interest rates for rental housing for the elderly and handicapped.
4 Below-market interest rate loans to higher educational institutions for housing and related facilities (including faculty housing and married student apartments).
5 Insured mortgages at below-market interest rates coupled with federal acquisition of the insured mortgage.
6 Below-market interest rate loans for rehabilitation of owner-occupied dwellings in urban renewal areas.
7 Partial grants to low-income homeowners in urban renewal areas for rehabilitation.

Economic Characteristics of "Assisted Housing" Programs

While this group of programs has the common economic characteristic that the housing for some period of time is provided to the occupant at less than the private market costs, the significant differences within the group may be categorized, tentatively, as: (1) differences in degree (level or proportion) of assistance; (2) differences in time pattern of gross and net federal outlay or cost; (3) differences in time pattern of benefits; (4) differences in the physical unit provided; (5) differences in total cost of the unit provided.

For purposes of this paper, it is necessary only to describe the range of these differences rather than the full array of them.

The degree of assistance can be as high as a partial contribution to operating costs plus the full capital costs of building new units as represented by the maximum annual federal contribution under low-rent public housing; it can be as low as a small fraction of the cost of a fix-up job as in the owner-occupant rehabilitation assistance programs. It may be as fixed as the maximum dollar limit for rehabilitation grants; it may be as indeterminate as the rent supplement payment which depends more on the future incomes of the tenants than it does on initial construction costs.

The time pattern of net federal outlays or cost can be as simple and as short as the one-check disbursement of a rehabilitation grant; it can be as long as the fifty-year maximum repayment period on a college dormitory loan; it can be as complex as the forty years of annually calculated net federal contributions to a low-rent public housing project plus the estimated federal loss on tax-exemption of the bonds sold to finance the project.

The time pattern of benefits can last as long as the housing unit stands in many cases; it could change or even terminate at the first annual tenant income reexamination of a rent supplement project; it can be linked to specific time periods as in the case of public housing leased units; or a residual part of it could be capitalized into the net selling price of a unit rehabilitated with great assistance when the property subsequently changes hands.

The physical units provided show large distinctions within each program group as well as between them—even when reduced from "structures" to "dwelling unit" terms. The range can be from the sleeping/study room shared by two or four college students to the multibedroom apartment for a large family in public housing or a rent supplement project.

Over and above the unit cost differences attributable to differences in average unit size, there are other major cost factors of great policy relevance. Quality of construction standards are among the most significant of these. Quality standards of size, equipment, and allowable amenities are administratively established pursuant to general legislative standards or guidance (e.g., "not be of elaborate or extravagant design or materials")[4] and thus differ most between programs which have been administered separately. The scope of "related facilities" included can also be significant as when a public housing project in-

cludes community rooms for recreational or social services activities. Equal size and quality units can be provided in large- or small-scale projects or in single units with greatly differing production costs. And, highly significantly, local land values and construction costs for the same product can differ within the nation by nearly 100 percent.

Relevant Policy Issues

Given a going concern which carries on, among its activities, a series of related programs with this range of diversity, the policy questions most frequently raised are likely to be along the lines of: What changes, if any, ought to be made in the multitude of administratively established constraints? What alternative devices could be proposed to better serve all or part of the objectives of this program group? And, most of all, what should be the incremental change in the relative proportions in which these related—and sometimes complementary—programs should be offered in the next annual budget?

The first of these questions is literally always relevant. The others become pressing on at least an annual cycle and become increasingly intense in those years in which a program exhausts its previously authorized time or money limits and must, in effect, have its option renewed. In each such policy question, varying degrees of partial goal reexamination and refinement are necessarily involved, but the complex nature of the composite goal mixture seldom permits abstract, total goals formulation except in the context of a policy issue along one of these lines.

At this stage of development, our approach to the assisted housing program group focuses on the income redistribution (housing cost savings to tenants) aspects which are their most common denominator but not necessarily the dominant goal of any one program nor of equal weights in the goal mix as between programs.

Measuring "Costs"

For present purposes, we believe it appropriate to measure "costs" of the assisted housing programs in terms of net federal payments, although more sophisticated measures may

---

[4] *Section 401(a), Housing Act of 1950 (Public Law 475, 81st Cong.; 64 Stat. 48).*

become more useful at later stages of analysis; e.g., in dealing with macroeconomic aspects of national housing investments. Our federal cost measure cannot, however, be restricted solely to direct outlays and recoveries of the Department. The nature of financing mechanisms used in this program group requires consideration of interest costs (only parts of which may be reflected in the agency's books) and the effects of exemption from federal income taxes. These factors are considered not for the sheer joy of complicating the analysis but solely out of the necessity that they be taken into account in reducing the disparate programs to a meaningful common basis.

The consideration of interest costs is present in another form when we attempt to make comparisons between the disparate time patterns of disbursement and repayment possible within this program grouping. Discounted present values are an obvious device for handling this problem, and the use of federal borrowing rates is an equally obvious first approximation of an appropriate rate of discount when we are comparing alternative federal methods of spending money to achieve the same or related ends. Again, more complex discount rate concepts, e.g., taxpayer's marginal value of consumption foregone, are only appropriate in the analysis of more aggregate aspects of the housing problem.

Measuring "Benefits"

Isolating the income-redistributional results of the housing assistance programs can be regarded as a first approximation of one aspect of the "benefits" of these programs, although we will most certainly want subsequently to look at the pattern of "savings" against the beneficiary income patterns to make a judgment on how well the income-redistributional results correspond to public goals. Initially, we may assume that the assisted tenants are those for whom income benefits are intended to accrue.

While the rents (or monthly housing costs for owner-occupants) of the units aided under the various programs are determinable, we need a base concept against which to compare these rents. Comparison with rents paid by the tenants in their previous housing has immediate but superficial attractiveness. It suffers from the defect that varying quality, size, and location of the previous unit make this comparison unreliable at best.

A better concept—which both avoids the uncertainty-of-previous-condition problem and adapts to the variety of factors influencing unit costs—is that of "private market housing of comparable quality." This standard has considerable flexibility in analysis and appears to be useful for a wide variety of comparisons, provided one keeps in mind the weakness of its implicit assumption that the tenant would have chosen housing of this size, quality, location, etc.

At its simplest stage, this standard can be applied to analysis of the pure cost differences to the federal government involved in its choices of financial devices. This can be accomplished by applying the financial assistance parameters of each program in turn to a standard housing unit to determine the variations in net federal cost and net rent savings yielded by each of them. This assumes that the unit would have cost the same to construct and would have served the same tenants under each of the programs compared.

The next stage would involve the assumption that private construction cost of the comparable unit would have equaled that experienced by the assisted unit. By holding unit costs constant and applying the financial parameters of the going private mortgage market (regular FHA mortgage insurance terms and conditions may be useful for this purpose), we may approximate the net rental savings to tenants for each of the programs in turn.

Since, in either case, these rental savings accrue over an extended period of time, they must also be aggregated in some way to compare the relative "rental savings per dollar of federal cost" efficiencies of the various programs. Because these savings are effectively felt by the recipients as the (reduced) rent becomes due, the temptation is very strong to ignore discount factors and simply add the savings over the period in which they are expected to occur even though the costs would be aggregated on a discounted basis. The natural compulsion toward symmetry and reversibility in analysis argues otherwise. In addition, it may be useful in evaluating income-redistributional effects of programs to consider the stream of benefits as equivalent to a stream of cash payments. Thus, by discounting rental savings also at the federal borrowing rate, we have automatically calculated the present value of a stream of payments which can be compared with the present value of the pattern of federal costs incurred to yield that income benefit through an indirect (or multiple-goal) device.

Subsequent relaxation of the "equality-of-cost" assumption will be feasible through successive stages of architectural-engineering analyses of the products of each assistance program to approximate more accurately the private reproduction costs of assisted units. As sufficient operating and maintenance cost data become available, it will also be possible and desirable to put overall construction and operating costs on comparable bases to evaluate differences in total life ("systems"?) costs resulting from differences in construction standards as between programs.

In any event, the relative values of private "rental savings per dollar of federal cost" among the various federal assisted housing programs provide one benefit-cost ranking—one that measures the income redistribution benefit. We may term the highest benefit-to-cost ratio "the income redistribution optimum."

In addition to the income redistribution effects, there are other aspects of the effects of assisted housing programs requiring equal attention, in their turn, such as the unit output/cost optimum or "most bang for the buck" target.

Over and above direct financial/cost benefit comparisons, there are differential benefits associated with the separate housing assistance programs in terms of how each program contributes or fails to contribute to the strategy of providing rebirth to dying cities or critical improvements to decaying neighborhoods. In short, if we were to give to the poor—through a negative income tax or some alternative device—the dollar equivalent of the income benefits they receive through these housing programs, we would still face the problem of saving our cities and neighborhoods; and this effort, too, would have its very substantial money cost.

Thus, should we identify two alternative housing programs which are comparable in their income redistribution benefits (or comparable in cost to the federal government), but

one makes a notable contribution to urban redevelopment or neighborhood improvement and the other does not, then clearly the one making the dual contribution is to be preferred on efficiency grounds.

Accordingly, we would next want to identify the nonquantifiable environmental impacts of the alternative housing solutions and the long-term versus short-term implications. By and large, this would consist of identifying the favorable and unfavorable consequences worthy of note for each relevant housing alternative, including implications with regard to meeting other urban objectives such as the creation of sound neighborhoods and economically viable cities. We would also assess the relative significance of these factors, considering such things as the relationship to overall area needs in terms of roads, facilities, and commercial establishments; the impact on the neighborhood subculture; the hostility or acceptance of nearby residents; the ease of assembling suitable real estate; the probable timing; and the number of persons affected, etc. This could culminate in the creation of a table of descriptive summary data along the following lines: housing alternative; cost disadvantage (over least total cost solution); unfavorable environmental consequences; favorable environmental consequences; significance of consequences.

The final stages of this approach to an optimum solution would consist of a new ranking from "most preferred" to "least preferred" which considers both housing cost/benefit factors and environmental consequences. The theoretical optimum at this stage may be defined as one of the following: (1) the "least total cost" alternative whose net environmental disadvantages are not sufficient to offset its cost advantage over higher cost alternatives, or (2) the alternative whose net favorable environmental consequences provide the most significant offset (nonquantitative judgmental offset) to its cost disadvantage. We will call this approximation the "environmental optimum."

The suggested handling of nonquantitative data is not a mechanical or arithmetic one, and it does not yield a numeric solution. For that reason, it will be unsatisfactory to some. We are all familiar with the horse and rabbit stew problem implicit in any decision involving both quantitative and nonquantitative data.

However, we believe that this approach provides the opportunity to quantify everything that can be quantified in a practical situation and to compare systematically alternative packages of concomitant net benefits associated with each alternative as offsets to cost factors.

The President has placed strong emphasis on the careful definition of program objectives and on careful analysis of alternative means for achieving these objectives efficiently. At the federal level, the general strategy in housing and urban development programs will almost certainly be (1) to encourage efforts by local governments to identify and pursue the most efficient local solutions, (2) to develop national data and analyses which identify the most effective overall programs and administrative practices, and (3) to seek expansion of these efficient programs and general and broad application of creative new approaches. We invite your attention to these matters and seek constructive suggestions on the analytical methods we have outlined.

READING 24

GOVERNMENT-INDUSTRY DEVELOPMENT OF A COMMERCIAL SUPERSONIC TRANSPORT *

Stephen Enke

The U.S. government is expected to spend $2 billion or more to develop a commercial supersonic transport (SST) that will be safe, profitable, and available for airline use around 1974.

Among the major policy questions now being raised by the U.S. SST program are: (1) Is a U.S. SST economically justifiable? (2) Why is federal assistance necessary? (3) How much of its expenditures on the SST should the federal government recover, and through what means? (4) How can government finance an SST monopoly, and yet protect the public interest without concerning itself with aircraft prices, flight frequencies, and passenger fares? (5) Are the benefits of the SST sufficiently general to justify a federal subsidy of its development and possible manufacture?

The answers to these questions are of very broad interest because the U.S. SST may be

* Reprinted with permission of American Economic Association from American Economic Review, vol. LVII, no. 2, May, 1967.

the first of several federal government programs to develop products of advanced technology for commercial use.

SST's Economic Justification

The President has declared that the U.S. SST must be safe and "profitable," but what is the interpretation of profitable and how can it be estimated far in advance?

Airline managements presumably will not buy an SST unless it can earn as much on its investment cost as can be earned on the advanced subsonics of the 1970's (e.g., the Boeing 747). Practically, this means that SST prices, flight costs, and receipts must permit a return of about 20 percent before taxes and interest. (Publicized "orders" for SST's are revocable until performance and prices are known.)

What airframe and engine manufacturers must ordinarily expect to earn from a new aircraft is more uncertain. Realizations have often been far worse than expectations, and several new commercial aircraft of the past ten years have lost money for their manufacturers (e.g., Convair 880). Expectations of profit must presumably be higher the greater are the sums to be risked and the greater the dispersion of possible financial outcomes.

If the U.S. government is initially to finance 80-90 percent of the U.S. SST's development costs, and if up to $4 or $5 billions of American resources must somehow be invested in development and manufacture before the program generates a net cash inflow from sales to airlines, an obvious economic test of the U.S. SST's justification is its ability to earn the 10-15 percent rate of return earned on an average by domestic resources employed in U.S. industry.

Whether the resource and money costs sunk in the U.S. SST's development and manufacture can earn a 10-15 percent rate of return depends upon: (1) costs of development, for airframe and engine; (2) costs of manufacture, for airframe and engine, as a function of production rate, cumulative output, and calendar date; (3) operating costs per plane mile, as a function of various performance parameters (e.g., specific fuel consumption) and permissible altitude of transonic acceleration; (4) operating receipts per plane mile, as a function of seating capacity, load factor (percentage capacity sold), and fare levels; (5) availability of supersonic passengers, as a function of number of long-haul passengers, subsonic passenger fares, willingness to pay more for less time in the air, and extent to which sonic boom nuisance restricts available routes and schedules. All of these factors remain shrouded in uncertainty.

Development costs of aircraft have often been underestimated by a factor of two—especially where the necessary state of art has yet to be attained.

SST operating profits are extremely sensitive to specific fuel consumption, lift-drag ratio (a measure of aerodynamic efficiency), and aircraft weight empty. Of its maximum gross take-off weight of maybe 650,000 pounds 10 percent or less will be payload and about 45 percent will be fuel. An X percent improvement in fuel economy, if translatable into greater seating capacity, could increase net flight receipts by perhaps $3X$ percent, proportionately increasing the selling price the aircraft can command.

Supersonics will have to compete with subsonics. Advanced subsonics may have costs per seat mile 20-30 percent below those of the U.S. SST. Airlines, unless they acquire SST's at subsidized prices, will hence buy relatively few SST's so that load factors are exceptionally high (e.g., 70 percent of seats are filled instead of the 55 percent typical of today's jets) and have to levy a surcharge (e.g., 10-20 percent) on SST tickets. No one knows how many long-haul passengers would be diverted to subsonics by such fare differentials. Estimates are that one-half may be lost.

The growth rate of passenger demand is also uncertain. Long-haul revenue passenger miles have increased at an average of 14 percent during the past ten years, but this rate is expected by most to decline. Continued growth will presumably vary with quality of service, per capita incomes, and population growth. The lowest estimate of passenger volume growth between 1966 and 1990 is five times.

Public acceptance or nonacceptance of frequent sonic booms by commercial aircraft remains doubtful. If commercial overland supersonic flight is not permitted by the U.S. and most foreign governments, no more than 40 percent of long-haul passengers remains to be shared with subsonics on the available routes over water. Conversely, as the SST's engines are "sized" for high altitude transonic acceleration (above 35,000 feet) and fuel consumption per mile at subsonic speeds is much higher, the economics of the SST are improved if it is permitted to cross the sound barrier at lower altitudes nearer to airport terminals. Unfortunately, as SST designs increase in gross take-off weight to permit more seats and hence lower seat mile costs, the severity of expected sonic boom increases and the possibility of operating restrictions (e.g., curfews on transcontinental flights) is increased. The prudent assumption, until more conclusive predictions can be made of public reaction to boom, is that commercial supersonic flights over populated land areas will be prohibited.

Anyone who has been intimately involved in econometric assessments of SST "profitability" realizes full well that its prospects will remain most uncertain at least until prototype flight tests and possibly until regular commercial operations begin. The total market for SST's to 1990 is probably somewhere between 150 to 600 aircraft. The profitability of the program is sensitive to numbers of SST's sold. Under certain sets of favorable assumptions the over-all rate of return could be 10-15 percent. But under other sets of equally plausible assump-tions the return is negative. Perhaps a best guess is an overall program rate of return of 0 to 5 percent.

The simple truth, however, is that such a complex and technically advanced aircraft must be an investment gamble in its first generation.

Necessary Federal Assistance

There is general agreement that, if there is to be a U.S. SST program, the federal govern-ment must finance it, past flight test and possi-bly certification, by means of outright grants, advances to be recouped later, and/or guaran-tees of borrowings by the airframe and engine contractors from the financial community.

Three of the principal manufacturers and their suppliers lack both the ability and will-ingness to provide $4 billion or so for the development and production funds required before the date around 1975 at which time net cash inflows commence. Their collective net worths, including that of some of their prob-able subcontractors, do not approach such a figure. Besides, even if able, why should air-frame and engine manufacturers risk such sums on an SST? They have alternative invest-ment opportunities involving fewer technical uncertainties, smaller investments, and shorter "dry" periods before recovery of principal. That one airframe and one engine manufac-turer are expected to be selected around Janu-ary 1, 1967, for continued development with government assistance, almost guaranteeing a limited monopoly of a usable design even-tually, is not enough apparently to evoke more than 10-20 percent participation in develop-ment costs by the manufacturers.

Potential airline customers are not expected to be a significant source of funds. No way remains of compelling the airlines to depart from their usual policy of "wait and see" be-fore purchasing. Firm orders cannot be ex-pected until after successful prototype flight tests in 1970 perhaps. And even then it seems unlikely that more than half the aircraft's fly-away price can be extracted through progress payments six to twelve months before delivery. (Although the first fifty or so SST's delivered

probably have a special premium value of sev-eral million dollars each, because of high load factors during their initial two to three years of service, the first hundred-odd U.S. SST's have already been allocated for refundable deposits of $100,000 each.)

The combination of high technical risks and large dollar magnitudes makes it most improb-able that the manufacturer, or indirectly the financial community, will provide the needed funds. Thus the federal government must either provide assurance against certain risks (e.g., accidental loss of a prototype) and/or become a sort of silent partner (providing say 80 percent of the net cash outflows and shar-ing say 80 percent of the net cash inflows). Such a scaling down of the private sums at risk to one-fifth of the total funds involved, with a commensurate scaling down of cash surpluses later, might be sufficient to evoke limited private financing despite the program's many uncertainties.

In addition to the funds required for devel-opment and production of an SST, safe and economical operation of SST's will be possible only if government expenditures are made for improved air traffic control, solar and cosmic radiation monitoring systems, and an improved meteorological forecasting capability.

The SST will cruise at 65,000 as compared to 35,000 feet for subsonics. The effects of wind and temperature on SST fuel consump-tion and the consequent impact on SST operat-ing costs and payload make better data on these parameters vital. At supersonic speeds more advance warning is required to maneuver around unfavorable weather. In the period from 1970 through 1990 meteorological im-provements alone could cost governments over a billion dollars.

These negative "externalities" should be considered part of the price of having an SST.

How Should the Government Recover?

The manufacturers will not risk even limited sums unless they and the government can agree on a financial plan that specifies at least the formula by which government will recoup its share of development and other "sunk" costs.

Unless there are significant and "external" national interests served by the program, a controversial issue discussed below, the federal government must be placed in a position to obtain the same rate of return on its investment as do the manufacturers if an impolitic and unwarranted subsidy is to be avoided. Thus if the program is continued because the $4 billions-odd worth of resources invested in it are expected to earn 10 to 15 percent before taxes or interest, and if the government were to accept say 5 percent on an 80 percent share of costs, the manufacturers would be expected to earn 30 percent to 55 percent on their investments. The only way government can avoid paying such a subsidy and still accept say 5 percent for itself, is to continue a program that prospectively wastes some of the nation's resources by promising a return less than that ordinarily obtained from domestic labor and capital used by industry in the U.S.

Thus government must be expected to share in profits if (1) the program appears economically justifiable and (2) unjustified subsidies to manufacturers are to be avoided. There is no logical escape. This requirement for government profit sharing has nothing to do with "socialism."

A major issue is whether government recovery should be either through some sort of tax or through sharing in net cash inflows as a silent partner.

Levies most often mentioned are:

1 A "royalty" or tax "off the top," added to the manufacturer's price of the aircraft: this would probably mean a 10 million tax added to say a $35 million manufacturer's price, and such a tax would lose sales to competing subsonics and possible supersonics.
2 An annual tax on SST aircraft operated by U.S. airlines: this would advantage foreign airlines, and a tax adequate for full government recovery plus an equity risk return would have the same present discounted value and incidence on price and sales as would an adequate royalty on delivery.
3 A tax of 10-20 percent on fares charged all SST passengers originating or terminating in U.S. territory: such a tax would further divert passengers to subsonic aircraft.

A tax on jet fuel purchased in the U.S. by all commercial supersonics may have to be reserved to pay for the special SST flight support services discussed above.

The alternative to a tax is sharing through a financial partnership or "pooling" arrangement. There could be one pool on the airframe and

another on the engine. In each case the selected manufacturer and the federal government would be the initial members—able to sell their shares later to financial intermediaries. They would contribute, quarter by quarter, development and production costs in some agreed upon ratio. And, when net cash inflows start around 1975, these would be shared by the contractor and the government in proportion to their credits in the pool. Such credits should include both advances and an equity rate of return, preferably the same for each partner, of from 10 to 15 percent compounded.

One advantage of pooling as against taxing is that there is less likelihood of handicapping U.S. SST manufacturers or U.S. airlines operating SST's.

Another potentially important advantage of pooling is that the self-interests of the airframe and engine manufacturers are made coincident with the interests of the federal government. If the contractor believes some design change will more than pay for itself, i.e., that it will earn a good rate of return on the extra cost of making a change, government will similarly be advantaged if the contractor knows his business. And ordinarily, because airframe and engine manufacturers are experienced in commercial air transport and presumably know the airlines' needs better than FAA officials, pooling could permit the federal government to give the manufacturers the maximum degree of private initiative possible. Such freedom may be needed to make the program an economic success. Certainly, the SST program should not be administered as though the U.S. were developing and procuring a bomber say, for hopefully it is airlines and not the federal government that will buy and use this aircraft.

Another recoupment issue is whether the government should share in manufacturers' receipts or net cash inflows forever or only until such time as the government has realized some previously stipulated rate of return on its outlays.

Making either the royalty or pooling claims to SST sales revenue transferable would enable the government to sell its rights to future revenues to the private sector if and when success of the program seems assured.

Why should government seek to recover all its advances from those who buy or use the SST, for are there not other broad national interests being served?

The most intangible and commonly suggested "external" benefits are (1) technological "fall-out," (2) contingent military use, and (3) national prestige, but each of these proclaimed grounds has been vigorously denied by others.

A more explicit argument is that the sale of U.S. SST's at $35 million or so each will benefit the U.S. balance of payments in the 1970's. Such claims ignore many substitution effects. Traditionally, half U.S. aircraft exports have been financed in the U.S. Each U.S. SST exported may mean at least one less U.S. subsonic exported. If the U.S. sells competitive aircraft to foreign airlines, U.S. airlines may lose passengers to them. Estimates suggest that, over five years from date of sale, the net balance-of-payments credit for the U.S. from the sale of an SST is no more than 5-10 percent of its U.S. export price (and may even be negative if increased U.S. tourist spending abroad is considered).

Nevertheless, some gross external benefits must exist, although not necessarily net of special high altitude meteorology costs, etc. In the end the program's Phase I and II (design competition) costs to the federal treasury might be "forgotten" as an alleged contribution of $300 million-odd to some vague "national interests." But beyond that, and starting with Phase III (prototype development) in 1967, the program should be treated as a commercial risk enterprise of manufacturers and government in partnership.

Mitigating the Monopoly

The federal government in early 1967 may select a single SST airframe and engine contractor to continue prototype development. The selected manufacturers will emerge with considerable monopoly power that could be of considerable value. How can the government use public funds to create a monopoly and yet protect the public interest without destroying the managerial prerogatives and efficiency of private manufacturers and airlines?

First, the monopoly will be limited, for there may be some competition from the supersonic Anglo-French Concorde; but more important should be the rivalry of growth subsonics, competition that compels the selected U.S. SST manufacturers to provide the best possible performance at a price.

Second, the selected prime development contractors will have many subcontractors, especially on the airframe. These subcontractors will acquire a competence that later could be used by a rival prime contractor. Also key employees have been known to transfer at higher salary to a rival manufacturer.

Third, the federal government is expected to have the right to license patents at zero cost, together with shop drawings, to any other airframe and/or engine manufacturers who might later seek to compete.

Hence, if a really large and profitable SST market were to prove itself, it is not evident that rival manufacturers could not materialize. The DC-8 did follow the Boeing 707. A first generation manufacturer is not always sure of developing a profitable aircraft that excludes competition.

A single airframe and single engine manufacturer for the U.S. SST should create other novel problems more easily overlooked.

One is division of the flyaway aircraft's price between airframe and engine. There is a very large range of indeterminacy. The engine for example might be priced almost down to its marginal production cost. But its price could be as high as the aircraft price minus marginal airframe cost. The maximum conceivable engine price could be three times the minimum. Previously an airframe company had some choice among engine firms to narrow the range of possible engine prices.

The airlines will be face to face with a limited monopolist able to charge variable (i.e., discriminatory) prices unless prevented by government. Some of the earlier deliveries, assuming they can maintain schedules, have potentially higher load factors and hence should command premium prices. Should the competition of Concorde and the subsonics prove minor, some airlines may ask for federal ceilings on U.S. SST prices.

This could be a dangerous step. If government regulates SST prices, should it not more energetically regulate SST fares so that airlines do not receive unjustified profits, and perhaps depress load factors through excessive competition in flight frequencies on approved SST routes? The situation of the U.S. merchant marine should be enough to deter any airline management from inviting government intervention.

The remaining alternative would be to develop two airframe-engine combinations—which practically would mean also producing two rival aircraft. This would double development costs. It would also lose some "learning curve" efficiencies in manufacturing. These extra costs would be justified only if, attributable solely to prolonged competition, operating costs were reduced by about a quarter.

Are the Benefits General Enough?

Costly public enterprises of great inherent risk are more easily justified if the spending of taxpayers' funds occasions widespread benefits. It is not enough that they provide employment and profits for a few localities and firms. How diffused are the benefits of the SST program likely to be?

About 85 percent of U.S. residents have never flown, those who do fly do not always take long-haul flights, and perhaps less than 5 percent of all Americans will ever fly SST's at their higher fares. Private, nonexpense account, long-haul passengers will mostly continue to fly subsonically. (It is not even certain that the federal government will reimburse its employees and those of its contractors for a supersonic surcharge.)

Further, American SST passengers will tend to travel to and from a few areas, such as New York, Chicago, Los Angeles, San Francisco, Seattle, Washington, D.C., and Miami. Americans living elsewhere may never use an SST except on international flights. But 100 million Americans may find themselves subjected daily to sonic booms if overland SST flights are permitted.

For all these reasons, and as the U.S. SST program is seen increasingly as a rival to expansion of Great Society programs, it is certain to become more controversial.

Conclusions

There are few modern instances of development with public funds of a technologically advanced product that is to be produced—very likely by a monopoly—and used commercially by private firms. Desirable guidelines in such cases are: (1) continuation only so long as the program is expected to earn a rate of return comparable to that expected by U.S. industry in making investments; (2) equal government sharing in such a rate of return, partly to avoid subsidization, but also to provide incentives for only economical design changes, etc.; (3) full recoupment by government, plus an equity or risk-taker's return, except insofar as there clearly are net "external" or national interests; (4) recoupment by government of its advances, not by taxes that reduce sales and use, but through some partnership (pooling) arrangement; (5) avoidance of special controls that will prevent the usual exercise of experienced management by the airframe and engine manufacturers; (6) use of public funds only to the extent that a private and excessively profitable monopoly will not be created; (7) no unrecovered government subsidies except where adequate benefits are likely to be diffused among a large fraction of citizens.

Finally, it is to be hoped and expected that a U.S. prototype of an SST will be flying well before the end of the 1970's, one that promises to be safe and profitable without being a public nuisance because of sonic boom. This means a state of art that will permit a rate of return of at least 10 percent on all resources invested in development after 1966 without supersonic flight over populated land areas. Until proposed designs can give this promise with more confidence it seems premature to begin construction of a prototype aircraft.

READING 25

AN APPROACH TO STRUCTURING TRANSPORTATION COST AND CRITERIA ANALYSIS*

Andrew V. Wittner

FOREWORD

In the coming decade, transportation investment decisions will begin to press even harder on government officials at the Federal, state, and local levels. As the scope and financial implications of transportation programs become more clear, the need for a systematic framework for guiding investments in research and facilities in those programs will be more pronounced.

The need for such a framework especially reflects the absence of any market mechanism adequate to elicit the resources required to support transportation programs. The massive capital inputs to regional transportation systems

° *Reprinted with permission of the author. This paper was written in early 1967 as part of an introductory study of the Northeast corridor transportation problem. Many of the ideas given in the paper were developed with the assistance of Dr. Gerald Higgins, now at the University of Texas. The author is presently on the staff of the Chief of Staff, U.S. Army.*

are simply too great for private funds to meet alone. If they are to emerge as realities, such transportation systems will probably have to be provided as a public commodity with resources in large measure provided by the government. And the government must be prepared to make these economic decisions without the guidance of a market mechanism.

This paper is intended for those engaged in seeking ways to come to grips with transportation investment criteria. It was not designed to be of use in the analysis of underdeveloped countries, although some sections may have application, but rather to persons concerned with the economics of transportation in the United States. There are few problems of economics and engineering more compelling, and the Federal Government is of course now engaged in establishing an expanding transportation post in the cabinet.

A reasonably complete overview of problem essentials does not seem to exist. We have apparently chosen to bypass sensible structuring of this problem, as with others, in our concern for the niceties of mathematical modeling and the supposed urgencies of rate making. This is not to argue against the need for sophisticated research technique and its potential application value, nor to imply that solutions to the many analytical problems embedded in relating, say, transportation to regional growth, or subsidy to self-sufficiency, will fall immediately from sensible structuring and orderly procedure. The point, instead, is that if such sophistication is to have value in application, we ought to be better advised as to which problems ought to be attacked, and in what order.

It is important to emphasize at the start that a rigid structure for transportation systems analysis is not proposed here. It is entirely possible that such a structure will never exist, or if suggested will be of little analytical value. What is attempted instead is the identification of key analytical issue, discussion of their economic and other dimensions, and suggestions for getting at these problems as study groups define their efforts. Hopefully, managers will find these ideas useful as they guide transportation research.

THE ELEMENTS OF TRANSPORTATION DECISIONS

Decisions to invest in transportation research and facilities will ultimately be governed by the following considerations:

Subsidy and/or regulation problems
Potential contributions to regional growth
Nonsubsidy Federal Government costs, and matching costs
Profitability, short and longer term
System growth potential and lifetime
Technical feasibility, including right-of-way availability
Manageability, if a large system
Prestige factor, if any
Vested interest

This set is neither exhaustive nor are all its elements mutually exclusive. The elements both interact and, clearly, may be rephrased or added to depending on one's viewpoint. Most important, each element *by itself* is extremely difficult to assess. And of course, the underlying problem is not so much establishing individual value measures relating to each factor, but finding some mechanism for tying all elements together such that a reasonably well-weighted decision may be made. The search for this means of integrating elements bearing upon transportation investment is tantamount, at this still early stage of transportation analysis, to a beginning search for criteria. It is well recognized that the development of these criteria will be difficult, as attested to by the Congressional hearings on the proposed Department of Transportation and the controversy concerning the provision in the initial bill giving criteria responsibility to the Secretary of Transportation. But criteria are critically needed, and they can be developed and communicated only through the logical and common sense evaluation of factors like those cited above.

WHY THOSE ELEMENTS?

The selection of these elements is not completely arbitrary. First, each element is itself composed of a set of subelements. These subelements are most often economic; but they are also political, social, technological, psychological, and perhaps other. In the vernacular, each factor is clearly multidimensional, and unfortunately there is even cross relation between the multidimensionality. Technological aspects of, say, a subsidy question can easily involve both economic and political backdrop.

It is this disciplinary multidimensionality, in some combination, that should, as analysis proceeds, characterize the way each factor is approached, dissected, and evaluated. But it is the economic dimension that will probably provide most of the quantitative decision-aiding information, although this will not come easy at first. This defines one of the two most important characteristics of the set: namely, that these factors, with the exception probably of only the last two given in this wholly arbitrary list, are all susceptible to economic analysis. There is much room, still, for improved economic analytical technique, in regional growth and its relation to transportation especially, but the framework for economic analysis is there. There exist costs, and this paper suggests ways to help measure them, and there will exist benefits, however difficult to define.

Underlying this entire question is the stark fact that there exists no clear market-directed mechanism that can now assist, or possibly will ever assist, in the efficient allocation of resources to large-scale transportation problems. Some elements of an economic market exist, but their interaction and lack of definition, coupled with prevailing nonmarket factors, seem to preclude the devising of an economically useful market analysis. Whereas most investment decisions in the private sector are made with thorough rate-of-return analyses, such analyses are likely to be of little value, presuming they might be accomplished, with regard to transportation systems. Uncertainties in the system are so dominant as to make rate-of-return estimating at this juncture little more than problem definition; useful in that sense probably, but not in a decision context. It is not so much the purpose of this paper to propose a surrogate or substitute for an economic market, but simply to look into matters that exert key influence on the total environment. In time, perhaps a surrogate market situation may develop.

Of more practical importance, probably, than each significant factor having an economic or other important dimension, is the straightforward notion that *those factors are the ones that will be framed into questions and asked* in some form or another by the persons most concerned. Here is where common sense appears to transcend analysis, the latter with its difficulty in communication and remaining underdeveloped ability to define and deal with these kinds of very broad problems. In short, we *know* that the factors cited above, or variations, are the important factors; what remains is to make them analyzable. And after all, there is not really too great a fundamental difference between common sense and application of economic analysis, so long as those persons applying the economics take continuing account of the present limitation of their art and those persons distrustful of economic analysis recognize that common sense cannot provide all the answers.

ASPECTS OF CRITERIA ANALYSIS

While the factors cited will undoubtedly bear on transportation criteria as they take shape, their importance and weighing will depend largely on analytical structuring. To rephrase, the importance of each factor will depend to a very great extent on how logically its economic (or other) composition is set forth. The follow-

ing key economic aspects, at least, will pertain to most factors.

Marginal costing—its potential and practicability
Joint cost or cost allocation—source or benefit
Remaining (or salvage) value measurement
Follow-on cost demand or implicit resource allocation, and spillover cost
Estimated total system cost, allocations among systems, and financing options

The above are cost aspects; the following are key benefit aspects.

Benefit definition—is the benefit as stated a true intended benefit or merely a convenient stopgap?
The benefit-time dimension—dynamics and discounting
Gross benefit measurement—does measurability exist?
Marginal and joint (spillover) benefit measurement—practical concepts or not?
Benefit weighting, given joint allocations
Choosing a desirable end-benefit, often without aid of previous analysis

Criteria aspects, some of which are given next, attempt to define relations between costs and benefits and provide a mechanism for choosing between alternative proposals; between alternative levels of resource (cost) allocation and hoped-for benefit realization. Criteria issues are relatively well-known and apply generally to both transportation and other problems, although, of course, in varying degrees.

Can a high level (more aggregate) cost-benefit criterion be chosen?
Are we unwisely relegating *absolute* accomplishment to secondary importance in an attempt to be efficient?
Can ratios, or perhaps a class of ratios, be useful criteria?
Do noneconomic criteria dominate?

In the process of early analysis, criteria discussions and criticisms per se should be set aside and cost and benefit questions should be tackled. From this, sensible treatment or derivation of criteria may come. Reversing things and backing into cost and benefit analyses by way of theoretical criteria study would be less likely to yield useful results or results that may be communicated to persons with less technical training.

This paper, then, is not so much an attempt to isolate criteria as it is an attempt to structure cost-criteria relationships and thereby shed partial light on how to select criteria. Some time is also devoted, in passing, to benefit-criteria relationships; this, of course, is conceptually at least as difficult as the cost aspect and is co-mingled with it.

The following section is directed at discussion of those cost and benefit aspects of criteria that are noted above. This is followed by a brief discussion of approaches to costing and how criteria may evolve.

CRITERIA-COST RELATIONSHIPS

1. Marginal Cost, Its Potential and Practicality

Clearly one would like to be able to pose in transportation analysis the typically sensible marginal query, "Is the additional expenditure a good idea or can I do better in some other way?" Given a cost-single-measure-of-performance function of the sort given by curve OM in Figure 25-1, certain analytical statements are possible.

At point A, where the slope of P-P′ is zero, no additional benefit is obtained at added cost. So if the additional expenditure C_1-C_2 were contemplated, some additional measure of benefit B_2 would have to result; in short, an additional dimension of effectiveness would have to appear at that point. It might perhaps take the functional form S-S′, but it is clearly not commensurable (or additive) with P-P′ as shown.

Of course, this merely indicates what has been known for some time: namely, that the postulating of a transportation "cost-composite benefit" function is exceedingly difficult. So, even if a family of "cost-single performance"

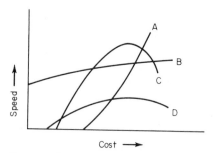

Figure 25-2   Different systems and a single performance measure.

functions for different proposed systems were conceived and drawn, as in Figure 25-2, the question of developing an overall criterion or criterion input is contingent not so much on marginal analysis relating to the *given* performance indicator, but rather to definition of co-mingled performance indicators. (Note: Systems A and B have interesting characteristics; A appears to offer unlimited speed, and B affords some speed at no expenditure. Most cost-speed functions will probably look something like C and D where the downward slope indicates the acquisition of an additional benefit or no added expenditure.)

But this is not to condemn marginal analysis, possibly in association with mathematical programming, as useless. Since the problem of defining all benefits of transportation systems will remain very difficult for some time, if not for always, where there is partial benefit definition (as with speed) there is room for useful marginal analysis. This is of course predicated on careful establishment and error bounding of the cost-single-benefit function. In short, attacking the cost-criterion problem in *stages,* by singling out measurable, individual benefits, should enable *and be encouraged by* useful marginal analysis. This should be a valuable aid to criteria development, at least in providing added insights. But care must be taken to ensure that little more than this is claimed, as yet, for marginal costing.

2. Joint Cost or Cost Allocation; Source and Service

Joint costs, simply defined are expenses incurred in the simultaneous production of two or more commodities or services. However, such costs may be viewed either from the "where generated" position or from the "where payoff"

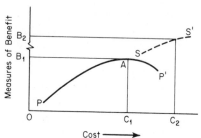

Figure 25-1   Cost-performance relationships.

position; that is, either from the *causing* system or endeavor (like R&D) or from the *caused* benefit or service. In either case, allocation problems must be dealt with early in the search for transportation criteria. Allocation, in the case of transportation systems, is more difficult when viewed from the benefit side. Both source-cost and benefit-cost allocation are discussed below.

As regards the allocation of not-yet incurred costs to alternative causing or planned systems, the problem is in structure like that faced in the military. A crude purpose or mission is hypothesized and a system (or systems) proposed to accomplish the mission. To the extent that costs are measurable, that is, that cost factors are derivable and that good system specification is possible, they may be allocated to that system. Analysis at this stage concentrates on careful specification and cost error analysis, and does not concern itself with subtle distinctions between system objectives, missions, purposes, or benefits. This point is important and often overlooked in a search for sophistication; careful system specification, based on knowledge of operation, is indispensable and must be sought early in the analysis. In fact, solid understanding of how a system functions should result in cost category structuring that will *both permit and facilitate* repeated re-allocation as purposes take on better definition and new systems are suggested.

There has been some question as to the handling of costs already incurred (for existing systems). These of course are sunk costs, yet certain of the more theoretically-minded argue that opportunity costs exist in the sense that previous commitments represent options foreclosed. It must be remembered that opportunity costs are not precisely costs, but rather benefits foregone as the result of taken action. As such, even if measurable, they are not readily combined with costs. Thus, the opportunity cost of an inherited asset is functionally related to both increasingly attractive benefit-cost criteria for present options (because of the cost being sunk), and to foregone benefits which may have resulted from past actions not taken.

These are logical and analytical imponderables, no matter how interesting. Granted that at a present decision point things (options) may be foreclosed because of past actions. But to state that their costs and benefits should be measured is to vastly over-complicate an already complicated problem and to imply that

measuring costs and benefits of still-existing options is easy. It is suggested, in transportation matters, that economists content themselves with trying to measure future streams for still-existing action possibilities. Success here will be reward enough.

In summary, then, from the standpoint of joint cost allocation to causing systems, in addressing the "where generated" allocation problem, there seems to be nothing unique to transportation problems. Note that "spillover" has not as yet been addressed. This is because spillover is defined here as a concept distinct from allocation, and is treated below in the section discussing implicit resource allocation. The following principles, not new by any means, are reemphasized here only because of the complexity of transportation analysis.

System specification, based on functional knowledge, is all-important to criteria development. Yet such specification must be parametric, and indicative of performance regimes in early stages of analysis.

Cost category structuring must relate closely to specification and still be flexible enough to permit re-allocation as designs and purposes are formed.

Sunk costs ought to be treated as they usually are, as sunk. Their opportunity costs are conceptually interesting but remain for economists of the next generation.

As regards allocation to benefits, in addressing the "where payoff" question, the problem cannot be so neatly structured. Benefit *measurement* or *definition* dominates the problem of *allocating* costs to benefits, as does the allocation of costs to benefits dominate the allocation for criteria purposes of costs to causing systems. (The above discussion of causing-system allocation naively assumes away the service or benefit aspect; and assumes away distinctions between services, products, objectives, and other forms of benefits.)

In summary, the whole question of benefit analysis pervades the question of cost analysis, and therefore of cost-criteria relationships. This is not a "finding" of this paper, but it is worth repeating as a warning to those who tempt logic by examining costs in a void. In the early years of military cost-effectiveness work, and still on occasion, the military variant of this was a major problem. Persons responsible for "effectiveness" studies would often seclude themselves, for security or administrative reasons, from persons concerned with resource analysis. A day or so before the due date, it would frequently be found that the two separate groups had produced separate and therefore useless products.

3. Remaining (or Salvage) Value Measurement

The concern here is not so much with how to make such measurements, but whether they are relevant to the decision context. How to make them is a complex question of purposes, estimating system lifetimes, and hypothesizing future buyers. But often they need not even be addressed.[1]

Suppose a transportation system exhibits an annual cost stream, over time, like that shown in Figure 25-3. At Time t the system is withdrawn from service and no further operating costs are incurred. But is the system "worth" anything sitting about idle? Hardly! And in some alternative use it would again begin incurring costs, as indicated by the dotted line. More important, except for modification or something similar, the system would have been "free" or available, an inherited asset, to the follow-on system. From this emerges the often overlooked rule that if a system has a place in a follow-on system, its remaining value at "follow-on time" (Time t above) is zero in any cost-benefit computation involving the new system; that is, remaining value is pertinent only in distinct and not related uses.

Unfortunately, for those who dwell extensively on the theory of remaining value, not too many carefully designed systems have distinct

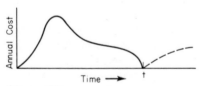

Figure 25-3

alternative uses (benefits). Even where such uses exist, prices users may be willing to pay are exceedingly difficult, if not impossible, to determine beforehand.

The important thread in this argument is the focus on use, or intended benefit. If, in alternative use, an older system can function, then that system is *inherited or free* except for modification[2] or add-on operating cost. As such, in that use, there is *no* remaining value. If it cannot function in that use, but may in some other, then nothing is inherited or free to the intended system (since it *cannot* "use" the older system). But perhaps there is remaining value if, for a different purpose, a buyer may be found.

However ... if there is remaining value, perhaps in the form of a Latin American entrepreneur or government, since it is by definition *not* related to the new or follow-on system, why should this value be credited to the follow-on system rather than elsewhere in the total economy? This question is interesting but ranges a bit beyond transportation criteria. The salient feature of the argument is to emphasize that residual value often has no meaning; it is not wise to set about such computation without asking why beforehand.

4. Follow-On Cost Demand or Implicit Resource Allocation, and Spillover Cost

These three ideas are often discussed as one, yet represent different sorts of resource allocation dangers. The definitions given below are arbitrary, but are designed to help point up specific problems:

Follow-on cost demand. The unexpressed requirement for allocation for resources at a *point in time* either explicitly beyond present planning or, although within the span of time being studied, so distant as to be obscured by more pressing problems. Careful scrutiny of the cost-time dimension may lessen the difficulty of estimating or bounding this resource requirement.

Implicit resource allocation. The unexpressed requirement for resource allocation caused by the *functional nature* of the transportation physical plant or overall complex.

---

[1] *Much has been written on the subject of computation. A good summary was provided by J. W. Noah then of the Center for Naval Analysis in his* Concepts and Techniques for Summarizing Defense System Costs. *He does not, however, seem to be specifically concerned with the question of alternative uses, as in this paper.*

[2] *Modification cost can be high.*

Spillover cost.   Cost or resource allocation sharing; induceable over time or functionally (as in the above two categories), or otherwise, and which, hopefully, is allocable.

Spillover cost has been used too often as a catch-all, to variously mean or suggest follow-on or implied costs, and joint costs. Yet one ought to avoid using "spillover"; it is not a useful analytical term. If a cost element or cost-causing factor does indeed "spill over" onto another, or to another resource source, it should be possible to postulate why this occurs.[3] Thus, spillover cost may be follow-on (time-related), implicit (functionally related), or have its basis in some concept of "jointness" falling outside either a strict time or functional dimension.

One such, for example, might relate to jurisdiction. A particular transportation concept might traditionally have involved participation of Federal, State, and local governments. Hopefully, percents contributed will somehow tie to anticipated jurisdictional benefits, and to call these "spillover costs" is to bypass the very fundamental idea that these costs somehow have roots in benefit/jurisdiction definition.

In summary, the notion of spillover cost as such is not a very helpful one. An effort designed to provide better definition of characteristics that will permit "spillover" to be broken into analytical components would be of considerable potential value in criteria structuring.

5. *Estimated Total System Cost, Allocations Among Systems, and Financing Options*

Possibly the most critical problem for the larger systems, from a practical viewpoint, will be that of raising sufficient capital from alternative sources to provide for whatever systems are chosen. All too often financial problems and methods have so pervaded transportation analysis as to overwhelm consideration of transportation needs and demands, and deter-

mine almost in and of themselves the form of transportation investment.[4]

Not only is the question of adequate total funding important, but the problems of how to relate potential sources to percentage contribution, and how to allocate among systems, are equally important. While the concern here is more with the first two of these questions, it is very important to emphasize that form of allocation will be a major determinant of total demand and distribution, and thereby of return to the various investors; it is in short an economic tool and one to be carefully evaluated.

Of much concern in recent months has been the question of user charges.[5] The three advantages usually cited in favor of such support which, incidentally, not only addresses the question of recovering outlay but also that of raising the money, are:

Users heretofore have often been able to avoid, by living outside the tax base area, a general tax levied by muncipalities to theoretically provide transportation funds.
User charges further enhance the ability of a transportation system to shape and respond to broader economic aims, through the pricing mechanism.
Governments, facing as they do many kinds of competing financial needs and obligations, are to a degree spared the problem of providing transportation funding.

These are compelling arguments. They are countered by those who cite the dangers of imbalanced user charges (equal charges for short versus longer distance), of user charges funding unrelated projects, and of user charges unrelated to demand or in fact causing demand overload (e.g., commuter discounts tending to

---

[3] *Postulating "why," as difficult as this may be on occasion, is only the beginning. This paper in its entirety is directed at suggesting ways to get at "how much."*

[4] *See Wilfred Owen, The Metropolitan Transportation Problem, Chapter V. Brookings, 1966. Owen concludes that present financial policies, as regards urban areas, are badly in need of study and overhaul. He favors a self-supporting system, and goes on to specifically suggest revision of state-aid policies, close ties between costs and charges, better use of the pricing mechanism, more efficient administrative arrangements, and attempts to improve integration and study of the "whole" transport system. His ideas are on the ascendancy.*
[5] *"Charges" and "taxes" are used synonymously here, although they are not precisely the same, to refer to the notion of a transportation beneficiary sharing in cost whether he has agreed to or not.*

encourage peak loadings). But these arguments are primarily management-related, not really bearing on the carefully applied validity of the user charge concept.

So self-support, judging from current discussions, will very possibly mean increased emphasis on user charges in the future; and this, clearly, can encourage investors to participate. Certainly no most-advisable financing or recovery method has stood out from among the many tried,[6] and as more proponents of self-support and newer resource allocation methodology are heard, the increased emphasis on "pay-as-you-go, but reasonably" is probably inevitable. Taxes, in so many cases, have not begun to recover costs associated with transport facility; and these costs over time have often required subsidy.

Since financing will be manifested in allocations to systems, and since these systems will generate use patterns, there exists a strong, if not clear, relationship between financing patterns and investment recovery. Cost structuring of proposed systems must take account of this process; it would not be wise to be wedded to a set of cost accounts (in a model structure) that could neither indicate which costs might be government-borne, or user-charge recoverable, or which cost elements are a direct function of use patterns of demand generated by charges within a certain pricing mechanism.

This is a factor of key importance in the planning of future transportation systems analysis. Much more work in seeking the relations between financing options and cost structuring is needed if decision criteria are to involve, as they should, costs as a function of financing possibilities.

WORKABLE CRITERIA AND APPROACHES TO COSTING

Approaches to costing.   By way of summarizing much of what has been said above, the following set of 14 questions is presented. The set, of course, is hardly all-inclusive, and as always the questions do often overlap. Yet

[6] *General and special taxes (e.g., real estate, personal property, gasoline) user charges (fixed and variable, often inequitable), equity and debt (in many forms, as initial capital), and combinations of all, with and without subsidy.*

each question, or a variant, ought to be thought of in considering all proposed sets of transportation system cost elements. There is no clear tie between the questions listed and the several conceptual issues previously discussed. Yet obviously there is strong relation, and a further attempt to integrate these "ways of looking at the problem" ought to be made early in any study effort. Many of the questions are applicable to most kinds of systems analyses, and some especially to transportation, but only explicit consideration can help to ensure that cost structuring gets off on the right foot by including or excluding appropriate cost elements.

1 Is the cost element likely to be significant, relative to total system costs?
2 What is the range of uncertainty about the cost element? How good are related data and experience?
3 Are the costs measurable? Do joint cost and allocation problems dominate?
4 May uncertainty be handled by cost-sensitivity analysis within a specified model structure? (Note: sensitivity analysis, in theory, enables analytical treatment of any cost uncertainty.)
5 Is the cost element common to different transportation systems?
6 Will an aggregate model, possibly with an "operator" function to zero-out inappropriate elements, be more efficient than a series of models?
7 Is the cost element "considered" important, perhaps for a specialized reason as for rate determination, by certain interests?
8 Is the cost element an input to other work and therefore needed in the interest of being responsive?
9 Is system operation or some other system-defining characteristic dependent on a certain, possibly unique, cost element?
10 Is the question of time-phasing, or following year costs, amenable to analysis? Related to this, are lag patterns tying *materiel* availability to *funding* availability desirable? In short, is the particular cost element in question especially time-dependent?
11 Is the cost element one that is marginally measurable? And marginally relatable to joint benefits and benefit measurement?
12 Does the element imply additional or subsequent costs? That is, will "implicit" or "follow-on" resource allocation be overlooked if an element is omitted?

13 Is the question of salvage or remaining value well understood? That is, is the relation between inherited assets, remaining value, and system functioning, with regard to the particular cost element, understandable?

14 Most important, what is the purpose of the costing exercise? The following are but four possible broad purposes of costing transportation systems:

> Understanding total system costs, over time[7]
> Establishing investment or rate-of-return-base
> Establishing basis for Federal government participation
> Providing a quick response answer to specific questions

These are the kinds of questions that should determine the emphasis given a certain cost element as study progresses. Approaches to costing can be roughly based on these questions and answers to them. The actual costing can both begin by building on the less conceptual approaches and the different data that derive, and later address the more subtle questions. The following chart roughly suggests several approaches, as different questions from among the 14 are addressed (Y = addressed; N = not addressed). Approaches 1 to 3 in general address fewer and less difficult questions, and may be somewhat shorter term efforts than approaches 4 to 7. However, both longer and short term efforts may involve difficult ques-

[7] *This could have many sub-purposes in itself. For example, focus might be on right-of-way payments or certain operational aspects.*

tions, as evidenced by questions 11 and 12 being tackled in several approaches.

A simple "yes" or "no" answer, unfortunately, will not provide the final judgment as to whether a given cost element should be included in a specific model format. For the first approach, as an example, although the chart above suggests that only six of the fourteen questions be directed at the proposed set of cost elements, a positive answer to but *one* question could mean including the cost element.

A glance at Question 14 will affirm this. If a cost element is important only because a desired cost estimate has a special purpose, then it must, for that reason alone, be included. These kinds of questions can help those costing large transportation systems to logically arrange their ideas, but the questions must be weighed intelligently.

Workable criteria. The thesis of this paper is that an overall procedure which pointedly addresses those cost-criteria problems very briefly sketched in each section, should help cut the criteria question to a size whereat some solid progress may be made. This is not to say that the suggested approach is as yet well integrated (that is, that the pieces tie together as best they might), that each problem is itself as clearly stated as it might be, or that other aspects of criteria-cost relationships could not profitably be singled out. Rather, the point is that study as suggested of each part of the problem is worthwhile in itself and should help provide basic knowledge as well as further guidance.

Preliminary criteria ought not involve too

Approach	Questions														
	1	2	3	4	5	6	7	8	9	10	11	12	13	14	*
1	Y	Y	N	Y	N	Y	N	N	Y	N	N	N	N	Y	8
2	Y	Y	N	Y	Ý	Y	N	Y	Y	N	N	Y	N	Y	5
3	Y	Y	Y	Y	Y	Y	Y	Y	Y	Y	Y	N	N	Y	2
4	Y	Y	?	Y	?	Y	N	Y	N	N	N	N	N	Y	8
5	Y	Y	Y	Y	Y	?	N	Y	Y	N	N	Y	N	Y	4
6	Y	Y	Y	Y	Y	Y	Y	Y	Y	Y	Y	N	Y	Y	1
7	Y	Y	Y	Y	Y	Y	Y	Y	Y	Y	Y	Y	Y	Y	0

Total number of questions not addressed in each approach.

many dimensions of benefit (yet speed often seems to overwhelm commercial transport planning), ought not to be too concerned with benefit *quantification* to the exclusion of benefit *definition,* and should have a firm foundation in sensible costing. In short, the search for transportation investment criteria ought to proceed as a search for resource allocation structure rather than for the criteria themselves. From an orderly structuring will probably derive useful technique application and theoretical insight.

Although benefits and theoretical benefit problems have been mentioned, the list of key benefit aspects given at the beginning of this paper has not been specifically addressed. The emphasis on costing reflects the notion that cost structuring, as difficult as it may be (especially since it is so interwoven with benefits), is easier than benefit structuring. This too might be attempted, but workable criteria are probably best found, in the author's opinion, if the analytical effort is tuned most to the development of cost relationships.

READING 26

THE APPLICATION OF COST-EFFECTIVENESS TO NON-MILITARY GOVERNMENT PROBLEMS *

Olaf Helmer

1. INTRODUCTION

In this paper an attempt will be made to set down general procedural guidelines for the introduction of a systematic cost-effectiveness approach to the budgeting problems of a Department of the federal government. The procedure to be outlined is, in principle, applicable to other cases—for instance to sub-sectors of a Department, to State or city government agencies, or to industry—subject however to obvious adjustments necessitated by considerations of scale and of specific constraints peculiar to each case.

It will almost immediately become apparent that the role of expert judgment cannot be neglected. Indeed, it plays such a dominant part that a portion of this paper will be devoted to a discussion of the efficient use of expertise and to the avoidance of its abuse.

* Reprinted with permission of The RAND Corporation, P-3449, September, 1966, The RAND Corporation, Santa Monica, California.

2. MANDATORY ALLOCATIONS

In allocating a given budget it will invariably be the case that some portions of it are already firmly committed, say for current operations, previously contracted obligations, pension payments, etc. For clarification, let it be understood that from here on we shall concern ourselves only with the remaining portion of the budget, that is, with that part which can be freely disposed within the constraints of feasibility and prudence. In particular, if there is a previous commitment to expend some amount on some particular measure or activity, but if the precise amount is subject to executive discretion, then the minimum amount required to be spent will be considered firmly allocated, while the question of what marginal amount above that minimum is to be allocated to that measure will be considered part of the budgeting process to be treated in this paper.

The conditions prevailing, or expected to prevail, at the beginning of the budgeting period, together with a statement of the mandatory allocations just described as well as of the amount of the freely disposable budget, constitute the initial situation on the basis of which the budgetary decisions have to be made.

3. PROGRAMS

In deciding how to spend a Department's budget (by which, as we noted, we mean the freely disposable part of the total budget), consideration has to be given to numerous competing measures.

Let us assume that

$$M_1, M_2, \ldots, M_z$$

is a complete list of measures worthy of such consideration. A measure M_i is rarely, if ever, of the all-or-nothing kind; that is, one can usually associate with it a degree, q_i, to which such a measure can be executed. As a rule, this is obvious. For example, salary raises, support of scientific research, agricultural subsidies, retraining programs, foreign aid, slum clearance, reforestation all are of this kind. But even in the case of seemingly unitary events, such as building a dam or landing on the Moon, there clearly are aspects under the planner's control —such as expected time of completion or size and quality of effort—which can be reflected in the "degree" of the measure's acceptance.

The construction of a program, then, may be considered to consist of the assignment of numbers

$$q_1, q_2 \ldots, q_z$$

to the above measures (where many of the q_i may be 0, indicating rejection of Measure M_i), such that the total cost of carrying out the given measures to these degrees is not expected to exceed the given budget.

The problem is to devise criteria under which alternative programs can be compared and to describe a procedure by which the preferred program can in fact be selected.

4. NOMINATION AND AGGREGATION

Before a program can be composed it is necessary to arrive at a list of measures deserving of consideration.

There is no hard-and-fast rule for the compilation of such a list. Good government policy depends not only on competent analysis and expert judgment but also on inventiveness and imagination. Therefore, in attempting to compile a list of measures for consideration, it is well to elicit suggestions representing as many different viewpoints as are relevant to the subject matter at hand.

Measures which are strictly complementary, in the sense that neither can be meaningfully adopted in the absence of the other, should be combined and listed as one measure. The measures thus nominated for consideration should be screened by an expert or, better, a panel of experts, in order to eliminate those which, upon closer examination, appear to be technically infeasible or expensive beyond all reason or fraught with highly undesirable incidental consequences. (The procedure for using a panel rather than a single expert, the opportunity for which will recur several times in the program budgeting effort, will be discussed separately in Sec. 10.)

If the total list thus obtained consists of no more than a few dozen items, it can be further processed as a whole. If it is larger, consisting perhaps of the order of a hundred or several hundred items, it is advisable first to aggregate all nominated measures under several subheadings in order to facilitate efficient processing by the planning staff. While a large set of potential measures usually lends itself to a rather natural categorization by subject matter, the precise manner in which this breakdown is achieved is immaterial, as long as items related by (partial) complementarity or by substitutability are relegated to the same subheading and each such category in turn contains no more than at most a few dozen items.

For the case where no such breakdown into categories is required we shall develop a method below of allocating the budget over the measures listed for consideration.

If, on the other hand, the number of measures to be considered is so large as to make a breakdown into, say, s categories,

$$K_1, K_2, \ldots, K_s,$$

advisable, then essentially the same allocation method may have to be used several times, as follows:

First, tentatively allocate portions B_1, B_2, ..., B_s of the budget, B, to K_1, K_2, ..., K_s respectively, where

$$B_1 + B_2 + \ldots + B_s = B.$$

Then solve the allocation problem of each B_i among the measures within K_i. The process of these sub-allocations may reveal that the original allocations of B_i to K_i require revision. Such a revision should be carried out by applying to the apportionment of B among B_1, B_2, ..., B_s precisely the same method that leads to the allocation of B_i among the measures listed in K_i. Let a revised, and thus improved, allocation be

$$B_1' + B_2' + \ldots + B_s' = B.$$

Now, for each B_i' which is actually different from B_i, a revised sub-allocation among the measures contained in K_i has to be carried through. If necessary, this process has to be iterated once again. (This sounds more complex than it is, since most of these revisions will be in the nature of minor marginal adjustments.)

5. REASONABLE ADOPTION BOUNDS

First of all, now, it is necessary to establish for each nominated measure M the unit in which its degree of adoption, q, is to be measured. Sometimes it may be easiest to describe the degree of adoption of a measure in terms of the number of dollars to be devoted to it, so that the dollar will be the unit of measurement. More often, a more natural unit may suggest itself, such as the number of items of a certain kind that are concerned by the measure (e.g., the number of acres to be reforested, the number of housing units or highway miles to be built, the number of workers to be retrained, etc.). The particular choice of unit is immaterial, as long as it is defined without ambiguity, so that "adoption of M to the degree q" has a precise meaning.

Regardless of just how the benefits derived from the adoption of M are to be assessed, its value V, as a function of the degree of adoption q, will typically be represented by an S-shaped curve of the following kind:

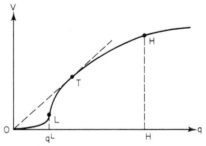

Figure 26-1

That is to say, up to a certain point L, roughly in the vicinity of the point of inflection, the degree of adoption of the measure, q, is too small to produce more than a negligible value, V. While beyond L the marginal value per added adopted unit begins to decrease, still the average value per unit increases up to the point T, where it reaches its maximum. Beyond T it begins to decrease, and from some point H on, the marginal returns decrease so fast as to make further investment in the measure under consideration appear definitely unremunerative.

While these points on the curve are not exactly determinable (nor even exactly defined), it will be possible, for each measure M under consideration, to establish by a panel of experts two approximate bounds, q^L and q^H, representing respectively the lowest and highest reasonable degrees to which the measure might, if at all, be adopted. The inherent conceptual vagueness of these bounds is immaterial; for practical purposes it suffices to obtain a consensus as to a value, q^L, below which the adoption of M would be pointless, and a value, q^H, above which marginal benefits are so small as to make a higher degree of adoption wasteful, or where the cost would exceed the entire available budget. It should be noted that among the causes for diminishing marginal return above q^H may well be nonmonetary resource constraints. That is, while increased adoption of M may eo ipso appear profitable, the entailed depletion of scarce resources may have a deleterious overall effect. This observation should serve to emphasize that, in appraising the value of a measure, a systems viewpoint must be adopted, giving due consideration to the overall effects rather than to the effects of M regarded in isolation.

6. COSTS

Next, the cost of each proposed measure has to be determined. Here we note at once that, since the costs in question are future costs, they are in principle not determinable with absolute accuracy but can only be estimated with a certain, limited, degree of reliability. Hence, while reasonable accuracy is desirable, an exaggerated display of supposed precision is misleading and, moreover, aggravates the planning process unnecessarily.

For most practical purposes it will suffice to estimate the costs, C_i^L and C_i^H, of each measure M_i at the levels of adoption represented by q_i^L and q_i^H respectively, as well as of the marginal costs per unit at each of these two levels of effort, and to assume that intermediate marginal costs can be obtained by interpolation. In extraordinary cases, where a sizeable deviation from such linearity is expected, a suitable annotation to that effect, indicating the need for later correction, will be sufficient at this point.

It is well known that the expected cost of a measure depends to some extent on what other measures are being enacted, and to what degree. This dependence on the systems context can often not be neglected, although it may be assumed to have only a secondary effect. Since at this stage an estimate must be supplied in ignorance of the remaining program, it is necessary to proceed by successive approximation. At this first stage, in fact, the cost of each measure should be estimated on the (fictitious) assumption that it alone be added to what has earlier been referred to as the initial situation. To aid the subsequent process of correcting for systems context, it may be well to annotate each item with appropriate indications as to

which other items, if adopted, would noticeably affect the given item's estimated cost-in-isolation.

The recommended procedure for actually arriving at the above cost estimates, C_i^L and C_i^H for each M_i (as well as corresponding marginal costs), is to have a staff of trained cost analysts prepare calculations of costs together with indications of, and reasons for, the degree of their own uncertainty associated with each. These are submitted to a panel of (subject matter and cost) experts, who form a consensus as to the acceptance or modification of the cost figures submitted to them. (For details regarding the operation of such a panel the reader is again referred to the last section of this paper.)

7. BENEFITS

The procedure for ascribing benefits (or effectiveness values) to contemplated measures is conceptually different but in fact not too dissimilar from that of ascribing costs.

The principal conceptual difference lies in the fact that no ready-made unit of measurement, comparable to the dollar in the case of costs, is available. It should be clearly understood that this is not just a temporary deficiency which the passage of time will eliminate. While certain consequences of the adoption of a measure may have objectively measurable effects (e.g., increased earning power resulting from retraining), any measure invariably has a multitude of effects which are in principle incommensurable because the relative evaluation of diverse effects will depend on individual subjective preferences among social utilities. Moreover, superimposed upon the subjectivity of these personal predilections is their inherent vagueness, due to the lack of explicit articulation characteristic of social attitudes.

The best that can be done in view of these circumstances is to resort, again, to the use of a panel of experts (taking care that all relevant aspects are represented). However, in order to make communication among them possible as to the values to be ascribed to various measures, it is necessary—as a minimum—to establish a unit of measurement, however vague. One way to do this (though not the only one) is by the following prescription:

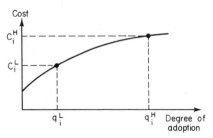

Figure 26-2

Take the initial situation, with no measures adopted (other than precommitted ones), as having zero value. Imagine the (unknown) budget allocation which the appraiser would regard as optimal to have a value of 1000. Assess the contribution of each measure M_i, at degree of adoption q_i, as the number of permills by which it, considered in isolation, would raise the value of the initial situation toward the value of the "ideal" situation (to which the value 1000 had been ascribed). Here again, as in the case of costs, it suffices to fix a few values, among them V_i^L and V_i^H (see Figure 26-1) to be ascribed to M_i if the latter is enacted at levels q_i^L and q_i^H respectively. It may be expedient, though not necessary, to determine the position of T (see Figure 26-1), where the ray from the origin is tangent to the curve. In view of the inherent vagueness of the value concept it is here even more justified to assume for all practical purposes that at intermediate levels the value can be calculated by simple interpolation.

The real value of a measure, even more so than its cost, depends on the systems context, that is, on the remainder of the adopted program. Thus, again, a successive-approximation procedure is indicated, allowing for correction of the values-in-isolation as the planning process zeros in on the finally adopted program. Annotations indicating the adoption of what other measures might particularly affect the value of a given measure would again be a helpful preparation to this effect.

8. COMPOSITION OF THE FIRST-APPROXIMATION PROGRAM

We are now ready to construct a first-approximation program, that is, a program which would be the optimal one, were it not for two considerations: (*a*) the true, systems, costs and benefits are not necessarily identical with the costs and benefits determined for each measure separately in isolation; and (*b*) both costs and benefits are mere estimates, based partly (in the case of costs) or wholly (in the case of benefits) on judgment, and thus subject to some revision as the planning process itself generates among the planners an increasing understanding of the implications of each decision under consideration.

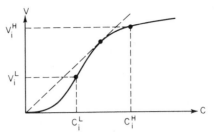

Figure 26-3

Disregarding these caveats for the moment, the matter of constructing an optimal program becomes one of straight-forward calculation, namely by maximization of marginal returns. Geometrically the solution to this problem can be visualized as follows: For each measure, M_i, represent the value, V_i, as a function of the cost, C_i (Figure 26-3), which under our assumptions will be an S-shaped curve similar (if not identical) to the representation of V_i as a function of q_i, but with the point of tangency, T', of the ray from the origin possibly farther to the right than in the latter case (due to the tendency of marginal costs to decrease).

Now represent the revelant parts of all of these curves on one diagram (Figure 26-4), where for simplicity a total of only 5 measures has been assumed, and consider a ray from the origin, with an angle α between it and the V-axis. All points above this ray have a larger benefit-cost ratio, V/C, than those below. Associated with each such ray is a program, obtained by selecting for each measure M_i the point on its curve that lies farthest to the right and on or above the ray. In the example, this program would consist in enacting the measures M_1, M_2, M_3, M_4, M_5 to the degrees $q_1, q_2, q_3, 0, q_5$ respectively (q_4 being 0 because

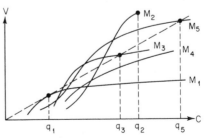

Figure 26-4

the corresponding curve lies entirely below the ray). Associated with this program will be a fixed cost C, where C is a monotonically increasing function of α. Thus, by rotating the ray through increasing values of α, the program cost can be increased until it equals the given budget, B. The resulting values of q_1, q_2, ..., q_z will furnish the desired first approximation to the optimal program.

9. REFINEMENT OF THE PROGRAM

Next, the process just described of obtaining costs and values and an approximate optimal program has to be iterated. However, costs and values are no longer determined on the assumption of measures being isolatedly added to the initial situation, but rather on the hypothesis that the adoption of each item is accompanied by the introduction of the other items at the levels indicated in the first-approximation program.

The result of this effort (which, because only marginal adjustments are called for, will be much simpler than that in the first round) will be a second-approximation program.

It is for the experts to decide whether the quality of this program is sufficient to be accepted as the final one, or whether another iteration is indicated. It may be expected that, while one iteration of the original process is indispensable for the production of a close-to-optimal program, further iterations may often not be required.

10. THE USE OF PANELS OF EXPERTS

As we stated at the beginning of this paper, and as must have become abundantly clear in the sequel, the reliance on expert judgment is an indispensible part of budgetary planning. In the particular type of case treated here, of budgeting the expenditures of a Department of the federal government, the range of required expertise is not likely to be provided by a single person; hence almost inevitably a variety of expert advisers needs to be consulted.

Experiments have shown that the best use of a panel of experts is not made by the traditional method of having the issues presented to them and debated in open discussion, until a consensus emerges or a group position has been agreed upon by majority acclamation. In order to avoid the inadvertent psychological drawbacks of such a procedure and to arrange a setting in which the pros and cons of an issue can be examined as systematically and dispassionately as its essentially intuitive character allows, it is preferable to proceed so as to minimize the effects of supposed authority and of specious oratory.

To this end, if time and facilities permit, it is expedient to provide for anonymity of the experts' opinions and of the arguments advanced by them in defense of these opinions. Such a procedure, at least until appropriately sophisticated computing machines come to our aid, is apt to be cumbersome, and compromises may have to be sought that do not violate the basic principle too much.

An anonymous debating procedure, aimed at contriving an eventual group position, might have the following form:

Let us consider the typical situation of having to arrive at a group answer to the question of how large a particular number N should be. (E.g., N might be the estimated cost of a measure, or a value representing its overall benefit, or the portion of the budget to be devoted to it, or an estimate of the smallest reasonable degree of adoption, or the reduction in cost due to the simultaneous adoption of some other measure.) One might proceed in the following steps: (1) Have each expert independently give an estimate of N. (2) Arrange the responses in order of magnitude, and determine its quartiles, Q_1, M, Q_2:

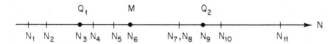

so that the four intervals formed on the N-line by these three points each contain one quarter of the estimates. Communicate the values of Q_1, M, Q_2 to each respondent, ask him to reconsider his previous estimate and, if his new estimate lies outside the interquartile range (Q_1, Q_2), to state briefly his reason why, in his opinion, the answer should be lower (or higher) than corresponds to the 75% majority opinion expressed in the first round. (3) The results of this second round, which as a rule will have a less dispersed distribution, are again fed back to the respondents in summary form, that is, by communicating the magnitude of the new quartiles to them. In addition, the reasons for raising or lowering the value, elicited in Round 2 and suitably collated and edited, are fed back to the respondents (always, of course, preserving anonymity as to the proponent). The experts are now asked to consider these reasons, give them what weight they are thought to deserve, and in their light to revise their previous estimates. Moreover, if their answer now falls outside the second round's interquartile range, they are asked to state briefly why they found the argument unconvincing that might have drawn them toward the median or beyond. (4) Finally, in a fourth round, both the quartiles of the third distribution of responses and the counter-arguments elicited in Round 3 are submitted to the respondents, who are now encouraged to make one last revision of their estimates. The median of these Round 4 responses may then be taken as representing the group position as to what N should be.

The above procedure can be refined by requiring each respondent in the first round to state how relatively expert he considers himself to be with regard to the particular estimate required of him. For example, if he is asked—as will normally be the case—to estimate not one but several quantities,

$$N_1, N_2, \ldots, N_z,$$

he may indicate, by assigning respectively A, B, C, or D to approximately one quarter each of the questions, how relatively competent he regards himself with respect to each question. On the basis of this information, it is possible to use as the group consensus, not the median of all fourth-round responses, but the median of only those responses that came from that third, say, of the respondents who had declared themselves relatively most expert with regard to the corresponding question.

The procedure described here would today require the use of questionnaires or of interviewers. Eventually it should be possible to have each expert equipped with a console through which he can feed his responses into a computer which would process these inputs, possibly augment them with relevant information automatically drawn from an existing data bank, and feed back the result to each respondent.

Until this day arrives—thus for another five years perhaps—the cybernetic arbitration procedure described above may be too time-consuming to be acceptable without modification. A simplified version, which preserves the anonymity of the estimate but not that of the proffered reasons, has already been tried successfully. This procedure is to have the experts meet in one room and to have each equipped with a device permitting him to select one of a set of numbers (say, from 0 to 10) by pushing an appropriate button. The set of these responses appears in scrambled order on a panel visible to all participants. They engage in a free debate, which produces reasons for raising or lowering the estimates as well as a critique of such reasons. This is then followed up by another (anonymous) vote, and the median is used as the group opinion. (Again, a refinement relying on self-estimates of relative competence, can easily be adjoined to the procedure.)

No matter which version of the technique is used, it may be expected that respondents with well-founded opinions on a subject will be swayed little by counter-arguments or by the opinion of the majority, whereas the opinions of those respondents who feel unsure of their positions will be influenced by valid arguments. The induced process of convergence therefore—one may hope—results from an increased understanding of the issue rather than from specious persuasion.

It is to be hoped that this technique of using expert opinions will be refined through future practice. Efforts at such refinements might aim at increasing either the efficiency, as indicated earlier, or the reliability of the method. But imperfect as it is at present, it appears to be the most promising approach available today toward the meaningful introduction of cost-effectiveness considerations into the operations of government agencies.

READING 27

ISSUES OF ANALYSIS IN COST-EFFECTIVENESS STUDIES FOR CIVILIAN AGENCIES OF THE FEDERAL GOVERNMENT*

John Haldi

The chief purpose of this paper is to discuss a few of the many current Government program issues requiring analysis and, hopefully, to stimulate additional interest in and study of Government programs. As the problems of modern society grow increasingly complex, and as Federal expenditures increase to overcome these problems, the payoff from analysis which helps us use our resources more efficiently will rise commensurately. Admittedly the tools of management science will not give us complete solutions to any of the Government's high-level managerial problems. Nevertheless, people trained to approach management problems objectively and quantitatively have a great deal to offer the Government's decision-making process.

In general, the issues to be discussed here are being raised in connection with the

* Reprinted by permission of the author. Paper presented at the meeting of The Institute of Management Sciences, Philadelphia, Pa., September 7, 1966.

Planning-Programming-Budgeting (PPB) System now being installed by all major civilian agencies in the Federal Government. Two important purposes of the PPB system are: (1) to stimulate more and better analysis of Government programs and (2) to see that the results of such analysis are reflected in budget decisions.

The initial instructions implementing PPB required that each agency (1) establish an output-oriented program structure, (2) within the context of this program structure, prepare a multi-year budget (usually for the next five years), and (3) establish new analytical staffs.

Although these instructions were comprehensive, it should not be inferred that Government agencies were completely lacking in all those areas. Rather, the impact varied among agencies. In passing, it ought to be noted that some Government agencies, chiefly on account of the two Hoover Commissions, moved towards program budgeting even before Defense did in 1961. And of course, all Government agencies had at least some in-house analytic capability (some rather well staffed) and all did some multi-year planning before the advent of PPB; in several instances, an agency's forward planning was and still is in excess of that now required by the PPB system. Nevertheless, the new PPB system appears to be having some impact on all agencies, and it is beginning to stimulate increased interest at high levels in the contribution that improved analysis can offer program decisions.

The most important single ingredient in the PPB package is more and better analysis of Government programs. Since Government programs cover such a wide variety of fields— health, highways, education, transportation, urban problems, etc.—the models, skills and types of analysis needed will vary from program to program and from agency to agency. To some extent, this will be illustrated by the examples which follow. First, however, a few general comments about most of the analysis which is being initiated under PPB. I do this because of certain misapprehensions which have been repeatedly brought to my attention.

We have *not* reached that golden millennium of cost-benefit analysis where we can make marginal comparisons, for instance, between hospital, highway and recreation programs. We have discovered no magic formula for quantifying benefits, and therefore, we have no studies underway or contemplated which will attempt marginal benefit-cost comparisons between entirely different programs. The shortcomings of the present state of the art of cost-benefit analyses have been well-summarized in a recent article by Prest and Turvey in *The Economic Journal*.[1]

The type of analysis receiving new emphasis from PPB can best be described as "cost-effectiveness" studies or systems analyses. Cost-effectiveness studies differ from cost-benefit studies in that: (1) certain basic objectives are taken as given and (2) no attempt is made to quantify all benefits in dollar terms. Thus, although cost-effectiveness studies fail to make marginal comparisons between radically different programs, the scope of the analysis is usually broader and somewhat more relevant to top-management problems than it has been in

the past. Two pragmatic reasons for being content with cost-effectiveness studies at this time are: (1) problems are more tractable at this level, and (2) there can be early and great payoff from such studies.

The examples that follow have been chosen to illustrate some of the various management-science problems that need analysis. There are many more like this and, in addition, a great many problems that can be described as "purely economic." A brief description of many of these "purely economic" problems is more or less available in an unpublished but rather widely distributed paper by Kermit Gordon, "Research Opportunities in Applying Rational Calculation to Federal Expenditures," (October 2, 1965), so here I will limit myself to (1) an attempt to present a few new examples in some detail, and (2) a brief mention of other subjects under study.

IN-DEPTH EXAMPLES OF ISSUES FOR ANALYSIS

Harbor deepening by the Corps of Engineers. The general practice of the Corps of Engineers in evaluating harbor improvements currently is to consider each harbor project as an entity. If the project shows a benefit/cost ratio in excess of unity, the project is justified. If the project is of a variable nature; i.e., if there is a range of improvements possible with corresponding ranges of costs and benefits, the project expenditure chosen is that which maximizes the difference between the present value of benefits and costs. In each instance, however, the particular harbor under consideration is analyzed separately from proposed improvements for some other harbor.

This approach is justified when improvements in one area will have no effect on other areas. For example, improving river port facilities along the Mississippi may have no measurable effect on harbor activity along the Northeastern States, and improvements in New York Harbor may have little effect on shipping at St. Louis. Such projects may be considered independent of each other.

But any one change may not be independent with respect to all other areas. Improvements in Boston Harbor may well have an impact on New York Harbor traffic and vice versa. When changes in one river or harbor will affect traffic in another, proposed projects in these competi-

[1] *A. R. Prest and R. Turvey, "Cost-Benefit Analysis: A Survey,"* The Economic Journal, *December 1965, pp. 683–731.*

tive areas may be viewed as interdependent. Analysis of interdependent areas will not yield maximum net benefits (present value of benefits-costs) if the projects for the areas are treated as separate (independent) problems. Current evaluation practice of improvement projects will bias decisions in the direction of over-investment when interdependent areas are considered independently.

Over-investment bias occurs for two reasons:

1 The area over which maximization of net benefits takes place is too localized. Of course, the nature of maximization of benefits will always be localized to some extent because it is not feasible to simultaneously compare and rank all Government investment projects; i.e., investment in moon projects, foreign aid, river and harbor projects, etc. But within an administrative subunit, and particularly with respect to a particular species of expenditure, maximization should be calculated over the broadest possible range, especially where competitive interdependence is large. Instead of maximizing the net benefits for a single harbor improvement, maximization should occur over several interdependent harbors. Such an approach could result in the abandonment of some projects which yield small net benefits even though the benefit/cost ratio for these projects exceeds unity.

2 Benefits are overstated because, when considering the anticipated benefits of a single harbor project, we ignore the impact of projects for different harbors that may currently be under consideration or that may come under consideration in the foreseeable future. Thus, the benefits anticipated as the result of an expenditure on harbor *A* may be eroded in whole or part by expenditures that may be made on harbors *B, C, D*, etc. If this erosion had been considered, a smaller total level of expenditure would have been justified.

Deepening East Coast harbors provides an excellent example of harbor improvement projects which are probably highly interdependent. Demand for deeper harbors, of course, arises from the larger ships now in existence, being built, or planned. A few specifics will give a better feel for the interdependencies. Over the past 10-15 years, there has been a marked trend towards bigger ships, especially tankers. Oil tankers have increased in size from 15,000-25,000 ton up to 200,000

ton giants, and still bigger ships are now on the drawing boards. In addition to oil, other bulk commodities such as bauxite, wheat and coal are beginning to move in so-called "giant" ships (currently up to 70,000-80,000 tons in the case of dry bulk cargo ships). These new ships may draw as much as 80-100 feet of water when fully loaded.

The Corps of Engineers currently maintains the depth of the channels in major harbors such as New York and Philadelphia at about 45-50 feet. This depth is adequate for the average dry cargo ship of 15,000-20,000 tons, but it will obviously be inadequate for these larger ships.

In New York and Philadelphia, existing channels have already been dredged down to bedrock, so that any further deepening will require underwater blasting and drilling—a somewhat expensive operation. In both the New York and Philadelphia harbors, the estimated cost of deepening only 10 additional feet is estimated at $300 million for each harbor; yet 10 additional feet will obviously be insufficient to handle fully loaded giant tankers. Furthermore, any underwater blasting in those areas might do far more extensive damage to the sea life and ecology than dredging has ever done, a disbenefit which any analysis must take into account.

Fortunately, a large number of alternatives and tradeoffs are possible. Since any given harbor usually requires further deepening for only one (or maybe two) specific commodities, it is proper for the analysis to take account of any special physical handling properties of the commodity in question. For discharging oil, for example, offshore loading facilities and lightering are both distinct possibilities at any given harbor. Moreover, consideration of pipelines introduces direct interdependencies and tradeoffs between harbors. Take the case of New York and Philadelphia. While we don't know at this time whether it is worth deepening either harbor, I do know that if we propose to deepen one of these harbors we should certainly investigate the cost of pumping oil 100 miles across New Jersey before committing ourselves to deepening the other harbor. Adequate pumping capacity may cost a lot less than $300 million.

If we broaden the analysis to include an additional stretch of the Eastern Seaboard, interesting possibilities may be available. One intriguing tradeoff possibility reaches from Philadelphia to Portsmouth, Maine. A cross-section profile of the harbor at Portsmouth shows that both the harbor and outside channel are both rather deep, but a substantial rock ledge at the mouth of the entrance restricts deeper ships from entering (See Figure 27-1). It might be possible to remove enough of this ledge, at a reasonable cost, to permit even the deepest tankers to use this harbor fully loaded.

Improving the Portsmouth harbor, plus construction of a large capacity pipeline to Boston, New York, and Philadelphia, might be a much more efficient way, economically, to supply overseas oil to the populous Eastern Seaboard than deepening the latter three ports.

The Corps' PPB unit has just recently begun a study of our East Coast harbor system. This study, far broader in scope than any done heretofore, will attempt to take account of the different commodity flows, usage, interdependencies, etc.

Forest Service timber cutting program. The U.S. Forest Service (FS) operates 154 National Forests encompassing 186 million acres. Virtually all National Forest (NF) land is managed for a multiplicity of purposes; e.g., timber, recreation, wildlife, grazing and natural beauty. However, current management practice by the Forest Service is to administratively "zone" all NF land according to its *primary* use. For example, land along highways and around lakes, up to the ridge line usually, is set aside for recreation or "natural beauty," and trees in this area are neither managed nor harvested for a commercial return. Any cutting that might occur on this land would be highly selective and would be aimed at enhancing beauty, enlarging campsite areas, or adding to trails for hikers.

Apart from this recreation land, a large amount, perhaps three-fourths of all NF land is designated primarily as "timber growing," and is managed primarily for commercial timber supply. In these areas timber is harvested regularly on a sustained-yield basis. ("Sustained-yield" is a conservationist measure which says, in essence, "don't cut more timber than you grow.") Last year, the Forest Service allowed approximately 12 billion board feet of timber to be cut from the National Forests on a sustained-yield basis.

For purposes of this discussion, let us completely accept the rather broad sustained-yield philosophy as just stated. A variety of interpretations are still possible. For example, the sustained-yield constraint can apply to the entire country.

On a country-wide basis, sustained-yield means "don't cut more timber than we grow nationally," and within this constraint it might be optimal to cut primarily in high productivity regions like the Pacific Coast and Southeast and use other regions as a sort of "strategic reserve" in the unlikely event that the country should ever be short of timber.

A regional constraint implies "cut no more than grows in each region," and a NF constraint says cut no more than grows annually in a NF. A "working circle," an area big enough to supply one modern mill, generally is somewhat smaller than any of our NF's. Thus the sustained-yield concept applied to the working circle is the most restrictive constraint.

Now if these different constraints could be applied to a programming model which included all timber land in the NF's, and if the objective function were to maximize revenues, then it seems reasonable to expect that revenues maximized under the tightest constraint would be less than revenues maximized under a looser constraint.[2]

Current Forest Service practice is to cut timber within the tightest of the four constraints discussed; i.e., each working circle is on a sustained-yield basis. This policy is followed for a variety of reasons, the most important being maintenance of stable employment in small communities heavily dependent upon timber.

[2] *This is a simplified presentation, of course. To be useful, such a model would have to take account of many other important restrictions, such as the difference between sawtimber (hardwood and softwood) and pulpwood.*

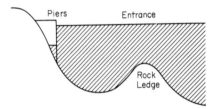

Figure 27-1   Profile of harbor at Portsmouth, Maine.

A major change in the present timber cutting policy of the Forest Service would probably result in changing the occupations of many individuals plus changing the population distribution and the future of many small towns. Resource decisions like this cannot ignore political realities, and these usually dictate that Government organizations take explicit account of the social costs attributable to change. Not only in the timber program, but in most other Government programs, the social costs attributable to change can generally be measured relatively easily in comparison to the difficulty involved in estimating the long-term gains that might flow from changing to other, more efficient practices. But such studies are not being made with sufficient frequency. Alternatives are not automatically more efficient. They must be subjected to in-depth analyses and their merits validated before responsible decision-makers, subject to a myriad of political forces, can seriously consider adopting new and better policies. The lack of good studies showing possible gains from more efficient policies all too often leads to bureaucratic inertia and stifling of desirable program changes. Since the amount of resources now allocated by the Government is so great, we simply cannot afford to assume that the current policy is optimal in any sense. This is where good systems analysis, aided by large computers, can be a significant aid to improved program management.

It should now be possible to comprehensively study the timber program and obtain good estimates of the gains to be derived by shifting harvesting to the most efficient timber-growing lands. With this knowledge in hand we could make a much more realistic reexamination of our present policies.

The post office network.   Currently there are over 32,000 Post Offices in the United States, and mail can originate at any office and receive final delivery from any office. In actual fact, of course, the great bulk of the mail moves between the few hundred largest offices. The volume of mail currently handled is staggering: 70 billion pieces per year. Letters comprise approximately 40 of these 70 billion pieces, with second, third, and fourth class mail making up the balance. Of these 40 billion letters, approximately 2 billion are now deposited as air mail by the senders, with many more moving by air on a space-available, nonpriority basis. Total expenditures by the Post Office are now approaching $6 billion per year, and the amount spent on processing and transportation alone is over $3 billion per year. Hence a 10 percent improvement in the processing-transportation network would yield annual savings of over $300 million.

Distribution of mail requires a great many small steps, each of which is very simple, but which represent a very complex network when considered in their totality. The procedures now used to distribute mail have evolved over a long period of time and are based on a great deal of experience and experimentation. For conditions of the past and the immediate present, these methods may possibly be near-optimal. However, prospective mechanization over the next 10–20 years will question and perhaps make obsolete centuries of time-tested methods, truisms, and tradition. Sophisticated network analysis will likely be required if we are to rapidly assimilate the full potential of improvements just recently available or now in development.

Before describing some mechanization and automation possibilities, let me first describe briefly how mail is currently worked. After collection, letters are simultaneously canceled and faced in the same direction. They then enter the sorting and distribution process. In large processing facilities, outgoing mail receives both a "primary" and "secondary" sort. Virtually all sorting is still done manually, in 49-hole (seven by seven) "cases." The rationale for the size of the case is simple: this is the convenient reach of an average person's arm.

In a major city like Washington or Philadelphia, the second sort customarily results in breaking down outgoing mail to about 2,000 destinations. This means, for example, that if a sufficient volume goes from Washington to Northern California, mail might be made up to San Francisco, Oakland, Sacramento, and "all other Northern California." Mail to each of these four destinations will then be tied in separate bundles up to 4–5 inches thick. If there are sufficient bundles to make up individual pouches or bags, this will be done, otherwise all bundles will go into one bag. Then upon arrival in San Francisco, the mail to Oakland and Sacramento is handled as bundles or bags (depending on how it was shipped), not as individual letters.

The current mail system has several major interdependencies. First, the primary rule of efficient letter-handling is: *always* preserve facing of letters (this undoubtedly is a good rule). Then, because mail is shipped in bags, it is tied into small bundles to preserve facing. And because it is time-consuming and expensive to untie bundled mail and put it back into the sorting process as loose mail, outgoing mail is made up into as many separate destinations as volume justifies, while still loose. (Breaking mail down to about 2,000 destinations tends to utilize secondary sorting clerks to capacity since the theoretical limit from breaking each of 49 initial sorts down another 49 ways would be 2,401 final destinations.)

Our shipping container, the familiar mail bag, is one of the important determinants of the process described. The great antiquity of the mail bag is attested to by the fact that it was reputedly first invented by the Phoenicians. In the Phoenicians' time, when labor was relatively plentiful and space on ships was scarce, the mail bag unquestionably made good sense. Even today no other container minimizes "cube" like the mail bag. However, relative scarcities have changed somewhat in the last 2,000 years, and minimization of space should no longer be presumed a desirable goal. Mail bags are not susceptible to mechanical handling by automatic equipment, and the amount of manual labor required to load and unload mail bags is now reaching enormous proportions. In the coming years, the Post Office will have to move to adopt other containers which can be handled more efficiently.

In addition to containerization, letter-sorting is now mechanizable in various degrees. The Post Office has recently begun experimenting with a "semi-automatic" letter sorting machine, where clerks sort letters by punching keys on a keyboard. This machine enables letters to be sorted about twice as fast as manually and, in addition, the first sort can be to about 225–250 locations, which seems to be the maximum "scheme" that clerks can remember.

By combining the capability of this letter-sorting machine with some kind of tray-like containers which preserve facing but don't require tying into smaller bundles, it might be considerably more efficient to have just a primary outgoing sort, and eliminate the secondary sort. For example, all mail to Northern California would be put into common trays, taken out to the airport and shipped to San Francisco as fast as possible.

A complicating factor which the Post Office lives with and which adds force to this suggestion is the fact that, in large cities, about 70–80 percent of all mail comes into the Post Office between 5:00 p.m.–7:00 p.m., while "late" planes tend to depart between 8:30 p.m.–10:30 p.m. Because of this, the Post Office segregates air mail and gives it first priority to meet the dispatch schedule. Eliminating the secondary sort would unquestionably make it easier to meet the schedule. When "priority mail" becomes a reality, and all long-distance first class mail moves by air, this peaking problem will be accentuated several-fold.

Any major switch in the present scheme is, of course, complicated by the fact that piecemeal experimentation is not possible. If all mail arriving in San Francisco had to be given extra processing, and San Francisco had to process all outgoing mail as it does now, it would be swamped and service would be worse, not better. The inability to experiment is all the more reason why a good systems analysis is virtually a necessary prerequisite to change and improvement.

OTHER EXAMPLES

On the basis of my experience to date, I would say that virtually all programs and all departments in the Federal Government are susceptible to and could profit from more in-depth analysis. In some areas the potential payoff is enormous compared to the investment. Even in programs where the payoff is less, good analysis will still pay for itself by a wide margin.

The poverty program is one of the biggest and most important areas now under study and it undoubtedly will be under study for some time to come. A variety of programs for dealing with poverty now exist (e.g., Job Corps, Neighborhood Youth Corps, Headstart, and VISTA) and many more programs will unquestionably be recommended in years to come. Since the resources available to fight the war on poverty are so small compared to the total need, it is imperative that we study the cost and effectiveness of each program before making major resource commitments.

Another problem area now under active study is motor vehicle accidents, a problem area that was highlighted in recent congressional hearings. It now appears that cost-effectiveness is a good tool for analyzing this problem. Some alternative ways to reduce auto accidents are: (1) improve safety features in cars, (2) improve driver training and driver licensing, (3) improve the driving environment, including better repair of existing roads and better construction of new roads, and (4) better emergency medical services. When these alternatives are reduced to specifics, the cost of each can readily be estimated, and, although subject to wider uncertainty, the effectiveness of each can also be estimated through careful systematic analysis.

Other areas which need the light of systematic analysis can be cited. (1) Water pollution: our current water resources policies seem to favor more expensive methods of reducing pollution over less expensive methods. (2) Other water resources policies encourage people to overbuild in vulnerable flood plains by building or promising flood control projects for such flood plains. (3) Our sugar subsidy program seems to cost three times as much as the total net income of sugar producers. (4) Our maritime policies include an operating subsidy whose structure creates a positive incentive to the overmanned ships. (5) Certain programs are bringing reclaimed land into production while other programs are designed to remove land from production. (6) We invest hundreds of millions of dollars annually to move passengers from airport to airport, but we have paid no attention to the leg of the trip between airport and final destination. The advent of an 1,800 miles per hour SST will make this deficiency in the system even more glaring. (7) We spend over ten times as much on urban roads as on urban mass transit without even examining the balance between these two types of transportation. (8) On different types of crime we spend widely varying amounts of resources on investigation, apprehension, and prosecution without any systematic study to determine whether significant improvements could be made by improving the mix.

This list of examples could be readily extended to include many more which come to mind. However, I believe it is sufficient enough to show that good imaginative analysis is capable of yielding great payoffs in terms of better Government programs. The important tasks immediately ahead are (1) to get our analytic capability organized so as to systematically attack these problems, and (2) to sell decision-makers on the value of good analysis and, in the case of Government programs, to also sell the public on the analytic results. How to accomplish this latter task could itself be the subject of a worthwhile analytic study.

INTERORGANIZATIONAL MANAGEMENT

An organization consists of an aggregation of resources—human and non-human. Such resources as exist require a meaningful relationship in terms of layout *and* authority—responsibility *relationships. Organizational structure takes many forms, from the simple one-man proprietorship to the complex matrix organization.*

As soon as the business firm involves more than one person, it has an organizational structure. Line *and* staff *provides the basic organizational dichotomy of the traditional bureaucratic model. Traditional function specialization and vertical hierarchy have been augmented in terms of the* project manager *who is given responsibility and authority to manage the development and acquisition of an* ad hoc *project requiring extensive crossing of the traditional lines of the organization. In the project organization, the authority and responsibility patterns take on vestiges of both the* functional *and the* project *organization. The traditional line-staff organizational arrangement is changed, for in such a case, the functional line manager may have to deal with many project managers whose projects are being supported in the line manager's department. Thus, in military and space projects and in the aerospace industry where large* ad hoc *projects are a way of life, the project organization becomes a dominant influence.*

The idea of project management has demonstrated its utility in a wide variety of Defense-Aerospace Industry contexts. So, too, are formal projects important to administration at the highest levels of the Federal government.

Witness, for example, the increasing emphasis being placed on special presidential missions and task forces and the consequent deemphasis of activities which are undertaken solely within a given cabinet-level department.

In the future, these concepts will undoubtedly be extended to such areas as urban renewal programs, transportation systems, and such related endeavors. Increasingly, these projects will have aspects of both business and government organization structure. Indeed, many of them will be performed on joint bases which involve elements of both functional and project techniques.

Again we emphasize that the new evolving theory of interorganizational management, *exemplified in the project environment, complements and refines traditional management theory. It is important to realize that management theory has much to gain from the project-management concepts, especially when one considers that project management is a move towards formalization of the many collateral contacts which are not explicitly considered in the traditional bureaucratic model.*

In this section the illustrations of interorganizational management serve to define the role and scope of applications of project concepts together with the difficulties involved in implementing project management.

READING 28

PROJECT MANAGEMENT*

Major David I. Cleland

Ultimate authority within the Department of Defense rests with the Office of the Secretary of Defense. This authority has its origin from Title II, The Department of Defense, the National Security Act of 1947 (Public Law, 80th Congress). This act reflects the intent of Congress to centralize and strengthen the management of the military, economic, and social aspects of national defense. Subsequent legislation in 1958, under stimulus of President Eisenhower's defense reorganization message, clearly portended subsequent recentralization of authority within the Office of the Secretary of Defense. This increasing centralization has been accomplished in an environment of:

1 Changing roles and missions of the military establishments with respect to the traditional separation of areas of operation; begining erosion and merging of parochial divisions of military operations into land, sea,

* Reprinted with permission from Air University Review, vol. XVI, no. 2, January-February, 1965.

and air employment; continuing unification of certain functions of the armed forces, with indications of a single national system of defense evolving.
2 Increasing and dynamic acceleration in the conception and development of weaponry.[1] Technical breakthroughs, incremental and protracted development cycles, and increasing costs stimulated the need for a distinct type of managerial innovation in the management of large development and production programs.

Within the national military establishment certain weapon acquisitions became so vast and demanding that it was impossible to assign to one single organization total responsi-

[1] Weaponry, *a general term, connotes the varied instruments intended to inflict damage to an enemy through the destruction of physical or mental capabilities. The term* weapon system *means a highly sophisticated weapon composed of a combination of equipment, skills, and managerial know-how, which as an integrated entity is capable of effectively destroying an enemy.*

bility for successful accomplishment of the objective. The increasing demands for more advanced weaponry and the increasing propensity of the Department of Defense to depend on the private industrial complex for research and development efforts intensified the requirement for a management philosophy that went beyond the traditional management theories.

Unfortunately expertise in the science and art of management lagged the state of the art in development and engineering. The military manager, engaged in the development and acquisition of weapons, was confronted with the coordination and integration of large aggregations of human and nonhuman resources, the greater part of which were outside the traditional concept of *line* command. Traditionally, management practitioners and scholars have approached the management function through the medium of the *line* and the *staff*. Line functions are thought of as those activities which have a direct and constitutional role in the accomplishment of organizational objectives. Staff, on the other hand, refers to the specialized assistance and counsel provided the line manager. Traditional management philosophy is pervaded with vertical flow of authority and responsibility relationships. Whatever horizontal relationships did exist were of a collateral and coordinating nature and did not violate the principle of unity of command. Traditional military and business organizations have functioned for the most part on a vertical basis and depend almost exclusively on a strong and inviolate superior/subordinate relationship to ensure unanimity of objective. The existing management theory was found lacking when it was realized that certain management relationships were evolving in the development and acquisition of large single-purpose projects whose development and production cut across interior organizational flows of authority and responsibility and radiated outside to other organizations that were managed as autonomous units. In particular, traditional management theory failed to provide a contemporary philosophy required for the manager to use in defense/industry ventures involved in the inception and development of advanced weapon systems. Singular elements of risk and uncertainty, extensive involvement of resources, and changing concepts in the employment of weaponry forced a management posture calling for a blending and unifying of many defense and industrial organizations directed toward a common objective. An existing multilayered and diffused management structure within the industrial and defense organizations concerned complicated the management function.

The basic objectives involved in the development and acquisition of a weapon system include divergent activities such as research, engineering, test, production, operational support, etc., all of which are time-phased over the life of the project. The result is an interlaced sequential managerial activity encompassing broad spectrums of personnel and resources extending over several years of time. The intimate superior/subordinate relationships found in recurring activities still exist, but the main focus of the task involves the unification and integration of complex input factors into a meaningful pattern of accomplishment. The functional approach, or traditional departmentation based on homogeneity of duties or geographical location, becomes meaningless when the task involves the coordinated single-goal effort of hundreds of organizations and people. Individual managers have a general affinity for identifying boundaries of responsibilities and specializing in these areas. When organizations were relatively small this provided no great problem, since the functional manager could maintain lateral staff contact to ensure mutual support and understanding of interfunctional goals. Traditional management thinking is built on these ideas; the emergence of multiorganizational objectives has shown the provincial management theory of Fayol and Taylor to be lacking.[2]

Since World War II there has been unprecedented acceleration in the advancement of technology in all phases of industrial and military management. Radical changes have occurred in the design and employment of weaponry. These profound changes have forced

[2] *Henri Fayol, a French industrialist, wrote a book titled* General and Industrial Management, *which appeared in 1916. No English translation was published in the United States until 1949 (New York: Pitman Publishing Corporation). Fayol is called by many scholars the father of modern management theory. His writings describe the job of the manager from the viewpoint of a single firm rather than from the unifying requirement demanded of a project manager in today's defense/industry environment. Frederick Taylor's writings appeared around the turn of the present century and described management at the shop level; he was concerned with the efficiency of workers and managers in actual production-line activities.*

innovation in Government- and Defense-oriented industrial organizations. In many cases weapons and strategy have evolved which do not fit the functional organization, and the result has been the emergence of new theories concerning management and organization. Attention is being given to molding the organization around the task. New terms have come into use, such as "systems management" and "systems engineering," which portend the need for a new type of managerial surveillance that has no organizational or functional constraints.

The size and complexity of contemporary and expected future programs discourage the development of a single *autonomous* element of the defense establishment to manage a program successfully. Rather what is required is a blending of the technical know-how of many functionally oriented organizations under one centralized coordinating and managing agency whose prime role is to synchronize and integrate an aggregation of resources. The *project management* philosophy has been developed by the military/industrial complex as a means to satisfy the requirement for the management of defense resources from inception to operational employment. How did this concept develop? Is it a further refinement of traditional management thought and theory, or is it a revolutionary new development which portends radical changes in organizational theory and in the management of activities by the functional approach?

In the aerospace industry/Government relationship there has developed a tendency towards greater and greater use of ad hoc offices concerned exclusively with the managerial integration of a single weapon system or subsystem. The increasing use of this managerial innovation indicates that it is becoming sufficiently ingrained in management thought and theory so that serious questions are being raised about the ability of the pure functionally oriented organization to manage more than one major project successfully. This is particularly so where nonrepetitive production programs are being conducted and in those military and industrial organizations where basic and applied research programs are undertaken. The establishment of a project manager in a functional organization permits managerial concentration of attention on the major considerations in the project or program. This concentration is particularly valuable when the producer is competing in a market

system where the product price is largely determined by reimbursement of costs actually incurred or where the contract involves, on the part of the producer, a total commitment of company resources over an extended period of time and, on the part of the buyer, a monopsonistic situation where an intimate dependence upon the producer to fulfill the contract commitment increases the risk and uncertainty factors. It is a market where the financial and managerial risks of the business center around only one or a few ventures. Consequently there is a much greater propensity on the part of the buyer to enter into the active management of the program in the seller's facility.

Characteristics of Project Management

In a sense project management is compatible with the traditional and functional approach to management, yet it has provided *a way of thinking* with respect to the management of highly technical and costly weapon systems, the development and acquisition of which have spread across several large autonomous organizations. The project manager within Department of Defense organizations has been established to manage across functional lines in order to bring together at one focal point the management activities required to accomplish project objectives. The project manager has certain characteristics which tend to differentiate him from the traditional manager:

1 As project manager, he is concerned with specific projects whose accomplishment requires a great amount of participation by organizations and agencies outside his direct control.
2 Since the project manager's authority cuts through superior/subordinate lines of authority, there is a deliberate conflict involved with the functional managers. The functional manager no longer has the complete authority with respect to the function; he must share the authority relative to a particular project with the project manager.
3 As a focal point for project activities, the project manager enters into, on an exception basis, those project matters which are significant to the successful accomplishment of the project. He determines the *when* and *what* of the project activities, whereas the functional manager, who supports many different projects in the organization, determines *how* the support will be given.
4 The project manager's task is finite in dura-

tion; after the project is completed the personnel directly supporting it can be assigned to other activities.

5 The project manager manages a higher proportion of professional personnel; consequently he must use different management techniques than one would expect to find in the simple superior/subordinate relationship. His attitude regarding the traditional functions of management must of necessity be tempered by increased factors of motivation, persuasion, and control techniques. For many professionals the leadership must include explanations of the rationale of the effort as well as the more obvious functions of planning, organizing, directing, and controlling.

6 The project manager is involved in managing diverse and extraorganizational activities which require unification and integration directed toward the objective of the project. He becomes a unifying agent with respect to the total management function. In effecting this unifying action he has no line authority to act per se but rather depends on other manifestations of authority to bring about the attainment of the objective. Thus the *directing* function is of somewhat less importance from the perspective of the project manager. What direction he does effect is accomplished through the functional managers who support him in the project endeavor.

7 The project manager does not normally possess any traditional line authority over the line organizations involved in creating the goods or services. His motivational tools become different than those available in the more prevalent superior/subordinate vertical relationship.

Evolution of Project Manager

One major difficulty in adjusting to the concept of project management is caused by a failure on the part of management to understand this new and evolving role. The concept of project management is still evolving. Its evolution has gone through stages where different titles and degrees of responsibility have been associated with the position. The construction industry early recognized the need for a management process which permitted the introduction of a unifying agent into the ad hoc activities involved in the construction of single, costly projects such as dams, turnpikes, and large factories and buildings.

During World War II when large aircraft contracts came to the airframe industry, a new method of management arose which integrated the many and diverse activities involved in the development and production of large numbers of aircraft. In the military establishment one sees evidence of the project manager in such endeavors as the Manhattan Project, the ballistic missile program, and the Polaris program.

The need for a unifying agent in these large projects motivated the development of a project-type organization superimposed on the traditional and functional organizational structure. This unifying agent idea reflects contemporary thinking about project management. The forerunners of project managers, designated project expediters, did not perform line functions but instead informally motivated those persons involved in doing the work. The project expediter was mainly concerned with schedules and depended upon his personal diplomacy and persuasive abilities to remove bottlenecks in the management process. The project expediter was perhaps the earliest kind of project manager. Slightly above him in terms of time and responsibility appeared the project coordinator, who had a more formal role in the organization and was concerned with the synchronization of organizational activities directed toward a specific objective in the overall functional activities. This type of coordinator had some independence, reflected by his freedom to make decisions within the framework of the overall project objectives, but he did not actively enter into the performance of the management functions outside his own particular organization. The project coordinator had specific functional authority in certain areas, such as in budgeting,[1] release of funds, and release of authority to act as in the dispatching function in the production control environment.

Today's project manager is in every sense a manager. He actively participates in the organic functions of planning, organizing, and controlling those major organizational activities involved in the specific project. He accomplishes the management process through other managers. Many of the people that feel the force of his leadership are in other departments or organizations separate and apart from the project's manager's parent unit. Since these people are not subject to his operating supervision and owe their fidelity to a superior line manager, unique conflicts of purpose and tenure present themselves. The project manager has real and explicit authority but only over those major considerations involved in the project plan. One of the project manager's biggest problems is how to get full support in the project effort when the functional people are responsible to someone else for pay raises, promotion, and the other expected line superior/subordinate relationships.

Authority and Responsibility of the Project Manager

Since the project manager acts as the focal point within the organization through which major decisions and considerations flow, he must be given a special kind of recognition with respect to the authority and responsibility involved in his relationships with other managers in the organization. Authority is the legal or rightful power to command, to act, or to direct. Ultimate authority derives from the society in which the organized effort exists. Authority is *de jure* in the sense that it exists by rightful title, i.e., specific delineations of the authority of an organizational position are contained in the unit's documents such as policy and procedural instruments job descriptions, and organizational charters.[3] Not to be neglected is the *de facto* authority that can be exercised by the project manager, i.e., the implied authority reflected in the organizational

[3] *Within the Air Force specific and forceful authority has been delegated to the project manager, or in Air Force parlance the system program director. Air Force Regulation 375–3, dated 25 November 1963, states:*

An SPD (System Program Director) is appointed by AFSC (Air Force Systems Command) for each system program not later than receipt of the formal document requiring application of system management techniques.

He manages the collective efforts of participating field organizations in preparing system program documentation, and revisions as requested.

His mission with respect to an approved system program is to:

(1) Manage (plan, organize, coordinate, control and direct) the collective actions of participating organizations in planning and executing the system program.

(2) Propose and/or prepare modifications of, or changes to, the system program within the limits of guidance received from participating organizations or higher authority.

(3) Make changes to the system program consistent with his authority, as required to maintain internal balance of the system program.

position. It is the intrinsic and necessary power to discharge fully the responsibilities inherent in the task or job. Thus an organization receiving public funds has *de facto* authority to create administrative policy stipulating how the funds will be maintained, to appoint a custodian to assume pecuniary responsibility for the safe-guarding and legal obligation of the funds, and to take other necessary measures to adequately control the expenditure of the funds within the specific authority granted when they were accepted. Other aspects of the *de facto* authority include the project manager's persuasive ability, his rapport with extra-organizational units, and his reputation in resolving opposing viewpoints within the parent unit and between the external organizations. Other factors that influence the degree of authority which the project manager can exercise include:

1 Influence inherent in the rank, organizational position, or specialized knowledge of the incumbent.
2 The status or prestige enjoyed by the project manager within the *informal* organizational relationships.
3 The priority and obligation existing within the organization for the timely and efficient accomplishment of the project goals.
4 The existence of a bilateral agreement with a contracting party for the completion of the project within the terms of the contract in such areas as cost, performance (quality, reliability, technology), and schedule.
5 The integrative requirements of the project manager's job in the sense that he has the sole responsibility within the organization to pull together the separate functional activities and direct these diverse functions to a coordinated project goal.

The project manager's authority and responsibility flow horizontally across the vertical superior/subordinate relationships existing within the functional organizational elements. Within this environment the authority of the project manager may often come under serious question, particularly in cases involving the allocation of scarce resources to several projects. Generally the project manager has no explicit authority to resolve interfunctional disputes through the issuance of orders to functional groups outside his office. However, since the project manager is the central point through which program information flows and total project executive control is effected, this individual comes to exercise additional authority over and above that which has been specifically delegated. His superior knowledge of the relative roles and functions of the individual parts of the project places him in a logical position to become intimately involved in the major organizational decisions that might affect the outcome of his project. As the focal point through which major project decisions flow, the project manager's input into the decision process cannot be ignored or relegated to a subordinate role. The unique position of the project manager inherently gives him knowledge superior to that of the personnel responsible for any subsystem or subactivity functioning as part of the integrated whole. (But this superior knowledge does not exist as the single authority within the total organization but only as the single authority with respect to the particular project involved.)

Organizational rank carries both explicit and implied authority. The project manager should have sufficient executive rank within the organization relationship to enable him to exercise a subtle and pervasive authority by virtue of his position or the trappings of his office. He should have sufficient rank (through evidence of seniority, title, status, prestige, etc.) to provide general administrative leverage in dealing with óther line officials, with supporting staff personages, and with those in authority but external to the parent unit. This implies that there should be some correlation between the rank of the project manager and the cost and complexity of the project he manages. The more costly the project, the greater the degree of risk involved; and the more complex the internal and external organizational structures involved, the higher the rank of the project manager should be. Within the military services there has been a tendency to increase the authority of a project manager's position by assigning higher ranking officers to it. A brigadier general would be expected to exercise more influence (and thus authority) over his subordinates, his peers, and extraorganizational elements than would a lieutenant colonel or major occupying a similar position.

Management literature has neglected any real definition or discussion of the authority of the project manager. This is to be expected because of the near universality of the functional approach to management education and practice. Until contemporary management thinking has fully conceptualized the unique nature of the project manager's role, extraordinary manifestations of authority will be required. It will be an uphill struggle because of the threat that project management poses to ingrained functional management practices and thinking.

The project manager requires a clear delineation of authority and responsibility in order to balance the considerations involved in the proper development and successful conclusion of the project objective. He is frequently faced with major and minor "trade-offs" involving factors of cost, schedule, and performance of the product. Many times these trade-offs lack clear-cut lines of demarcation and foster internal and extraorganizational conflicts of purpose. Referral of the problem for resolution to the proper functional managers may not resolve it in the best interests of the project, since the functional manager tends to be parochial (and rightly so) in his view and less concerned with individual project objectives than with providing the services of his particular function across all the projects.

The creation of the position of project manager in an organization requires careful planning to prepare existing management groups. Certain criteria are offered for delineating the authority and responsibility of project managers:

1 The charter of the project manager should be sufficiently broad to enable his active participation in the major managerial and technical activities involved in the project. He should be given sufficient policy-making authority to integrate the functional contributions to the project goals.
2 The project manager must have the necessary executive rank to ensure responsiveness to his requirements within the parent organization and to be accepted as the unquestioned agent of the parent organization in dealing with contractors and other external entities.
3 He should be provided with a staff that is sufficiently qualified to provide admistrative and technical support. He should have sufficient authority to vary the staffing of his office as necessary throughout the life of the project. This authorization should in-

clude selective augmentation for varying periods of time from the supporting functional agencies.

4 He should participate in making technical, engineering, and functional decisions within the bounds of his project.

5 The project manager must have sufficient authority and capability to exercise control of funds, budgeting, and scheduling involved in the project accomplishment.

6 Where the project management task involves the use of contractors supporting the project effort, the project manager should have the maximum authority possible in the selection of these contractors. After the contractors are selected, the project manager should have direct involvement in the direction and control of the major contractors involved in his particular project. His should be the only authority recognized by the official in the contractor's organization who is charged with contractual actions.

Focal Position of the Project Manager

The typical relationship that would be desirable for a situation involving two organizations having a mutuality of interest in a large project is shown in Figure 28-1. The establishment of a special project office in both the buyer's organization (e.g., the Government) and the seller's organization (e.g., an aerospace company) permits a focal point for concentration of attention on the major problems of the

project or program. This point of concentration forces the channeling of major program considerations through a project manager who has the perspective to integrate relative matters of cost, time, technology, and system compatibility.

This managerial model is not meant to stifle the interfunctional lines of communication or the necessary and frequent lateral staff contacts between the functional organizations of the defense contractor and the military organization. Rather, what is intended is the establishment of a focal point for critical decisions, policy-making, and key managerial prerogatives relating to the project manager when trade-offs between the key elements of the research or production activity are involved. By being in a face-to-face relationship the two project managers can control and resolve both interfunctional and interorganizational problems arising during the course of the project. This organizational relationship precludes any one functional manager from overemphasizing his area of interest in the project to the neglect of other considerations.

Organizational Arrangements for Project Managers

The organizational arrangements for management of industrial projects can vary considerably. One example is the functional organiza-

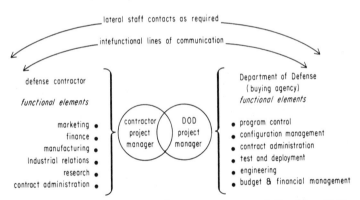

Figure 28-1 Interorganizational project manager relationships. Critical decisions involving policy and managerial prerogatives are directed through the central focal point. Decisions involve cost and cost estimating, schedules, product performance, (quality, reliability, maintainability), resource commitment, project tasking, trade-offs, contract performance, and total system integration.

Figure 28-2   Functional organization with project manager in a staff capacity.

tion with the project manager reporting to the company president or general manager in a staff capacity (Figure 28-2). Under this concept the project manager functions as an "assistant to" the chief executive officer in matters involving the project, relieving him of some of the burdensome detail of the project. As a staff official the "assistant to" type of project manager investigates, researches, analyzes, recommends, and coordinates relative to the project. Major decisions are made by the chief executive officer. Although the project manager does not function in a line capacity in this arrangement, he usually has wide use of functional authority and by being in close proximity to the chief executive wields significant influence with respect to the project.

Placing the project manager in a staff capacity degrades his ability to function as a true integrator and as a decision-maker with respect to the major factors involved in the work of the project. With this arrangement there is the risk of having the project manager's responsibilities exceed his authority. If he is relegated to a staff position, his ability to act decisively depends almost solely upon his grant of functional authority, his personal persuasive abilities, or some specialized knowledge he has.

A functional organization exists in which the project manager reports to the chief executive officer in a line capacity (Figure 28-3). In this organizational and authority relationship the project manager's immediate office

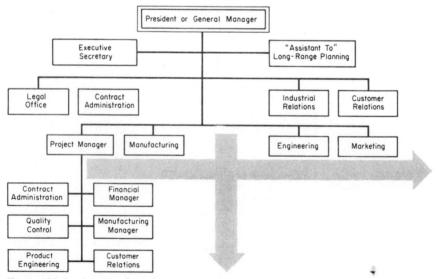

Figure 28-3   Functional organization with project manager in a line capacity. This organizational structure allows for vertical flow of functional authority and responsibility.

staff may vary from a single manager to several hundred people, depending upon the degree of centralization of the project activities. As the project manager's responsibilities increase and more and more of the operating facets of the project are centralized under his control, the organization may seem to have a new company or organizational division formed to manage each major program or project independently. The project manager has authority over the functional managers with respect to the *when* and *what* of the project activities. Functional managers in turn are responsible to both their functional supervisors and the project manager for adequate support of the project.[4] The authority of the project manager in this organizational relationship flows horizontally throughout the organization. It is tempered, however, by direction from the functional managers, who are concerned with the *how accomplished* portion of the project.

The type of functional organization, the size and complexity of the project, and the philosophy of management held by the chief executives of the firm will affect the type of project management to follow. The proponents of total project management would desire to have all project people working directly for the project manager. The choice of organizational arrangement, whether pure functional, completely projectized, or an organizational form in between these extremes, should be made after the effects of the unique environment on the particular project are evaluated as to basic advantages and disadvantages.

[4] *This appears to violate the scalar principle described by Henri Fayol in* General and Industrial Administration. *Fayol envisions the scalar chain as the chain of superiors ranging from the ultimate authority to the lowest rank with the line of authority following every link in the chain. He also discusses the unity of command principle, i.e., an employee should receive orders from one superior only. The author of this article believes that these principles can easily be upheld in small organizational arrangements where the management process operates through the vertical superior/subordinate relationship. In today's large organizations where the management of a single project may cut across many internal functional lines of authority and extend into outside organizations, these management principles lack ubiquity. What is required is a discrete differentiation of managerial functions between the functional manager and the project manager as to respective spheres of influence.*

Project Management in DOD

The Department of Defense has something over 100 weapon and support systems managed by project managers. Practically all these project managers are officers with the rank of colonel or lower, though in some of the larger programs (e.g., the F-111 System Program) the project manager has the rank of brigadier general. As military officers, these project managers are subject to permanent change of station in and out of the system program offices. Usually their tenure in any one project manager position is considerably shorter than the four to eight years required for the development and acquisition of a major weapon system. Ostensibly, these project managers plan, organize, and control the activities involved in the development and acquisition of weaponry. They are supported by subsystem managers and other project managers throughout the research, development, and production complexes of both Governmental and industrial organizations. Within the Governmental structure, project managers are identified as the symbol of leadership of the project. Unfortunately, in some cases this leadership is symbolic only, because of the active participation in upper organizational echelons of advisers, delayers, debaters, inspectors, and coordinators. These specialized staff personnel become involved in providing such support as budget, audit, contract surveillance, technical advice, programing, procurement review, facilities control, etc. The proliferation of these special support agencies leads one to fear that the project manager is becoming merely a symbol of leadership for whom there is a lack of authority and responsibility, in both degree and clarification.

The project manager may be located in an organizational position several echelons down the managerial hierarchy of the Department of Defense. In this position he finds it difficult to be selective in the acceptance of the abundant special staff assistance that is made available—and in some cases directed—to him. The increasing trend toward centralization in the Department of Defense and the establishment of certain thresholds in the expenditure of Defense funds have placed constraints on the project manager. The delegations of authority to the project manager vary widely in their charters and perhaps even more widely in practice. One could not reasonably expect the project manager to have complete control of his funds or the final decision on technical problems when his project is part of an overall defense development effort. Logically, a superior organizational unit that has a greater perspective of the total resources to be allocated should retain sufficient control over the project manager to ensure unanimity of national goals. What does become suspect is the use of multilayers of line managers and staff specialists between the project manager and the point of decision in the Department of Defense.

The use of project management techniques had its inception in the military/industrial complex. It has enabled the management of large aggregations of resources across functional and organizational lines directed toward unifying all effort to the common objective. Project management is a relatively recent phenomenon; as business and military organizations continue to become larger and more interdependent, the role of the project manager will come into clearer focus.

MAKING PROJECT MANAGEMENT WORK*

John M. Stewart

Late last year [1964], with a good deal of local fanfare, a leading food producer opened a new plant in a small midwestern town. For the community it was a festive day. For top management, however, the celebration was somewhat dampened by the fact that the plant had missed its original target date by six months and had overrun estimated costs by a cool $5 million.

A material-handling equipment maker's latest automatic lift truck was an immediate market success. But a few more successes of the same kind would spell disaster for the company. An actual introduction cost of $2.6 million, compared to planned expenses of $1.2 million, cut the company's profits by fully 10 per cent last year.

A new high-speed, four-color press installed by a leading eastern printing concern has enabled a major consumer magazine to sharply increase its color pages and offer advertisers

unprecedented schedule convenience. The printer will not be making money on the press for years, however. Developing and installing it took twice as long and cost nearly three times as much as management had expected.

Fiascos such as these are as old as business itself—as old, indeed, as organized human effort. The unfortunate Egyptian overseer who was obliged, 5,000 years ago, to report to King Cheops that construction work on the Great Pyramid at Giza had fallen a year behind schedule had much in common with the vice-president who recoils in dismay as he and the chief executive discover that their new plant will be months late in delivering the production on which a major customer's contract depends. The common thread: poor management of a large, complex, one-time "project" undertaking.

But unlike the Egyptian overseer, today's businessman has available to him a set of new and powerful management tools with the demonstrated capacity to avert time and cost overruns on massive, complex projects. These

* *Reprinted with permission from* Business Horizons, *Fall, 1965.*

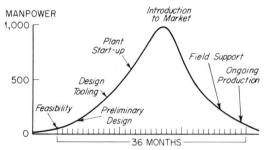

Figure 29-1 Manpower commitment to a new-product introduction project.

Figure 29-2 Manpower commitment to a merger project.

tools, developed only recently, are not yet in common use outside the construction and aerospace industries, where such projects are a way of life. But there is already solid evidence that they can be successfully applied to a host of important, nonroutine business undertakings where conventional planning and control techniques fail—undertakings ranging from a new-product introduction or the launching of a national advertising campaign to the installation of an EDP system or a merger of two major corporations (Figures 29-1 and 29-2).

PROJECT MANAGEMENT ORGANIZATION

Commercial project management is usually a compromise between two basic forms of organization—pure project management and the more standard functional alignment. In the aerospace and construction companies (Figure 29-3), complete responsibility for the task, as well as all the resources needed for· its accomplishment, is usually assigned to one project manager. In very large projects, the organization he heads, which will be dissolved at the

conclusion of the project, resembles a regular division, relatively independent of any other division or staff group. Outside the aerospace and construction industries, however, the project manager is usually not assigned complete responsibility for resources (Figure 29-4). Instead, he shares them with the rest of the organization. He may have a project organization consisting of a handful of men on temporary assignment from the regular functional organization. The functional managers, however, retain their direct line authority, monitor their staffs' contributions to the project, and continue to make all major personnel decisions.

Reluctance to adopt new tools is typical in any industry; thus, one should not expect the tools of project management to gain instant acceptance. Outside the aerospace industry, few business executives appreciate their value and versatility. Fewer still are able to recognize the need for project management in specific situations, nor do they know how to use the powerful control techniques it offers. Meanwhile, the few companies that have grasped the significance of the new management concepts and learned to apply them enjoy an extraordinary, if temporary, advantage. They are bringing new products to market faster than their competitors, completing major expansions on schedule, and meeting crucial commitments more reliably than ever before.

Project management, however, is far from being a cure-all for the embarrassments, expenses, and delays that plague even the best-managed companies. First, project management requires temporary shifts of responsibilities and reporting relationships that may disturb the smooth functioning of the regular organization. Second, it requires unusually disciplined executive effort.

Basic to successful project management is the ability to recognize where it is needed and where it is not. When, in short, is a project a project? Where, in the broad spectrum of undertakings between a minor procedural modification and a major organizational upheaval, should the line be drawn? At what point do a multitude of minor departures from routine add up to the "critical mass" that makes project management operationally and economically desirable? Senior executives must have methods to identify those undertakings, corporate or divisional, that cannot be successfully man-

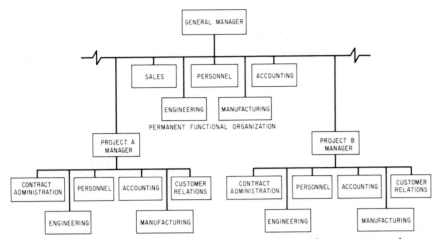

Figure 29-3   Typical project organization in the aerospace and construction industries.

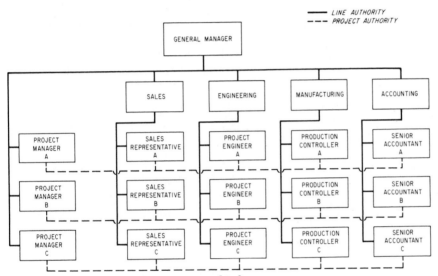

Figure 29-4   Project organization in general industry.

aged by the regular functional organization working with routine planning and control methods. Although there are no simple rules of thumb, management can determine whether a given undertaking possesses this critical mass by applying four yardsticks: scope, unfamiliarity, complexity, and stake.

Scope

Project management can be profitably applied, as a rule, to a one-time undertaking that is (1) definable in terms of a single, specific end result, and (2) bigger than the organization has previously undertaken successfully. A project

must, by definition, end at an objective point in time: the date the new plant achieves full production, the date the parent company takes over operating management of the new acquisition, or the date the new product goes on sale in supermarkets across the nation, to name a few.

The question of size is less easily pinned down. But where substantially more people, more dollars, more organizational units, and more time will be involved than on any other infrequent undertaking in the organization's experience, the test result is clearly positive. Such an undertaking, even though its component parts may be familiar, can easily overwhelm a divisional or corporate management. Project management forces a logical approach to the project, speeds decision making, and cuts management's job to a reasonable level. For example, a large service company, with years of experience in renovating district offices, established a project organization to renovate its 400 district offices over a two year period. Even though each task was relatively simple, the total undertaking would have swamped the administrative organization had it been managed routinely.

In terms of the number of people and the organizational effort it involves, a project could typically be charted over time as a wave-like curve, rising gradually to a crest and dropping off abruptly with the accomplishment of the end result. Consider, for example, the introduction of a new consumer product. The project begins with a few people studying the desirability of adding a product to the line. After some early decisions to proceed, perhaps a few dozen engineers are employed to design the product. Their work passes to scores of process planners, tool makers, and other manufacturing engineers, and finally involves entire manufacturing plants or divisions as the first month's production gains momentum. This momentum carries into the field as salesmen increase their effort to introduce the product successfully. Finally, the project effort ebbs as the new product is integrated into routine production and marketing operation.

Again, a merger typically shows a similar "growth and decay" project pattern. Initially, a few senior executives from each company may be involved in discussing the merger possibility. As interest grows, financial and legal advisors are engaged by both sides. Key inside executives are added to the task force to assist in planning. Then, as the deal moves toward completion, widening circles of executives, technical people, and analysts become involved in identifying the changes required after merger. Once the merger has been approved by the directors and stockholders of the two companies, the process of meshing the philosophies, structures, policies, and procedures of the two organizations must begin, possibly requiring the active participation of hundreds or even thousands of people. Eventually, as most of the changes are accomplished, employees return to their normal duties, and the corporation resumes its orderly march toward the end of the fiscal year. The merger project is at an end.

Unfamiliarity

An undertaking is not a project, in our sense of the term, unless it is a unique, or infrequent, effort by the existing management group. Lack of familiarity or lack of precedent usually leads to disagreement or uncertainty as to how the undertaking should be managed. In such a situation, people at the lower management levels need to be told more precisely what they are to do, while senior executives are justifiably troubled by a greater than usual sense of uncertainty about the realism of initial cost estimates, time commitments, or both.

Thus, though a single engineering change to one part of a product would not qualify for project management by this criterion, the complete redesign of a product line that had been basically unchanged for a decade would in most cases call for project management treatment. Individual managers could accomplish the first change easily, drawing on their own past experience, but each would have to feel his way by trial and error through the second.

Complexity

Frequently the decisive criterion of a project is the degree of interdependence among tasks. If a given task depends on the completion of other assignments in other functional areas, and if it will, in turn, affect the cost or timing of subsequent tasks, project management is probably called for. Consider the introduction of a hypothetical new product. Sales promotion plans cannot be completed until introduction dates are known; introduction dates depend upon product availability; and availability depends on tooling, which depends in turn on the outcome of a disagreement between engineering and product planning over performance specifications. There are many comparable interdependencies among marketing, engineering, manufacturing, and finance. If, as seems likely in this situation, no one person can produce a properly detailed plan on which all those concerned can agree; if estimates repeatedly fail to withstand scrutiny; or if plans submitted by different departments prove difficult to reconcile or coordinate, the critical mass of a project has probably been reached.

Stake

A final criterion that may tip the scales in favor of project management is the company's stake in the outcome of the undertaking. Would failure to complete the job on schedule or within the budget entail serious penalties for the company? If so, the case for project management is strong.

The corporate stake in the outcome of a project is commonly financial; that is, the failure of a $50,000 engineering project might jeopardize $12 million in annual sales. But it may also involve costs of a different kind. As more than one World's Fair exhibitor can attest, failure to meet a well-publicized project schedule can sometimes do real harm to a company's reputation. Again, failure to meet time and cost objectives may seriously disrupt corporate plans, as in the case of an equipment manufacturer who was obliged to abandon a promising new product line when a poorly-managed merger soaked up earnings that had been earmarked for R&D on the new line. In all such cases, the powerful controls of project management offer a much firmer prospect of meeting the time, cost, and quality objectives of the major one-time undertaking.

The specific advantages of project management for ventures that meet the criteria just discussed are easily summarized. Project management provides the concentrated management attention that a complex and unfamiliar undertaking is likely to demand. It greatly improves, at very small cost, the chances of on-time, on-budget completion. And it permits the rest of the organization to proceed normally with routine business while the project is underway. But these benefits are available only if top management clearly understands the unique features of project management, the problems it entails, and the steps required to make it work.

THE NATURE OF PROJECT MANAGEMENT

With respect to organization, project management calls for the appointment of one man, the project manager, who has responsibility for the detailed planning, coordination, and ultimate outcome of the project. Usually appointed from the middle management ranks, the project manager is supplied with a team, often numbering no more than half a dozen men for a $10 million project.

Team members, drawn from the various functional departments involved in the project, report directly to the project manager. For the duration of the project, he has the authority to insist on thorough planning, the freedom to challenge functional departments' assumptions and targets, and the responsibility to monitor every effort bearing on the successful completion of the project.

Within the limits of the project, the project manager's responsibility and authority are interfunctional, like that of top management for the company as a whole. Despite this similarity, however, his function cannot safely be superimposed on a top executive's normal workload. Every company I know that has tried giving operating responsibility for the management of a complex project to a division manager has found that he is soon swamped in a tidal wave of detail. Most projects call for more and faster decisions than does routine work, and clear precedents are usually lacking. Thus, a general manager who tries to run one of his own projects seldom has any guidelines for making reliable cost and time estimates, establishing cost control at commitment points, or setting adequately detailed targets for each department. Lacking precedents, he is obliged to invent them. This procedure may drain off far more of his time than the division can afford, without really providing the project with the concentrated attention it needs. He may well find that he is spending better than half his working time trying to manage a project representing less than a tenth of his division's annual budget, while divisional performance as a whole is slipping alarmingly. For these reasons, few projects are ever successfully managed on a part-time basis.

The essence of project management is that it cuts across, and in a sense conflicts with, the normal organization structure. Throughout the project, personnel at various levels in many functions of the business contribute to it. Because a project usually requires decisions and actions from a number of functional areas at once, the main interdependencies and the main flow of information in a project are not vertical but lateral. Up-and-down information flow is relatively light in a well-run project; indeed, any attempt to consistently send needed information from one functional area up to a common authority and down to another area through conventional channels is apt to cripple the project and wreck the time schedule.

Projects are also characterized by exceptionally strong lateral working relationships, requiring closely related activity and decisions by many individuals in different functional departments. During a major product development, for example, a design engineer will work more closely with the process engineering manager and the product manager from marketing than with the senior members of his own department. He will need common sense and tolerance to succeed in the scramble for available resources, such as test-cell time or the help of metallurgical specialists, without hurting relationships of considerable importance to his future career.

Necessarily though, a project possesses a vertical as well as a horizontal dimension, since those who are involved in it at various stages, particularly those who make the technical decisions that determine costs, must often go to their superiors for guidance. Moreover, frequent project changes underline the necessity of keeping senior executives informed of the project's current status.

SPECIAL SOURCES OF TROUBLE

Understandably, project managers face some unusual problems in trying to direct and harmonize the diverse forces at work in the project situation. Their main difficulties, observation suggests, arise from three sources: organizational uncertainties, unusual decision pressures, and vulnerability to top-management mistakes.

Organizational Uncertainties

Many newly appointed project managers find that their working relationships with functional department heads have not been clearly defined by management. Who assigns work to the financial analyst? Who decides when to order critical material before the product design is firm? Who decides to delay design release to reduce unit cost? Who determines the quantity and priority of spares? All these decisions vitally concern the project manager, and he must often forgo his own guidelines for dealing with them. Unless he does so skillfully,

the questions are apt to be resolved in the interest of individual departments, at the expense of the project as a whole.

Because of the number of decisions or approvals that may arise in the course of a large project, and the number of departments that have an interest in each, innumerable possibilities always exist for interdepartmental conflicts. Besides coping with these conflicts, the project manager must juggle the internal schedules of each department with the project schedule, avoid political problems that could create bottlenecks, expedite one department to compensate for another's failure to meet its schedule, and hold the project within a predetermined cost. Moreover, he must do all this single-handed, with little or none of the experienced top-management guidance that the line manager enjoys.

Unusual Decision Pressures

The severe penalties of delay often compel the project manager to base his decisions on relatively few data, analyzed in haste. On a large project where a day's delay may cost $10,000 in salaries alone, he can hardly hold everything up for a week to perform an analysis that could save the company $5,000. He must move fast, even if it means an intuitive decision that might expose him to charges of rashness and irresponsibility from functional executives. Decisions to sacrifice time for cost, cost for quality, or quality for time, are common in most projects, and the project manager must be able to make them without panicking. Clearly, therefore, he has a special need for intelligent support from higher management.

Vulnerability to Top-Management Mistakes

Though senior executives can seldom give the project manager as much guidance and support as his line counterpart enjoys, they can easily jeopardize the project's success by lack of awareness, ill-advised intervention, or personal whim. The damage that a senior executive's ignorance of a project situation can create is well illustrated by the following example. A project manager, battling to meet a schedule that had been rendered nearly impossible by the general manager's initial delay in approving the proposal, found functional cooperation more and more difficult to obtain. The functional heads, he discovered, had become convinced—rightly, as it turned out—that he lacked the general manager's full confidence. Unknown to the project manager, two department heads whom he had pressured to expedite their departments had complained to the general manager, who had readily sympathized. The project manager, meanwhile, had been too busy getting the job done to protect himself with top management. As a result, project performance was seriously hampered.

EXECUTIVE ACTION REQUIRED

Because of the great diversity of projects and the lack of common terminology for the relatively new techniques of project management, useful specific rules for project management are virtually impossible to formulate. From the experience of the aerospace and construction industries and of a handful of companies in other industries, however, it is possible to distill some general guidelines.

Guideline 1: Define the Objective

Performing unfamiliar activities at a rapid pace, those involved in the project can easily get off the right track or fall short of meeting their commitments, with the result that many steps of the project may have to be retraced. To minimize this risk, management must clarify the objective of the project well in advance by (1) defining management's intent in undertaking the project, (2) outlining the scope of the project, that is, identifying the departments, companies, functions, and staffs involved, and the approximate degree of their involvement, and (3) describing the end results of the project and its permanent effects, if any, on the company or division.

Defining management's intent. What are the business reasons for the project? What is top management's motive in undertaking it?

A clear common understanding of the answers to these questions is desirable for three reasons. *First*, it enables the project manager to capitalize on opportunities to improve the outcome of the project. By knowing top management's rationale for building the new plant,

for example, he will be able to weigh the one-time cost of plant start-up against the continuing advantage of lower production costs, or the competitive edge that might be gained by an earlier product introduction. *Second*, a clear definition of intent helps avert damaging oversights that would otherwise appear unimportant to lower-level managers and might not be obvious to the senior executive. One company failed to get any repeat orders for a unique product because the project team, unaware of the president's intent, saw their job only in terms of meeting their schedule and cost commitments and neglected to cultivate the market. *Third*, a definition of the intent of the project helps to avoid imbalance of effort at the middle-management level, such as pushing desperately to meet a schedule but missing cost-reduction opportunities on the way.

Outlining the scope of the project. Which organizational units of the company will be involved in the project, and to what degree? Which sensitive customer relationships, private or governmental, should the project manager cautiously skirt? By crystallizing the answers and communicating them to the organization, the responsible senior executive will make it far easier for the project manager to work with the functional departments and to get the information he needs.

Describing the end results. Top managers who have spent hours discussing a proposed project can easily overlook the fact that middle managers charged with its execution lack their perspective on the project. An explicit description of how a new plant will operate when it is in full production, how a sales reorganization will actually change customer relationships, or how major staff activities will be coordinated after a merger, gives middle managers a much clearer view of what the project will involve and what is expected of them.

Guideline 2: Establish a Project Organization

For a functionally organized company, successful project management means establishing, for the duration of the project, a workable compromise between two quite different organizational concepts. The basic ingredients of such a compromise are (1) appointment of one experienced manager to run the project full-time, (2) organization of the project management function in terms of responsibilities, (3) assignment of a limited number of men to the project team, and (4) maintenance of a balance of power between the functional heads and the project manager. In taking these steps, some generally accepted management rules may have to be broken, and some organizational friction will almost inevitably occur. But the results in terms of successful project completion should far outweigh these drawbacks and difficulties.

Assigning an experienced manager.   Though the project manager's previous experience is apt to have been confined to a single functional area of the business, he must be able to function on the project as a kind of general manager in miniature. He must not only keep track of what is happening but also play the crucial role of advocate for the project. Even for a seasoned manager, this task is not likely to be easy. Hence, it is important to assign an individual whose administrative abilities and skill in personal relations have been convincingly demonstrated under fire.

Organizing the project manager's responsibilities.   While some organizational change is essential, management should try to preserve, wherever possible, the established relationships that facilitate rapid progress under pressure. Experience indicates that it is desirable for senior management to delegate to the project manager some of its responsibilities for planning the project, for resolving arguments among functional departments, for providing problem-solving assistance to functional heads, and for monitoring progress. A full-time project manager can better handle these responsibilities; moreover, the fact that they are normally part of the executive job helps to establish his stature. A general manager, however, should not delegate certain responsibilities, such as monitoring milestone accomplishments, resolving project-related disputes between senior managers, or evaluating the project performance of functional department managers. The last responsibility mentioned strikes too close to the careers of the individuals concerned to be delegated to one of their peers.

For the duration of the project, the project manager should also hold some responsibilities normally borne by functional department heads. These include responsibility for reviewing progress against schedule; organizing for, formulating, and approving a project plan; monitoring project cost performance; and, in place of the department heads normally involved, trading off time and cost. Also, the senior executive must encourage the project manager to direct the day-to-day activities of all functional personnel who are involved full-time in the project. Functional department heads, however, should retain responsibility for the quality of their subordinates' technical performance, as well as for matters affecting their careers.

Limiting the project team.   Functional department heads may view the project manager as a potential competitor. By limiting the number of men on the project team, this problem is alleviated and the project manager's involvement in intrafunctional matters is reduced. Moreover, men transferred out of their own functional departments are apt to lose their inside sources of information and find it increasingly difficult to get things done rapidly and informally.

Maintaining the balance of power.   Because the project manager is concerned with change, while the department head must efficiently manage routine procedures, the two are often in active conflict. Though they should be encouraged to resolve these disputes without constant appeals to higher authority, their common superior must occasionally act as mediator. Otherwise, resentments and frustrations will impair the project's progress and leave a long-lasting legacy of bitterness. Short-term conflicts can often be resolved in favor of the project manager and long-term conflicts in favor of the functional managers. This compromise helps to reduce friction, to get the job accomplished, and to prepare for the eventual phasing out of the project.

Guideline 3: Install Project Controls

Though they use the same raw data as routine reports, special project controls over time, cost, and quality are very different in their accuracy, timing, and use. They are normally superimposed upon the existing report structure for the duration of the project and then discontinued. The crucial relationship between project time control and cost control is shown graphically in Figure 29-5.

The project in question had to be completed in twenty months instead of the twenty and a half months scheduled by a preliminary network calculation. The project manager, who was under strict initial manpower limitations, calculated the cost of the two weeks' acceleration at various stages of the project. Confronted by the evidence of the costs it could save, top management approved the project manager's request for early acceleration. The project was completed two working days before its twenty-month deadline, at a cost only $6,000 over the original estimate. Without controls that clearly relate time to cost, companies too often crash the project in its final stages, at enormous and entirely unnecessary cost.

Time control. Almost invariably, some form of network scheduling provides the best time control of a project. A means of graphically planning a complex undertaking so that it can be scheduled for analysis and control, network scheduling begins with the construction of a diagram that reflects the interdependencies and time requirements of the individual tasks that go to make up a project. It calls for work plans prepared in advance of the project in painstaking detail, scheduling each element of the plan, and using controls to ensure that commitments are met.

At the outset, each department manager involved in the project should draw up a list of all the tasks required of his department to accomplish the project. Then the project manager should discuss each of these lists in detail with the respective departmental supervisors in order to establish the sequence in the project in relation to other departments. Next, each manager and supervisor should list the information he will need from other departments, indicating which data, if any, are habitually late. This listing gives the project manager not only a clue to the thoroughness of planning in the other departments but also a means of uncovering and forestalling most of the inconsistencies, missed activities, or inadequate planning that would otherwise occur.

Next, having planned its own role in the project, each department should be asked to commit itself to an estimate of the time required for each of its project activities, assuming the required information is supplied on time. After this, the complete network is constructed, adjusted where necessary with the agreement of the department heads concerned, and reviewed for logic.

Once the over-all schedule is established, weekly or fortnightly review meetings should be held to check progress against schedule. Control must be rigorous, especially at the

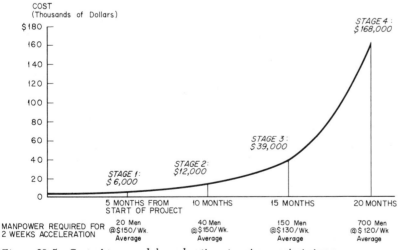

Figure 29-5   Cost of two weeks' acceleration at various project stages.

start, when the tone of the entire project is invariably set. Thus, the very first few missed commitments call for immediate corrective action.

In critical path scheduling, one of the major network techniques, the diagram is similar in principle to that of Figure 29-6 for a very simple hypothetical project.

In the diagram, each arrow represents a defined task, with a clear beginning end, and time requirement, that can be delegated to a single manager or supervisor. Each circle, or node (except the "start" node), represents the completion of a task. Task A, for example, might be "Define the technical objective of the project." The numeral 1 indicates that the allotted time for its completion is one day.

The arrangement of the arrows is significant. As drawn here, B depends upon A; that is, it may not start until A is complete. Similarly, C may not start until B is complete. Also, while B and E may start at different times, neither may start until A is complete. Further along, G may not start until both D and F are complete. This diagram, then, is one of *sequence* and *dependency*.

The time required for the project corresponds to the longest path through the network from Start to Complete in terms of the time requirement associated with each task. In the diagram above, A-E-F-G is the critical path. To meet the over-all schedule, each of these tasks must begin as soon as its predecessor is completed and must end within its allotted time. To shorten the schedule, one or more of the tasks on the critical path must be accelerated.

There are other more complex varieties of network scheduling. Critical path method calculates both normal and crash schedules (and costs) for a project. Program evaluation and review technique (PERT) allows the use of multiple time estimates for each activity. PERT/Cost adds cost estimates, as the name implies. RAMPS (resource allocation and multiproject scheduling) adds the further refinement of a tool for allocating limited resources to competing activities in one or more projects. All, however, rest on the basic network concept outlined above.

Cost control.   Project cost control techniques, though not yet formalized to the same degree as time controls, are no harder to install if these steps are followed: (1) break the comprehensive cost summary into work packages, (2) devise commitment reports for "technical" decision makers, (3) act on early, approximate report data, and (4) concentrate talent on major problems and opportunities.

Managing a fast-moving $15 million project can be difficult for even the most experienced top manager. For a first-line supervisor the job of running a $500,000 project can be equally difficult. Neither manager can make sound decisions unless cost dimensions of the job are broken down into pieces of comprehensible size. Figure 29-7, which gives an example of such a breakdown, shows how major costs can be logically reduced to understandable and controllable work packages (usually worth $15,000 to $25,000 apiece on a major project), each of which can reasonably be assigned to a first-line manager.

Cost commitments on a project are made when engineering, manufacturing, marketing, or other functional personnel make technical decisions to take some kind of action. In new-product development, for example, costs are committed or created in many ways—when marketing decides to add a product feature to its product; when engineering decides to insert a new part; when a process engineer adds an extra operation to a routing; when physical distribution managers choose to increase inventory, and so on. Conventional accounting reports, however, do not show the cost effects of these decisions until it is too late to reconsider. To enable the project manager to judge when costs are getting out of control and to decisively take the needed corrective action, he must be able to assess the approximate cost

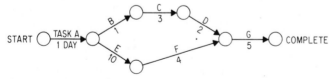

Figure 29-6   A simple critical path network.

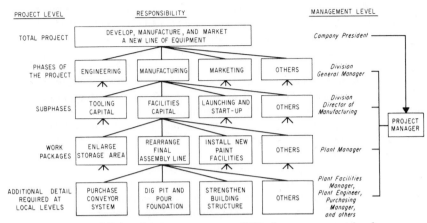

PROJECT LEVEL RESPONSIBILITY   MANAGEMENT LEVEL

Figure 29-7 Breakdown of project cost responsibility by management level.

effect of each technical decision. In other words, he must have cost commitment reports at each decision stage.

Almost without exception, experience shows, 20 per cent of the project effort accounts for at least 80 per cent of the cost to which the company is committed. With the aid of a detailed cost breakdown and current information on cost commitment, the project manager is able, even after the project is underway, to take people off less important activities in order to concentrate more effort where it will do the most good in reducing costs. One company cut its product introduction costs by over $1 million in this way between the dates when the first print was released and the first machine assembled.

Quality control. Experience with a wide variety of projects—new-product introductions, mergers, plant constructions, introduction of organizational changes, to name a few—indicates that effective quality control of results is a crucial dimension of project success. Quality control comprises three elements: defining performance criteria, expressing the project objective in terms of quality standards, and monitoring progress toward these standards.

The need to define performance criteria, though universally acknowledged, is generally ignored in practice. Such quality criteria can, however, be defined rather easily, that is, simply in terms of senior executives' expectations with respect to average sales per salesman, market penetration of a product line, ratio of accountants to production workers, processing

time for customer inquiries, and the like. If possible, these expectations should be expressed quantitatively. For example, the senior executive might expect the project to reduce emergency transportation costs from 15 per cent to 5 per cent of total shipping costs. Or he might expect a 30 per cent reduction in inventory costs following installation of a mechanized control system.

Since achievement of these quality goals is a gradual process, the project manager should review progress toward them with the general manager monthly or quarterly, depending upon the length of the project. Sometimes there will be little noticeable change; in other cases major departures from expectation will be apparent. Here, as in the case of time and cost controls, the importance of prompt action to assure that the objectives will be met cannot be overemphasized.

MANAGING THE HUMAN EQUATION

The typical manager in a commercial business who is handed his first project management assignment finds adjustment to his anomalous new role painful, confusing, and even demoralizing. Lacking real line authority, he must constantly lead, persuade, or coerce his peers through a trying period of change.

Too often, in these difficult early weeks, he receives little support from senior management. Instead, he is criticized for not moving faster and producing more visible results. He may be blamed for flaws in a plan that, through the fault of top management, had to be rushed to completion mere days before the project began. Senior managers need to recognize that naming and needling the project manager is not enough. By giving him needed support at the start, by bringing a broad business perspective to bear on the over-all project plan, and by giving the project manager freedom in the details of the doing, the senior executive can greatly enhance his prospects of success.

Another critical point comes at the conclusion of the project, when its results are turned over to the regular organization and the project manager and his team must be returned to their permanent assignments. By virtue of the interfunctional experience gained under pressure, the project manager often matures in the course of a project, becoming a more valuable manager. But he may have trouble slowing down to a normal organizational pace. His routine job is likely to seem less attractive in terms of scope, authority, and opportunity to contribute to the business. Even the best project manager, moreover, can hardly accomplish his project objectives without antagonizing some members of management, quite possibly the very executives who will decide his future. In one instance, a project manager who had brought a major project from the brink of chaos to unqualified success was let go at the end of the project because, in accomplishing the feat, he had been unable to avoid antagonizing one division manager. Such difficulties and dissatisfactions often lead a retired project manager to look for a better job at this time, in or out of the company.

To retain and profit by the superior management material developed on the fertile training ground of the project, senior executives need to be aware of these human problems. By recognizing the growth of the project manager, helping him readjust to the slower pace of the normal organization, and finding ways to put his added experience and his matured judgment to good use, the company can reap a significant side benefit from every successfully managed project.

READING 30

MULTIPLE LADDERS IN AN ENGINEERING DEPARTMENT*

F. J. Holzapfel

Despite the rapid rate of change in technology and products, industry's organization concepts all seem to be variations of the traditional organization of a fighting force such as was used in ancient times. The principle of organization then, as now, was authority.

McGregor[1] sums up the conventional conception of harnessing human energy to organizational needs as "Theory X." This theory states that management directs and controls the efforts of people, modifying their behavior to fit the needs of the organization. Further, this theory implies that without this active intervention, people will be passive or resistant to organization needs and hence must be persuaded, rewarded and punished.

Where this theory is practiced, most people will want to be managers, rather than managed. Oratory about dual ladders or the

equivalence of managerial and technical jobs is hypocritical in such cases. The day-to-day actions belie the words.

In noting that managerial, professional and technical employees have become the largest group in our workforce, Peter Drucker has commented[2] that a different organizational philosophy may be in order. He suggests that we have to organize an information and decision system (that is, a system of judgment, knowledge and expectations) rather than a system of authority, responsibility and command.

As an alternative to Theory X, McGregor suggests "Theory Y." An important element of this theory is that the essential task of management is to arrange organizational conditions and methods of operation so that people can achieve their own goals by directing their own efforts toward organizational objectives. Peter Drucker has called this "management by objectives" in contrast to "management by control." This organization philosophy should not be confused with "permissive management," because attainment of objectives can be the most demanding taskmaster of all.

WHY THE DISSATISFIED ENGINEER?

The literature is full of articles about dual ladders of promotion (manager vs. technical specialists).[4-9] Surveys repeatedly indicate that most engineers are less than satisfied. In my opinion, the engineers are really dissatisfied with the "command and control" organization philosophy that prevails. They recognize that under such circumstances any pronouncements about dual ladders or equivalence of technical and managerial jobs are intended to salve the ego of those who haven't been anointed.

Basically, the various "multiple paths of progression" plans are salary administration devices. Most companies use a salary administration system that divides the entire salary spectrum from office boy to president into a series of overlapping salary ranges. Within broad limits, individuals in the same salary range are considered to be of equal value to the company. It is convenient to assign titles that suggest the type of work done by the individuals.

Very often, administrative or managerial titles are bestowed as status symbols, even though the direct line supervisory aspects of the job occupy only a small part of the man's time. Here too it is necessary to have an intimate knowledge of the particular company, and even of the particular department, since practices vary widely.

Where the "Theory Y," or "Management by Objectives" philosophy, is practiced, the distinction between the two rails of the dual ladder become a matter of degree, rather than of kind. The ability to listen, motivate, and persuade are not only desirable attributes of administrators. The technical specialist will derive greater satisfaction and be more likely to influ-

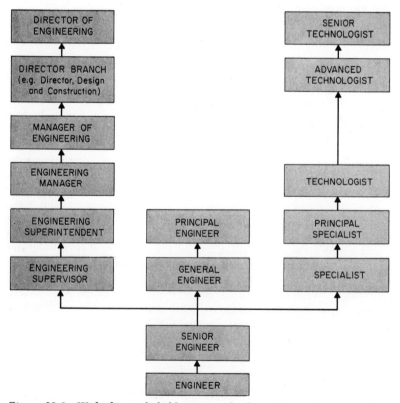

Figure 30-1 With this triple-ladder approach, the senior engineer can choose (or be chosen) for the managerial, generalist, or specialist route to advancement. It is possible to switch from one ladder to the other—e.g., for a qualified principal engineer to move over to the managerial side.

ence events to the extent that he learns and practices these same skills.

A SPECIFIC EXAMPLE

So much for generalities. Let's see how management by objectives applies to the Central Engineering Dept. of Monsanto Co. This department was created in 1965 by the merger of the separate and autonomous engineering departments of the firm's seven operating divisions. Its principal assigned job is the design and construction of all major (more than $100,000 each) capital projects for the entire company. The total capital program has been at the $150 to $200 million per year level.

The long-term objectives of consolidation are to:

Achieve greater organizational flexibility, so that personnel may be shifted to handle large projects faster.
Develop greater technical skill in the many new specialties that are becoming important in engineering.
Have a broad enough base to develop in-house consultants, refresher training programs, etc.

Figure 30-2 shows the basic administrative scheme of Monsanto's Central Engineering Dept. To achieve organizational stability, to provide for continual technical training in order to combat obsolescence, and to facilitate career counseling and salary administration, the organization is made up of technical sections—such as electrical design, construction, and so on.

Each of these sections is administered by an engineering manager, who must provide adequate numbers of people trained in the particular technical specialty of his section (e.g., electrical design) and who must assign men to provide such specialized design for each project. In the case of his younger men, and those whose technical skills are less than his, the manager must review the work for technical adequacy.

However, the department is really a job shop. Its function is the design and construction of capital projects—some 100 to 150 at any one time, which vary in size from $100,000 to $30 million. Efficient execution of any one project requires that each have a "project manager," and that project management of each of the various simultaneous projects be superimposed upon the basic organization. The real-life organization is thus a "matrix." Figure 30-3 attempts to show this schematically. As far as the usual administrative or managerial role is concerned, the project manager has no

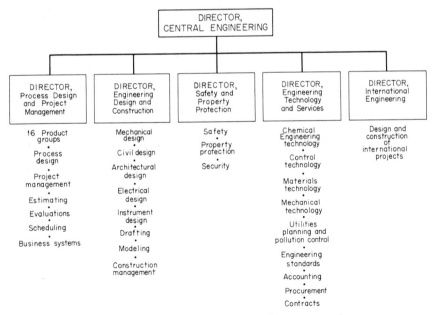

Figure 30-2   Basic organization of Monsanto's central engineering department.

one who reports to him directly, unless it is a large project and he needs one or more assistant project managers. He is not responsible for anyone's salary administration, career counselling, training, or discipline. If his is a small project, he may be a relatively young engineer. On larger projects, his "salary administration" title may be senior engineer, general engineer, principal engineer, specialist, or even engineering supervisor, superintendent, or manager (see below). The project manager title is in effect an assignment, rather than a position, for the duration of the project only. The scope and objectives of the project are established in discussions with the client—the operating division.

Here is the definition of project manager that we have given to our personnel:

> The *Project Manager* is ... charged with primary responsibility for a project so that its engineering objectives are attained within established cost and schedule limitations. He is the chief representative of the Central Engineering Dept. to the client.
>
> Responsibility for the performance of various functions is divided among the different sections of Central Engineering. The Project Manager makes arrangements with each such section for assignment of personnel and execution of its portion of the work, and monitors progress to insure that actions are taken and

decisions made in a fashion that will best satisfy total project objectives. Line authority for the performance of the members of a functional section and for the technical adequacy of their work remains with the manager of the functional section.

There will be occasions where compromises must be made in the interests of achieving total project objectives. The Project Manager is expected to make a reasonable effort to reconcile differences and to minimize the need for compromise, insofar as time and good judgment permit. However, where concurrence cannot be obtained, the project manager shall make such decisions as are required. The various functional sections are expected to implement such decisions. They may appeal the decision through their line organization to the extent that conviction and good judgment dictates, but work is to continue in line with the Project Manager's decision while appeal is pending.

On paper, this system may seem cumbersome. It lacks the comforting hierarchy of decision-making and command. But it does work. In his technical specialty, each man is subject only to his technical superior. The administrative group must set goals for each project. With goals established, each man is able to use judgment to arrive at decisions in his

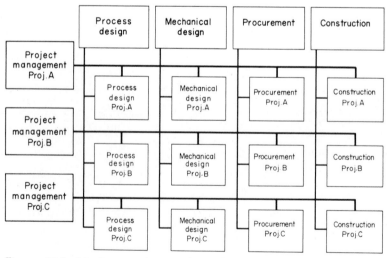

Figure 30-3 Matrix organization shows how project work is handled within the department.

area of expertise. For the most part, conflicts between technical areas can be resolved in the best interest of the project by objective discussion among peers, and few problems need to be arbitrated by the administrative groups.

PERSONAL ADVANCEMENT: THE LADDERS

In the Central Engineering Dept., we are attempting to practice management by objectives, and we do have a "dual ladder" title and salary administration scheme. Figure 30-1 shows the titles used. There are approximately 1,000 people in this department. Of these, about 650 are engineers or members of one of the other professions.

Note that this chart shows the starting engineer at the bottom center. He progresses as a "general practitioner" to senior engineer. From here, he may elect, or be chosen for, an administrative job (shown in the left column), or may decide to concentrate on some technical specialty (shown in the right column). However, he may prefer or be better suited to general practice. The center column indicates that he may make further advances in salary and influence.

The titles that appear on the same horizontal line are in the same salary range. In this connection, it is worth noting that the administrative line of progression is characterized by a series of discrete steps because of the nature of the organization units, whereas the specialist line of progression is really a continuous spectrum of ability.

At periodic intervals, each man should perform an agonizing self-appraisal to establish the type of work from which he derives most satisfaction, the amount of sacrifice he is prepared to make to achieve his goals, and the amount and nature of the competition. If properly done, semiannual or annual discussions between the engineer and his "administrator-coach" can be very helpful in establishing goals, indicating desires, and mapping out plans for achieving such desires. At the earlier stages in a man's career, it is easy to arrange for transfers and temporary assignments, so that the younger engineers may have a taste of each of the types of work.

Maloney, in his articles on ladders for technical status seekers,[3] has some down-to-earth advice that bears rereading. In some cases, an engineer may find it interesting to subject himself to a series of psychological tests that have been validated on engineers and are administered and interpreted by a competent psychologist.

The existence of a multiple-path progression plan, or of an enlightened organization philosophy, will not relieve any engineer of the need for the soul-searching outlined above. Where both exist, however, the conscious choice of one of the nonadministrative roles is less difficult to make. The nature of our modern technology-dependent organizations is such that we must have more people on the technical side. Their work will be more rewarding both to themselves and to the corporation if they have elected this choice, rather than if such choice were by default.

References

1. McGregor, D., "Leadership and Motivation," M.I.T. Press, 1966; also "The Human Side of Enterprise," McGraw-Hill, 1960.
2. Drucker, P. F., "Management and the Professional Employee," *Harvard Bus. Rev.;* also "Managing the Educated," unpublished address.
3. Maloney, P. W., "Ladders for Technical Status Seekers," *Chem. Eng.,* Sep. 13 and Sep. 25, 1965; also "Reward Systems for Technical Men," *Chem. Eng.,* Aug. 2 and Aug. 13, 1965.
4. "Dual Ladder—Theory or Practice," *American Engineer,* Aug. 1966 (staff article).
5. Murdick, R. G., "The Three Jobs of the Technical Specialist in the Engineering Organization," *American Engineer,* Mar. 1966.
6. Campbell, R. O., "Climbing Three Ladders to Success," *Oil & Gas J.,* Nov. 2, 1964.
7. "Three Ways Up at Calresearch," *Chem. Eng. News,* Nov. 13, 1961.
8. Trader, W. D., "Professional Job Levels," *Machine Design,* Sep. 13, 1962.
9. Raudsepp, E., "Engineering or Management," *Machine Design,* Dec. 21, 1961.

READING 31

THE ROLE OF PROJECT MANAGEMENT IN SCIENTIFIC MANUFACTURING *

Keith Davis

Summary—A survey was made of various types of project management organizations used to achieve some measure of managerial unity. Four principal types were identified.

The project expediter achieves unity of communication, the project coordinator gets unity of control, the project confederation achieves unity of direction, and project general management accomplishes the ultimate unity of command. Furthermore, project management may disregard existing levels and functions in superimposing its own structure on the existing organization.

Project organization requires a project manager with considerable role adaptability. He must balance technical solutions with time, cost, resource, and human factors. He is an integrator and a generalist, rather than a technical specialist; and he devotes most of his

* *Reprinted with permission from* IRE Transactions on Engineering Management, *vol. 9, 1962.*

management time to the functions of planning and control. Both the project manager and his superiors may need to give more emphasis to the **management** aspects of his job. To be an effective project manager, the technical man needs to be intellectually sophisticated in the field of management and also to have an attitude which gives some priority to the management aspects of his job.

Project management has become a major device for better management in scientific manufacturing during the last two decades. The project manager generally has complete managerial, budget, and technical responsibility for directing a specialized research or development project. The mix of his group is tailored to fit one specific job, and when that job is finished, he is returned to his "permanent" job or to another project, usually with a different mix of specialists, depending on the requirements of the new project. In this manner, each new project has a separately constituted work group drawn from their permanent or "home-base" assignments within the organization. An arrangement of this type achieves a necessary measure of stability through permanent attachment to the organization, while permitting greater flexibility to adjust each work group to fit the specific manpower requirements of that one job.[1]

PROJECT MANAGER'S ROLE AND FUNCTION

Project management gradually developed in manufacturing as a device for achieving better management of complex development and manufacturing projects. Probably it evolved somewhat from the construction industry, which had practiced something similar to it for years. In the construction of dams, air bases, and factories, separate project organizations were established under a project director. When the job was completed, the project group disbanded to be assigned to other activities of the parent organization. When large manufacturing contracts came to the air frame industry, its members were quick to notice the similarity and to develop a type of project management suited to their own needs for better management. Some of the first companies to make major use of it were Douglas, Lockheed, Martin, and Chance-Vought. Similarities between heavy construction and air frame manufacture may be observed. In each case there is a major job, substantially separate in itself, of finite duration, for one or a very few customers, involving something at least slightly different from what has been done before.

ORGANIZATION FOR PROJECT MANAGEMENT

Fundamental to the project management concept is some form of organization which will help project accomplishment. Emphasis is upon structures and procedures which will integrate the many diverse activities involved in today's complex scientific projects. Each project must be *administratively* tied together in the same

way that its end product must be *physically* put together before it is a workable whole. It follows that *the primary reason for project management organizations is to achieve some measure of managerial unity*, in the same way that physical unity is achieved with the product. Without project organization, the project's activities remain functionally separated in the traditional functional areas of the business, such as production, research, and engineering, and are unified only in the general manager or his equivalent. However, some scientific projects are of such vast complexity or so unique in nature that one general manager is unable to devote the required time to performance of the unifying function; therefore, he establishes a separate unifying agent to perform this function for him. This agent is some form of project organization.

My research with manufacturing firms in the West discloses that there are several types of organization which are sometimes designated "project management." At least four types are readily distinguished. The first type has only a *project expediter*. He does not perform primary management functions, such as directing people, but he does perform two other activities essential to good management. First, he is supposed to expedite the work by dealing with all persons involved to assure that schedules are met; however, he has no power other than persuasion and reporting back to his superior. This reflects his second function, that of serving as a center of communication to be able instantly to report to general management on the *whole* of the project and thus relieve general management of the tedious task of keeping up with all the details. Accordingly, he accomplishes unity of communication, a key necessity in the complex world of advanced technology. Furthermore, he serves as interpreter and translator of complex scientific concepts into the cost, market, and other business interests which general management has.[2] In some cases, he expedites technical aspects only, in which case he is the scientific equivalent of the old production expediter on the factory floor. In other cases, he expedites the whole project, serving more as a staff assistant to a general manager.

[1] See Paul O. Gaddis, "The project manager—his role in advanced technology industry," Westinghouse Engr., vol. 19, pp. 102–106, July, 1959.

[2] For example, see T. Burns, "Research, development and production: problems of conflict and co-operation," IRE Trans. on Engineering Management, vol. EM-8, pp. 15–23, March, 1961.

A second type of project organization is directed by a *project coordinator*. He has independent authority to act and is held responsible therefore, but he *does not* direct the work of others. He is more of a staff leader, exercising his leadership through procedural decisions and personal interaction, rather than through line authority. For example, he can independently, or in discussion with others, determine a schedule change and issue procedural changes relating thereto, somewhat like a production control department in a factory, but he cannot direct or discipline others. As another example, his signature may be necessary for release of budget monies, like a controller, but he does not originally set the budget. His control of the budget is perhaps his greatest strength. This forces a unity of control, in addition to the unity of communication which existed in the first type, the production expediter. Like the expediter, the coordinator may cover only the technical aspects of the project, or he may co-ordinate the entire project.

The third type of project organization is headed by a manager who actually performs the full range of management functions from planning to controlling the work of others; hence, he may properly be called "manager." However, those persons he directs are mostly working in other departments spatially removed from him and are, consequently, not subject to his operating supervision throughout the work day. Though they are assigned to his project, they remain in their permanent departments. In some cases, they may be assigned to the project only part time, but in most cases they are assigned full time. A typical situation is the following one. The project manager determines budgets for his employees, issues instructions to them, sends them on trips, assigns their work, and so on, but much of their housekeeping services and routine supervision are supplied by their permanent departments. Often each person looks to his permanent department for technical leadership also. Since he continues to be a part of his permanent department, he has recourse through his own departmental chain of command to the project manager's superior in case of an irresolvable dispute. Thus, each can administratively go around his project manager without committing the organizational sin of bypassing. The project manager may select his personnel or they may be assigned to him on the basis of

specifications he sets. In either case, he may remove one of them from the project because of poor performance but this act merely returns that person to duty in his permanent department.

This third type of organization is a *project confederation*. In addition to the unity of communication and of control found in types one and two, the confederation achieves a unity of *direction*. All operations, though spatially separated, are focused toward one objective under the *general* direction of one person. In small projects, the project manager manages his departmental people without any intervening level, no matter what level they occupy in their permanent departments. In larger projects the project manager directs *departmental* project managers who then supervise on a face-to-face basis the persons assigned to the project. The project manager may be assisted by several employees and sub-managers working directly with him in his office.

The fourth type of project organization has the ultimate organizational objective of unity of command, which basically means that each person is responsible to one manager only. Persons are temporarily withdrawn from their departments and wholly assigned to the project under the project manager. He is their chain-of-command manager until they are removed or the project plays out. This fourth type is *project general management*. Its manager directs virtually the complete project. He is in many respects a separate branch manager with profit authority and responsibility, subject to general direction by his superior. This type of organization is especially suitable for major projects lasting one year or more.

The four types of project organization which have been discussed represent important differences, but there are many further variations within each type. The concept of project management is a complex one, permitting infinite variations in management design. In all cases the basic objective is some measure of managerial unity. The project expediter achieves unity of communication; the project coordinator gets unity of control, the project confederation accomplishes unity of direction, and project general management accomplishes the ultimate unity of command.

For project unity, there appear to be three avenues open to the chief executive of a firm. One is that he can perform the unifying function himself. Another is that he can have a committee do it, but projects require managerial action rather than deliberative thought, so a committee is rather unfit for managing or coordinating the whole project. This leaves the third choice—a separate project manager or coordinator. My research has disclosed an interesting example of the failure of committee project management. As shown in Figure 31-1, Project Roger was originally designed to be coordinated by AA and BB, who were in separate chains of command. GG was also part of the coordinating "committee," but it was felt that his status was lower since he worked at a lower level in the organization. The project soon bogged down under the weight of coordination problems, lack of authority and responsibility, and red tape. As stated by one of those involved, "I found it simply unworkable. It could not provide the requisite experimental controls, proper procedures, and generally could not keep things going smoothly."

Finally a revised organization was designed for Project Roger as shown in Figure 31-2. The revised organization had the chain of command centering in a project manager. In addition, LL was brought in to provide additional routine task and paperwork coordination, leaving the project manager free to make major decisions. This new organization worked effectively.

It is apparent that *project organization may disregard existing levels and functions in superimposing its own structure on the existing company organization*. It establishes a structure of its own based upon each person's ability to

contribute to that specific project, regardless of his permanent organizational location. Project Roger illustrates this development.

Figure 31-3 shows the permanent organizational assignment of persons in Project Roger. In this chart, AA and BB are at the same level, but in the revised project organization (Figure 31-2), AA is superior to BB. Similarly, GG is ordinarily one level lower than BB, (Figure 31-3), but in Figure 31-2, he is at an equal level with BB in the project. KK and MM are normally at the same level with LL, and in a different chain of command, but in the project (Figure 31-2) they both report to LL. Earlier in the project, (Figure 31-1), KK reported to II, who in the permanent organization was his equal and in a different chain of command.

In one company which used type 3 of project organization (the project confederation), the project managers reported directly to the general manager, even though in their "permanent" organizational assignments they were at least two levels removed from him. They freely admitted that at the end of the project they expected to return to lower levels in their firm. Project management in this firm was looked upon as a testing ground and a broadening experience for promising middle managers.

THE PROJECT MANAGER'S ROLE

Indeed, project management is broadening. It requires a wide range of abilities, judgment, and communication. It may require skills of talking science with a physicist, as well as costs with the general manager and general business relationships with the customer's purchasing agent, engineer, or vice president. It is evident that *project organization requires a project manager with considerable role adaptability*. If he cannot adapt to quick changes in level, function, and interest, in his relations with others, then his multitude of contacts may

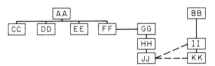

Figure 31-1 Project Group Roger, original design. (Three chains of command loosely coordinated.)

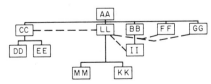

Figure 31-2 Project Group Roger, revised design. (The chain of command with added task coordinator LL.)

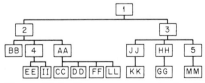

Figure 31-3 Permanent organizational assignment of men in Project Group Roger.

be ineffective. He cannot insist on being an engineer or a physicist all the time, because he is dealing with many other types of people and situations.[3]

The importance of role adaptability is shown in Figure 31-4, which reports 485 minutes of observation of three project managers who directed project confederations (type 3). The data show that project managers during this brief period had a broad range of contacts from the general manager to vendors and from the research to the sales function. During frequent trips which the observer could not record, they were also contacting customers, the home office, and the general public.

Column 2, Number of persons interacting, excluding the manager being observed.

	Minutes	Per Cent
0	103	21
1	199	41
2	53	11
10	38	8
12	92	19

Column 3, Activity.

	Minutes	Per Cent
1. Communication	481	99
2. Contemplation	4	1
3. Personal time, excluding discussion with observer	0	0

Column 4, Interactor level.

	Minutes	Per Cent
0. No interacter	103	21
1. General Manager	1	*
2. Departmental managers	11	2
3. Functional managers (middle management)	156	32
4. Supervisors (operative supervision)	96	20
5. Employees (operative workers)	110	23
6. Vendor	6	1
7. General public	0	0
8. Home office personnel, any level	0	0
9. Field personnel, any level	0	0
10. Not classified	2	*

Column 5, Interacter function.

	Minutes	Per Cent
0. No interacter	103	21
1. Own department (immediate subordinate or superior)	1	*
2. Other in department	0	0

[3] See S. Marcson, "Role concept of engineering managers," IRE Trans. on Engineering Management, vol. EM-7, pp. 30–33, March, 1960.

	Minutes	Per Cent
3. Research	16	3
4. Engineering	92	19
5. Production	8	2
6. Sales	91	19
7. Finance	0	0
8. Personnel	0	0
9. Other staff	72	15
10. General management	7	1
11. Miscellaneous, not classified	95	30

Column 6, Communication technique.

	Sending	Receiving
0. No Interacter	3	0
1 or 11. Oral telephone	38	9
2 or 12. Oral face-to-face, two persons (31 per cent)	88	64
3 or 13. Oral face-to-face, over two persons (38 per cent)	73	110
4 or 14. Written letter	0	17
5 or 15. Other written	5	78
10 or 20. Other	0	0
Per cent sending and receiving	43	57

Column 7, Management function.

	Minutes	Per Cent
0. No interacter	3	1
1. Planning	123	25
2. Organizing	1	*
3. Directing	1	*
4. Controlling	341	70
5. Not classified	16	3

* Less than one half of one per cent.

Figure 31-4 Code for dimensions, showing times in minutes and per cent of time for each dimension.

Figure 31-5 provides further evidence of the need for role adaptability. It reports interview responses rather than observations. The respondents are departmental project managers operating under type 4, project general management. Figure 31-5 suggests that the extradepartmental contacts of the project managers are considered time consuming and important. Again contacts ranged widely from customers to operating personnel. (Observe, however, that in all instances the most time was taken in direct supervision of a particular subordinate.)

It follows that *the function of project manager requires a balancing of technical solutions*

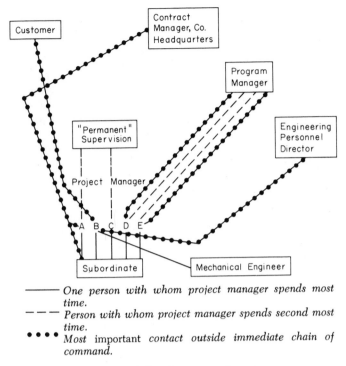

——————— *One person with whom project manager spends most time.*

— — — *Person with whom project manager spends second most time.*

• • • • *Most important contact outside immediate chain of command.*

Figure 31-5 Contacts of five departmental project managers.

with time, cost, resource, and human factors. *The project manager is an integrator and a generalist, rather than a technical specialist.* In the various contacts reported in Figure 31-4 the project manager is largely working with others to achieve a balance of all interests in the project. For example, scientific department X has worked out a bid price for a unit of the project. The project manager points out how the price is out of line with competitors and the unit's heavy weight will cut into the weight allowance for other units of the project. In another case, a technical department insists that a unit cannot be "done right" and still meet the deadline. It demands more time to completely check out all bugs before proceeding. The project manager shows how the reality of deadlines will not permit standard procedures and that "checking bugs" must proceed concurrently with further work on the unit. In the middle of this discussion the customer telephones concerning a proposed conference with the customer about the project.

It is probable that project managers, having mostly a technical background, do not realize the vital significance of broadness and versatil-

ity, rather than specialty, in performing as a project manager. Top managers probably do not realize how difficult it is to get a competent technical man to give genuine first priority to his *management* job when he is a project manager, and accordingly *they* fail to take the time to convince him of the first priority of management.

Reference to Column 7 of Figure 31-4 shows that *project managers devote most of their management time to the functions of planning and control.* Four hundred and eighty-five minutes is a limited period of observation, but the data consistently emphasize planning and control. Referring back to the conclusion that managerial unity is the basic purpose of project management, it is evident that planning and control are organic in achieving this unity. Organizing is primarily a commitment resulting from plans, and it takes very little time. The directing function is mostly achieved in the operating departments, leaving the project manager more involved in controls to assure performance and to report performance. Thus the first and last items in the sequence of management functions—planning, organizing, directing, and controlling—are the functions which require the most project management time and may be of most significance.

CONCLUSION

The primary reason for project management is to achieve some measure of managerial unity. There are four principal types of organization to achieve this objective.

The project expediter achieves unity of communication, the project coordinator gets unity of control, the project confederation achieves unity of direction, and project general management accomplishes the ultimate unity of command. Furthermore, project management may disregard existing levels and functions in superimposing its own structure on the existing organization.

Project organization requires a project manager with considerable role adaptability. He must balance technical solutions with time, cost, resource, and human factors. He is an integrator and a generalist, rather than a technical specialist; and he devotes most of his management time to the functions of planning and control. Both the project manager and his superiors may need to give more emphasis to the *management* aspects of his job. To be an effective project manager, the technical man needs to be intellectually sophisticated in the field of management and also to have an attitude which gives some priority to the management aspects of his job.

SECTION 8

PROJECT PLANNING AND EVALUATION

Managerial controls provide the manager with the tools for determining whether the activity being carried on under his guidance is efficiently proceeding toward the planned objective. Controls provide a means for comparing actual with expected performance. Feedback, the essence of management control, consists of data, arrayed in various forms, which has a predictive value for the manager. In a project, the factors of time, performance, *and* schedule *provide a basis against which control can be exercised. Control is the constant matter of seeking an answer to the question: "How well am I doing in terms of accomplishing that which I set out to do?"*

In the development and acquisition of a major project, such as a weapon system or a new product, progress towards the deadlines and cost targets require control techniques that are frequently more advanced than those found in the more traditional commercially oriented firm. As a result, the aerospace industry and the Department of Defense has devoted considerable effort in recent years in advancing methods to track the cost, performance, and schedule of development progress. This section will examine and compare some of these techniques as related to the more conventional methods of control.

READING 32

AN ANALYSIS OF MAJOR SCHEDULING TECHNIQUES IN THE DEFENSE SYSTEMS ENVIRONMENT *

J. N. Holtz

I. INTRODUCTION

The Weapon System Acquisition Environment

The aerospace industry, faced with time deadlines and using sophisticated technology, requires scheduling techniques that are frequently more advanced than those of the more traditional commercially oriented firms. Consequently, the industry has devoted considerable effort in the past decade to advancing the scheduling state of the art. The devices discussed in this Memorandum, however, are not applicable solely to defense-oriented systems. Several are used by industrial firms on various commercial products, and these firms are increasingly adopting the more advanced techniques.

This Memorandum attempts to survey, compare, and evaluate the major scheduling

techniques currently available to project management, and to suggest areas for further research that may lead to improving these techniques. To provide a framework for this analysis, the nature of the weapon system acquisition environment must be clearly understood. The following discussion describes several critical dimensions of this environment: the life cycle of a weapon system—its built-in uncertainties and dynamic character—the numerous firms involved in a given project, and the hierarchies of project management existing in corporations and agencies.[1]

The life cycle of a weapon system.   Most, if not all, commercial products have a life cycle. Fad items—hula hoops, for example—have a very short life cycle. Other items—such as stoves or refrigerators—have a longer cycle. Each new product must be conceived, re-

* Reprinted with permission of The RAND Corporation, RM-4697-PR, October, 1966, The RAND Corporation, Santa Monica, California.

[1] Readers already familiar with this environment may prefer to turn directly to the subsequent material.

searched, designed, tested, produced, sold, and serve its function before it becomes obsolete.

Defense systems likewise have a life cycle, but their period of usefulness is limited by changing operational requirements and advances in technology. This life cycle usually consists of several phases: (a) conceptual, (b) definition, (c) acquisition (including development and production), and (d) operation.

From a scheduling standpoint, perhaps the most significant characteristic of the life cycle is the change in the type of work performed in each phase. In the conceptual and definition phases, emphasis is on specifying the performance characteristics and hardware configurations that will eventually result for the system. Here the effort is primarily analytical, and activities are usually unique and varied.

In the development phase, the design, fabrication, and testing of a limited number of prototypes are usually the primary functions. Frequently, the vehicles used to test individual performance characteristics may be quite dissimilar. The activities in the development phase, although not highly repetitive, have reached the stage where enough information is available to permit the scheduling of resources to specific functions. In a large weapon system development, interactions among the activities are likely to be numerous, complex, and consequently, formidable to manage. A comprehensive scheduling system is therefore required to permit efficient management of the project.

When performance has been demonstrated by the prototypes, production operations usually follow. Contractors are required to produce quantities of the same item on a scale that on occasion approaches mass production. By this time, most of the design uncertainty has been overcome, and reasonably final production drawings exist for the components. It is thus possible to make detailed subdivision of production operations and to control the use of resources on these operations.

Eventually the completed systems, and spares, are turned over to the using commands —Strategic Air Command (SAC), Tactical Air Command (TAC), etc.—which are responsible for their deployment and operation until the systems become obsolete.

Managerial decisions affecting the project must be made throughout all phases of the life cycle. The diverse nature of the activities in each phase requires a variety of scheduling information. This Memorandum will attempt to determine whether any single scheduling technique is sufficiently versatile to be used throughout the entire life cycle of a project.

Numerous industrial suppliers.   The development of a new product frequently requires diverse technologies. An example is the recent commercial development of petrochemicals, which was accomplished by forming joint subsidiaries combining technologies adapted to petroleum and chemical firms. Yet the development of defense systems is substantially more complex than the development of most commercial products. The technologies required generally exceed the feasibly attainable capabilities of any one firm. Consequently, defense firms frequently form arrangements similar to a joint venture. The simplest arrangement involves the designation of one firm as a weapon system prime contractor, the other firms being affiliated with it as subcontractors.

Another common arrangement is where several large firms become associate contractors, each being responsible for developing a major segment of the weapon system. For example, one associate contractor is responsible for guidance, another for airframe, another for propulsion, etc. Frequently each associate contractor subcontracts a portion of his project to another firm; the subcontractor may sub-subcontract a smaller portion to yet another firm, etc. Such subcontracting frequently involves thousands of industrial firms in the system development effort.

A third arrangement is one similar to the associate contractor system but with the addition of an integrating contractor whose function is primarily to coordinate systems engineering and checkout for the entire weapon system.

Many governmental agencies often furnish personnel, facilities, or material to develop a system. Each industrial firm and governmental agency, in turn, has more than one level of internal management. The levels vary in number from firm to firm but range in scope from first-line supervision to top management. Consequently, for a significant weapon system there evolve a substantial number of managerial interrelationships. Each managerial group must be informed of plans and progress relating to its sphere of responsibility.

Program monitors.   It is obvious that in this environment some group or agency should be responsible for management of the entire project. In the Air Force a System Project Office (SPO) is established in the appropriate division of the Air Force Systems Command (AFSC) to provide this function. The SPO is responsible for the project throughout the weapon acquisition phase. Upon completion and delivery of the hardware, the remaining responsibilities of the SPO are transferred to a weapon system manager in the Air Force Logistics Command (AFLC). Responsibility for operation of the weapon system in the field rests with one of the using commands (i.e., SAC, TAC, ADC, etc.). The SPO, in conjunction with AFLC and the training command (ATC), coordinates the planning for training and for the maintenance and supply which will be required in the operational phase of the system.

If many firms are to make portions of the system, some mechanism should exist to ensure that all components will mate (interface) and function properly in the completed system. The SPO has this responsibility and accomplishes it with technical support either from in-house systems engineering laboratories (those at Wright Field, for example) or from nonprofit engineering concerns.[2]

In defense contracting, the industrial firms deal with only one consumer, the Government, and more specifically with the program manager designated by the Department of Defense. The importance of national defense, coupled with this monopsony (one buyer) situation, naturally leads the Government to take a very active interest in the progress of the system. The SPO is primarily responsible for directing the program, while AFSC, Headquarters USAF, and the Office of the Secretary of Defense (OSD) are also involved in reviewing its progress. In addition, the Bureau of the Budget, Congressional committees, and even the President may become involved in a particular program from time to time.

Again, it is essential that the information systems used for analyzing program status be capable of directing pertinent information to each of the appropriate agencies and individuals concerned.

Dynamic nature of the environment. To be useful in this environment a scheduling sys-

[2] *The MITRE Corporation, Aerospace Corporation, etc.*

tem also must be responsive to extensive changes in the projects. The project life cycle generally lasts a period of several years; frequently, development effort alone will require four or five years. A mix of various weapon systems is necessary to accomplish the objectives of national defense. From time to time the assessment of the threat to our national security may be modified, which in turn may alter the relative priority of a given project in this mix or affect the amount of funds allocated over time to the project. These factors often result in either an accelerated schedule or a program "stretchout."

Likewise, general technological advances and experience on a specific project frequently lead to design changes that affect the project schedule. The scheduling system must respond to these changes if it is to be useful to management.

Criteria for Comparison of Alternative Scheduling Techniques

It is difficult, if not impossible, to prepare a quantitative assessment of the utility of a particular scheduling technique. It is possible, however, to isolate features that are desirable and then to assess the extent to which these features are satisfied. Although, conceptually, it is possible to assign weights to each feature and thereby construct an index of relative usefulness, this additional step, being inherently subjective, will be left to the reader.

The following criteria are not intended to be comprehensive but are sufficiently basic to be helpful in estimating the strengths and weaknesses of each technique. The discussion in the subsequent sections should indicate the usefulness of these criteria in assessing various systems.

1 *Validity.* The information contained in the system and presented to the appropriate levels of management should reflect genuine progress. For example, suppose a guidance system is required to keep a missile on course, and a gyroscope is an integral component of this guidance system. If the gyroscope is improperly designed, a bias will be introduced into the measurement of spatial relationships. Measurements used in the guidance system will be invalid, that is, they will not reflect the true state of affairs.

2 *Reliability.* The data contained in the system should be consistent regardless of who

obtains them or when they are obtained. In the above example, suppose that the gyroscope were properly designed, and thus capable of providing a valid measurement of attitude, but that electrical pulses, external to the gyroscope, frequently altered its motion and generated inconsistent readings. Readings used by the guidance system would then be unreliable. Relating this example to scheduling techniques, the system may be well designed, and consequently valid, yet subject to error because of weaknesses in data collection, and therefore unreliable. Or the reverse, that is, reliable yet invalid results are also possible.

3 *Implementation.* A large number of personnel are likely to be involved in furnishing inputs to and using outputs from a scheduling system. Thus the technique should be easy to explain and understand, and simple to operate.

4 *Universality of Project Coverage.* Ideally, one scheduling system should be sufficient from beginning to end of a project life cycle. All levels of management should be able to use the information in the system, and all relevant factors to be controlled should be encompassed by the one system.

5 *Sensitivity Testing (Simulation).* Since management decisionmaking involves selecting one course of action out of alternative possible courses, it is desirable to assess the scheduling implications of these alternatives. A system that enables management to simulate the impacts of alternative courses of action can facilitate the selection process and lead to better decisions concerning the project.

6 *Forecasting.* One purpose of collecting data is to assess the probability of accomplishing future tasks. Some scheduling systems are oriented more explicitly toward longer term operations than others.

7 *Updating.* Program decisions in a dynamic environment must be based on current data. The scheduling system should be capable of incorporating rapidly, and with ease, information on project progress.

8 *Flexibility.* A desirable feature in a scheduling technique is its ability to adapt easily to changes in the project. This feature is closely related to a simulation capability. The system must be flexible if simulation of alternatives is to be possible, but a system may be flexible without emphasizing simulation potential.

9 *Cost.* The scheduling system should provide the required information at the lowest cost. Cost is a difficult factor to measure for several reasons. First, scheduling costs are not usually uniformly recorded by industry and government, probably because the functions attributable to collection of data in support of the system vary among contractors. Also, total scheduling costs are needed to compare techniques. In a Gantt system, for example, time standards are as much a part of the cost as is chart preparation, yet this factor frequently is not included in estimates of schedule cost.

Second, systems that are the most useful in terms of the above criteria generally involve greater cost. Consequently, the appropriate cost statistic is not total dollar cost, but rather cost per unit of utility, or benefit. This cannot as yet be precisely measured.

Finally, cost is largely a function of the size of the program, and implementation of each system involves both fixed and variable costs. Thus, techniques with high fixed costs tend to be relatively less expensive in large-scale applications and relatively more expensive in small projects.

Missile System Development Example

A hypothetical missile system has been selected to facilitate a comparison of alternative scheduling techniques for the development phase of a project. Although the example is greatly abbreviated, it will suffice to demonstrate the major characteristics of each technique. Various nonstandard illustrations are used in describing applications to production processes.

Table 32-1 contains all the basic data—events, activities, and time estimates—needed to compare the scheduling techniques for the missile system development example. The discussion in the various sections throughout the Memorandum will draw upon this table.

Project status is measured by the accomplishment of *events* representing significant points of partial completion of a project. *Activities,* on the other hand, occur over a time horizon. Each activity is defined by a starting and an ending event. Resources are consumed by activities rather than events. Decisions made by project management may alter the levels and qualities of resources applied to activities. Estimates of the time required to accomplish each activity are given in Table 32-1. These estimates are indicated as "optimistic," "most likely," and "pessimistic,"[3] and serve as the schedule data for the example.

---

[3] *The meaning of* optimistic, most likely, *and* pessimistic *times is explained in Section V.*

Generally, the events and activities required to complete a component or subsystem are *dependent* upon the results of the preceding activities in that subsystem. Frequently, information generated through performance on an activity in one subsystem also is essential to the definition and performance of activities in a different subsystem. For example, information concerning the size, weight, etc., of a missile must be obtained from the missile design before the launching equipment can be designed and fabricated. In general, fabrication of launching equipment is separate from fabrication of the missile except for this information requirement. This relationship makes the activities interdependent. Such interdependencies must be considered in scheduling projects. The relevant interdependencies are identified in footnotes to Table 32-1.

II. GANTT AND MILESTONE CHARTS

Gantt Technique

The Gantt technique was the first formal scheduling system to be used by management.[4] The cornerstone of the technique is the Gantt

[4] *Developed by Henry L. Gantt in the late 1800s, the technique was based on the scientific management approach of Frederick W. Taylor. Prior to the twentieth century, management of productive operations was loosely organized. Few standards existed by which performance could be gauged. In the 1880s, Taylor altered the process of management by attempting to substitute "scientific management" for "opinions" and "hunches" based on little factual data.*

This "scientific method" involved identifying tasks and subtasks to be performed in the productive operations of the plant. The subtasks were refined into elementary work movements, which were "timed" to determine how much time each movement should require under normal working conditions if performed by a "typical" operator. The elementary operations were then assigned to an operator and their accumulated times became a standard by which the operator's performance was measured. The variance, if any, between work planned for the day, week, etc., and work completed for the period was analyzed to determine the factors responsible for underperformance (or overperformance), so that corrective action could be prescribed.

Gantt met Taylor in 1887 and became actively involved in the scientific management movement. Gantt made numerous contributions to management philosophy, but he is remembered primarily for his graphic technique, which he devised to display data required for scheduling purposes.

chart, which is basically a bar chart showing planned and actual performance for those resources that management desires to control. In addition, major factors that create variance (i.e., overproduction or underproduction) are coded and depicted on the chart.

Application to production operations. The Gantt chart was designed for, and is most successfully applied to, highly repetitive production operations. Normally, it assumes that time standards are available for each operation and that the objective of management is to obtain "normal" output from each major resource employed, especially labor and machinery. If, for example, it has been established that an average of 60 seconds (including personal time)[5] is required for a "typical" worker to assemble a cigarette lighter, then each man assigned to that task should be scheduled to assemble 60 per hour and he should meet this quota. Reasons for underperformance should be established.

A similar example can be given for machinery. If a drilling machine is rated as requiring 30 seconds to drill six holes in a two-barrel carburetor, then that machine should be scheduled to perform this function on 120 carburetors per hour. Again, reasons for any variation in performance should be established.

The Gantt charts applicable to these two types of production operation are called "man-loading" and "machine-loading," respectively. An example of a man-loading chart is given in Figure 32-1. The machine-loading chart is similar, except that machine time rather than man time is scheduled. The chart shown in Figure 32-1 provides the following information:

The "✔" indicates that the chart was based on actual production through Friday, July 10.

The space shown for each day represents the output scheduled for that day. The thin line indicates the output actually produced by the worker for the day. In the example, Mr. Braden failed to produce his scheduled output on Monday, Tuesday, and Wednesday. His underproduction on Monday and Tuesday was due to material troubles (M) and Wednesday's underproduction was traced to tool troubles (T). On Thursday, Braden met his scheduled output, and on Friday he ex-

[5] *An allowance for coffee breaks, wash room, etc.*

TABLE 32-1 DATA FOR THE MISSILE SYSTEM DEVELOPMENT EXAMPLE

Event No.	Events	Activity No.	Activities	Estimated Time Required (weeks)		
				Optimistic	Most Likely	Pessimistic
1	Begin project	1-2	Assemble maintenance equipment fabrication facilities	1	3	6
2	Start maintenance equipment fabrication	1-3	Assemble training facilities for operating personnel	3	4	5
3[a]	Start training of operating personnel	1-4	Assemble ground equipment fabrication facilities	0.1	0.2	0.5
4	Start ground equipment fabrication	1-5	Assemble installation and check out equipment fabrication facilities	0.1	0.2	0.5
5	Start installation and check out equipment fabrication	1-6	Assemble missile erection equipment fabrication facilities	1	3	6
		1-7	Assemble missile transportation vehicle fabrication facilities	5	7	8
6	Start missile erection equipment fabrication	1-8	Assemble missile fabrication facilities	0.1	0.2	0.5
7	Start missile transportation vehicle fabrication	1-9	Assemble emplacement fabrication facilities	4	5	6
		1-10	Assemble training facilities for maintenance personnel	1	2	3
		1-11	Assemble site construction facilities	3	4	5
8	Start missile fabrication	2-12	Fabricate maintenance equipment	14	19	26
9	Start emplacement equipment fabrication	3-13	Train operating personnel	16	19	20
10[b]	Start training of maintenance personnel	4-21	Fabricate ground equipment	16	19	21
11	Start site construction	5-14	Fabricate installation and checkout equipment	4	6	7
12	Maintenance equipment fabrication completed	6-15	Fabricate missile erection equipment	2	3	5
13	Training of operating personnel completed	7-16	Fabricate missile transportation vehicle	8	9	12
14	Installation and checkout equipment fabrication completed	8-17	Fabricate missile	27	30	54
15[c]	Missile erection equipment fabrication completed	9-19	Fabricate emplacement equipment	26	28	31
		10-29	Train maintenance personnel	8	9	10
		11-30	Construct launch site	18	21	25
16[d]	Missile transportation vehicle fabrication completed	12-25	Transport maintenance equipment to site	0.1	0.2	0.5
		13-23	Transport operating personnel to site	0.1	0.2	0.5
17	Missile functional test completed	14-20	Test installation and checkout equipment	5	7	8

No.	Event	Activity	Description			
18	Missile fabrication completed	15-26	Transport missile erection equipment to site	0.1	0.2	0.5
19	Emplacement equipment fabrication completed	16-27	Deliver missile transportation vehicle to site	0.1	0.2	0.5
20	Preliminary check out of installation and checkout equipment completed	17-18	Correct deficiencies in missile	8	10	11
		18-27	Transport missile on missile transportation vehicle to site	0.1	0.2	0.5
21	Ground equipment fabrication completed	19-28	Transport emplacement equipment to site	0.2	0.4	1.0
22	Installation and checkout equipment on dock at site	20-22	Transport installation and check out equipment to site	0.1	0.2	0.5
23	Operating personnel at site	21-24	Transport ground equipment to site	0.1	0.2	0.5
24	Ground equipment on dock at site	22-32	Install checkout equipment at site	0.1	0.2	0.5
25	Maintenance equipment on dock at site	23-32	Operating personnel install ground equipment	0.1	0.3	1.0
26	Missile erection equipment on dock at site	24-32	Ground equipment installed at site	0.1	0.2	0.5
		25-31	Install maintenance equipment	1	2	3.5
27	Missile on dock at site	26-33	Install missile erection equipment at site	0.2	0.4	1.0
28[e]	Emplacement equipment on dock at site	27-33	Install missile at site	0.1	0.2	0.5
29	Maintenance personnel at site	28-33	Utilize emplacement equipment to install missile	0.6	1	2.0
30	Site construction completed	29-33	Perform maintenance operations on missile site	0.1	0.2	0.5
31	Installation of maintenance equipment completed	30-34	Check out site construction	0.1	0.2	0.5
32	Installation of ground equipment completed	31-34	Check out installed maintenance equipment	1	2	3.5
33	Missile installation completed	32-34	Check out installation of ground equipment	0.1	0.2	0.5
34	Launch site completed	33-34	Check out missile installation	16	24	34
35	First operational unit completed	34-35	Transfer responsibility for operational unit to using command	0.1	0.2	0.5

NOTE: Footnotes a through e indicate interdependencies between events. The meaning of interdependency is explained on page 321.

a Must be completed before event No. 20.
b Must be completed before event No. 20.
c Must be completed before event No. 17.
d Must be completed before event No. 17.
e Must be completed before event No. 34.

ceeded it. The overproduction on Friday is indicated by a second thin line.

Braden's performance for the entire week is shown as a heavy, solid line immediately beneath the thin lines representing his daily performance. It can be readily seen that his cumulative output for the week was less than scheduled. Each worker's performance is analyzed in a similar way.

Because the foreman is responsible for the output of those working under him, the chart records the scheduled output of his combined work force. In the example, the shaded line opposite his name indicates that Mr. Allen did not meet the scheduled output for the week. The reasons for this underperformance can be traced to specific employees on specific days.

The general foreman is responsible for the overall production of the department and thus the row opposite his name represents the scheduled output for the entire department. In the example the solid bar indicates that the output of the department did not meet the week's scheduled production. Consequently, the factors responsible for the poor performance and the areas in which they occurred will need to be determined.

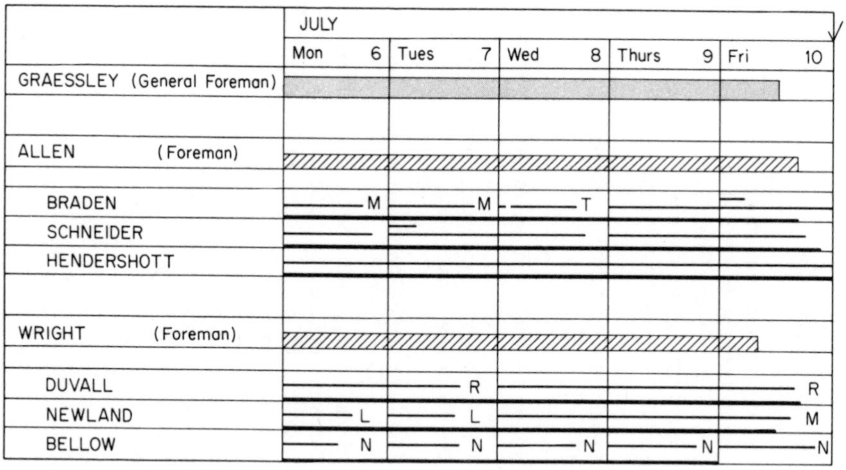

	JULY				
	Mon 6	Tues 7	Wed 8	Thurs 9	Fri 10
GRAESSLEY (General Foreman)					
ALLEN (Foreman)					
BRADEN	— M	— M	— T		—
SCHNEIDER					
HENDERSHOTT					
WRIGHT (Foreman)					
DUVALL		— R			— R
NEWLAND	— L	— L			— M
BELLOW	— N	— N	— N	— N	— N

LEGEND

A. The ordinate (y axis) comprises a discrete listing of the names of employees in a department. The abscissa (x axis) represents a time horizon.

B. Other characteristics

    1. | | Width of daily space represents amount of work that should be done in a day.

    2. ———   Amount of work actually done in a day.

    3. – – –   Time taken on work on which no estimate is available.

    4. ▬▬▬   Weekly total of operator. Solid line for estimated work; broken line for time spent on work not estimated.

    5. ▨▨▨   Weekly total for group of operators.

    6. ▭   Weekly total for department.

    7. Reasons for falling behind:
      A = Absent
      N = New operator
      L = Slow operator
      R = Repairs needed
      T = Tool trouble
      M = Material trouble
      Y = Lot smaller than estimated

Figure 32-1 Gantt man-loading chart.

In a similar manner, the work performance of several departments can be combined on a single chart to show aggregative accomplishment. Charts can also be prepared for various managerial levels so that performance can be depicted and responsibility traced throughout the organization. The graphs are normally maintained on a daily basis to provide up-to-date control.

Frequently, even in production operations, workers perform tasks for which there are no time standards, such as tool repair, housekeeping, etc. The amount of time spent on such tasks is usually represented by a dashed line. This type of effort is not indicated in Figure 32-1, but the line is identified in the legend.

Gantt charts need not be organized along departmental lines only. For example, instead of showing quantity of output for one department, the chart could depict the progress of various departments striving simultaneously toward completion of a *component* or some other appropriate unit. This latter type of chart is more appropriate for prototype development and testing. Its application is discussed below.

Application to Development Operations.

To demonstrate the application of a Gantt chart to nonrepetitive operations we will use the hypothetical missile system development example presented on page 320. A schedule of *planned* activities (taken from Table 32-1) is shown in Figure 32-2.[6]

In constructing such a schedule, it is important to keep in mind that when activities must be performed in series, they cannot be scheduled to begin before their predecessors are completed.[7] Assuming available resources and a desire to complete all activities as soon as possible, the tendency would be to schedule each activity at its *earliest start time*,[8] i.e., as

soon as the prior activity is scheduled to be completed. Only certain "critical" activities need be scheduled in this fashion; most others can be delayed as long as the scheduled completion of the project is not jeopardized.[9]

Unfortunately, the degree of flexibility which exists in scheduling a project cannot be readily ascertained through the use of the Gantt charts because relationships among activities in a project are not clearly revealed. For example, in Figure 32-2 activities 2-12 (fabricate maintenance equipment), 3-13 (train operating personnel), and 8-17 (fabricate missile) are all scheduled to be completed before activity 17-18 (correct deficiencies in missile) is scheduled to begin. That activities 8-17 and 17-18 are in series, i.e., have a formal predecessor-successor relationship, is not revealed by the chart.

Figure 32-3 is a typical Gantt chart used by management to control activities after the schedule is completely prepared and actual operations are under way. The chart assumes the project has been in operation for 20 weeks and is scheduled for completion in an additional 40 weeks.

The chart indicates that activity 9-19 (fabricate emplacement equipment) and activity 11-30 (construct launch site) are, respectively, four weeks and one week ahead of schedule. However, activities 2-12 (fabricate maintenance equipment) and 4-21 (fabricate ground equipment) are, respectively, two and three weeks behind schedule. On the basis of the information in Figure 32-3, it is not obvious whether the project will be completed on schedule. Actually it is possible to complete the fabrication of maintenance equipment and the fabrication of ground equipment as late as the 60th and 64th week, respectively, and still complete the project on schedule.[10] Since the chart does not provide this information, it is necessary to use other techniques to establish interrelationships and to compute the earliest start and latest completion dates for each activity. A Gantt chart incorporating all of this information would be too cluttered to be easily read and understood.

A Gantt chart based on earliest start times

---

[6] *Activities with a most likely time of less than 1.0 week add little to the illustration at this point and are omitted, reducing the number of activities listed from 43 to 22.*

[7] *Managers do occasionally assign resources to portions of later activities in a series before earlier activities are completed.*

[8] *This term was not formally introduced into the scheduling literature until the critical path technique evolved. However, since it simplifies the description, it is used here in explaining the basis for construction of the Gantt chart.*

[9] *In subsequent discussion of scheduling techniques, such latter points are called* latest start times, *and the flexibility in scheduling certain activities are termed "float" or "slack."*

[10] *The method for computation of latest completion dates is given in Table 32-7 in Section IV.*

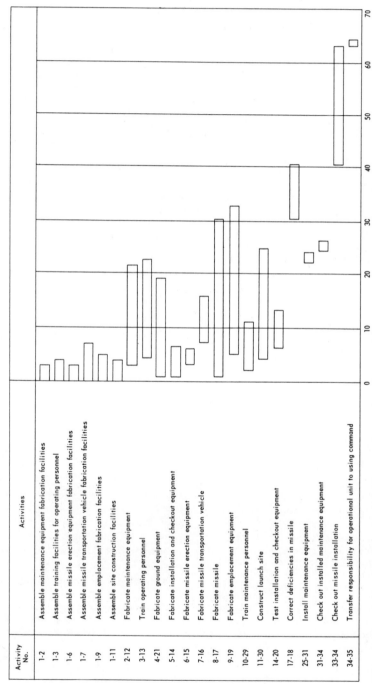

Figure 32-2   Gantt chart showing plan for missile system development.

...

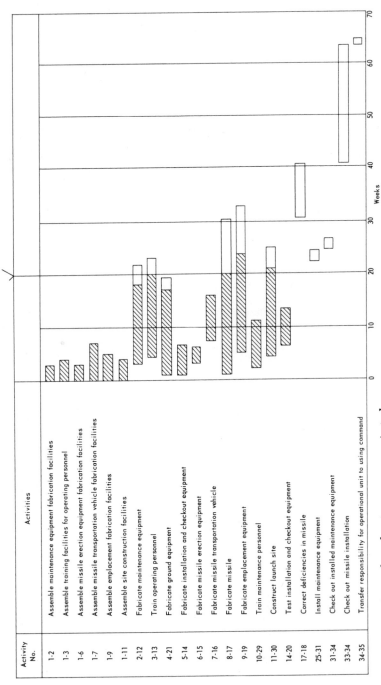

Figure 32-3 Gantt chart showing progress against plan.

combined with a transparent overlay based on latest completion times would provide more of the information useful for scheduling but would still not depict the interrelationships existing among activities.

The Gantt technique was devised originally for use by first-line supervision on repetitive production operations. It is an excellent tool for this type of operation because (1) good estimates of normal production times can be obtained when work is performed repetitively; and (2) production responsibility of first-line

supervision is normally limited to a few operations. Thus, significant interrelationships, if any, are obvious at this level. The complex interrelationships evolve when information on many facets of an overall project must be presented to higher levels of management. The large amount of detailed information accumulated at the foreman level must then be compiled and summarized into fewer activities.

The most important strengths and weaknesses of the Gantt technique are summarized in Table 32-2.

TABLE 32-2   GANTT TECHNIQUE—STRENGTHS AND WEAKNESSES

Criteria	Strengths	Weaknesses
1. Validity	Good in production operations. Because of short time duration of each measured operation, only small errors in measurement are likely to occur.	No explicit technique for depicting interrelationships, which are especially important in development.
2. Reliability	Simplicity of system affords some reliability.	Frequently unreliable, especially in development stage, because judgment of estimator may change over time. Numerous estimates in a large project, each with some unreliability, may lead to errors in judging status.
3. Implementation	Easiest of all systems in some respects because it is well understood. (System implies existence of time standards.)	Quite difficult to implement for the control of operations in development phase, where time standards do not ordinarily exist and must be developed.
4. Universality of project coverage	Can comprehensively cover a given phase of a life cycle. Effective at the resource or input level of control.	Less useful in definition and development phases of life cycle.
5. Sensitivity testing (simulation)		No significant capability.
6. Forecasting	In production operations, good technique to assess ability to meet schedule on a given activity if based on good time standards.	Weak in forecasting ability to meet schedule when interrelationships among activities are involved.
7. Updating	Easy to update graphs weekly, etc., if no major program changes.	
8. Flexibility		If significant program changes occur frequently, numerous charts must be completely reconstructed.
9. Cost	Data gathering and processing relatively inexpensive. Display can be inexpensive if existing charts can be updated and if inexpensive materials are used.	The graph tends to be inflexible. Program changes require new graphs, which are time consuming and costly. Frequently expensive display devices are used.

NOTE: Recall that this table is intended only as a summary of certain qualitative information on the relative usefulness of the scheduling technique. As indicated previously, a more formal quantitative evaluation of the extent to which the criteria are met was considered infeasible in this study.

Milestone Technique

The milestone scheduling system is based largely on the same principles as the Gantt system but the technique of displaying project status differs. The milestone system is usually applied to development projects and is frequently used at several of the higher-management levels, for example, corporate, SPO, AFSC, and Hq USAF.

A milestone represents an important *event* along the path to project completion. All milestones are not equally significant. The most significant are termed "major milestones" usually representing the completion of an important group of activities. (Also, events of lesser significance are often called "footstones" and "inch stones" at least in conversation if not in the formal literature.) In reality, of course, there are many gradations of importance.

Events that are designated as milestones vary from system to system. Attempts are currently being made to establish milestones common to all programs, especially within major systems. For example, events such as "Contractor Selected," "Equipment Delivered," and "Final Acceptance Inspection Completed" are common to all systems, while "Aircraft Flyaway" is common to all aircraft systems, but not to missile systems. It is anticipated that milestone standardization, if successful, will be of significant help to program monitors in comprehending the status of the program, as well as in comparing progress on various programs.

Milestone chart. Systems management requirements currently specify that schedule data be furnished in milestone form by the System Project Office (SPO) and various contractors. In the planning phase, milestones are established for the total life cycle of the program. Major milestones are included in a comprehensive development plan, i.e., the System Package Program.[11] Progress in accordance

[11] *Described in* System Program Documentation, *Air Force Regulation 375–4, Department of the Air Force, Washington, D.C., Nov. 25, 1963. Progress information is reported in accordance with a procedure sometimes referred to as the Rainbow Reporting System. When initiated the Rainbow System required status information on cost, manpower, facilities, and technical performance, as well as schedule information. The system was called Rainbow because each type of information required was described on a card of a designated color, the assembled package being not unlike a rainbow.*

with the plan usually is reported for two time periods: (1) milestones scheduled to occur in the current fiscal year and (2) milestones scheduled to be completed during the current month.

A chart showing selected milestones for our hypothetical missile system is presented in Figure 32-4. The milestones are designated by their event number as given in Table 32-1 and are for the current year. The project status is shown as of April 30, 1966. On that date five milestones had been completed on schedule. The milestones for event 16 (missile transportation vehicle fabrication completed) was completed two months behind schedule. Also, it was anticipated that event 19 (emplacement equipment fabrication completed) would not be completed by August as scheduled, but would lag a month; thus it should be rescheduled to be completed in September. The remaining milestones are expected to be completed on schedule.

Collection and reliability of data. The method of collecting and organizing data is similar to that for the Gantt technique. Only the graphic presentation is different. Accordingly, the strengths and weaknesses of the milestone technique are very similar to those summarized in Table 32-2 for the Gantt technique. The milestone reporting system can be automated with relative ease. Data on changes in status can be read into a computer, which prints the required format depicting progress on the appropriate milestones. This innovation tends to reduce the costs of the system and also to improve the timeliness of the data.

III. THE LINE OF BALANCE TECHNIQUE (LOB)

Application to Production Operations

The line of balance technique (LOB) was developed to improve scheduling and status reporting in an ongoing production process. Essentially the technique consists of four elements:

1 The objective,
2 The program or production plan,
3 Measurement of progress, and
4 The line of balance.

The objective. The first step in scheduling production is to obtain the contract delivery

Event No.	Milestones	1965			1966												1967		
		O	N	D	J	F	M	A	M	J	J	A	S	O	N	D	J	F	M
12	Maintenance equipment fabrication completed			↑															
13	Training of operating personnel completed			↑															
14	Installation and checkout equipment fabrication completed				↑														
15	Missile erection equipment fabrication completed				↑														
16	Missile transportation vehicle fabrication completed				⇧	◆													
18	Missile fabrication completed											⇧							
19	Emplacement equipment fabrication completed												⇧	◇					
20	Preliminary checkout of installation and checkout equipment completed							↑											
21	Ground equipment fabrication completed								⇧	◇									
30	Site construction completed									⇧									
33	Missile installation completed																		⇧
35	First operational unit completed																		⇧

LEGEND

↑   Action completed on schedule (completed action)

◆   Action not completed on schedule (actual slippage)

◇   Anticipated delayed accomplishment of future action (anticipated slippage)

⇧   Scheduled (or rescheduled) action

Figure 32-4   Milestone chart applied to missile project.

schedule. The objective of the production operation is to meet a schedule based on cumulative deliveries. Figure 32-5*a* illustrates this *objective* as used in LOB. The chart shows the cumulative number of units scheduled to be delivered and the dates of delivery. The *contract schedule line* represents the cumulative quantity of units scheduled to be delivered over time.

The program.   The second step is to chart the *program*. The program, also called the production plan, comprises the stages in the producer's planned production process and consists, essentially, of key manufacturing and assembly operations sequenced in a logical production scheme over the time period required to complete. A sample program is presented in Figure 32-5*b*. Time is shown in working days remaining until each unit can be completed. Symbols and color schemes can be used to depict different types of activity, such as assembly, machining, purchasing of materials, etc.

Measurement of progress.   To illustrate the control function, let us assume that production has been in progress for a month. We are then able to measure the status of the components (units) in the various stages of completion.

Program progress data are obtained by taking a physical inventory of the quantities of materials, parts, or sub-assemblies that have passed through a series of control points in the production plan. The data are then plotted on a bar chart illustrated by Figure 32-5*c*. For example, if control point 15 in chart *b* were selected, the inventory might reveal that 29 units were completed on that date and hence 29 would be shown on the bar chart, which thus represents actual production progress.[12]

Line of balance.   The last step is to construct the line of balance, which represents the number of units that *should* pass through each control point at a given date if management can reasonably expect the objective, i.e., the delivery schedule, to be met.

The line of balance is constructed in the following manner:

1 Select a particular control point, for example, 15.[13]

[12] *The legend also utilizes shading in parts b and c to indicate the type of material or function involved. This assists in identifying general areas of responsibility.*

[13] *Actually one would probably start with the last control point (42) and work back through the project. For our purposes here control point 15 is of special interest in illustrating the usefulness of the technique.*

2 From the production plan (Figure 32-5*b*) determine the number of days required to complete a unit from the control point to the end of the production plan (i.e., 27 days).

3 Using this number determine the date the units should be completed. (October 29 plus 27 working days is December 8.)

4 Find the point corresponding to this completion date (December 8) on the contract schedule line and ascertain the number of units (35) that should be completed on that date if the delivery schedule is to be met.

5 Draw a line on the production progress chart (Figure 32-5*c*) at that level (35 units) and over the control point (15).

6 Repeat this procedure for each control point and connect the horizontal lines over the control points. The resulting line is the line of balance. It indicates the quantities of units that should have passed through each control point on the date of the study (October 30) if the delivery schedule is to be met.

The production progress chart shows the status of a program at a given point in time. Thus management can determine at a glance how actual progress compares with planned progress. Where actual progress lags planned progress, the variance can be traced to the individual control point(s).

In the example described above, it is evident that without management action the delivery schedule will not be met because several control points, including the last one, are behind schedule. By using both the production plan and the program progress chart, one can begin at the end control point (42) and trace back through the series to find the source of the delay. Working *backward,* we see that control point 37 is a critical point of delay. If 37 were on schedule, then it is quite likely that all the succeeding control points would be on schedule. In trying to determine why 37 is behind schedule, we see that control points 35, 31, and 30 are also behind schedule. Control point 35, however, is in series with 31 and is presumably held up because 31 is not on schedule, which in turn is held up because control point 30 is not on schedule. We note that the control points preceding operation 30 are on schedule and therefore assume that the difficulty probably lies within operation 30 itself. The initial difficulty, however, lies in the sequence of activities preceding operation 31, so that 31 is behind schedule because 15 is behind schedule. Thus control point 15 is the

bottleneck. It is reasonable to assume that with more management surveillance, and perhaps with more resources devoted to operations 15 and 30, operation 31 will be on schedule, and as a result so will 35, 37, 38, 39, 40, 41, and 42.

Application to Development Operations

Although LOB has been widely applied to production operations at the prime and associate contractor level, a variant of this technique can be used in the development stage of a weapon system where only one complete system, or a small number of complete systems, is to be produced. In this case, control of the quantity of items through a given point is not relevant as it is in production operations. Instead, monitoring of progress is directed toward major events, that is, the completion of significant activities in the development process. In our discussion, we assume the development of a single unit using the hypothetical missile system described in Sec. I.

As applied to the development phase, the four elements of the technique are essentially the same as those for production scheduling and control, but their composition is altered.

The objective.   Instead of scheduling many units, the delivery schedule is based on the production of a single unit or on a limited number of units. The objectives chart will thus show the required percent completion of individual activities, rather than number of systems through each control point. Figure 32-6 illustrates this possible adaptation of LOB to the hypothetical development project.[14] Supporting data are given in Tables 32-3 and 32-4.

The scheduled starting date of the component begins in the appropriate week at a point on the abscissa representing zero percent completion. The scheduled completion date of each activity is represented in the appropriate week at a point on the abscissa which represents 100 percent completion. A straight line is drawn between these two points. This straight line assumes that the same rate of progress will occur throughout the activity period. If the scheduler has reason to doubt that progress will proceed at a constant rate, the line can

[14] *The list of activities has been condensed for purposes of illustration.*

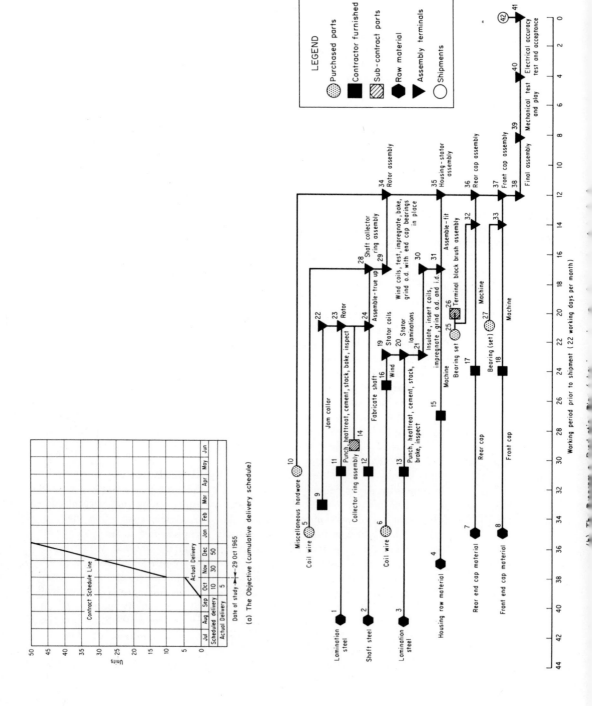

(a) The Objective (cumulative delivery schedule)

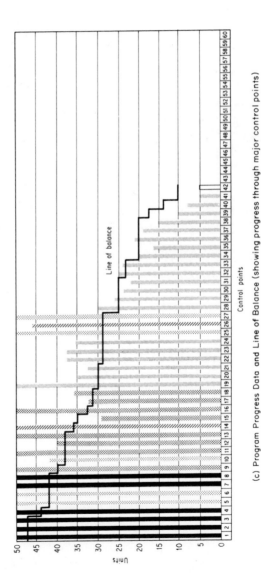

(c) Program Progress Data and Line of Balance (showing progress through major control points)

Figure 32–5   The line of balance technique.

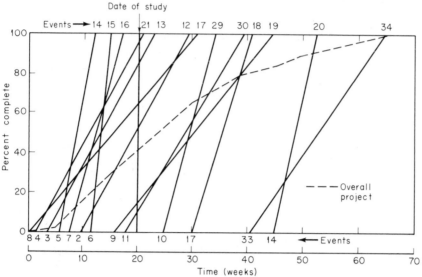

Figure 32-6   LOB prototype development objectives chart.

be drawn in any shape that management feels will correctly depict the expected progress.

Using the data in Table 32-4, an overall project objectives curve can be constructed as follows:

1 Summarize the weeks estimated to complete each activity and thus obtain the total activity-weeks of effort to be involved dur-

ing each incremental time period. (Computations were made for five-week intervals in the example.)

2 Compute the cumulative activity-weeks of planned effort through the end of each time period.

3 Compute the ratio of (1) over (2) for each time period. This ratio is the percent of the project planned to be completed at the respective points. The line connecting these

TABLE 32-3   SUPPORTING DATA FOR FIG. 32-6

Activity No.	Activities	Estimated Activity Time (weeks)	Scheduled Dates	
			Start	Complete
2-12	Fabricate maintenance equipment	19	10	29
3-13	Train operating personnel	19	4	23
4-21	Fabricate ground equipment	19	2	21
5-14	Fabricate installation and checkout equipment	6	6	12
6-15	Fabricate missile erection equipment	3	12	15
7-16	Fabricate missile transportation vehicle	9	8	17
8-17	Fabricate missile	30	0.2	30.2
9-19	Fabricate emplacement equipment	28	16	44
10-29	Train maintenance personnel	9	25	34
11-30	Construct launch site	21	18	35
14-20	Test installation and checkout equipment	7	45	52
17-18	Correct deficiencies in missile	10	30.2	40.2
33-34	Check out missile installation	24	40.6	64.6
Total		204	—	—

TABLE 32-4   DATA FOR OVERALL PROJECT OBJECTIVES CURVE

Time Period (Identified by Final Week)	Estimated Activity-Weeks Required During Period	Cumulative Activity-Weeks to Date	Percent of Planned Completion[a]
0	0	0	0
5	9	9	4.4
10	21	30	14.7
15	30	60	29.4
20	28	88	43.1
25	24	112	54.9
30	24	136	66.6
35	19	155	76.0
40	14	169	82.8
45	9	178	87.2
50	10	188	92.1
55	7	195	95.6
60	5	200	98.0
65	4	204	100.0

[a] Information in this column is basis for dotted line in Figure 32-6.

points is the overall project objectives curve. The completion date of the last activity should coincide with the completion date of the overall project.

The development plan.   A flow chart showing the development plan of the hypothetical missile system is given in Figure 32-7. Procedurally, the development plan chart is taken as a control point for the progress chart (see Figure 32-8). The development plan chart in

our example does not show connections between the activities because only 13 activities out of the 34 given in Table 32-1 are included. If all 34 were shown, the activities would follow in sequence to the completed missile system.

Determination of progress.   There is no technique available to determine true overall program status where considerable uncertainty exists concerning completion dates. The origi-

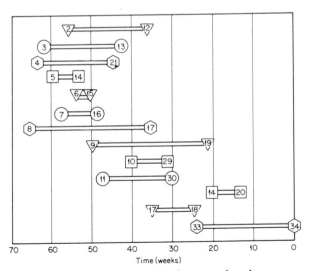

Figure 32-7   LOB prototype development plan chart.

nal estimated time to complete an activity, the length of time devoted to it to date and the current physical state of completion all may be known. However, the actual time required to complete it is not known and must be estimated by the responsible project engineer. The LOB technique for approximating the status of the program is as follows:

$$\text{Percent completion} = 1 - \frac{d}{A}$$

where d = the number of weeks required to complete a particular activity, and A = the gross number of weeks originally estimated for the entire project. As an example, suppose that the time originally required to complete the development phase was 10 weeks, that 8 weeks have already elapsed, and that the current estimate of the time to completion is 4 weeks. According to the LOB formula, the development phase is 100 $(1 - (4/10)) = 60$ percent complete.

Two alternative techniques could also be used to estimate percent completion. For example, if it now appears that the total time required for the development phase is 12 weeks, when 4 weeks remain to completion one can consider that the development is actually 8/12 or 67 percent complete, and not 60 percent complete as revealed by the LOB formula.

A second alternative would be to place the 8 actual weeks of effort over the original time estimate (10 weeks); this would indicate that the phase was 80 percent complete.

While the major reference material on LOB discusses the second alternative, it selects the basic LOB technique as the preferable one because "while the prescribed method requires one additional mathematical step, it helps compensate for inaccuracies in the initial estimate of time required for the entire phase."[15] However, in some respects the first alternative appears to be the most realistic because it is based on current information rather than on the original estimate.

On the other hand, it is obvious that no simple algorithm alone can be expected to solve the problem of precisely determining the actual percent completion of a complex project.

The procedure recommended in the LOB technique is applied to our hypothetical missile system in Table 32-5, and the program progress is shown in Figure 32-8. (Control points are the ending events for the activities.)

To determine total project status, sum the estimated weeks required to complete each activity (d), and divide by the total number of weeks originally estimated to be required for the entire project (A). This gives the percentage not completed $(d \div A)$. Subtract the percentage not completed from 100 percent, and the result is the percentage of the total project completed $[1 - (d/A)]$.

[15] Line of Balance Technology, *op. cit., p. 19.*

TABLE 32-5 SUPPORTING COMPUTATIONS FOR FIGURE 32-8 (PERCENT COMPLETION: 20TH WEEK)

Activity No.	Activities	d	A	$1 - (d/A)$
2-12	Fabricate maintenance equipment	12	19	37
3-13	Train operating personnel	4	19	79
4-21	Fabricate ground equipment	4	19	79
5-14	Fabricate installation and checkout equipment	0	6	100
6-15	Fabricate missile erection equipment	0	3	100
7-16	Fabricate missile transportation vehicle	0	9	100
8-17	Fabricate missile	11	30	63
9-19	Fabricate emplacement equipment	24	28	14
10-29	Train maintenance personnel	9	9	0
11-30	Construct launch site	17	21	19
14-20	Test installation and checkout equipment	7	7	0
17-18	Correct deficiencies in missile	10	10	0
33-34	Check out missile installation	24	24	0
Total		122	204	40

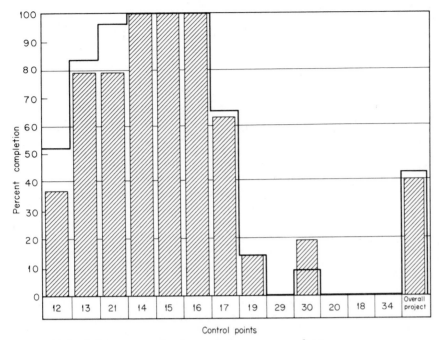

Figure 32-8   LOB prototype development phase progress chart.

In the example (Table 32-5), the total activity-weeks originally estimated were 204. In the 20th week of the project, it is estimated that 122 activity-weeks will be needed to complete the project. Accordingly, the estimated percentage of the overall project completed is $1 - (122/204) = 40$ percent.

Although the LOB technique does not provide any sophisticated way of guiding personnel in the process of estimating time remaining to complete a project, one method frequently used by schedulers is to divide a major phase into a number of individual technical tasks and then relate the number completed to the total. However, such a method has the limitation of assuming that all tasks are of equal difficulty. An alternative, of course, is for the estimator to draw more generally on his own experience in determining estimated time to completion.

The line of balance.   An additional step is necessary to complete the analysis of program progress. That step is "striking the LOB." On the objectives chart (Figure 32-6), construct a vertical line perpendicular to the abscissa at the date of the study. This vertical line will intersect several, if not all, of the percent completion lines for the individual events at a

point representing their currently scheduled completion status. Then draw a horizontal line at the percent completion point on the progress chart (Figure 32-8), above the respective events. Thus, both the scheduled status and the actual status of the events and of the overall project are shown for the date of the study. Notice that in the development phase, the line of balance does not necessarily descend continuously in a stepwise fashion as it must in the production plan.

Evaluation of LOB Technique

The LOB technique, like the Gantt technique, was originally designed for production operations. The Gantt technique focused on providing management with information relating to the efficient utilization of resources. Machine and manpower inputs to the production process were emphasized. On the other hand, the LOB technique is *product* oriented. Its information centers on the extent to which the planned production of a quantity of items is actually being realized. It is not directly concerned with the efficient utilization of resources. Its key usefulness is that bottlenecks in the production process are emphasized.

Management must then take appropriate action, generally increasing the level of resources at these bottlenecks. Consequently, Gantt and LOB are complementary techniques.

The LOB technique has some applicability in prototype development when a limited number of components, or operations, are to be controlled. The LOB development plan chart is capable of depicting interrelationships, although seldom is the effort made to include all such relationships.

The LOB technique has several limitations. The inability to precisely state the percent completion of components is one area that can lead to weakened managerial control of the project.

In addition, if management wishes to examine the impact of alternative approaches to overcoming a bottleneck, the LOB affords no simulation capability for this purpose. The determination of the time to complete a component is left up to the judgment of an engineer, and LOB is silent as to how this estimate should be made. Consequently, inconsistencies occur and reliability is impaired. Finally, the technique is rather inflexible. If there is a change in the development plan, the entire chart system may need to be reconstructed; the

TABLE 32-6   LOB TECHNIQUE—STRENGTHS AND WEAKNESSES

Criteria	Strengths	Weaknesses
1. Validity	Uncertainties surrounding completion times in production operations are minimal; consequently LOB affords management a sound technique for judging status of operations.	Uncertainties encountered in the development phase impair judgment on actual project status. The techniques for estimation of percent completion can lead to erroneous decisions concerning project development.
2. Reliability	Compares favorably with Gantt technique.	
3. Implementation	Only slightly more difficult to comprehend and to implement than Gantt technique.	
4. Universality of project coverage	Capable of covering a system life cycle.	Does not emphasize resource allocation directly.
5. Sensitivity testing (simulation)		No significant capability for simulating alternative courses of action.
6. Forecasting	Depicts status of project well in production stage and can forecast whether or not schedule will be met.	Offers no technique to handle uncertainty in development phase.
7. Updating		Considerable clerical effort required to update graphs.
8. Flexibility		Inflexible. When major program changes occur, the entire set of graphs must be redrawn.
9. Cost	Data gathering and computations can be handled routinely. Expense is moderate and largely for clerical personnel and chart materials.	Charts require frequent reconstruction, which is time-consuming.

NOTE: Recall that this table is intended only as a summary of certain qualitative information on the relative usefulness of the scheduling technique. As indicated previously, a more formal quantitative evaluation of the extent to which the criteria are met was considered infeasible in this study.

up-dating of program progress requires extensive chart changes. Table 32-6 further identifies the strengths and weaknesses of the LOB technique.

IV. THE CRITICAL PATH METHOD (CPM)

Application of CPM[16]

The critical path method (CPM) was the first technique designed specifically for complex, one-of-a-kind operations. Although initially used to plan and control the construction of facilities, it applies equally well to development of new weapon systems and is designed to interrelate diverse activities and explicitly depict important interdependencies. The construction of a chemical plant, for example, requires coordination of numerous functions and activities. A well-coordinated construction schedule can shorten the project by months and thereby significantly reduce project costs. The CPM technique utilizes a network approach and a limited time-cost trade-off capability for organizing data on these types of interactions. Accordingly, the basic elements in CPM are:

1 The flow diagram or network,
2 Critical time paths,
3 Float (scheduling leeway), and
4 The time-cost function.

Network. The development of a network or flow diagram that embraces all events and activities and explicitly recognizes major known interdependencies among activities is an important element in the CPM. It is based on the following simple concepts:

1 An activity (or job) is depicted by an arrow:

2 Each arrow is identified by an activity description:

develop engine

[16] *The basic development is attributable to M. R. Walker who was with the Engineering Service Division of E. I. DuPont De Nemours & Company Inc., and J. E. Kelley, Jr., Remington Rand Univac (now Sperry Rand Corporation).*

3 A sequence of activities is indicated by linking arrows:

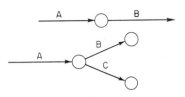

4 Events link activities:

An event occurs at a point in time and signifies either the start or completion of an activity.

5 A grouping of activities and events forms a network. Networks may be either activity- or event-oriented. In activity-oriented networks, the activities (arrows) are labeled; in event-oriented networks, the events (circles, or other symbols) are labeled:

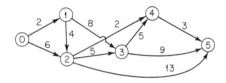

There are certain rules to follow in constructing a network; e.g., no looping is allowed:

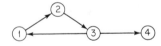

Looping indicates not only that event 1 must be completed before event 2, and event 2 before event 3, but also that event 3 must be completed before event 1. It is logically not possible to require the start of a preceding event that depends on completion of a succeeding event.

6 The length of an arrow has no significance; it merely identifies the direction of work flow. Also, time estimates which are secured for activities represent elapsed or flow time and are not identified—at least initially—with calendar dates.[17]

The critical time paths. In a complex project, involving multiple activities and events,

[17] *The distinction between flow time and calendar (or scheduled) time will be clarified further under the subsequent section on the PERT system.*

sequences or paths of activities can be identified. These paths vary in length according to the time required to accomplish the component activities. The path or paths requiring the longest time are called the critical paths. When a critical path has been determined, management is advised to devote resources to those activities along this path in an effort to reduce the time requirement and thus shorten the overall program. Of course, as one critical path is shortened, another eventually becomes critical.

Float.   Some leeway exists in scheduling activities not on a critical path. This leeway is called float. The technique for determining float is as follows:

Starting at the beginning of the network, determine the *earliest occurrence time for each event in the program.* Since the first event (which has no preceding activities) must occur before any succeeding activities can begin, assign it an earliest occurrence time (*ES*) of zero. Add to this time the duration of the activity leading to the next event; this yields the *ES* for that succeeding event. If several activities lead to a given event, then its *ES* is the highest value obtained by adding the duration of each predecessor activity to the *ES* of the activity's beginning event. *Thus when an event is a part of two or more paths, the longest path to the event must be completed before any subsequent activities can be started.* Continue the process until the final event has been reached; its *ES* becomes the earliest completion time·for the project.

To determine the latest occurrence time (LC) for each event, begin with the time estimate for the completed project, obtained from the *ES* procedure above, and assign this as the *LC* for the final event. Then subtract from this the time duration of the immediate predecessor activity to obtain the *LC* for the activity's beginning event. If an event has several succeeding activities, its *LC* is taken as the smallest value obtained by subtracting the duration of each of these activities from the *LC* of its ending event. In this manner calculate the *LC* for each event, starting at the *end* of the network and working backward along activity paths until the beginning event is reached, which will have *LC* = 0.

If for each event both the earliest and the latest occurrence time are available, the float or leeway in scheduling each event can be readily calculated. Those events and activities with zero float are necessarily on the critical path.

The actual procedure for computing float is as follows: Let i = an event signifying the origin of an activity, let j = an event signifying the termination of the activity, and Y_{ij} = the activity time duration. Note that an activity's earliest start time (ES_{ij}) equals ES_i, the earliest occurrence time of event i; and the activity's latest completion time (LC_{ij}) equals LC_j, the latest occurrence time of event j.

Construct a matrix by entering the Y_{ij} for each activity in the proper cell. For example, using the network shown in item 5 above, a matrix can be constructed as follows:

ES		i\j	1	2	3	4	5
0		0	2	6	-	-	-
2		1	-	4	8	-	-
6		2	-	-	5	2	13
11		3	-	-	-	5	9
16		4	-	-	-	-	3
20							

0	2	6	11	17	20	LC

Computing Earliest Occurrence Time. The procedure for computing earliest occurrence time (*ES*) is as follows:

1 Enter a zero in the first cell of the *ES* column, which represents the starting time of the project.
2 Add the corresponding values of Y_{ij} to the *ES* values column by column. In our example, $ES_0 = 0$ and $Y_{01} = 2$; hence $0 + 2 = 2$, and we enter 2 in the *ES* column below the zero, indicating that 2 weeks are required before the activities immediately after event 1 can be started.
3 Continue this procedure for each column. For example, the values in column 2 of the matrix are 6 weeks and 4 weeks. The corresponding values in the *ES* column are 0 and 2 weeks. Adding $6 + 0 = 6$ and $4 + 2 = 6$, we see that by either path it will be 6 weeks before event 2 can occur. Consequently, we enter 6 in the *ES* column opposite event 2.
4 Where different times result from this summation process, select the *longest* time

(path) and enter that number in the ES column. For example, column 3 of the matrix has Y_{ij} values of 8 and 5; the corresponding ES values are 2 and 6. By adding $8 + 2 = 10$ and $5 + 6 = 11$, we see that 11 is the longest time path and place it in the ES column.

Computing Latest Occurrence Time. The procedure for computing latest occurrence time (LC) is as follows:

1 Enter the longest time path in the project (i.e., 20 weeks, taken from the last cell in the ES column) in the last cell of the LC row.
2 Subtract the corresponding values of Y_{ij} from the LC values row by row. In our example, $LC_5 = 20$, and $Y_{45} = 3$; hence $20 - 3 = 17$, and we enter 17 in the LC row to the left of the 20 weeks. This means that event 4 must occur by the seventeenth week if the project is to be completed in 20 weeks. Continue this procedure for each row.
3 Where different times result from the subtraction process, select the *shortest* time (path) and enter that number in the LS row. For example, row 3 of the matrix has Y_{ij} values of 5 and 9; the corresponding LC values are 17 and 20. By subtracting $17 - 5 = 12$ and $20 - 9 = 11$, we see that the shortest time path is 11 and enter that number in the LC row.
4 The last entry in the LC row should be a zero, corresponding to the zero in the first cell of the ES column.

Identifying Events on the Critical Path. Every event that has an equal ES and LC time is on the critical path. In our example, event 1 has an ES of 2 and an LC of 2; hence it is on the critical path. Event 4 has an ES of 16 and an LC of 17; hence it is not on the critical path. Accordingly, the critical path includes events 0, 1, 2, 3, and 5.

Identifying Total Float. Total float for an activity is the amount of time available for an activity less the amount of estimated time required to complete the activity. In our example, total float for an activity equals $(LC_j - ES_i) - Y_{ij}$. Thus, for event 3, $LC_3 = 11$; $ES_1 = 2$; $Y_{13} = 8$; hence $(11 - 2) - 8 = 1$ week of float.

Other Types of Float: Free, Interfering, and Independent. It may be desirable to know how much a preceding activity may be delayed (if at all) without interfering with the earliest start of the succeeding activity. This is called *free* float. At this point, it is necessary to introduce data on an activity's completion time (EC_{ij}). EC_{ij} is derived by adding the estimated time required for an activity (Y_{ij}) to the activity's earliest start time (ES_{ij}). To compute free float: Let ES_{12}, EC_{12}, LC_{12}, and Y_{12} apply to the preceding activity and let ES_{23}, EC_{23}, LC_{23}, and Y_{23} apply to the succeeding activity. Then $ES_{23} - (EC_{12} + Y_{12}) =$ free float for activity 1-2.

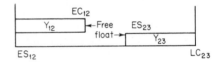

Interfering float is total float minus free float. The concept also can be presented in a diagram. For example, any delay in activity 1-2 beyond the ES date of activity 2-3 will delay or interfere with activity 2-3. Hence, part of the total float for activity 1-2 is free float $(ES_{23} - EC_{12})$ and the remainder is interfering float $(LC_{12} - ES_{23})$.

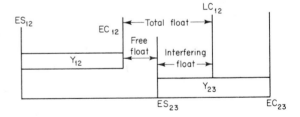

Independent float is computed as $ES_{34} - LC_{12} - Y_{23}$. For example, if all activities prior to activity 2-3 are completed by the LC_{12} date, and all activities succeeding activity 2-3 are started at the ES_{34} date, then $ES_{34} - LC_{12}$ is the amount of time available to perform activity 2-3. Subtracting the actual time required to perform the activity from the available time gives the independent float; i.e., the activity can be displaced forward or backward within this time interval without interfering with any other event.

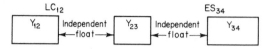

Time-Cost function.   The contribution to system management embodied in the CPM does not end with the time parameter. It also provides a technique to aid management in making time-cost trade-off decisions.

The technique is quite simple, requiring only four estimates: (1) normal activity time, (2) normal activity costs, (3) activity times on a "crash" basis, and (4) cost on a "crash" basis. These estimates are based on the principle of the time-cost curve, illustrated in Figure 32-9.

In this example, the normal activity time estimate would be six weeks and the cost estimate would be $10,000. On a crash basis, the activity time would be four weeks and the cost $20,000. A simple assumption would be that cost and time are related inversely and linearly (i.e., for each reduction in time there will be a corresponding increment of added cost). For example, according to Figure 32-9, shortening the time by one week (from six to five) would cost $5,000. The decision-maker can compare the costs of shortening the schedule by allocating additional resources to an activity (or activities) on the critical path for which marginal cost is less than for any other activity. Thus the time required on any path can be shortened at least cost. Assumptions other than an inverse linear relationship can also be introduced by properly reflecting them in the shape of the time-cost curve.

The task of calculating these time-cost trade-offs can be quite formidable to accomplish manually if the project becomes even moderately complex. A computer program assuming linear time-cost relationships has been developed that will automatically schedule the project for the least cost activities. This computer routine requires at least the two time-cost data points—i.e., assuming normal and crash programs for each activity. Non-linear assumptions are more difficult to treat in large projects.

It is not the purpose of this Memorandum to explore time-cost relationships; however, this mechanism is usually considered a component of CPM and should be mentioned when comparing CPM with PERT.[18]

Application to the Model

The CPM can be applied to the hypothetical missile system described in Sec. II. Figure 32-10 represents the planned sequence of activities in network form. The numbered circles correspond to the events in Table 32-1. Note that interdependencies are depicted in the network. For example, event 3 must occur before event 20 can be completed. Such interdependencies can be readily ascertained from the CPM network but would not be clearly evident in a tree diagram or in a Gantt or milestone chart.

It could be argued that engineers responsible for development are usually aware of these interrelationships when the Gantt chart is used, and nothing is gained by the network presentation. This may indeed be the case in simple or small-scale projects. However, when a number of managers are involved in planning and measuring the progress of a complex system, they may not be aware of the effect of interdependencies beyond their immediate sphere of interest. It is possible that a subcontractor

[18] *Several scheduling techniques have since been expanded to incorporate cost considerations, e.g., PERT-Cost, RAMPS, SPAR, etc. See especially PERT-Cost System Description Manual, vol. 3, U.S. Air Force, December 1963; Jack Moshman, Jacob Johnson, and Madalyn Larsen, RAMPS—A Technique for Resource Allocation and Multi-Project Scheduling, Proceedings 1963 Spring Joint Computer Conference; and J. D. Wiest, The Scheduling of Large Projects with Limited Resources, Research Memorandum No. 113, Graduate School of Industrial Administration, Carnegie Institute of Technology, Pittsburgh, 1963.*

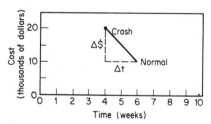

Figure 32-9   CPM time-cost trade-off.

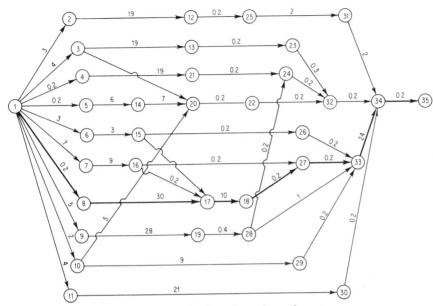

Figure 32–10   CPM network applied to hypothetical missile system.

may be well aware of those relationships within his control, and yet not realize that his schedule is in jeopardy because another department will not be able to deliver its portion of the project on time, or, conversely, that a component he is developing may, if not completed on time, retard another subcontractor and hence the entire project. In making the relationships explicit, the network serves as a communications device to ensure that all parties concerned are aware of the overall plan and their responsibilities in view of the plan.

The problem of keeping the planning and control information system attuned to actual development operations is common to all managerial techniques. A major advantage of the network-type presentation is that it enables the manager to cumulate the activity times along a given path to determine the total estimated time per path. The longest time path is the critical path. In Figure 32-10, for example, the longest time path is 64.8 weeks and is composed of events 1, 8, 17, 18, 27, 33, 34, and 35. All other paths are estimated to be completed in less time. If the tasks are scheduled to take the estimated time, then all paths other than this critical path contain float. Any path on which estimated completion time is greater than, or equal to, the time remaining before a scheduled project completion date is called critical. Hence, there may exist *the* most critical path, the *second* most critical, etc. In Figure 32-10, events 1, 9, 19, 28, 33, 34, and 35 would comprise the second most critical path (58.6 weeks).

Table 32-7 presents the matrix of task times needed to compute the *ES* and *LC* times for each activity in our hypothetical missile system. For example, activity 14-20 has an earliest start time of 6.2 weeks from the beginning of the project. It must be completed in the 64th week or the activity will "float" the succeeding activity beyond the project completion date. Thus we can compute the various float concepts for activity 14-20:[19]

1 Total float
$$= (LC_{20} - ES_{14}) - Y_{14\text{-}20}$$
$$= (64 - 6.2) - 7 = 50.8$$
2 Free float
$$= ES_{20\text{-}22} - (ES_{14\text{-}20} + Y_{14\text{-}20})$$
$$= 13.2 - (6.2 + 7) = 0.$$
3 Independent float
$$= (ES_{20\text{-}22} - LC_{5\text{-}14}) - Y_{14\text{-}20}$$
$$= (13.2 - 57) - 7 = -50.8$$

[19] *For clarity, and to be consistent with the explanation on pages 40–41, LC and ES values are identified by the appropriate activity designator which in turn is composed of both the starting and ending event numbers. Technically, however, ES can be fully defined by the starting event and LC by the ending event number.*

Table 32-7 — 35 × 35 matrix (rotated on the original page). Column index $i = 1 \ldots 35$ across the top with the row "LC" giving the column values; row index $j = 1 \ldots 35$ down the side with the column "ES" giving the row values.

i \ j	1	2	3	4	5	6	7	8	9	10	11	12	13	14	15	16	17	18	19	20	21	22	23	24	25	26	27	28	29	30	31	32	33	34	35	ES
1	0																																			0
2		3																																		3
3			4																																	0.2
4				0.2																																0.2
5					0.2																															3
6						3																														7
7							7																													0.2
8								0.2																												5
9									5																											2
10										2																										4
11											4																									22
12												19																								23
13													19																							2
14														6																						4
15															3																					6.2
16																9																				6
17																	30																			16
18																	0.4	10																		30.2
19																	0.2		28																	40.2
20																				5																33
21																				5	19															13.2
22																				7		0.2														19.2
23																							0.2													13.4
24																								0.2												23.2
25																									0.2											33.6
26																										0.2										22.2
27																								0.2			0.2									6.2
28																											0.2	0.4								40.4
29																													9							33.4
30																														21						11
31																															2					25
32																																0.2		0.2		24.2
33																																0.3	0.4	2		33.8
34																																0.2	0.2	0.2		40.6
35																																	1	24	0.2	64.6
LC	0	41.4	44.9	45	51	26.8	21	0.2	11.2	31.4	43.4	60.4	3.9	57	29.8	30	30.2	40.2	39.2	64	64	64.2	64.1	64.2	60.6	40.2	40.4	39.6	40.4	64.4	62.6	64.4	40.6	64.6	64.8	

TABLE 32-7

1 *Total float.* Assuming that there are no project changes, and that activity 14-20 is started at the earliest possible date and completed at the earliest possible time, 50.8 weeks will elapse before activity 20-22 will have to be started. Consequently, freedom exists to allocate resources to other more critical tasks up to a maximum of 50.8 weeks before the scheduled completion of activity 14-20 is jeopardized.

2 *Free float.* If activity 20-22 were to start on the earliest possible date, no freedom would exist to allocate resources to other tasks. In other words, there would be no free float in the scheduling of activity 14-20. As mentioned previously, total float can be subdivided into free float and interfering float. Interfering float would delay (interfere with) the start of the subsequent activity (20-22) beyond the earliest start date. In the above example, all of the float for activity 14-20 is interfering.[20]

3 *Independent float.* In the illustration a negative value (−50.8) was obtained and therefore there is no independent float. This negative statistic does indicate that there would be no time available to perform activity 14-20 if the prior activity (5-14) were delayed until its latest completion date and if scheduling the subsequent activity (20-22) on its earliest start date was contemplated. In fact, the latest completion date for activity 5-14 significantly postdates the earliest start date for activity 20-22. This, of course, is of no real concern here because the earliest start date of activity 20-22 (also identified by LC_{20}) can be delayed substantially without jeopardizing project completion. In other words, total float exists, but independent float, being a very restrictive concept, does not in this case.

Evaluation of CPM

The network concept of CPM is an excellent device for explicitly depicting significant interrelationships among events. The flow of all activities is on paper so that those concerned can analyze the work plan and approve or disapprove it. Communication of planned activity is thus facilitated.

Since time estimates lead to the determination of a critical path, the attention of management is focused on the activities along the path so that resources can be applied to them, perhaps by reallocation from other activities where float exists.

One criticism of CPM is that emphasis on critical path activities may obscure the fact that some activities on a second path may be very close to being critical and would become so with slight changes in values. However, this possibility can be alleviated by determining the first most critical path, the second most critical path, etc., and *then* determining the critical activities within this broader context.

The time-cost function, although not fully implemented in actual systems, can provide trade-off information on the relative cost of reducing scheduled time in various activities. This trade-off feature linking cost and schedule is beyond the scope of this study but nevertheless is an important element of the CPM method.

CPM does not provide a capability for handling schedule uncertainty. For example, the development of a component may involve a major engineering improvement, and there may be considerable uncertainty regarding the time required for its accomplishment. In CPM, the responsible individual must provide management with his single best estimate of the time requirement. He may not reflect his uncertainty in terms of a range of estimates. The single value is incorporated into the network and the critical path determined. If the estimate is in error, then the critical path may be incorrectly drawn.

The strengths and weaknesses of CPM are summarized in Table 32-8.

V. PROGRAM EVALUATION AND REVIEW TECHNIQUE (PERT)

PERT Methodology

The program evaluation and review technique (PERT)[21] was formulated at approximately the same time as the critical path method (CPM). Like CPM, PERT is designed for scheduling activities in the development phase and is not directly suitable for application to repetitive

---

[20] *If these resources were allocated, it would be at the cost of delaying the start of task 20–22. This may, nevertheless, be a wise decision since activity 20–22 may be delayed a maximum of 50.8 weeks and the project can still be on schedule.*

[21] *PERT was developed by C. E. Clark, W. Fazar, D. G. Malcolm, and J. H. Roseboom, working with the management consulting firm of Booz, Allen and Hamilton, the Navy Bureau of Ordnance, and Lockheed Corporation.*

TABLE 32·8   CPM TECHNIQUES—STRENGTHS AND WEAKNESSES

Criteria	Strengths	Weaknesses
1. *Validity*		No formula is provided to estimate time to completion; consequently, the technique is as valid as the estimator. The margin of error is generally less in construction than in development.
2. *Reliability*		Numerous estimates in a large project, each with some unreliability may lead to significant errors in judging project status.
3. *Implementation*		Relatively difficult to explain, especially if the various concepts of float are utilized.
4. *Universality of project coverage*	Very good for single-shot activities, such as construction or development projects.	Weak in the production phase of a weapon life cycle. The technique is not well adapted to scheduling production quantities.
5. *Sensitivity testing (simulation)*	Excellent for simulating alternative plans, especially when coupled with the time-cost aspect.	
6. *Forecasting*	Strongly oriented to forecasting ability to accomplish future events on schedule.	
7. *Updating*	Good capability. Activities are clearly identified and time estimates can be obtained as needed.	
8. *Flexibility*	Portions of the network can be easily changed to reflect program changes.	
9. *Cost*		Considerable data are required to use CPM as both a planning and status reporting tool and a computer is almost invariably required. Therefore, the cost outlay can be fairly extensive.

NOTE: Recall that this table is intended only as a summary of certain qualitative information on the relative usefulness of the scheduling technique. As indicated previously, a more formal quantitative evaluation of the extent to which the criteria are met was considered infeasible in this study.

production operations. Both CPM and PERT are based on the network concept; both identify a critical path; both isolate float or slack. CPM, however, pioneered simple time-cost trade-off relationships. PERT, on the other hand, used a more sophisticated approach to the problem of treating schedule uncertainties.

Since the events, activities, and network concepts embodied in PERT are the same as those described for CPM, our discussion of PERT will cover only the major differences between the two techniques.

The PERT planning phase: estimated time. It is essential in the PERT planning process to secure estimates of the amount of time required to complete each activity. PERT recommends that three estimates be obtained rather than a single point estimate:

1 *Optimistic time, a,* (only 1 percent of the time would the activity be completed more quickly),*

* *This 1 percent requirement is frequently relaxed in practice.*

2 *Most likely time, m* (mode),
3 *Pessimistic time, b,* (only 1 percent of the time would more time be required).[22]

This estimating method has the following advantages. First, estimators usually make more valid estimates if they can express the extent of their uncertainty. Range-of-time estimates are more realistic and informative than a single point estimate. They are particularly worthwhile assuming that the burden of preparation does not become excessive.

Second, a single point estimate is likely to be the mode. In estimating activity time, the mean is generally considered a more representative statistic than the mode. It more nearly represents all possible values in the time distribution because it is based on all the information relative to the distribution, rather than being merely the most frequent single estimate.

The beta (β) distribution is used in the PERT estimation process.[23] A formula approximating the mean of the distribution, called the expected time (t_e), can be derived based on the three time estimates and the beta distribution. For example:

$$t_e = \frac{a + 4m + b}{6}$$

Letting a = 5 months, m = 7 months, and b = 15 months, we obtain

$$\frac{a + 4m + b}{6} = \frac{5 + 4(7) + 15}{6} = \frac{48}{6} = 8 \text{ months}$$

Note that the midpoint of the range is $(15 + 5) \div 2 = 10$ months. The mode is 7 months. The mean (t_e) is 8 months. The mean lies one-third of the distance from the mode to the midpoint of the range.

The critical path.   After the expected time has been determined for each activity in the network, it is possible to compute the critical path, which is simply the longest path of expected times in the network. When more than one time path leads into an event, the longest time path leading into that event establishes the expected time for the event.

Calendar time.   The scheduler is now ready to schedule the start and the completion of each activity, based on the expected time estimates. Several concepts have been developed to aid management in monitoring progress and allocating resources to the activities. The first is that of the earliest expected occurrence date of an event (T_E). Normally, the start of a project is associated with a specific calendar date, and then the elapsed time for an activity is added to that date to determine the calendar date of the next event. This procedure is followed for every event on the PERT network. In working from the start to the end of the project—i.e., the forward pass—the expected earliest occurrence dates for each event can be determined.

After the earliest completion date has been established for the end item in the project, the latest allowable occurrence date (T_L) for each event can be determined by proceeding backward—the backward pass—from the earliest completion date,[24] *or from a promised due date,* and subtracting expected times. The T_L represents the latest date that an event can occur and not jeopardize the project completion date.[25]

It is now possible to determine the amount of *slack* in the project. Slack is the time flexibility available to management in scheduling resources to a given activity and is defined as $T_L - T_E$. If T_L is later than T_E, then positive slack exists and management has some freedom in scheduling the event. If T_L is earlier than T_E, negative slack exists and completion of the project is in jeopardy. The path with the most negative slack, or the least positive slack if there is no negative slack, is necessarily the longest time path—the critical path.

---

[22] *This 1 percent requirement is frequently relaxed in practice.*
[23] *The beta distribution has two interesting characteristics: (1) The range precisely equals six standard deviations (i.e., the "tails" of the distribution do not approach infinity), and (2) using the PERT approximation, the mean of the distribution lies one-third of the distance from the mode to the midpoint of the range. Also, in practice the skewness of activities tends to be toward the right.*

[24] *If the earliest completion date is used as the project completion date (due date) in performing the backward pass, earliest and latest completion dates will be identical for events on the critical path.*
[25] T_E *and* T_L *correspond to the ES and LC measures for events in Sec. IV. A different symbol has been selected to emphasize that the event occurrence times in the PERT model are probabilistic measures—the sum of* expected *activity duration times.*

Negative slack should not exist in the planning phase of a project. If the T_E and T_L were computed as described above, negative slack could not exist, and the critical path would contain, at a minimum, zero slack. Frequently, however, under pressure from the customer or in eagerness to obtain a contract, a contractor will agree to complete a project in less time than is indicated by the preliminary estimates.[26] This directed completion date is then entered on the calendar as the scheduled completion date (T_S) and, in the backward pass, new T_L dates are computed based on the directed date. Thus, negative slack may exist.

Negative slack must be remedied in one of two ways if management expects to complete the project on schedule. First a portion of the resources can be withdrawn from noncritical activities and allotted to critical activities. This, of course, implies that such resources—i.e., skills, equipment, or facilities—are transferable. Second, management can increase the overall level of resources devoted to the project.

From a project management standpoint, an ideal situation would exist if there were zero slack on all activities. Adequate resources would then be optimally allocated, given the completion date of the program.[27]

After analysis of possible trade-offs of resources, acceptable scheduled completion dates (T_S) can be determined and the activities scheduled. As one might suspect, in general T_S should occur between T_E and T_L.

The PERT operating phase. The acceptance by management of the T_S means the acceptance of a plan of action and the end of the initial PERT planning phase. The authorization of work to be performed as scheduled begins the PERT operating phase. Essentially, this phase involves reporting program status and acting on this information. The following information is reported during the operating phase:

1 Completed activities and their completion dates.

[26] *It also should be noted that such estimates usually are made with a specified level of funding in mind and are subject to modification if the anticipated funding level is revised.*
[27] *This assumes that the cost-time relationship for individual activities is a continuously decreasing function to the right, as illustrated in part in Figure 32-9.*

2 Changes in activity time estimates.
3 Changes in schedule.
4 Event and activity additions and deletions.

Input data are prepared and computer printouts of status are distributed periodically (generally every two weeks) to the appropriate levels of management.

The PERT-Time system cycle, with the interrelationships between the planning and the operating phases, is shown in Figure 32-11.

Various types of data are contained in the PERT system. Thus far, the most important use of operating data for control purposes appears to be through the analysis of slack. The amount of slack (often negative) is charted periodically so that management can follow the trend from week to week. Normally, with good control the amount of negative slack on a path should decrease over time. This decrease is generally attributable either to greater management attention to activities on that path or, as described below, to the lessening of uncertainty concerning completion times.

The standard deviation (σ) of an activity. By using three time estimates for each activity, the scheduler can apply probability theory in determining uncertainty in scheduling activities. Assuming that the beta distribution is a valid representation of the distribution of the estimates, the standard deviation for an activity can be approximated by the following equation:

$$\sigma = \frac{b - a}{6}$$

thus the range $(b - a)$ is six times the standard deviation.

To illustrate the standard deviation of an activity, let $a = 10$ months, $m = 13$ months, and $b = 16$ months. Then

$$t_e = \frac{10 + 4(13) + 16}{6} = 13$$
$$\sigma = \frac{(16 - 10)}{6} = 1$$

A common interpretation of this statistic is that a 67 percent chance (67 out of 100 times) exists that the activity will be completed within one standard deviation (12th and 14th months); a 95 percent chance between 2σ of the mean (11th and 15th months); and a 99 percent

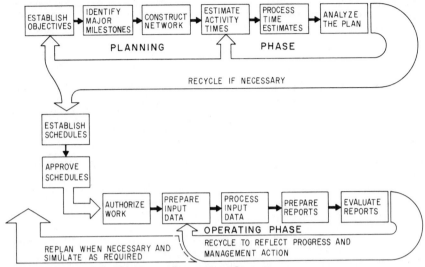

Figure 32-11   PERT: Planning and operating phases.[28]

chance between 3σ of the mean (10th and 16th months). This interpretation is misleading because the above applies to a normal, and not to a beta distribution. Depending on the skewness of the beta distribution one σ from the mean may contain considerably more or less than 67 percent of the observations. The σ has no inherent meaning in quantifying uncertainty for an individual activity; however it is used to compute the σ of an event which is described in the following subsection.

Probability of meeting scheduled date or of having positive slack.   The probability of meeting the scheduled date or, alternatively, of having positive slack can be determined by using the concepts of slack and standard deviation of an activity. While this probability statistic can be computed for any event in the project, the *ending* event is used in the following example.

First, compute the length of the longest path leading into any specific event (T_E), and then compute the standard deviation of that event's earliest occurrence time (σT_E). The σT_E is defined as the square root of the sum of the activity standard deviations squared (σ^2), i.e., the variances of the activities lying on the longest time path leading into that event. Here the

event time (path length) is generally assumed to be normally distributed,[29] not beta distributed. The probability of meeting the scheduled date can then be determined by using tables of the areas under the normal curve.[30] The formula for this normalized statistic is

$$\frac{T_S - T_E}{\sigma T_E}$$

If we assume that an event is scheduled to be completed in 10 months, but the earliest expected date is 12 months from now, and the standard deviation of that event is 1 month, then

$$Z = \frac{T_S - T_E}{\sigma T_E} = \frac{10 - 12}{1} = \frac{-2}{1} = -2$$

From tables of the area under a normal curve we find that a Z of minus two (-2) is associated with 0.0228 of the total area under the curve; in other words, only two times out of

[28] *Taken from* PERT-Time System Description Manual, *vol. 1, U.S. Air Force, September 1963, p. V-3.*

[29] *Through invoking the central limit theorem. Also, the assumption must be made that the activities are independent. This assumption has been challenged on numerous occasions, since many activities are interconnected and also frequently appear on more than one path in a network.*
[30] *Tables of areas under the normal curve can be found in virtually every basic statistics textbook. They are also included in the* PERT-Time System Description Manual, *Appendix B.*

100 would management expect to complete that event on schedule. Since this represents a small probability, it is clear that the program schedule is in difficulty.

Unfortunately, management usually does not employ this probability measure because of a feeling that too much uncertainty exists in the entire estimation and planning process for this statistical calculation to have meaning. It also appears that management in general is not familiar with probability theory.

Actually, similar information can be presented to management without using formal probability theory. The scheduling section in the Dynasoar (X-20) Program Office derived an interesting surrogate for such probability statistics. A "recovery ratio" was computed that was simply a ratio of the negative slack to the length of the critical path. For example, path A in a project may require 20 weeks to perform and contain 5 weeks of negative slack. Path B may require 3 weeks and have 1 week of negative slack. Slack calculations alone would indicate that Path A was most critical (i.e., 5 > 1). The recovery ratios for path A would be $(5 \div 20)$, $\frac{1}{4}$, or 0.25; for path B they would be $(1 \div 3)$, $\frac{1}{3}$, or 0.33. This would indicate that in reality path B is more critical than path A, since only 3 weeks would remain to pick up 1 week of negative slack, whereas on A, 20 weeks are available to pick up 5 weeks of negative slack. The recovery ratio is easier to compute and to understand than the probability distribution, and is worth serious consideration by management.

Types of PERT networks.   The fact that various levels of management and numerous interrelationships among firms, agencies, and military offices that are involved in weapon system acquisition was brought out in Sec. I of this Memorandum. In such an environment, with its variety of demands, a single network often will not suffice. Accordingly, variations have been evolved to handle various aspects of the planning and control process.

1 *Detailed and Operating Level Networks*
    Generally, each prime or associate contractor constructs and uses a network that covers his individual sphere of program responsibility. If a portion of the project is subcontracted to another firm that subcontractor in turn may be required to construct and use a network for his portion of the project. These networks are constructed in considerable detail and frequently comprehend even relatively minor activities and events.[31] Such networks are utilized by operating managements and are termed operating networks, or detailed networks. In addition, since they often cover only a fragment of a project, NASA has referred to them as fragnets (*fragmentary networks*).

2 *Integrated Project Networks*
    The detailed operating networks prepared by the separate firms and agencies may be combined or integrated, generally at the SPO level, into one comprehensive network encompassing all events in the entire project. Although perhaps not directly involved in detailed operations, the SPO can exercise management surveillance over the progress of the entire project through use of this integrated network.

3 *Condensed or Summary Networks*
    Generally, detailed networks contain too much operating data for top project management or other interested parties (i.e., DOD, Headquarters USAF, etc.) monitoring the progress of the program on a more aggregative basis. To accomplish this, a summary, or condensed network is constructed which eliminates much of the detail, yet retains the events of major significance. Such networks frequently are displayed in project control offices.

Accurate translations of activity time estimates must be made when the operating networks are either integrated or condensed. The integration and condensation processes involve identifying, recording, coordinating and storing interface events.[32] Various computer routines are being developed to accomplish this complex and vital task. The relationship among these various forms of networks is indicated in Figure 32-12. This diagram depicts condensation of networks prior to network integration. Either condensation or integration can occur first depending on the requirements of the levels of program management.

Information usually is abstracted from the condensed network and forwarded to agen-

[31] *It is evident that the level of detail may vary among contractors.*
[32] *An interface event signals the transfer of responsibility, end items, or information from one part of the project effort to another.*

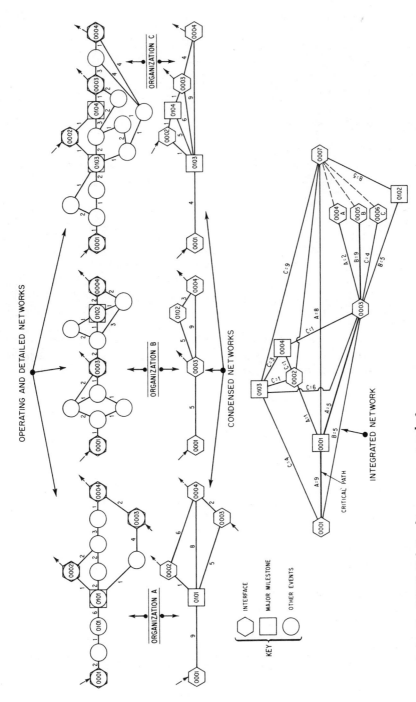

Figure 32-12 PERT: Relationships among networks.

* Adapted from Planning and Control Techniques and Procedures (PCT), Headquarters, U.S. Army Material Command, AMC Regulation 11–16, vol. 2, August 1963, Fig. 11-3-5.

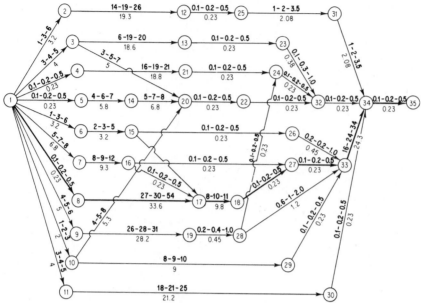

Figure 32-13   PERT network applied to hypothetical missile system.

cies above the SPO in milestone form. The current procedure of selecting information from the networks and listing this information in line item or narrative form appears to have limitations. One relatively simple improvement would utilize the network concept and its relevant information on interrelationships at top project levels. Perhaps this could be accomplished by including a requirement that summary networks be incorporated in the System Package Program[33] and that project progress be reported against these networks.

Application of PERT to Hypothetical Missile System

The PERT network shown in Figure 32-13 for our hypothetical missile system is a summary network. The events and activities are identical to those used in the network illustrating the critical path technique in Sec. IV, and the same "rules" are followed. In each case the work flow envisioned at the time is the same, and thus the networks are the same. However,

[33] *As mentioned previously, the System Package Program is the basic management document for major weapon systems programs.*

in the PERT network, three time estimates are used for each activity: optimistic, most likely, and pessimistic. These estimates (taken from Table 32-1) are displayed in bold on Figure 32-13 to emphasize the major difference between CPM and PERT.

The expected times as derived from the three time estimates in PERT frequently will differ somewhat from the single time estimates recorded in CPM. As described above, the mean is conceptually a more comprehensive measure incorporating the extreme (optimistic and pessimistic) values and in this sense reflects the range of uncertainty revealed by the three time estimates. The mean used in PERT will vary from the mode used in CPM in those instances when the time interval between the mode and the optimistic time differs from the interval between the mode and the pessimistic time estimates. The mean and mode will coincide where there is equal uncertainty in positive and negative directions, since the mode will bisect the range between the optimistic and pessimistic times.

Once the expected time for each event has been computed, the techniques are identical in their method of identifying the critical path. In our missile system example, the critical path for PERT is identical with that for CPM (i.e., events 1, 8, 17, 18, 27, 33, 34, and 35). However, the time to complete the project has been lengthened from 64.8 weeks to 68.6 weeks. This difference is the result of the fact that in the estimates for individual activities prepared using the PERT technique, the range between the optimistic and expected times was less than the range between the pessimistic and expected times.

In this simple example, the difference of 3.8 weeks in a project of 69 weeks' duration is only moderately important. It would be difficult to state clearly which estimate (PERT or CPM) was the more accurate. The PERT technique is more sophisticated in that it does attempt to deal with uncertainty. However, various mathematicians have questioned certain of the simplifying assumptions used in the PERT estimation process.[34]

If, in scheduling the activities for our hypothetical missile system, we assume a directed date of 65 weeks from now, that becomes the scheduled date for completion of the project. If the length of the critical path is 68.6 weeks, we have negative slack of 3.6 weeks. Because of the uncertainty inherent in the activities as shown by the estimation intervals, management may require some "feeling" for the likelihood of the project's being completed on schedule. Using the concept of zero slack, this likelihood can be ascertained by computing (1) the standard deviations of the activities on the critical path (σ), (2) the standard deviation of the final event (σ_E), (3) the Z statistic, and, finally, (4) the probability of positive slack. These computations are given in Table 32-9.

Note that the probability is only 0.25. A gambling management might be content to proceed and see what develops, but most managements would probably require at the very least a 50 percent chance of meeting schedule. This would then call either for shifting resources from noncritical events to critical events or for employing a higher level of resources. If positive slack exists, management frequently is content to assume that the project will be completed on schedule.

[34] *An analysis of the significance of these arguments is found in K. R. MacCrimmon and C. A. Ryavec,* An Analytical Study of the PERT Assumptions, *The RAND Corporation, RM-3408, December 1962.*

TABLE 32-9   COMPUTATIONS REQUIRED FOR PROBABILITY OF POSITIVE SLACK

(1) Standard deviation and variance of critical path activities:

Event Number on Critical Path	Standard Deviation of an Activity $[(b-a)/6]$	Variance of an Activity (σ^2)
8	$\dfrac{0.5 - 0.1}{6} = 0.07$	0.0049
17	$\dfrac{54 - 27}{6} = 4.5$	20.2500
18	$\dfrac{11 - 8}{6} = 0.5$	0.2500
27	$\dfrac{0.5 - 0.1}{6} = 0.07$	0.0049
33	$\dfrac{0.5 - 0.1}{6} = 0.07$	0.0049
34	$\dfrac{34 - 16}{6} = 3.0$	9.0000
35	$\dfrac{0.5 - 0.1}{6} = 0.07$	0.0049

Total variance along the critical path. . . 29.5196 or 29.52

(2) Standard deviation for the final event = $\sqrt{29.52}$ or 5.43.

(3) $Z = \dfrac{T_S - T_E}{\sigma T_E} = \dfrac{65 - 68.6}{5.43} = \dfrac{-3.6}{5.43} = -0.662.$

(4) Probability of positive slack. Referring to tables of the area under the normal curve, the Z statistic corresponding to the number −0.662 is approximately 0.25. This means that only 25 times out of 100 could management expect to complete the project on schedule.

Evaluation of PERT

Since its formulation, PERT has been received both favorably and unfavorably. Those who favor it recognize it as a good planning tool. Others feel that it has been offered as a panacea for all scheduling problems. Still others think that the technique is "basically nothing new." PERT, however, does offer several concepts not previously incorporated in scheduling techniques.

Unfortunately, PERT, as conceived by its developers, has never been applied in total to any major system. In particular, the three time estimates and the probability computations have never had a thorough test throughout a full project cycle. Perhaps the most complete attempt was the use of the three time estimates on the Dynasoar program, but that program was cancelled before completion.

Obviously, it is difficult to make a satisfactory comparison between CPM and PERT if the factors unique to PERT—its three time estimates and use of probability theory—are not implemented. Since use of the beta distribution in the PERT technique has been attacked by mathematicians, and engineers have been reluc-

TABLE 32-10   PERT TECHNIQUE—STRENGTHS AND WEAKNESSES

Criteria	Strengths	Weaknesses
1. *Validity*	PERT, like CPM, is capable of depicting work sequence. The use of three time estimates should make it more valid than any other technique.	
2. *Reliability*		On the other hand, securing three time estimates for each activity requires more information which would tend to introduce additional error.
3. *Implementation*		The complete PERT system is quite complex and therefore difficult to implement.
4. *Universality of project coverage*	Very strong in development phase.	Requires adaptation for application to production operations.
5. *Sensitivity testing (simulation)*	Since PERT is usually mechanized, it has good potential for simulating the impact of various resource allocations on the schedule, or the various ways of sequencing work.	
6. *Forecasting*	PERT is strongly oriented to forecasting the ability to accomplish future events on schedule.	
7. *Updating*	Activities are clearly identified and elapsed times can be obtained as needed.	Estimation of activity times is quite time-consuming, and calculation of expected times requires use of a computer.
8. *Flexibility*	As the project changes over time, the network and new time estimates can be readily adjusted to reflect changes, especially if present experimental efforts on automatic plotting of networks are successful.	
9. *Cost*		More data and more computations are required than in any other system; hence the system is more costly.

NOTE: Recall that this table is intended only as a summary of certain qualitative information on the relative usefulness of the scheduling technique. As indicated previously, a more formal quantitative evaluation of the extent to which the criteria are met was considered infeasible in this study.

tant to make the three time estimates because they believe them to be too time-consuming, the probability calculations have usually been abandoned, perhaps justifiably. However, any new system that is to be used by numerous firms requires time to implement. Perhaps PERT should be implemented a portion at a time. Further study might indicate that in most cases expected time estimates do not vary significantly from single point estimates and therefore multiple estimates are not justified in view of the added inconvenience and cost. On the other hand, the problem of dealing with uncertainties in estimates remains. This issue is as yet unresolved.

At first, PERT had no cost-estimating capability. Now the network and critical path features of PERT-Time have proved their worth, and attempts are being made to extend the concept to the cost and reliability aspects of project management. The first full-scale application of the PERT-Cost technique was made on the TFX program. It is important to note that the PERT-type network provides a common framework for incorporating these other factors, and thus PERT provides the basis for a more completely integrated management system.

PERT has earned widespread acceptance in industry and government, and undoubtedly will be the dominant scheduling system for major development programs for some time to come, especially since attempts are being made to integrate it with companion techniques for planning and control of cost. In addition, it appears likely that a related effort will be made to utilize it in the planning and control of technical performance.

Some of the strengths and weaknesses of PERT are summarized in Table 32-10.

READING 33

MANAGING RISKS FOR MORE EFFECTIVE PROGRAM CONTROL*

James R. Polski

Engineers and scientists usually are the world's greatest optimists. In some respects they need to be, in order to ride the waves of opposition while pursuing their intuition into uncharted waters. The Wrights, the Edisons and the Goddards are the classical models of this tenacious breed.

The present day confreres of these titans are urged to temper bubbling optimism with equal doses of realism—regarding the risks of failure —to meet commitments of megabuck magnitude without overruns.

Inherently, the risk of failure to meet objectives shadows all design and development programs. Yet, because it is a negative aspect, the incidence of risk is quite often overlooked in the glare of optimism. Or, even where it is not ignored completely, it may be appraised but not deeply enough, or perhaps not often enough to serve as a significant input for decision-making.

* Reprinted with permission of General Electric Company, Missile and Space Division, from Aerospace Management, vol. 1, no. 1, Spring, 1966.

Risk is a prime variable in a design and development program. It can be defined as the probability that the work being done will miss the triple target of cost, delivery schedule, or technical performance. Reducing this probability is as healthy to a contractor as the reduction of a beltline is to an overweight. Coincidentally, in both cases the achievement of success depends upon discipline.

In the management of a design and development program, the discipline consists of identifying and evaluating the elements of risk on a continuous basis. To use elements of risk as inputs for decision-making, the General Electric Company, Missile and Space Division has developed the Risk Appraisal of Programs System (RAPS). Basically, RAPS provides both a framework for identifying the risks and a comparative measure for expressing the extent of risk associated with each hardware end-item or task.

In general problem-solving, the identification of the problem is the first step to its solution; this holds true also in risk appraisal. A good point to remember, however, is that the RAP

System is not aimed at eliminating risks, but rather at balancing risks across the program. For, better program value is provided if one does not spend money on elaborate attempts to lower risk in one area while excessive risks are going unheeded in another.

An accurate appraisal of risk can serve both the customer and the contractor; first as a planning tool, it can provide bases for trade-offs; secondly, it can function as a communication medium between customer, program manager, and the program team; lastly, when practiced during the course of development, it can be used for assessing the changes in program risks and for verifying conformance to plans.

FACTORS AFFECTING RISK

The many factors which affect risk in a development program can be grouped in two broad categories: (1) factors stemming from resource limitations such as funds and time, as well as from specific mission requirements; (2) factors bearing on the conduct and management of the total task.

For each hardware subsystem "Resource Limitations" risks are appraised using a checklist—from the viewpoint of individuals responsible for the end item. Seven fundamental aspects are considered: inputs, capabilities, knowledge, reliability, margins, schedules and funds.

Based upon the lack of a given resource factor, risk-level estimates may be assigned. These limitations may comprise a lack of capability with respect to critical skilled manpower, or a lack of inputs such as design requirements data on a subsystem.

The risk-level gradation for each of the seven aspects is identified as "High, Moderate, Minor, or Low."

A "High" risk estimate is a judgment that the particular resource limitation could jeopardize the successful fulfillment of the program. This, in effect is a "signal" for management action. "Moderate" risk implies an attenuation of this signal; whereas "minor" signifies a normal amount of risk incident to this type of work; and "low" indicates that additional risk could be assumed in this area—for trade-off purposes.

Where limitations are adjudged to be "High" or "Moderate," substantiation is furnished by providing an explanation and recommendations

for lowering to "Minor"; as well as a rough cost-estimate of direct labor and materials that may be required to lower the risk level.

This substantiation is the guiding philosophy of the RAP System. For it motivates people to focus on potential problem areas and to formulate solutions—without losing sight of cost-time-technical-risk trade-offs. This requirement then, counteracts the natural human tendency to "over-control" in reacting to risks.

INFLUENCE OF MANAGEMENT PRACTICES

Program Risk can also be varied with the use, or lack of use, of certain proven management methods and practices for conducting the work in all the principal functions. Management practices to be followed may differ from program to program. The practices to be used may vary with the nature of the development, the extent of the funding, the criticality of the schedule, as well as the influence of other customer requirements. A point to remember here is that the disciplined approach to risk appraisal is primarily an insurance against the omission of certain practices through oversight. Application of rigorous management practices to the conduct of work can serve to substantially lower the risk.

Risk appraisal for "Management Practices" is conducted on the basis of selected key areas from the various functions. Such key areas include Design Review, Qualification System, Procurement Management, Quality Controls and Schedule Management. Typical examples of proven low-risk practices from these areas are:

Use of outside consultants for Design Reviews.
Incorporation of Qualification requirements in the equipment specification.
Employment of vendor-capability analyses in Procurement Source Selection.
Use of the Quality Audit technique.
Regular reporting of Schedule information for current program status.

SELECTION OF KEY AREAS

A question may be raised at this point, as to how the key areas for management practices, and the practices themselves were selected for risk appraisal, in the first place?

Methods and practices of the greatest practi-

RESOURCE LIMITATIONS
RISK ESTIMATE CHECKLIST

PROGRAM:_____   DATE:_____

ITEM:_____

Based upon your experience and judgement in reference to a program of this nature and based upon the present plan for technical analysis, design, hardware, fabrication, testing and evaluation indicate the Risk due to any lack of the following

Risk Level Estimates
HIGH   MOD.   MINOR   LOW

1. INPUTS – Based upon the clarity and firmness of available customer requirements and/or interface definitions, drawings, or study results, what level of risk is imposed on the program?

2. CAPABILITIES – Considering the need for suitably skilled and experienced manpower and of appropriate facilities for conducting the work, as compared to the availability and allocation of these capabilities, what level of risk is involved?

3. KNOWLEDGE – Based upon the availability of fundamental and accurate information on the environment, technologies, or techniques involved; or upon the test results available or planned, what level of risk is imposed on the programs?

4. RELIABILITY – Considering the degree of proven reliability of parts or components available, as judged by failures and problems that have persistently reoccurred in similar equipments, what level of risk is involved?

5. MARGINS – Based upon the stringency of the reqt. vs. the state-of-the-art supplemented by development plans, what level of risk is involved? (Examples: weight limit in view of past actuals and present research; materials specified in view of fabrication difficulties.)

6. SCHEDULES – Considering the programmed time for significant portions of the work in the current phase or throughout the total development, what level of risk is imposed on the program?

7. FUNDS – Considering the funding available and/or allocated to this work for the immediate period or for the total task, what level of risk is imposed on the program?

The limitations which are adjudged to be of "High" or "Moderate" Risk must be substantiated on the following page by a brief explanation of the action that might be taken and a rough estimate of the cost of such action.

Name/Title Estimator:_____
Form A

Figure 33-1

cal significance were selected in the light of cumulative experience at General Electric and the Air Force. First a study was made, within the General Electric, Missile and Space Division, to earmark practices which consistently contributed to the successful conduct and control of past development programs. Secondly, the chosen practices were compared with the Air Force Systems Command findings reported in AFSCP 375-2, entitled "A Summary of Lessons Learned from Air Force Management Surveys." This report highlights the most repetitive management deficiencies encountered in the aerospace industry, grouped as follows:

Program and Contract Functions
Engineering Functions
Production and Quality
Assurance Functions
Purchasing and Material Functions
Product Support Functions

Correlating these Air Force findings with in-house studies, twenty-one management practice areas were identified as most significant for managing development programs. These are:

Specifications
Design Stage Release System
Design Review
Reliability Plan
Reliability Design Analysis
Qualification System
Make-or-Buy Plan
Material Control
Manufacturing Process Control
Procurement Management
Quality Control & Test Plan
Quality Controls
Failure Analysis
Value Engineering
Configuration Management
Data Management
Logistics/Support Management
Facilities Management
Cost Management
Schedule Management
Audits

Now, as any seasoned manager in a customer or contractor organization knows, when it comes to a management practice, what counts most is not "what's up front" on its label, but what's in it to ferret out program weaknesses and to lower the risks of failure. To this end, the following five fundamental questions are addressed to each management practices area:

What actions are involved?
Who is responsible?
When are these actions to take place?
What format is to be followed?
What follow-up action ensues?

Accordingly, each of the twenty-one management practices are appraised by filling in a checklist of significant requirements. Space has been provided on each checklist for commenting on mitigating circumstances; the overall risk for the function under consideration is then judged, based on the answers to the detailed questions. The same four gradations of risk are used here as in the risk appraisal of "Resource Limitations." The checklist concept used here serves the same purpose as checklists used by pilots in various phases of their flight, or the item-by-item checkout approach used in launch operations.

RAPS IMPLEMENTATION

When should RAP System Implementation begin? As soon as the program team has been organized and operating. The implementation starts with an "Initial Appraisal" that establishes a plan by the Program Manager, and a Risk Appraisal by the program team. Subsequent re-appraisals are made on a periodic basis, generally quarterly. The risk levels and the actions taken to attenuate major risks can then be displayed in reference to the basic plan.

Essentially, here's what the "Initial Appraisal" does:

(1) Establishes a Risk Plan by the Program Manager, as to the risk level acceptable for the "Resource Limitation" factors, and the extent to which the low-risk management practices are to be used. These risk levels together make a "profile" line on the RAPS presentation.

(2) Determines the level of risk for each major hardware end item (generally a subsystem) by "Resource Limitation" factor; also determines the level of risk in each management practices area. Risk levels are assigned depending on the extent the low-risk practices are planned for use.

All appraisals are made by the team members responsible for the hardware item or function involved. "Resource Limitations" checklists are completed for each subsystem by each responsible person in Engineering, Manufacturing, and Quality Control. These are consolidated by subsystem, to review the commonality of the risk estimates and consistency of recommendations made to deal with them.

One of the attributes of the RAP System is that it lends itself to summarization and to tab runs. The data may be recorded on cards so that tab runs can be made by:

Hardware end-item or technology
Resource limitation factor
Gradation of risk
Organization function submitting the data

As a result, the similarity between symptoms, problems and recommendations can easily be recognized and generalized for discussion. The Risk Appraisal for the total program is then formulated by aggregating and summarizing the subsystem appraisals.

Appraisal data is arrayed on a chart with columns set up for each of the four risk levels; the left hand side defines the dual look at risk —the seven Resource Limitations factors followed by the 21 Management Practices areas; the field displays the Program Manager's Plan as a profile line and the percent of appraisals at a given risk level in tabulated form. Percentages exceeding the plan are shaded for emphasis. The scheme for reading the RAPS chart is shown below. This chart is a typical example of a Risk Appraisal. The adjacent RAPS chart is used as a part of the Program Appraisal and Review (PAR) System presentation. As evident in the right half of this data chart, analytical comments are confined to terse statements on risks, as well as the action planned for reducing them.

This chart initially concentrates management attention on planned risks and the basis for the plan; and later it focuses on the extent to which the appraised risks differ from the plan.

BENEFITS, PRESENT AND FUTURE

In essence, then, the benefits of the RAP System can be summarized as follows:

Helps focus management attention on major risk areas.
Provides an opportunity for offering recommendations to lower excessive risks.
Assists management in evaluating how the overall job is being done.

There are also additional side-benefits to performing risk appraisals on a formal, written basis: it improves communications with program management and provides that often-needed memory jog to follow proven practices. Also when problems and suggested solutions are committed to paper, these are less suscepti-

ble to being swept under a carpet of complacency.

The RAPS management system has been used on seven programs in the Division and on the entire activities of the Mississippi Test Support Department. Furthermore it is planned for use on all new major or critical programs in the Division.

This type of look has resulted in program adjustments to accomplish additional analyses, reallocate hardware for qualification, and change funding release dates. In the words of Bob Hammond, Manager of Ballistic System Programs, Re-entry Systems Dept., who has used RAPS on two programs in his Section: "RAPS highlights problem aspects which are not always readily visible. Particularly in view of time limitations this structured approach to looking at a program's problems can be a real help. My program managers are, of course, extremely close to their programs, but even for them this technique may present the problem in a fresh light and in total, provide a useful checklist for the program."

RAPS can provide an effective tool for communicating the risk picture on a program to the customer. It offers the opportunity to jointly review the risks—be they inherent or imposed. RAPS can thus promote full understanding of the approaches and methods to be used to achieve program objectives.

Possibly among the unexplored areas of activity which may in the future furnish fertile grounds for customer applications of this basic idea, are Source Selection and Program Definition. If used in connection with Requests for Proposals, RAPS might improve the definition and presentation of development and management plans. This could contribute to the further refinement of "tools" used in evaluating and comparing proposals.

Systems Program Management procedures are now being required on many of the new contracts awarded by the DOD. The "Self-auditing" feature of the RAPS technique is particularly adaptable to Systems Program Management, for example in identifying compliance with the Air Force 375 requirements, RAPS could be used both by industry and System Program Offices, in addition to independent surveys for identifying compliance with 375.

Presently, the Management Practices check-

DESIGN REVIEW
RISK ESTIMATE CHECKLIST   DATE:_____

PROGRAM:_____

ITEM: _____   _____
    (System, Sub-System, Component or Other Name)   Drawing No.

1. At what point in the program was design review scheduled and conducted?
  a) Before Stage Release I. . . . . . Yes ( ) No ( )   c) Before Stage Release III. . . . . Yes ( ) No ( )
  b) Before Stage Release II . . . . Yes ( ) No ( )   d) Before Stage Release IV. . . . . Yes ( ) No ( )

2. Were advanced checklists sent to the engineer and properly completed?. . . . . Yes ( ) No ( )

3. Were suitable data supplied to the Design Review Office by responsible parties a reasonable
  time before the review? (Check One)
  a) Yes. . . . . ( )   b) Data not timely. . . . . ( )   c) No. . . . . ( )

4) Was item definition provided to design review participants early enough to permit study? (Check One)
  a) Yes. . . . ( )   b) Marginal. . . . . ( )   c) No. . . . . ( )

5. Which of the following technical items were covered adequately during the design review?
  a) Basic approach or features. . . . . . ( )   m) Maintainability analysis. . . . . ( )
  b) Relation to "state-of-the-art". . . . . ( )   n) Parts Application Review . . . . ( )
  c) Anticipated problems . . . . ( )   o) Design safety factor analysis . . . . ( )
  d) Development required . . . . ( )   p) Tolerance analysis . . . . ( )
  e) Development plans . . . . ( )   q) Utilization of specification design
  f) Aerodynamic analysis . . . . ( )   standards applicable to program . . . . ( )
  g) Stress, vibration & other   r) Development tests . . . . ( )
    mechanical analyses. . . . . ( )   s) Qualification tests . . . . ( )
  h) Thermal analysis . . . . ( )   t) Manufacturing plan . . . . ( )
  i) Electrical analysis. . . . . ( )   u) Schedule information . . . . ( )
  j) Life analysis . . . . ( )   v) Cost information . . . . ( )
  k) Reliability analysis . . . . ( )   w) Quantity control plan. . . . . ( )
  l) Trade-off analysis, including costs. . ( )   x) Test plan . . . . ( )

6. Was the design review attended by the following technical personnel?
  a) Design Engineer . . . . Yes ( ) No ( )   f) Producibility. . . . . Yes ( ) No ( )
  b) Next Product Level Designer . . Yes ( ) No ( )   g) Manufacturing . . . . Yes ( ) No ( )
  c) System Engineer . . . . Yes ( ) No ( )   h) Qualified Consultant (not
  d) Reliability . . . . Yes ( ) No ( )   working on this Program). . . . Yes ( ) No ( )
  e) Quality Control . . . . Yes ( ) No ( )

7. Were minutes and action item records published? (Check One)
  a) No . . . . ( )   c) Yes, usually in 1 to 2 weeks. . . . . ( )
  b) Yes, usually in over 2 weeks . . . . . ( )   d) Yes, usually within 1 week . . . . ( )

8. Did the design review accomplish or provide:
  a) Assurance of design feasibility? Yes ( ) No ( )   e) Assurance that input and output
  b) Adequate producibility? . . . . . Yes ( ) No ( )   requirements and tolerances are
  c) Reliability assurance? . . . . . Yes ( ) No ( )   compatible with next design
  d) Proper consideration of trade-   level . . . . Yes ( ) No ( )
    off factors . . . . Yes ( ) No ( )

9. What has been the response to action items from prior related design reviews? (Check One)
  a) Performance is always timely and   c) Performance is sometimes
    effective . . . . ( )   inadequate . . . . ( )
  b) Performance is usually adequate   d) Action item response is generally
    technically and timely. . . . . ( )   unsatisfactory . . . . ( )
                                           e) Not applicable. . . . . ( )

COMMENTS: (Use Reverse Side or Additional Sheets if required)

DESIGN REVIEW – OVERALL RISK ESTIMATE _ _ _ _ _ _ _ _ _ _   HIGH   MOD.   MINOR   LOW

                                                                   ☐   ☐   ☐   ☐

Name/Title Estimator:_____

Form E

Figure 33-2

list used in RAPS is being expanded to cover the 375 procedures. This same approach could possibly be used by a System Program Director and his staff to assess the overall risk in the early phases of a program. Both the System Contractor and the System Program Office could thus complete their separate appraisals and compare their risk profiles. The incorporation of key procedural requirements in checklist form could prove a valuable aid to the Contractor's Program Managers and to the System Program Offices alike.

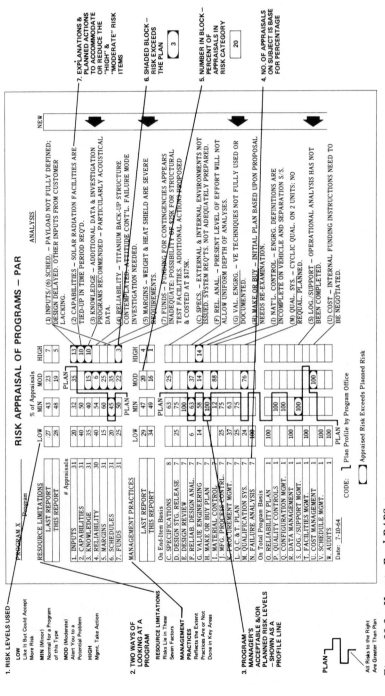

Figure 33-3   How to Read RAPS.

SECTION 9

ORGANIZATION CHARTING

The development of traditional management theory has involved a constant search for a universal organizational concept. Much of the controversy reflected in the literature centers around the attempts to perpetuate the hierarchical model of the organization. Verticality of management practice is apparent in such principles as unity of command, parity of authority and responsibility, the scalar chain, and functional authority. Advocates of the hierarchical model are characterized by their dependence on a nucleus of principles designed to preserve the sanctity of the vertical organization. The concept of the informal organization has been used to explain the unstructured community of people having reciprocal peer relationships in the organization.

There is a growing awareness in management literature of the propriety of peer-colleague relationships in accomplishing organized effort. We have not suddenly discovered these relationships, but we are beginning to see evidence of attempts to develop charting techniques to formalize them.

One might well question the value of the traditional charting methods as a means of analyzing organizational relationships. Perhaps the most frequent complaint about pyramidal organization charts is that they fail to portray the interrelationships of people in their day-to-day activities. But we must remember that the pyramid chart has considerable value in showing how the organization is functionally structured.

The value of linear responsibility charts, systematized linear charts, and the other techniques discussed in this section lie in the fact that such methods go beyond functional, formal lines of authority. These newer methods provide a means of displaying the coordinative interrelationships that unify the basic functional activities.

READING 34

ROLES AND RELATIONSHIPS: CLARIFYING THE MANAGER'S JOB*

Robert D. Melcher

Far too many companies cherish the myth that the publication of organization charts and position descriptions will resolve the majority of problems relating to the role each manager plays in relationship to his work group and to the organization. The organization chart does show basic divisions of work and who reports to whom, but it does not depict detailed functions and how individuals relate to these functions; in other words, it does not show how the organization actually works. The position description delineates the detailed task to be performed, but it cannot show how the organization really functions, either. Position descriptions are far more concerned with defining an individual's tasks than with how, in carrying out his responsibilities, he interacts with his colleagues. The way in which management positions are described often indicates com-

* Reprinted with permission from Personnel, vol. 44, no. 3, May-June, 1967. Copyright 1967 by American Management Association Inc.

plete independence from other positions—and, more often than not, independent action instead of group participation is encouraged. As a result, there is no opportunity to build a framework that can be used to relate and integrate each manager and the work he does to the organization and its goals.

The human-relations approach to resolving problems relating to interpersonal and intergroup relations concentrates primarily on behavioral approaches and experiences involving sensitivity training sessions, group problem-solving and goal-setting courses, and similar techniques. The primary purpose of the behavioral approach is to develop an awareness within each individual of his own behavioral characteristics, to increase his understanding of the underlying cause of intergroup conflict, and to develop techniques and approaches that can in some way help improve the individual's working relationships.

Unfortunately, many of these human-relations approaches do not involve the work group. Even when the work group is involved, the subject matter seldom relates specifically to the various working roles and relationships of the members of the group. Hence there is little opportunity for the group to focus on their work interface problems and put to productive use the techniques and skills gained through human-relations training experiences —and when experiences cannot be put to use, their value is soon lost.

PLANNING AND PARTICIPATION

A sound and successful organization development process requires a planned, systematic approach that encourages management involvement and participation. In order to meet these criteria and strengthen the organization development process, a number of companies have utilized an approach that enables each manager to actively participate with his superiors, peers, and subordinates in systematically describing the managerial job to be done and then clarifying the role each manager plays in relationship to his work group and to the organization.

The tool that evolved has been called the Management Responsibility Guide. Its development was sparked by a linear charting technique, developed by Ernest Hijams and Serge A. Bern, that is used to relate management positions, functions, and responsibility relationships to each other. Although their Linear Responsibility Chart can be used to describe roles and relationships, its use seems to be somewhat limited, because the functions are not systematically structured and the approach does not actively involve members of the work group in resolving their roles and responsibility relationships. Without a planned and systematic approach, it is very difficult to group and relate managerial functions in the manner best suited to aid an organization to objectively solve its organizational problems. And without the active involvement of the work group, there is little opportunity to actually resolve differences and improve communications. It was out of the recognition that the mating of a behavioral sciences approach to a systems framework was essential, if role and relationship resolution was to take place, that the Management Responsibility Guide approach evolved.

Within every organization there exist specialized managerial tasks or functions that must be acted upon if the organization is to attain its objectives and goals. At the higher management levels, these managerial functions tend to be described in objective-oriented terms; at each subsequent lower level, these functions are broken into more detailed functions and are defined in more task-oriented terms. To be meaningful, these functions must be structured and phrased in a manner that not only describes the managerial functions but highlights the role and relationship problems that need to be clarified and resolved by each work group. Only after the objective delineation and definition of these essential managerial functions have been completed should each manager's responsibility relationships be developed. How each manager's view of his responsibility relationship to each function and each person is resolved determines how effectively the organization works—or does not work.

SEMANTIC SOLUTIONS

One of the primary problems impeding the process of role and relationship resolution is that of developing a set of terms that describe the various responsibility relationships in a way that is meaningful and acceptable to the group. Although there are many responsibility relationship terms that could be developed for a specific organization, the following seven definitions seem to meet the communication requirements of most organizations and, along with the defined functions, serve as a common focal point for the work group:

A. *General Responsibility*—The individual guides and directs the execution of the function through the person delegated operating responsibility.
B. *Operating Responsibility*—The individual is directly responsible for the execution of the function.
C. *Specific Responsibility*—The individual is responsible for executing a specific or limited portion of the function.
D. *Must Be Consulted*—The individual, if the decision affects his area, must be called upon before any decision is made or approval is granted, to render advice or relate information, but not to make the decision or grant approval.

E. *May Be Consulted*—The individual may be called upon to relate information, render advice, or make recommendations.
F. *Must Be Notified*—The individual must be notified of action that has been taken.
G. *Must Approve*—The individual (other than persons holding general and operating responsibility) must approve or disapprove.

It is obvious that a format is required that can be used to relate the organization's managerial functions, positions, and responsibility relationships to each other—and this is where the Management Responsibility Guide format makes its contribution.

DEVELOPING THE GUIDE

How the Management Responsibility Guide is developed by the work group is as important to its successful completion as the elements that it comprises. The first and perhaps most important step pertains to how the work group views and relates to the process that is to take place. Ordinarily, someone outside the work group is needed to work with the group as a consultant in developing the functions and serving as a resource. More often than not, there is a high degree of skepticism within the work group regarding the role of the consultant and his ability to actually help them, as well as considerable concern on each person's part as to how his status will be affected. Because each member of the work group must be afforded the opportunity to understand the process and to express his feelings, a group briefing session should first be held to explain the entire process and ground rules. Questions about the process and its underlying concepts and purposes should be encouraged by the manager of the work group and the consultant.

The functions of the work group can now be developed. Each member of the group is individually interviewed and given the opportunity to describe his job and any problems he wants the consultant to be aware of. In this fact-gathering and problem-definition phase, it is essential that the focus be directed toward objectively describing and grouping managerial functions that logically belong or relate to the same family, regardless of who presently is responsible. If responsibility relationships are also discussed at this time, emotion and subjectivity enter the picture and the probability

of objectively delineating what needs to be done is poor. When questions relating to responsibility relationships are raised, the person raising them should be advised that he will have the opportunity to express his views fully at a later stage in the process.

A DOUBLE CHECK

After the key functions have been defined to the satisfaction of each manager, the consultant reviews all the defined functions with the managers' superior and, if necessary, revises the definitions to the satisfaction of the superior and each of the subordinates concerned.

The point has now been reached where the responsibility relationships can be developed. Each individual within the work group is given, in the Management Responsibility Guide format, a list of all functions developed for the group and is requested to enter the relationship code or codes that best express what he thinks his responsibility relationship to each function should be. He is further instructed that if he assigns an operating responsibility (B) to himself for a function, he should enter what he thinks should be the responsibility relationship of all other managers who should have a relationship to that function. In addition, he is requested to review each function and make whatever change in the wording he deems necessary.

After the forms are completed, they are returned to the consultant and the various points of view are entered on a master copy. The chart in Figure 34-1 shows how the master copy might look after the views of all members of the group have been entered on it. (In this case, the group concerned is a large division of the company; other charts would break down each of the functions in more detail and would list managers at lower levels of the organization. This division, in turn, would represent one of the functions on a chart indicating top management's roles and responsibilities.) For each function, the top line of symbols represents the point of view of the person who has indicated that he holds operating responsibility (B) for that function. The symbols in the second line represent the point of view of the person whose position title appears at the top of the column. Since two people considered that they had operating responsibility for the

MANAGEMENT POSITION

NUMBER	FUNCTION	Vice President Aerospace	Vice President Manufacturing	Director Engineering	Manager Technology	Manager Quality Assurance	Manager Marketing	Manager Contracts	Manager Master Scheduling	Manager Financial Services
10.1	Coordinate division budgeting & financial planning activities & communicate financial information to division management.	A / AF	EF / DF	EF / E	EF / F	EF / EF	EF / E	E / D	B	
10.2	Develop project & program schedule requirements, establish, coordinate & control schedules & report on status.	A / A	EF / D (○)	EF / DF	EF / C	EF / D (○)	EF / D	B	EF / E	
10.3	Direct contract activities & evaluate & approve contract provisions of all division sales proposals & contract documents.	A / A	E		E	EF / D (○)	B	EF / DF (○)	EF / C (○)	
10.4	Plan & coordinate divisional marketing activities so as to secure the business necessary to maximize division's capabilities.	A / AD	EF / F	EF	E	B	DF / CG (○)	EF / CD (○)	F / F	
10.5	Develop & design new, & improve existing, electronic & electro-mechanical aerospace products & processes.	A / AF	F / E	B	E	E / DG				
10.6	Secure materials & tools, coordinate manpower & manufacture products to specified quantity, time & cost requirements.	A / A	B	E	F / CD (○)	EF / E	EF / E	F / F	EF / E	
10.7	Establish quality assurance policies, procedures & controls to insure that products meet applicable standards & specifications.	A / A	DF / DG (○)	E / E	B	F / E	EF / D	EF	F	
10.8	Develop & design proprietary products & processes utilizing proven technology specifically adapted to industrial automation.	A / AF / A	C / B / E	B / DF (○)	E	E / EF / DF	D / E / EF / DF	F / E / F	F / F	

RELATIONSHIP CODE

A GENERAL RESPONSIBILITY
B OPERATING RESPONSIBILITY
C SPECIFIC RESPONSIBILITY
D MUST BE CONSULTED
E MAY BE CONSULTED
F MUST BE NOTIFIED
G MUST APPROVE

ORGANIZATION IDENTIFICATION	NUMBER		DATE	PAGE
Aerospace	200	MANAGEMENT RESPONSIBILITY GUIDE © R. MELCHER 1967		NO 1 OF 1
Aerospace Division		APPROVAL		

Figure 34-1

function on line 10.8, the first two lines represent their points of view, and the third line represents the views of the individuals at the tops of the column. The symbols that are circled indicate major conflicts between the viewpoints of the person with operating responsibility and those at the tops of the columns.

RESOLVING CONFLICTS

After an analysis of the responses has been completed, a determination must be made as to how best to resolve any divergent points of view that have been brought to the surface. At this stage the personalities and backgrounds of the people in the work group influence what is to be done.

One approach is to allow each member of the work group to review the varying points of view, then bring them together at a group meeting to collectively clarify and resolve differences. This approach has the distinct advantage of getting the full participation and involvement of each member of the work group. Ordinarily, interpersonal differences related to the day-to-day job content never get aired; this process permits each member of the group to present his position, and more often than not the individuals themselves resolve differences without their superior's having to intervene or make a decision.

This process is highly educational; it gives each member of the group a better understanding of the interaction that must take place in order for the group to function effectively. Moreover, the superior has an opportunity to sit back and view how his organization operates and how the members of his staff relate to one another.

Of course, there may be sensitive situations that are better handled or resolved on a superior-subordinate basis, but, for the most part, group participation and involvement seem to be more effective. No matter what approach is taken, the objective should be to get differences into the open and encourage the individuals themselves to clarify and resolve their roles and responsibility relationships.

The same general approach is used to resolve differences between work groups. After the group members have reached agreement on their roles and responsibility relationships, other individuals or groups are asked to indicate what they think their responsibility relationships should be to each of the functions. As before, differences between the groups that have been brought to the surface can then be resolved, and copies of the form indicating the agreed-upon roles and responsibility relationships are then issued to each member of the work groups as well as to other members of management within the company. Figure 34-2 shows how the chart might appear after divergent views have been reconciled and the relationships with managers outside the work group have been entered.

The Management Responsibility Guide, as its name indicates, is only a guide; it reflects the work group's view as to how they agreed to work with one another at a specific point in time. Conditions continually change and the Management Responsibility Guide, like any other management tool, should be periodically reviewed and updated.

SOME APPLICATIONS

Because the Management Responsibility Guide serves to clarify and resolve problems relating to working relationships, it can be a means of solving problems relating to duplication of effort and overlapping of responsibility; conversely, it can be used to identify responsibility gaps within the organization. It provides an objective way to bring sensitive relationship problems into the open and helps establish a common understanding of each function and each individual's or group's role in the organization.

The guide can also be used as a means of instituting managerial controls and pinning down responsibilities. Since objective consideration can be given to an individual's strengths and weaknesses, in relation to each function, management is able to tighten or loosen controls as well as clearly determine who is responsible for a given function.

As an organization analysis tool, there are a number of uses. For example, in a management audit, the Management Responsibility Guide can be analyzed to determine workload balance, pattern of delegation, and shifting of responsibility due to cutbacks, additions, or other changes in the workload. Since functions and responsibility relationships are delineated in an orderly and systematic manner, management is able to evaluate the impact of

NUMBER	FUNCTION	President	Vice President Aerospace	Vice President Manufacturing	Director Engineering	Manager Ind'l Technology	Manager Quality Assurance	Manager Marketing	Manager Contracts	Manager Master Scheduling	Manager Fin. Services	Treasurer & Controller	Vice President Earth Sciences	Vice President Test Laboratories	Manager Ind'l Relations	RELATIONSHIP CODE
10.1	Coordinate division budgeting & financial planning activities & communicate financial information to division management.	A-F	E-F	E-F	E-F	E-F	E-F	E-F	D	(B)	D-F					**A** GENERAL RESPONSIBILITY
10.2	Develop project & program schedule requirements, establish, coordinate & control schedules & report on status.	A	D-F	D	D-F	D-F	E-F	E-F	(B)	F						**B** OPERATING RESPONSIBILITY
10.3	Direct contract activities & evaluate & approve contract provisions of all division sales proposals & contract documents.	A-F	E	E	E	E	D-F	(B)	E-F	F	E-F	E	E			**C** SPECIFIC RESPONSIBILITY
10.4	Plan & coordinate divisional marketing activities so as to secure the business necessary to maximize division's capabilities.	A-D	E-F	E-F	E-F	E	(B)	D-F	D-F	F	E-F	E				**D** MUST BE CONSULTED
10.5	Develop & design new, & improve existing, electronic & electro-mechanical aerospace products & processes.	E-F	E-F	E	E	E	D-F			E				E		**E** MAY BE CONSULTED
10.6	Secure materials & tools, coordinate manpower & manufacture products to specified quantity, time & cost requirements.	A	(B)	E	E	D-F		E	E-F	E	E-F					**F** MUST BE NOTIFIED
10.7	Establish quality assurance policies, procedures & controls to insure that products meet applicable standards & specifications.	A	D-F	D-F	E	(B)	E-F	D-F	E-F	F						**G** MUST APPROVE
10.8	Develop & design proprietary products & processes utilizing proven technology specifically adapted to industrial automation.	A-F	E	E	(B)	E	E-F	D-F	E-F	F						

ORGANIZATION IDENTIFICATION	NUMBER 200	MANAGEMENT RESPONSIBILITY GUIDE © R. MELCHER 1967	DATE	PAGE
Aerospace Aerospace Division		APPROVAL		NO. 1 OF 1

Figure 34-2

major staffing changes and, accordingly, can quickly realign functions and responsibility relationships.

EVALUATING PERFORMANCE

One of the more difficult aspects of evaluating performance is establishing the criteria on which performance is to be judged. Since functions and relationships are systematically delineated, it is possible to use the Management Responsibility Guide as a basis for evaluating performance. The systematic delineation of functions has similar advantages in the field of systems and procedures. At the lower echelons of an organization, functions tend to be described in task-oriented terms; hence, the job of the analyst is simplified, for with the clarification of responsibility relationships, the analyst need only describe the work in greater detail.

Position guides, at best, describe the general responsibilities of a position and generally do not consider organization levels or specific management relationships. Manually, or through the use of data processing techniques, a new type of "guide" can be prepared—one that can be updated instantly and that simultaneously considers organization level, functions, positions, and responsibility relationships. In a similar manner, programs relating to managerial experience inventories and the cross-referencing of similar or identical functions can be instituted.

PARTICIPATION IS THE KEY

Over the past five years, the Management Responsibility Guide has been used in some 30 organizations ranging from large to small, in industry and government, as an aid in solving a variety of management problems relating to managerial roles and relationships. One of the primary reasons for its success is the fact that managers at all levels were drawn into the process and actively participated in resolving problems in which they were personally involved. In each organization, this approach has provided a dynamic means of objectively describing the work to be done and clarifying the role each manager plays in it—and it has proved to be a major factor in improving management communications and interpersonal and intergroup relations.

READING 35

WHAT'S NOT ON THE ORGANIZATION CHART*

Harold Stieglitz

Organization charts come in various sizes, colors and even textures. Most are black and white and printed on paper. Some are affixed to office walls—and made of materials that are easily changed. Some charts are highly detailed; some are very sketchy. Some are stamped *confidential* and secreted in the desks of a chosen few; others are broadly distributed and easily available. Despite these and other variations that might be noted, all organization charts have at least one thing in common: they don't show how the organization works. Or, as some people say, they don't show the *real* organization.

Such a statement, which usually emerges as a criticism of organization charts, goes beyond the fact that the organization chart, like milk, may be dated but not fresh. For it is increasingly understood that no organization chart is 100% current. Rather, the criticism is that

even the most current chart is utterly inadequate as a diagram of the organization.

Few organization planners, even those whose major preoccupation is drawing charts, argue too vehemently against this criticism. They just go on drawing their charts. Most often, the charts they draw are of the conventional type made up of boxes and lines. These usually end up in a pyramidal shape with a box (generally larger) at the top to represent the chief executive.

However, behind the preparation and issuance of the chart, there is, presumably, this basic understanding: An organization chart is not an organization. And there is far more to an organization—even in the limited sense of an organization structure—than can ever be put on a chart.

But while the chartist himself may be aware of it, this knowledge is seldom pervasive. Some companies recognize this and attempt to underscore the fact that a chart is just a two-dimensional representation by placing the following caution at the bottom of the chart:

* Reprinted with permission from The Conference Board Record, *September, 1964. Copyright 1964 by National Industrial Conference Board.*

Level of boxes shows reporting relationships and has no significance with regard to importance of position or status.

Such a caution or demurrer is seldom sufficient to quiet the critics or unruffle ruffled feathers, and is quite often taken with a large grain of salt—sometimes because the chart does show some of the very things that the demurrer may say it doesn't. If nothing else, for example, the head of a unit that doesn't appear on an organization chart can be reasonably sure that his unit is not rated important enough to merit inclusion.

Actually, the conventional organization chart (see the chart) shows very little. It implies a little more than it shows. But the inferences that are drawn from it are limited only by the experience, imagination and biases of the beholder—in or outside of the company. In other words, one of the troubles with charts seems to be the people who read them.

WHAT IT SHOWS

The organization chart of most companies shows—indeed is designed to show—just two things:

1 Division of work into components. These components may be divisions or depart-

ments or they may be individuals. Boxes on the conventional chart represent these units of work.

2 Who is (supposed to be) whose boss—the solid lines on the chart show this superior-subordinate relationship with its implied flow of delegated responsibility, authority and attendant accountability.

Implicit in these two are several other things that the chart is designed to show:

3 Nature of the work performed by the component. Depending upon the descriptive title placed in the box, what this shows may be specific (Facilities Engineering), speculative (Planning) or spurious (Special Projects).

4 Grouping of components on a functional, regional or product basis. This is also conveyed to some extent by the labels in the boxes.

5 Levels of management in terms of successive layers of superiors and subordinates. All persons or units that report to the same person are on one level. The fact that they may be charted on different horizontal planes does not, of course, change the level.

It is rather difficult to pinpoint anything else about a structure that is actually shown on an organization chart. Some may argue whether, in fact, even the few items above can be read directly from any or some charts.

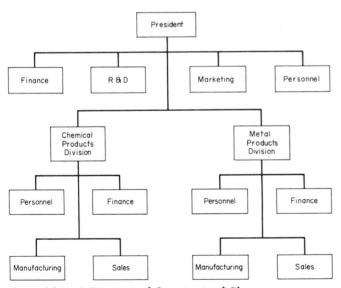

Figure 35-1 A Conventional Organizational Chart.

WHAT THE CHART DOESN'T SHOW

What an organization chart doesn't show is often the most interesting part of the chart—at least to the internal personnel. And it is the inferences that arise from what's missing which companies attempt to deal with in their demurrers or cautions. The demurrers, as already suggested, don't always scotch the inferences. In many cases, the warnings may be erroneous or incomplete.

Degree of Responsibility and Authority

Take, for example, this caution: "Size and position of boxes do not indicate degree of responsibility or authority." Well, it is quite possible that they do. Indeed in the mere process of showing superior-subordinate relationships, the chart does clearly imply varying degrees of responsibility and authority. This is implicit in the process of delegation.

A possibly more accurate demurrer might be "any relationship between size and position of boxes and degree of responsibility and authority may be coincidental, accidental or just plain odd." For what the chart clearly does not show is the degree of responsibility and authority exercised by positions on the same management level. Two persons on the same management level may have vastly different degrees of authority. A man on the third level may have more or less authority than a second-level manager in a different chain of delegation.

Of course, because the chart cannot adequately begin to depict varying degrees of authority, it cannot show the degree of decentralization. Decentralization, organizationally speaking, has relevance only in terms of delegation of decision-making authority. Almost by definition, it refers to the level at which decisions are made.

Inferences about decentralization are often drawn from charts; the company chart that shows activities grouped into product divisions or regional divisions as opposed to a purely functional grouping is often referred to as decentralized. That may or may not be the case. The view from the top may be of a highly decentralized company; the view from the bottom or intermediate layers may be quite the opposite. And a functionally organized company can be as highly decentralized as a divisionally organized company. It all depends on the level at which decisions are being made. The chart cannot depict that, nor can it depict the extent of the restrictions—in the form of policies, budgets, procedures, reports, audits— that make for more or less decentralization.

Staff and Line

Distinguishing between staff and line is an arduous, hazardous, and so far as some organization planners are concerned, an academic chore. Attempting to determine line and staff from an organization chart presents similar hazards. Titles or functional labels alone won't do it. What one company considers line may be staff to another. Again, it depends on the responsibility and authority delegated to the units.

Of course, the nature of the company's business may have clues to what is staff or line. In a manufacturing company, for example, certain functions are traditionally viewed as staff: personnel administration, public relations, legal and secretarial, and finance are examples. In a services company the arrangement may be quite different. But reliance on the nature of the business can be misleading. In manufacturing, for example, divisionalization has brought into being staff units with labels such as manufacturing and marketing—labels that typically would belong to line components in a functionally organized firm.

In some companies, charting methods are used to attempt to distinguish what these firms consider to be line and staff (or service and operating) units. Sometimes the so-called staff units are charted on one horizontal plane, line on another. Other companies use skinny little lines to connect staff, healthier looking lines to connect line or operating units. Still others add labels to underscore this visual aid.

With all these visual distinctions, a chart reader might readily infer what is obviously being implied: there is a difference between the two types of units. To try to interpret these differences in terms of line-staff responsibilities, authorities, and relationships presents the same difficulties as reading the degree of decentralization from the chart.

Status or Importance

To some people, inclusion on the organization chart is, in itself, a status symbol. The physical location on the chart—the linear distance from the chief executive—is viewed as a measure of importance. And there's the rub. Given the limitations of a piece of paper, not everyone can be charted equidistant from the chief executive. Reassurances like "size and position of boxes do not reflect importance or status" are seldom reassuring enough. The incumbent charted in a particular spot may realize the truth of this statement; but he may fear that the "other fellows may not," or vice versa.

There is little question but that position on an organization chart, in some companies, does imply relative importance and status. But it has the same limitations in implying (or covering up lack of) importance as do size of office, titles, parking lot space, etc. Most people still rely on the pay envelope as a more accurate reflection of relative importance. And the organization chart just isn't designed to reflect the pay structure of the company.

In short, the organization chart may imply relative importance or status, but, to rephrase a caution that might appear on a chart, "Any inferences drawn from this chart regarding relative importance or status may or may not be correct."

Lines of Communication

Another caution that shows up is: "This chart does not indicate channels of contact." Actually it does. What it doesn't show is *all* the channels of contact or communication. Possibly a more appropriate warning might be: "This chart indicates a few of the major channels of contact—but if the organization sticks to only these, nothing will get done." For it is a truism of organization that no one unit or individual operates in isolation from all the others. All are linked by an intricate network of communication. (Maze may be a more apt term than network.) Proper organization performance relies on this network and on each unit and individual becoming party to it. To chart the total network is practically impossible. To attempt to chart it—and thus introduce certain rigidities into it—might easily frustrate its workings.

Relationships

In a real sense, lines of communication are really relationships. "You can't have one without the other"—and the picture of either that

shows up on the chart is that of only a few key links in the total network.

Any organization is a hotbed of relationships. Not all of them, of course, necessarily grow out of the nature of the work of the company. Even those that do, however, do not show up on the conventional or even unconventional organization chart.

On occasion a company has noted: "This chart shows relationships only and does not represent levels of management." The caution may have been on the wrong chart, for on the chart in question the opposite seemed true.

More frequently the company notes: "This chart shows reporting relationships only. . . ." Even this seems questionable—it is accurate only if the phrase reporting relationships is understood to mean superior-subordinate reporting relationships.

Organizational relationships—as opposed to social, etc. relationships within a company—grow out of the division of work and delegation of responsibility and authority. A number of functional relationships, authority relationships, staff-line relationships, and just plain work relationships may come into play in reaching any decision or in completing any given piece of work. Most companies long ago gave up any attempt to even begin to show all of these relationships on a chart.

The "Informal" Organization

To some people, that mystical entity known as the "informal" organization is the *real* organization. *It* is how things really get done.

The *it* referred to, however, may be any number of things, depending upon the point of view. To narrow it to just two types—there is the "informal" organization and the *informal* organization.

The "informal" organization, in this makeshift dichotomy, encompasses all relationships and channels of communication that mature, reasonable people are expected to develop and use in order to meet organizational objectives. As mature, reasonable people, they are expected, of course, to also respect their superior's need to be kept informed of matters affecting his area of accountability. This "informal" organization is viewed as a logical and necessary extension of the formal organization. It is informal only in the sense that nobody has found it necessary to inundate the organization with memorabilia that fully spell out its workings.

The *informal* organization, on the other hand, encompasses all the relationships, communication channels, and influences or power centers that mature, reasonable people develop because a lot of other people in the organization are not mature and reasonable—"especially the bosses who needn't be informed because they'll only say 'no.' " Rather than being a logical extension of the formal organization, it comes into being because the formal organization is viewed as being illogical or inflexible or inefficient or just plain inconsistent with the personal and possibly organizational objectives being worked toward. This *informal* organization, according to "informal" organization specialists, gets work done in spite of the formal organization.

Neither shows up on the organization chart: the "informal" because it's too complex to be reduced to a two-dimensional chart; the *informal* because that would make it formal—a heresy that would immediately give rise to another *informal* organization.

For those not fully satisfied with this dichotomy, there may be a third type—the INFORMAL organization. It includes parts of the "informal" and *informal*. By definition, it covers everything not shown on the organization chart; by definition, it can't be charted.

THE INADEQUATE CHART

Attempts to revamp the conventional organization chart in order to overcome these and other limitations have produced many examples of modern, nonobjective art (Alexander Calder's mobiles have been mistaken for organization charts.) There is the circular chart (and its variants) designed to better convey internal relationships and to better camouflage "status." There is the chart with the vertical lines between boxes stretched to reflect similar levels of responsibility or similar levels of pay (scrapped after first attempt—required too long a sheet of paper). There is the chart with the pyramid up-ended to reflect the true flow of authority—from subordinates to superiors (scrapped after first attempt—"That's rubbing it in").

Despite all its limitations, the conventional chart is increasingly used to depict the skeletal structure of the organization. For more complete documentation of what this chart means, companies rely on position guides, linear responsibility charts, statements of general responsibilities and relationships—indeed, the whole organization manual.

The essential value of the chart seems to lie in the fact that it does strip the organization to the skeletal framework. In so doing, it serves a useful purpose both as a tool of organizational analysis and a means of communication.[1] As a complete picture of the organization, it is recognized as being completely inadequate. But it evidently is less inadequate than most substitutes.

---

[1] See "*Charting the Company Organization Structure*," Studies in Personnel Policy, *No. 168, for detailed description of charts and their uses.*

READING 36

LINEAR RESPONSIBILITY CHART—NEW TOOL FOR EXECUTIVE CONTROL *

Alfred G. Larke

Every now and then, somebody comes up with an idea so obvious that everybody understands it, and many good men ask themselves, "How could I have overlooked it?" Some, in fact, always wonder if anything so simple could be good, just because it is simple.

The originators of a new and graphic method of analyzing and recording organizational structure, job content, and functional operating responsibilities, seem to have come up with just such a simplification of a number of management control devices.

Called the Linear Responsibility Chart, it compacts within the limits of a single sheet of graph paper much if not most of the information that normally would require dozens of pages of organization manual, organization charts, operating or responsibility flow charts, and job description write-ups to record by usual methods.

The mere packing of a lot of information into a small space does not, of course, necessarily make it more readily available or easier to comprehend, as anyone realizes who may have tried to read the Lord's Prayer engraved on the head of a pin.

The virtue of the new type of chart is that, in presenting much in little space, it presents it in visual rather than verbal form, making good on the fabled Chinese picture, so often said to be worth 1,000 words, but so seldom proven to be.

Whether the Linear Responsibility Chart replaces the many forms of organizational information records whose data it summarizes is open to question.

The Serge A. Birn Company, Louisville, Ky., consulting management engineers who introduced the new chart (a simplification of a European device of similar nature), think it can completely replace at least the usual bulky organization manual.

The Controller's department of Corning

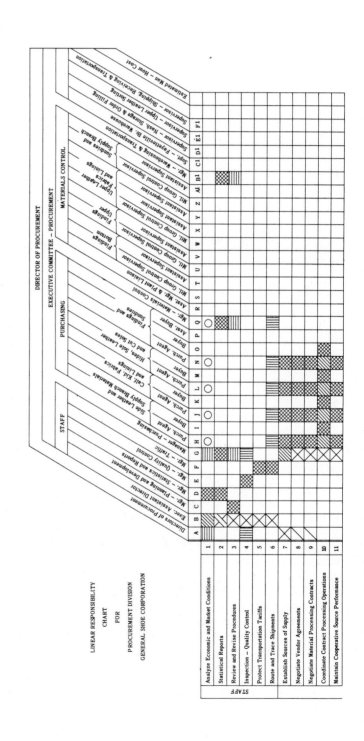

LINEAR RESPONSIBILITY
CHART
FOR
PROCUREMENT DIVISION
GENERAL SHOE CORPORATION

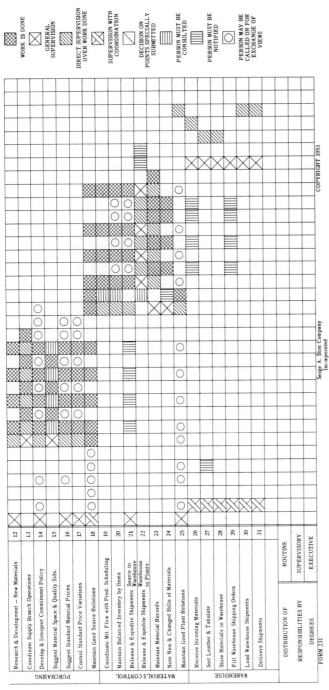

Figure 36-1 Typical Linear Responsibility Chart is this single-sheet description of Purchasing Division of General Shoe Corporation, Nashville, Tenn. A tentative study proposal, rather than a chart of the situation now in effect, it shows how LRC is used. General Shoe study was aimed at (1) More clearly defining authorities and responsibility; (2) Reassigning present personnel to jobs that company experience and testing showed them best fitted for; (3) Providing for an orderly progression of advancement; (4) Pointing up where on-the-job training is needed to fit others for advancement. Note that symbols (see key) in any vertical column describe the job at its head; in any horizontal row, show operating responsibility for function at left. Other charts have been used with quantitative symbols to tally time or to make interplant comparisons of methods. In most applications it has been found to be both clear and concise.

Glass Works, Corning, N.Y., which has worked out variations of its own on the basic chart, sees the LRC rather as a summary of information from many sources, handier to use than the original material because it is compact and visual.

"It does not replace (other) accepted techniques of functional and organizational control," says a Corning Glass internal memo on the subject. "Rather, it is an important supplementary tool which supervisory and other management individuals can use advantageously because it affords the opportunity quickly to scan and assess the actual relationship which exists between an operating group's employees, their functions, and their workloads." (Corning Glass has introduced a quantitative feature into its .version of the Linear Responsibility Chart.)

Another consulting engineer, exposed to Birn's LRC idea for the first time, described the chart as "a very handy tool" for executive control but was doubtful it could completely replace older methods of charting organizational relationships.

No company has abandoned the organization manual as a result of adopting the LRC, but that is inconclusive, since the charts have been in use in this country only a little more than a year, and among a very limited number of companies. Some have never had a manual, some are so small it is doubtful they could afford to set up one or, having set it up, afford high-grade talent needed to keep such a manual up to date.

What the Linear Responsibility Chart is, and how it presents its information, are best understood by looking at a typical one, like that made during a study for General Shoe Company (see Figure 36-1).

In its basic form, it uses eight symbols, as shown, to indicate eight relationships that may exist between any position in an industrial organization and any function or piece of work with which he may be associated as policy-maker, supervisor, co-ordinator, or do-er.

On a specially designed sheet of charting paper, the job titles in the department or unit of the company are listed along the horizontal axis, at the top. The functions performed by the organizational unit are listed along the vertical axis, at the left. In the square where job title and function meet, the relationship is indicated by the appropriate symbol. If the job

has nothing to do with the function, the square is left blank, of course.

S. H. Durst, works manager of Gamble Brothers, Louisville, Ky., manufacturers of dimension lumber and machined wood parts, gives this description, from his use of the Linear Responsibility Chart:

"On most charts, as you look at the chart, you see the man's name, his department, and to whom he is responsible. The duties that he performs are a separate set of instructions, usually carried in a procedure manual. With the Linear Responsibility Chart, you see the man's duties, what he is responsible for, and to whom he is responsible.

"I think a good example of this chart would be to compare it to a curve sign on the highway. Although the sign says there is a curve, you are in doubt how fast you can take your car around the curve. If you add to that curve sign (the notation) 45 miles per hour, you then have a complete explanation, that there is a curve and that you can proceed around it at a safe speed of 45 miles per hour.

"Thus, a man can look at the Linear Responsibility Chart and also pick off the duties that he is responsible for."

Replacement or supplement, the LRC has a great many uses in which its virtues are to save time and money, or to throw a bright spotlight on an organizational situation that needs study—or both.

Here are some of the uses (in its brief history of use in this country, the LRC has been put to most of them):

1. To simplify and speed up the making of a management audit.

Initially an advantage to the outside consultant making the audit, this is, of course, of advantage to the corporation under study, because a saving in time in making the audit will be reflected in a saving in the cost of making it.

Instead of having to make lengthy notes as he interviews executives, and of then having to study them as he converts them into a verbal description of the organization, the man making the audit can chart his facts on the LRC graph as he gets them—altering them, if need be, as he receives conflicting or additional facts.

Birn and his associates use this method regularly now; it constitutes a kind of organizational shorthand that need not be transcribed.

2. To simplify executive control and speed executive decisions.

The executive wishing to determine responsibility for something that has gone amiss is unlikely to want to ruffle through many pages of an organizational manual every time the need occurs but he will find it simple to check responsibility on a one-page chart that he can keep in his desk, or his pocket.

The president of one sizable company, who has used the LRC for nearly a year now, is jovial about this use. "It used to be," he says, "that when something went wrong, it was almost impossible to pin it on anyone. Now I keep the chart in my desk—these men helped make it; it represents exactly how things are done. So, now when anything goes wrong, I simply open my drawer and take it out. There can be no argument, and there never is."

3. To spot organizational errors, and to make them easy to correct by making their faultiness obvious to everyone concerned.

The "before" charts made in almost any organization the consultants have studied are much more interesting than the "after" charts, but with becoming modesty, no management seems willing to demonstrate how greatly it has improved matters between "before" and "after." The mockup chart (Figure 36-2), a disguised version of a real-life before-and-after set, shows, however, how these faults are detected and remedied.

The "before" chart of this pair shows a situation that had grown up gradually over a long period and worked well so long as the company was operating under large, long-run contracts. Too many production superintendents, however, shared authority to make binding decisions on sequence of operations and other processing details. Time spent in reconciling differences was great—often two hours per man weekly for as many as fifteen men. But, when competition forced the company to go out for new business aggressively, the old methods became suicidally cumbersome.

Bids were late, friction increased among the many men who had authority to decide. Eventually, one week, it took six meetings, totalling twelve hours, for each of those involved, to come to a common decision. At this point, the Linear Responsibility Chart made clear why the company was falling behind.

The conditions had existed before. Management knew something was wrong. But *what*

was wrong, and in what way, did not become clear until a graphic display like this *made* it clear. The "after" chart, concentrating decision in a few hands—the proper ones—and giving only consultative authority to the others, straightened the problem out.

One measure of the method's success was the reduction in "steps required" to settle methods from 41 to 21. Hours saved were almost geometrically proportional.

4. To facilitate changes in assignments of duties and authorities when a change in leading personnel occurs.

Because a new top man usually handles his job differently from his predecessor, delegating some things he did himself and taking on responsibilities he assigned to others, a shift in the work of lower-ranking management is required, too. This is the point at which maintenance of an unwieldy organization manual is first apt to break down. With responsibilities and authorities recorded visibly on a single sheet, as in LRC, the necessary changes are easy to make.

5. Realignment of tasks when activities are expanded or contracted because of varying business.

6. To check on whether a given executive is putting too much time or effort into routine activities—or supervisory—instead of executive.

7. To compare methods and operation of similar departments in a multiplant operation.

Corning Glass Works did this kind of comparative study of accounting departments in fourteen plants with the expenditure of about ten man-weeks of time. Using symbols of its own devising, instead of those proposed by Birn, it was able to get a quantitative measure of time spent on the various functions listed at the left of the chart, as well as of the work done by each individual in the vertical columns.

When the charting survey was finished, data was available for changes: Time per employee spent in payroll preparation varied from plant to plant, as did also total accounting personnel per employee.

These results spotlight areas for further study: Are the wide variations justified in each case, or can a better method be picked up from one plant and made standard procedure in all plants?

The charting, as R. C. Koch of Serge A. Birn Company points out, aids in an effort to make

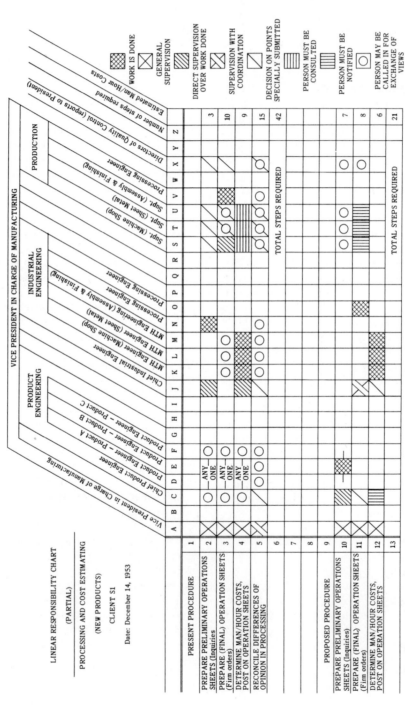

Figure 36-2 Before-and-after charts, disguised, but from a real plant, show how organizational faults are detected, remedied. See text.

accounting "a dynamic, not a static function" in the company's business, to "take a hand in making its history, not remain satisfied with recording it," as is often the case.

Other uses of the new chart suggest themselves to almost every executive who begins studying them. One feature of their adaptability is that although they record facts in a dramatically usable way, the facts may be used in pursuance of any organizational theories the user may favor; they do not require adherence to any given type of policy.

One additional fact needs to be stressed, however. Despite the apparent simplicity of the charting, it still requires expert knowledge to construct. The Birn organization is supported in this warning by the experience of Corning which says: "It should be strongly emphasized that serious thought and attention must be given to the selection and phrasing of the descriptive categories shown (on the left of the chart) so that conclusive but not overly detailed descriptions are employed. Otherwise, serious misrepresentations of the true and factual situation can result."